Mind of State

Conversations on the Psychological
Conflicts Stirring U.S. Politics & Society

Edited by
Betty Teng, Jonathan Kopp, Thomas Singer

CHIRON PUBLICATIONS • ASHEVILLE, NORTH CAROLINA

www.ChironPublications.com

Cover design by Nancy Kruger Cohen
Interior design by Danijela Mijailovic
Printed primarily in the United States of America.

ISBN 978-1-68503-197-8 paperback
ISBN 978-1-68503-198-5 hardcover
ISBN 978-1-68503-199-2 electronic
ISBN 978-1-68503-200-5 limited edition paperback

Library of Congress Cataloging-in-Publication Data Pending

Acknowledgments

Many people have contributed to the creation of *Mind of State*, first as a podcast and then as a book. None of it would have been possible without the extraordinarily generous support of Rebecca Mayne, cofounder and sponsor of the podcast.

Alletta Cooper and Jenny Woodward were creative and resourceful producers of the podcast during season two (2020–2021), greatly improving on our already strong model. Michael Epstein was a cohost and coproducer of season one (2019). Rowan Hair edited our interview transcripts, so that we could display them on our website, and Anne DeMare contributed to aspects of graphic design.

Nancy Kruger Cohen created the *Mind of State* logo, which perfectly captures the intention and spirit of the project; she also designed this book's cover. Matt Gaul provided invaluable legal counsel throughout all phases of the project.

In the production of this book, LeeAnn Pickrell and Allison Tuzo helped us manage all the complex aspects of getting more than thirty different contributors to meet timelines as well as copyediting all the episode transcripts.

We are profoundly grateful to all for the skills, talents, and energies they lent to *Mind of State*. Its strength comes from the vibrant energy of this collective.

BETTY TENG, COHOST & COFOUNDER

Betty P. Teng, LCSW, MFA, is a psychoanalyst and trauma therapist who has worked with survivors of sexual assault, domestic violence, and childhood molestation at Mount Sinai Beth Israel's Victims Services Program in Manhattan. She is one of the authors of the *New York Times* bestseller, *The Dangerous Case of Donald Trump*. Ms. Teng has spoken and written on trauma and its impacts for various conferences and media outlets, such as *Slate* and *Vox*. She currently sees couples and adults in private practice.

JONATHAN KOPP, COHOST & COFOUNDER

Jonathan Kopp is a communications strategist specializing in issue and positioning campaigns for candidates, causes, companies, and countries. He is a partner at FGS Global, a leading strategic communications and public affairs consultancy, helping clients navigate complex environments. Jonathan was a member of the Obama for America 2008 National Media Team, the Opposition Research & Rapid Response Team of the 1992 Clinton/Gore "War Room," and the Clinton Administration White House staff.

THOMAS SINGER, COFOUNDER

Dr. Thomas Singer is a psychiatrist and a Jungian psychoanalyst who trained at Yale Medical School and the C. G. Jung Institute of San Francisco. He contributed a chapter to the *New York Times* bestseller, *The Dangerous Case of Donald Trump*. In addition, he is the author/editor of many books and articles that include a series of books on cultural complexes that focus on Australia, Latin America, Europe, the United States, and Far East Asian countries. He has also coedited another series of books featuring *Ancient Greece, Modern Psyche*. He serves on the board of ARAS (Archive for Research into Archetypal Symbolism) and has been the coeditor of *ARAS Connections* for many years.

Contents

Introduction

This collection is based on a series of conversations from the *Mind of State* podcast (2019–2021), untangling stories that make up our daily news diet. This diet overstuffs us with details of culture wars, political stalemates, and legislative stunt shows—essentially infotainment mixed with serious reports of our rapidly deteriorating climate, increasing tensions between identity groups, and our diminishing trust in facts and data—such that we begin to lose sight of what is real and true. How do we take all this in, never mind make sense of any of it? How do we contend with our growing fear that we just might be headed for oblivion—either through nuclear war, pandemic, climate change, or a combination of all three?

Our goal with *Mind of State* is to attempt to make sense of such sociopolitical nonsense by exploring the relationships between psychology and politics in contemporary American society. This approach is not easy; so much of what is called political is, in fact, psychological, and so much of what is psychological has become political. The boundaries between the two are porous and yet, when you talk to politicians about psychology, they go blank—and when you try to talk to psychologists about politics, they share the human tendency to veer towards the dogmatic. The reality is a paradox: politics and psychology are all mixed up with one another and, at the same time, conversations about politics and psychology mix like oil and water. In spite of this, we committed to having such an exchange many times over. Across 29 episodes, we did our best to tease out and better understand the intersection of what we like to call *psyche* and *polis*, or psychology and politics. In the process, we found that it is highly useful, if not critical, to ask questions that show just how mutually influential psychology and politics are. Questions like: Why do we vote for the people we vote for? What emotions drive our political behavior? And how might this allow—or prevent—us from fruitfully living together?

Relevance

Why go to the trouble of putting a book together now, based on conversations that occurred three or four years ago? What possible relevance could they have today?

Certainly, the monumental events of the recent past—be it the COVID-19 pandemic, George Floyd's murder, the Black Lives Matter and #MeToo movements, a myriad of climate disasters, or the January 6, 2021 white-nationalist-led insurrection—all of it can start to blur. We have difficulty holding on to them; they can be poorly remembered. Did they occur in the distant past, or just yesterday? This is likely a consequence of our flooded mental and emotional states—the quick sequence and convergence of historical cataclysms are overwhelming, such that one catastrophe can quickly cancel out our memory of the last. We begin to live in an eternal *now*—lurching from moment to moment between dramatic occurrences lacking meaning since they feel disconnected from past or future. Or, our anxious desire compels us to quickly move on; we give ourselves no time to reflect.

Yet, it is crucial to create the space to remember, and that is why these episodes became a book. Only by remembering can we make meaning out of all that is happening to us. Thus, we spent a good deal of time going back to think about the relevance of these conversations from 2019–2021, and we discovered that they remain not only highly relevant, but also, at times, even prescient. This may be because at the core, most of the issues our society struggles with are thematic and remain unchanged. So although the details of an issue's specific context may have evolved, its underlying resonance remains as timely today as it did a few years ago.

Circumambulation

Considering the mutual impact of psyche and polis, we made a key discovery from these conversations we started four years ago: perhaps the best way to untangle the vexing, interrelated problems we now face in the U.S. is to circle around them again and again. Only then can themes and patterns be recognized because to make sense of difficult and seemingly unanswerable psycho-political questions, time is required—and lots of it.

To fully appreciate the individual topics and consider how their various themes are interwoven, we needed to go over our questions and responses at different times— to see them from different angles and various perspectives.

By engaging in such a process, we recognized previously unseen links, not only within one conversation, but also between various episodes as well. One example—among many—of the interconnections we discovered, is the braiding together of conspiracism, mass shootings, and racism. Only upon our return to them, and only by considering all 29 together as a whole, have these *Mind of State* episodes revealed multiple layers of meaning that were not as apparent when we first recorded them.

We call this approach *circumambulation*—a form of repeatedly walking around the same issues until a sharper picture emerges that embraces the complexity and multidimensional answers to thorny, vexing questions. Here are the major arenas of concern that emerged for us after *circumambulating* the interviews, individually and as a whole:

- Acknowledging Death, Trauma, Loss
- Why Truth Matters
- Anxieties of Race and Dominance
- Democracy at Risk
- The Importance of Myth in Politics

We organized this book into sections based on these themes and made each of the podcast transcriptions an individual chapter and placed it in one of the sections. Often, an individual conversation chapter could have easily gone into a different section, as the themes inevitably overlap. While our choices could be debated, we created this structure to organize the myriad topics and to show the connections. To further aid in organizing and locating these discussions in time, we also created a visual timeline to graphically represent the intermingling of cascading events with the conversations we were having about them. This was all to serve our goal—and frankly, our yearning—to make meaning and sense of psychopolitical nonsense.

On Conversation

We would be remiss not to share an essential observation we made in our circumambulations around these *Mind of State* episodes: the benefits—if not to say the gifts—of conversation itself. We found that when facing opaque, charged, and consternating sociopolitical issues, engaging with others in dialogue is a highly useful tool for distilling and digesting what is extremely difficult to think about alone. These dialogues and what they contain were spontaneous co-creations between people who cared, not only about the topic we came together to discuss, but also about the exchange itself. We cared about hearing from each other, sharing our thoughts and grappling with our confusions in a forum of respect and openness. Moreover, we cared to invite listeners to think right along with us.

While rereading these transcripts and listening again to the conversations, we were struck by the fact that while each episode featured an expert guest—whose ideas and writings we were eager to explore—there isn't one "author" to any of these discussions. Instead, each episode was an improvisational trio—or, sometimes, a quartet—in which we, along with our guest, interwove the themes and attitudes of psyche and polis, without taking sides. What was—and is—delightful was that some of our most politically minded guests came up with the most psychologically astute insights, and some of our most psychological experts issued extremely political assessments. In many cases, this interplay of psychological and political perspectives allowed us each to make surprising connections, syntheses— and even some groaningly bad puns—that we would not have otherwise come up with. These collaborative exchanges could not be reproduced— and this is the ephemeral beauty of conversation, of dialectic, of making links together. Taking a step back to look at this series of sand-painting-like collaborations, we see these conversations as microcosms and models of collective expression, which we, as a society and a democracy, seem to both crave—and yet also be in danger of losing.

Reflection as Prayer

Over time, the spirit of this book has also been informed by words of the Polish Nobel Prize–winning novelist Olga Tokarczuk, who wrote in *Drive Your Plow Over the Bones of the Dead*:

> It's a good thing that God, if he exists, and even if he doesn't gives us a place where we can think in peace. Perhaps that's the whole point of prayer—to think to yourself in peace, to want nothing, to ask for nothing.[1]

---

[1] Tokarczuk, O. (2018). *Drive Your Plow over the Bones of the Dead.* (A. Lloyd-Jones, Trans.) Penguin Random House. p. 232.

Tokarczuk unveiled to us that our larger goal in putting this book together has been to create a place where we can think in peace—where we have room to think. Thinking in peace truly becomes a form of prayer, whether a God or gods exist or not. Our American tendency—perhaps informed by our historical traumas—is to discard or forget anything from the past,[2] and we seem to be adopting increasingly ahistorical mindsets. Perhaps this is why Heather Cox Richardson's *Letters from an American* have become so popular, as a compensation for our "mindless now." She, too, has carved out time and space to seek perspective and contemporary relevance in our past history, which again, allows for thinking and reflection. This is the goal of this published collection of conversations as well. For in our reconsiderations, we have discovered that thinking and reflection are essential to fostering spiritual health, which in turn promotes individual and collective growth and well-being. Given the stagnation and fragmentation created by the psychopolitical and environmental extremes of these times, nurturing the strength and compassion of our human spirit is necessary now, more than ever.

---

[2] See our conversations with Pauline Boss in Chapter 3 and Betty Sue Flowers in Chapter 27.

Sampling of Significant Political, Cultural
Natural Events and Mind of State Podcasts
from 2017-2021

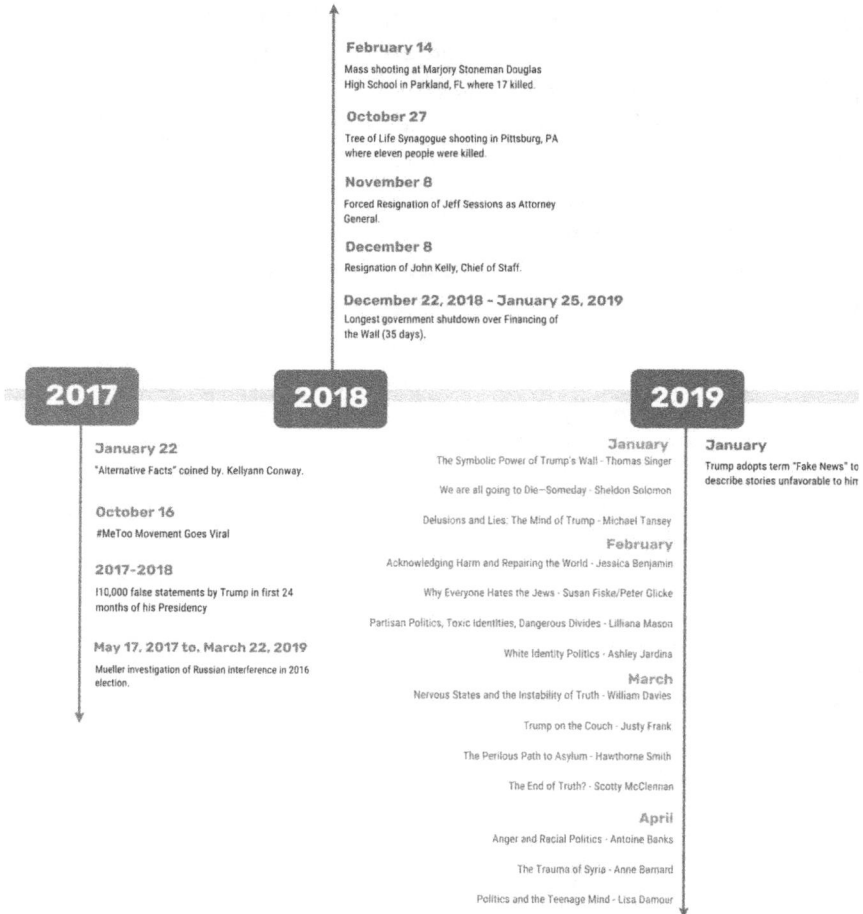

February 14
Mass shooting at Marjory Stoneman Douglas
High School in Parkland, FL where 17 killed.

October 27
Tree of Life Synagogue shooting in Pittsburg, PA
where eleven people were killed.

November 8
Forced Resignation of Jeff Sessions as Attorney
General.

December 8
Resignation of John Kelly, Chief of Staff.

December 22, 2018 - January 25, 2019
Longest government shutdown over Financing of
the Wall (35 days).

2017

January 22
"Alternative Facts" coined by. Kellyann Conway.

October 16
#MeToo Movement Goes Viral

2017-2018
110,000 false statements by Trump in first 24
months of his Presidency

May 17, 2017 to, March 22, 2019
Mueller investigation of Russian interference in 2016
election.

2018

January
The Symbolic Power of Trump's Wall - Thomas Singer

We are all going to Die—Someday - Sheldon Solomon

Delusions and Lies: The Mind of Trump - Michael Tansey

February
Acknowledging Harm and Repairing the World - Jessica Benjamin

Why Everyone Hates the Jews - Susan Fiske/Peter Glicke

Partisan Politics, Toxic Identities, Dangerous Divides - Lilliana Mason

White Identity Politics - Ashley Jardina

March
Nervous States and the Instability of Truth - William Davies

Trump on the Couch - Justy Frank

The Perilous Path to Asylum - Hawthorne Smith

The End of Truth? - Scotty McClennan

April
Anger and Racial Politics - Antoine Banks

The Trauma of Syria - Anne Barnard

Politics and the Teenage Mind - Lisa Damour

2019

January
Trump adopts term "Fake News" to
describe stories unfavorable to hin

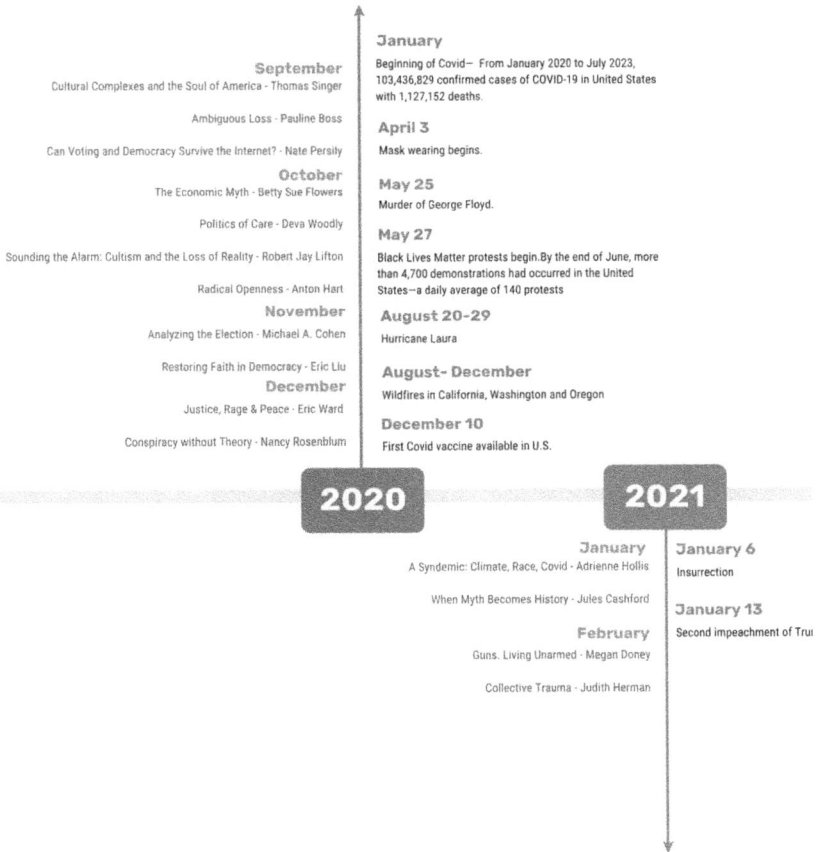

September
Cultural Complexes and the Soul of America - Thomas Singer

Ambiguous Loss - Pauline Boss

Can Voting and Democracy Survive the Internet? - Nate Persily

October
The Economic Myth - Betty Sue Flowers

Politics of Care - Deva Woodly

Sounding the Alarm: Cultism and the Loss of Reality - Robert Jay Lifton

Radical Openness - Anton Hart

November
Analyzing the Election - Michael A. Cohen

Restoring Faith in Democracy - Eric Liu

December
Justice, Rage & Peace - Eric Ward

Conspiracy without Theory - Nancy Rosenblum

January
Beginning of Covid— From January 2020 to July 2023, 103,436,829 confirmed cases of COVID-19 in United States with 1,127,152 deaths.

April 3
Mask wearing begins.

May 25
Murder of George Floyd.

May 27
Black Lives Matter protests begin.By the end of June, more than 4,700 demonstrations had occurred in the United States—a daily average of 140 protests

August 20-29
Hurricane Laura

August- December
Wildfires in California, Washington and Oregon

December 10
First Covid vaccine available in U.S.

2020

2021

January
A Syndemic: Climate, Race, Covid - Adrienne Hollis

When Myth Becomes History - Jules Cashford

February
Guns. Living Unarmed - Megan Doney

Collective Trauma - Judith Herman

January 6
Insurrection

January 13
Second impeachment of Tru[...]

FRAMEWORK

Chapter 1
Cultural Complexes & the Soul of America

Guest: Dr. Thomas Singer
Episode Aired: September 2, 2020

Dr. Thomas Singer is a psychiatrist and a Jungian psychoanalyst who trained at Yale Medical School and the C. G. Jung Institute of San Francisco. He contributed a chapter to the New York Times bestseller, The Dangerous Case of Donald Trump. *In addition, he is the author/editor of many works including a series of books on cultural complexes that have focused on Australia, Latin America, Europe, the United States, and Far East Asian countries. He has also coedited a series of books featuring* Ancient Greece, Modern Psyche. *He serves on the board of* ARAS *(Archive for Research into Archetypal Symbolism) and has been the coeditor of* ARAS Connections *for many years.[1]*

In late 2019, when we decided to launch a second season of Mind of State, *we felt we needed a framework to more consciously organize the themes emerging from the 15 conversations that we had recorded in Season One. When our partner and cofounder Tom Singer introduced us to his Jungian concept of cultural complexes and listed the seven he saw as instrumental to determining our cultural attitudes in the U.S., it was as if we had discovered a hidden framework for* Mind of State *that we had been following all along.*

---

[1] Singer, T. (Ed.). (2020). *Cultural Complexes and the Soul of America.* Routledge. Other books in the Cultural Complex Series include *Cultural Complexes of Australia: Placing Psyche* and *Latin American Cultural Complexes: South and Soul,* which are being reissued by Routledge in late 2023; *Cultural Complexes in China, Japan, Korea, and Taiwan: Spokes of the Wheel* (Routledge, 2021); and *Europe's Many Souls,* originally published by Spring Journal Books in 2016, with an updated edition forthcoming from Routledge.

We therefore begin this volume with the conversation that established the framework by which we thematically organize the twenty-nine transcripts that follow. The first section, Acknowledging Death, Trauma & Loss, *is a series of conversations on the American cultural complex of* trauma and loss, *best encapsulated by Dr. Pauline Boss's statement that "we are a nation founded upon unresolved grief." This is followed by the section,* Why Truth Matters? *relating to the cultural complex of* speech, truth, and falsehood. *We consider the roots of a decline of our faith in truth, facts, and reality in recent years and the serious threats this poses to our liberal democracy. The third section,* Anxieties of Race & Dominance, *focuses on the cultural complex of* race, gender, and ethnicity *and considers the meaning, importance, and struggles of power, identity, and difference which have stressed U.S. society for generations. The fourth,* Democracy at Risk, *considers the cultural complex of our relationship to the collective and explores the increasing tensions that imperil our ability to govern ourselves collaboratively. Finally,* The Importance of Myth in Politics *touches upon three cultural complexes—our relationship to commerce, free speech, and "the other" by also considering the role myth and symbolism play with relationship to politics.*

In September 2020, our conversation with Tom launched our second season and marked the midpoint of the 30 episodes that comprise Mind of State. *At that moment, much of the United States was still in lockdown due to the ongoing COVID-19 pandemic, we were headed into the most intense period of the 2020 Biden/Trump presidential election season, and climate disasters such as deadly hurricanes and forest fires plagued the South and the West. While it had been our ongoing objective with* Mind of State *to join with experts in politics and psychology to collectively make psychological sense out of sociopolitical nonsense, we could not predict how grounding we would find these conversations as we navigated what would become an incredibly volatile period for American democracy.*

Interview

Betty: Jonathan, welcome. I'm very excited to dive into season two with you.

Jonathan: So great to be here with you.

Betty: We are in some intense and interesting times.

Jonathan: Interesting times, indeed. We relaunch this conversation amid a lot of turbulence—the COVID-19 pandemic, an economic crisis rivaling the Great Depression, and racial tensions as intense as those during the civil rights movement of the 1960s. If only there were some sort of psychological frame that would help us make sense of all the chaos.

Betty: Exactly, this is why we're here, isn't it—to make some psychological sense out of sociopolitical nonsense. This brings us right up to what we'll be talking about with Tom Singer, who is our cofounder and a psychoanalyst and an expert on psychology and politics. Tom introduced both of us to the idea of a *cultural complex*, which just might be the frame for more effectively considering what to make of these volatile times. Because a *complex*—or we might say a *preoccupation* or an *obsession*—is something a person, or even a society, has about a particular issue, identity, or ideal over time. Society struggles with these phenomena—these cultural complexes—as a way of defining its character and reflecting on what it prioritizes and values. Considering which cultural complexes have gripped—and are gripping— the United States will give us a guide to talking about our current political state and help frame our thoughts and feelings about them.

Jonathan: It's such a great way to begin. I'm eager to get us started. Welcome to *Mind of State*, Tom. It's great to have you here.

Tom: Thank you. It's good to be here.

Jonathan: I feel like I need to lead off with an observation. I think, secretly, if it had been up to you, *Mind of State* might have been called *Psyche and Polis*.

Tom: That's absolutely right.

Jonathan: So I want to start off by asking you to talk to us about *psyche* and *polis*. Can you help us understand the distinction between *psyche* versus *mind* and *polis* versus *state*? Are they the same—or are they different? Are they just the Greek translations of English terms?

Tom: First, I love the name *Mind of State* for our show. I think it's perfect. But I also prefer to use the old Greek words, *psyche* and *polis*, to evoke the living reality of how we actually experience *mind* and *state*, if that makes any sense. *Psyche* is the root of "psychology," of course. *Psyche* is also the Greek word for *soul*. And *polis* is the Greek word for *state* or *city-state*. But my preference for *psyche* and *polis* is not only about being a Hellenophile and wanting to go back to some nice, old elitist-sounding names. I do find the words *mind* and *state* rather concrete and heavy. There's not a lot of life or movement when you say *mind*. I don't think of something that's living and breathing. I don't think of something that's moving and shifting all the time, winding its way through individuals and groups of people. To me, *mind* is a little bit more mechanical in what it evokes. I think of neurons firing off if I think of *mind* at all. And *state* is the same way. When I think of *state*, I tend to think in terms of bureaucracies and rather lifeless or sterile organizations that aren't breathing and don't have movement in them. So, for me, *psyche* is, by contrast, filled with movement and vitality, and *polis* is as well. If the Greek city-states were anything, they were alive. And I think sometimes we drain the life out of things when we talk about *psychology* or *mind* or *state*. So, that's why I prefer using those Greek words.

Jonathan: I think a lot of the American public and maybe the public beyond the U.S. would agree with you about conversations of *state* boring them or there being a quality of lifelessness when you come to talking about politics. I find politics to be the arena of ideas, but sometimes it just gets reduced to either partisan bickering or data downloads from a bunch of bureaucratic bean-counters. And that's not what we're here to talk about, is it?

Tom: No, we're here to talk about the very unpredictable and fluid movement of how, when individuals gather together in groups, this *mind*—by that, I mean our *collective psyche*—is very alive and ever-shifting. Today it's shifting on a daily basis, according to whatever the news may be. So, that's also why I prefer *psyche*.

Betty: From your comments, Tom, on *psyche* and *polis* as compared to the more fixed or concrete *mind* or *state*, what I get is that there's flow to those words. There's an energy to *psyche* and *polis* that suggests what may be going on in our souls and in our interactions with each other in our civic lives and government. It *is* a very dynamic thing. I think that's really important because right now, as Jonathan says, everything is volatile and in dynamic movement, with so much going on with the pandemic, with the economic crisis, with the presidential election coming up, and with race relations being what they are. This flow and energy and dynamism is very electric right now, in an almost shocking way. Sometimes it's even hurtful, but it's consistently unpredictable and unknown. Is that an accurate reflection of what you're expressing?

Tom: Yes, it is. Another piece of why I prefer *psyche* and *polis* versus *mind* and *state* in this kind of conversation is that we tend to experience these flows or dynamics in a subjective and inner way. *Psyche* really refers to how things get experienced inside or between us. We really don't talk about "experiencing mind." It's a more objective statement about the structure of the brain. And *state* is likewise an objective term for the structure of government. That's not how we take in our government, or the *polis*. That's not how we *live* it. That's not how we *relate* to it. And it's the same with *psyche*. Right now, everything seems remarkably fluid in the day-to-day unfolding, as psyche moves and winds its way through us. It seems as if everything is unpredictable. And yet, paradoxically, there are some ongoing themes in the *psyche* and *polis* of the United States that have been with us for the 250 years that we've been around as a nation. On the one hand, there's this tremendous sense of dynamism and fluidity, and then, on the other hand, there's a tremendous sense of repetition and even static sameness. If you're a Black person engaged with Black Lives Matter, for example, today probably feels little different from how it did in the 1960s. Over time, the issue of racism, or the issues around gender, or the issues around the economy tend to appear to be more static than fluid, although they may feel very fluid in the moment.

Jonathan: What I'm hearing is that there are these major psychological and sociological themes that flow through our collective consciousness and drive our society. They shape or influence our identity and the ways that we relate to each other, and we might manifest them in different ways. There are different moments that bring them to light and different terms of art that we might use to describe them. But what I hear you saying is that there are thematic throughlines that link what we're experiencing now to similar circumstances Americans might have experienced 100-, 200-, 300-plus years ago, because they're part of our psyche. Is that right?

Tom: That's very well said. There are thematic throughlines. Rather than labeling it as psychology or sociology, I think of it as an *inner sociology*. And what I mean by that is that these ongoing thematic issues that the country has been facing for a long time, they actually exist *inside* of us. They exist inside of us as individuals, and they exist inside of us as members of groups, or as members of competing groups. So, exactly as *sociology* implies—it's inner sociology.

Jonathan: Inner sociology, but collective, right?

Tom: But collective. Yes.

Jonathan: Somehow it's within me. It's within you. And yet it's also flowing through all of us. How does that work?

Betty: We're trained as psychotherapists to look at patterns of behavior in people. They come to us to consider these patterns because they might not want to keep doing certain things over and over again. Many times folks ask me, "Why do I keep doing this? I want to understand what it is that I'm doing, so that I can have more agency over this, rather than have these things keep happening over and over again." Some say the definition of insanity is to keep doing the same things over and over again and yet expect different outcomes. And as groups of people, we also have the historical experience of repeating the same patterns over and over again—whether it be about race, or the economy, or gender, just to name a few issues. What makes us repeat these behaviors, some of which lead us to conflict or harmful outcomes? I think that gets to the core of what a cultural complex is. It offers a way to decode recurring patterns in politics and psychology. This will be a theme for not only today, but also the entire season. So, can you tell us more specifically what a *cultural complex* even is, Tom?

Tom: Yes. First, let me space things out for a minute, in terms of how to think about this. If you were an amphibian living 400 million years ago and you were crawling out of the sea for the first time and you had to survive on land, you might think that the first thing you'd need to survive would be to have lungs. But Homer Smith, who wrote a wonderful book called, *From Fish to Philosopher*, focused on the kidney as the key to survival on land.[2] Because you need to filter what's going inside and outside your body in a way that a fish living in the sea doesn't. The kidney is a filter that maintains a constant internal environment. The kidney maintains a sea inside us with just the right balance of chemicals. It is able to do this by excreting those chemicals that would be toxic to us if they remained inside. Now, think about the psyche. Think about human beings needing filters that help us differentiate what to

---

[2] Smith, H. (1961). *From Fish to Philosopher*. Anchor Books/Doubleday.

retain and what to excrete, what to keep inside and what to eliminate. I think of cultural complexes as the kidneys of the collective psyche.

Now, that's a mouthful. But we have filtering systems that allow us to process thoughts, images, emotions, memories—all sorts of things that are part of our everyday living. This is actually a very complex process by which all of what we take in is being filtered. This happens in the individual psyche and in the group, or collective psyche. We have a filtration system. I think of cultural complexes as being collective psychological filtering systems for both individuals and groups. And they allow us to maintain a relatively stable internal environment in relationship to a very complex outer world. They filter things on the basis of memory, on the basis of feelings, on the basis of thoughts, on the basis of images. And what happens historically is that different groups of people, living in different places, develop different cultural complexes that determine, as groups, how they think, feel, behave, and remember. I've been studying this for about twenty years, literally all over the world and, most recently, in the United States. I would argue that we have six or seven cultural complexes that have determined our history and our politics. This may sound grandiose—and it's just one way of looking at things. But I have observed that these cultural complexes determine how we think and feel and behave about a variety of ongoing "thematic throughlines," as you referred to it, Jonathan. And I call them *cultural complexes* because they operate more unconsciously than consciously.

Jonathan: Tom, can you give us an example? You've been studying cultural complexes for decades, all over the world. But to me, they are still sounding very abstract, and I would love for you to ground it a little bit more.

Tom: Well, one powerful cultural complex we're experiencing right now is racism. Racism has been part of our history for as long as we've been a nation, for some 250 years or so. It has all sorts of fixed simplistic ideas and thoughts attached to it as well as repeating memories, behaviors, and attitudes. These are deeply ingrained in white people and Black people, people of color. Everybody has racial complexes. I want to clarify that individual complexes or cultural complexes are not abnormal; in fact, they're actually normal in the sense that they're quite common. That's how we filter the world. In our country, the cultural complex of race has determined a great deal of our history, and most of it has been unconscious. It activates intense and frequently destructive emotions. In general, cultural complexes are characterized by unbelievably raw, primitive emotions and very simplistic ideas that tend to be literally black and white and divide things into opposing positions. They are, therefore, highly reactive. Once you trigger them, the emotion that's released is unbelievable. We've just seen that with what's happened following George Floyd's murder. His brutal murder expressed and activated the oldest, most virulent, potent, and destructive cultural complex in American history.

Jonathan: You're bringing up something that gets right to the core of *Mind of State*. What you just did in talking about cultural complexes and *psyche* is that consciously or not, you lapsed into *polis*, or politics. You started talking about George Floyd and the political processes, ideas, and issues that are welling up and boiling over all across this country.

People are not out marching in the street about a cultural complex, right? Nor are they marching in the street thinking about either *psyche* or *polis*. They are marching in the street about inequality and injustice. But it's the emotion that they're bringing to it, the anger and the frustration that taps into this primal human conflict over race. It's that relationship between mind and state, between psyche and polis, that you've landed us on.

Betty: And to key off of what you just said, Jonathan, there's something in the culture that has been triggered. And seeing it as a cultural complex or seeing it as a movement or a linkage of how our minds are driving our state—or how our minds are reacting to situations happening in our state—is really not *just* political, but psychological, sociological, and cultural as well. So, it's a blend. Maybe this allows us to look at, better understand, and maybe even break the mechanisms of the cycle perpetuating, in this example, racism due to inequalities and injustices in our *polis*.

Why can't we see how these cycles repeat themselves? Is it because the emotions are so high they blind us? Is it because there's some resistance that the cultural complex brings forth? How, Tom, can we use our awareness and understanding of this cultural complex, or filtration system—which, from what you just said, is a way people and groups self-regulate? We talk a lot about self-regulation in trauma treatment because traumatized individuals suffer from extreme mental and physical states due to being out of modulation from the harmful event they experienced. Often, in reactions to trauma, systems get severely dysregulated. Recapturing the ability to self-regulate is so important. Just as the kidney is an organ that regulates and maintains balance, I wonder what you can say about how a cultural complex, if it is a filter, tends to regulation or dysregulation in groups?

Tom: That's a really good, interesting, and difficult question. When a cultural complex has been activated and all of that raw emotion gets discharged, there's not much regulation going on at all. And these cultural complexes tend to be highly repetitive. That is, they recur over and over in time. They're also autonomous. They seem to have a life of their own in the psyche. And, as with all the protests and outpouring of rage following George Floyd's killing, when the cultural complex is triggered, all of the pain and anguish and suffering that's accumulated since the time of slavery discharges itself. In those moments, it is meaningless to talk about homeostasis or self-regulation, because cultural complexes are not self-regulating and they're not homeostatic. On the other hand, if you take a different view, I do think the psyche tends to compensate for its excesses and does have a homeostatic function. Maybe we're beginning to see that in our country right now with the beginnings of a movement against Trump. But the highly repetitious, highly autonomous, and tremendously emotional, reactive nature of cultural complexes makes them almost impenetrable when they've been activated.

Jonathan: Tom, you got me excited when you started talking about Trump losing momentum. And I have no doubt that we're going to talk a lot more about race through this whole season. But let me stop you a second, because we're just getting started and these are still new terms. You gave us one example of a cultural complex in the U.S.—that being racism. Are there others?

Tom: Actually, all of this began with a paper I wrote on the eve of the 2008 election. I was asked to reflect on politics and the soul. And at the time…

Jonathan: That was a soulful election, for sure.

Tom: I thought I was an idiot to take on the task of trying to reflect on the relationship between politics and soul. But as I began to work on it, I defined seven different areas where I think cultural complexes have been determinative or formative of American history. And I went on to argue that it is in what we do with these cultural complexes that the soul of our nation gets forged. So I was and am really connecting two separate concepts or realities—cultural complexes and soul. The tension we experience when these cultural complexes get activated, and then we engage with them, creates the cauldron in which soul can get made or soul can get undone.

Let me very briefly run-through the seven cultural complexes that I think are determinative of our political processes and our historical processes. Of course, this is just one model, and we can add to it, subtract from it, or throw it out the window. But I do think soul gets made in this process. And I'll just give you this list. I posit that cultural complexes form around a series of relationships. So, there is our relationship to money, commerce, and consumer goods. That's definitely a cultural complex. There is our relationship to the natural environment, which is clearly the most pressing cultural complex, on which the survival of the human species is now dependent. There is our relationship to the human community, including family life, social life, and the life cycle from conception to death. That's a great big thing. But how we relate, or don't relate, to our community, as a cultural complex, is one of the most divisive forces in our society these days.

Jonathan: Particularly relevant in this era of pandemic and social isolation, right?

Tom: Absolutely. I mean, if we don't think we're responsible members of the community and the virus isn't real, we don't put on a mask. It's about as concrete as you can get.

Jonathan: All right, so, that's three...

Tom: There is our relationship to the spiritual realm. And that's always been an important part of American history and how we define ourselves. I would argue that it's still incredibly important in terms of what we do with the spiritual values and aspirations and the meaning or meaninglessness in our life. That's a cultural complex.

Betty: Tom, does religious freedom come into that?

Tom: Absolutely. Religious freedom is a fundamental building block of our society. The very foundation of our American history was based on the fight for religious freedom. Then there are cultural complexes formed around the relationship to race, ethnicity, and gender. All of the so-called "others." What do we do about gender, race, and ethnicity? Putting them all together is probably a stupid thing to do. But it's about the "other." And it's what we do with people who aren't like us or are different from us. Then, here's a really important cultural complex, which is particularly unique to American history: our relationship to speed, height, youth, progress, and celebrity.

Jonathan: That's a big bucket.

Tom: There are a lot of big buckets. And actually, these cultural complexes overlap with one another. They are not as pure forms as I'm articulating them. But we are all about speed, height, youth, progress, and celebrity. That's the deal. We're not about age. Let those old people die of the pandemic in the old folks' homes because they really don't count. They are just numbers. I'm not saying that's how I feel. Rather, that's how I think the cultural complex about our relationship to aging in our culture can lead us to feel. And finally, the seventh cultural complex would be about the relationship to the world beyond our borders. How do we feel about the United States in relation to other countries? And we're in the midst of a huge fight about that, a huge cultural complex that generates all kinds of emotion and simplistic ideas. If you want to look at simplistic ideas as a defining characteristic of cultural complexes, look at our policies toward other countries at this time in our national...

Betty: The shortenings of visas, the challenges to visas on all levels, just absurd, you know?

Jonathan: Well, our place in the world is in chaos right now, right between putting up walls...

Betty: ...and travel bans.

Jonathan: Banning travel and pulling out of the WHO (World Health Organization). This is incredibly fraught. And what's interesting to me, Tom, is when I hear you list these seven cultural complexes, my mind immediately goes to cabinet agencies or committees of Congress or landmark legislation—because that's what I'm hearing in every single one of them, whether it's the Civil Rights Act or the Equal Rights Amendment or the Department of Commerce or the Foreign Affairs Committee. When you say, "cultural complex," I think politics and government. And that's exactly why I think you are the human embodiment of *Mind of State*.

Betty: You know, there's one thing that I wanted to say about the cultural complex on race—and the words that can signify "other"—such as *gender* or *ethnicity*. When we say, "different from 'us'" it is important that we frame this as meaning different from an *assumed* centrist idea of what or who "us" is. Because when we refer to the "other" as women, or immigrants, or people of different races other than white, there is a presupposition as to what "us" versus "them" is. And I think it is key to highlight and clarify this.

It is no less useful, however, to see that this complex stirs us. And because I fashion myself a good student of your teaching, Tom, and since we've been talking about this over the past few months as we planned out the show, I have thought a lot about this and wanted to add to the list of cultural complexes our *relationship to speech*. We are a country singular in the world in our pride in freedom of speech and how we defend it legally. It's protected by the First Amendment. But right now, we challenge speech on both sides of the aisle. We challenge calling Trump a liar because we want to be impartial in the press. Yet we also are grappling with "cancel culture" and the language of what is right and what is wrong. It amplifies the polarization from what first emerged as political correctness.

Jonathan: Liberal liberalism became illiberalism pretty quickly.

Betty: And now there is such importance placed on speech—how we say things, what we say, and where we say it. The speech on MSNBC or Fox News seems to be tilting toward extremism, perhaps on both sides. And we can think of our relationship to speech as a cultural complex. We claim speech to be so open and protected here in the United States, when really it can also be quite dogmatic.

The other cultural complex that I would add to the mix is the cultural complex of our *relationship to loss and trauma*. I don't know if it's because I'm a trauma therapist, but I tend to see everything through this lens. I would say that we are a nation built on loss. It may be an unacknowledged loss, which is troublesome because when we don't acknowledge the loss, we can't heal it. There is a lot of talk about loss around what has emerged from the loss of George Floyd in such a very brutal fashion. But many who embrace "Make America Great Again" are also feeling a deep sense of loss about our country and a yearned-for past. They harken back to a real or imagined way of being that was better then. What about the losses that are clear or unclear that we keep replaying as a type of cultural complex? What do you think about these two additions to your list of American cultural complexes—our *relationship to speech* and our *relationship to loss*?

Tom: I think they are excellent, essential additions. What I like to do when I try to use the notion of cultural complex with some precision and clarity is to look at the defining characteristics of cultural complexes and see if they are present. For instance, if we are going to say that how we handle loss in America is a cultural complex, I would ask if the following characteristics were met:

- That our powerful emotions about loss as individuals and groups of people in the country are autonomous, that they have a life of their own.
- That they are repetitious, that they go on inside of us, often without our conscious awareness, and that they recur over and over again. So, they are autonomous, and they are repetitious.
- That they collect experiences and memories that validate their own point of view. For instance, with regard to loss, the phrase for denying loss as an entrenched cultural complex is "move on." It's a trigger word or phrase to deny loss. We are actually in a culture that right now is trying to deny the loss of hundreds of thousands, if not millions, of people to COVID. Again, the complex collects experience that validates its own point of view.
- And finally, the thoughts that go along with a cultural complex are often quite simplistic or black and white. Complexes don't like complex or nuanced thinking.

If those criteria are met, then I think you can speak of a cultural complex. And I think that's true both of loss and speech for the U.S. I might add to our list of cultural complexes the idea that *thinking* itself in our country seems to be frozen in a complex. The quality of thinking in our country is very low. It hardly seems as though we think at all. Everything has become simplistic. Not only is the quality of speech far more inhibited and limited than we think, but the quality of our thought has, in my opinion, deteriorated into simplistic black-and-white assertions for which there is no real response.

Jonathan: Well, our politics have become reductionist, right? It's down to bumper stickers and memes. And if you can't say it in a TikTok video, then it's no longer relevant. No one is reading the long form feature article. And that has a way of pushing people to the extremes, of crowding out nuance, doesn't it?

Betty: And I think these things are pitched in shorter time frames as technology speeds everything up. We are not reflecting. We're surfing. We're clicking. We're going from one thing to the next to the next to the next. One thing I wanted to ask you about, Tom, was when something is "autonomous" and acts on its own, what do you mean by that?

Tom: *Autonomous* means that something has a life of its own without conscious control. If you think of the vegetative or autonomic nervous system, which controls heartbeat, respiration, and digestion, we don't think about having to do any of those activities. They're autonomous. They function on their own without our having to think about them.

Betty: So, are they like assumptions?

Tom: They are assumptions. They are ongoing psychic processes akin to vegetative biological processes that go on and have a life of their own, whether we think about them or not. And what I'd like to add, because we've done a very quick run-through of the notion of cultural complexes, is that in our thinking about *Mind of State* over the next many episodes we present, we have used this model of the cultural complex as a bit of a framework. Many of the issues that I've touched on very briefly are going to be the topics of much more in-depth conversations as we go along.

Jonathan: This is a great framework. It makes me think how much better our political process would be if the actors in it, if our politicians, our government officials, were more psychologically aware. I mean, they are living out; they are experiencing. They are expressing cultural complexes and they don't even know it.

Tom: Absolutely, Jonathan. It used to be my assumption that because politicians are very good at reading the mind or the psyche of the population—as that's what they're trained to do—one would think there would be a natural conversation between those of us thinking about cultural complexes and politicians who are tuning into them and responding and resonating to them every day. You would think it would be a very natural conversation to have between politicians and psychologists, or students of cultural complexes. Unfortunately, what I've discovered is that the language, the thinking, and the approaches of politicians and psychologists tuned into the psyche of groups of people are really like oil and water. They don't go naturally or easily together, although one would assume that they would.

Betty: I think this show exists to encourage all of us to think more about our politics, to think further about our state, and to think about our state of being—to consider "where are we?" with respect to our individual and collective needs. If we can do that, then maybe we can shift some assumptions or shift some of these autonomous processes in our minds, in our culture, and in our politics that repeat and, therefore, seem stuck.

Tom: Since we are encouraging people to think, then I would encourage people to think about the cultural complexes that they can identify, that they can recognize in themselves even though they tend to be unconscious. Cultural complexes are naturally occurring phenomena, and we are all moved by them, and right now in our society, we are drowning in them.

Betty: If our objective as psychoanalysts is, in part, to make the unconscious conscious, so that people can alter repetitive thoughts, feelings, and behaviors, rather than behave out of group complexes because they're just operating within us without awareness, then *Mind of State* might be a useful offering to those who want to think about the mind of our states and the states of our minds.

Tom: A really interesting exercise is to look at the daily newspaper and identify each of the headlines by the cultural complex that is driving them. You'd be amazed. They are the same ones over and over again, every day.

Jonathan: All day, every day, we are being bombarded by the moment, the crisis, the outrage. What we are doing here at *Mind of State* is giving people an opportunity to think about more long-term trends and cultural complexes that have been with us and will continue to be with us for a long time. So, if we can pull people back from the edge to be a little bit more reflective and introspective, we'll have done something.

Betty: We really do want to stop the spin. We want to give people an opportunity to step out of the twenty-four-hour, seven-days-a-week news cycle and think about things that are happening rather than just feel, as you say, Jonathan, bombarded.

All right. So, Tom, our partner, our cofounder, thank you so much for joining us on the show and framing up what is going to be a very exciting season two of our podcast.

Tom: It's a great pleasure to join the two of you in this really stimulating discussion. I get very excited—and it's fun.

Jonathan: Thanks for joining us on *Mind of State*. And thanks again to our guest, Tom Singer, whose latest book, *Cultural Complexes and the Soul of America* can be found anywhere you get your books.

ACKNOWLEDGING DEATH, TRAUMA & LOSS

Chapter 2
We Are All Going to Die—Someday

Guest: Dr. Sheldon Solomon
Episode Aired: January 29, 2019

Sheldon Solomon is Professor of Psychology at Skidmore College. His studies of the effects of the uniquely human awareness of death on attitudes and behavior have been supported by the National Science Foundation and Ernest Becker Foundation and are featured in the documentary film Flight from Death: The Quest for Immortality. *He is coauthor of* In the Wake of 9/11: The Psychology of Terror *and* The Worm at the Core: On the Role of Death in Life. *Sheldon is an American Psychological Society Fellow, a recipient of an American Psychological Association Presidential Citation, a Lifetime Career Award by the International Society for Self and Identity, the Association of Graduate Liberal Studies Programs Annual Faculty Award, and a Career Contribution Award by the Society for Personality and Social Psychology.*

We recorded this conversation with Sheldon Solomon during the first weeks of January 2019. At the time, there was a government shutdown underway, which was the result of a dispute between President Trump and congressional Democrats over funding of a proposed wall along the U.S./Mexico border to keep illegal immigrants from entering the U.S.—a campaign promise Trump declared he would deliver as a part of his extreme anti-immigration platform in 2016. This turmoil was happening concurrently with the ongoing Mueller investigation, a Justice Department inquiry into allegations that Trump had colluded with Russian spies to influence the 2016 U.S. presidential election in his favor,[1] along with myriad firings and resignations of top members of his administration,

---

[1] Beavers, O., Thomsen, J., & Samuels, B. (2019). The Mueller Probe: A timeline from beginning to end, *The Hill.* https://thehill.com/policy/national-security/435547-mueller-probe-a-timeline-from-beginning-to-end/.

including the dismissal of Attorney General Jeff Sessions and resignation of White House Chief of Staff John F. Kelly, all of whom Trump deemed to obstruct his authority.[2] *We turned to Sheldon Solomon to discuss how his research on how our human existential anxieties about death and safety can unconsciously fuel whom we choose to lead us—and whom we vote for—in times of crisis and perceived threat.*

Interview

Michael: Sheldon, your work helped me understand more about the 2016 presidential election and all of the turmoil and the chaos of the Trump presidency than anything else I have read. The campaign really did predict the kind of president we got. People thought that he would elevate in the office and...

Betty: ...Pivot.

Michael: Right. But, we have had no pivot, no elevation. And, Sheldon, your insights gave me an intellectual framework to see what was going on in the media and with Trump himself—as well as with Trump's supporters. I think of the angry, ugly, and incredibly divisive debate that we're having right now as a country over immigration. So it's great to have you with us so we can discuss these insights and share them.

Sheldon: Well, thank you, Michael and thank you, Betty. It's a great honor to be here.

Michael: Your work is death focused. What is it about death that is so difficult for us to accept as human beings? This is not a new idea. We all know we're going to die, right?

Sheldon: Absolutely.

Michael: What's the big revelation here? Why haven't we gotten past it by now? Why are we unable to accept the finite nature of a life?

---

[2] Lu, D. & Yourish, K. (2020). The Turnover at the Top of the Trump Administration. *The New York Times.* https://www.nytimes.com/interactive/2018/03/16/us/politics/all-the-major-firings-and-resignations-in-trump-administration.html.

Sheldon: A great question. That's where Ernest Becker comes in. In 1973, he wins a Pulitzer Prize, ironically, a few weeks after he died, for the book *The Denial of Death*.[3] Becker argued that this is the central cog in humankind's psychological apparatus. As he put it, if we're genuinely interested in understanding why people do what they do, we need to understand two things: one is that, in many ways, we're not any different from any other living creatures. We're the products of evolution, and we're exquisitely designed over millions of years to persist at all costs. So, fundamental to Darwin's ideas is that all living things share a basic biological predisposition toward self-preservation. We want to survive. Living things like to stay alive. And I like that because, in most places, that's a relatively noncontroversial assumption.

Michael: If a lion is going to attack the wildebeest, the wildebeest is going to run. And same thing with us.

Sheldon: Absolutely. That then raises the question of how are we distinctly and uniquely different? And Becker points out that we're "smarter." Let me note that intelligence is vastly overrated, unless it's complemented by a host of moral and ethical sensibilities that we seem to, at times, be lacking. But Becker's point is, we've got this enormous forebrain. It gives us the capacity to think abstractly and symbolically to the point where we can literally imagine things that don't yet exist, and then we have the audacity to take our dreams and render them into reality.

Michael: We have the ability to communicate complex ideas.

Sheldon: Absolutely.

Michael: So, I could say, "Hey, Sheldon, I was down at the river this morning and I saw a lion. Don't go there cause you're going to die."

Sheldon: Absolutely. It is profoundly adaptive to be able to speak symbolically, to be able to reflect on past events that help us anticipate the future. And all of this for Becker is bound up with the fact that we're so smart, and as Kierkegaard noticed, that we actually realize that we exist. A lot of people think, "Well duh, obviously we know that we're here." But

---

[3] Becker, E. (1973). *The Denial of Death*. Free Press.

Kierkegaard's point is that we take self-awareness for granted because that's our default cognitive apparatus. You wake up in the morning and can say to yourself, "I woke up." You're walking to work and you say, "Here I am walking to work."

Michael: Well, worse, you're thinking about your awful boss. You're thinking about getting your kids to school. You're thinking about how you want to stay in and sleep. You're thinking about everything else *but* your existence.

Sheldon: That's quite correct. And Kierkegaard's point was, very simply, it takes a ridiculously sophisticated cognitive apparatus to make yourself the object of your own subjective inquiry. English translation: rose bushes are here, but they don't know it.

Michael: Well, what about my dog? My dog has emotions.

Sheldon: Yes. Dogs are unique, and we may have to come back and do another session just on them. But basically they were savvy wolves a couple hundred thousand years ago feeling, "God, I'm cold and hungry. I'm going to hang out with these primates and hope that they'll give me a bone." But dogs in the wild, I would insist, have no idea of their own existence.

Michael: Molly, my dog, doesn't know she's going to die.

Sheldon: That's correct. At least in circumstances where she's not directly threatened.

Michael: Right, that's an instinctive thing.

Sheldon: Absolutely.

Michael: Every animal has that instinct to fight or flee. "I'm going to run, or I'm going to push back."

Sheldon: The question is, "So what?" And Kierkegaard says, "Look, if you're smart enough to know that you're here, that's both exhilarating and terrifying. It's exhilarating to be alive and to know it." I try to emphasize that to myself all the time, in part to remind myself how grateful I am to wallow in the spontaneous exuberance of life itself. It's art.

Michael: I keep relating this to my dog because she's twelve. My wife, who loves her way more than me and for good reason, is already mourning her death. Now, Molly is perfectly healthy. She's vibrant. She jumps. She could be six. But my wife is already anticipating mourning her. She can even make herself depressed by thinking about our dog's mortality.

Sheldon: That's it. Psychologically, that's the crux of the matter. Because it's not only that we realize we will someday die. We realize that we can die at any time, for reasons that we can't anticipate or control.

Betty: And what your wife is doing, Michael, is protecting herself by inserting herself into the imaginary future of your dog's inevitable demise. By mourning Molly now, she protects herself; even though this also destroys her in-the-moment enjoyment of Molly's healthy existence. And that is what Sheldon seems to be saying—by fearing the inevitable, we truncate our present to protect ourselves against this terror of nonexistence. Gets back to Kierkegaard.

Sheldon: Sure does.

Michael: And maybe it partially explains the culture that we then create to deny our nonexistence?

Sheldon: That would be Becker's point. If death is all we thought about, we all would literally be paralyzed with a debilitating existential terror. What if all our thoughts were, "I'm going to die. I could walk outside and get hit by a comet. I'm just a breathing piece of defecating meat"? You would be cowering under the table, a twitching blob of biological protoplasm, yearning for large sedatives. But most of us are able to stand up and walk around every day. How do we do so? The answer is culture.

What Becker hypothesizes is, what our ancestors did very cleverly, although quite unconsciously, is to develop views of the world, cultural worldviews that are beliefs about the nature of reality that we share with people in our group. This reduces death anxiety by giving us each a sense that life has meaning and that we have value. And this, in turn, gives us a gateway to immortality, either literally, through the heavens and afterlives of the world's great religions, or symbolically, as the ancient Greeks told us, "You may know you're not going to be here forever, but you're comforted by the prospect that some aspect of you will persist, nonetheless." Maybe this is from having kids, maybe from writing a book, maybe from doing a great podcast.

Michael: It's like the old Woody Allen joke: "I don't want to live on through my work."

Sheldon: Yes, I want to live on by not dying. So, obviously the preferred form of immortality would be to not die in the first place. But the critical point here is, according to Becker, what we humans do to manage the existential terror that comes from the uniquely human awareness of death, is that we envelop ourselves; we embrace cultural worldviews that tell us what life means and what we're supposed to do while we're here. These worldviews enable us to feel good about ourselves by meeting or exceeding the standards of value associated with the social roles that we inhabit.

Michael: All right. So let me shift gears a little bit. We've now established, at least in these writings, the notion that we are aware of our death, and that this does certain things to us. As a response, we create all manner of cultures. That culture can be Christianity; it can be Islam; it can be Hinduism or Judaism—and it can be nationhood, right?

Sheldon: Absolutely right.

Michael: It does not need to be religion. It can be anything that makes sense of the universe and gives us a place in it. So, it can be nationalism.

Sheldon: Absolutely.

Michael: What happens to us, and how do you measure what you call "mortality salience"? What is *mortality salience* and what happens to us when we're reminded of our death?

Sheldon: Great question. First, let's back up for a second. Becker wins a Pulitzer Prize, and he couldn't get a job as an academic. People said, "You're an amusing clown. You're an entertaining lecturer. These ideas are just speculative nonsense." They're soft. They come from existential philosophy and psychoanalysis. There's no evidence for them, nor can there be. And here's where we egghead experimental social psychologists come in. We wrote a paper about Becker. We said, "These ideas are important." We sent it to *American Psychologist*. It was rejected with this one-line review: "I have no doubt that these ideas are of no interest whatsoever to any psychologists, alive or dead." Now, we're like, "Wow!"

Michael: How old were you when you got that?

Sheldon: We were in our early thirties. But being brash, we approached the editor at a conference. I had a drink with one of those little umbrellas in it. Braced by ethanol-infused beverages, I said "Dude, you know, you should publish our paper." And he's like, "That's 'Doctor Dude' to you. Show some respect." He adds, "You guys should get some evidence." To his credit, he granted, "Look, these are interesting ideas, but no academic psychologist in North America or Europe will take you seriously until you can prove it in the traditional sense of the word." And so that's what we did; we came up with a very simple paradigm. And unfortunately, this is a discredit to the profession of psychology, but you have to have jargon for everything. So we thought, "Okay, let's see if Becker's right. If his argument—that your beliefs about reality serve to minimize death anxiety—has merit, then let's see what happens if we bring people into the lab and we remind some of them that they're going to die and others of something unpleasant, but not fatal. Like, you have your leg cut off in an accident. You need a root canal on your teeth. You failed an exam."

Our view is "Okay, Becker's right. When you're reminded that you're going to die, you should cling more tenaciously to your cultural belief system." And we should be able to detect that by measuring your reactions, either to people who share your beliefs, or people who are opposed to them, or people with beliefs merely different from them.

Michael: So you're measuring what people believe, if confronted with their death?

Sheldon: That's right.

Michael: Facing death, people will respond to someone outside their group differently than to someone within their cultural group.

Sheldon: Yes, that's better. I like how you put it. You will like and support people in the in-group and you will hate and harm people in the out-group.

Betty: Under threat of death?

Sheldon: That's correct. When existential threats are aroused. Now the question is, "All right, now, how do we do that?" The answer is, we create jargon. We're going to call that *mortality salience*. That's just a fancy phrase for reminding you that you're going to die.

Sometimes we do it in a pretty straightforward fashion. We bring people into the lab. We give them a little questionnaire. And one of the questions is "Write down your thoughts and feelings about your own death or write down your thoughts and feelings about being in pain." At other times, we go outside the lab. We stop people in front of a funeral parlor, and we stop others 100 yards to either side. Again, the logic is, "Well, if you're in front of a funeral parlor, death might be on your mind. But you might not even know it." And then the most subtle paradigm we use involves subliminal death prompts. I have you come to my office at Skidmore to read your email. And while you're doing that, we flash the word "death" on-screen for 48 milliseconds, so fast that you don't even know that death is on your mind.

Michael: So just standing in front of a funeral parlor is enough?

Sheldon: That is correct. These effects are incredibly subtle. And for them to happen, you need not know that death is on your mind. One of the very first studies we did was in Arizona. We had Christian participants. They were either reminded that they were going to die or told to think about something unpleasant. And then we asked them to rate other students in the room. The class consisted of those who identified as coming from Christian families and some who identified as coming from Jewish families. All we wanted to see was whether or not their impressions of people varied as a function of their religion, depending upon whether death was on their minds. And the results?

First, the good news. In the control condition, the Christian participants rated the Jewish and Christian students equally, thus restoring my faith in humanity, if only momentarily. On the other hand, when they were reminded of their mortality, they liked fellow Christians a lot more, and they hated the Jews. And this has nothing to do with Christianity. To be silly, the five Jewish people who live in Arizona were busy that day, so we couldn't do that experiment. But over in Israel, if you remind Jewish people they're going to die, they love Jewish people and they hate Arabs and Christians, and so on.

Betty: So, the more extreme the situation you put yourself in—such as "your death is imminent"—the more polarized you become in your beliefs?

Sheldon: That's correct. And it will lead to innumerable potential reactions. It's not only about attitudes. For instance, when German people are reminded that they're going to die, they sit closer to people who look like they're German and they sit farther away from people who look like they're immigrants. When Iranians are reminded that they're going to die, they become more supportive of suicide bombers and more willing to become one. Americans are more pragmatic. We're not going to blow ourselves up, but we're happy to blow up other people. So when we remind Americans of their mortality, they become more supportive of the preemptive use of nuclear, biological, and chemical weapons.

Michael: And you did these experiments with judges, too?

Sheldon: That's correct.

Michael: And that one blew my mind.

Sheldon: It should. Astonishing. This was actually the first study, Michael. We reminded municipal court judges of their mortality. And then we asked them to set a bond for an alleged prostitute. And in the control condition when we didn't subtly suggest their mortality, the bond was 50 dollars, which was the typical bond at the time. After being reminded of death, the judges set an average bond of over 450 dollars. And why this is striking is that judges are trained to administer the law in a fair and dispassionate way. When we told the judges what we had done, they responded, "There is no way your stupid questionnaire could have influenced our judgment."

Michael: Because I'm a rational person.

Sheldon: Because I'm a rational person.

Betty: This is also where the legal system, and the rest of us, take for granted that the prefrontal cortex, the thinking brain, is a more powerful operating system than the evolutionary brain, or the midbrain. And I don't think any of us really understand how powerful the evolutionary brain or the primal brain is.

Sheldon: Well put, Betty. And of course, Daniel Kahneman, the great Nobel Prize–winning psychologist at Princeton, makes this point. He posits that there are two systems. One is rational and reflective: "I'm going to step back and think about things." But that's not our default mental state. We occasionally lapse into rationality and coherence, but for the most part, we are quite driven by limbic and midbrain processes.

Michael: So we are not ruled by the intellectual, but rather the emotional.

Sheldon: Absolutely.

Michael: Right, it's not that you're sitting here like we are, with headsets and microphones and having this nice intellectual chat about it. You experience it as a physical thing.

Sheldon: Oh, absolutely. When I was here in Manhattan on September 11, 2001—I was at Brooklyn College at the time and saw the Twin Towers go down—I was deeply shaken: "People are dying." Even those of us who purport to be dispassionate scientists trying to figure out the so-called truth, when push comes to shove, as Nietzsche put it, we're all too human.

Michael: Do you feel that these ideas about Terror Management Theory and how we deal with our mortality have a direct relationship to understanding Donald Trump, Trumpism, and the moment we live in right now?

Sheldon: Trump comes down the escalator in 2015 with all the rental humans supposedly cheering him on and declares immigrants, specifically Mexicans and Muslims, to be drug dealers and rapists. And this doesn't make me a savant, but I turned to my family, and I said, "He's going to win."

Michael: Why? Every media outlet at that point was saying, "We're not going to cover him because he's a joke."

Sheldon: Everyone. Because that was the same thing that people said about Hitler. Then people got to know Trump a little better. Most people in New York were saying that Trump is a vulgar, sadistic, vindictive, pathologically narcissistic, sociopathic, misogynistic, racist, xenophobic, functionally illiterate, Twittering Mussolini Cheez Doodle impersonator. And there's no ambiguity about that. To many of us, this guy was appalling as well as grotesquely ignorant.

Michael: And who in their right mind is going to fall for that?

Sheldon: That's right. And with no disrespect to the people who did fall for it because we're all human. They were not in their "thinking" minds, as it were.

Betty: So we need to give more respect to the evolutionary brain.

Sheldon: That's correct. I think Hillary Clinton was unfortunate when she said these folks are "deplorables." They may have been wrong and are lamentable in some ways, in that I now hold them more accountable than others for our current malaise. But 2016 was not the same as 2001 because nobody had literally attacked us. What Trump did masterfully was to create threats or magnify them. "There are immigrants storming the southern border. There are Islamic terrorists who are going to parachute into Buffalo and rape our daughters and eat our chicken wings. And China is raping us." And his point was that we are weak.

He appeals to a segment of the American population that is no longer able to subscribe to the American dream. We all need a compelling narrative, and for a large chunk of Americans, white guys after World War II, those were the golden days. If you had a high school education, you could get a well-paying job. Your kids could go to college. You could have a boat and a car and so on. And life was good.

Michael: And going back to Terror Management Theory, the culture reinforces all that in the Cold War and in the arms race.

Sheldon: That's right.

Michael: And in the midst of that, there is a narrative of nationalism—America, God, and country.

Sheldon: I'm going to make America great again. And so Trump did what all populist leaders do: you turn existential fear into rage. And you direct that rage toward an external enemy: immigrants, Muslims, Chinese people. And, having defined the threat externally, you then come back and say, "I am the only one who can keep you safe."

Michael: I'm going to play a speech that Donald Trump gave in Ohio in 2016 about terrorism.

[AUDIO]

> **Donald Trump:** *It's great to be with you this afternoon. And today we begin a conversation about how to make America safe again. In the 20th century, the United States has defeated fascism, Nazism, and communism. Now a different threat challenges our world. Radical Islamic terrorism. This summer, there's been an ISIS attack launched outside the war zones of the Middle East. Hard to believe every eighty-four hours. Here in America, we have seen one brutal attack after another. Thirteen were murdered and 38 wounded in the assault on Fort Hood. The Boston Marathon bombing wounded and maimed 264 people and ultimately left 5 dead, including 2 of our great police officers. In Chattanooga, Tennessee, 5 unarmed marines, unbelievable people, by the way, were shot and killed at a military recruiting center. Last December, 14 innocent Americans were gunned down at an office party in San Bernardino. Another 22 were very gravely injured. In June, 49 Americans were executed at the Pulse nightclub in Orlando. Another 53 were badly injured. It was the worst mass shooting in our history. And the attack by far the worst on the LGBTQ community. And I'll tell you what. We can never, ever allow this to happen again.*

Michael: The speech goes on for another five minutes. A long laundry list of attacks. So, what's the point of doing that?

Sheldon: Well, two points. One is that he's exploiting a very common kind of mental bug, if you will, that Daniel Kahneman identified. It's called the *availability heuristic.* Basically, you bring an Islamic terrorist attack to mind. And second is the *representativeness heuristic.* By citing a particular event, you swap baseline information. An immigrant or an Islamic person killed somebody. That's bad. But that fact can only be rationally interpreted relative to baseline information. English translation, "It's terrible when anybody gets killed. All right, but the most common way of dying in America is falling in your bathtub." If your real interest is in preventing tragedies, then we'd be adding nonstick bottoms to our bathtub. I'm being silly, right?

But not really. What Trump does, and he does it every time, is talk about how an immigrant killed an innocent person. And the next thing you know is that he suggests that all immigrants are killers.

Michael: An immigrant killed this innocent person.

Sheldon: And therefore, all immigrants are killers.

Newt Gingrich said it perfectly during the Republican National Convention when Trump was nominated. Gingrich was being interviewed on national television and he started blabbering about rampant crime in America and Trump is going to come in and make the world safer. And the interviewer corrected him and said, "No, wait a minute. Violent crime is actually down." And Gingrich said, "No, it's up in Chicago." And she said, "Yeah it's up in some places, but it's actually as low as it's been in a long time." And then Newt said, "Well, you know, you liberals, you're hung up on facts, and we're more concerned about how people are feeling. And I'm telling you that people are feeling threatened. And as a politician, I'll take feelings over facts any time." Of course, he's being cynical, but he is absolutely correct, except for not pointing out that they are the ones creating the fear in the first place.

Michael: Do you think that it's manipulative?

Sheldon: Oh, absolutely, in my estimation. Because, back to Trump for a minute, we did the same studies in 2015 and 2016 that we did in 2003 and 2004 (where we demonstrated that death reminders increased support for charismatic leaders in general and President George W. Bush in particular) with the same outcome. American respondents preferred Hillary Clinton to

Donald Trump in a benign state of mind. But if they were reminded of their mortality first, then their affection for Trump and their stated intentions to vote for him, increased dramatically.

Michael: Hence, the strategy of warning that the barbarians are coming to rape and pillage.

Sheldon: Absolutely. Because what we also found in other studies is that when we asked people to imagine a mosque being built in their town or an immigrant moving into their neighborhood, that brought death thoughts more readily to mind and that, in turn, increased support for Trump. Think about this for a moment: just being asked to think about immigrants coming to your neighborhood or a mosque being built in your town is sufficient to bump up support for President Trump.

Betty: What scares me about this is that it is a recipe that works.

Sheldon: It does.

Betty: We can't change the uncertainty of our times: climate change, globalization, the Internet age. It's a really complicated time. And jobs have gone overseas because it's been too expensive to maintain the industries we had that would keep people employed in the Rust Belt. And there is the shadow of 9/11 upon us, which introduced an actual threat to our homeland. Homeland Security was created then. How do you keep people focused on facts—say about the actual number of immigrants who are drug dealers, rapists, and murderers? Because obviously you can't deny people their emotions. And they do drive us. How do we disrupt such reactivity and encourage more reflection?

Sheldon: Whoever can answer those questions is worthy of a Nobel Prize. But I see no harm in at least delineating the scope of the problem. Eric Hoffer wrote a book called *The True Believer* in 1951.[4] He pointed out that once you have a group of people devoted to a populist leader, a "fact-proof screen" develops between the supporters and their leader. If you think that

---

[4] Hoffer, E. (1951/2010). *The True Believer: Thoughts on the nature of mass movements.* Harper & Row.

you're going to get anywhere by appealing to facts, you're sadly mistaken. Hoffer would say, "Look, if you have two politicians and one is a populist leader spewing slogans and the other is a thoughtful and able, effective leader who has actual policies, you're doomed because you're going to be putting out complex and sophisticated arguments and position papers and the populist is going to lock her up, build a wall, and make America great again."

Michael: The paradigm becomes: Republicans stand up and say, "You are special."

Sheldon: That's right.

Michael: And the Democrats stand up and say, "I am competent."

Sheldon: That's correct.

Michael: The Democrats' messaging is terrible. Competence will rarely move you in the same way as "you are a special person, and you are under assault. And I am going to protect you and preserve your specialness." You said the following: "Trumpism is a new world view and supporters' self-esteem is bolstered by belonging to it."

Sheldon: Absolutely.

Michael: And supporting the sacred mission it promotes. Mr. Trump's supporters now have something to live for.

Betty: And in the face of uncertain times, when people feel really beleaguered and pressured by uncontrollable circumstances, what is real? It's real enough that Trump's slogan gave his followers something to believe in and live for. That part is real. But then what? How do we stop superseding reality with these imagined nonfactual slogans?

Sheldon: It's going to take a lot.

Michael: Well it's going to take a leader on the other side who offers a better, more powerful story.

Sheldon: Precisely. And so we're going to need a very special kind of human who, on the one hand, can step back and reflect on what's happening. But it also can't be an academic egghead like me who wouldn't be able to get up in front of a crowd of Trump supporters and convince them by this kind of discourse.

Michael: We're really only speaking to ourselves, preaching to the choir, at this point.

Sheldon: Although the fact is, my first talk about the George Bush studies was in Wasilla, Alaska, where Sarah Palin had just been elected mayor. And it was a largely conservative audience. But these were real conservatives because they were pissed until I started showing them data. And then they began to see that reminding people that they're going to die, increases support for Bush.

Michael: Well, on the left, they certainly feel the mortality salience of Trump.

Sheldon: Absolutely. And Betty, you make that point that it's easy to say, "Okay, I get it. The Trump supporters tend to be blue collar white people whose world view was shattered by modernity. All right, but what about those of us who didn't vote for Trump?" Well, our progressive worldview was ground into dust because here we are naively, even if well-intentioned, subscribing to the Enlightenment tradition that people can be rational, that democratic outcomes can be decided by deliberations.

Michael: And that time leads to progress.

Sheldon: Exactly. And that's really a huge point. That's correct.

There's a philosopher in England, John Gray, and he basically says, "Look, this is the Enlightenment idea. Progress is just a de-theistic version of Christianity, where at the end of the road, things will inevitably be better." And while that was true for most of American history, it surely is no longer true.

Michael: And Trumpism confronts you in that same way.

Sheldon: That's exactly right.

Michael: It confronts you with your mortality. It is...

Betty: The end.

Michael: Well, it is much like putting a Jew in a cathedral and saying, "Okay well, what are we going to do with this narrative that doesn't accept Christ as savior, in immortality, and heaven as a path to it?" Trump is like that person sitting smack dab next to me saying, "The story that you tell about yourself and your culture is now challenged and wrong."

Betty: And I have a lot of patients who are in chaos, for want of a better word. The systems that they believed in and that they operate under have been thrown into chaos. How did this come to pass? And they want to become anarchists. And they know that they can't. But they struggle internally with this.

Sheldon: Well, it's a tough one. And I think you've both identified where we now stand and why it's such a vulnerable moment, because we're surrounded by mortality salience. This is why we're in an escalating cycle of perseverating problems—death is in the air. And, so, you have the Trump people clinging to Trump who has no trouble denigrating anyone who doesn't believe in him.

Michael: Well, every single utterance out of him is "we're going to die if you don't do what I say."

Sheldon: But apropos of Betty's point, here we are on the other side of things, reminded of our mortality. And it becomes all too easy, myself included, to then just denigrate reflexively the people who support Trump.

Betty: So we're devolving into an "us versus them" culture.

Sheldon: I think it was Martin Luther King who said, "An eye for an eye makes us all blind."

Michael: Right now, politics does seem to be about two bare-fisted fighters in a ring going at each other with no bell to call the end of a round. And the fuel to the fight is made up of immediate and constant reminders in our culture of our death. And that seems to be the driver for you.

Sheldon: You know, I think it is.

Betty: When I read your paper and thought about your work, Sheldon, I was astounded. I felt like I have been naive with my faith in facts and my faith in reason. I have become more aware that I am not driven by my knowledge alone, but also my feelings and faith in reason. We are obviously driven by emotions like fear, and we need to pay more attention to that.

Michael: Yes, exactly. What we didn't get a chance to talk about yet is the environmental crisis.

Betty: There's definitely mortality salience in that.

Michael: Right, the mortality salience of climate change. The environmental crisis delivers the same kind of existential threat to those of us on the left that the immigration crisis creates for those on the right. We had analyst Tom Singer on the show, and he talked about climate change denial as behaving as a kind of psychological wall.

Sheldon: I couldn't agree more. That's what we're doing now, empirically. And the only difference is, we are about twelve years away from climate disasters that will make Godzilla movies look like Mary Poppins.

Betty: Which will increase the immigration crisis—and crises of all kinds.

Michael: Maybe you can join us in a couple of months on an episode titled, "Death and the Environment, the sequel."

Betty: That happy tale. Thank you very much, Sheldon Solomon, for your most provocative and enlightening insights.

Chapter 3
Ambiguous Loss & the 2020 Pandemic

Guest: Pauline Boss
Episode aired: September 16, 2020

Dr. Pauline Boss is professor emeritus at the University of Minnesota and a fellow in the American Psychological Association and the American Association for Marriage and Family Therapy. Dr. Boss coined the term "ambiguous loss" in the 1970s and is the foremost expert on the topic. She authored the widely acclaimed Ambiguous Loss: Learning to Live with Unresolved Grief. *At the end of 2021, she released* The Myth of Closure: Ambiguous Loss in a Time of Pandemic and Change, *a book about ambiguous loss in the context of the COVID-19 pandemic.*

Our conversation with Dr. Boss was posted on September 16, 2020, about six months into the pandemic, and during a period when, across the United States, airlines had reduced their volume of flights, schools and institutions closed, and in-person group events and gatherings were discouraged or canceled. Almost overnight, video-conferencing platforms like Zoom, typically used in corporate work settings, became ubiquitous tools not only for businesses, but also for schools, universities, and medical providers as well as for families and social gatherings. In many states, due to the absence of a COVID-19 vaccine or any medication effective for treating its symptoms, mask-wearing in public spaces was mandated. It was not until early 2021 when a working vaccine became widely available in the U.S. By January 2021, due to the coronavirus, the country had a total death toll of more than 432,000.

Currently, in 2023, while a working vaccine and medications like Paxlovid vastly reduce the most harmful consequences of COVID-19, American citizens continue to struggle with the disruptions a positive COVID test can bring. We have only begun to reckon with the permanent losses of loved ones, milestone celebrations, key social interactions, professional opportunities, educational lags, and a sense of security in how we regulate our public health.

Interview

Betty: This week, we're talking about ambiguous loss, which is a perfect topic for us on *Mind of State*, because it has to do with both mind and state. On the mind side of things, loss is something that everybody's grappling with in this pandemic—we are losing ways of life, losing events, losing contact—but in a very ambiguous, or indirect way.

Jonathan: On the political side, ambiguous loss is also an apt topic for this moment. On the one hand, we're in election season right now, where it's all black and white; there are only extremes, and there's no room anymore for conversation about ambiguous or nuanced topics in politics and loss in the political space. We're dealing with a lot of loss—loss of jobs, loss of lives, loss of the ability to congregate in common spaces, where we would talk about our ideas for improving public health and civic life. So ambiguous loss in a political context is rich.

But first, I think, Dr. Boss, it's important for us to start with asking, how do you define ambiguous loss?

Pauline Boss: It has a simple definition. It's simply an unclear loss that has no verification. There's no death certificate. There's no evidence of a body—there's no proof. And so, it's an unclear loss, an abstract loss. And there are two different kinds—the first is physical. That's the first kind of ambiguous loss I studied in the 1970s, with families of soldiers missing in action in Vietnam. Soldiers were physically missing but kept psychologically present because their families didn't know whether they were coming back or not. Sometimes they did return, yet most of the time they did not.

The second kind of ambiguous loss—which I studied in the '90s—was present in families where a member had Alzheimer's disease. They were physically present, but psychologically absent because of dementia. And so this kind of uncanny loss, where there's a disconnect between knowing and not knowing, is more common than we think. The one thing about this theory is that people tend to almost immediately plug in their own ambiguous loss. And most of the time, they're absolutely right.

Jonathan: So ambiguous loss refers to circumstances where we're unable to have closure?

Pauline Boss: Yes, but I'm going to add a caveat. I don't like the word *closure* anymore. I think it's very cruel for people who have lost someone to talk about it in this way because we like to remember the people we've lost. We don't really close the door, but *closure* is a handy word that is unfortunately used too much. So I would rather say it this way—*ambiguous loss* is a loss that has no possibility of resolution.

Betty: Considering our current situation of being in the midst of a global pandemic, we thought it especially apt to talk with you about ambiguous loss in relation to everything that people are experiencing right now.

Pauline Boss: There are many ambiguous losses right now—it's overwhelming. First of all, we're facing an enemy, and we can't see it. We don't yet know enough about it to control it, so we've lost control over our own destiny. In a sense, we've also lost trust in the world, because the people who are supposed to be advising us and leading us—aren't. And so we're in a tailspin about what to do and who to trust. So that's loss of trust in the world, loss of faith in having our everyday connections, loss of gathering with the people we love, loss of going to big events like football games or concerts. Sometimes the losses are not ambiguous—that would be loss of finances, loss of your house, or something tangible. But many of the losses are more abstract, more ambiguous.

Betty: And the unknown is persistent—we thought in the spring that the pandemic and its constraints were temporary, but now they're not. We don't know when exactly this is going to end.

Pauline Boss: And that's ambiguous, too.

Betty: In the many decades of research and work you have done with people around ambiguous loss, how do you help people deal with such ambiguity and uncertainty?

Pauline Boss: There are ways to do so. But let me preface it by saying that the United States is a particularly mastery-oriented culture where we feel that the world is what they call "a just and fair place"—one where if we work hard enough, we can solve anything. Well, now we have a problem we can't solve as of yet, and we're very anxious about that. The uncertainty is driving people crazy. Some cultures are less mastery-oriented than we are, and they will—how can I say—roll with the waves more easily than we might. So because we are a culture that wants to solve problems—we'll put a person on the moon, a rover on Mars, etc. I don't want to denigrate that at all, but when we're faced with a problem that has no solution, I think we are particularly inept at dealing with it because of our culture.

Jonathan: It's a fascinating conflict, a fascinating tension that you're raising here. First of all, there are things that we can do, right? We might not have a vaccine, but we can wear masks. We can social distance. Yet I wonder, how do we tend to our daily lives while we're grappling with this ambiguity?

Pauline Boss: Well, two things. First, I think you have to find something you can control because being in control of our own destiny is essentially associated with sound mental health. We have to be able to control something, so we can control our external life right now. And perhaps that's why we have heard about so many people baking bread or doing meditation—or doing physical exercise or writing or something. They're cooking together as a family because there's a finality to that—you work for a couple hours and you have a beautiful outcome, a tasty outcome, or you have a better body for what you've been doing.

So we have to find something small that you can control. And, of course, meditation is in our control. Since you can't control the outside world right now, you can control your breathing and your inner self.

And the second thing is that we have to change our way of thinking. And that is, you can do more "both/and" thinking. You can find the middle ground. This is very un-American because I don't think we've been trained to do this. I've learned this primarily from Native Americans in northern Minnesota, and from my Asian colleagues. I don't use the term *dialectical thinking* with people I work with, but it has its roots in that.

So, you think about the situation, the stressor that's facing you in a nonbinary way. We say something .like, "this is terrible. This is both a terrible time in our history—and we may get stronger for it." Or you could say it more present tense: "This is terrible. I can't go out. I can't see my family—and we can gather together on Zoom and in other ways." So that nonbinary way of thinking will lower stress when you're stuck with uncertainty and ambiguity and when you can't change the situation you're facing.

Betty: Dr. Boss, what you're talking about is something I see a lot with my patients. I work with trauma survivors, and we often talk about externals being things you cannot control. But what we can control is our internal selves—and that's what we have jurisdiction over. What you say about cultivating a nonbinary way of thinking causes me to think about what is happening in politics—which is very polarized right now.

Pauline Boss: Yes.

Betty: The binary freezes us. Combating this kind of rigid thinking seems to apply not only to how we survive a pandemic, but also to how we survive our current state of politics. I wonder if opening our minds might lower our stress a bit.

Pauline Boss: I agree with you, and I think the answer is, yes. We have to find a middle ground. Before I dealt with ambiguous loss, people were saying people are either dead or alive. They can't be both—people are either here or gone. Well, actually yes, they *can* be both, when there's no proof of one thing or the other. In the mind's eye, they are "both/and."

And so when we have the politics of today, some are saying things are either "good" or "bad." And here's the one I like to focus on—you either win or you lose. You can't be both. Certainly, regarding human relationships, that's a very dysfunctional way of thinking. People in our lives are absent and present at the same time all the time. And in everyday life, as well as in more extreme and catastrophic situations, people are never 100 percent present or 100 percent absent. So giving it this extreme binary is very dysfunctional in human relationships, but I believe it's also dysfunctional in community and national relationships as well.

Jonathan: How do we make sense of the polarized nature of the response to the pandemic? Where some are embracing a full lockdown, social isolation—they are advocating for masks and shaming people if they don't wear a mask—and yet others express an extreme response in the opposite direction, saying, "Mask mandates are authoritarian tyranny that gets in the way of my ability to live my free life." It seems like we're not embracing the "yes/and" that you're suggesting.

Pauline Boss: No, they aren't. The people who have that absolute rigid feeling about masks are seeing one thing. They're seeing their liberty, their right to liberty and freedom—which I also value. But when you have an outside predator, in a virus that could harm so many people, we need to think not only of ourselves, but also of how we might do harm to our neighbor or the other person in our household. That takes a more mature way of thinking, or you could call it something else, some more empathic way of thinking. You're not just thinking about "my freedom, my way—I'm going to do it my way, others be damned"—versus saying, "I don't like to do this. I don't even feel good in a mask. I don't like to give up my freedom to breathe freely outdoors and to do what I want, but I will pay attention to it because I don't want to harm my other family members and my neighbors." Some people haven't gotten there yet.

Betty: This is my psychoanalytic lens, but I feel like when people feel that there's only one way to think about something, it's cutting something off.

Pauline Boss: It's a zero-sum game.

Betty: Yes, it's a zero-sum game with no other options. But there's something that's being avoided. I think people are avoiding—or in denial—about death because they're thinking, "I'm going to live. I'm going to live forever. I don't need a mask. This virus isn't going to defeat me." This is what some people protesting on the steps of state capitols declared earlier in the year.

You've said, "We are a nation founded on unresolved grief. As a result, we don't like to talk about death, and we don't like to talk about ambiguous loss." So there's something to this mask-wearing and the avoidance of it in some people. Maybe it's the avoidance of death itself that might be echoing. I wonder if you're seeing that, and if you can talk a little bit about how we are a nation founded on unresolved grief.

Pauline Boss: I think you're right. It's really a denial of loss. It's a denial of the possibility of loss. It's the denial of death, which Ernest Becker wrote about a long time ago in *The Denial of Death*.[1] Yes, I have written about our being a nation founded on unresolved grief. And I do still believe that. I got that idea first from historian Drew Gilpin Faust who wrote the book *This Republic of Suffering: Death in the American Civil War* in which she states that our nation is founded on the suffering of unresolved loss from the Civil War.[2] I agree with her—and I would go further and say it's not just the Civil War. It's what we did to the Native Americans when we first came to this land and uprooted them, if not tried to obliterate them. It's what we have done to slave families who were separated on the selling block, one from another.

If I can go even further, we're a nation of immigrants who have been separated from family members across the seas. This was before there were communication possibilities and airplanes to go back and forth, so that there is much unresolved loss in this nation that is never talked about, except now during COVID. And we could go into why it might have happened during this year of lockdown. Suddenly racial tensions come to the forefront with George Floyd's killing and what happened here in Minneapolis. It may be because we've been less distracted, having to stay at home all the time, that we suddenly are paying attention. I would confess, I was not previously aware of the unresolved losses that are coming to the fore right now. Black lives do matter. But it's clear that they haven't mattered. And there's been poverty that we haven't paid attention to. I've been astounded by how many people don't have healthcare—and so on.

So we're a nation that doesn't want to pay attention to loss. We like winners. We like to pay attention to winners. Even our TV shows are so often about the upper-middle-class—like *Downton Abbey*, how we love to see all those jewels and things. That's not how people live in this country now. And unfortunately, too many are living in poverty and without just the basic needs. And certainly Black Lives Matter is something that finally has been noticed as something that has to change.

Betty: I'm so glad that you mentioned the impact of our unresolved relationship to slavery and what Drew Faust talked about with the Civil War—the many unresolved traumas of American history, inclusive of the unacknowledged traumas of immigrants leaving their own traumas in

---

[1] Becker, E. (1973). *The Denial of Death.* The Free Press.
[2] Faust, D.G. (2008). *This Republic of Suffering: Death in the American Civil War.* Alfred A. Knopf.

homelands that forced them here, or the trauma of just leaving home and having to reestablish themselves in a wholly new place.

Pauline Boss: And it was traumatic. Did you know that the Irish girls who left to come and be maids in New York and other cities were given funerals before they left? They were at their own funerals, and they were told not to come back because it was too painful to say goodbye again. Ambiguous loss is often a traumatic loss. Trauma surrounds it. So, you have trauma plus uncertainty and ambiguity, which is immensely stressful for people. It immobilizes them.

Betty: Yes. Traumas echo or bring forth past traumas. It's so interesting to look back—just a few months of quarantine here in the United States brought forth a massive reaction to the George Floyd murder and this big referendum nationwide—and globally—on Black Lives Matter. As you said, all of these pressures were amplified because we were home with more focus on what's going on, and we also felt more of a direct impact because we were all suffering in our own ways, whether or not at the same pitch. Now that we are all destabilized like this, it seems like there's also an opportunity here.

Pauline Boss: Yes, I would add, in chaos there is opportunity. Before change can happen things have to shake up. Boy, are they shaking up right now. I'm an optimist—I don't see that as terrible, although it's terrible if people are dying and being killed, that's of course tragic. But having things unstable for a while means that change is afoot. Change is coming and hopefully it's change for the better.

Jonathan: Change brings to my mind the notion of the election. In November we're going to have the 2020 presidential election, arguably the most important election in our lifetimes. We often like to think of elections as a binary choice. It's either change or more of the same. Clearly, we're in such a tumultuous moment. But how do political leaders grapple with ambiguous loss in a world where politics is about the binary? It's about the black and white. It's about the zero-sum game.

Pauline Boss: I don't know that it is. Certainly, with our accountants and our banks, we want the binary. There are many places where we want the binary. In politics they always say you're either blue or red—you're this or that. But in the end, compromise is the only thing that makes the government work. They have to find the middle ground. And what we see now is they have not. And that brings about a stalemate, immobilization. So, it seems to me that, yes, when we go into the voting booth, we check one box or another. That's true. And that's binary. But when people legislate, when people govern, when people lead, when we parent our children, when we run a household, things are never black and—well, let me edit that. Things are *rarely* black and white. You have to make decisions that are in the gray area, and sometimes you see the good and the bad in the same location.

Jonathan: Right. So politics is all about the art of the compromise. But in the bumper sticker slogan, it's either say, Black Lives Matter or Blue Lives Matter. So our political discourse drives us to a binary, even if ultimately the good, smart, and deft politicians have to get us to compromise. I guess I wonder how politicians, how elected officials, as individuals, process ambiguous loss? And how might it translate to their ability or inability to lead with clarity?

Pauline Boss: You know, the first person I voted for was Eisenhower. I grew up as a child during the Roosevelt era. And, with Mr. Roosevelt, if you read about his life, he had one way of thinking, but his wife, who was not a quiet woman, had another way of thinking. And you get the idea that the binary was softened because of that kind of interaction. Now, bringing it up to today, or any time in more modern history, I like to look at politicians to see their humanity. Is it there? Can they shed a tear? Can they show empathy? Have they had personal experiences that have knocked them around a bit? And have they survived? How have they survived? Have they gotten harder, or have they gotten more open to differences?

I don't want to name names, but we can see the differences in the politicians today in how they live their own lives. I find that can be an extraordinarily valuable piece of information for how they will lead. If they have had tragedies and it hardened them, then they will be more binary thinkers, more black and white, more absolute. If they have had tragedy, if they have had trauma, and somehow have found resilience from it, then they'll be really good leaders because they've been through it. They know what suffering is. And so when they see it, they won't just turn their head away. A lot of our people are suffering. And our leaders have got to start seeing that.

Jonathan: I think they will. I think they do. I think that the compassion and the empathy that we're hearing from some elected officials and some would-be elected officials is getting a response from the American public that indicates that there's a need, there's a yearning, for that sort of compassion, that empathy.

Pauline Boss: Absolutely a hunger for it. And it must be, because governing is not just managing budgets and rebuilding roads and things like that. It's making life better for people. It's a human task for humanity to improve it, so you have to have that part.

Betty: In terms of the losses that we may or may not see our politicians expressing empathy with—be they losses due to the global pandemic, the economic crisis, the referendum on racial injustice, or all of the above—there seems to be, even before March 2020, here in the United States, this question about change embedded in the "Make America Great Again" slogan. In it, there is an underlying implication that we are different now. We want to go back to the way we were before, or we want to recapture the greatness we had before. And I want to know whether you have any thoughts on that in terms of this denial of loss—how you might see that being addressed in the "Make America Great Again" slogan.

Pauline Boss: For one thing, I love America. My father was an immigrant, and he flew the American flag every day of his life in front of the house. He came from Switzerland in the 1920s and never was able to go back for decades because of the Depression and World War II. So he was an immigrant by default, but such a patriot. He taught us that as well. But I feel that America is a democracy, and a democracy never reaches 100 percent perfection. It's a work in progress. And so we need to be careful about saying things like "make America great again." I think it was both—always great and always imperfect. Again "both/and"—but we need to change. In fact, I believe we're in a paradigm shift right now, which is very chaotic and painful and traumatic. And it's being exacerbated by COVID, by the pandemic and all the other things that have surfaced during this pandemic. The Black Lives Matter issue, the poverty issue, the lack of healthcare issue, the economic crisis, the systemic racism that has caused so many inequities in our systems.

So suddenly we're in chaos and a mess. But that is what happens in a paradigm shift. And you can't be thinking in binaries—that this is good or bad. It's bad because there are many deaths. There is suffering. Children are not getting enough food. It is good because it may bring about change, and change is needed. But first, we have to understand why we have this denial of death and loss before any good change will happen. And this is a country that's had its head in the sand about loss, about trauma, about unresolved losses. We need to face them and do some reconciliation about them. We need to acknowledge those losses from long, long ago.

Jonathan: It sounds like what you're saying is—look, we've got a multigenerational grappling with ambiguous loss and that we were founded, in fact, on grief …

Pauline Boss: That's right. Unresolved grief.

Jonathan: Do you think that ambiguous loss is baked into the American DNA? It was written in the founding documents that we are in pursuit of a more perfect union. We recognize that we are never fully resolved.

Pauline Boss: That's right.

Jonathan: And so is it baked into our DNA? And if so, if we seek to exert control over our lives, how do we wrestle with something that is part of our DNA?

Pauline Boss: I think we have to both value and acknowledge it, that it may need to change now and then. Our reaction to this Constitution that we have—which I think is unbelievably wonderful—we have to change our reaction to it, our interpretation, every now and then. Mostly, we've been sailing along for quite a while. We had a paradigm shift in World War II. We had a paradigm shift in the 1960s. And with the women's movement, we had some paradigm shifts that perked up at the turn of the century and then again, in the '60s, '70s, and maybe now, regarding the #MeToo movement. We have to be more acknowledging of the need for change on all these different fronts and come together as a community, as a nation, instead of always seeing what it is in it for me. Yes, our Constitution is, I believe, the only one based on the individual. I like that we are big on individualism here, but we also need to balance it with paying attention to our neighbor.

Betty: How would you say we need to reckon with our losses in order to be more collective? How can we own the head-in-the-sand thinking that you spoke about earlier? It can self-perpetuate, meaning the more you stick your head in the sand, the more you don't want to pull it out.

Pauline Boss: That's right.

Betty: This seems to be a time where we can't ignore our losses—due to the pandemic, economic crisis, and racial injustice. This is all telling us something; it's reflecting something back to us. And it seems accurate to say that it's telling us we have to deal with our losses, and we have to deal with all that we lose—and all that we have lost. We're not just winners—nor can we be a binary state. No government can. So how do we deal with what's been cut off for so long?

Pauline Boss: I think we have to start at home. I think we have to start with ourselves, review our own losses. Clinically sometimes I use symbols like river rocks, little stones that I've collected, and the person will put them on the floor to represent the losses they have had since they can first remember, the losses that really stick with them. And sometimes that line of pebbles and stones gets really long. We have to acknowledge the losses we have had since childhood that have shaped us, and many of those are unresolved. And by the way, I've found out that for some people, the loss of a pet belongs in that string of losses as well. It could also be the loss of a home. It could be loss of something abstract that you loved. Everybody should face their own losses and then talk about them with their intimates, either their family or friends, whoever is important to them, share them with someone else. Don't keep them to yourself. Share them with a therapist. Try to resolve your own losses, so they don't impinge on your feelings about the larger community because that's what's stuck in all of us, our own unresolved losses. We don't see it, and we certainly don't see it on a larger scale if we can't see it on our personal scale.

Jonathan: Do you think our political leaders are capable of leading us on that exploration, on leading us through that reckoning and that reconciliation with loss?

Pauline Boss: That may be above my expertise just to answer that. I think the leaders we have who have done that reckoning in their own lives and, frequently, if you read their books and so on, you can tell who has and who hasn't. If they haven't done that kind of reckoning about their own personal losses and haven't dealt with them—I don't mean, by the way, closure. I don't believe in closure. That they have reckoned with and acknowledge their own losses and their feelings about it and are able to hold the "both/and" in their mind. There, my loved one is gone, but I still remember them. They can carry on with their life without being stuck and without having that chip on their shoulder. Then, I think those are the leaders that can bring us forward. What I'm saying is, read their book and watch their movements, watch how they interact with people, and you will see who the leaders are who can take us out of this thicket that we're in. There has been great loss. We see in the papers every day how much loss there is. And the numbers are going up worldwide and also in the United States. And, you know, the financial losses, the losses of jobs, the losses of business, the losses of all of these things are just monumental. So we need a leader who understands loss.

Jonathan: An empathetic leader for sure.

Pauline Boss: Yes.

Betty: One thing that I would say about this is that we as citizens can ask this of ourselves—to reckon with loss—and ask this of our politicians, to see if they can, as people, reckon with their own losses and then help us reckon with ours—as a society.

Pauline Boss: Yes, it has to start at the bottom.

Betty: That makes sense. It seems doable, which is key. Because so much of what I see in the clinical room is that people feel overwhelmed with the monumental nature of what they don't have control over.

Pauline Boss: Right. Right.

Betty: One last question, Dr. Boss—I often hear from patients that they don't want to reckon with loss because it's so painful.

Pauline Boss: It *is* painful.

Betty: However, what I know from experience and what I also hear you saying is that when a person talks to somebody about their losses, they don't isolate them. They open them up, and so therefore, their burden is shared.

Pauline Boss: That's right.

Betty: So, for those listening who really are grappling with losses and don't want to turn toward their losses because they find it too severely painful, what would you say is the function of reckoning with loss? Does it put it to rest?

Pauline Boss: No.

Betty: Does it give it some space?

Pauline Boss: It doesn't put it to rest. The research shows now that there will be ups and downs, that you will learn to live with loss. You don't get over it. There is no closure. There is no ending to it. What you're hoping to do, if I can use a less therapeutic word, you're learning to manage the pain of loss over time, and that now and then it will still rear its painful suffering. Let's say there's an anniversary or there's—if you lost a child—a time when they would have graduated, their class is all together and they're not there. Those kinds of things bring back pain again, and that is normal grief.

The other thing the public does not know is what's normal and what's abnormal. We cannot pathologize sadness and grief. There's a big difference between sadness and depression, and not all grief is depression. The minority of people who are grieving are depressed in a clinical sense. The majority of people are sad. And the intervention, the treatment for sadness, is human connection. So, you need to tell your story to someone else. It could be a friend, a family member, or a therapist, or you could write it. You need to tell your story to someone else. Your story of loss. Painful as that is. It is more painful not to tell your story.

Jonathan: And human connection in this time of COVID, with social distance, is all the more challenging. But, as we have shown here, whether it's over Zoom or phone or with masks and at social distance, we can still connect and we can still have conversations and we can still share. Dr. Boss, thank you so much for joining us. It's been a pleasure. We've learned a lot and I hope our listeners have too.

Pauline Boss: Thank you. It was my pleasure too.

Chapter 4
Our Collective Trauma

Guest: Judith Herman
Aired: February 17, 2021

Dr. Judith Herman is a professor of psychiatry at Harvard Medical School. For thirty years, she was the director of training at the Victims of Violence Program at Cambridge Hospital in Massachusetts. She is the author of two award-winning books, Trauma and Recovery: The Aftermath of Violence—from Domestic Abuse to Political Terror *and* Father-Daughter Incest, *both are seminal to the field of trauma-informed mental health treatment and continue to be foundational texts in university and trauma clinics nationally and internationally. Her most recent book is* Truth and Repair: How Trauma Survivors Envision Justice.

When we spoke with Dr. Herman in February of 2021, much was astir in the U.S. Eleven months after the country went into lockdown to prevent the spread of the COVID-19 virus, working vaccines had been developed by pharmaceutical companies Moderna and Pfizer and were being administered across the country. While Joe Biden had begun his first month as president, the country was still reeling from the impact of the January 6, 2021, siege on the U.S. Capitol, when over 2,000 Trump supporters, encouraged by Trump's false assertions that the 2020 U.S. presidential election had been stolen from him, attacked a joint session of Congress to prevent ratification of Joe Biden's election. On January 13, 2021, one week before he was to leave office, Donald Trump was again impeached by the House of Representatives, this time for inciting insurrection. This was just thirteen months after he was first impeached in December 2019, for abuse of power and obstruction of investigations by Congress of Trump's attempts to pressure a foreign nation—Ukraine—to smear his presidential opponent, Joe Biden.[1]

Against this backdrop of intense social and political instability, we were lucky to access Dr. Herman's depth of experience and wisdom about trauma and its impacts upon a collective. By pointing out that the United States had yet to reckon with the traumatic legacy of the Civil War, never mind the COVID-19 pandemic, she reached deep into U.S. history to point out the roots from which many of our current psychological and political conflicts have grown. Pointing out the similarities between the white nationalist groups who stormed the Capitol and the Ku Klux Klan of the 1920s, Herman notes, "We recognize that those militias were not invented on January 6." In this, she connects American trauma to white nationalism, ambiguous loss, the Black Lives Matter movement, and antisemitism. Our conversation with Dr. Herman is thus closely linked to our discussions with Eric Ward (Chapter 14), Pauline Boss (Chapter 3), Deva Woodly (Chapter 22), and Susan Fiske and Peter Glick (Chapter 16). By pointing out trauma's antidote—reckoning with the truth—she provides a crucial key to both psychological and political health.

Interview

Jonathan: Betty, in your work as a trauma therapist, you focus on the individual, right?

Betty: Yes, absolutely.

Jonathan: As a student of politics, I keep thinking about our collective experience and about collective trauma. It feels, from a layperson's perspective anyway, that we are experiencing some serious collective trauma.

Betty: Absolutely. Right now we are in the midst of a natural disaster, a biomedical crisis.

Jonathan: And not only that, we are simultaneously experiencing a number of crises.

---

[1] Astor, M. (2021). The Impeachment Proceedings That Came Before. *The New York Times*. https://www.nytimes.com/2021/01/13/us/politics/which-presidents-have-been-impeached.html.

Betty: Right. We sit in the middle of these intersecting crises that are having a compound impact. Our whole lives have been derailed—and they remain derailed a year out from the onset of COVID-19. People are fraying in myriad ways.

Jonathan: And that's individually true, but it's also true of our societal collective. We are wrestling with multiple traumas: physical, economic, racial tensions.

Betty: Yes, political *and* societal pressures…

Jonathan: …bubbling up and mixing together all at once. While this describes our present moment, it's also multigenerational. We can go back over generations of suffering and trauma, and it's an awful lot for us to be processing at this moment.

Betty: So much. It's really too much. And for that reason, we are really lucky to have trauma expert Dr. Judith Herman here to speak to us about how we might apply some of the tenets of trauma treatment to ourselves as a society, as we go through these crises.

Jonathan: Welcome to *Mind of State*, Dr. Herman.

Judith Herman: My pleasure.

Betty: Dr. Herman, there has been what some people consider the four-year trauma of having Donald Trump as our president, and now we are looking at societal, sociopolitical traumas of monumental proportions. Not only are we suffering through a pandemic, but also an economic crisis, a referendum on racial injustice, stress about climate justice, and anxiety over climate change. Can we go through the framework of trauma-informed treatment to see how we can apply it to such a tangle of crises?

Judith: The place to start is to see trauma not simply as an individual problem, but as a social problem. And this is particularly true of the multiple traumas that ensue when you have a social structure defined by dominance and subordination, such as systemic racism or patriarchy. The Black Lives Matter movement now challenges us to reckon with the legacies of slavery.

The #MeToo movement comes out of a reckoning with the oppressions of patriarchy. And then we have all the economic injustice issues. You can think of the pandemic as a virus that not only attacks the weak spots in an individual's immune system, but also the weak spots in society's immune system, so that all of the injustices, inequalities, and inequities of our society are exposed and made worse.

Jonathan: They are like preexisting conditions, aren't they?

Judith: Yes, and so our society fractures along those lines, and we see, for example, Black people being more exposed to COVID and getting sicker because of racial disparities in healthcare and so death rates of Black Americans are much higher…

Betty: …four to five times higher…

Judith: …than white people. So, trauma, to me, is never a personal issue. It's a social issue. And that means that the healing is not just a personal matter; it's a social matter. And that's why, for example, groups are so important and social support is so important in healing from trauma. We have very good data showing that social support is a powerful predictor of resilience—meaning not developing post-traumatic stress disorder (PTSD) in spite of being exposed to a deadly stressor. Also, in individual treatment, we have very good data that applies not only to trauma but also to psychotherapy in general, showing that the therapeutic alliance is the single greatest predictor of recovery and for prevention in developing post-traumatic syndrome.

Jonathan: For us laypeople, can you define *therapeutic alliance*?

Judith: It refers to a relationship of trust where a person feels safe and free to speak her mind. So in talking about trauma recovery, psychotherapy is really the bedrock of trauma treatment. We don't have medication that makes trauma go away, although people self-medicate with alcohol and all sorts of other substances for that reason. It makes the pain go away temporarily. So, the first stage of trauma treatment is developing a safe, trusting relationship. The problem is that for people who have been exploited and abused, the first thing that's destroyed is trust. You can't just assume that the person coming into your office is going to trust you. It has to be earned. And so we talk about building a *therapeutic alliance* or building a trusting relationship.

Jonathan: So the therapeutic alliance is between the mental health professional and the patient?

Judith: Correct. That's the beginning of trauma treatment. Then, I define three basic stages of treatment, and they're neither rigidly defined, nor do they have a rigid timetable. I still get questions, especially from the bean-counter types: "Well, how long does the treatment have to go on? Can we get it done in three weeks? Six weeks?"

Jonathan: Right. They want to know the program. They want to know the end goal. They want to know the timing.

Judith: Absolutely.

Jonathan: But it's a more fluid, organic process.

Judith: Absolutely, and it depends to a large extent on how severe, how prolonged the trauma was. A single incident is not the same as being abused starting when you're 5 years old and going on until you're 17 when you then run away from home. So, the first step—when you've built, or you've started to build, a relationship—the first goal of trauma treatment is safety.

And that means if you're working with a battered woman this is crisis intervention: you have to know how to get a restraining order, where the safe houses are, how to figure out how to get somebody some money. It's all about survival at the beginning, and about establishing at least a perimeter, a defensive perimeter. You can't really go back and talk about the past until there's some degree of safety in the present. And that's not just a therapeutic challenge. That's a social problem.

Jonathan: Right. You need physical safety before you can start to address the mental and emotional.

Judith: Exactly. And this is an issue, for example, with refugees and people in conflict zones after they've gotten to a refugee camp. If it's run by a mafia, there's still no safety. And yet you're trying to build social support, you're trying to build at least a small space where the person doesn't have to be hypervigilant all the time. And *hypervigilance* is being on alert constantly, expecting danger at all times. That's one of the major symptoms of post-traumatic stress disorder. It means that your adrenaline is going all the time. You can't sleep; you have nightmares; you startle at the smallest sound; and you're constantly watching the door or scanning the environment.

Jonathan: In mentioning doors, I recall an episode with our guest Megan Doney (Chapter 6), who was a survivor of a school shooting, and she said that ever since escaping out the emergency exit door, she sees doors differently, and she probably will for the rest of her life.

Judith: You can see when people have PTSD. If you meet them in a coffee shop, for example, they'll want to sit near the door or sit where they can see everything. And they'll check out all the exits.

So safety really is the first challenge. And, as I say, it's not just an individual problem, because nobody can be safe in isolation. It means you have to know who you can trust. You have to have some social support system. If you don't have it, you need to build it. One of my colleagues at Cambridge Hospital used to say to patients: "Our first order of business is to make sure you have a friend because I can't be your 24/7 support system. I'm a limited human being, so you have to have at least one friend, and if you don't have a friend, then our first job is going to be making a friend."

That's stage one, and it doesn't mean we don't talk about the trauma. We do, but we talk about it more in terms of its impact on the symptoms that the person is having now. Understanding PTSD means understanding the feelings of shame and anger and terror that go along with trauma and naming them. It means understanding how the feelings impact you, how they're experienced in life now. For our early-recovery patients, we have what we call our Trauma Information group. And that's a 10-week weekly meeting with a very fixed structure. Each session has a topic, and we have an information sheet for each topic such as "What is PTSD?" or "Safety and Self-Care," which is our second topic. We read a paragraph from our information sheet and then people discuss. "Oh yeah, I have that symptom too," or "Oh you have nightmares, too?" "Oh, you know, when I go out and I just want to withdraw and hide." "Oh, I do that too."

Jonathan: So, part of the treatment is understanding that you're not alone in the symptoms that you're experiencing, that there is common human experience and response to trauma?

Judith: Exactly. And that it has a name, and it doesn't mean you're weird or crazy which is what a lot of people fear. It just means something terrible happened to you, and this is a normal response. And so being in the group and feeling understood is a tremendous relief for people who feel isolated, ashamed, and that no one will understand, or no one will believe them. That's the early stage of trauma recovery, where it's about safety and self-care because if you don't feel safe in your body, or if you are a danger to yourself, then you can't be safe anywhere.

Jonathan: And when you talk about the feeling of isolation, you're speaking predominantly about mental and emotional isolation, that you feel like you're experiencing this alone. But in the case of this pandemic, where we are actually physically isolated as a way of remaining safe, how does physical isolation feed into the experience of the traumatized person?

Judith: Of course, it exacerbates both the feeling of being alone and also the danger many harmed people are in. Globally, there's been a tremendous increase in domestic violence reported since the pandemic lockdown because if husbands are home…

Jonathan: Oh, right. You're isolated, but unfortunately, you're isolated with the person who's causing the harm.

Judith: Exactly. And we're not getting a big increase in child abuse reports, but people are worried that's only because kids are not going to school, and they don't have teachers they might be able to confide in—or they're not going to their regular pediatrician's appointments. So, they're not only not getting immunized for ordinary things like measles, mumps, and rubella, but also they're not having opportunities to be out of the home where somebody else might be able to intercede. And, of course, teachers and doctors are what we call mandated reporters. We are required, if we suspect child abuse, to let Child Protective Services know, but that's not happening as much in the pandemic. So the isolation is both emotional, with a big increase in demand for mental health support, and it's also physically dangerous for many people.

Betty: In talking about the macro impacts of trauma upon ongoing sociological situations like abuse in the home, what are we to do in terms of establishing safety for individuals and society?

Judith: Let me go through the other two stages, because I think that will help us think about how we can do this on a macro level. Once safety is established, then what generally comes next is a reckoning with the past—going back and talking about what happened. And reliving what's happened, not just the facts of what happened, but the emotional impact and the bodily sensations and the thoughts such as "it's all my fault"—which is so common—and the shame, the self-blame, the sense of being different, of not belonging, of not deserving to belong, and sometimes of not deserving to live. And so all of that has to be revisited from this place of greater safety so that you can make a distinction between "that was then" and "this is now." And we don't do that as an exorcism. People often think they just want to vomit it out to get it all purged, but that doesn't really work very well. That's what they used to do with combat veterans, using hypnosis or sodium amytal, when they wanted to return them to combat. But that's not how you recover and live the rest of your life.

So we do it a little at a time. We process each little bit of the person's experience or experiences of harm, and we keep it within the range of emotional tolerance so that people are not retraumatized by being compelled to pour out more than they can emotionally handle. And then there is a process of grieving because you can't go back to the person you were before this happened. You can't have the life that you might have had if you had not been abused as a child, or if you had not been made to be a child soldier. You are changed by what happened to you, but as you grieve, you also come to realize that the trauma is just a part of your story; it's not the whole story. It's part of you, of who you are, but it's not all of who you are. As people come to realize that, then they begin to have more of a sense of the future.

Then, in the third stage of recovery, people begin to emerge from their grieving. It becomes more about possibility and expansion. Instead of existing within a safe defensive perimeter, life can be lived from an expansive sense of taking on new challenges, developing more intimacy, and of daring to do things or to imagine who you can be, not just who you were. That's a most rewarding moment in trauma recovery—when people really are able to embrace all of who they are. And some amazing survivors develop what my colleague and friend Robert Jay Lifton calls a "survivor mission," which is to redefine the meaning of the trauma by making it a gift to others in some way—by joining with others to try to prevent this from happening to other people.[2] And people will say things like, "You know, if I can prevent one person from getting assaulted, or if I can help one person be safe, or if I can help change the laws so survivors are better cared for and some of these injustices can be corrected, then it won't have been in vain and maybe this is what I was meant to do."

Jonathan: A sense of mission, a sense of purpose.

Judith: Yes.

Jonathan: I know, Judith, that you've also written about collective PTSD, of systemic political violence. You've written about some of the direst situations in the world: dictatorships, civil wars, genocide, things that, frankly, most of us have not experienced in the United States. Many refugees from other parts of the world do bring their personal experiences to the U.S. But, collectively, here in the United States, we have not experienced a modern civil war or a genocide or these terrible traumatic experiences that are occurring in other parts of the world. So, as we apply this framework of trauma and post-traumatic stress to the collective experience, how would you apply your approach to collective PTSD to the experiences that we've had in the U.S. during this pandemic that feel very traumatic?

Judith: I would argue that we are still dealing with the legacy of our Civil War.

Jonathan: Oh, that's interesting.

Judith: It's not clear who won the Civil War. The Union was preserved, and slavery was abolished in the Constitution. But once the federal forces were withdrawn from the South, we had a century of Jim Crow—which I would argue was a system of state terrorism by which an enslaved population was

---

[2] Lifton, R.J. (2001). Giving Meaning to Survival. *The Chronicle of Higher Education.*

basically and functionally re-enslaved. And the political structure that we developed involved tremendous compromise with what I would call the one-party dictatorships of the South. A compromise developed that also implicated the north in financing the cotton industry and the other cash crops that were grown by, if not literal, slave labor...

Jonathan: ...then indentured servitude, certainly.

Judith: Yes. I think we do need to come to terms with that legacy in a much deeper and more widespread way than we have to date. I do think that we might be due for a "truth and reconciliation commission," for example, as a kind of stage one of the sort I outlined for the treatment of individuals suffering PTSD. Or I would call it more a "truth and repair commission" because I think repair has to precede reconciliation. I think one of the big strengths of the Truth and Reconciliation Commission (TRC) in South Africa was that it put survivors at the center. And their testimony was widely broadcast, mostly on radio, so that their stories were central. It really became impossible to deny, even though apparently the Afrikaners called it the "lying and crying commission." Because of this testimony, it became impossible to reframe apartheid as a benign system, which is what happened with the *Gone with the Wind* hagiographic narrative in America that reframed slavery as benign.

Putting the survivors' testimony at the center was a big success because it did not allow minimizing the effects of apartheid in South Africa. The other big success was that they traded amnesty for confession so that some of the major perpetrators of state-sponsored violence did confess in order to avoid trial. But South Africa didn't have any kind of reparations built into the Truth and Reconciliation Commission. And I think they are still very much suffering in their society from the fact that it's still such an unequal society where all of the capital that was created by a subordinated group has advantaged the oppressors. And there has never been any compensation for the oppressed. So we need to think about that. I wonder if we can create enough safety to embark on something like the Truth and Reconciliation Commission in the United States.

Jonathan: Right now we have disaster relief to avoid a very immediate near-term economic collapse associated with the COVID-19 pandemic, and these funds have nothing to do with reparation for the injustices that remain as a result of slavery and the Civil War in the 19th century.

Judith: Right. In collective trauma, as in individual trauma, you have to focus on safety first—and right now, that means safety from the pandemic. A lot of the disaster relief money is about trying to roll out a competent vaccination program that's centralized and equitable and gets people to herd immunity quickly. So that's what we mean by "safety first" in the case of collective trauma. We also need to plug those fundamental holes, so people don't suffer mass evictions and hunger. As with those suffering individual trauma, collective trauma requires food, clothing, and shelter first.

Betty: Yes, all the basic needs must be met.

Jonathan: I want to come back to my question about the things that we've experienced here in this modern moment of pandemic and economic crisis and racial injustice, which are so real and visceral. We're living them right now. Can you apply the collective PTSD treatment approach that you've written about for survivors of genocide and modern civil wars to the things that we're experiencing here and now in America?

Judith: Sure. But you have to start with stage one, which is to establish safety.

Jonathan: Right.

Judith: And then we have a reckoning. I would argue that talking about the storming of the Capitol doesn't make sense right now unless you understand its white supremacist roots. Scholars of the Ku Klux Klan say that the group that stormed the Capitol is very similar to the Ku Klux Klan of the 1920s, both of which consisted of Evangelical Protestant Christians, white supremacists, and militias. And both groups were widespread throughout America, not just located in the South.

Jonathan: And we saw that on display on January 6, right, with...

Judith: ...with the Confederate flags...

Jonathan: ...nooses...

Betty: …swastikas.

Jonathan: Right, swastikas, and Holocaust denial on sweatshirts—all of that. And so the reconciliation, the bearing witness to that experience, has to take into account the historical underpinnings they carry forth?

Judith: Right. We recognize that those militias were not invented on January 6. That would be my argument about stage two. It's crucial to get the truth out there, make it known, so we can process and grieve it and then do something to fix it. I think it'd be a lot easier to start talking about how to fix it once you have a very widespread process.

You know, there was a commission appointed after many of the Black ghettos had uprisings in the late 1960s. It was called the Kerner Commission Report, and it talked about two Americas, separate and unequal. The report was excellent and many of its recommendations would still be very pertinent today.[3] Martin Luther King, who praised the report, was assassinated a month after the report's release.

Jonathan: You raise an interesting point because I've been wondering, in reading your work and listening to you, about how politicians and elected officials respond to collective trauma. And there's certainly a component of bearing witness, but I wonder about the balance a politician, it seems, needs to strike—they will bear witness, but then typically they'll try to pivot and …

Judith: …they'll say "let's move on. Let's move on."

Betty: Right. They'll say, "Let's not dwell."

Jonathan: But then we had Joe Biden, President Biden, expressing tremendous empathy, bearing witness to the death and the illness and the trauma that people have experienced throughout the pandemic, dedicating the night before the inauguration to the purpose of bearing witness and then launching into …

Betty: …which his predecessor did not.

---

[3] Kerner Commission. (1968). *Report of the National Advisory Commission on Civil Disorders.* https://www.hud.gov/sites/dfiles/FHEO/documents/kerner_commission_full_report.pdf.

Jonathan: Right. So we had one president who was in denial and then Joe Biden, his successor, in contrast—marked contrast—bearing witness for the world.

Judith: And then wanting to move on. I totally understand that he has a lot of work to do and not much time to get it done. So, of course, he wants to push forward. On the other hand, we need to have a reckoning with someone who basically incited an attempted fascist coup. This is like the Beer Hall Putsch of 1923.[4] The siege didn't succeed, but it could be a portent of things to come. And not just here, but in Europe and other democracies.

I think what politicians can do depends very much on what people know, on whether the truth is out there. The big mistake of the Kerner Commission, fifty years ago or more, was that it was a big written report— and how many people read it? It needed to be publicized and the testimony of survivors needed to be the main event so that everybody could understand what it was we were dealing with. It's not just a problem over there. It's our problem too.

Jonathan: And you've written that recovery requires remembrance and mourning and that you can't move on in your stages, in your framework, until we first get to safety—to name it and grieve.

Judith: Yes.

Betty: And what you're saying, Judith, reminds us of Pauline Boss (Chapter 3) and what she has said to us—that we are a nation founded upon unresolved trauma.

Judith: Exactly.

Betty: This goes back to what you said about the Civil War and your referencing South Africa as a country that tried to come to grips with its

---

[4] The Beer Hall Putsch, also called the Munich Putsch, was a failed coup d'état by Hitler and the Nazis in Bavaria. The coup d'état launched in a beer hall where the state commissioner was speaking. Once the Nazis had taken over Bavaria, they planned to march on Berlin and take over the Weimar Republic. Hitler was sentenced to prison for treason, but he would serve less than a year. In 1933 he was declared Chancellor of Germany.

past—that it is imperative to get the truth out and mourn the pain, suffering, and loss. What I find most interesting about what you said about South Africa's truth and reconciliation process is that it put survivors at the center and did not privilege the powerful.

Judith: Exactly.

Betty: It privileged those harmed.

Judith: Yes.

Betty: And in moving forward, we place huge demands upon politicians. Biden doesn't have a lot of time. He must do almost two stages at once. Do the safety and the recognition and the repair in this accelerated fashion. But, as we know in trauma treatment, time is our ally. It's one of our tools and so, in both the macro of collective trauma and the micro of individual trauma, how do we make this effort for ourselves and support the efforts of our leaders who are attempting to move us through this trauma? What are your thoughts on that?

Judith: I would say don't try to do anything alone. That's what I tell therapists and certainly people who are involved in political work. Find your squad, find your support system, find the people who you trust and try to work together with them. And if you're trying to reach out of your comfort zone a little bit and do something you have never done before, run for political office or that sort of thing, know who your buddies are. Don't do it alone.

Jonathan: Judith Herman, thank you so much for joining us on *Mind of State*.

Judith: Well, thank you for having me.

Chapter 5
Acknowledging Harm & Repairing the World

Guest: Dr. Jessica Benjamin
Episode Aired: February 5, 2019

Dr. Jessica Benjamin is a supervising faculty member of the New York University Postdoctoral Psychology Program in Psychotherapy and Psychoanalysis and a founder, board member, and faculty member of The Stephen Mitchell Center for Relational Studies. Dr. Benjamin is a major theorist in the field of relational psychoanalysis and one of the most influential psychoanalysts of the last four decades. She is one of the most influential women analysts who introduced feminism and gender studies into psychoanalytic thought, integrating the clinical with the societal. She is the author of several books, including The Influential Bonds of Love *and, most recently,* Beyond Doer and Done To: Recognition Theory, Intersubjectivity, and the Third.

In early 2019, we asked Dr. Benjamin to consider the psychological roots of political impasses. While political gridlock had plagued Barack Obama during both his terms in office, the election of Donald Trump further intensified political partisanship, creating divides that became highly emotional and personal. After 2016, disputes and splits between family members and couples over politics were common and amplified Americans' levels of stress.[1] Moreover, when we spoke with Dr. Benjamin, the United States remained in the longest government shutdown in its history. Lasting from December 22, 2018 to January 25, 2019, and impacting the livelihoods of over 800,000 federal employees, the shutdown grew out of an entrenched conflict between Donald Trump and the Democrat-controlled House of Representatives over funding for a wall he insisted on building along the U.S./

---

[1] Chatterjee, R. (2019). Stressed Out by Politics? Here's How to Keep Caring Without Losing Your Cool. *NPR.* https://www.npr.org/sections/health-shots/2019/09/25/764216567/is-politics-stressing-you-out-heres-how-to-keep-caring-without-losing-your-cool.

Mexico border. It was an example of what one of our later guests, Boston Globe political columnist Michael Cohen, would observe—that political polarization, and not foreign threat, is what imperils American democracy the most.[2]

With all this in mind, we asked Dr. Benjamin the question: How do we move out of a political discourse of blame and shame into one that acknowledges past and present harm done and the need to repair it? She first pointed out the roots of polarization and illustrated the mechanisms of the shame/blame dynamic between opposing parties, describing such conflicts as rigid "doer and done to" binaries where each side believes the other is in the wrong and no one takes responsibility for any harm done. As a result, the ensuing struggles both perpetuate abusive systems of racism, injustice, inequality, and economic exploitation and distract us from recognizing their underlying causes. To jump us out of this spin, Dr. Benjamin proposes creating a third space in which we are able to acknowledge and repair such harm, while taking account of the powerful forces of fear and resentment that have prevented such recognition:

> My argument is that in order to have a vision of a societally embraced third space where we can carry out conflicts, we also need to have a vision of repair, what you called redemption. We have to have a notion that these things that we're talking about that are so problematic in our history that we, collectively as Americans—both those who did participate in slavery and genocide through their ancestry and those who did not—have to take responsibility for reparation, for making amends, for making sure this doesn't happen again, for changing what's happening...

Here Dr. Benjamin agrees with Judith Herman (Chapter 4), Pauline Boss (Chapter 3), and Scotty McClennan (Chapter 9); all assert that for true communication between opposing parties to occur—be they individuals or groups—both sides must recognize the loss or harm underlying the dispute. Denial of this vulnerability results in a dismissal of the other's humanity and a perpetuation of zero-sum power struggles. This not only blocks useful collaboration within a society but hinders its healthy movement and growth. Judging from the extreme partisanship that infused every one of the momentous social and political events that would impact the U.S. in the ensuing two years—from Donald Trump's first and second impeachment trials; to the spread of the COVID-19 pandemic; to the murder of George Floyd triggering the Black Lives Matter movement; to the 2020 presidential

---

[2] See our conversation with Michael Cohen in Chapter 25 along with his book, coauthored with Zenko, M. (2019). *A Clear and Present Safety.* Yale University Press.

elections; to the January 6, 2021, siege on the U.S. Capitol—as Dr. Benjamin suggests, the health of American society requires a vision of a "societally embraced third space" to recognize and reckon with our deepest conflicts, so that we may find true redemption and repair.

Interview

Betty: Thanks so much, Jessica, for joining us on *Mind of State*. We are honored to have you here.

Jessica: I'm excited to be here. Thank you.

Betty: To refer to your most recent book, *Beyond Doer and Done To*, we have an audience here that might not know about your very influential concept of "the third." And you've used it very elegantly to talk about how we might move beyond this entrenched political impasse we are experiencing in the U.S., between the right and the left. Can you explain your theory of *the third* and the *doer and done to* concept?

Jessica: To put it most simply, most binds that we get into are ones in which, rather than carrying through on a conflict in a way that allows both sides to express themselves, there is a lack of a certain kind of space in which a disagreement or an opposition can be held. So, if you think of the conversational space or the space of dialog between, say, two partners, if that space closes, then you get into a kind of *doer and done to complementarity* where each person feels that the other is shutting them out; each person feels "my reality is the *only* reality," or each person feels like they *think* their reality is the only reality—that kind of thing. So that space in which you can imagine that there are two different points of view, or two different but equally deserving and equally…

Betty: …valid?

Jessica: …valid, but also equally *valued* persons, is the space of the third. And you can think of it as a metaphor of space, very literally, in the sense that when that third space is open, each person puts their ideas or their feelings into the middle, the way you would throw your chips into a game. And their contribution counts. And when that space closes, it seems like there's nothing—there's nowhere to go with any kind of conflict or opposition except banging up against each other.

Michael: So, this sounds to me very much like a situation in couples' therapy.

Jessica: It could be. But the way that I look at it comes less from couples therapy and more from developmental studies—say, of infants and their parents. In lieu of "parents," I'll say "mother" here, just for short. And in all the early studies of mothers and infants, and in the later ones as well, what we noticed was that a certain kind of accommodation pattern, a certain kind of adjustment would be going on between the two partners. But it was not a pattern of action and reaction. It wasn't, for instance, the mother stimulating the infant, and the infant reacting. Rather, the two of them would get into a groove, into sync, and create a rhythmic pattern that each of them could, at times, change or even violate in order to make things more interesting. But within the context of this pattern, they were recognizing each other's moves. The important thing is that, when you get something like that going, you go beyond the idea of simply creating or coexisting in a space; you have a pattern that you can in some way rely on, but in some way, it is also novel and outside both people's control. It starts to take on something of a life of its own if it's good.

Michael: And if it's bad? In terms of your patients, Betty or Jessica, help us ground this in the real for a second.

Jessica: Right, if it's bad, you get an action and reaction pattern. For instance, what we saw with mothers and infants was something called *chase-and-dodge*, where if the mother didn't recognize that the infant needed to slow down, which the infant shows by, say, looking away from the mother because it's too stimulating, then the mother moves in even more, she looms in. And if the infant twists their body and tries to get away, and then the mother looms in even more—we call that the *chase-and-dodge pattern*. And that would be an example of the kinetic, early experience of having a "doer and done to" relationship. What the infant feels, on some level, is "I'm helpless, I can't get away from this person." But the mother also feels helpless because she doesn't know what she's doing wrong. She doesn't know how to get her infant back online.

Michael: And she yearns for the connection from the infant?

Jessica: Exactly. She's getting more anxious, so then, both people are getting more anxious. So that would be an example of how, rather than creating a third, you get this negative pattern. And this negative pattern closes down both people's opportunities to co-create and be active together in a good way.

Michael: And it sounds to me that then it's sort of self-propagating. Which is to say, it must be very hard to stop that "doer and done to" dynamic without intervention.

Jessica: Yes. Interestingly, though, some very simple interventions often help a great deal. Mothers can learn to be more aware, let's say, and things will calm down. And this is very important: Things calm down. People need to calm down—that is, not to be what we call *hyper-aroused*. Because the more hyper-aroused people get, the more the back-and-forth intensifies; and the more they calm down, the more they can give each other space.

Betty: And it seems that what you're saying, Jessica, is that the resonance that a mother and child can have—or lose—with each other in this most basic, original sense, is what we can use as a framework, even when looking at very complex adult interactions such as the kinds we experience right now. With the ongoing shutdown, we are currently experiencing the concretization of an impasse that has shut down the Federal government for a historic amount of time. So it's useful to consider developmental theory to look at how resonance and attunement works between people.

Jessica: If you stop there, however, the picture is incomplete in a very essential way. And I want to interject that now if I can. There's another piece to this idea of a kind of basic rhythm and a basic set of principles of interaction. And that has to do with what I call *lawfulness*. That is to say, that you set up certain patterns, or you can expect certain patterns with the other. And let us say that now, from the child's perspective, the pattern that I expect from you has been violated. What do you do when that pattern is violated? Ideally, you acknowledge the violation. So, we have something called *rupture and repair*, where many little things go wrong in the life of a baby or a small child. But those many things can be continuously acknowledged by the adults. "Oh, that hurt." Or "Oh, you bumped your head," and so on. Or, those things can be denied, particularly if they're things that the parent caused, like discomforts that we necessarily cause children, not to mention deeper kinds of pain that we cause. The less acknowledgment, the less there is what we consider to be *repair*. So, this is going to lead into what I think is politically crucial in the resolution of impasse, which is, you can't simply restore attunement. You have to repair the disruption of it. And that means you have to acknowledge what actually went wrong. And if you do not, that's where people are going to start to fight again.

Michael: So, in layperson's terms, *own it?*

Jessica: Yes, own it.

Michael: Can I ask you, before we move into the political space—and I guess this is for both of you—if you see this dynamic in a patient, in private, how does it manifest, or how does a child then carry this into adulthood? What are the consequences of the dynamic you're speaking about in someone's life?

Jessica: Well, I will slant this somewhat toward the political by saying that one of the basic consequences has to do whether we can trust authority figures—people with power whom we depend upon—to right the wrong that they have done or to acknowledge the wrong that someone else has done, that is, whether we grow up with the basic sense that they'll never really admit anything that happened; they'll never feel empathetic to our suffering or injury.

And so, the assumption can be, "I'm all on my own when it comes to this, and I have to either constantly rage against it or shut it down completely or just walk around in the world expecting no one to really ever understand anything about how I see the world." In a way, such a person can think "other people are crazy, but maybe I'm crazy." All of those things go on if you do not get acknowledgment and if you aren't in the presence of people who think, "When something goes wrong, we try to put it right." Or, if we can't put it right—for instance, we really can't pick the ice cream off the sidewalk after your cone falls—then we acknowledge what a painful thing that is. It really can start with someone having the littlest things, the smallest hurts recognized, versus somebody being told to just suck it up.

Betty: Or, being told that it's their fault or they are to blame, so that the process of mini-mourning the dropped ice cream cone is not possible for the child. They've got to suck it up, as you said. And in my field of trauma treatment, that sets the tone of silencing, which can really have some deleterious effects where people don't know their own boundaries, meaning they don't have an inner sense or voice that says, "It's okay to have my wrongs acknowledged." Or "It's okay to put up limits to where I end and the other begins." It creates a very unconscious entrenchment of a habitual state of mind, which can get people into trouble later on when or if they meet with threatening or unsafe circumstances in the future.

Jessica: Exactly. Where they feel that they can't protect themselves. Going back to my illustration of the child and the parent, an important point is that if your protest about something that hurt you or that felt wrong to you is silenced in the way that you're describing, then one of the main things that happens is that not only do you lose a sense of your true agency—your ability to protect yourself—but you also do not see the world as having a kind of lawful order. Instead, the world is made up of power relations, which have nothing to do with lawfulness. By lawfulness, I don't just mean the things that we institutionalize legally, but all kinds of unspoken rules of behavior regarding fairness, and so forth. The reason that those can all go out the window for some people is that they've never experienced anything but naked power. They've never really seen this kind of respect, not only for the person or the other, but also for the patterns that you and I have established together, our expectations of each other. They've never seen that kind of respect for a certain type of order. Their idea of order is a top-down imposition of power, and whoever doesn't have that power just has to knuckle under.

Michael: This is fascinating, and I can already hear how it resonates in today's political environment. So I have some questions. The first is, what do you say to somebody who says, "Yeah, but that's my reality. I'm an African American male, and I'm a doctor, and I get stopped by police thinking I'm a criminal"?

Jessica: But even if the person is not a doctor, the most ordinary person who gets stopped in that way has a sense that this is not lawful.

Michael: Correct.

Jessica: The whole point is that they are not lacking an internal representation of what is lawful and whether they got it from their parents, or the church, or the school they went to; they have a sense of what is right and wrong. When power is exerted in that way, they understand that something unlawful is being done. Now, at the same time, they also understand that if they were to protest about that, they could come into more harm.

Michael: Exactly.

Jessica: So, they're in a bind. They have to be able, in effect, to hold on to their own idea of right and wrong while being cunning enough to protect themselves from somebody who might shoot them while they take their driver's license.

Michael: Because you both are obviously empathetic to the victims in this situation, you're not suggesting somehow that the burden is on them, right? It's a burden on us. So how do we, Jessica, how do you take your ideas then and find practical application in the political space?

Jessica: Well, just to go back for one moment to what Betty said, because it's right: we want to give people practice in being able to disagree with us or complain to us or accuse us without our retaliating. The most important thing for people to get is a recognition of their protest without retaliation. So, now, if you look at the societal level where we have a high degree of mass incarceration and this punitive discourse of blame—you get what you deserve—that is really overwhelming. Compared to any other civilized country, it is just shattering to realize how intense it is—when you can see that the idea of punishing, rather than recognizing what is behind someone's behavior, must be something that is extremely widespread and acceptable to a large majority.

Michael: Otherwise, we wouldn't allow it.

Jessica: We would say, "Wait a minute, you've got a sixteen-year-old who's committed some kind of crime, but we understand that he's just a kid. We have to find out what's going on. We have to take care of this person. We have to help them." But that's not the attitude in our society. We just have this notion of there being superpredators, this notion that they are bad seeds or destructive people. All of that can be seen from a psychoanalytic viewpoint as a kind of projection of badness onto a certain population. Sometimes it's just onto an individual, sometimes onto populations. You're basically saying, "These people, who are acting out of anger over their circumstances, need to get in line like the rest of us. We've knuckled under. We've had to suck up things that have made us angry. Yes, we've had to give in to things that harmed or thwarted us. We've had to submit to authority our whole lives. We went to public school and had to submit to authority. Why don't they submit to authority the way we do?"

Betty: And why don't they comply? Why don't they accommodate the social structure?

Jessica: The idea is really that people deserve to be punished when they step out of line. Because the more authoritarian your own upbringing is, the more you think other people should be punished.

Michael: It's fascinating to me because what it doesn't consider is the humiliation. I mean, forget the practical injustice of having to succumb to a power structure when you're at the bottom, and the emotional component of the humiliation—of being completely negated, overlooked, denied. It strikes me as funny that I keep coming back to Trump, who strikes me as this guy who is guilty of all the things that we've discussed, which is to say his relationships are all about power. He sees them all in a zero-sum game dynamic. There is no third space for him. And you are, as you say, Betty, required to succumb. And he turns other people into criminals. Is that an inappropriate leap?

Jessica: No, I think that's a very good leap. And the point is that we all assume that Trump had a very authoritarian upbringing, that his father was pretty frightening and humiliating, and that his older brother was frightened and humiliated, and that led to his alcoholism. We all pretty much make the same assumptions about that. The issue is, why is his appeal so widespread? And that has to do with the fact that he, on the one hand, has learned these techniques for overcoming humiliation that other people admire. They admire that he's been able to reverse the humiliation, to put it onto the others who are weak, or feminine, or in some way deserving supposedly of this shame and humiliation. So that makes people who feel a lot of shame and humiliation very happy that they can identify with this guy who's learned how to throw it over onto the other, all while projecting.

Michael: Can you unpack that a little bit more for us, if you don't mind? Because I think it's really essential that we understand what you mean by "projecting" and what Trump's doing by placing his own personal shame on women, for example.

Jessica: Well, I think you just expressed it. There isn't that much more to it. At the simplest level, *projection* is when you take something that is unwanted by the self because it is either shameful or felt to be destructive, and you put it into someone else. So, Trump, for instance, not only puts things that are humiliating, like, bleeding or being in some way, physically exposed...

Betty: ...or unattractive.

Michael: ...or disabled, in the case of the handicapped reporter who he famously mocked.

Jessica: Right. Any form of weakness. But there's another aspect that is also involved in his projection, and that is these other people at the border are gang members—dangerous, rapacious predators. This projection of the dangerous predators is, in a way, more interesting to me because, whereas I think the media was able to pick up on the obviousness of how he's shaming other people, I think the media was more helpless in the face of Trump's projection of harm onto these poor few immigrants—as opposed to owning the way in which the United States government and the powers that he represents have done more harm in the world than these people could ever even imagine.

Betty: On a far, far larger scale.

Jessica: On a monumentally larger scale. I think it has been harder for the media because the media doesn't want to talk about mass incarceration in that way. They don't want to talk about drone warfare in that way. They don't want to talk about the violence of constantly slicing things from the federal budget, like heating for old people, like nutritional support for poor people. They don't want to talk about those things as violent, so that the predation is being constantly projected. And I think that leads us into the theme that we hope to get to today, which is the constant refusal of Americans to own any predatory aspects. And at the same time, Trump celebrates his successful predation even as he is projecting it onto others.

Michael: It's a source of pride.

Jessica: He's always talking about how he's really getting the better of other people. And that contradiction, which isn't experienced as contradiction, is, I think, part of his attractiveness to certain people. And part of, of course, what horrifies others.

Michael: It's funny, as you were talking, Jessica, about the media's unwillingness to look at our own predatory behavior, I was thinking about this in terms of those people seeking asylum. It occurs to me that they are not immigrants; they are people.

Jessica: Right. I meant to say that myself.

Michael: They're seeking asylum from an untenable, violent situation. And I was thinking about it mostly in the context of Honduras, which is a violent mess of a country for which both George Bush and Barack Obama...

Jessica: ...bear responsibility.

Michael: And the total absence in this entire debate about a "caravan," which is not a caravan. Even the way that the media adopts the language of the user, but the lack of any reporting about our complicit actions to create the problems in Honduras that are forcing these people out, seeking asylum and safety for their families, it's nowhere to be found, at least not in the press that I consume.

Betty: And Jessica, you pointed to this in your writings, this allowance that Trump gets to both celebrate his strongman status, and yet project this predatory persona onto those who do not have it, all the while denying the enormous scale of predation that he and his colleagues and business associates have exhibited. There is a link between how people wanting to feel better about themselves and their own situation might want to identify with this leader, particularly in times and states of uncertainty. I was wondering if you could draw those lines a bit more clearly for us, that link between someone feeling low or weak preferring the strongman to be their leader because they identify with him, even if it is at the cost of their own well-being.

Jessica: I think that the identification with the strongman leader is more complicated than people want to admit. Because in the studies I've looked at, a large percentage of those who supported Trump, for instance, were not economically insecure people. They were not even what we would consider working class. And by many definitions, they were people with a substantially secure income in sales or management.

Betty: Absolutely.

Jessica: Of course those people are not free from being economically threatened. The economic crisis in 2008, in particular, was no doubt frightening to all kinds of people who are or aren't wealthy. But I think what caused financially secure people to embrace Trump wasn't economic uncertainty. I really think it's the uncertainty of white male identity on the one side, and on the other, the uncertainty of not knowing what we are responsible for in the world. In other words, a person—an American—is being accused, and they should be accused in a certain sense, but they don't know what they're being accused of because, as you point out, nobody's actually telling them what happened in Honduras, nobody is telling them what happened in Afghanistan or Iraq in a meaningful way. So, all of these accusations that are flying around that America has done something wrong, going all the way back to Vietnam, make no sense to people who are not, shall we say, inducted.

Michael: And they aren't if they have no exposure to it.

Jessica: Yes. If you're not inducted into a whole panoply of ideas and information that our media shut out, then these people don't have a way of knowing what they did wrong. And they also don't have anybody offering to show them a way to make it right.

Let's go back to my original point. If you do something wrong, and you know that you did, but you're able to acknowledge it and put it right, that's very important, not just for the other person who gets the acknowledgment from you. It's important for you. Otherwise, you walk around feeling destructive and like you're harmful.

Betty: Without even knowing why. It's very anxiety-producing.

Jessica: Exactly. So now you've got this person who says, "Oh no, we're not destructive. We're great. But they're telling us we're destructive. And what we actually have to do is be stronger and be even more powerful." And there are many different reasons for this, but among other things, I really hold responsible a very intentional media conspiracy to keep people in the dark about what they're actually responsible for and to obfuscate the harm that America has perpetrated for many reasons, especially economic reasons. I don't hold the individuals as such responsible, although of course they are used to a certain pattern of authority relations.

Michael: Okay, so the classic media analysis is that the 2007 economic crisis made people feel marginalized and created economic insecurity. The liberal or neoliberal elite didn't pay attention to the rising income inequality and therefore, you end up with Trump. And that may be part of the equation for you.

Jessica: It is.

Michael: But you're also saying it's more. You're saying there are other elements involved as well?

Jessica: There are elements that have to do with trying to understand why the neoliberal elite ignored the inequality and ignored the suffering of the American people. And what I think is really important to underline is that the elites did not want to confront certain kinds of responsibility for harm.

Now, if you don't mind, I'm going to make a leap here, because I want to get to this idea. You've used the word *impasse* a number of times. I don't think what we have is an *impasse*. Not really. I think what we have is a deliberate attempt by a certain part of the American ruling elite, led by Mitch McConnell, to make sure they stay in power by any means necessary. And the means that they have chosen, as we all know, is to starve the beast of government, making sure government is dysfunctional, making sure the government doesn't give people what they need. And so they're willing to cause any amount of suffering in order to be able to manipulate perception in this way. That's been going on for quite a long time. What concerns me is the inability of the other side—whichever part of the other side you belong to, except for a very small, very small group of determined people who are now becoming much more vocal—to confront or deal with Mitch McConnell. Obama, in particular, could not say Mitch McConnell is evil. And I don't mean to say he should have literally gotten on television and said, "Mitch McConnell you're evil," but ...

Michael: It would've been nice.

Jessica: Something close to that. And Obama was much more eloquent than me, so he could have figured out a really good way to say it—and he didn't. But then, the other piece that we should consider is that those people who we are designating as the "elite" have something else, which is they have access to the big power. They have access to the big wealth by being their most trusted servants. They are what we call "implicated subjects."[3] And they don't want to lose that position. There is a lot of investment in not calling out the harm. But at the same time, there's an internal conflict because many of those people who are liberal and educated really don't want to do harm.

Michael: You know, as I was reading some of your papers, as a layperson I came back to the idea that so much of this is about the stories we tell about ourselves and the stories that we're capable of telling about ourselves. It's very hard to tell a story about yourself, whether as an individual or as a nation that...

Betty: ...that we're the bad guys. That we've done wrong.

---

[3] Rothberg, M. (2019). *The Implicated Subject: Beyond victims and perpetrators.* Stanford University Press.

Jessica: Excuse me, but it's not just hard; it's also wrong politically to go around saying "we're the bad guys." That has had a very deleterious effect, which people like Trump can use …

Michael: Correct, that's the left's narrative, which is we're the bad guys—and Jessica, you're saying we are not going to win anybody over with that?

Jessica: Right, you have to win people over with the idea of saying "harm has been done historically, but we're going to make it better and we can make it better. And there is enough to go around, so we don't have to fight in this way."

Michael: Which is to say, it seems to me that what we've lost is the possibility for redemption. Redemption does not negate the facts, but it allows for a path forward. Maybe this is the third space that you're talking about. As you were speaking, I was thinking about my daughter, who just went through waves of early decisions for colleges. And I personally hate them because they are, to my mind, engines of economic inequality. First of all, you have self-selecting wealthy people who can afford 65,000 to 70,000 dollars a year for tuition. On top of that, often they're products of private schools or well-funded suburban public schools as well as of tutors and classes to help students raise their test scores. But when that decision comes in, they don't see it as a function of privilege or a driver of economic inequality. They see it as validation of their own merit—that they earned it. And that paradigm, that conflict, is that what you're talking about?

Jessica: Yes, thank you. I'm talking about the distinction between the individual and systemic points of view. And what I'm saying is that the systemic point of view is not being presented in a way that makes it something that people can own because, as you say, there's no redemption. There's no way for them to really get out of just being an exploiter or privileged person. So that is an extremely destructive way of putting it. But I actually think that Bernie Sanders and people who are now gathering around him are finding a much more positive way to put this so that it's not primarily about blame.

Betty: And this goes back to your point that there is no space for acknowledging that one can be both self-interested and supportive of the collective at the same time. What I think about, when I think about all of these things, is time and how we exist in a 24-hours-a-day media cycle that promotes or privileges conflict.

Jessica: No, not conflict. It promotes and privileges certain kinds of disruptions and certain kinds of excitement, but doesn't actually allow the underlying conflicts that are involved to be analyzed and worked on.

Betty: Maybe a better word is *drama*. The news-media cycle promotes the drama of reactivity but allows no space or time to even get to what we need to acknowledge.

Jessica: Yes. Drama, thank you, drama. And in psychoanalysis, we call that *enactment*. So the drama enacts the conflict, but the actual conflict that's behind that drama that is being enacted never gets revealed. So you never actually find out why the actors are motivated in the way that they are. And we never find out why McConnell is motivated in the way he is. We find out, for instance, that Cheney had all the oil executives come into the White House and tell him what their needs were for an energy plan. But nobody ever actually looks at that as a conflictual situation, where the other people's side is presented—the other people being the whole rest of the society whose interest is in keeping fossil fuel limited so that we don't burn up the planet. You're not allowed to actually have that conflict be presented. Instead, you have a pseudo-conflict, which is "Well, why shouldn't he be allowed to bring those people into the White House? Why are you negating his right to do that?"

Betty: What I appreciate about psychoanalysis is that we can apply it—as a different lens—to look beneath the enactment or to look beneath the drama of what's happening, because there's a lot of drama. There is something else going on in the ping-ponging back and forth. I think you've even used that language, Jessica. But this back-and-forth baton, the baton of blame, of back-and-forth, of "I'm blaming you, you're blaming me," is even, itself, a signifier that something more than what we see is in play.

Jessica: Right. It seems to be about blame rather than actually about, for instance, being able to say, "Well there are different interests involved here and legitimately there's an opposition between those interests. And you, the American people, should get to decide which you think is your interest."

Betty: And I see this as a traumatogenic, or trauma-induced response. We're frozen. We're frozen in this wordless spin of not being able to speak to these wounds.

Jessica: Or we're frozen in fear of the powerful people who would really come down on us if we tried to do this. I'm not sure whether we can leave out of the trauma the fact that it could happen again. Powerful, abusive figures frighten people. They frighten them unconsciously, in a certain way, but they frighten them. And I'm not sure exactly how to think about what to do collectively about such figures, other than saying we have to become a *we*, not an individual, when facing them. In order to not be frightened, you have become part of something larger. But there's a level at which people are frightened of being shamed. This is what happened with Kavanaugh and the hearing for his Supreme Court appointment. That a woman comes forward, Christine Blasey-Ford, and says, "I'm not going to let myself be frightened here. I know that everybody's going to try to shame me and frighten me and attack me if I come forward and say that one of these denizens of power really was a destructive person." Now, I think that there are all kinds of problematic things about singling out somebody who is a part of a whole culture of destructiveness, but nonetheless, he was a Supreme Court nominee.

Michael: He's going to have real power.

Jessica: Right.

Betty: And he still holds power to ascend.

Jessica: That's right. So Blasey-Ford's idea of speaking truth to power—if you look at the way that was treated, you see a part of how her efforts were vitiated and undermined had to do with the notion that what she was saying was *unfair* to him. That he, as a powerful person, should have his shot. He should get to have his day. He gets to have his interview, as it were, for his job without somebody coming along and ruining it for him. So this attitude has to do with people identifying with the king, with the powerful person, and not wanting their power to be spoiled.

Michael: So how does the narrative in the case of Dr. Blasey-Ford and Brett Kavanaugh factor in when you hear people say things like, "Well, now anybody can just come out and say anything." This notion that it's uncorroborated and it was an event that happened a long time ago—not that I'm ascribing to this—but the argument against Dr. Blasey-Ford being, there's no center of gravity anymore. Anybody can say anything and ruin anybody's life.

Jessica: But those kinds of arguments are sophistry. I'm interested in what's underneath this sophistry, which is an appeal to a certain mentality within American culture that says what was being done to him was unfair. And that's what I'm trying to look at. I'm trying to look at what happens when you try to ask somebody who has done harm in a culture that is so built on this kind of harming, upon patriarchal sexual harming—especially in this case, alongside all the other harming we've talked about—when you ask them to bear the onus individually of having done this. It's like saying to them, "Well you know, you're the great, great grandchild of slave owners, so you really can't be on the Supreme Court." It's like asking someone to bear the onus of a historical responsibility that the society at large is not taking upon itself to remedy.

Betty: And the stakes are that high.

Jessica: Yes. Then people start to feel like you can't put this enormous burden on any one person. But the problem with that is that the link between that burden of harming and the actual political policies that this individual Kavanaugh plans to carry out were thus undermined and made invisible by the media in the way that they portrayed this, because they simply refused to connect the dots and say, "Look here's a guy who's obviously against a women's right to choose." This is not unrelated to how he treated women. You cannot, in fact, separate them. And so that's part of the splitting that I'm talking about.

Betty: And if we don't take the time to consider connecting the dots, we're going to perpetuate this behavior.

Jessica: That's right.

Michael: And then Dr. Blasey-Ford is re-traumatized, assaulted yet again.

Betty: And other survivors who are watching her and identifying with her are re-traumatized themselves.

Michael: Right. So how then, if we look back at Kavanaugh's confirmation hearing last year and all of the anger, the sense of powerlessness—even the way that Lindsey Graham responded, ranting, and then women who were accosting people in the halls of the Senate.[4]

Jessica: I wouldn't call that accosting. I would say confronting.

Michael: Confronting. Fair enough.

Jessica: They were legitimately confronting lawmakers. And that's what I mean. That legitimate confrontation with lawmakers, in the hands of those less powerful, is confused with a form of attack.

Michael: Okay, I will own that. In the notion of actually trying to find a third, I will own that.

Jessica: But wait. That's a perfect example of how something deteriorates into the "doer and done to" framework. You see, that's how we get into the "doer and done to" complementarity, where the accuser is felt, by the accused, to be hurting him. And, so now, the accuser is also a harmer. And now everybody feels caught in this cycle of harming. So then the American people say, "Well, Blasey-Ford is also harming him." And that's what I was trying to get at before, which I didn't articulate.

And then you have what you are calling an "impasse." But, in reality, that impasse looks like it's a "doer and done to" conflict—and nobody's right and nobody's wrong and both people are harming. But in reality, there has been harm done.

[4] Shear, M.D. (2018). Furious Lindsey Graham Calls Kavanaugh Hearing "the Most Unethical Sham." *The New York Times.* https://www.nytimes.com/2018/09/27/us/politics/lindsey-graham-kavanaugh-hearing.html; Stanglin, D. & Simon, C. (2018). "Rise Up, Women!": Angry crowds flood Capitol Hill to protest Brett Kavanagh hearing. *USA Today.* https://www.usatoday.com/story/news/2018/09/28/brett-kavanaugh-hearing-protesters-christine-blasey-ford/1453524002/.

Michael: Correct.

Jessica: And I'm just going to assume, for the sake of this argument, that Dr. Blasey-Ford was definitely right. So, harm has been done, but you can then turn that around into a "doer and done to" situation where you now can say, "Well, everybody's being harmed, so forget about it."

Michael: Then the harm goes without being addressed, and a false moral equivalence is created.

Jessica: Which our media specializes in creating because they're hooked on the "doer and done to" mentality, by which I mean, in the "doer and done to" mentality, anybody who protests, anybody who opposes injustice, will be sucked into being a part of the problem, not the solution. In other words, because they're accusing someone, you see, their protest is seen as an equivalent form of harming rather than an appeal to a lawful third position.

Michael: Okay, so in the hope of trying to ground this for our listeners, it feels like an impasse. It feels like we are arrested. What do you see as a path forward? What can we do differently or what should we be demanding differently of the media, of ourselves, of our politicians, to break this very destructive dynamic?

Jessica: My argument is that in order to really have a vision of a societally embraced third space where we can carry out conflicts, we also need to have a vision of repair, what you called redemption. We have to have a notion that these things that we're talking about that are so problematic in our history that we, collectively as Americans—both those who did participate in slavery and genocide through their ancestry and those who did not—have to take responsibility for reparation, for making amends, for making sure this doesn't happen again, for changing what's happening. In a sense like the Germans did after World War II. But the thing that is vital in making this work is to keep saying, "We can do this." We don't have to sit with this system of mass incarceration like the one we have. We don't have to keep attacking other countries in the way that we are. We don't have to keep using fossil fuel the way that we are. We can make all of these changes, if we agree that the point is not about blame, but about responsibility.

And to do this there will be conflicts of interest that we have to carry out. But let's say that on "our side" we are completely, legitimately interested in making solutions available that will probably be friendly to the majority of people. And those solutions will involve fighting tooth and nail against those who are profiting from not having those solutions. That's unavoidable. We need to face the fact that people are going to want to keep harming us and we're going to have to nonviolently stand up to their harming. We need to take inspiration from those Standing Rock water protectors.[5] We need to think about how we can take an idea of protection that's not about "only one can live" or "them versus us," but an idea of protection that really is so much more embracing of the Earth and of all people. And that has to do with believing that there really are some original instructions[6] that are given to us about how to conduct life on Earth.

Betty: What you're both speaking to is that there's an anxiety in this stuck dynamic and there's no movement forward.

Jessica: There's no taking responsibility.

Betty: And as difficult as taking responsibility can be in the short term, in the long term, it's a relief. It's a way to move. It gives motility.

Jessica: Right. And that's very good.

Michael: I think this is great because we are recording this on the day of the celebration of Dr. King's birthday, and he seems to have pushed us toward what you're talking about. His is a narrative that is that third space.

Jessica: He had an inclusive narrative. He believed that when white people gave up doing these things that they were doing, that they would actually be the happier for it. He didn't believe this was just Black people making white people do this thing that they would hate and that would make them

---

[5] The Standing Rock water protectors joined to protest the route of the Dakota Access Pipeline, just north of the Standing Rock Sioux Reservation. However the pipeline became functional in 2017 and despite an initial ruling that the pipeline be shut down and emptied of oil and a further ruling by the Supreme Court affirming an environmental review, the pipeline remains operational. See "Treaties Still Matter: The Dakota Access Pipeline," Native Knowledge, https://americanindian.si.edu/nk360/plains-treaties/dapl.

[6] A Cheyenne idea described by the Indian psychologist Eduardo Duran.

---

unhappy. He actually thought white people would be happier if they saw the light about how we need to treat each other, what kind of society we need to create. And he was able to actually convey, with conviction, this vision such that against all odds, he was heard by many people who otherwise would not have heard this message. And we have to remember that he was killed. But whoever killed him did it precisely because he was giving the one message, shall we say, the one message that could really help us to save ourselves.

Michael: Making America live up to its promise.

Jessica: I wouldn't call it that because I think its promise, as you pointed out earlier, was flawed from the beginning. At the same time, he understood that some people are going to have to take responsibility for painful realities. It wasn't that we just had to live up to our promise. We had to live up to facing our own history and our own painful reality.

Betty: While it is time, we thank you so much for joining us, Jessica.

Michael: Jessica, that was great. Thank you very much.

Jessica: Thank you.

Chapter 6
Living Unarmed

Guest: Megan Doney
Episode Aired: February 3, 2021

Megan Doney is a professor of English at New River Community College in Virginia where she and her students survived a school shooting in the spring of 2013. Since then, Megan has written and spoken extensively about that experience; her work has been published in Inside Higher Ed, Earth & Altar, *and* Creative Nonfiction, *as well as the anthology* If I Don't Make It, I Love You: Survivors in the Aftermath of School Shootings, *and in the forthcoming anthology,* Allegheny. *Her essay "The Wolf and the Dog" was nominated for a Pushcart Prize.[1] Megan serves on the board of the Virginia Center for Public Safety.*

When we spoke with Megan Doney in early February 2021, social and political events in the U.S. were swirling at a fever pitch. Jonathan's summary at the beginning of our interview captured some of the spin:

Within the span of three weeks, we went from insurrection to impeachment to inauguration, and now we're back to having the same debates over gun control that we've been having for the past 40 or 50 years. But it's now gotten to the point where armed insurrectionists are carrying AR-15s into the halls of Congress and members of Congress are refusing to go through metal detectors because of their freedom to carry a gun.

---

[1] Doney, M. (2020). The Wolf and the Dog. *Creative Nonfiction,* no. 73. https://creative-nonfiction.org/writing/the-wolf-and-the-dog/.

We sought Megan out to talk about her experience as a survivor of an active shooter incident, so we could hear from someone directly impacted by gun violence in the U.S. In our conversation, she pierces generalized schemas of how single-shooter events "typically" occur with precise, personal memories: how she wrote her witness statement in red ballpoint ink, how sirens in April have become perpetually painful, how she has become hyper aware of the location of doors. Megan's sensory details bring us close to the haunting and enduring disorientation of such trauma.

Against the backdrop of our national struggle over gun control, and the unforgettable images of pro-gun seditionists wielding semi-automatic weapons in Congress, Megan's clarity and attention to detail about her experience gave us a poignant close-up view of the long-term psychological harm gun violence wreaks. The power of her descriptions of how her life was forever changed by her struggles to heal from the shock show us how difficult, crucial—and essential—it is to pay close attention to such experiences of trauma.

Interview

Jonathan: About a month ago, we all remember vividly that the U.S. Capitol was stormed by a murderous, seditionist, white-supremacist, antisemitic mob. They were armed with guns and knives and bear spray and pipe bombs and nooses and all the rest. They came to fight; they were wearing their MAGA hats, waving Trump flags, carrying QAnon signs. And in the time since, Donald Trump was impeached, and Joe Biden has been inaugurated. We have a new president, but we also have new members of Congress, including Marjorie Taylor Greene and Lauren Boebert, who is fighting for her right to carry a concealed weapon onto the House floor. That's where we are at this moment.

Betty: It's really incredible, isn't it?

Jonathan: Within the span of three weeks, we went from insurrection to impeachment to inauguration, and now we're back to having the same debates over gun control that we've been having for the past 40 or 50 years. But it's now gotten to the point where armed insurrectionists are carrying AR-15s into the halls of Congress and members of Congress are refusing to go through metal detectors because of their freedom to carry a gun.

Betty: It really is remarkable how guns are being brought into spaces intended, and solely designed, for civic discussion, collaboration, and negotiation. And that just says something in a symbolic way right there, doesn't it, about what is happening nationally. The insistence on these brute weapons of force in spaces where we're supposed to be talking and collaborating, where we're supposed to negotiate our differences with language. I don't think it can be starker than that.

Jonathan: When you combine the force and the intimidation that is present when guns are present with the irrationality of false-flag conspiracy theories, which assert that the shootings we have witnessed are somehow "false-flags," or fictions concocted by anti-gun activists looking for justification to take away people's guns, it becomes mind boggling. We are in a period when it seems like there is no way for one side to argue meaningfully with the other, because, of course, what we see as rational, the opposition considers irrational and vice versa.

Betty: With all that you're addressing, Jonathan, it's a particularly great opportunity for us to talk to somebody who has been a survivor of a school shooting. She's gone through it firsthand.

Jonathan: Yes, indeed. Thank you so much for joining us, Megan Doney.

Megan Doney: Thank you so much for inviting me. This is an incredible honor. I really appreciate it.

Betty: So, Megan, just to orient us, you are a person who has survived a single-shooter incident, and that is, for a lot of us, beyond a worst nightmare. It must be hard for you to talk about, so we want to make sure you're feeling contained and okay. When people come to me with a traumatic experience, I say to them, "You don't have to say anything that you don't want to." I know that you've been speaking and writing on this, but every conversation and every interface is different. And I also know that every conversation about this incident can have its impacts. So I want to ground ourselves in that knowledge.

That said, given that we are awash in too many of these random mass-shooting incidents, can you tell us about yours and when it happened? Perhaps you can give us a sense of what you went through.

Megan: So I struggle with the pronouns. I don't always know whether I should call it "my" shooting or "the" shooting or "our" shooting, but "my" shooting happened on April 12, 2013, at the mall site of the community college where I'm a professor in Virginia. And when I say the mall site, that refers to a satellite campus that is literally in a shopping mall. So, in addition to the campus that's in that building, there's also an actual shopping mall there. At the time of "my" shooting there was a food court and other shops. On the afternoon of April 12, 2013, one of our students entered the building with a shotgun and opened fire. He shot a student and one of our staff members. They both survived, thankfully, but they were badly injured.

I was in class with my students that afternoon, and right around two o'clock, we heard the first gunshot and one of my students said, "What was that?" I initially thought it was a car backfiring. And I walked across the room from the instructor console to the door to the classroom, and I opened it for a moment. And then I heard two more shots. And, at that point, I knew what it was. I thought to myself for just a second, "Should I close the door? Do I lock us in here?" But this classroom was adjacent to an emergency exit, and so I opened the door wide and turned to my students and commanded, "Get out!" And they were just gone. They were out the door. As a trauma therapist, I am sure you understand that in moments like that how time stops making sense; it stops working.

Betty: Yes.

Megan: And so it seemed like it happened so quickly. And many of them left all of their stuff in the room. They were over the tables and out the door. Some of them jumped in their cars and peeled off. Some of them were just standing out there. I was baffled because as we were standing out there, I could still hear the gunfire from inside. I thought, "Why isn't everyone else coming out? Why are we the only ones out here?" And I thought, "Is he killing everyone? Did I make a mistake?" And then, I thought for a moment that maybe I had completely misread the situation and had traumatized my own students for no reason. I remember so clearly standing there in complete bafflement, not understanding what was really happening. But then the sirens started, and that was another confirmation that this was real.

And some of my students and I, we hid behind cars in the parking lot for a little while, and there were some women who herded us into their car. They let me use their cell phone because I didn't have anything on me. I had left all of my stuff in the building. At this moment, I just couldn't make sense of what was happening. Years later, one of my students asked me if

I was scared. And I said I wasn't scared until afterward. I was frightened afterward. Almost immediately the media was there. While we were still standing out in the parking lot, reporters were coming up and sticking their microphones in my face and saying, "Tell us what just happened." And I was saying, "Get away. Who are you? What?"

And finally, the injured women were taken away by emergency health personnel. The shooter was subdued by an unarmed off-duty security officer who had shouted at him to put the gun down, and he did. He was arrested. Then people started coming out of the building. I could see and hug some of my other students and colleagues who were still in there. I remember giving a statement to the police at the end of the day. They wanted witness statements, and I remember using a red ballpoint pen to write out my statement—I remember that very clearly. But I was not able to say very much. I recall hearing the police talk about me, saying, "She's in shock. You need to get her something." And I was thinking, "Oh, they're talking about me, aren't they?"

The shooter was arrested and, a year later, he was sentenced to 38 years in prison. He was 19 at the time of the shooting.

Betty: I know you've written about it, and you've spoken about it. But this time, how is it to tell it?

Megan: My heart is pounding, and my hands are freezing.

Betty: I want to make sure you're okay to keep going because this is the impact of such an event.

Megan: Yes. This is very familiar. I expected the physical sensations. I have learned to expect this. So it's not a problem.

Betty: You had mentioned that the media showed up and they were sticking microphones in your faces, and we see so much of that scenario on national media. What we don't see is the riot and disorientation of what's going on with each survivor internally.

Megan: Yes.

Betty: This happened in April 2013. So it's many years ago. As you said that day started like any other day and then it became a very different and significant day. How has it been since then? How did it change you?

Megan: Well, I'm a very good student. My way of trying to cope with most things is to read. But one of the worst parts of the aftermath was being failed by literature. That was actually devastating. As a professor, I have access to every academic database that you can think of. And I searched for hours for a scholarly article about what happens to professors who survive a school shooting or who witness a school shooting. And just for additional context, at that time, I lived in Blacksburg, Virginia, which is where Virginia Tech is. So "my" shooting was the second school shooting in this county in a five-mile radius.

One might think there would be a lot of literature about educators who had been through this—and there was almost nothing. I found a PhD dissertation from Finland and one dissertation from this country. There was no scholarly research about the impact of a random shooting on professors. I found all kinds of stuff about students: how to support students, how to improve organizational culture, descriptions of safety measures and all that. But I needed someone to say, "Here's what's going to happen to you. This is what it's going to be like three months out, six months out—a year out. This is the percentage of teachers who are still able to go back to the classroom. Yes, you are normal." I really needed someone to say what you're feeling is normal and you are going to be alright. And when I didn't find that, I thought, "Oh maybe I'm not going to be alright."

And I have books about travel, divorce, loss of a child, loss of a sibling, loss of a pet. I had memoirs about everything that you could think of. And there were no memoirs about an educator surviving a school shooting. So I thought, "I guess that's what I have to do. I guess that's the book that I'm going to have to write." I needed to write my way out of this and to say, "You will live. You will be able to go back to the classroom. You will be able to find that joy with your students again. And you're going to make it through this."

Jonathan: I'm struck by what you're saying, namely that "yes, you are normal." Although that's meant to be comforting, it's also quite disturbing that being a survivor of a school shooting is somehow a new normal— that this is an occurrence we have had to learn to live with through the first-person experiences of people like yourself and the proliferation of such accounts, from within your county and all across the country, from Columbine to Sandy Hook to Parkland.

Betty: And myriad other sites in between.

Jonathan: Megan, you went from being Megan who is picking up the groceries and prepping for the class and interacting with her family and her neighbors and living her life, to Megan who has survived a school shooting. Can you talk about how your own perception of yourself and your place in the world has changed?

Megan: In my essay in *Creative Nonfiction* one of the things that I mentioned is a new awareness of doors. One of the ways that my perception of architecture has rearranged itself is that I now pay attention to where the door is wherever I go, and I never paid attention to that before. Now I look for something like that first. I remember a later moment at the library when I saw a teenager with his hands in the pockets of his hoodie. I just immediately thought of the gun he might have in his pockets. Of course, it turns out that he's just got mittens in there. Whenever I hear a siren now, I assume that it's a school shooting, especially in April. Because April was the month of the Virginia Tech shooting, of my shooting, of the Columbine shooting. I just assume that if there's a siren in April, it must be a school shooting. I have been working on a poem in my mind in which all other emergencies are canceled in April. There's no other reason for a siren in April. It can only be a school shooting.

So those are some of the terrible ways that things are different now. The wonderful ways are that I know that that day made me so much less afraid of life. I don't know that I would have had the courage to do so many things, not least of which is to marry again. I was going through a divorce when the shooting happened, and I don't know that I would have been brave enough to marry again. It's a brave thing to be able to say "yes" to love. And my husband has given me so much courage in every way that he has said "yes" to me. He's made it possible for me to say "yes" to living, to say "yes" to not being scared. That Friday was a beautiful April morning. It seemed like a Friday. My dad was coming down to visit me that weekend. I knew he was going to probably be at my house when I got home. But I ended up that day writing a witness statement in bright red ink.

Once I learned how that day was to go, I discovered paradoxically that it's hard to be afraid of other things. I used to be a terrible hypochondriac. If I had a headache, it had to be a brain aneurysm. I was a catastrophizing thinker. For some reason, that day cured me of that kind of thinking in a powerful way.

Betty: It sounds like you met an extreme, and on the adaptive or positive end of things, it really adjusted all of your fears in an organizational manner. It gave you something even as it took things away. As a serious student of trauma, which you are now, and not by choice, you activated your brain to ground yourself. The brain isn't going to wait around to associate. For instance, when April sirens go off, you know it signals a special danger. Your active decision of "I'm going to write my way out of this" allowed you to discover and use your voice. At that point, the personal has become political in your writings.

So what's it been like to move into using your voice in this way as you see similar things happen to other people in school settings, to other teachers, to people in the Capitol just recently? How does that impact you, given that you're one of the people who has actually been in their shoes?

Megan: It's shattering to see it happen at other schools. I wrote an essay "A Most Beautiful Country in Ruins." I had just lost my dog, an incredible creature that grounded me through my own shooting. She died February 3, 2018, and February 14 was the Parkland massacre. And that was the first school shooting since mine that I had to live through without her. And it was awful. I heard it on the radio coming home from work. I heard the news reports, and I had to pull over because I thought to myself, "I know how this is going to feel. I can picture the scene in the parking lot." That's one of the things that is particularly awful for anyone who has been wounded by gun violence. And I'm using the word *wounded* to mean psychological, spiritual, and physical injuries. I don't think you ever get a break because not only does it keep happening in actuality, it also happens over and over and over again in your mind. It feels like there's no respite.

Sometimes people have asked, "Why are you doing this? Why are you writing this? Why are you engaging in activism?" The only reason is because I have had to write a document called "Post-Shooting Lesson Plans" and I don't want anyone to ever have to write that document again. Full stop. No teacher should have to have a Word document called "Post-Shooting Lesson

Plans." And I can't make it any clearer than that. There's nothing noble in this. I don't want anyone to do that. It's terrible. It's terrible.

Betty: It sounds like you're making sense out of nonsense. "Post-Shooting Lesson Plans" is like a symbol for you. It's absurdist to have lesson plans that are organized modes of pedagogy designed to transmit knowledge and then labeling it, "Post-Shooting." It turns it completely upside down.

Megan: Educators have been taught to organize their lesson plans with the acronym *SWBAT*, which stands for "students will be able to." That's how you plan. So I just called "Post-Shooting Lesson Plans" my SWBATs. By the end of the day after coming back from the shooting, my students will be able to do the following: They will know that they don't have to talk to the media if they don't want to. They will know that they can take their grades where they are and just be done with the rest of the semester if they want. They will know that those random people wandering around the school are counselors from the county. It's lunacy that this document even has to exist.

Jonathan: Megan, kids go through active shooter drills at school—and this reminds me of the famous Mike Tyson quote: "Everyone's got a plan until they're punched in the face." How much does planning matter when you're in the moment and rationality and the ability to think and reason go out the window?

Megan: This was 2013. I don't know whether my students then had grown up having active shooter drills. I'm not sure they did, actually. I certainly never had one. And I can't know what training would have done for me. I remember an episode of *This American Life* from a few years ago in which they interviewed a number of teachers from Marjory Stoneman Douglas High School who talked about the training that they went through.[2] And on the day of the massacre, they still did something different from what they had been trained to. They were told to close your classroom door and lock it. And then they had kids coming up to the door and begging to be let in. They're not going to say no. Of course, they opened the door and let those kids in.

[2] Semien, R. (2018). Act One: Ready as you'll never be. Before the next one. *This American Life*, WBEZ Chicago. https://www.thisamericanlife.org/659/before-the-next-one.

My husband was a military officer, and he says that people who make claims about what they would do in such a situation exhibit "the bravery of being out of range." He goes on to say that if you've never been in the fog of war, you don't have any idea what you're going to do. You don't have any idea how you'll react. If someone had asked me at eight o'clock that morning, "What would you do if someone opened fire at your school?" I can't imagine what I would have said. In that moment, I think that maybe we have an idea about what fear feels like. But I think for me, whatever the fear was, the most powerful feeling I had was an incredibly pure, cold, utterly rational urge that said, "Just do what I tell you, and that is get out right now." That's it.

Jonathan: I want to try to shift from your personal experience to the political dimension, which is my role here at *Mind of State*. I'll tell you, Megan, I so appreciate you being on this show. I've been a gun control activist since 1981, when I was 15 years old. I'll date myself—it was when Jim Brady was permanently disabled from the gunshot wound during the attempted assassination of Ronald Reagan. Back then, our focus was on handguns. And now, 40 years later, the weapons are more lethal, more numerous, more available. The politics have shifted so dramatically in ways that I could not have possibly imagined.

Megan: Yes.

Jonathan: You've been out on the front lines of advocacy from a personal experience, and you've turned political. We have David Hogg calling on the Biden administration to appoint a gun safety czar, a similar approach to what he's taken on climate. Are you more optimistic? Less optimistic? We've been let down time and time again, yet the vast majority of the American public supports common sense gun reform.

Megan: Right. They do.

Jonathan: What do you see and what are you feeling?

Megan: I think that there is reason to be hopeful and that a lot of changes happen on the local level; they happen on the small scale. And because of that, since they're not on the national radar, I think it's easy for some people to despair and say, "Oh well, if Sandy Hook didn't change everything, then, there is no hope." The lack of national response after that is unforgivable.

However, there are states that have made incredible changes in gun regulation and Virginia is one of them. Lucy McBath, whose son, Jordan, was killed at a gas station, is now in Congress. She's representing a district in Georgia.[3] So those changes are happening. And I think that by having hard conversations with one another, there can be change. But the conversations are incredibly difficult, and there are many people who are resistant to having them. Policies are one thing, but we as Americans need to be having far more difficult conversations about what it means to be a man, what it means to be safe, what it means to be free. And those are not questions that are going to be answered with one or many laws.

Betty: Say more about that, Megan. When you say we need to have more difficult conversations on what it is to be a man, what it is to be safe, and what it is to be free—how does this relate to gun control?

Megan: School gun violence, in particular, is almost exclusively perpetrated by men. And I get very frustrated when I read reports of school shootings in the news, and they talk about the shooter or the perpetrator or people, in general. It's not people, in general. It's a boy or it's a man. I'm sorry to be blunt about that, but the research bears that out.[4] Something like 99 percent of the people who do this are male. There are others in this country who want to blame this on medication, on video games, on the demise of the nuclear family, and any other thing that you want to talk about. However, girls and women also take psychiatric medication; they also play video games; they also have the same access to firearms; they also watch the same movies; they also grow up within the same family structures; and they do not take AR-15s to school and kill everyone. They just don't.

[3] Lucy McBath represents Georgia's 7th Congressional District. After her son was killed in 2012 she dedicated her life to activism. After the Marjory Stoneman Douglas massacre, she decided to run for Congress and was elected in 2018.

[4] Schmall, E. (2023). Most Mass Shooting Suspects Are Male. *The New York Times.* https://www.nytimes.com/2023/03/27/us/woman-shooter-nashville.html. See also The Violence Project at https://www.theviolenceproject.org/. DeMarco, N. (2019). Nearly All Mass Shooting Are Committed by Men. Why Isn't Masculinity a Bigger Part of the Debate? *The Washington Post.* https://www.washingtonpost.com/podcasts/post-reports/nearly-all-mass-shootings-are-committed-by-men-why-isnt-masculinity-a-bigger-part-of-the-debate/.

Betty: Right.

Megan: Women are probably more likely to take out their agony and aggression on themselves. They engage in self-harming behaviors—and men and boys take it out on other people. So, from my perspective, that is a conversation that men need to have among themselves. They need to talk about why boys and men decide that an appropriate way of exercising their need for control is to murder other people. And many school shootings have an element of gender retribution in them. We know this because the shooters leave behind artifacts that say, "This is why I'm doing it. This woman wouldn't have sex with me."

I have no patience with people who say "it's because there are all these gun free zones. There was no one else there to shoot them." Not a single shooter, to my knowledge, has said, "I picked this place because it was a gun free zone." They said, "I picked this place because this woman wouldn't sleep with me, they wouldn't pay attention to me, and now I'm going to make them all pay attention to me." Culturally, we're really resistant to listening to the people who perpetrate these murders, and they tell us why they do it. Maybe that's what we ought to listen to.

Jonathan: You're absolutely right, of course. But now post January 6, with the insurrection in the Capitol …

Betty: Of which the perpetrators were predominantly male.

Jonathan: Absolutely.

Megan: Yes.

Jonathan: Stormed by murderous, seditionist, white-supremacists—who were mostly armed men. Yet, the debate has now shifted to a woman, Marjorie Taylor Greene, who wants to carry a concealed weapon into the Congress.[5] And she is now one of the leading voices in this debate over gun control, and *freedom* is the word that she constantly invokes. And yet, Lucy

---

[5] Lauren Boebert also promoted carrying a gun on Capitol Hill. Flynn, M. (2021). In Ad, Lawmaker Vows to Carry Her Glock around DC and on Hill. *The Washington Post.* https://www.washingtonpost.com/local/legal-issues/boebert-capitol-guns/2021/01/04/a59f70f8-4e9d-11eb-83e3-322644d82356_story.html.

McBath, also from Georgia, is on the other side of this debate. So, I wonder how gender is going to impact the debate going forward.

Megan: I do, too. And, you know, there are a lot of women who have bought into this idea that guns are protective. But again, the evidence is overwhelming that a gun in the home endangers women more than men, by factors of hundreds. It does not keep women safe. As a woman, you are much more likely to be shot by your partner with that gun. And again, I think that we need to have some much more challenging conversations about what *safety* really means. Or *freedom*. I do an exercise with my students where we talk about the word *freedom*, and you can follow up qualifying the word with *freedom from, freedom to, freedom of.* We try to fill in a lot of those blanks in order to think and see what we are actually talking about. For instance *freedom of speech* or *freedom to associate*, I want my students to unpack what sort of values and beliefs are embedded in the way in which we complete those phrases. But there has to be a *freedom from random terrorism* in our schools, in the movie theater, at the concert, at church. I mean, what public venue hasn't been the scene of a mass shooting so far? I'm not sure that I could name one. I just think that those questions about what it truly means to be safe are much more difficult and much more challenging than hammering out legislation. Not that I've ever hammered out legislation.

Jonathan: Writing policy is certainly hard, but in a world where the politics are fraught with emotion and a lot of irrationality, it's that much more difficult. I'm struck by listening to you that you are so rational and thoughtful and evidence-based and nuanced. And I wonder how proponents of gun reform can possibly engage, when the opposition defending the Second Amendment is being fueled by arguments supported by false-flag conspiracies, crazy theories, a lack of logic, a lack of evidence, and an unwillingness to even engage in the consideration of data and evidence. What's your experience been when you're coming from the rational and confronting the irrational?

Megan: Honestly, I don't feel like I can do that anymore. I'm not sure what the point is in trying to engage. Earlier in my journey through the activism world, I went to some gun shows and I brought my now husband with me. I thought, if you're going to have an activist role, you should know what happens at a gun show. You should have firsthand experience with seeing things. What we saw were people in the parking lot selling guns out of the back of a truck. We saw vendors at that gun show selling Nazi memorabilia and swastika flags. Even at gun shows, there are private sellers who will sell an AR-15 for cash. I'd ask, "Do you mean to say that if I write you a check for $1,700 right now, I could walk out with this?" And they'd say "yeah!" And under the law, that means I'm a responsible gun owner.

Jonathan: You could drive a truck through the loophole.

Megan: Right. Because I bought that legally. I don't see any point anymore in trying to have a conversation with someone who says to me, "You should have had a gun that day or if you get raped, that's your own fault, because you weren't carrying." I can't do that. And so I think that the best thing for me personally is to be as good of an advocate as I can for the things that we do know make a difference: lock your guns up, keep them away from children. We know that background checks work. We know emergency risk protection orders work. These are not things that take away anything from anyone.

Jonathan: Progress is being made, even if we have to measure in glacial terms. The NRA is in retreat. They are moving from New York to Texas. Still, Second Amendment activists are wearing swastikas and carrying nooses and wearing sweatshirts with antisemitic Holocaust denial slogans. The sides are showing pretty clearly who they are. Hopefully we are seeing some progress, even if too late and not enough. Hopefully we are getting there because of the bravery of people like yourself who are sharing their experiences.

Betty: And Megan, you speak from a position of experience and common sense, which is in short supply these days. As you move forward through this journey, this transformation as you've called it, where are you now and where are you going to take this, if you can even say?

Megan: I continue to show up when I can. I'm not affiliated with any particular group or organization right now. I certainly speak up at meetings when something related to gun violence prevention is on the floor. What I have been working on the most is a collection of essays about life after the shooting. I try to interrogate this question of "safety" and what it means to live knowing that nowhere is safe. The working title of the collection is *Unarmed*. It has multiple meanings. I choose to live unarmed. I don't carry a gun. I don't have one in my home. I can't think of a situation that is going to change my decision to do that. But I also want to live unarmed with the meaning that I want to say "yes" to what might happen. I don't want the day of "my shooting" to control every decision that I make from now on. I want to be open. I want to be vulnerable. I want to love and be hurt and to accept whatever happens. I know now that safety is an illusion. So why not walk gratefully into whatever is ahead of you?

Betty: Spoken like a true survivor. Megan, thank you so much for speaking with us and sharing your insights. They are invaluable.

Megan: Thank you so much for having me. It was a great honor to be here.

Chapter 7
The Trauma of Syria

Guest: Anne Barnard
Episode aired: April 9, 2019

Anne Barnard is a veteran reporter and Middle East correspondent who led the New York Times's *coverage of the war in Syria for six years as Beirut bureau chief, from 2012 to 2018. She has reported on conflicts around the world for the* Times *and other outlets, from Syria, Iraq, Lebanon, Turkey, Libya, Gaza, Russia, Haiti, Pakistan, Afghanistan, and, of course, the United States. When we interviewed her in 2019, she had recently moved back from Beirut to New York and was serving as the 2018–19 Edward R. Murrow Fellow at the Council on Foreign Relations.*

At this time, in 2023, four years after we spoke with Anne about the impacts of the Syrian civil war, this excerpt from our conversation stands out:

Betty: …There is a conflict going on under the surface [in Syria], the United States and Russia are involved in it, and I wonder if it is going to surface at some point.

Anne: We are in pretty deep denial, and it will get closer and closer the longer that we deny it. Syrians have said, "If this is allowed to happen here, it will happen in the West." When I used to hear them tell me that, I thought they were being a little rhetorical or histrionic. And that doesn't sound as over the top to me now as it used to … How far will it go? We have authoritarianism in Hungary. We have Trump talking about journalists the same way Assad does, to be quite frank.

Betty: The Nazi Party is on the rise in Germany.

Michael: The 20th-century conflict ultimately was not between capitalism and communism, but ultimately between liberalism and authoritarianism. That's what we're seeing now.

These comments tempted us to retitle this episode, "The Lesson of Syria." Another war, sparked by Russia's unprovoked invasion of Ukraine in February 2022, has now raged on for over 18 months, with no end in sight. That our 2019 discussion—focused on the psychological impacts of the denials and falsehoods obscuring the traumas of the Syrian war—should unwittingly contain predictions of Putin's authoritarian attempt to annex Ukraine three years later, reveals how crucial it is to pay attention to trauma and its impacts. The trauma of Syria has indeed become its lesson to the entire world.

This affirms what Pauline Boss (Chapter 3), Judith Herman (Chapter 4), and Jessica Benjamin (Chapter 5) have asserted in their Mind of State *discussions regarding the corrosive repercussions that the denial of harm can bring. Be it individually, interpersonally—or, as our conversation with Anne shows—geopolitically, engagement with trauma and its truths is crucial to avoid repetitions of historical abuses and atrocities enacted by perpetrators intent on obscuring reality.*

While we place this episode with Anne Barnard on "The Trauma of Syria" at the end of this section on Acknowledging Death, Trauma & Loss, *we note that we could have also placed it in our following section,* Why Truth Matters? *because so much of this discussion centers on the consequential truths and falsehoods about the Syrian war and its long-term global impacts. We use it as a bridge, to underscore how interwoven trauma and truth are.*

Interview

Betty: I'm proud, honored, and delighted to introduce this week's guest who is one of my oldest and dearest friends. Welcome to *Mind of State*, Anne.

Anne: Thank you so much.

Betty: Anne, we started this conversation off-mic, after you had listened to a couple of *Mind of State*'s first episodes and started to consider, in a manner of speaking, the mind of Syria, which you've covered for the past few years. It made sense to invite you to talk with us because Syria is a state that impacts so many other states, politically and psychologically as well. You've covered this civil war in Syria for almost seven of its soon-to-be eight-year-long conflict—including from Syria, but often remotely from your base in Beirut, Lebanon. Can you say why that was and what the challenges of covering a civil war remotely were for you?

Anne: Well, on the one hand, Syria may be the most documented conflict in history. But it also poses unique challenges because it is both a police state and a conflict zone. And reporters often deal with one or the other, but it's not that often that we're in the middle of both at the same time. So, at the beginning of the conflict, it was hard to operate in Syria because the government was very controlling of journalists' movements and who they would allow into the country. Later, when rebels gained some territory, some reporters would go in there—and that was extremely risky due to the massive bombing by the government of rebel-held areas and also, especially later, because of the threat of kidnapping. So, one team would go in there, and I was part of the team that would go in whenever possible to the government-held areas. But again, you couldn't always go. You couldn't always get a visa. Much of what we did to supplement was to work with sources who we knew from meeting them in person previously in Syria or elsewhere, but keeping in touch with them online, and to work with other sources who we eventually met online through them. And the war became very much documented by Syrians themselves, from all sides and perspectives on the conflict. They would video and upload and contact people outside the country and tell their own story to us.

Betty: So, social media played a huge factor, or was a big tool, in reporting on this story for you guys outside of Syria?

Anne: Exactly. It was a tool of direct one-to-one communication with people. And also people would be broadcasting things that we would then try to verify.

Betty: In that regard, what was it like to have access, not just when you were in the country, but all the time? Because one of the functions of social media and the internet is that you're accessible to information constantly. And verifying information must be pretty challenging. But it must have seemed endless, just as any online channels are limitless.

Anne: Exactly. In addition to the traumatic events that we would witness in person when inside Syria or when you meet with someone and they describe the harrowing things they've been through, we also had a 24-hour flow of front-line images and messages even when I was physically safe in Beirut, at my home or in my office. I was in constant touch with people who were being bombed, who were in very dangerous situations, and who were taking big risks to talk to me. We think of war correspondents as people who go to the war and then they come back. But we were always in the war zone in a way and also always struggling with a bit of guilt over being in touch with these people when we were in a safer place.

Michael: A virtual correspondent.

Betty: It's a 21st-century war correspondence that you went through. We, with the 24/7 news cycle, often talk about how we're sipping water from a firehose, in terms of taking in information. You're sipping toxic information and material from a firehose. And now you have been looking at this conflict in Syria for years. The numbers are staggering: an estimated 500,000 Syrians killed and 100,000 imprisoned without knowledge of where they are.[1] Family members are looking for them. So millions of family members are searching for loved ones, and people are imprisoned in a gulag-like system.

Anne: Half the country's population has been displaced: 5 million outside the country, something like 9 million or more inside the country. I wouldn't say that 500,000 rebels have been killed, but the estimate is that a total of 500,000 Syrians have been killed.

Betty: These numbers are massive. You talk about hundreds of thousands of people killed, millions displaced, which is half of the population of Syria. You're covering this, and it must seem overwhelming.

Anne: It is overwhelming. I really should add that everything we've gone through as journalists, humanitarian workers, those trying to engage with the conflict, it's actually nothing compared to what Syrians themselves are going through. It's their family members and themselves who are being tortured

---

[1] This figure includes rebel and government fighters and civilians and is an estimate as the UN stopped counting early in the conflict. It is likely an undercount.

and bombed. On top of that, they are constantly sharing information on their cellphones. They too multiply their own exposure to traumatic events by sharing this information and reacting to it, in addition to what they've experienced directly.

Betty: In that regard, the trauma is exponential and refracted and mirrored in many different ways. And in Assad, there is a mass perpetrator—if we might call him that. And the international situation in terms of the UN Security Council is intensified by Russia's conflict with the United States. The United States is exhausted by its conflict in Iraq, so it does not want to expand its intervention, maybe for good reasons. In covering this massive conflict, have things changed over the six years or seven years that you have been observing it?

Anne: The only thing that has changed is the depth and the volume of the human disaster. It started as a popular uprising, mostly peaceful. Then, there was a huge crackdown, and some people took up arms. Then, what we saw changing was the level of violence. There were terrible atrocities by all sides of the conflict. But when we're talking about the state and the mind of the Syrian state—it has the greatest responsibility under international law. It operates all the machinery of violence that is at the disposal of the state. And it uses all of it. We were shocked the first time there was an artillery attack on a neighborhood that had supported the rebels. Then we were shocked to see helicopters bombing neighborhoods. Then we were shocked to see warplanes bombing neighborhoods and Scud missiles and naval bombs being dropped and then chemical weapons used. Each person has a deep, unbelievable story, and then you multiply that by millions. It did become overloading for the public as well as for the people trying to assimilate that horror and explain it to the public. How do you get across both the magnitude of this war and the human individual scale of it at the same time? That was our challenge.

Betty: And that is a trauma happening that is, as you put it, hard to digest. The massive numbers, the overwhelming information, the magnitude of destruction—and then the individual stories that are excruciating to read, like that of the fourteen-year-old boy crying outside of a hospital because he just found out his mother had been shelled and may have died in the hospital, after he had just lost his father the week before.

Anne: Yes, that was when we were reporting on the ground in Aleppo.

Betty: How do you decide who to focus on? How do you do this on a daily basis? How do you orchestrate a team to cover this and then think? How do you maintain the capacity to think in all this?

Anne: Yes, getting time to think and step back is always hard in daily journalism, even more so when the material is so beyond human scale. I think some of it is serendipity, when you come across a story that not only is very compelling, but also the person is willing to talk to you, and they are able to go through the verification process of …

Betty: And they are risking their lives to talk to you, right?

Anne: In many cases, yes. Or they've fled to relative safety, but they're nervous about the safety of people who are still back in Syria, family members. Those people who have an amazing story that plugs into some larger issue, that's what really makes us commit to an in-depth report. But, of course, we had many daily news stories where we would just quote whoever we could reach who was a witness to a certain situation, and then we would move on. We've probably talked to thousands of individual Syrians over the course of the conflict.

Betty: And in terms of a micro-narrative like an individual's story, and how it might connect to a larger issue that's going on, did you experience frustration that these stories were not moving the international political scene?

Anne: Yes, I think we all as journalists understand that our primary role is to document and to tell stories and have them be heard. And that, by itself, is meaningful. At the same time, I think what we all hope for is that the information will matter to government decision-making. And, if there are atrocities going on, we have been trained to expect that we expose atrocities and abuses of power not just to air them, but ideally to prompt action to stop them. Now, of course, as you mentioned, Syria was in a complicated situation, and there was major debate in other countries' governments about how and whether they could intervene. But it ended up being a proxy war. Other countries, including the U.S., got involved and much of that involvement only seemed to make things worse. At the same time, the world as a whole seemed impotent. We have this ideal of an international system that is supposed to be able to stop such horror and ensure there is a "never again" to such horror. We are not comparing this directly to the Holocaust in scale, but this is a massive atrocity perpetrated by a state, and it happens with impunity. And if that authoritarian state wins, other authoritarian leaders can look at that and say, "Oh wow. That's a good system to have. That's a good way to respond to civil unrest."

Michael: I think people missed out on how important Libya was to the beginning of this, with respect to what Putin took from Gaddafi's and Obama's failure in Libya—and Obama's subsequent failure in Syria. I'm curious—what do you think people in the West misunderstood or missed or didn't connect with about this conflict? We seemed to see it as "other," as outside of "us." And that seems to be a moral failing on the West's part. As someone who was on the ground, what do you think we misunderstood about the beginning of the Syrian civil war and how it evolved, and what lessons have we learned—or not?

Anne: Well, I always say that one problem with the U.S. response was that Obama talked loudly and carried a small stick—which was the opposite of Teddy Roosevelt's advice. So, he spoke as if he were going to fully support this uprising and Syrians believed that and took larger risks as a result. One thing that we missed in our understanding was that words from the president are taken seriously. As much as there's a lot of resentment toward the United States in the Middle East, people do believe that the United States, even if rhetorically and very inconsistently, still supports ideals of self-determination, civil rights, freedom, and democracy. That's a big reason why the Syrians took a risk to talk with us journalists. They thought that by getting their message out to the world through us, something would change. I'm not saying that they all wanted a massive U.S. intervention, not at all. But somehow, abstractly, they thought the world wouldn't let this go on when all they were asking for was dignity, citizenship, and a little more freedom and self-determination in their lives.

Betty: When I'm thinking about the mind of Syria and the mind of the world toward Syria in terms of Obama's "speak loudly and carry a small stick," it occurs to me that the U.S. disconnect in Syria may have been a by-product of the conflict in Iraq, which was so messy and maybe ill-conceived.

Anne: Maybe!!!

Betty: As a trauma therapist and as somebody who is involved in thinking about trauma in many different ways, there seems to be a certain disassociation, a certain numbness, and a certain unwillingness to go there. There is an unwillingness to face these atrocities, to meet this challenge maybe because of exhaustion, or perhaps due to previous traumas. We don't, of course, know if a state has the capacity to disassociate because it's a collective of people and they are not all thinking in the same way. But there's some echo, or some tracer, of this for me. I don't know if this resonates with what you have observed.

Anne: Well, it's interesting, when you were just talking about dissociation, I thought about our dis-association from allies and from engagement around the world. That is something that our state is doing. We have to go back to what Michael said about the "other." To me, this is the absolute heart of the situation. There's always been some racism and Islamophobia in people in America and the West in their perception of the Middle East. "It's over there. Violence is just what they do. It's not our problem." And then after 9/11, it was "This is a threat to us. We are afraid of these people. We don't think they are regular people." People are so afraid of the threat of Islamist terrorism, which, in fact, is not that common in the West. We are willing to see almost *any* number of atrocities against Muslims and people of color in the Middle East as long as it's done in the name of fighting terrorism. And that's exactly the card that Assad has been playing.

Michael: And has been allowed to play. That's the horror. The irony for me of both Iraq and Syria—and I do think Libya is the forgotten third piece of this—is that Bush's response to 9/11 was a profound moral failing and an illegal act, but Obama's failure to act more decisively in Syria was equally as bad a moral failing, if not worse, in some ways. It's as if Obama learned the worst possible lesson from the war in Iraq—which is to do nothing in the face of these profound human tragedies. And we bundle all of that up into separating ourselves from a Middle Eastern "other," which justifies our indifference to the suffering we have caused.

Anne: And we [the U.S.] did a lot to change the norms around warfare …

Michael: Absolutely.

Anne: Such as the drone wars and civilian casualties and Guantanamo and all these things. But I also want to say that the piece about overestimating or inflating in one's mind the threat of Islamic terrorism versus other threats in the world, is that there are a lot of psychological explanations for how different biases contribute to the thing that scares us the most. The media covered ISIS's atrocities far more than those of the Syrian government. But as horrible as ISIS atrocities were, they do not compare to the magnitude, the scale, of atrocities committed by the Syrian government. But most casual consumers of the news didn't grasp that. And that misconception doesn't only affect Syria, it affects the global political climate and its growing shift toward authoritarianism.

Betty: Related to the notion of disassociation is the isolationism that we experience here in the United States under Trump. But it is also impacting Western Europe, and they, too, are attempting to disassociate from this massive conflict in Syria. As you have put in your writing on how Syria changed the world, the Syrian conflict has tipped a lot of dominoes in Western Europe. And it is mirrored here in the U.S., too. Yet I don't think many in the U.S. have made this direct connection. Can you connect some of those dots for us?

Anne: A lot of people have just blanked out the details of Syria—and who can blame them, really? But in their minds now, Syria is just all about ISIS— *"it's a battle between ISIS and the government of Syria"*—which was never true and isn't true now. It's much more complicated than that. So, when they think about refugees coming from Syria, they mix it all together as if those refugees are the perpetrators of violence, as if they're ISIS, as if they're so "other," we can't possibly understand them. The reality is so far from the truth. Those people are fleeing *both* ISIS and the government. Those people are people like you and me. I can tell you that because I've spent the last years with them and, of course, one of my main missions as a journalist is to show that there is no "other." If we don't understand a place or a people, we need to go there, learn their language, talk to them, speak with them, understand them. And what you find is a lot that you can relate to.

Syria used to be a middle-income country with high levels of education and culture. It's been a civilization for 5,000 years. Its cities existed in biblical times. It is a wellspring of culture for the whole world. And we act like this is a country of dangerous hordes of people coming to invade Europe. In fact, only maybe a million Syrian refugees came to Europe as a whole, compared to the one-and-a-half to two million Syrian refugees in Lebanon, where I lived, which is a country of four million people. The level of freakout in Europe about these refugees is really out of proportion. It has to do with that "otherizing" and the over-inflation of an Islamic threat.

Michael: The irony, though, is that on the left, the people who rightly recognize the Syrians as a people who are in crisis and in need of refuge don't understand why they are refugees in the first place. There is a lack of connection to the way in which we all are responsible for their plight. And I see the inaction in Syria as potentially destabilizing NATO.

Anne: Absolutely. The reaction to the wave of refugees has led to the rise of the right in Europe. It has driven Brexit. It has, to some degree, driven the rise of Trump, which is bizarre because the number of Syrian refugees who were let into the United States, even under Obama, was minuscule. But it really has contributed to Trump's rise. You can see actual connections between far-right people online in the U.S. and Europe who support Assad. They see him as a white knight against these brown people. And the moral injury that comes from this for Syrians is enormous.

Michael: Which we should talk about.

Anne: People around the world are affected by this, but it is especially the Syrians who have paid the ultimate price. The world talked about universal human rights, and the Syrians opposing Assad took the world at its word and they took incredible risks. They did incredible things. They made lots of mistakes, too. But they put their money where their mouth was. And the world gave them less than nothing.

Betty: To speak to your comment on NATO, Michael, the UN Security Council is deadlocked and the Geneva Convention…

Michael: …but it's only because of Russia that they're deadlocked. It's Putin.

Betty: But it speaks to the ineffectual nature of the UN Security Council now. It is an institution whose effectiveness is being questioned. The Geneva

Conventions, which originated in 1864, were updated in 1949 after the horrors of World War II, and it was something that we held up as the rule of law to hopefully regulate these civil conflicts, these atrocities happening around the world. But its effectiveness is also being called into question because Assad is getting to perpetrate great harm, unfettered. And, as you both said, the magnitude of the numbers is increasing. It's happening as we speak. Confused with this are the images of ISIS beheading journalists and other captured Westerners. These images are affecting more than just one generation. I have a friend here in New York whose young son was instructed in art class to illustrate his greatest fear. He drew a picture of a member of ISIS beheading a person. The boy was 11 or 12 at the time. These images of violence and "otherism" are permeating down to our kids.

Anne: And remember, those images started in Iraq with al-Qaeda, the predecessors of ISIS. This has been happening across more than one generation.

Betty: The viral nature of these atrocious images causes them to become disassociated from their origin and thus fragmented; they float around the internet like psychological free radicals.

Anne: And people assume Syrians are the terrorists. But, in fact, ISIS, the very people who are victimizing both Iraqis and Syrians, are the true terrorists.

Betty: This speaks of the power of fear. Fear shuts down thinking and freezes the mind. Then we react. In our first *Mind of State* interview, social psychologist Sheldon Solomon spoke about what happens when people are reminded of their mortality. Unconsciously when reminded of their demise, people prioritize their in-groups and even think negatively of those outside their tribe. These images of ISIS beheadings, disaggregated from their origins, get passed around the internet and assigned, willy-nilly, to the conflicts of others—to the conflict of the "other," out there, in the Middle East. In a fear-dominated mind, which can't think, all Syrians, Iraqis, members of al-Qaeda and ISIS get lumped together as the "other" to be feared and kept out. I wonder if that is something you see as valid.

Anne: Absolutely. Moreover, those terrorist groups, like ISIS, do this on purpose. They know the psychological effect such images have. It magnifies their power in people's minds. It prompts overreactions. Al-Qaeda's attacks on 9/11 were designed to prompt an overreaction, and the United States fell right into that. We played into their hands completely, and we're still doing it.

Betty: It was a massive success on so many levels.

Anne: Yes. And I think it's not a coincidence that it was aimed at New York. And so, even liberals—the "New York elite"—felt personally in danger and didn't speak up at the very beginning when all these mistakes began. ISIS did that on purpose…

Michael: And that's the whole point of terrorism, to show you have no power.

Anne: And Assad was able to exploit it. And I don't want to downplay the horror and criminality of those attacks in any way. But it is in our power to choose how we react. This is a psychological concept: you can decide how you react to something.

Betty: Yet, it is only after a conflict or crisis, that trauma, or the reactions to the terror and the harm, sets in. And that's something you have to work through. But as you're working through it, you want to bring meaning into it and you want to assign words to the chaos because it makes no sense. Terrorism is chaotic. It's a driver of chaos. Terrorists are nihilistic. They often do not have any ideological basis for the violence they create. They aim to foment the most disorganization possible. And this disorganization, in a psychological sense, is insanity—meaning a state of not being able to regulate oneself. And it seems, in a certain sense, Syria is deeply dysregulated. And when a country is dysregulated, there is this chaotic churning of crisis. You can define trauma as something that's post-crisis—it seems Syria's not even there yet.

Anne: Yes. Instead of post-traumatic stress, I call it chronic traumatic stress.

Betty: Right. It's a state of complex and persistent stress.

Anne: Because the adrenaline rush never stops. And even more so, to continue the psychological metaphor, after abuse by trauma, you are supposed to be safe from the abuser and only then, can you start dealing with it. But in Syria, the most prolific abuser remains in power; he still has all the state's tools of perpetration and is now coming back around for the dissenters he forgot to arrest in the first place. For those people who are still in Syria, we are talking about literal and psychological repression, because people will not be able to work through their fears, let alone have a truth-and-reconciliation or transitional justice process. They will not be allowed to even speak of it publicly.

Michael: What in your mind is the future, then, for those people, or for Syria? What's your sense?

Anne: A dark period because that trauma does not go away. It is just politically, physically and psychologically repressed. Syria has been through this cycle before, with the uprising in 1982 in the city of Hama, a Muslim Brotherhood uprising that used violence and was put down with more massive violence. Many random, innocent Syrians were punished for that, and the city was leveled.

Michael: That was under Assad's father and predecessor, Hafez al-Assad.

Anne: Yes. Now it's happened on a much more enormous scale. And why would we not expect another round of this in another generation? Meanwhile, the whole country is impoverished. It's de facto occupied by Russia and Iran, plus, in the east, U.S. troops supporting a Kurdish faction. People I have talked to, even government supporters, are very upset. Even some who were personally involved in the government's war effort feel like it was for nothing. They feel like all these people died and the victory is hollow. The country is destroyed. The leaders are exposed as incompetent and uncaring...

Michael: And as criminals.

Anne: And as criminals. So, what to do?

Michael: And that's the problem, which is that it is a vassal state of Putin's Russia and of the mullahs in Iran. And that is also true of Iraq.

Anne: Iraq is an interesting example because there is still some political flow in Iraq. There is some give and take. There is a political process. I'm not saying it's a great situation, but Baghdad is much safer and more livable and alive than it was a few years ago now. It's weird to say, but it's a relative bright spot in the region.

Michael: Well, certainly the fever of their civil war broke, but when ISIS went through Anbar and other cities, Saddam's old Sunni generals took up arms.

Anne: The trauma cycle is continuing in Syria because the security forces are still torturing and doing extrajudicial executions. We've seen this cycle before.

Michael: I have read that people are just being randomly assigned death sentences inside the courts.

Anne: People have trials that last one minute, and they're assigned to execution.

Michael: As a journalist, do you find it hard to not shift over into advocacy from pure reporting? How do you deal with knowing all of this, experiencing it, seeing it, and then at the same time coming back here to the United States and seeing the dissociation and the indifference?

Betty: Also, Anne, you've spoken about the losses in your local team that have impacted your colleagues and the people who you have relied on.

Anne: I could talk for a whole hour about your questions, Michael and Betty. I have many different roles in this catastrophe. One is to discover and convey information with humanity and empathy. At the same time, I do not want to lose journalistic rigor and strategic context. I'm proud of what my team has done in placing these events in a context, to giving words and thoughts to the events without forgetting to convey the horror, for trying to marry these different things. But to do that does bring a high cost to me and my team. It is hard to keep all those things in mind, especially the things that the mind wants to just blank out, having experienced them chronically over years and years. It takes a toll. And then there's a literal toll. As I was telling you before, my team is comprised exclusively of people from the region, except for Ben Hubbard, who is my colleague and who speaks great Arabic and is American. And we have one of the most amazingly connected journalists on Syria: our main Lebanese colleague, Hwaida Saad, who is a survivor of the Lebanese civil war and has had to relive it all through this war. And we had a parade of wonderful Syrian reporting assistants who came through our bureau and worked for us, some of them for many years. All of these people have had their own personal traumas related to war and that's part of what makes them great at what they do. We all had to make a commitment not to go into advocacy because that's not our role. I tell them: Sometimes just telling the story is advocacy, and that's the way we do our advocacy. I can't tell you how many of our sources have died or disappeared or been imprisoned or tortured or been displaced.

Michael: For being sources?

Anne: Maybe some of them, yes, for speaking out in general but we tried to avoid being the direct cause of harm. We tried to take precautions so that we won't get them in trouble. Most have suffered, not because they spoke with us, but just from being Syrians. One of our Syrian staffers came to me after having been in prison for a year and a half. He was tortured [in Syria by security agents, then fled to Lebanon where he worked for us] and then driven out of Lebanon because the authorities were not sympathetic to Syrians like him who were former activists. He'd been a civilian activist who went to some demonstrations and brought medical supplies to people injured in the demonstrations. That is considered terrorism by the Syrian government. He made a commitment to moving to journalism. He spoke to people on all sides and empathized with them and told their story. He went through a lot of stress. He broke down crying when he was translating Assad's victory speech after a rigged election victory in the middle of the war.

And that's when our colleague realized he had to leave. He went to Europe and has returned to advocacy, using some of his new journalism skills. He is a videographer for MSF, or Médecins Sans Frontières—Doctors Without Borders in English—and he goes around the world and videos other refugees in situations like his. And that's part of MSF's communications about their work. I have another colleague who hasn't seen his family in six years. They are still in Syria. He was in Turkey; now he's in Berlin. I don't want to go into detail about other people's personal stories, but let's just say I don't know a single journalist who has covered Syria for this amount of time who hasn't struggled with their own reactions to the trauma, whether that's through physical or mental symptoms, or both. It is really difficult.

Michael: Do you think you're going to stop being a journalist at some point and shift over into some other voice? Is journalism an adequate voice for you at this point, or is there something else needed, do you think?

Anne: At this point, I need to write a book about Syria because there is so much. It's impossible to hold all this in mind and imagine trying to put it into 1,200-word stories. There's so much that we haven't explained. There are so many connections between the geopolitical and the personal. The story of the Syrian war really did touch me personally. I feel like I'm not done talking about it, but I came back to New York in August [2018, eight months before this interview], and it has taken some time to process and to heal and recover a bit before I could even begin to take another step. But I do have a big project coming out, not a book scale, but a big newspaper investigation about one aspect of this conflict that I find may be the most important.[2]

Betty: Looking at the Syria story and pointing to the facts and debunking the fake news, or the information wars by documenting it, seems to be a most important task in this recalcitrant situation. We can put words around a vortex of chaos and ground the facts in words. In that regard, it's a double-edged sword for you, Anne. You have to look at the terror and find some way to corral your mind not to be frozen by these horrific stories and situations of torture and bring out the details so that other people can see the horror in order to react to it and move. How do you thread that needle?

Anne: I feel like my team and I are like a funnel. We take in this huge amount of horror, and we try to analyze it, and we try to make it into a story that's digestible. We actually had a rule in our bureau which said that we should not *all* watch every video documenting death, violence, torture, and the like. If a source sends you a video, just watch it and write a description of what's in it and send us the description and the link. If other team members have a

---

[2] Barnard, A. (2019). Inside Syria's Torture Prisons: How Bashar al-Assad crushed dissent. *The New York Times.* https://www.nytimes.com/2019/05/11/world/middleeast/syria-torture-prisons.html.

need to watch it, we watch it. But otherwise, I ordered my team not to watch every video. We took turns watching these videos.

Betty: Because?

Anne: Because the volume is too much and it's affecting us. It's affecting our health. And data is now showing that video materials can have the same kinds of traumatic effects as in-person experiences.

Michael: Did you ever become numb to it? I mean, did you ever stop connecting or caring?

Anne: Not really. Some people do. That's one way of coping. I became very depressed sometimes and very enraged at other times.

Michael: Do you have survivor's guilt?

Anne: Of course. I had survivor's guilt while it was happening because often I'd be in my home office at night. I'd be talking on the phone to a mother in Syria while putting my own child to bed. You know how when your kids are a certain age, they think they might die in their sleep and they want your reassurance. They think there might be kidnappers outside, and they want to know that they're safe. So, I'm tucking in my little kid and I'm telling her I'm here and that she's safe. And the woman on the other end of the phone is telling her kids the same thing, but she knows she's lying because they could be bombed overnight. And I just did that day after day and night after night. I would see pictures of children's bodies ripped apart in ways that you just can't imagine—children the same size as my own child.

Michael: It seems that our indifference is an essential ingredient to this ongoing war. Assad couldn't do any of this without our indifference. None of this happens without our indifference.

Anne: Imagine the betrayal for the Syrians who trained themselves to become videographers, who risked their lives, who died in great numbers, bringing the story to others. We sometimes get sources who tell us that they are not going to give us information anymore. I just came back from Germany where I met with a lot of Syrians who I've known from many different walks of life who ended up there. They all went into a deep depression as soon as they were safe there. Some were doing drugs, drinking, partying. They are all people who have done extraordinary things to survive or to be part of efforts to keep civil society alive. Some of those who resisted Assad were rebel fighters, and some of them were against the use of violence. But the point is, most have done extraordinary things and took huge risks for a big ideal—and lost. And now nobody cares. And they're still only 27 or 28 years old. What's notable is how they're still trying to do things. Some of them are looking for ways to keep on helping Syria. Some of them are trying to put Syria aside for the moment. They say to themselves, "I have to work on myself because I survived. It's my duty to do something with my life."

Betty: This mirrors the work that I do in the consulting room. It is a different kind of trauma. They are survivors of sexual assaults, childhood molestation, and domestic violence. But Assad could be seen as a domestic violence perpetrator writ large, and the Syrian nationals could be seen as the abused partner in which a cycle of violence continues and continues and continues, and in which the perpetrator is constantly present. You have to find a way to live. There is resilience, and the psyche finds ways to protect itself, sometimes through numbness or disassociation or whatever means necessary to forget it, or to act. That can be the way forward for individual people. As for the way forward for the world, in terms of the impact of the refugee crisis and in terms of what immigration means now, it's the thing that Trump rises and falls on in the United States.

Anne: He likes to say that there are lots of terrorists coming from Central America or wherever.

Betty: He capitalizes on fear. The projection onto Syria may be something like "Let the brown terrorists duke it out among themselves and we should stay out of it." However, if we don't recognize that this is happening and think about it and do what we can to slow this thing down, it's going to proceed unfettered. There is a conflict going on under the surface, the United States and Russia are involved in it, and I wonder if it is going to surface at some point.

Anne: We are in pretty deep denial, and it will get closer and closer the longer that we deny it. Syrians have said, "If this is allowed to happen here, it will happen in the West." When I used to hear them tell me that, I thought they were being a little rhetorical or histrionic. And that doesn't sound as over the top to me now as it used to. There is an accomplished Syrian human rights lawyer, Mazen Darwish, who survived many years in prison. He survived torture, and he is now trying to take Syrian officials to court in Europe for war crimes. Darwish has since testified in war crimes trials of Syrian officials in Germany. He said years ago that the violent repression of Syria's uprising would send a mass of refugees to Europe, that this would affect the political situation in Europe, and that this would erode the norms of democracy that were fought for after World War II. Someone from the European Parliament recently called him and said, "When you said that back then, I thought you were crazy, but I see that you were right." The wider public didn't react when all these people were tortured in Syria. People reacted a little bit when Jamal Khashoggi, the Saudi journalist, was brutally killed by his own government, which is a tightly embraced U.S. ally. And still, it turns out there are no consequences for the Saudis. How far will it go? We have authoritarianism in Hungary. We have Trump talking about journalists the same way Assad does, to be quite frank.

Betty: The Nazi Party is on the rise in Germany.

Michael: The 20th-century conflict ultimately was not between capitalism and communism but ultimately between liberalism and authoritarianism. That's what we're seeing now. How do you organize your government? Where do your rights come from? Do your rights come from the government? Did your government grant you rights? We reject that notion. We grew up out of the Enlightenment that said you have natural rights, and it doesn't matter what country you come from. The fullest expression of that was the Universal Declaration of Human Rights.

Anne: And this is the problem with the UN system—that it's based on state sovereignty. The state can do basically whatever it wants to you. The Universal Declaration of Human Rights was supposed to balance that or leaven that. Of course, if you take the principle of state sovereignty completely away, you get the invasion of Iraq. How do we balance all this as a world, not just as a country? What about climate change? How do we act together as a world on climate change when we can't even stick to things that we already agreed on 70 years ago?

Betty: I think that fear becomes part of this issue here because fear shuts down reason. The Enlightenment principles are being assaulted by more primal fears.

Anne: There's a scholar on Syria who has a classic work about Assad's father. It's called *Ambiguities of Domination.*[3] Her concept goes beyond traditional gaslighting. This is a situation where the authoritarian leader imposes his truth, which everybody knows is a lie. And he knows that you know it's a lie. He also knows that you have to perform for him as if you believe it's true, even when you know it's a lie. This is an expression of power that actually goes beyond brainwashing you. You are actually forcing people to act "as if." And the son has continued the same system. I don't want to take the metaphor too far, but some of the stuff we are hearing from the White House is along those lines nowadays. A big difference between Assad and Trump is that Trump cannot kill you or jail you if you don't go along with the lie. And we want to make sure it stays that way.

Betty: Right. But he can declare a national emergency for no reason.

Anne: And he's revoking press passes.

Michael: He's an awful leader. Horrendous. But there are still institutions, like the newspapers that I read daily. Even the Senate is rebuking him for his declaration of a fake national emergency. There were midterm elections. Hitler never had a midterm election after 1933. Stalin never had a midterm election. Along with Assad, none of these people have had meaningful democracies. Theoretically, Nancy Pelosi is a meaningful check on his power. I just don't like the parallels. Trump is somebody who idealizes and romanticizes authoritarianism. He wishes he could be like Erdoğan or Putin ...

Betty: ...or Kim Jong Un.

Anne: Let me bring this back to the personal again because it goes directly to what you're saying. My children grew up in Beirut surrounded by people, family, and friends, who had been through the Syrian conflict, and they

---

[3] Wedeen, L. (1999/2015). *Ambiguities of Domination: Politics, rhetoric, and symbols in contemporary Syria.* University of Chicago Press.

expressed a fear when we were moving back to the U.S. that my husband and I, who are both journalists, could be put in jail if we end up writing something the president doesn't like. They understood that, in the Middle East, we had a certain immunity as foreigners. And also we lived in Lebanon, where the government is mostly too chaotic to bother arresting people who criticize it. But they understood that Syrian journalists were jailed for writing things that "the president" didn't like. As far as my children knew, by moving back to America, their parents could be in danger [from the U.S. president]. That's something to think about.

Betty: And I think in terms of impact, the intergenerational transmission of trauma is significant here. Whereas even if everything were to roll to a stop right now, a generation of people and their children are going to be living with this and passing it on in many different ways for generations to come, as Holocaust survivors and grandchildren of Holocaust survivors and great-grandchildren of Holocaust survivors can attest to. Trauma is not something that just happens in the now and then ends.

Anne: Especially since there isn't going to be a Nuremberg, at this rate, right?

Betty: Right.

Michael: I was trying to think of the town that we just "freed" in Iraq from ISIS ...

Anne: Mosul.

Michael: Mosul. The Battle of Mosul last year or the year before was beyond indescribable.

Anne: You talk about gaslighting. My husband was just at the Sulaimaniya conference where Haider al-Abadi, the former prime minister of Iraq, said to Jane Arraf, one of the most experienced journalists covering Iraq, that in Mosul only eight women and children were killed in the whole thing.[4] And

---

[4] An annual conference in Sulaimaniya (city name is transliterated various ways) in the semi-autonomous Kurdish region in Northern Iraq.

Jane was like, "Are you kidding? I personally saw more than eight bodies of women and children in one hour in Mosul," and he argued with her about it back and forth in front of an audience. It was so crazy.

Michael: So, what about you? How do you manage?

Anne: I'm trying to figure that out. I've been covering the aftermath of 9/11 and conflicts in the Middle East for ten or eleven of the last fifteen years. And I have loved doing it. It's the work of my life. That said, and I'm very open about this because I think it's really important for journalists to be open about it, I had to take three months off for medical leave in the summer of 2017 because of traumatic stress.

Michael: How did it manifest itself?

Anne: I started to have this feeling of "weirdness." I wanted to do my work, but I couldn't do it all the time. I couldn't focus. I couldn't put narratives in order in my writing. My brain didn't work. And some of it was conscious; some of it was unconscious. And, at the same time, I was doing a lot of mission-driven work. And when it came to gathering the information, interviewing, I could still do that. It was very much related to everything we've been talking about. I felt fine when I was doing that.

Betty: That's a neuroscience impact of trauma on the brain. Higher order functions get compromised. In a colloquial way of putting it, you are flooded. The brain is too overwhelmed and basically shorting out.

Anne: In hindsight, that makes perfect sense. That's what it felt like. Like I was shorting out. And it happened after a very intense six months of covering the siege of Aleppo. That's when I was having those nightly conversations with people that I described earlier. I went to the government side of Aleppo during that time. It was a police-state situation in which we were getting shelled and seeing victims of shelling. Then there was a quiet period, which is exactly when this weirdness started to manifest itself. Right when I was struggling with this, there was the sarin attack on Khan Shaykhun in Idlib.[5]

---

[5] Sarin is a nerve agent, an internationally banned chemical weapon. The attack took place in Khan Shaikhoun, a town in rebel-held Idlib province in northern Syria.

We had tried to minimize our exposure to the trauma of such events. We had learned lessons such as not watching all the videos. But in that case, we had to watch, over and over again, multiple videos of children suffocating to death. We were trying to evaluate the evidence by looking at the timelines and geolocations. After that, I really felt affected. I had a shortness of breath and faintness. It didn't occur the day of watching the videos, but a couple days later. For the first time in my career, I had to call up and say, "I can't finish this piece on deadline." It wasn't a news story. It was an analysis piece. But even the news piece had been harder than usual for me to do.

A couple of months later, I realized that I needed to ask for time off. That also happened on another assignment. I was scrolling through my entire photo roll because I was looking for past pictures. I looked through six years of photographs of the conflict, things that I had seen in person, things that I saw online, people I talked to, people who are dead now. The photos were mixed with those of my family life, including the parts of my family life that I had missed because of all this work and travel. Viewing pictures of my children growing up in the Middle East, which was the only home they knew, I had another one of those times where I couldn't breathe and the room was closing in on me. Having the time off was really great. Thank God that I have a full-time job so that workers' comp for work-related stress could come in. What about freelancers? They don't have that. I wouldn't say that I'm done working through this. But, as journalists, we have to normalize working on processing trauma. And we have. In the field, the peer support is excellent. Everybody's been through a version of this.

Michael: Can I ask you how your daily rhythms have changed? For instance, has what time you wake up altered?

Anne: I've always been a night owl, so those late nights would be normal for me. But one thing that happened to me when I was in the thick of it was that I would finish interviewing and writing and I couldn't go to sleep. Syrians stay up late anyway and also sometimes they didn't have internet except late at night. They were using generators, and they were conserving them. They would only turn them on when they needed to put on lights. So I would finish with this work very late at night and I couldn't go to bed right away. My husband was asleep. My children were asleep.

Betty: You were exhausted, but you couldn't go to sleep.

Anne: How could I go to sleep directly from that? I would just stay up in these long hours of the night reading the newspaper, drinking a glass of wine, spacing out—like, I don't know what I was doing.

Michael: At three o'clock in the morning.

Anne: Yes. Regularly, three o'clock in the morning. Now that I'm back in the U.S., the one thing that was relatively easy to fix was getting back to a much more normal sleep schedule—this didn't last, insomnia is an ongoing problem—and a much more normal schedule of daily life and interacting with my family. I'm on a fellowship, so I don't have to do daily news reporting. I'm also not in a seven-hour time difference from headquarters where they are still working at 6 p.m. and it's 1 a.m. for me, and I would still have to work.

Betty: Well insomnia is one of the main symptoms of PTSD because you're overstimulated and your brain literally cannot rest or shut off. Is there any institutional help given regularly in terms of therapy or trauma therapists on staff at your newspaper?

Anne: *The New York Times* has more support than some institutions have. There is an expert on journalism and trauma who's a psychiatrist in Canada, and he is available to talk to correspondents to educate them on trauma, self-care, and mental health. It's not officially therapy because, as I understand it, his Canadian licensing doesn't permit that remotely.[6]

Betty: So, there's not a regular check-in with him? Journalists call when they feel like they need to, in the midst of their busy schedules?

Anne: Occasionally, an editor would call me after a particularly stressful assignment and say, "You should call the doctor, just to check in." But I would say the industry, as a whole, needs to work on having these things be much more routine, so that no boss or journalist needs to take it upon themselves to say this or that person needs help now. It would be nice to have more regular care. There is a protocol at ABC Australia, which was

---

[6] Barnard was diagnosed with PTSD in January 2019. When this interview was recorded in March 2019, she had not yet disclosed that to her employer. Since then, she has spoken about it publicly in advocating for trauma awareness, support, and destigmatization in journalism.

developed by the Dart Center for Journalism & Trauma at the Columbia University Graduate School of Journalism, that makes it part of the routine to have certain check-ins among peers and managers before you access the level of a psychiatrist. You can mitigate a lot of things in advance, both in the way that you manage people and in the way that you normalize interacting around these issues. You don't want to force anybody to disclose things they don't want to disclose. But just making it a normal part of the conversation before, during, and post-assignment allows issues to come up organically. And that is something that institutions are working on.

Michael: It's got to fly in the face of the romantic notion of being a tough war correspondent. The people I know who are war correspondents almost take pride in being battle-hardened.

Anne: Yes and no. It's definitely changing now that so many of us have been covering these "forever wars" for ten or fifteen years. And it's the 21st century. People are much more open about things like therapy, health, and mental health. Among peers, there's a lot more discussion of this now. But we all react with black humor, too, and a lot of us drink and smoke—it's not that we don't still use the old-fashioned coping mechanisms. But not everybody.

But also, I think there's an evolution in how we talk about these things. There are many more women involved now. I'd say the majority of bureau chiefs in the Middle East during my time there were women. It's become easier to talk about these things, and the trauma is being dealt with a little more openly—instead of being allowed to manifest itself in being so hard and numb that you don't care or you act like you don't care. But this is not only among women. I'm talking about everybody.

It's happening not only in journalism but also in other human rights and humanitarian organizations. It's an evolving understanding of how we interact with the world. It's no longer the colonial model where somebody pops into the war and then goes home. Journalists and other humanitarian professionals are living in regions of conflict. Oftentimes, the journalists are members of the societies where it's happening, so they're not going to leave. And then you add in the video, audio, and online 24/7 aspect of the work. We have to consider, "How do we manage the fact that this is now the air we breathe and not a limited assignment?"

Betty: In trauma treatment, we clinicians have to check in with our supervisors and our colleagues weekly. Sharing the burden of these overwhelming stories is a necessary protector against secondary trauma. Research has shown that if a person, having suffered a sexual or physical assault, can talk to somebody right away, the long-term effects of the trauma are significantly mitigated. That is why, in New York City, by a New York State Department of Health mandate, they place trained advocates in ERs to respond to sexual assaults as quickly as possible. With immediate acknowledgment and care, survivors suffer fewer somatic occurrences, less chronic pain, less insomnia. Otherwise, a lot of somatizations of these overwhelming events happen unconsciously because the brain can't process the magnitude of the traumatic event and that's the beginning of dissociation.

Anne: There's another interesting point about people who incur secondary trauma in the course of their work. There's data that shows that if they feel supported by their institution, especially since the institution sent them on the mission that led to their suffering the trauma, if they feel supported by that institution, not just in terms of trauma, but in terms of the way they are treated—meaning by their compensation, by their sense of satisfaction in the work—they have better, fewer adverse trauma outcomes and can recover faster. That's something I think all institutions should look at because that's an opportunity.

Michael: Well, listen, Anne, I have to say thank you very much, because the thing that we always swim upstream from is a lot of the indifference to these horrific events. Hearing your stories and your point of view is ...

Betty: ... invaluable.

Anne: Thank you.

WHY TRUTH MATTERS

Chapter 8
The Case for Radical Openness

Guest: Dr. Anton Hart
Episode Aired: October 28, 2020

Anton Hart, PhD, FABP, FIPA, is a training and supervising psychoanalyst and faculty at the William Alanson White Institute in New York. He's a member of Black Psychoanalysts Speak and recently served as co-chair of the Holmes Commission on Racial Equality in American Psychoanalysis. Dr. Hart is on the faculty at Mount Sinai Hospital, New York Presbyterian Hospital, The New York University Postdoctoral Program in Psychoanalysis, and at other psychoanalytic institutes in New York and other cities. He is in full-time private practice in Manhattan.

We begin this section on the importance of truth with Dr. Anton Hart's reflections on his concept of radical openness. *Although Dr. Hart conceived of* radical openness *as a way by which a psychoanalyst or a psychotherapist could cultivate the greatest receptivity in themselves for truths to emerge in dialogue with a patient, we invited him to speak with us about its applications beyond the session room and in the realm of political discourse. Specifically, we asked:* How might radical openness help us navigate communication breakdowns and foster constructive dialogue between politically polarized individuals or parties?

When we spoke with Dr. Hart in late October 2020, the presidential debates between Joe Biden and incumbent Donald Trump had just concluded. The first, held on September 29, 2020 was viewed by many to be a "disaster" due to Trump's constant interruptions and belligerent, disrespectful conduct toward opponent Joe Biden and moderator Chris Wallace.[1] As the Washington Post editorial board noted, "Mr. Trump

---

[1] Gambino, L. (2020). Trump Plunges Presidential Debate into Chaos as He Repeatedly Talks over Biden. *The Guardian.* https://www.theguardian.com/us-news/2020/sep/29/

has nothing but contempt for the values and norms that are essential to democracy: among them, truth, civility and respectful disagreement.'² While Trump's 2020 debate conduct was extreme, it nevertheless mirrored the devolving, polarized mud-slinging in American political exchange that was occurring at all levels—in Congress, in the media, and interpersonally.

It was against this troubling backdrop that we turned to Dr. Hart for his wisdom on fruitful exchange. What ensued was a lively discussion, not just about what constitutes the best circumstances for open communication, but also on the intricacies of truth and the conditions it requires. Thus, our conversation with Dr. Hart is particularly apt to launch this section on Why Truth Matters. *Through our fruitful dialogue, we touched upon the perils, difficulties, and the necessities of open and honest exchange and arrived at its core: it is a very human way to take care of one another.*

This central notion of care *as an undergirding of* truth *usefully frames all of our conversations on the American cultural complex that has formed around speech, truth, and falsehood—be it about conspiracism with Nancy Rosenblum (Chapter 10), elitism with William Davies (Chapter 11), or the distinctions between delusions and lies with Michael Tansey (Chapter 13). That it also points to our conversation on* The Politics of Care *with Dr. Deva Woodly (Chapter 22) in Part 5,* Democracy at Risk *reveals how crucial* care *and* truth *are to healthy self-government, for individuals and societies alike.*

Interview

Betty: Jonathan, with Dr. Anton Hart joining us, we are two psychoanalysts squaring off against you—the lone political strategist!

Jonathan: You got me outnumbered, two to one! Tell me how you came to stack the deck against me?

Betty: The thing that inspired me to ask Anton to join us was actually a quote from Joe Biden. At a campaign speech in Gettysburg, he quoted

us-debate-trump-biden-latest-2020-presidential-news; Montanaro, D. (2020). Trump Derails 1st Presidential Debate with Biden, and 5 Other Takeaways. *NPR.* https://www.npr.org/2020/09/30/918500976/trump-derails-first-presidential-debate-with-biden-and-5-other-takeaways.
² Editorial Board. (2020). The Debate Was a Disgrace. It Showed Us Trump's Assault on Democracy is Escalating. *The Washington Post.* https://www.washingtonpost.com/opinions/the-debate-was-a-disgrace-it-showed-us-trumps-assault-on-democracy-is-escalating/2020/09/30/2e7e075c-033c-11eb-b7ed-141dd88560ea_story.html.

Abraham Lincoln in saying, "A house divided against itself cannot stand."[3] Then later, in other venues on the stump, he channeled Obama by saying, "No red states, no blue states, just the United States."[4] Yet such unity feels like a hard challenge these days. I see this in sessions with my patients, some of whom can't talk to relatives about politics anymore.

Jonathan: For sure.

Betty: This brings up the relevant questions, micro to macro, of "How do we go forward as a society together? How do we talk with and understand each other?" It seems that our health as a democracy depends on this. The psychoanalytic concept of "radical openness," which we'll talk with Anton about, seems to offer a way. Now, we can get a bit heavy theoretically, so I'm going to ask our listeners to bear with us, because I think the conversation does bear fruit. Don't you think, Jonathan?

Jonathan: I actually do, Betty.

Betty: I will add, Jonathan, that although both you and I value communication highly—we are in fact both professional communicators—we approach and engage in communication from very different angles. Your focus is on public communication, whereas I engage in very private and personal exchanges. The Venn diagram overlap of our professions can be found in the question, "How do we best communicate with one another?" Political strategists and psychoanalysts are constantly asking, "How do we talk to each other? How do we listen? What language do we use?"

Jonathan: Yes. And psychoanalytic concepts and theories have direct application in our political context, in discourse, and in other societal settings. I think this is a great time to bring on our guest, Dr. Anton Hart. Welcome to *Mind of State*, Anton.

---

[3] "Joe Biden: Gettysburg Campaign Speech Transcript, October 6," Transcript Library, @Rev, https://www.rev.com/blog/transcripts/joe-biden-gettysburg-campaign-speech-transcript-october-6#:~:text=As%20we%20stand%20here%20today,in%20each%20other%20is%20ebbing.

[4] Blitzer, R. (2020). Biden Channels Obama in Declaring there are "No Red States, No Blues States, Just the United States. *Fox News*. https://www.foxnews.com/politics/biden-channels-obama-in-declaring-there-are-no-red-states-no-blue-states-just-the-united-states.

Anton Hart: Thank you. I'm glad to be here.

Jonathan: We wanted to bring you on *Mind of State* to talk about this concept that you have described, called "radical openness." Would you start out by defining radical openness?

Anton: *Radical openness* is a concept I have been developing that pertains to the situation of psychoanalytic psychotherapy and psychoanalysis. It has to do with how the analyst or therapist listens to the patient, and how the analyst or therapist takes in what the patient says and thinks and feels, giving these things serious consideration and being as open as possible to the truths that reside in the patient's experience. Rather than focusing primarily on traditional notions of transference in the psychotherapeutic process—meaning that the patient is bringing things from their past into the present moment with the analyst—radical openness proposes the idea that the analyst could be listening as if the patient is telling something true, even and particularly if it sounds strange to the analyst, if it sounds foreign, or if it sounds like it's coming from someplace else.

It's at those times that the analyst could really listen in a different way—allowing for what the patient says to sit with them and to affect them, both cognitively and emotionally, so that the truth that resides in what the patient is saying and experiencing could really be considered—even if it seems like distortion, even if it seems like projection.

Jonathan: First, I'm curious: Because I'm not a psychoanalyst, it sounds funny to me, frankly, that the notion of listening to a patient and taking their words at face value would be a departure from the traditional approach of psychoanalysis. Betty or Anton, talk to me about how listening with radical openness is different from other forms of listening in the psychoanalytic tradition?

Anton: Well, Jonathan, to be clear, I am not proposing the same thing as taking things at face value. This is about taking things seriously, taking them to heart, if you will. Sometimes patients say things to their therapists, to their analysts, that seem like distortions. There's been a whole body of thought in the psychoanalytic perspective that says we're trying to listen for those distortions, also referred to as *transferences*. We're trying to listen for what the patient is importing into the analytic relationship. Through noticing the ways the patient is seeing us—ways that really, we're actually *not*—we can learn something about the patient's conflicts, issues, dynamics, history, and traumas.

Radical openness proposes an alternative, or a counterpart, to this way of viewing things. It says that there are two people in the room—and *both* of them, analyst and patient, have an unconscious mental life and an irreducible subjectivity, not just the patient. Because of that, neither participant in the therapeutic process could be the ultimate arbiter of what's going on, of what's true. And so, instead, the analyst could do well to listen in such a way that takes very seriously the strange things the patient tells the analyst about him-, her-, or themself. That means I try to sit with things that might feel like they have nothing to do with me, to have an open mind and to invite the feeling, the consideration, that they *could* have something to do with me. Almost like the patient is my therapist, the patient is my analyst, and the patient may have access to things about me that I don't have access to, by virtue of my human unconsciousness.

Betty: Now, Anton, something out of what you're saying, which is really taking it down to basics for me, is that there are two very different people in the room, and they are each coming from very different perspectives and different experiences, whatever their identities. And that radical openness proposes a certain kind of a bridge, a way to say, "You know, I don't assume that I know anything about you. You're telling me something. And I, as the therapist, and you, as the patient, we're entering into an environment where we are going to have a conversation where we get down to those basics and try to bridge that gap." Anton and I talk to different people all the time; and Jonathan, you do too, as a political strategist. You know, you're talking, Jonathan, in a very public way. Anton and I talk in a very private way. Is radical openness a means to acknowledge how different we are from the other?

Anton: Yes, sure, Betty. You're onto something. You've captured something about the essence of radical openness. It's derived from Gadamerian hermeneutic phenomenology.

Jonathan: Wow, wow.

Anton: Hans-Georg Gadamer is a philosopher who is arguably the father of hermeneutics in philosophy, which is about the meaning of interpretation.[5] And Gadamer has a lot to say about the process of understanding oneself, understanding other people, and understanding text, originally. He proposes that when you read a piece of text—a book, an article, a newspaper, scripture, anything—read not just what's on the page, but what surrounds it, what its context is. Who wrote it? Who are they speaking to? Who is ignored and marginalized in this speech? Who is included? What kind of knowledge is privileged? What kind is ignored? Things like that are part of the hermeneutic orientation. Hermeneutics puts itself on the track of dialogue, and dialogue becomes this central, important thing. We enter into dialogue not only to understand others more fully, but also to understand ourselves. And we can't understand ourselves unless we're in conversation from this perspective. And, also, we enter into dialogue to discover how much we don't understand—about our dialogic partners and about ourselves.

So, Betty, you're talking about finding a way of bridging, and Gadamerian hermeneutics talks about the "fusion of dialogic horizons." That's just a fancy way of saying that as we enter into conversation with each other, as we find ways to listen to each other without presumption, without *foreknowledge*, as Gadamer put it, and as we speak to each other *with the other in mind as we're speaking*, our horizons start to fuse.[6] We start to become part of each other, entangled with each other emotionally and psychologically. It's not simply that we understand better the content of what the other person is saying, we start to actually be changed by the kind of listening and speaking that we do when we genuinely enter into dialogue.

So that's the crucial thing, and that is a kind of bridging. And hermeneutics says one more thing—I don't want to go on too long—but hermeneutics says that what we do when we enter into a genuine conversation is we try to think—not about what we can gain, or what we can do; not about what knowledge we can get from the other person; instead, it asks us to consider what we can *lose* as we participate in the conversation. What can

---

[5] Malpas, J. (2022). Hans-Georg Gadamer. *The Stanford Encyclopedia of Philosophy*. (E. N. Zalta & U. Nodelman, Eds.). The Metaphysics Research Lab, Stanford University. https://plato. stanford.edu/archives/win2022/entries/gadamer/. See also: George, T. (2021). Hermeneutics. *The Stanford Encyclopedia of Philosophy*. (E. N. Zalta, Ed.) The Metaphysics Research Lab, Stanford University. https://plato.stanford.edu/archives/win2021/entries/hermeneutics/.

[6] Gadamer, H.G. (1975/2004). *Truth and Method*. (J. Weinsheimer & D.G. Marshall, Eds.). Continuum.

we relinquish that we thought we knew? What kind of foreknowledge, what kind of presumptions, what kind of prejudices can we loosen our grasp on and let go of as we try to take in the other person?

Jonathan: First, I definitely did not have *hermeneutics* on my bingo card for today! So, I appreciate you bringing a new word to my consciousness. I'm open to it. I'm *radically* open to it! More importantly, what I'm hearing is that when you say *openness*, it sounds like what you're really referring to is opening your own mind and opening your own thought process to the other person's ideas and context, and letting that permeate your mind. Radical openness is your mind's openness to the other person's words and context, rather than being open about your own thoughts with someone else.

Anton: Precisely. Radical openness has nothing to do with being extra self-disclosing. It has to do with being open to the other. And as you put it, open to their words, their thoughts, their context. I would add to that list, to their *being*; being open to the other's being as another human subject whom you can listen to—be with—and *take into your care* as you're listening. Taking the other into your care is a way of putting it that comes from Emmanuel Levinas, a French philosopher and theologian. Here's the idea: I listen, taking what the other says, feels, thinks into my care; and in taking them into my care, I'm a different kind of listener than the listener I might be if I'm just trying to listen to the argument the person is making so that I can come up with a reply, or come up with a counter-argument, or a rebuttal, or something like that.

Jonathan: So, by taking what they say into your care, that suggests to me a duty of trust, a responsibility to give a benefit of the doubt perhaps, to the person to whom you're listening.

Anton: Yes.

Jonathan: In other words, bringing respect, a dignity to what they're saying, rather than a prejudgment or a critical analysis, and giving full consideration to the things that the other person is saying.

Anton: Yes, *full consideration*, both intellectually and emotionally. That's precisely right. Levinas said that when we turn toward the face of the other, we feel a calling, an ethical calling, to take the other's experience respectfully, openly, and caringly into our consideration, into our care. And that amounts to, just as you're describing, a way of listening as openly as possible, as deeply as possible, as fully with all of our being as possible. That's how we become more fully human ourselves, to listen in this manner.

Betty: What I love about this, Anton, is that it is so humanistic. It embodies the definition of humanistic psychoanalysis, by putting the human we listen to at the center. What's also amazing about it is, while I have my own assumptions about dialogue, what you just said—that entering into a radically open dialogue with somebody has the goal of *loss* in it—I think that's incredible. So in a certain sense, you gain by losing? By the way, Jonathan, I think you're going to get a psychoanalytic training out of this before this session is done!

Jonathan: Oh but wait—because I'm going to bring it to politics, I promise you!

Betty: We are still *Mind of State*, but we're deep in the "mind" side of things here! But to go back to this effort of *losing to gain* in dialogue—which comes from putting the human at the center and turning to the face of the other and really taking them into our care—are we then creating something new through radical openness?

Anton: Yes. The hope is that something new will be created or will emerge. But the tricky part is—and this is one of those paradoxes that often characterizes psychoanalytic thought—you can't go into it saying, "I'm going to lose something *in order* to gain something. I'm going to lose my preconceptions and my foreknowledge, and I'm going to be open in order to gain something out of this contact and out of this conversation." Because as soon as you start to think about your gaining something, then there's a way in which you start to depart from the kind of openness to which we aspire. Between you and me, on the side, I'll say yeah, there's probably a gain there that might be around the corner. But you go into it, not with your eye on the gain, but with your eye on the loss. Like, what can I relinquish? What can I give up in order to take the other person in? And then, how do the two of us become something new together and allow for the "merging of our dialogic horizons," as Gadamer put it.[7] How does that happen? We can't say in advance that it's going to happen, that it's guaranteed. We have to aspire to it, aspire to losing what we thought we knew. And then something might start to form, and it might be good, but we don't know what it's going to be in advance.

Jonathan: So, it's sort of like when we say an altruistic act also has a thread of selfishness in it, right? Because although it feels good to do something altruistic, we don't go in with a selfish intent. We go in altruistically, and the byproduct might end up making us feel good, but the altruism is what comes first.

I do want to make this shift out of the therapy room and into politics for a second, because I think there's a great application of what you're talking about for the nonclinical world. When I first heard the notion of *radical openness*, it actually brought to my mind a notion that we talk about in politics and even in corporate communications, which is *radical transparency*. And *radical transparency* is the notion of a leader cutting through the pabulum and jargon and instead being human in their expression; rooting themselves in empathy, being straight with their audience, respecting them enough to be honest, even if it involves admitting errors and shortcomings, or demonstrating some sort of weakness. It's the weakness that's actually a strength, rather than hiding behind the bluster. I think when you get a *radical openness* of listening with a *radical transparency* of being forthcoming, then we start to get into a flow that I think could be applicable to the political and community conversations we need to have, particularly around very divisive issues that are creating a lot of conflict in society right now.

Betty: And what prompts radical transparency, Jonathan? When do you guys turn toward it, or how did it come about in strategic communications or political communications?

Jonathan: You know, generally we counsel our clients, whether it's a candidate or an elected official or a corporate executive, to be radically transparent when it's clear that there's doubt or skepticism in the audience. People can feel it when there is inauthentic communication or when there is

---

[7] Gadamer, H.G. (1975/2004). *Truth and Method.* (J. Weinsheimer & D.G. Marshall, Eds.). Continuum. p. 306.

stonewalling, when there is legalese or jargon that people are hiding behind. With radical transparency you say, "Put that aside, put the talking points aside, and talk like real people." When you see that something's not working and that you're at risk of your mission going awry, that's when…

Betty: Is that when people stop listening, in a certain sense?

Jonathan: That's right.

Betty: When they start to feel like you're not being true, and your words are not authentic?

Jonathan: That's right.

Betty: And they're turning away from you. They're turning their faces away from yours.

Jonathan: That's exactly right.

Betty: That's interesting.

Jonathan: And we see it all the time. We see it when the politician is caught in a hot-mic incident or in an illicit or inappropriate relationship. They need to come clean, and they have a moment when they either come forward, demonstrate that they have humility, that they are going to speak with candor, that they're going to learn from the experience, and that they're going to level with the public—or forever lose that trust.

Betty: Anton, what do you think about *radical transparency* versus *radical openness* since you're the expert on radical openness for us?

Anton: Here's the interesting thing that radical transparency makes me think of, Jonathan and Betty. There's a way in which there is quite a parallel between *radical openness* and *radical transparency*, as you're describing it. However, I'm concerned about the notion of "transparency." For me the word implies a kind of elimination of the human element, like the human desire to hide a human imperfection. It seems to say, "I'm not going to be mysterious in the various ways that I might be. I'm going to be transparent." As if the ideal then becomes transcending one's own humanness. I know that's not all that radical transparency implies, as you've described it. But the use of the word *transparency* concerns me because transparency is language combining *secret-keeping*, on the one hand, and *secret-divulging*, on the other. And that's something that already takes us down the path of not being in good faith from the very beginning.

Jonathan: Yes. Well, when there's so much distrust, it's almost a way of saying, "Look, I'm actually not going to translate this at all. I'm not going to filter it. I'm just going to open up the book and let you see the records for yourself. You be the judge. I will not be a filter."

Anton: Yes, right.

Betty: Here's the thing: *radical openness* may depend on a private conversation, a truly confidential conversation—as it is between a patient and an analyst or a therapist and a client. What Jonathan describes about *radical transparency* has to do with a public openness.

Anton: Yes.

Betty: And so, there's a politician or a public figure, and this closed or private thing happens to them. Maybe it's a scandal. Or maybe it's a hidden record of taxes not paid. Not that I'm thinking of anybody in *particular*.

Jonathan: No, no.

Betty: And there is almost an assumption on the part of a public figure that they're hiding something. So, as you're putting it, there is a challenge for them to be transparent. But can we flex? Is it possible to flex radical openness—I'm making a leap here—into the public sphere?

Anton: You know, my hope is that our politicians would be open. But I don't start with their openness about their own bank accounts, or taxes paid, or holdings in foreign governments or countries. I instead am focused on their openness to the other person—the other people that they're elected to govern.

Jonathan: The empathy.

Anton: Yes, the empathy, but I want to take it further than empathy because it's not just the signature Clintonian comment, "I feel your pain." It's the openness to the idea that you could be hearing something that sounds very foreign, that you could think very differently about, but you could be receptive to it anyway and see what it does to you as you sit with it, rather than try to respond to it right away. That's one of the crucial aspects here—which is, in the therapeutic situation and outside of it, this could be a constant—that we try to listen in such a way that we sit with what we hear for a while. We take it in. We take it into our care. We let it affect us. Perhaps to *move* us—is the language that I prefer. And we may be moved in such a way that our perspective changes; that we may let go of ideas and thoughts and ways of organizing the world that we had previously clung to with all our might. That's the kind of openness that I'd like to see from politicians, which has nothing to do with them coming clean about who they're having sex with or where their money is going.

Jonathan: Right, so empathy suggests that you can relate to someone else's pain or circumstance. Openness doesn't necessarily suggest that you would relate through your life experience, but that you're open to being *moved* by their experience, even if it's radically different from yours, and that you grow from your knowledge of their experience. You grow from your sharing a moment with someone and getting insight into their experience, right?

Anton: That's right. I would prefer to say, you grow from your *receptivity* to their experience, rather than your knowledge of their experience.

Betty: Anton, this prompts me to think about a burning question that I have about polarities and polarization in our country's dialogue right now.

Anton: All right, I've been sitting on the edge of my seat.

Betty: You're talking about radical openness and how with it, you don't make an assumption about the other. We're in a place societally in the U.S. where people are making all sorts of assumptions about all sorts of people, without making any kind of inquiry. There are a lot of information silos on the internet and within social media. There are a lot of silos within legacy media as well. The left and the right are *not* radically open to each other. Is there a way in which we can prepare people, or convince people, to communicate with radical openness? Maybe it's because I'm also a psychoanalyst, but this seems fantastic. It really seems like what we desperately need in order to have a democratic conversation.

Jonathan: Right. How do we condition people for dialogue?

Anton: Yes. But see, Jonathan, your instinct to do something to people to get them to be better goes against radical openness in a certain sense. You're wanting to condition them. And I don't know if that'll work. Here's the problem: We want people to be curious about each other. Curiosity is so crucial. But as psychoanalysts, we know that curiosity is precarious. From the beginning of life, babies are born curious. They come into the world—they reach out, they touch things, they taste things, they look at things. All their senses are alive, and they're curious about everything. Unfortunately, the process of growing up involves a curtailment of a lot of human curiosity over time. It's as if it's too dangerous to remain curious—at least as curious as we were when we were babies.

Jonathan: Right, right.

Anton: So, we have to learn to avert our eyes. We have to learn to narrow our curiosity down and be able to have "normal" conversations. "Normal" as in "Hi, how are you?" "I'm fine." "How are you?" "I'm fine." "Good to see you." "Bye." That's an incurious conversation, but we are socially *conditioned* to do that—to use that word, Jonathan—as a way of getting through life and feeling relatively self-contained and as if things can continue as we expect them to. Curiosity represents a threat to this. It's not this nice thing, like "Oh, I'm curious." "Oh, you are? Great. Let's explore your curiosity." Curiosity threatens to take us into territory that is unfamiliar and that may mess up the way we've organized our understanding of ourselves and of the world. So that's the challenge in radical openness—we're trying to enter conversations and to be very, very curious about each other, as curious as babies are about the world. And that's arguably a dangerous thing to do. And that's what makes it hard to tell people, "Hey, be more open. Be more open to each other. Relinquish your preconceptions. Let go of the things you thought you knew and enter into the conversation as if you don't know all the things you thought you knew."

Jonathan: Right. It's like, "Hey come on into the arena, but leave your armor outside."

Anton: Exactly. Leave your armor.

Jonathan: This is the conundrum: We want people to enter into a more open dialogue, but we understand the fears. We understand the risks in doing so and in going in open and unprotected. So how do we engage in unscripted dialogue and in open listening and taking people in when language can be loaded, when we are conditioned to protect ourselves and to avert risk? How do we go there?

Betty: I'll add to what Jonathan says, Anton. Right now, we're in a place of great instability. We're in a pandemic, we're facing climate change, we're facing a referendum on racial injustice, we're facing economic crises. There's a lot pushing us to play it safe. And yet maybe this is also a time of opportunity because we can also say, "What do we have to lose? The situation is desperate." But being open does go against an evolutionary impulse to protect oneself.

Anton: I don't know if the impulse is evolutionary, but I think it is really part of the challenge of being a human being in relation to other human beings. Babies learn that they can't be too curious about things, or they might make their parents anxious. So, the baby has to learn to manage such anxiety so as not to drive their parents crazy. So, the challenge is, how can we help people enter into open dialogues? How can we get people to practice radical openness, perhaps not just in the psychoanalytic or psychotherapeutic context, but in life?

Now, one thing that experience seems to show—because I do consulting and hold workshops about issues of diversity—and one of the things that seems to be the case is if you get people talking to each other, something good happens. You get people talking to each other with fairly banal questions—questions like, "When were you first aware of your race?" or "When were you first aware of your gender?" Just simple questions. People start to talk with each other and feel things that they don't usually allow themselves to feel. Of course, there's always the risk of things getting polarized and people feeling hurt or rejected in such conversations. But those risks can't be avoided. They can't be escaped. Having these kinds of conversations involves risk. It's a risk worth taking, I would argue, but we can't take out risk. One of the things that drives me crazy these days is the notion of a *safe space*, like, "This is a safe space. We're going to have a conversation in a safe space." And my feeling about that notion of a "safe space" is that it is nonsense. No space can be proclaimed safe. You can only find your way to that through the process of trying to be open to each other and having a good faith effort to have a conversation, to have a dialogue with each other.

Jonathan: I wonder, does radical openness work in all settings? Should we consider radical openness equally applicable in work, in school, and in community settings? Or are there places where we shouldn't be as open?

Anton: That's a great question. I think that it really does require a kind of protected setting where we're coming to talk to each other in good faith and where we can agree on the aspiration toward openness. A lot of that has to do with who our leaders are and how our leaders are acting, quite frankly. If you have leadership all the way to the top and the leadership says, "I don't listen to other people; I know, I already know; you don't need to tell me because I already know"—then that's frankly the opposite of radical openness. That might be *radical ignorance* …

Betty: A breakdown.

Anton: If I may.

Betty: You may.

Anton: Whereas if a leader says, "Huh, I don't know everything, I'm willing to listen just as much as I'm willing to talk. And in my listening, perhaps to be influenced and affected and to have my perspective changed," then that's an example that is likely to make its way into ordinary conversations that are not just in the psychotherapeutic context. Jonathan, the place where things can't really work well when it comes to radical openness—where it doesn't apply—is when people are debating each other. Debate is very different from the kind of conversation that we're hoping to have.

Jonathan: Right.

Anton: Another context where it doesn't work is where people are lying. Quite frankly, lying interferes with and breaks down this process totally.

Jonathan: I would imagine.

Anton: Because that's an attempt to manipulate the other person, to mislead them, and to send them off in a direction that has nothing to do with the truth or with you. In that case, being radically open to a lie is not going to lead to the kinds of change that we're talking about.

Jonathan: The trust has to be on both sides of the fulcrum, obviously. You referenced that if the leaders are not open, then it's going to signal something that's going to break down the openness of the system. But these days, I wonder if there's not also a responsibility by those who are being led; because it seems that in some organizations or in some settings—whether it's employees or constituents or those of us marching and protesting in the streets—we're coming in "loaded for bear." We're called the "PC police," or we're ready to call out people if they make an error, particularly our leaders. We're looking for an error. We're looking for a lie. And that, too, can shut down a process, can't it?

Anton: Absolutely. You know, instead of that term "calling out," as in "calling people out," I strongly prefer the notion of *calling people in*. When there's a problem, *call them in* to dialogue. So, if we've got a problem and I say, "What you're saying is hitting me in this way, and I'm seeing it differently; or it's hurting me in this way, or it's even making me angry—can we talk about this?" That's an attempt at conversation, rather than the notion of calling people out, which is shame-based and implies, "I'm going to shame you for what you're saying."

Betty: Anton, the topic of shame really makes me think, because of what you and Jonathan were saying about the trust required for openness to be possible, about what our last guest, Robert Jay Lifton (Chapter 21), was talking about as the breakdown of communication between the Democrats and the Republicans. Lifton is a historian and a psychiatrist who has been studying authoritarianism for seventy years, and he sees our democratic process as being contingent on the notion of there being a *loyal opposition*, meaning that, even if you disagree, you have respect for those opposing you. You do not demonize them. You do not think of them as an enemy. You're in this together. And that is two sides of a debate—which is not radical openness—but it causes me to think about *trust*, which is a container for a lack of shame. Meaning trust is an antidote for shame. Or it does away with the conditions that create shame.

And I think that trust is what's lacking right now. And so how do you create a situation of calling people in? Because they're going to need to know they're not going to be shamed. And I think in these conversations, particularly around race and diversity and prejudice, there's a lot of shame in the subjects themselves. These topics create anxiety—and people assume they're going to do the wrong thing.

Anton: Yes.

Betty: So how do you use radical openness—and I think it is very potent and perhaps key in helping us discuss high-octane topics—to call people in, in good faith, so that they're not afraid they will be shamed around a really difficult subject?

Anton: Betty, it's such a challenge. Because when people have traumas in their lives that make them sensitive to shame—which virtually every human being has—then it's almost impossible to convey to that person that they're not going to be shamed. They can even hear it in your telling them, "You know what, I'm not going to shame you." "Oh, well, why are you telling me that? You think I'm sensitive to shame? I'm not, you know! I don't care about that."

Betty: Right. That sounds like a callout.

Anton: There's a kind of malignancy to the sensitivity to shame and a shame-based orientation, which is very hard to overcome. The best we can do, I think, rather than saying, "I'm not going to shame you," is to conduct ourselves in ways that convey openness; in ways that convey a willingness to listen thoughtfully and as openly as possible—without giving in to our own human internal reflexes to rebut, or to counterargue, or to, frankly, shame the other person—especially when we hear things that we just can't stand to hear.

Jonathan: Are there times that are more suitable to radical openness than others? Do you think that we're in a period where language is so charged and emotions are running so high that it's not possible to be radically open?

Anton: Yes, the more anxious people get, the more polarized they get, the harder dialogue becomes. That's a fact of life. We need to cool things down. We need to deescalate the ways in which people in the United States are at each other's throats. And you're absolutely right that dialogue can sometimes be impossible, or at least feel that way. The challenge that we have is when dialogue feels impossible, can we find some small way of restarting the conversation? That's what I believe is a good starting point. We can't avoid those breakdowns of communication when we're not listening to each other and we're not speaking to each other. We can't prevent that from ever happening. But what we can do is see the breakdowns of communication as opportunities. Inevitably, they're going to come. But what do we do when the conversation breaks down? How can we find a way to start talking again, even if the conversation that we're restarting is going to be awkward and bring up bad feelings again, how can we get it going again? Because that, frankly, is our only way of getting through this together. If we're going to be human beings residing on this Earth, we're going to have to figure it out together. And so, we're going to have to restart conversations that break down.

Betty: What you're saying reminds me of what you said earlier about care, that you enter into dialogue because you care. Would it be useful, then, to transmit that we engage because we care and that's why we listen—not because we want to attack or to shame or to hurt. And that with acknowledgment perhaps that we each hurt—because I think we all do—so that we would want other people to see this and understand that we, too, need care. So that there's an accountability on all sides to using this communication, not just to mediate a peace, but to advance taking care of each other.

Anton: Yes, caring is crucial. We must find ways to care about each other. But there are no guarantees that we're going to be able to behave in caring ways all the time because sometimes we won't be conscious of the ways in which we're treating another person that aren't so caring. So, what we're called upon to do is to listen with radical openness so that we can hear the ways in which what we're doing is not caring and might be hurting the other person. That's our ticket to getting back on track with dialogue. "I'm trying my best to participate in this conversation. I'm trying not to attack or hurt you. But you know what? I might wind up unconsciously attacking you, or you might notice an attack that I didn't even think of. And when you do, let me take that thought very seriously rather than telling you, 'No that's not what I was doing. No, I didn't mean that. No that's not what I said. You're twisting my words.'" Better, from a radical openness standpoint, to say, "Oh all right. I'm thinking about that. I'm sitting with that."

Jonathan: How explicit are you suggesting we be? Do you name the phenomenon as it's happening? Do you say, "Am I saying something that's offending you? I think I'm saying something that's causing you concern?" Or is it an internal voice?

Anton: I think we all can have our different styles. And much of this is internal. Much of it is based, not on what you actually say, but on how you're processing the moment. And people can sense when you're listening in a receptive way versus not. But of course, having said that, I'll say, of course, it can be useful to say, "Wait, how is that sinking in? How is that hitting you, what I'm saying? How is that coming across? Is there a problem with it?" Or "I see some distress on your face with what I said. Tell me about that." When we express interest like that, then maybe we'll hear something interesting that can have an impact on us. It can have, dare I say, a therapeutic impact on us that can enhance our growth to make us a better participant in the dialogue.

Betty: Anton, what you're saying is something that I've said to my patients, who come from all sorts of identities and socioeconomic backgrounds and ages and ethnicities, immigration statuses. I tell them that, although I work with all different kinds of people, the one thing that does unify them is the wish to see and be seen. And what I hear you saying, is that when we reflect that we are seeing the other, we show them that they are in us, that we are reflecting them and that we care—again here's that word *care*—and I'm thinking as we go through the upcoming presidential election, we all hope, at least on this podcast, that it will go a certain way. But things will not …

Anton: We hope that the most *open* person will win.

Betty: Yes. That's perfect. May the most open person win. But there will be a lot of work to be done and a lot of conversations have been collapsed. As I was saying before, many opinions have become siloed. And, so, can we start to see these ways of being radically open, beyond this moment of where our current president is very, very closed and telling us that he knows everything and modeling an opposite view—a radical ignorance?

Anton: The debates are over now—the presidential debates—but imagine if the debates weren't debates, but presidential *conversations* where the candidates had to sit in a room and talk to each other. And we would be listening to how they do that and how able they were to listen to each other, as much as how articulate they could be about their points. Imagine if that was prioritized. That would be a much more interesting thing to watch than what we've seen, I daresay.

Jonathan: Anton, I think we are going to have to get you onto the presidential debate commission.

Betty: On that note—may the most *open* leader win.

Betty: Thank you so much, Anton, for coming on and giving us your time.

Anton: It's been my pleasure. Thank you, Betty, and thank you, Jonathan.

Chapter 9

The End of Truth?

Guest: Scotty McLennan
Episode Aired: March 25, 2019

Scotty McLennan is an ordained Unitarian Universalist minister, a lawyer who has specialized in poverty law, and a lecturer at the Stanford Graduate School of Business, where he teaches in the areas of ethics, spirituality, and business. From 2000 to 2014, he was the Stanford University Dean for Religious Life. Before that, he was the University Chaplain at Tufts University for sixteen years. He is the author of several books, including Jesus Was a Liberal: Reclaiming Christianity for All.

When we spoke to Scotty McClennan in March 2019, the terms fake news *and* alternative facts *were commonly used by Trump and members of his administration.* Fake news, *coined by Donald Trump in late 2016, was a term he used to discredit any unfavorable news stories about him or his administration, whereas* alternative facts *was popularized by Trump's former campaign manager and senior counselor Kellyanne Conway, who used the term to legitimize false claims made by the administration, from the outsized numbers of people who attended Trump's inauguration to false incidents such as the* Bowling Green massacre, *a fictional Islamic terrorist attack used by Conway to justify Trump's 2017 executive order banning immigration and travel from several Muslim countries. Such manipulations and abuses of truth, which continued throughout the Trump administration, caused us to ask Scotty, an expert in law, mediation, and religion, to help us think about the various uses, meanings, and functions of truth in society and how its manipulations impact us interpersonally, emotionally and psychologically.*

Interview

Betty: Scotty, with a colleague, you teach a course at Stanford titled "Ethics of Truth in a Post-Truth World." And, from your point of view as a minister, a lawyer, and a professor, you look at truth from different positions. There's a lot of talk in the media about "alternative facts" and our "post-truth" world. Can you tell us some of your positions on truth—or what do we mean by *truth* when we say that word?

Scotty: Well, in the course I co-teach, we look at truth through a number of different lenses—journalistic truth, scientific truth, law and the way truth comes out in the courtroom, religion and its claims on having the truth, and personal authenticity.

We ask, "What does it mean to be true to yourself?" And in the process, we realize that we live in a postmodern world where—putting aside for a moment all the things we hear on the news about fake news and alternative facts and is there any truth anymore—it really is quite difficult to talk about truth since it tends to be in the eye of the beholder. So, if you're talking about history, for example, what is the historical fact or reality that you might be looking at? Well, it depends, from a postmodern perspective, as to whether you are low income or high income, what your race is, what country you're from, and so on. It is hard for students to grasp what we mean by "truth." Then, when you proliferate the arenas in which we talk about "truth," it gets even more difficult.

Betty: But in the news and in politics, truth is something that's really up for grabs these days. I'm thinking right now of the story consuming this moment's news cycle—of television actor Jussie Smollett (from the popular show, *Empire*) who claimed he was attacked by MAGA supporters because he was black and gay.[1] Now it has come out that he allegedly faked this attack, and it's created another stir. I'll add that Smollett has been charged and awaits a court hearing. From your multiple positions of expertise, Scotty, can you weigh in on this—how the truth or falsehood of Jussie Smollett's story has occupied the front pages of many of our major news organizations for the last two weeks? This story—which is about polarization, race, sexuality,

---

[1] See "Jussie Smollett Hate Crime Hoax," on Wikipedia, at https://en.wikipedia.org/wiki/Jussie_Smollett_hate_crime_hoax, where you can also access some of the many articles written about the case. In March 2023, he filed an appeal challenging his conviction.

power, and victimization—has also set off a furor of commentary on social media. How do we get to the truth when, on social media, everybody has an opinion, and everyone claims to have authority? Everybody takes what they hear and runs with it. What do you think of all this in terms of how we manage the truth in the digital age?

Scotty: Well, at the first level, you've already distinguished between journalistic truth and legal truth; I appreciate you using the word *allegedly*. The fact is that in this country, you're presumed innocent until proven guilty in a court of law. So, from a legal perspective, it's very important to use the word *allegedly* and to not prejudge when somebody has been criminally charged, how something is going to come out at trial. On the other hand, in terms of journalism, we need to be careful to report only what we know— when it's not entirely clear, or when there might be a counter perspective— and to make sure that other viewpoints are presented. And I do worry about opinion being confused so often with journalistic integrity and in reporting facts. Many of our students don't often know the difference between opinion and factual reporting.

Michael: What do you mean by that?

Scotty: Well, take the *Wall Street Journal*, for example. It's often seen as a very conservative newspaper because if you look at its editorial pages and its opinion pages, you'll get a conservative perspective. But they have some of the best investigative journalism in the country, where they really dig in and make sure they are presenting what's true, factually, regardless of what one's opinion may be of those facts.

Betty: And when you say, "dig in," do you mean they fact check, and they confirm sources and quotes, and they present a balanced view? They don't take just one person's comments about a reported situation?

Michael: All of the things people don't do when tweeting, basically.

Scotty: Exactly. You do need journalistic ethics, which people used to take seriously when they called themselves journalists. And you make sure that you have more than one source, that your sources have been checked, that you have, ideally, other kinds of evidence available to you than just what somebody might say. If you are reporting as a journalist and complying with traditional journalistic ethics, you wouldn't just be—as you say—tweeting out something that you like or don't like, based on your bias.

Michael: It's interesting, too, because I think there can be a presumption that journalists, filmmakers—I'm a documentary filmmaker, and I teach documentary journalism—can slip into seeing themselves as advocates. And that's a slippery slope because when you advocate, you have a bias. But, Scotty, it seems to me that this malleability of truth is, in many ways, a product of the New Left, mostly out of the Sixties. They attacked the order of that day, the academy, the Michel Foucaults of the world.[2] They said you can't really know anything, and you can't judge other cultures. Your truth doesn't extend to somebody else's truth. And all of this relativism, both in terms of moral relativism and moral truth…

Betty: Go for it, Michael.

Michael: … I'm starting to sound like a Fox News commentator here— has, in some ways, come back and boomeranged on them. And so now you have folks, like Donald Trump or Kellyanne Conway, saying, "Hey, there is no truth. There's only truth which is a function of power." And, therefore, I look at the left in academia as having eroded the notions of truth for generations. This is Harvard historian Jill Lepore's point. She says we've spent a generation saying, "It's all your truth; you can't take Western culture and impose it on someone else." But then you're left with no center of gravity—so what about that?

Scotty: If we go back to your earlier point about advocacy and that being confused with journalism, we have the problem that I, as an attorney, see all the time, which is you need two sides when you walk into a courtroom. You can't just have one person advocating for her or his own client. There are the other perspectives and an advocate present for the other side. And you have a neutral fact-finder in the middle—a judge and/or a jury. While they don't necessarily come up with the truth, they try to get to the truth

---

[2] Michel Foucault (1926–1984) was a French philosopher, historian, writer, and critic. Foucault's theories primarily address the relationships between power and knowledge and how they are used as a form of social control through societal institutions.

beyond a reasonable doubt, by a preponderance of the evidence or by clear and convincing evidence. There are rules and a process by which to do that.

So that's quite different from—let's take another realm for a moment—religion. Most religions think they have the "capital-T" truth and that this whole postmodern way of looking at truth is fundamentally flawed because it doesn't understand the genuine nature of reality, which is "capital-U" Ultimate, "capital-R" Reality. So, yes, there are very different ways of coming at what truth is.

I do think it's dangerous when you begin only using approaches like *advocacy* or you apply a pure postmodern analysis, where there is no truth except from the mouth of power. We then lose our legal notion of truth. We lose our religious notion of truth. And let's go to another area—science. What is scientific truth? And that's one area where I think our students are usually clearest. They say, "Well, if we can't find an absolute truth anywhere else, at least we can find it in science. There are these natural laws that are discoverable. If you jump out of a 10-story building, there is a law of gravity and you're going to die." And you are not going to argue about that. So, that's the one clear arena really, and, of course, now that gets undercut too, because science keeps progressing and there are new theories. Now we go from Newton's law of gravitation to Einstein's theory of general relativity to quantum theory and so on.

Michael: Can I go back to Betty's query earlier about Jussie Smollett? Because that ends up playing something out about what truth is. We should frame this by saying, in this country, you are always innocent until proven guilty, and accusations are not the same thing as guilt.

Betty: But a lot of things get adjudicated in the newspapers.

Michael: Well, that's the point.

Betty: That's what I think happens.

Michael: That's exactly your point. In light of getting at our topic of what determines the "truth"—this whole narrative is fascinating to consider. Trump supporters are asserting about Jesse Smollett: "You, the left, rushed to judgment. We are vindicated."

Many people covered the Jussie Smollett case as fact. Presidential candidates Kamala Harris and Cory Booker came forward in support of Smollett, and now, people who support Donald Trump feel vindicated in *their* truth. Similarly, people who are victims of real hate crimes feel uniquely vulnerable. They worry that Smollett's false story might cast doubt on their true testimonials of being physically harmed or racially slurred. Their legitimate claims won't be listened to. What I find disturbing in all of this is the speed with which we determine truth—and then the danger, for all of us, when that rush to judgment turns out to be...

Betty: Precipitous. Too fast.

Michael: And that's a kind way of saying it.

Betty: And perhaps—although we're talking about truth, and we're saying the word *truth*, we actually mean something else. We mean *opinion*.

Michael: Well, we're using the word *truth* as a club to beat other people. That's what we do. That's where I get to the notion of advocacy. I'm curious what you think about that, Scotty.

Scotty: Well, we've said a lot about it—it's opinion versus fact, etc. But when it's all claimed as facts and truth, it's important to use words like *alleged*, again to note that we don't yet know. And the Mueller investigation is doing quite a good job of this. Everybody keeps saying, "Well, we don't really know yet. We've got to be patient. We've got to hear how this comes out." That's a really important thing for us to keep reminding ourselves of—we don't know yet. We don't have the whole story. Another thing we need to do more of—because we're so siloed in our partisan worlds—is to genuinely listen— to empathetically listen to each other, rather than being quick to shut each other down.

Michael: (*laughing*) We can't even do that on this podcast, Scotty.

Scotty: I mean, I find it really astounding—given that we don't have Walter Cronkite, who was the epitome of the network news anchor, to tell us both sides out of one person's mouth—that anyone can watch the news at night and not watch *both* Fox News and MSNBC (or CNN or whatever). Both sides are necessary if we want to have any possible understanding of what's going on.

Michael: Betty, do you watch the news?

Betty: I don't. I admit that I don't.

Michael: Scotty, do you?

Scotty: Yes, I do.

Michael: How do you watch it?

Scotty: I do exactly what I said. I watch Fox and I watch MSNBC and I watch PBS. And I'm hoping that somewhere in that, I can sort it out and find something close to the truth. But you're not going to get it from one channel.

Michael: When you tell people in your community you listen to Fox, what do they say?

Scotty: Because I'm on the left, a lot of people are appalled. They can't believe it. And I go the other way and say, "I can't believe you're not listening to Fox. How can you possibly live in this country, where, somewhere close to—we'll call it over 30 percent—of viewers see Fox as the lens through which they look at the world?" And, of course, MSNBC has all of its own biases. How can you possibly grasp our reality without watching both? Would that we had Walter Cronkite back—but we don't.

Betty: Scotty, you're going to both sides of the news spectrum to get to the truth. But a lot of people are not going to the news to get at the truth, but instead they are seeking to reaffirm their tribe, their identity—their belief systems. So, they gather around Rachel Maddow, or they gather around— um...

Michael: ...Sean Hannity.

Betty: Ah, Sean Hannity. Right. Thank you.

Michael: You're so Fox illiterate.

Betty: I really am. I would fail the "Fox News anchors" quiz. And I would also fail the "MSNBC anchors" quiz, although I do have a fangirl feeling for Rachel Maddow.

But back to what I was saying, people are going to these news sites and channels to affirm themselves, to find their group, to gather around these camps, and reify their belief systems and their values. They're not necessarily looking for the truth. They're looking for a way to feel better about what's going on, to hear their side of it on a national cable news channel. And, no, we don't have a Walter Cronkite or a three-channel system anymore where we're getting all of our news from very specific and centralized sites. So, you're talking about a centralized versus a decentralized dissemination of information. How do we ground ourselves in this fragmentation and spin, which has emerged over decades with cable news giving way to the internet's takeover of how information is spread?

Scotty: Well, we're forgetting democracy. We're forgetting our civics lessons from fifth grade. We're forgetting that we put our hands over our hearts on a regular basis and pledged allegiance to a flag and talked about a republic, one nation, indivisible, with liberty and justice for all. How do we do that at one point, and then forget that that's what we're all about. We're all Americans. Obama said this back in the 2004 Democratic convention: "There's another ingredient in the American saga. A belief that we are connected as one people…It's what allows us to pursue our individual dreams, yet still come together as a single American family. *E pluribus unum.* Out of many, one." He went on to say, "The pundits like to slice and dice our country into red states and blue states… We are one people, all of us pledging allegiance to the stars and stripes, all of us defending the United States of America." So, we're not blue states and red states; we're the United States of America. We know from our revolutionary history the quote, "United we stand, divided we fall." What's happened to our understanding of democracy that we find the need to stick with our own tribes? We know that's a recipe for disaster. We know that's a recipe, ultimately, for revolution.

Michael: Scotty, you're talking about listening to MSNBC as one piece of a truth or Fox as another piece. However, I don't think either of them traffic in facts or truth. As an example—Mueller has not come out with anything.

He's had some indictments. Those indictments are very specific. And yet, every time there's an indictment, pundits on Fox and MSNBC—on CNN as well—pontificate on what it all means, which they actually don't know yet.

Betty: What Michael points out prompts me to ask you, Scotty, to comment on the form in which truth gets packaged—or the way opinion and truth gets packaged. Because we lend authority to the Walter Cronkite–type news anchor on a major TV network, or to a host of a TV show on a cable network that gets disseminated all over the world, and we believe in what they are saying. Or you see the printed word on a website or—in the old-fashioned sense—in a newsprint journal. Is that something we need to be careful about now, given that there are now many of these online journals and many of these news websites? With some of them, we know where their information comes from—as you said, we know *The Wall Street Journal*, in their investigative reporting, does an extensive and in-depth job of checking sources and presenting both sides of a story. But not every journalist, not every news organization does this.

Michael: I think that that's one of the problems with Trump. He's attacked news organizations so spectacularly that we don't even have faith in journalism anymore. But journalism is not the same thing as opinion.

Betty: No, it's not. But now that people are thinking what they get on Facebook is equivalent to news…

Michael: That's Facebook's problem.

Betty: Well, it's our problem too, because many of us buy it. We buy what we're seeing.

Michael: That's why everybody should go off Facebook.

Betty: You're in the minority position there.

Scotty: And it's not just Facebook. It's Google. It's Wikipedia. It's wherever you're going for information, but you're not digging down to the sources that underlie what you're getting. And it is this confusion between opinion and journalism. And part of it is that we need journalists and schools of journalism to remind us about journalistic ethics. What is a journalist? Why is it a profession and not just a business to make money off of? What does it mean to be a profession? What does it mean to have a code of ethics? What does it mean to care about your clientele? Who are your readers, as they are your number one constituency—not yourself, nor your business? I think we need to return to a real understanding of professional ethics across the board—in law, in medicine, as well as in journalism, to name a few. We need to get back to that center and to have people respected because they actually are professionals who uphold value systems and ethics in service of their field and those who rely on their expertise.

Betty: You identified the basic American values of democracy and unity, citing *E pluribus unum*. In a recent podcast, I quoted the Declaration of Independence as having grounding principles and central tenets that we can return to and that remind us of what we're all about as Americans. But these guideposts seem to be getting drowned out by the signal-to-noise ratio of our digital age. So, how do we clarify? How do we focus ourselves and remind ourselves of democracy when even our president—the person sitting in the highest office of power in the United States, the leader of the free world—is now advocating for authoritarian policies that are very much against our principles of democracy?

Scotty: We need to defend our institutions. We need to make sure that courts are courts and have somebody like Chief Justice John Roberts say, when the president talks about "Obama judges," that we don't have Obama judges. We have judges in an independent court system. We need to defend our—and I never thought I'd say this having been on the left for my whole life—but we need to defend the CIA and the FBI and their ability to do a thorough and neutral investigation. We need to defend our institutions, like Congress, and realize we have a separation of powers, and Congress needs to exercise its duties to make sure that it, not the president, has the power of the purse.

Ultimately, this country is only an idea. It is the Declaration of Independence, and that is our creed as a nation. And we've had some good leadership in the past.

I think of people like Martin Luther King Jr., who was able to advocate for his tribe and talk about people who were oppressed and about racism and poverty, all while tying it back to our common connection to the

Declaration—that there are certain self-evident truths that all people—although it actually said "men" originally—are created equal. And there is somebody who is able to say, "Yeah it did say *men* originally, but now we mean *women* too; we mean not just white men. Go back to those original documents, to that original vision, because otherwise America has nothing." We're not an ethnicity, like a lot of countries are. We're not a religion, like a lot of countries are. But we are an idea.

Michael: We're an aspiration. The thing about King is that he was consistently asking us as a country to hold ourselves to our own standard. That America, in King's vision, was capable of living up to its own words. Although it had failed, it could still succeed in its promise of ensuring human rights and dignity to each of its citizens. What I think is so fascinating is that it seems we've lost that vision, and we've lost that articulation. We are now telling two competing stories. On the right, the narrative is to "make America great again." The right tells a story in the past tense. They say, "Looking back, we once had glory. We have to get back to that." And when you do that, you don't include immigrants. You don't include equal rights for women. You tend to also be exclusionary because "going back" means returning to a time when whites were even more dominant.

Betty: It's past tense, with the past defined by those people who want to characterize it in a certain way.

Michael: On the other hand, the left does not tell a story about America that has any hint of redemption in it. The left's vision of America is one where America is implacably evil and can't be redeemed. It's always going to be racist. It's always going to be sexist.

Betty: Well, I don't know if that's exactly the argument on the left, but …

Michael: It feels that way to me.

Betty: I think the left wants, as you, Scotty, put it, a plurality and a recognition of all different voices. I do feel, in that way, it's lost an ability to unify those voices.

Michael: I think that's because there's no redemption in its narrative.

Betty: Actually, I think there's no link. And it goes back to an interesting point about Jussie Smollett if I may. There's another point about that story, which is underlying the actual actions and opinions that are swirling around it, which is that here is a Black, gay young man who was walking down the street on his own. And if he allegedly created this situation, what in him created that narrative? Why did he need to tell this story of being subjugated by people who were MAGA supporters? Was he making concrete something that was implied, if not imposed, ideologically?

Michael: Well, my sense is that he did it for his own selfish reasons of trying to get more money. At least this is the allegation at Fox.

Scotty: Allegedly.

Michael: Yeah. Allegedly. This is the allegation that the motivation was simple.

Betty: For attention?

Michael: For greed. He was not getting the part he wanted, and he didn't get the money he wanted, and that's why he did it. That is the nightmare of this thing.

Betty: So to clarify, he wanted to create greater celebrity around himself, so he would be more valued on the TV show?

Michael: Correct. That's the allegation—an unproven allegation. That is not the truth. In theory, the motivation is a deeply selfish and destructive one. And that's the danger in all of this. We're spending time on it because it causes real harm to a lot of people. But chief among them are people who are the true victims of hate crimes in this country. But those people who are deemed complicit because they are MAGA supporters of Donald Trump—they are now feeling not just vindicated, but triumphant. That's what Twitter went crazy with when this story broke. What we end up with as a consequence, however, is all conflict, zero truth. Nothing to hold on to. All sand that runs right through your fingers. And now everybody is using whatever piece of that narrative that they want.

Betty: What do you think of all this, Scotty?

Scotty: I'd like to go back to what Michael said—that we don't have a vision of redemption. That's a really important point. It moves me to speak from another realm of my life, which is religion. Obama offered a redemptive vision of how America might be—one not of blue states or red states, but of the United States. His was a message of hope and a vision of an America that was grounded in these founding documents, even if not yet realized. And I want to say something positive about identity politics, which we've been talking about. If you move from the realm of selfishness that we've been talking about, to one where you feel the pain of other people along with the hope and the aspirations of others—if you can keep building those concentric circles out and resist circling the wagons, ultimately, you can get a vision of the whole and you can arrive at a redemptive vision.

And historically, that's what religions have done. They've done a lot of harm. I used to preach a sermon every year titled, "Does Religion Do More Harm Than Good?" And obviously religion does a lot of harm in terms of creating divisiveness and violence. This has resulted in holocausts, pogroms, and holy wars. But a lot of spiritual communities talk about some vision of the next world—whether it's based in Christian ideas of redemption, or Jewish concepts that we've been exiled, or Muslim notions of getting beyond your own pride and submitting to God to return to a promised land with a larger vision and a different kind of hope. Buddhism also considers ego attachment and selfishness as the core problem of human suffering. How do you advocate for a vision of compassion and a vision of bringing together all living beings, all sentient beings, as one?

My sense is that we need to build these circles out and keep building, with messages such as Jesus delivered, "Love your neighbor," with the Hebrew Bible on his lips. But he went on to say, you need to "love the stranger," which is also a Jewish concept. But beyond that, Jesus advocated, "Love your enemy." And you need to love your enemy because the blessed community includes everyone. And that vision of redemption is one that Martin Luther King Jr. talked about all the time.

Michael: He was a minister, and he understood the power of redemption. If you deny yourself or others redemption, you deny the other person humanity. And ultimately that is where we have gone. We don't see the humanity in the other anymore.

Betty: Something that you mentioned, Michael, about Jussie Smollett and something that you mentioned, Scotty, about redemption and what multiple religions say about how we are redeemed, brings to mind the dialectic between materiality and spirituality. So, when we talk about Jussie Smollett—he did what he did, allegedly, for personal gain by creating a plausible story that relied on our assumptions about MAGA supporters and what they might do to a young, gay, Black man walking down a street alone at night. And then later, there came an extra added element complicating his reasons for telling this story, which is about celebrity, money, and materiality.

So, we're talking about truth, we're talking about words, and we're talking about words mattering. But when every sentence possibly becomes something to garner yourself a million likes, then words become currency, and saying something true becomes less important than saying something that everyone will pay attention to. Because attention translates into material power. This influences politicians, who now aim to tweet something everybody will pay attention to, giving them the spotlight. But there is a lack of spirituality in this. Because the truly spiritual doesn't have a dollar sign next to it, and this is something that we also desperately need—expressions that are earnest and not transactional. We are limited creatures on this Earth. We're going to die. And, as one of our first interviewees, social psychologist Sheldon Solomon said, the thing that carries us across the anxiety of death is meaning, culture, and art. And meaning, culture, and art are all elements of spirituality. Would you agree with that, Scotty?

Scotty: Every word. I mean, this is the beauty of not having to preach if somebody else can do it for you. Just beautifully stated.

Betty: From therapist to the pulpit. I'm moving on up, Michael.

Michael: Reverend Teng.

Betty: Amen.

Michael: Scotty, how do you see the role of religion in our society right now? There seems to be a great deal of skepticism toward religion. One of the things that unfortunately has happened is that people who are deeply religious, for whom God is an integral part of their life—especially devout

Christians—feel as though they have no home on the left. Their feeling is that, among progressives, there is a condescension toward the very religious.

Betty: We are ever more divided along religious lines.

Michael: Well, religion has been politicized. But I also think that the left looks down on those who are very devout, with progressives thinking, "Frankly, you must be stupid if you are so religious." *Not educated* is a nice way of saying it.

Betty: Scotty, you told me a story about when you were a chaplain at Stanford or Tufts. I think that it could be an interesting metaphor for what we're going through right now as a society around difference. Could you tell some of that story about all the different student groups that came to you while you were a university chaplain?

Scotty: Well, this happened both when I was a chaplain at Tufts for sixteen years and then when I was the Dean for Religious Life—or chaplain—at Stanford for fourteen years. So, across thirty years of having several dozen different religious groups on campus—from Christian Evangelicals, Orthodox Christians, Roman Catholics, Jews, Muslims, Buddhists, Hindus, Bahais—it goes on and on. And then at Stanford, we even had this wonderful group called AHA!—with an exclamation mark—which stood for Atheists, Humanists, and Agnostics!

Betty: That's awesome. I want that group's t-shirt.

Scotty: So, every one of those groups would come into my office at one time or another. We'd close the door; they'd sit down; and they would tell me how discriminated against they were and how much they felt at risk and how the whole community thought they were—yes, Michael, "stupid." They would come in and say, "I'm an Evangelical Christian and nobody thinks that I have any intelligence." Or "I'm a Roman Catholic and Catholicism has always been attacked within the academy." Or "I'm a Jew and let me tell you about the levels of antisemitism that are rife in this university." Or "I'm a Muslim and I've actually had death threats, and people say, how can you wear that headscarf and be a modern woman in a university?" They all came in, and they all told me how discriminated against they were and how they tended to not know that everybody else was coming in and saying virtually the same thing.

And then one thing I really used to love was having all these religious groups talk about being under the umbrella of a secular university and how you can't talk about religion in the modern university because it's all rational… it's all anti-religious…it's all science. And then I would have the AHA! group, or any collective of humanists come through the door and complain, "The problem is you cannot be an atheist at a university. It is so religious. It is so spiritually oriented. We have this church sitting at the middle of the campus. And when I graduate and I want to go into politics, I can never say I'm an atheist. There's no way you can go into politics or attain acceptance in America as an atheist. Consistently 95 percent of Americans surveyed by an annual Gallup poll say they believe in God." The non-religious groups also felt so discriminated against and that U.S. society is a religious environment and there's no room for secularity. So how do you put all that together?

Betty: From your position as university chaplain, did each group have a legitimate claim to feeling so subjugated?

Scotty: Absolutely. Every one of them had a factual—and I'm going to say that again—*factual* basis for their claims. And they could point to evidence and to experience that backed up what they were saying. Absolutely.

Betty: So that illuminates something about the identity politics on both the right and left here in the U.S. Everybody has a legitimate claim to their feelings of being subjugated. We were talking last week to a political scientist whose research investigated white identity politics—and even mainstream whites feel aggrieved. So, if everybody has a legitimate claim to feeling discriminated against, what is your answer to these groups? What did you say to them?

Scotty: Part of my answer is to let them know that, by the way, five minutes earlier or five weeks earlier, the exact person you say is oppressing you walked through the door and told me how oppressed they were. So this is a generalized phenomenon of—call it, religious affinity, identity politics, community identity. That's one thing that I do—I let people know that. The second thing is to say, "Gee, if you would actually listen to each other"—and I tried to create some constructed cross-group events, like having people participate in discussions over very controversial subjects, where you could not speak until you had summarized what the previous speaker had said in a way that the previous speaker could accept that you understood their position. So you would summarize their view and they'd say, "No, you didn't quite hear what I said. I said this." Then you'd have to try again. Not until you could adequately summarize to the other's satisfaction what had just been said could you speak.

This method helps people really listen to each other and listen empathetically. And you begin to see how much similarity there is and how much shared pain. But you also see the uniqueness of every group's issues and how it really is for them. Antisemitism really isn't the same as Islamophobia—and neither is what Evangelical Christians experience by being denigrated in the academy, etc. I advocate being able to figure out how to get people to listen empathetically to each other. And then, at the far end of it, you say, "All of your traditions talk about a vision of unity. They all talk about the commonality, that we're all creations of the same God. And, we have this fundamental document in the U.S. that states there are truths that we're all created equal, and we're endowed by a creator to have certain inalienable rights." And that's it.

Betty: So, people could only earn the right to speak if they had proven they truly listened to their opponent—or the person who spoke before them. They should do this in Congress.

Scotty: One exciting thing in Congress is there are beginning to be some of these groups. There is a veterans' organization called With Honor that I'm trying to follow a bit. It is putting money up for both Democrats and Republicans who have come out of the military and who have a sense of a nonpartisan America and who have a sense of the basic values of being an American and the importance of talking across the aisle. And they sign a pledge to do a number of things that are kind of abstract, but then some concrete things, like to sponsor one piece of bipartisan legislation a year and to co-sponsor several one-on-one meetings with somebody from across the aisle on a weekly or monthly basis. We need to be able to return to these underlying Pledge of Allegiance, Star-Spangled Banner, Declaration of Independence, America the Beautiful values that we all talk about, especially in Congress, our lawmakers.

Betty: Something that you were talking about earlier quoting *E pluribus unum*. We have lost, it seems, the *unum*—or we're losing sight of *unum*, or unity.

Scotty: Right.

Betty: We have a lot of diversity and increasing diversity in American society. Things are heating up in our arguments with each other over our different identities and our different voices. What MAGA supporters say about what "made us great" could be seen as a reaction to this increasing diversity—that we were "great" because we were one race, one religion, one creed, and one kind of people.

Scotty: We're all WASPs. We're all White Anglo-Saxon Protestants ...

Betty: ...who eat apple pie.

Michael: Only, we never actually were.

Scotty: Of course not.

Betty: We were founded upon a system of slavery and that was a hidden history.

Michael: And we fought a civil war with 800,000 deaths.

Betty: Yeah, but to say that, and to consider there are people in the country who think racism is nonexistent, who deny the Civil War and our history of slavery and genocide...

Michael: I listen to all this, and I think to myself, we have yet to come out of the upheaval of the second civil war, which was the civil rights movement, a largely peaceful civil war that remade the country. And yet, when we lost King, we lost a visionary. He was murdered for his actions. Let's not forget that we have not, in the generations since his death, been able to find a single individual man or woman who can articulate a narrative like Lincoln did at Gettysburg—"of the people, for the people, by the people"—where you are judged by the content of your character and not the color of your skin.

Those are the insights of forward-thinking visionaries. Jefferson, flawed though he was...

Betty: ...articulated that "all men are created equal."

Michael: And Ben Franklin made those truths "self-evident." They were originally written with the use of the word *sacred*—they were "sacred truths"—and Franklin came in with his black pen and turned them into "self-evident truths." Thank you.

Betty: Thank you, Enlightenment.

Michael: I think we're hungry for a visionary. And I think we are lost in the wilderness without, if you'll excuse the religious metaphor, a Moses to lead us forward.

Scotty: That's so true. Yet, on the other hand, we can't wait around for Moses. This is on each of us—on a daily basis. I think this should be a citizen's matter. This should be taught to all as Civics 101. This should be part of what defines citizenship. This should be what we stand for with our neighbors, who we have over to dinner, what news we watch each night—as we were saying earlier. This is on every one of us. And we can't just look for the visionary leader.

Michael: When you were talking earlier about the news, one of the realities is that we lost legislation. We lost the Fairness Act, which the FCC removed. One of the reasons why Cronkite was Cronkite was there was a time when we legislated fairness on the public airwaves, and we got rid of that. And the consequence of that is what you were talking about earlier regarding the biases rampant on Fox and MSNBC. So, one way to solve the Rachel Maddow/Sean Hannity bifurcation is to re-legislate fairness.

Betty: And also maybe to not put journalism in the realm of capitalism. To not put it in the hands of profit.

Michael: There is NPR. There's one place in America that's not driven by profit.

Scotty: Right.

Michael: And PBS being the other. They have to survive with our good grace and donations as well as our tax dollars. They can't survive on the public dole, so they're constantly fundraising.

Scotty: That's why I give them money all the time.

Michael: Betty, you're right. The economic model of news and truth needs to change. I think the legislative model of news and truth needs to change.

What's missing is fundamental civics. People don't know the Constitution. People have not read the Declaration of Independence. The Greeks knew that their society couldn't function without ethics and rhetoric. And we've just completely decided there's no value in the humanities.

Betty: I totally agree that we need ethics education too. And I totally agree we need civics education. I mean, I think part of the reason the principles of the Declaration of Independence and *E pluribus unum* and the Bill of Rights are disappearing is because we lack civics education. Arts education is important too. I believe that there is a deeper meaning to the arts. That arts are, what we call in the psychoanalytic world, transitional objects in object relations. They hold us together across the gaps—the gaps being maybe the fear of death, the gaps being separation from the other. You have a piece of art or a piece of music...They unify you to other people. You know, you could communicate better with somebody—a MAGA supporter—if you found out they love the same art or music you do.

We go back to my original sermon, which is the spirituality and the materiality. You go one to one. You learn coding to get a job. You learn civics to understand how to better become a politician or manage yourself in the world. That's great and that's useful. But you also have to tend to the spiritual, which is a part of the mind. And we are mindful creatures who have spirituality, who need to know that there is meaning. Otherwise, life is boring. If you just mind your "to do" list, you just mind your "bottom line," you just mind your bank account, it's deathly dull. And this is what people in the rat race suffer from. They don't have anything that connects them to a different, a higher order. And it's something that's more idiosyncratic to them. Everybody looks at a color differently. Everybody sees and tastes things differently. And if you can explore that through aesthetics, then you come to a better understanding of yourself and ground yourself in this.

Scotty: Why can't we see education as having a number of different goals, including, obviously, getting you a job someday, but so much more. That's critical. And certainly, civics is critical to being a citizen. You're being educated not only to get a job, but to be a citizen, and you're being educated to be able to relate to other people. So, talk about psychology or whatever, you're being educated in order to have an aesthetic dimension to your life, to be able to appreciate, to smell, to taste, to be able to understand music and drama and literature and so on. There are a lot of reasons why we educate. And we've got to be careful to not just limit it to one. And that's why we have universities, ultimately. We're supposed to take all of this and turn it into one. We don't want to have somebody graduate from a university where all they did was get these various siloed topics, such as computer science, and not understand its connection to all the rest of human knowledge.

Betty: Or a confusion of subjects that don't link together into one unified curriculum.

Scotty: Back to *E pluribus unum*.

Betty: Scotty, our time is up, but this has been wonderful. Thank you so much.

Michael: Thank you, Scotty.

Scotty: Thank you for what you are doing. It's really important, and I appreciate it. I hope everyone in the world hears what you're saying here.

Chapter 10
Conspiracy Without Theory

Guest: Nancy Rosenblum
Episode Aired: December 23, 2020

Nancy L. Rosenblum is the Senator Joseph Clark Professor of Ethics in Politics and Government emerita at Harvard University. Among other books, she is the coauthor of A Lot of People Are Saying: The New Conspiracism and the Assault on Democracy, *published in 2019; and author of* Good Neighbors: The Democracy of Everyday Life in America; *and* On the Side of the Angels: An Appreciation of Parties and Partisanship, *which received the Walter Channing Cabot Fellow Award from Harvard in 2010 for scholarly eminence. She lives in New York City.*

At the time of our conversation with Nancy Rosenblum in early December 2020, the U.S. was still in the grips of the COVID-19 pandemic and settling down—somewhat—after a tense and divisive presidential election season resulting in Joe Biden's win over Donald Trump. In a fall 2020 report on Americans' sense of uncertainty and conflict surrounding the presidential elections, the non-partisan Pew Research Center cited heightened awareness of, and opinions about, conspiracy theories as a key source of uncertainty and split between Republicans and Democrats.[1] Other conspiracy theories prevalent at the time included "Birtherism" assertions that Barack Obama was not born in the U.S. and, therefore, was fraudulently elected president; claims that widespread

---

[1] Mitchell, A., Jurkowitz, M., Oliphant, J.B., & Shearer, E. (2020). Most Americans Who Have Heard of QAnon Conspiracy Theories Say They Are Bad for the Country and That Trump Seems to Support People Who Promote Them. Pew Research Center; Cox, D.A. & Halpin, J. (2020). Conspiracy Theories, Misinformation, COVID-19, and the 2020 Election. Survey Center on American Life and the Center for American Progress.

election fraud in the 2016 presidential elections meant that Donald Trump, and not Hillary Clinton, captured the popular vote as well as that of the Electoral College; and allegations that the COVID-19 virus was manufactured by the Chinese government as a biological weapon.

The rise in attention on conspiracy theories and how they stirred up in the 2020 elections prompted us to access Nancy Rosenblum's expertise on what she observes as the phenomenon of "conspiracism," or conspiracies that are unmoored from theory—and its dangers. Chillingly, not a month after we spoke with Nancy, the January 6, 2021 siege on the U.S. Capitol occurred, where alt-right groups openly touted slogans and statements drawn from conspiracist assertions, such as "Stop the Steal"—where Donald Trump insisted that the presidency was "stolen" from him due to poll tampering—and the "Great Replacement Theory," which claims that immigrant and nonwhite voters are imported from abroad to "replace" white voters and their political agendas.[2] Equally alarming, in May 2022, 18-year-old Payton Gendron—a white nationalist—cited the Great Replacement Theory in his 180-page screed justifying his shooting rampage at a supermarket in a Black neighborhood of Buffalo, New York, killing ten people and wounding three others, most of whom were Black. These crises point to the imperative that we must pay attention, not only to the social and political impact of conspiracism, but also to its psychological roots, if we are to keep ourselves—and our practice of democracy—safe.

Interview

Betty: Hi, Jonathan. What's on your mind today?

Jonathan: Space. Space is on my mind, Betty.

Betty: Okay—space?

Jonathan: I'm clear eyed, I'm lucid, and I'm thinking about aliens—and here's why.

Betty: (*laughing*) Okay—

---

[2] Jones, D. (2022). What Is the "Great Replacement" and How Is It Tied to the Buffalo Shooting Suspect? NPR. https://www.npr.org/2022/05/16/1099034094/what-is-the-great-replacement-theory.

Jonathan: Because I read recently—you might have seen this—that a former Israeli space security chief has told the press that aliens exist, and we don't know about them only because humanity is not ready.

Betty: Oh wow. The Israeli space security chief…

Jonathan: He says we have known, we've been in touch, and the Galactic Federation is out there—and Trump is going to spill the beans.

Betty: Jonathan, do you know what this is? I'm not going to hide my interpretation—it's a conspiracy theory. Am I bursting your bubble?

Jonathan: Hey, I love a conspiracy theory—whether it's about the Bermuda Triangle, the Kennedy assassination, or that the moon landing was fake.

Betty: Why? What do they do for you?

Jonathan: There are some wonderful things about a conspiracy theory. One, it's taking the dots and connecting them, right? It's taking evidence and putting it together. Two, is the notion that there is a story out there that would explain a lot, if only it were true. And so that gives us hope that the things that we don't understand are actually understandable.

Betty: I see, so a conspiracy theory gives meaning to what might be unknown, or chaotic.

Jonathan: It does, but unfortunately, I think we're seeing that conspiracy theory is seeping into politics these days—and that's where it gets a little more disconcerting.

Betty: It's seeping into politics—and families. Folks that I've been seeing have been running into some real conflicts with family members who subscribe to conspiracy theories—ones not as charming as your aliens with the Galactic Federation. It has polarized families and split them apart. They can't agree on the facts because there are no facts. This brings us to our next guest, Nancy Rosenblum, and I'm so excited to speak with her. Thank you so much for joining us today, Nancy.

Nancy Rosenblum: It's a pleasure to be here.

Jonathan: Nancy, I wonder if we could just start with some basics. Can you, for our listeners, explain the difference between what I might describe as a good old-fashioned conspiracy theory and the more recent phenomenon of what you call *conspiracism*?

Nancy: Yes, but before I do my definitional stuff, let me just remind everybody that some conspiracy theories are true. However, the way that people talk about conspiracy theory and conspiracism today is as if they're all, by definition, fantastic concoctions. I want to put that on the table first.

Jonathan: So if someone's following you, you might be paranoid, but you might also be right.

Nancy: Right. And we know that there are a variety of conspiracies—conspiracies by governments and conspiracies by corporations, and so on.

Old-fashioned conspiracy theory—and it's still with us—says that things are not as they seem, and we can reveal the nefarious plot behind events. We do this by following all the dots and seeing that the dots create a pattern. The example I like to use is the Declaration of Independence because everybody knows it. It begins with "all men are created equal" as a self-evident truth. But what wasn't self-evident was that the British were trying to enslave the colonies. So, the Declaration of Independence has a long list of grievances—stating, "Here are all the grievances, here are all the things the Brits are doing, and they're all tending the same way. There is a pattern." And because they can show this pattern, they can convince the colonists that there should be a war of independence. And that's a conspiracy theory. It works. And if you read about the conspiracy theories of 9/11, or of the Kennedy assassination, they are like this. They're full of evidence—scientific evidence. They mimic research. If you go to a website—my favorite is *Architects and Engineers for 9/11 Truth*—it's all about the temperature of jet fuels and the speed of airplanes.

So they're researchers. They're like social scientists or scientists and so on. But conspiracy theories are theories in a second sense—which is that they're political theories. Because to identify the danger of some sort of plot or action, you have to know what is being threatened, what is the injustice being done, what is the law that's being broken, what needs saving, or what needs creating. The point of the Declaration of Independence was to say this should not be a war that would just bring us a redress of grievances—this has to be a war of independence. All of these things have to show such a tight pattern that there can only be one outcome—and that is a war of independence. That is a classic conspiracy theory, an explanation, like any other explanation. Now, should I go on to conspiracism?

Jonathan: Yes, please.

Betty: Please.

Nancy: *Conspiracism*, that's the word current scholars use, *decouples* conspiracy and theory—that's all. It's no longer providing an explanation. It dispenses with all evidence and argument, even in court, as we have seen with these last electoral challenges. And it simply makes a bare assertion, with just one word—*hoax*, for example, or—*rigged*. And what validates this conspiracy charge is not evidence or argument, but repetition and affirmation. That is why the title of my book on conspiracism is *A Lot of People Are Saying*. Trump used to say this all the time: "A lot of people are saying that George Soros is secretly funding the migrants who are crossing the border."

Jonathan: Yes, of course.

Nancy: That is the basic difference. This is conspiracy without the theory. It's sheer assertion. And one of the things we have to figure out is why people need to do this, and why people assent to it.

Betty: I have a question, Nancy. When you're talking about conspiracy theory in the classic sense, you're talking about something that is connecting the dots. So it's a meaning-making endeavor. And to make meaning is a very human impulse. So, a conspiracy theory also has a purpose. Taking the Declaration of Independence as an example—it's meant to be a protest; it's a justification for taking action. Conspiracism, these bare assertions, however, seem to decouple not only the conspiracy from the theory, but also the form from its function. What is conspiracism's objective—is it a protest? Is it arguing against something, or is it trying to prove something? Does it operate in the same way as a conspiracy theory?

Nancy: That's a great question. I think you're right, that a classic conspiracy theory is a call to action. Exactly that. In fact, it is a dramatic call to action. It says that the moment to act is now, and if we don't act now, all will be lost. For the most part, the kind of conspiracism that we've seen coming from the Oval Office, from Trump's followers, and, in some ways, from the bulk of the Republican Party—does the same thing. It's claiming that some injustice is being done to them, that there is some grievance. But it's not quite a call to action. And that's something I haven't really thought through, but you're quite right to say that. It's not clear what it's saying should be done.

Now in the electoral context, we have seen the apogee of this conspiracism with the 2020 election and with the COVID-19 pandemic. In the election context, there was something to be done. That is, you could hire lawyers to take cases to court, and you could try to convince Republicans in the state legislatures to undo the vote count, even not to count the votes, or to decertify votes, and so on. But for the most part, the conspiracy charges that have been made don't call on followers to take any action. What does happen—and it's less dramatic than a call to revolution, as with the Declaration of Independence—what does happen is that you have a president with a conspiracist mindset and a compromised sense of reality with the capacity to impose his sense of reality on the nation's institutions. That's been the main focus of my thinking. It is a call to action, but it's an action that only Trump takes.

Jonathan: But, Nancy, here's where it gets confusing and even absurdist for me. It strikes me that conspiracy or conspiracism would typically emanate from the powerless as a weapon against the powerful. So how on earth does the most powerful person in the world, the president of the United States, continue to maintain an outsider perspective and posture, railing against the system that is fighting against him?

Nancy: First of all, I would quarrel with your initial statement. That is, very often conspiracy claims or conspiracy theories come from the government itself. For example, the big lie that the Jews were responsible for Germany's loss of WWI came from Hitler, the leader of the government.

Jonathan: Yes. Good point.

Nancy: In fact, very often it comes from governments. But you're right that the typical notion of the conspiracy theory is by people who are powerless—who are outside, who are looking in, and who see some sort of elite or powerful agents opposed to their interests doing them in. And your question is, how it is that Trump seems to embody protest for people who might have grievances against the government he leads? And I think that, first of all, when you have a conspiracist mindset, you always see the opposition as an enemy and the worst possible one. So Trump's always aggrieved. He's aggrieved all the time, and he represents himself always as a victim. Remember that even after he won the 2016 election, he went on and on and on about how the election was rigged and he had really won the popular vote. It shows a mindset where Trump believes that enemies are constantly after him. Many people followed him in this belief—people who may have true grievances or who may simply be of the same disposition. This is typically American and, moreover, it's a very American thing to see elites who are opposed to you.

There's a generalization you can make about all conspiracies, which is that the circumstances under which they arise and become powerful and influential in a society is when there's been some social change and when there's been a status loss by a group. But in the United States and in democracy, there is a constant substrate of the discontented because there's such a deep-rooted anti-governmentalism and anti-elitism.

Jonathan: If conspiracy can be found everywhere, then there are conspiracy theorists on the left and conspiracy theorists on the right. It seems that the conspiracism you have talked about is more of a phenomenon of the right. I'm wondering what you would say to those who try to apply a "both sides-ism," to that assertion.

Nancy: I would say that they're wrong. And you can parse the text and look at recent history and see that they're wrong. I absolutely acknowledge that there are conspiracy theories coming from the left. All you have to do is listen to the first two years, day in day out, of Rachel Maddow on the Russian case. But she was doing the classic thing: Here are the dots; I'm following the dots; there must be a pattern. She never came exactly to the conclusion that he was a Russian agent or that he wanted to build something in Moscow, but this was classic conspiracy theory, and it went on every night—for years. So, the left does it. Sometimes when the left does it, it's even correct. For instance, read Jane Mayer's book on dark money (*Dark Money: The Hidden History of Billionaires behind the Rise of the Radical Right*), or Naomi Oreskes on the tobacco industry and the fossil fuel industry (*Merchants of Doubt: How a Handful of Scientists Obscured the Truth on Issues from Tobacco Smoke to Global Warming*), and the conspiracies they construct.

So, conspiracies can be true, and they do, sometimes, come from the left. This sheer assertion, bare assertion, dispensing with the evidence and argument practice of conspiracism, however, is a phenomenon of the right. Now the question is why? I think that the answer is—or one piece of the answer is—that a classic conspiracy theorist wants to bring the evidence and argument to bear because it's important to convince you of these facts. They want you to think that their interpretation of events is true. That's not going on with Trump. If you look at his avalanche of lies—these are ephemeral, they're easily disproved, but that doesn't bother him. Because he's not concerned with whether or not you think it's true. He's concerned with your assenting to his view of reality. And that's exactly what's going on with these charges that the 2016 election was rigged.

Jonathan: That explains him. But how about the people on the right who buy into it?

Nancy: Exactly. I think the same thing is true there. That is, there is a congruence here—that belief is not the best way toward understanding. For people who assent to and "like" and retweet and spread and—in some cases—even try to act on these conspiracy claims that come from above— for them, objective evidence isn't necessary. In fact, it's not a matter of believing the facts of the matter. But on the other hand, it's not a matter of repeating something they know is factually false but they say is true anyway. What they believe is that this claim has a deeper truth. The deeper truth is that these people on the left are trying to change the nature of America; they want to deny that it is a Christian nation or a white nation.

You remember the conspiracy claim about "Pizzagate"—that Hillary Clinton is running a child sex-trafficking ring out of the basement of a pizza parlor in Washington, DC? Well, there were no facts to be had. There was no event. There were no screams. There were no predators coming at night. There wasn't even a basement. But it was *true enough* and it was true enough because Hillary Clinton was so evil, and, in some views, she was so satanic—she'd already murdered two people, so she *could* be running a child sex-trafficking ring.

The best example of this—one of these conspiracist claims that is "true enough"—was from Sarah Huckabee Sanders [now the governor of Arkansas] when she was the press secretary. There was a video going around of a Muslim immigrant assaulting someone—and it turns out it was not a true video. And she was confronted at a press conference with this fact: "This is a phony video that you're passing around," and she said, "Whether or not it's a real video, the threat is real." It's true enough.

I will give you one more example of this—because I think it's so important to get. There was a congressman who was talking about George Soros paying migrants to come over the border, and he said, "I'm not saying it's true, but I'm saying that it is completely plausible. It's completely plausible." It's true enough.

Betty: Nancy, on so many levels, it seems there is a fear that people are fomenting and expressing via conspiracism that doesn't jive with reality or rationality. Fear is irrational—it's a driver of irrational thought, and it makes me think of the disorientation that you've spoken about—how conspiracism disorients us. But it also exhibits an aspect of groupthink, which says, "My group of people is threatened by another group of people, so I'm going to make these bare assertions, which don't need evidence because it's really about our fear, and our fear is justified by these assertions that then get repeated over and over." So I just wanted to ask—if Trump is an embodiment of a presidential conspiracist—now that he's voted out of office, are his conspiracist claims going to be weakened, or have they taken hold, like a MRSA superbug?[3] Are we stuck with conspiracism virally infecting us relentlessly—like with COVID?

Nancy: You've said so much here and asked so much. Let me try to take it apart. Put aside for the moment what happens when Trump leaves office, and let's just talk about your initial statements. They really are interesting. You began by saying that conspiracism is fear—that it's irrational fear. I think that there are probably some cases where that's valid, but I see the

---

[3] Methicillin-resistant Staphylococcus aureus (MRSA) is a staph infection that is resistant to antibiotics.

assent to conspiracist charges more akin to performative aggression. I think it's much more aggression than fear.

But the other half of what you said is absolutely correct and important. And that is what's happening when you assent to these conspiracy charges—either that the election was rigged or that COVID is a hoax—it's not you personally and alone that's assenting. It's a signal of your identification with a collective group, with a collective "we." It's tribal in that way. I think you're exactly right. And by assenting and spreading these conspiracist claims, what you're doing is creating and avowing this group identity. And, in fact, it's viewed by the people who do it as a form of political participation. The interesting question for us is—*is* it a form of participation? Is it actually any kind of collective agency or act at all? Or is it some sort of uncoordinated and unorganized and—in a sense—unpurposive venting?

Jonathan: I get the notion of wanting to belong, to be tribal, to go along, but then it gets to the point where individual citizens are buying QAnon shirts and signs and parading around …

Betty: Well, that's signaling they're part of the same team.

Jonathan: As if it's their team.

Betty: They're saying, "I'm on the QAnon team."

Jonathan: Right, but it's taken to such a degree—there are people profiting from this. There are people willingly playing into it, and it almost seems as if they're thumbing their noses at those who might know better and saying, "Disprove it, buddy."

Nancy: The one thing I want to say—almost as an aside here—is that part of what's going on now is not just about Trump and his followers and Republican officials. It's that we now have a universe of conspiracy entrepreneurs. That is, people who are out there on YouTube and the internet who make money off this. I've written a piece on Alex Jones who has gotten very, very rich selling his vitamins and his erectile dysfunction remedies and so on. So there are people out there making money on it and sucking other people in. And to be an Alex Jones follower is like being a Trump follower. That is, it doesn't even have to be aimed at Trump, but there's an industry out there doing it. I think QAnon is a very good case for questioning political participation and tribal identity. Because unlike most of the other conspiracies that get liked and retweeted and become part of the political atmosphere, QAnon, the QAnon people are out there in public. They go out; they don't stay virtual ...

Jonathan: And they get elected to Congress.

Nancy: They go out, and they see themselves as a group. They have these slogans, *Where We Go One, We Go All,* and they have their paraphernalia that identifies them. And they are interested in intimidating people—not just demonstrating to themselves that they're intimidating. I've talked a lot about QAnon because people have suggested that maybe it isn't just a political group—maybe this is a cult, with their chanting and so on—or is it a new religion? How we categorize QAnon is a difficult matter; it's something that's in flux. But I dissent from the view that sees them as a religious cult, although it does have cultish qualities. QAnon is apocalyptic. It asserts that there is going to be a "storm at which point everybody's going to be arrested; John F. Kennedy Jr. is going to come back from the dead; and the Satanists will all be killed." And Trump is their leader. So QAnon has certain cult-like qualities, including some scary ones—like this apocalypticism. Others describe it in a similar way, as a sort of new religion. But I think not. I think we've seen it morphing away from being cult-like toward greater participation in politics. The question is, is this going to turn into a movement, like the Tea Party movement—which was grassroots and did start electing people and organizing, especially at a local level? Now will we see these Q people such as Marjorie Taylor Greene from Georgia and Lauren Boebert from Colorado in Congress? Again, I don't think so.

Jonathan: What gives you such optimism? Please share.

Nancy: First of all, there's reason to think that the Qs who run for office—like other Republicans—and maybe we'll get into that story—are playing to their constituency. They're playing to their states—and who knows what they really think. I mean, it's too bizarre, although they may, in fact, work in reverse. Meaning, they were elected because they are convincing. The other thing is—they have no politics. There's that. The Tea Party movement grew in two ways. It was both grassroots and funded massively from above by

Big Conservative money. And they funded it because the Tea Party had an agenda of small government, being against deficits, and lowering taxes. They had an agenda that corresponded with the most conservative agenda, and they followed it.

Jonathan: It was political from its origin. The very name, *Tea Party*, evokes ...

Nancy: It was a bona fide political movement and remains something of a bona fide political movement, whereas QAnon doesn't appear to have a politics. It's morphed. It wanted to get more political, so it has admitted all these anti-vax people because they seem to be organized, but—and I have been criticized a lot for diminishing their significance—but I'm skeptical that they're going to be important in politics.

Jonathan: I guess the question is—are they going to be? You have suggested at times that when Trump leaves office, conspiracism is going to somehow retreat to the fringes from whence it came. But now I wonder—is the genie out of the bottle?

Betty: And this echoes my question—is this going to fade with Trump's exit or has it become stuck here as a superbug—a political superbug?

Nancy: There's no way of minimizing the fact that there will be a change. The fact that the president with a compromised sense of reality and the capacity to—and we haven't even talked about what he's done—the capacity to delegitimate foundational institutions will be gone. The damage has been done in large part, not because of his followers, but because of the unusual authority and power that the man had and because of the submissiveness of the Republican Party. At some point maybe we can talk about that.

But in that sense, everything will change. Now, the question is, what's the scenario? Will he retain a government-in-exile in Mar-a-Lago and run again? If so, then conspiracism will continue to be very central to electoral politics and public life. If not, there are still more negative scenarios, and I'm not fatuous in this regard. The Republican base will continue to like this conspiracist stuff, and if they can't link Trump to it, they can see him as a martyr. They will urge other officials and the next presidential candidate, or other candidates, to follow it. I also think there are lots of lower-level appointments—positions in the agencies and in government—who will be very difficult to remove. They have created, in a sense, their own deep state to do this stuff. But the main point is, in America and abroad, that the utility of these conspiracism assertions has been established.

Jonathan: What keeps a conspiracist on the left from succeeding?

Nancy: Well, we don't know that anything would stop a conspiracist on the left. We just haven't had one yet. If you look at the Democratic primary candidates, none of them really fit that bill. I guess Bernie Sanders comes to mind...

Jonathan: In other words, is it merely circumstantial that conspiracism has been from the right, or is it because there's some characteristic of the right that makes them more susceptible to conspiracism?

Nancy: That's a great question. I don't think it's just circumstantial. I was being too simple-minded. I think that there are two things: one, the Democratic Party is a coalition party, and when you have a coalition party like that, you can't rely on a single, fantastical, made-up universe in which you own reality to unify groups around. There are too many realities within the Democratic Party to do that. The other thing is, the Democratic Party—and perhaps I should have said this before—is a party that wants to govern. And that's partly because its constituencies want things. And so the Democratic Party has to try—as best it can under difficult circumstances—to govern, to do things. And I think that conspiracism is a substitute for governing. That's true, certainly true, of Trump, who, even under the circumstances of the pandemic—or especially under the circumstances of the pandemic—threw up his hands, absolved himself of responsibility, and didn't want to govern.

As for why Republicans go along with this—I think they go along for a lot of different reasons. Some are simply supine. Some thought they could control Trump, manage him, and use him to their purposes. Some perhaps have confidence in him and want to ride his coattails for electoral purposes. But I think what's been missing from the conversation about Trump and conspiracism has to do with this governing piece—that the Republicans don't want to govern. That is, they want as little government as possible. There is a congruence between the craziness of Trump's conspiracism, which disrupts the agencies and takes people who have capacity and expertise out of play—and that has been true of the Republicans for twenty or more years. They want to cut taxes, but that's about all they want. They want deregulation. The chaos is not exactly what they want. They would like to do it in a more planned way, but they don't want a government, an active government. So there is this very deep alliance—and "a going-along-with" between these forces.

Betty: Nancy, from what you were saying about Trump and QAnon and even the Republicans right now—it seems that there's this bald-faced power. It's almost like power and governance has been decoupled under politics, that politics has become just a sheer grab for power, which a pluralistic group, like the Democrats, is not going to be interested in and able to capture. And I know you also have written on pluralism. By demographics, we are becoming far, far more pluralistic in terms of population and in our separate identities. Can we wait this out, or has the impact of Trump, his conspiracism, and the delegitimation wrought irreparable damage? I want to go back to what you think Trump has done to us—or what he and his followers have done in their delegitimating institutions. To refer to one of your pieces, *The Assault on Democracy*, how has our democracy been assaulted?

Nancy: To address your initial point about the power of delegitimation, I'll stick with one thing that has been delegitimated by the Republicans—and that is the notion of a loyal political opposition. Let me explain. Political parties are the foundational institution of representative democracy. They are how you have a peaceful change of power, and that only happens because you assume that the opposition is legitimate. You may disagree with it in all sorts of ways, but you don't think that it has no claim to power if it wins elections. At every election, the losers may claim, "Oh he cheated; he lied; he had too much money; he had too little money." But they don't challenge the legitimacy of the person who won the office.

What we have with the Republican Party—and it has been true before Trump, but Trump has brought it out further—in fact, he's illuminated a lot. What was going on before, is that Republicans—being a minority party and wanting to hold onto power—were willing to do it by any means, and at any cost, beginning with voter suppression and now, the bolder attempt to actually erase votes that have been cast. It's the only way that they can continue to hold power as a minority party. And to be clear, what I mean by "delegitimation" is to refer to the delegitimation of *parties*. I want to underscore this because the word is everywhere, and it's being used promiscuously. *Delegitimation* is not mistrust. You don't mistrust an institution that's been delegitimized, and you don't doubt its operation and cast doubt on it. So *delegitimation* has a very specific meaning. It means that this institution—for example, the Democratic Party—no longer has any meaning, any value, or any authority. And because of these things, what *delegitimation* of an institution means is that it has no claim on your consent, or your compliance. To delegitimize something is an invitation to disobey or exercise rogue violence upon it. Now, that seldom happens.

Betty: So it's a justification of it, right?

Nancy: It's not only a justification; it's a license. That's exactly what it's about. It's when Trump says, "If Biden is inaugurated, we can't call him a 'president.' We have to call him 'a person in the office of the presidency.'" If, by Trump's assertion, Biden has no claim to authority, he also has no claim to obedience. And we see around the fringes now, the rogue violence that follows from that. We see the not-so-rogue violation of democracy, like voter suppression and voter erasure. But that's what delegitimation is. It's not about mistrust. Mistrust behaves differently. When people say, "Well, we now mistrust the CDC, how can we regain our trust in the CDC?" We know that kind of mistrust. You mistrust something if it doesn't operate to your advantage or if it's corrupted in some way. And those things can, over time, be corrected—and trust regained. But delegitimation is a deeper, very different and more troubling phenomenon.

I'll end by saying that social scientists and historians know a lot about how democratic institutions got legitimated—and what gave them authority over time. We are now seeing, in front of our eyes, the delegitimation of these institutions—what's sometimes called democratic backsliding. We have no idea how to re-legitimate delegitimated institutions.

Betty: That was our next question.

Nancy: Well, I think this actually prompts not one, but two questions. And Betty, maybe this speaks to it, maybe it doesn't. One of the questions is, how do we combat this conspiracism? But the other, harder question is, how do we re-legitimate the institutions that have already been degraded?

Betty: Right, in other words, a) how do we stop the virus, and b) how do we make the body healthy again?

Jonathan: Particularly when we've democratically chosen to put people in place who are corroding the very notion of government from the inside.

Nancy: Right. They want power, but they don't want to govern.

Jonathan: They want the power to not govern.

Betty: It's inherently unraveling. There's so much we could say about the outrageousness and the drama of conspiracism that draws so much attention. Something you said, Nancy, in response to how disorienting this all is, and what we need to do struck me. You said we need to be "startled into thought." Now that's a really great, interesting, and powerful phrase, because this stuff can really shut down thinking. I hear about things like Pizzagate and Hillary Clinton running a pedophile ring, and my mind just freezes. I cannot compute. And I can't imagine what people who actually believe such things are thinking. And, in response to such phenomenon, you're saying we need to be *startled into thought*. Can you say more about what you mean by that?

Nancy: Well, I can speak for myself. This project began after the inauguration when…

Jonathan: In early 2017…

Nancy: Right. It was right after the 2017 inauguration when Trump claimed he had the "largest inaugural crowd in history," certainly larger than Barack Obama's. But the photographs from the National Park Service came back and showed only a modest crowd that was not, in fact, the biggest crowd in history. Trump's immediate response was that the photos were doctored. Now, I was startled. I mean, I was completely startled. What did this mean? It was so disorienting—and different from a lie because it's a lie plus a charge of conspiracy, that these silly photographers in the National Park Service were doing something malign. I began thinking then about the significance of this conspiracy claim and why it was so disorienting. First of all, it was an assault on common sense. And if you have, ongoing, an absurdity assaulting common sense, you get turned upside down.

Betty: Absolutely. Which describes the last four years of Trump's presidency.

Nancy: But then, if you can actually think about what's really behind this disorientation that we are talking about, two things emerge. One is the deep, deep question: What does it mean to know something? What does it mean to know that the photographs were doctored or not doctored—or that the election was rigged or not rigged? And what we have here is a divide that's much more treacherous and much deeper than just a partisan divide—although it tends to follow the partisan divide. It is this epistemic divide about what it means to know something. And unless you can bridge that divide—which we have not been able to do—you can't argue, you can't persuade, you can't negotiate, you can't even disagree, because there's no common basis on which to do so.

Jonathan: So, it's like the old expression, "You're entitled to your opinion, but you're not entitled to your own facts."

Nancy: Exactly. That was Daniel Patrick Moynihan's famous phrase.[4] And, you know, facts are disputable, whether they're accurate or not is disputed, and the significance of fact is disputed. But without some basis of even arguing about facts, you can't have any kind of government. You can't have any kind of policy. And this leads to the bigger thing that's happened. I spoke of the delegitimation of foundational democratic institutions, where one key example is the delegitimation of political parties and the notion of a loyal opposition, and the other—and we've all seen this for four-plus years now—is the delegitimation of knowledge-producing institutions. From the FBI, at the outset of the Trump administration, to the Environmental Protection Agency, to now, the delegitimation of the CDC. While this is probably more reparable than the attack on political opposition, it's going to take a long time to repair because these agencies have been hijacked. They've been diverted from their purposes. They've been circumvented.

---

[4] Daniel Patrick Moynihan (D-NY) was a storied senator who served in the U.S. Senate between 1977–2001. He first said this in his article "More Than Social Security Was at Stake," in The Washington Post, January 18, 1983, A17, column 5.

Trump loyalists have been put in positions, so that these agencies have been altered in what they do. I think that the reestablishment of the legitimacy and proper functioning of these knowledge-producing government agencies is the first order of business for the incoming Biden administration. We see Biden going about this already, because you cannot govern without, for example, information from the Bureau of Labor Statistics or the census—it makes no sense.

Jonathan: Right. It's the technocrats, the bureaucrats. They provide the stuff of government that we need. We need data. And we need facts. My question is, do you think that the task of restoring our faith in democracy and in government—of getting past conspiracy and getting back to faith in evidence—is something that an elected president (Joe Biden or anyone else) is able to accomplish, or is that more the job for a cultural social figure or movement? You know what I mean?

Betty: Yeah, is this a grassroots thing, or is it a top-down thing—or both?

Nancy: I think it is both. It is a deeply social thing. But more immediately and practically it is a political question. And I would divide my answer to you into two categories. First, I think that the COVID pandemic, which was so riddled with conspiracy, partisanship, and ungovernability—with no attempts at governing it—made it so that reality bites.

Betty: Well said.

Nancy: I think reality bit back hard and cost Trump the election. Then, there is a broad social—not just a political—entrée for the Biden administration to go back to resurrecting knowledge-producing institutions and using their evidence, their facts. This path is probably a traversable path. I'm quite hopeful about that.

On the other side, there is the political side, which involves shifting the attitude that the Democratic Party is an enemy and not a loyal opposition, and therefore any Democrat can be kept from office by any means. Moreover if any Democrats are elected, you obstruct them by any means so they can do nothing. I don't see that attitude, which is becoming entrenched, disappearing. I will be very surprised if it did. In the short run, they reach a bipartisan COVID agreement because even Republican voters are dying and need help. But I think it will take a long time to repair the party system. And a representative democracy can't work without a party system.

Jonathan: I could keep geeking out on this topic for so long. I keep wondering, is this music to my ears because I happen to be a Democratic partisan who agrees, or is there objective truth here? Am I just buying my own accusation of their absurdity, or can we still believe in an objective right and wrong—and have a political left and a right?

Nancy: Well, something bad has happened, that is objectively true.

Betty: And it's serious. It's intense to hear you lay this out—really intense. This assault on democracy is happening on so many levels. It is really like a bad virus infecting and damaging our political body and its systems of democracy.

Nancy: I appreciated your final question—which we didn't get to talk about—where you mentioned pluralism. I do think that's part of the answer to all of this. I just think that when we talk about the destruction of knowledge-producing institutions and the legitimacy of facts, of data and so on, I don't want to go too far to the other side. I think democracy requires skepticism about these things.

Betty: Of course.

Nancy: Experts can be wrong, biased, and corrupt. And there are lots of reasons to mistrust them—not to delegitimate them altogether—but to mistrust them.

Jonathan: Well, that's why we have watchdogs and ombudsmen and independent inspectors general and everything else.

Nancy: And above all—and this is getting back to Betty's point—above all, what we have is a pluralism of institutions. If you don't have plural sources of knowledge, then you can never be certain that the knowledge that you have is not—leave aside "true"—but useful for our purposes, or not. So, pluralism is key to all of this—a pluralism of political parties and a pluralism of knowledge-producing institutions. Certainly what conspiracists and, in fact, what the Republican Party have done in recent years, is to build itself a sort of edifice of certainty and the opposite of pluralism, of monism or totalism, or whatever you want to call it.

Betty: Well, there's a lot of work to do. And the ability to think is a worthy weapon. And you have given us that, Nancy, seriously. So, thanks for joining us.

Nancy: It's been fun. Great fun.

Chapter 11
Nervous States & the Instability of Truth

Guest: Dr. William Davies
Episode Aired: March 5, 2019

William Davies is a professor in political economy at Goldsmiths, where he is director of the Political Economy Research Centre. He is author of This is Not Normal: The Collapse of Liberal Britain; Nervous States: How Feeling Took over the World; The Happiness Industry: How the Government and Big Business Sold Us Wellbeing, *and* The Limits of Neoliberalism: Authority, Sovereignty and the Logic of Competition. *He writes regularly for* The Guardian *and* London Review of Books.

What prompted us to seek out William Davies was a powerful 2018 article he wrote for The Guardian, *"Why We Stopped Trusting Elites." In it, he points out a key component of a growing breakdown of faith in facts and expertise:*

To understand the crisis liberal democracy faces today—whether we identify this primarily in terms of "populism" or "post-truth"—it's not enough to simply bemoan the rising cynicism of the public. We need also to consider some of the reasons why trust has been withdrawn. ...By focusing on trust, and the failure of liberal institutions to sustain it, we get a clearer sense of why this is happening now.[1]

---

[1] Davies, W. (2018). Why We Stopped Trusting Elites. *The Guardian.* https://www.theguardian.com/news/2018/nov/29/why-we-stopped-trusting-elites-the-new-populism.

Because this helped explain a baffling—and alarming—tolerance for manipulations of truth and disregard for facts and data in Trump and Trumpists in the U.S. and Brexit supporters in the UK, we turned to William to help us better understand the roots of this erosion of trust in facts and information. What resulted was a far-ranging conversation on his 2019 book, Nervous States *and how our faith in knowledge itself has become unstable, in part due to the barrage of news and information we are subject to via constant access to the internet.*

Four years later, in 2023, William's insights have only become more relevant. Three years of the COVID-19 pandemic and social distancing has exponentially increased our dependency on digital media. Moreover, extended isolation, coupled with a current COVID death toll of over 1.1 million lives in the U.S. and 6.9 million lives worldwide, have raised existential concerns about the fragility and meaning of our lives.[2]

Our discussion with Sheldon Solomon on our tendencies to emphasize in-group affinities and to turn to strongmen in the face of death anxieties combines with William Davies's observations that "what nationalism offers people, which liberal technocracy never offers and cannot ever offer, by its very constitution, is to treat them as feeling beings, as communal beings, as beings who are recognized for the fact that each life counts." Together they point to the deep-seated fears of vulnerability and insignificance which nationalistic, authoritarian leaders assuage with promises of dominance and agency over scapegoated groups—be they immigrants, experts, or anyone of minority status.

What is striking is that these 2019 discussions offer psychological explanations both for historic political events that occurred just before these conversations—such as 2016's Brexit decision and Trump's election—as well as for major events that took place long after we spoke to William as well—stark examples such as the January 6, 2021 siege of the U.S. Capitol, and the February 24, 2022 Russian invasion of Ukraine. The timelessness of these topics alert us to how crucial it is for us to tend to our psychic needs for significance and security in order to preserve—and ever expand—a collective experience of civic freedom.

Interview

Betty: Michael, can I make a confession?

Michael: Sure, go ahead.

---

[2] COVID Data Tracker, CDC (as of July 24, 2023), https://covid.cdc.gov/covid-data-tracker/#datatracker-home; WHO Coronavirus (Covid-19) Dashboard (as of July 26, 2023), World Health Organization, https://covid19.who.int/.

Betty: I have Headline Stress Disorder.

Michael: You have what?

Betty: Headline Stress Disorder. It's a term coined by Steven Stosny in 2017 to describe a phenomenon where the news upsets you.[3] But that's all people want to talk about. My patients, my family, my friends. I can't get away from it.

Michael: I don't think you're alone in this. That said, what do you do? You're the shrink. You're helping other people with Headline Stress Disorder, but you suffer from it yourself.

Betty: I'm going to try something new today. I'm going to turn to a political economist. I think these are the people who can help psychoanalysts deal with their Headline Stress Disorder.

Michael: I like this. A political economist to the rescue.

Betty: So, without further ado, I'd like to bring Dr. William Davies on to join us. All banter aside, he's got many insights to share from his book, *Nervous States,* which captures not only the political, the economic, and the historical, but the psychological drivers of what stirs us in the headlines right now. Welcome to *Mind of State,* William.

William: Thank you very much.

Betty: William, the *New York Times Book Review* called your book "an interdisciplinary masterpiece."[4] "Interdisciplinary" is what captured our attention in this comment from the *Times,* although, of course, "masterpiece" is a hard word to miss. You are a political economist, but with a title like *Nervous States,* your book clued us into one of the angles that you take on

---

[3] Stosny, S. (2017). Overcoming Headline Stress Disorder. *Psychology Today.* https://www.psychologytoday.com/us/blog/anger-in-the-age-entitlement/201703/overcoming-headline-stress-disorder?_gl=1*au9i0b*_gcl_au*MjA5ODE2MjkxMy4xNjg3Mzc2MzMy.

[4] Green, M. (2019). Three Authors Consider Contemporary Politics, Anxiously. Review of *Nervous States: Democracy and the decline of reason,* by Davies, W. *The New York Times Book Review.* https://www.nytimes.com/2019/01/18/books/review/william-davies-nervous-states.html.

politics—namely, psychology, or *mind*. The title of our podcast is *Mind of State*. That puts us in the same boat as you and your thoughts on nervous states. So I want to start by asking, why did you choose this book title? What, in your view, is a *nervous state* and what compelled you to write about them?

William: Well, there's a pun in the title, which is to say that "states" in a political sense are in a nervous condition at the moment. Partly, there is a deep uncertainty that runs through the constitutions and futures of many Western liberal democracies that has been widely discussed in terms of the future of liberalism in Europe, North America, and around the world. And there's a kind of fear that peace itself is not quite as secure, as we took this for granted for much of the late 20th century.

So that's one aspect of it. The other aspect is that much of the book is about what is happening to knowledge, expertise, and truth in our society, a topic that's been widely analyzed and discussed in the context of the Trump presidency and Brexit in my own country. And what I really wanted to understand, or grapple with, was the way in which our condition is not just about a declining respect for objective fact, truth, and expertise—although I think that is happening—but it is also about becoming increasingly adapted to forms of real-time reactivity. That is to say our forms of subjectivity, our form of self that is emerging in the digital age, is one that is acutely attuned to what is going on right now, which is a nervous state. We have fantastic infrastructures that allow us to remain in very close contact with emerging trends, with real-time developments, with the news of the last half hour. And as we develop greater and greater capacity to react, to stay in touch in real time, to be constantly monitoring change—which is what our nervous system itself is so brilliantly designed to do—our other types of cognitive, psychological, and ethical capacities to reflect in a more dispassionate, more critical, more distanced way on things seems under threat.

Michael: So, the idea is that if you have news alerts on your phone, and you can update your online life immediately, and you can see someone else's social media updates in real time, you live totally in the present tense—that does something emotionally and psychologically to us.

Betty: And there's no time to reflect on other things, to take in all this information and engage in a deeper process of thinking about them, in order to integrate them.

William: That's right. One of the things I try to do in the book is talk about some ways in which our contemporary society is being refashioned— as is happening, for example, in the financial sector—where the greatest profits do not go to those who are making slow and informed analyses of changes in the real economy, but rather to hedge funds or high-frequency traders who are making huge amounts of money from anticipating very, very small but very, very rapid changes in prices. Or money is being made on developing technologies or even on experiments in things like brain supplements to try to create an edge over competitors, so that reactions to change can be as quick and as decisive as possible. In that sense, the areas where the most societal progress has been made technologically, politically, culturally over recent decades—and Silicon Valley is, I suppose, the absolute pioneer of these efforts—have been all about enhancing and supplementing our capacities to react, to anticipate, and to detect change as it happens. Yet our very idea of what it means to know the world and to live in it has perhaps not been enhanced by this.

Betty: What you're speaking about causes me to think in terms of neuroscience, which tells us that states of reactivity truncate the functioning of our prefrontal cortex. Because if we react in a very emotional way, we draw on our fear centers and our limbic brain reflexes. I wonder if all this progress points to a paradox—where, while we are quicker to react to information, we are not actually responding thoughtfully by using the most advanced parts of our biological brains.

But how does that point to how people are fearing what's going on? We're in this fear state, a reactive state, and our politics, our policies, and our economics are being driven by this incessant information cycle. What prompted you to take your observations of our nervous states and expand it into a book? What were you seeing?

William: Well, the book began with the massive political rupture in my own country, which was the Brexit referendum in the summer of 2016. And we still haven't quite found out where that's all going to lead. But it doesn't seem to be going anywhere.

I think we've only just begun, that's the worry. But one of the things that many on the pro-European side were horrified by was that it seemed that people had won by telling lies in some way. That was where this whole concern with post-truth and fake news came from. We also began to wonder if there'd been interventions by Russian robots and troll farms—the same sort of suspicions that circulated around the U.S. presidential election of 2016.[5]

Michael: And in England, it was mostly about how much money the National Health Service would be getting.

William: Right. There were these particular numbers that were bandied around.[6]

Now I'm a pro-European; I voted to remain in the European Union, and I'm pretty unhappy with the way things are going—but what I was trying to do was to understand what was going on without simply throwing up my hands in horror. I think that there was a certain naïveté at the heart of the pro-Europe side that echoes what went wrong with parts of the Democratic campaign in the U.S. later that year, which was that people trusted in expert accounts of the world, that people will vote in their own economic interests, and that, although people may not be getting significantly better off under the status quo, they're not going to risk everything by throwing all the cards up in the air.

And clearly, there was a certain impulse in many at the moment to throw all the cards up in the air and precisely do violence to the status quo. What I was initially interested in examining with the book was this apparent decline in the authority of expert claims about the world—of particular facts and statistics that economists produced—along with a seemingly greater emotional dimension and a more combative element to politics.

One of the things that statistics and facts from economists and experts aspire to do is to provide a minimal basis for consensus between otherwise opposing sides of an argument. That way both can say, "Well at least we agree that this is what's going on in this situation right now. We can agree on the size of the economy or the unemployment rate, whatever it might be." But when people show total disregard for those numbers, or they are prepared to just invent their own, then you're in a totally different type of politics

---

[5] Russia also interfered in the 2020 election as well, according to an intelligence community assessment. See Barnes, J.B. (2021). Russian Interference in 2020 Including Influencing Trump Associates, Report Says. *The New York Times.* https://www.nytimes.com/2021/03/16/us/politics/election-interference-russia-2020-assessment.html.

[6] "Brexit Will Be Bad for the NHS, Survey of UK Doctors Reveals," *BMJ.* https://www.bmj.com/company/newsroom/brexit-will-be-very-bad-for-the-nhs-survey-of-uk-doctors-reveals/.

altogether. So, the book attempts to tell the long history, first, of where these centers of expertise originated from and what their initial political pitch was going back more than 350 years. And then it looks at some forces that are pitted against these centers of expertise, very prominent of which is the rise of the real-time information cycle and the rise of reactivity-based politics.

Michael: It's funny. As you're talking, I thought of my friends in Virginia, close friends who are Republicans who have told me many times that they'll only ever vote Republican. I mean, it could be anybody. It could be an empty glass jar...

Betty: Or a reality TV host?

Michael: Well, when I went down to stay with them, my friend said, "You know, Trump's doing exactly what we want. We wanted it all shook up. We wanted the chaos. He's delivering what we needed."

Betty: How does anybody want chaos?

Michael: She felt as though the system had failed them. William, it sounds like some of what you're talking about in your book is how the liberal elite assumes that rationality and a social contract based on the English model prevails. That is our Declaration of Independence. We borrowed it from you all, from John Locke.[7] And, to a lesser extent, from Scots like David Hume.[8] All of us have inalienable rights. And our government's job is to protect those rights. That's the contract. I think people like my friend see a total breakdown of that social contract because they don't care about that ideal. They expect a different contract, which they feel is broken, which is to say, they don't have work. They've done the hard work. They've gone to get their high school, technical college, or even college education. They go to work.

[7] John Locke (1632–1704) was referred to as the "father of liberalism." See Uzgalis, W. (2022). John Locke. *The Stanford Encyclopedia of Philosophy*. (E. N. Zalta & U. Nodelman, Eds). The Metaphysics Research Lab, Stanford University. https://plato.stanford.edu/archives/fall2022/entries/locke/.

[8] David Hume (1711–1776) was a Scottish Enlightenment philosopher. See Morris, W.E. & Brown, C.R. (2022). David Hume. *The Stanford Encyclopedia of Philosophy*. (E. N. Zalta & U. Nodelman, Eds). The Metaphysics Research Lab, Stanford University. https://plato.stanford.edu/archives/sum2022/entries/hume/.

They show up. Yet they lose jobs, and the system is indifferent to them. They say, "Well, nobody's talking about how the system has failed me." So chaos is better than stasis, which feels deeply immoral to them.

Betty: Is this what you're seeing, William?

William: Yes. I recognize this. One of the issues with Brexit, as an example, was it always perceived and presented England's being part of the European Union as doing some economic harm. John Locke and David Hume, absolutely, are a part of this, and there's a very important concept that came into political and economic thinking in the 17th century that the historian of economics, Albert Hirschman, writes about—which is the idea of interests and that people have interests.[9] And even if people don't know what their interests are, someone else—say, a benign technocrat—can uphold those interests for them. And out of having interests, we are a little bit richer each year, a bit healthier, we live a bit longer—these are the things that obviously everybody wants. And this is the founding principle of the philosophy of utilitarianism, which says that we can all get a little bit more of everything over time. And I think both because people have not been getting a little more and also because there's something rather soulless about this, as a form of politics, it doesn't speak to certain aspects of humanity.

What struck me when I began work on the book in the summer of 2016, was that what seemed to emerge was a joy of sabotage. There was an upsurge of a different spirit of humanity that part of me respected in a strange way—a breaking free of technocracy. What we're dancing around here is the notion of nationalism. Because what nationalism offers people, which liberal technocracy never offers and cannot ever offer by its very constitution, is to treat them as feeling beings, as communal beings, as beings who are recognized for the fact that each life counts. I talk a bit about early nationalism in the book and of how the origins of nationalism lie in the aftermath of the French Revolution. What happened was people became part of this nation, this popular mass that could be mobilized— later in the Napoleonic Wars as well. People could become part of a mass community that hadn't existed in any recognized way before. This bestows a sense of meaning to life that markets and liberal technocracy cannot. So,

---

[9] Hirschman, A.O. (1977). *The Passions and the Interests.* Princeton University Press.

I think this is what runs through Brexit, which might have resonances with certain political groups in the United States.

Michael: Oh, for sure.

Betty: Absolutely.

William: But there's a sense that liberals are not upholding national traditions. They've almost colonized a proud nation in some way. And these technocrats in Washington, DC, or Brussels are a foreign power who are imposing a style of politics upon people that comes from somewhere else altogether. You hear this from Steve Bannon on the more radical right, those who refer to the *globalists*, the people who work in the IMF (International Monetary Fund) or who go to Davos.[10] They are a circuit of nationless people. It's got antisemitic undertones or even overtones. They critique a type of politics that seems to have broken free from any sort of territorial or national or cultural base. Now, this energy can be used in various ways. On the one hand, it can point toward some extremely frightening forms of nationalism. On the other hand, it also taps into some understandable instincts that people have—to be recognized, to be heard, to not have their lives disrupted. And what those of us who have more liberal sympathies than national ones are struggling with at the moment, is how to understand some of these instincts without justifying them or giving them more authority than they already have.

Betty: What you're both alluding to is something our first guest, social psychologist Dr. Sheldon Solomon, highlighted.[11] He talked about our human need for meaning and culture, which we use to combat our fear of death. Solomon, referring to Kierkegaard's observations, notes that what makes us human is that we are aware that we're going to die, that we have limited time on this Earth. And our human condition and existential anxiety is in wondering, if not doubting, if anything makes us more than an animal or, to quote Solomon exactly, "a twitching blob of biological protoplasm." So, as you observe, people leaning toward nationalism are in a desperate search for meaning, for a narrative, for some kind of organizing principle against this

---

[10] The World Economic Forum is held each year in Davos, Switzerland. World leaders, CEOs, academics, and other delegates attend.

[11] The interview with Sheldon Solomon appears in Chapter 2.

cold global technocracy controlled by foreign powers, Jews, immigrants—strangers who cannot connect with us in our cozy communities, who cannot care about our well-being because they don't know us, and we don't know them. So, if that is the case, if it's a dearth of meaning that has created this skepticism about technocracy, about technology, about expertise, about facts, and therefore about reality, how do we grapple with this?

William: This is the great dilemma. Understanding it is obviously the first step. I think there is a certain mass psychoanalysis that is underway, which, hopefully, can move us through some of this. There's work to be done in unpacking this. One of the things that I talk about in the book is the appeal for war—the lure of heroism. One way of understanding this search for meaning and how it's manifested itself in the modern world, is to see how it draws groups toward violent conflict. Wars are a context within which it is possible for a person to attain some sort of immortality through extreme heroic acts, which is worth the sacrifice of living a shorter life.

One of the great existential lies or myths of liberalism dates back to Thomas Hobbes in 1651, who said that human beings only want to live as long and as safely as possible.[12] Well, that might be true of most people, but it's not true of everybody. There is an aspect of the human condition that desires something more than just a nicer, safer, more prosperous life. And that is clearly what is flowing through our democratic politics at the moment. These desires—for meaning, for heroism, for immortality—come from somewhere real and somewhere even quite dark, but it is something that needs to be understood.

One thing that I think is interesting is whether that energy can be diverted anywhere else. The obvious answer could be toward the war on climate change. To speak of yearnings for narratives of heroism and mutual sacrifice, what all of these Brexiteers in Britain are obsessing over at the moment is the Second World War. They're endlessly saying, "Oh wouldn't it be great if we ran out of food, and we'd need the army to help the food get into the country. It'd be just like 1943 all over again." Indeed, over the next hundred years, there will be real demands placed on us to make sacrifices and give up some of our prosperity. The question is whether some of these

---

[12] Thomas Hobbes (1588–1679) published *Leviathan or The Matter, Forme, and Power of a Commonwealth Ecclesiasticall and Civil* in 1651. It was written during the English Civil War and argues for a social contract and absolute sovereign.

psychic needs and drives could be diverted toward such real threats rather than the mythical or conspiratorial threats people like Trump or Brexiteers point toward.

Betty: The challenge in this is how to get people to recognize that climate change is even a serious problem, which throws us back to the current controversy over facts. You speak about facts as being in the realm of elites, and that there is a debate between elites and populists in your country about the legitimacy of facts. It does mirror a debate that's going on here in the United States. Can you say more about that skepticism, that facts are now in the realm of a group—and if you're not a part of that group, you're not going to subscribe to those facts? That facts are not objective. How did facts and loyalty to one's group get stuck together?

William: I tell some of the history of this in the book, which is that facts have always belonged to a group, actually. We have to recognize that there is a core truth to some of the populist critique. This isn't to say that facts are not real or true, but throughout the history of modern expertise—dating back to the late 17th century—the ability to make objective, dispassionate, consensual claims about either nature, in the form of the natural sciences, or about society, in the form of statistics and the social sciences, has always been something that self-appointed groups of experts, scholars, and gentlemen engaged in. Some of them were merchants and some of them were more like data geeks, but they pioneered these mathematical techniques and experimental methods in the late 17th century and began to circulate their findings within a fairly niche group of people—fairly tightly controlled groups.

These groups weren't democratically elected. They were self-appointed. And there remains a suspicion that has lurked ever since, that there are certain professions—including journalists, politicians, academics, and other forms of experts—who have seized a monopoly on the ability to make claims about the world. And when they are challenged by people outside of that cartel, they can be quite sniffy about it. So, there is a political problem here. It's not the populists who invented the fact that experts are not democratically accountable. In a simple way, this is a genuine problem. Now there is a whole field of science studies and science policy studies that tries to grapple with this and talk about how scientists should engage with the public and how they can become better at deliberation and democracy.

But to bring it much more up to date, one thing that has happened over the last thirty years is the distinction between these different elite groups has started to blur in important ways. The professionalization of politics, where it's not clear who's an expert adviser and who's a politician, has been a real problem in Britain. The rise of spin doctors who are former journalists who then go and work in politics, or the revolving door between Goldman Sachs and the White House, gives the sense that "oh, they're all the same—they all went to the same Ivy League colleges, and they all know each other." This is also a huge problem in French politics, where the people who work for *Le Monde* newspaper are the same people who go to Macron's dinner parties. There is this sense of a cloistered, unaccountable elite. It's a real sociological phenomenon, and it's not imagined.

So that's one ingredient in how facts lose objectivity and become tied to a group. In addition to that professionalization of a technocratic elite, the second ingredient is social media. Until ten or fifteen years ago, you might have had all of these thoughts about these elites as you were sitting on your sofa watching *CNN* or reading the *New York Times*. But you had very few ways—other than going down to your local bar and mouthing off—of connecting with other people who had similar thoughts about all of this. So, technologically, the monopoly on the capacity to report on the world has been broken by YouTube, Facebook, and by people like Alex Jones and Infowars and others. So the technological monopoly on the capacity to tell the truth about the world has been broken. That, I think, is what's happened over the last thirty years or so.

Betty: So, there's a divide between social media and legacy media—legacy media being in the realm of the elites in this exclusive club, who are all of a high socioeconomic class. There's power in the realm of a high-class group and—there's populist rule on the internet.

Michael: Or mob rule.

William: The question is, what kind of dialogue is possible between the so-called elite and the so-called mob?

Michael: With Mark Zuckerberg as the fulcrum, that's a problem.

Betty: That's also the issue, social media is driven by economics right? There are big profits to be had from any attention-getting incendiary language, conflict, fearmongering, and controversy.

William: In my utopia, these platforms get closed down overnight.

Betty: The impact of social media is very serious in all realms now. You know, even as a trauma therapist, I have patients who encounter their perpetrators online—not their choice. And then they're also stirred by events in the media because they have their notifications on and these news clips about Weinstein or about Cosby, name the perpetrator of the week. Things that stir people in extremely harmful ways, from the micro to the macro. Say some more about social media—how you would close down these platforms if you could?

William: At the end of the book, I raise this thought experiment: Imagine it was 1945, and we had just come out of a long war, and we could plan a postwar peace in the way that the Bretton Woods meetings of 1944 did, which set up the postwar financial system.[13] What would you demand? What would you do? And quite unambiguously, I think that Facebook and Twitter are of no social value. I mean, what do they sell? They take friendship, the oldest social value of them all, and they claim to repackage it and sell it back to us. It's absurd, really.

Betty: They are also channels for advertisements. They are really using people's information to sell to other corporations to make Facebook profitable.

William: Of course, sorry—obviously that's their commercial product. But we know that some of their former employees have come out and said that they're frightened by the extent to which platforms like Facebook seek to

---

[13] The Bretton Woods Conference, officially known as the United Nations Monetary and Financial Conference, was a gathering of delegates from forty-four nations that met from July 1 to 22, 1944, in Bretton Woods, New Hampshire, to agree upon a series of new rules for the post-WWII international monetary system. The conference led to the creation of the World Bank and the IMF. See Library of Congress Research Guides, "Bretton Woods Conference & the Birth of the IMF and World Bank," https://guides.loc.gov/this-month-in-business-history/july/bretton-woods-conference.

cultivate addictive behaviors and exploit insecurities by the way in which they sell advertising space.[14] You know, there was a leak in the Australian Facebook, bragging about how it could identify insecure and anxious teenagers and target messages directly at them.[15] These are malign institutions.

Michael: It seems to me that part of what you're discussing here is this notion that there's no way in which Facebook sees itself as responsible for the content it disseminates. They talk about being a platform without value, meaning it doesn't value one thing over another.

Betty: It's "neutral," so to speak.

Michael: But there's then no civic, liberal—in the way we think of it—responsibility. And ultimately, what you have to do, then, is somebody has to regulate the content, whether Facebook regulates it, or, per your vision of a perfect world, William, the liberal elite do so by shutting it down. And this gets back to what you've been talking about, which is, at the end of the day, who has a say? And as you were talking earlier, about Bannon, Trump, and globalism, there is a clear sense that this liberal experiment—to grant universal rights to all—is under assault: the idea that it doesn't matter what nation you were born into, that we all share inalienable rights. If we go back to your postwar model, the great document that comes out of the Second World War is the Universal Declaration of Human Rights, which is the apogee of the liberal experiment.[16]

And what's emerged recently is an attack against communitarianism—the idea that human beings are asked to have the same moral duty to a stranger as to one's own child, which isn't possible. The liberal experiment is too reason-based. And this is where we are right now. People who are upset with Trump for, say, denying refugees entry to the U.S.—which is, by the way, a denial of the Universal Declaration of Human Rights—they hold onto the liberal notion of universal rights. Yet the people who support Trump—and who drive Brexit in your country—reject the notion of communitarianism.

---

[14] "Facebook Whistleblower Testimony," *The New York Times,* October 26, 2023, https://www.nytimes.com/live/2021/10/05/technology/facebook-whistleblower-frances-haugen.

[15] Levine, S. (2017). Facebook Told Advertisers It Can Identity Teens Feeling 'Insecure' and 'Worthless.' *The Guardian.* https://www.theguardian.com/technology/2017/may/01/facebook-advertising-data-insecure-teens.

[16] See "Universal Declaration of Human Rights," United Nations, https://www.un.org/en/about-us/universal-declaration-of-human-rights.

They say my moral obligation is to my family, to my wife, my children, my husband, my neighborhood, my country.

Betty: In other words—loyalty to my group.

Michael: Yes, to my group. This question of whether we as a nation espouse these esoteric elite values—this seems to me the fight that we are in right now. Is that what you're talking about?

William: That is a fair take on what's going on. In fact, my book is split into two halves and their titles address this shift. The first half is called *The Decline of Reason* and the second is called *The Rise of Feeling*. In the first half, it's about how that liberal edifice stopped functioning properly. And then, the second half is about how this vision of political heroism, of leadership, and of belonging surged in its place. I think liberalism also did some damage to itself over the late 20th century by escalating inequality. Just to give an example, I discuss the decline in the credibility of statistics in the book.

Betty: How is a decline in the credibility of statistics an example of escalating inequality?

William: You take a statistic, which is one of the most prominent numerical indicators in public life these days—gross domestic product (GDP), for example. In the U.S., GDP has grown roughly by 2 or 3 percent a year— every year over most of the 20th century, but fairly steadily since the 1970s. But we now know, thanks to the work of French economist Thomas Piketty, that 50 percent of Americans have had no increase in their real income since the late 1970s.[17] This means that while the headline indicators keep going up and up and up in a fairly steady fashion, 50 percent of people have actually not had any increase in their prosperity or their quality of life in the last forty or so years. Meanwhile, you've also got these other indicators heading in precisely the wrong direction in recent years, such as a frightening rise in midlife mortality rates that Case and Deaton detected in the United States.[18]

[17] Piketty, T. (2013). *Capitol in the Twenty-First Century*. (Trans. A. Goldhammer). The Belknap Press of Harvard University Press.
[18] Case, A. and Deaton, A. (2015). Rising Morbidity and Mortality in Midlife among White Non-Hispanic Americans in the 21st Century. *PNAS 112*(49). pp. 15078–15083. https://doi.org/10.1073/pnas.1518393112.

So aspects of the liberal project have concealed the fact that just under the surface, things have not been nearly as good as some of the macro stories have made it out to be. Now, none of that in itself directly explains Trump. We know that in 2016, your average Trump voter was actually richer than your average Clinton voter. I think what that does show is that the credibility of some of the stories that liberalism tells about itself have gradually been falling apart.

The other thing that I think is worth mentioning in terms of what you said regarding the communitarian and the liberal—and seeing liberalism as an abstract defense of universals, which is absolutely right—has occurred well outside the realm of philosophy. If you consider the Iraq War and the rise of neoconservative foreign policies in the late 20th and early 21st century, the U.S. and its allies effectively treated liberalism, not as a set of abstract universal ideals or philosophy, but instead as a set of Western values to be aggressively defended, asserted as a weapon, and dropped on countries from 10,000 feet.

This is similar to the way in which certain figures of the so-called intellectual dark web, bullish defenders of the new atheists, people like Ben Shapiro, Richard Dawkins, and Christopher Hitchens, basically say, "Yeah, actually, the West is best, and I can show you how the West is best." And this always teeters on the edge of Islamophobia. Thus liberalism started to mutate into something that was itself rather a hostile, identity-based phenomenon before this rise in populism.

Betty: Something that you've highlighted, William, with respect to this growing need in people for mobilism and aggression, and also for violence and heroism, points to something that British psychoanalysts D. W. Winnicott and Melanie Klein pointed out. This is that aggression is actually an expression of libido. We, as human beings, want to be mobilized. We don't want to be frozen in anxiety. We don't want to be passive. So perhaps we might mobilize toward aggression, maybe not even toward our own best ends. But it is a means of showing to ourselves that we are alive. And it seems like this might inform what is going on, in addition to what's being shown from an economic point of view.

William: Sure.

Betty: These two perspectives combine to point to a trend that is complex and alarming.

William: Yes. The language in all of this is quite interesting. We use the word *mobilize*. The term *to move* means we can move physically, but we also talk about *emotion* as moving. And *emotion* itself has motion in it, so *to emote* is to move outward. That type of liberalism, as you just said, treats us as a static object—a particular unit in a big statistical data set. Maybe the data set is expanding from year to year in terms of population growth, GDP growth, or life expectancy, but other than that, it's static. And the task of government from a liberal perspective is to represent, so you take this mass of people who are all getting on with their private lives—getting a job, having a family, and so on—and as a government, you represent their interests in a parliament, or a congress, or in the legal system, and the way you do that is you uphold peace. I mean, these are the core rudiments of a liberal ideal of government.

Whereas the alternative—which is the populist ideal—the point of representation is to move people. You will move people both in an emotional sense and in a physical sense. You'll move them onto the streets; people will come together and move from point A to B. All of the language of populism is about emotion in some way. For example, Jeremy Corbyn in my own country is what you might call a left populist. He's the leader of the Labour Party. The organization that was set up to support him, because he was such an implausible candidate to start with, is called *Momentum*. It's about trying to create momentum around Corbyn, this constant movement, so that in some ways, he's constantly in campaigning mode.

So that's one thing. The other thing—which is telling about what's going on in our public sphere right now—is that for Twitter users, when you decide you want to connect with someone, you don't "like" them or tune into them or read them, you *follow* them. They are effectively becoming your leader in some way—you are going where they go. And all of these metaphors and non-metaphors of movement, emotion, momentum, leadership, followership, etc. tell us about a very different idea of what politics is. It's very separate from that static ideal of representation that you find in the liberal tradition.

Betty: I think you're right. Earlier this season, we talked to political scientist Dr. Lilliana Mason (Chapter 18) about the reasons for increasing partisanship between Democrats and Republicans here in the U.S. She noted how Republicans use such conflict to mobilize their base. And interestingly, this language of mobility correlates directly with my work in trauma treatment, with the very words "fight, flight, freeze." They describe the physical responses we have to crisis or threat—so the different words or aspects of mobility are also the words associated with survival. *Freeze*, for example, describes the most extreme state of terror in a life-or-death situation. We freeze when we're terrified because the brain floods with cortisol and we can't move. Under extreme threat, any mammal's body will shut down because if the animal determines that they can't outfight the predator, they may freeze and "play dead" on the chance the predator will pass by a carcass. *Fight* and *flight* describe the ways we deal with attack or threat; all are ways we react to crisis. So, like you, Dr. Mason pointed out that political groups in the U.S., particularly those on our populism front, are mobilizing according to emotions rather than policies in order to self-mobilize and feel alive.

William: I'm not a psychologist, or even less so a neuroscientist or evolutionary neuroscientist, but I think what's interesting there is what you've said about the so-called fight-or-flight mode. It taps into a form of subjectivity and, no doubt, an aspect of the brain that is very different from the reflective, thoughtful one. It is a response from the instinctive, reactive one.

Betty: Absolutely.

William: And that's the same aspect of the brain that interface design is constantly concerned with—in relation to your smartphone, or a social media platform, or, to go back to my previous example, for high-frequency traders, a Bloomberg trading screen. This is what Silicon Valley is obsessed with, how to create the interfaces by which we can act without having to really think. Of course, this has all sorts of immediate conveniences and entertainments. It means that we can dial up a pizza just by asking Alexa. Or your eyes get drawn to the bit of the screen that seems interesting, and you click on it because your emotions are hooked, or you click on something else because you're appalled by it. But this kind of thinking, or non-thinking, is concerning. This is where Hannah Arendt's work on the threat of totalitarianism becomes relevant. She stresses that totalitarianism and fascism prosper through a lack of thought. And a lot of what she talked about was in relation to the famous work on the Adolf Eichmann trial in

Jerusalem—for here was someone who had lost the ability to think.[19] This politics operates via a fight-or-flight, instinctive, reactive, nervous state, supported by interfaces that are so perfectly attuned to the movements of our eyes and the sensations of our fingers in the way we swipe on a screen that we have lost the spaces for thinking and reflection. Now, I'm not someone who says we need to save reason. I'm not Steven Pinker saying that Western rationality is under threat, and we need to aggressively fight back.[20] But what is under threat, I think, are those times and spaces in which thought, dialogue, and reflection can take place, within which I would include the space of psychotherapy. And this is what we need to defend right now.

Betty: I think you're right. This is something that I've reflected on about Trump; his aggression and his language and his constant tweeting really creates an atmosphere of non-thinking. It's a cycle that goes back and forth and back and forth. We can't look away from him because he's so outrageous and what he says and does seems dangerous. But we can't look away either because if we did, something could happen. Additionally, he's such a spectacle that it's hard to look away. But then, we're stuck in this cycle of non-thinking. All of this combines with the objectives of Silicon Valley corporations that employ neuroscientists to hack our brains. They are literally finding ways to create dopamine surges by doing things like aggregating all the "likes" on your social media feed to create a greater, more pleasurable impact. We become addicted to our social media channels, going back again and again, like Pavlov's dog, to get that desired rush of seeing that all these people approve of us.

William: There's also a major commercial problem here that the media faces as well. There has been some good work done by people like journalism scholar Jay Rosen. He and some populism scholars have tried to put out advice on how the media should deal with Trump. And one of the main parts of that advice is not to get drawn into the hour-by-hour commentary, all the tweets. You have to try to ignore it.

Of course, that's difficult given the financial pressures that the media is under and the rise of rival clickbait channels. They need attention, these

---

[19] Hannah Arendt was the author of *The Origins of Totalitarianism* (1951) and *Eichmann in Jerusalem: A Report on the Banality of Evil* (1963).
[20] Pinker, S. (2022). *Rationality: What it is, why it seems scary, and why it matters.* Penguin Random House.

legacy media outlets, but ultimately Rosen's critique is very important and needs to be taken to heart.

One of the other things that led me to write this book was—probably about five or six years ago—I was looking at different forms of interface design, and I became very interested in the rise of what I described as "dashboard culture." If you think of the way facts were reported in say, the 19th century, you would have a quarterly shareholder report and a book of accounts and the daily newspapers and so on. All this was true up until the late 20th century.

Whereas now, particularly in the United States, when you turn on the TV, there's about five things going on on-screen all at once. There's stock information; there's the weather forecast; there's someone speaking to another talking head somewhere; there are headlines running along the top or bottom of the screen. It's this babble, really—like a river that's constantly running through your living room in real time. And the dashboard is a metaphor for how we get information. The most common idea of a dashboard is the car dashboard. It's this instrument panel of constant feedback on how things are going, with different indicators, different lights flashing, different things telling you certain numbers are up, certain numbers are down. But it's not really a way of getting an objective view of the world. What it is, is a means of navigation—again we return to metaphors of mobilization and movement—and it is a way of finding out "how is this right now?" But what that doesn't provide you with is an account of the world, or a story about the world that actually has any narrative arc, or any greater meaning. Instead, all it does is provide a comforting blanket that allows us to say, "I think things are okay right now..."

Betty: William, to me, what you're pointing out is the impact of fragmentation. On our devices and screens, we are exposed constantly to all these bits and pieces of information, which, at best, function to reassure; maybe at worst, distract and create noise. We've talked with other interviewees about all the drama that's going on in the news, but the question is—what's underneath the drama? We don't have the time or space to think about what's going on underneath this conflict, agitation, and strife because it's constantly spinning, and we're perpetually bombarded by these random bits and pieces of information.

Michael: We don't even know where to look. If you're watching the news there's the ticker or running text at the bottom of many news channel screens, which became ubiquitous in the aftermath of 9/11. There's no way to fully assimilate the information you're being given; if you're listening, you're not reading, and if you're reading, you can't listen. What ends up happening is you're going back and forth between the two. Nothing has any meaning anymore because…

Betty: …nothing is permeating.

Michael: Well, one kind of information doesn't have primacy over the other. This sounds like part of what you were saying, William, about shutting down Facebook, which I think is a great idea.

This also gets back to what you were saying at the beginning of the conversation, how the old model has been blown up and a new model, which we don't fully understand, has taken its place. In the old models, we were consumers of culture. We would read a book or watch a TV show, and we often did that in groups. In this new model, we're all producers of content, and we're constantly broadcasting our own lives, turning our lives into content and programming. And ratings come in the form of "likes." Kim Kardashian might be the very best at this new model. I have two young daughters whom I love dearly, who, when they were in middle school, would obsess over how quickly it would take them to get a social media post to acquire a certain number of likes and how many likes they had compared to other people. It was like, "Oh my God, you're like a Hollywood executive, talking about your overnights."

Betty: And that is the impact of the dopamine hits that their young brains are getting attached to.

Michael: And when you live in a culture of 300 million programmers, all competing against each other, how do you determine fact?

Betty: How do you even navigate all that information?

Michael: And where is your leader through it all? That's some of what you're talking about, isn't it, William, with respect to the assault on elitism and this notion that we've all been Balkanized down to the individual.

Betty: But in terms of shutting off Facebook, we can still do it for ourselves, as you did Michael. We can still exercise agency in this world.

Michael: Oh, but it comes at a cost. And for sure, I feel better.

Betty: Exactly. There's not a plus without a minus. No minus without a plus. So, maybe, William, what you're pointing out is, whereas globally, we could shut down Facebook so it's not available—in reality that's a very long-term prospect if it's even feasible. But individually we still do have agency. And if we are aware of what all this media bombardment is doing to us—and we have to take time to think about it rather than react, which is a challenge—but if we do conclude it's blocking us more than helping us, we can mobilize ourselves to stay off Facebook and the like, which is a certain kind of action.

But in terms of our nervous states—this wonderful pun—we do live in a nervous state where we're constantly clicking; we're constantly being bombarded by fragments of information. We live in nervous societies that are beset with battles between elitism and populism. Here in the U.S., it's battles between conservatism and liberalism, Democrats and Republicans. Where do you see us going? How do we navigate this?

William: I think you're right about agency. I think that we have to defend the spaces that already exist, which have not been permeated by some of these forces. And we still have the capacity to build new types of defense mechanisms that protect both our human relationships and our time and space separate from these forces. Of course, that requires political work. Some of these divides seem extremely intractable, but I do think that we need to be very clear about what the threat is. And I think the threat is neither emotion as such, nor is it emotion versus reason. It's fast versus slow. That's the key takeaway or conclusion in my book—rather than saying we've got these rational elites versus these emotional, ignorant mobs, the question is this: how can we defend slowness, including emotional slowness? This is how caring, loving relationships are cultivated and endure, whereas transactional relationships happen very, very quickly and are not nearly as meaningful.

I talk a bit about some of the ways in which the communication of something like climate science is changing. The effort is to try and get scientists to act in a more emotional, grounded, and human way about what confronts us. Events like the March for Science, where scientists mobilized on the streets of Boston and Washington, DC, and around the U.S. after the beginning of Trump's presidency, was probably the right step. It's quite a risky thing to do. But science, and scientists have to become more humane and more honest about the fact that it is a community. It's not a transcendent set of unquestionable truths. And there are these interesting experiments in trying to get scientists, in relation to things like climate change, to open up more about how scared and worried they are and what they think this really means to them. This is actually a fight for humanity. It's not just about abstract laws of nature and mathematics.

I think that's a key—to humanize the truth. And one of the things that is really fascinating—and this is a pleasant note of optimism—is that if you look across various societies, including the United States, at these surveys on trust that are done, they show that trust in politicians and the media is disastrous. It's been plummeting for years, whereas trust in certain parts of the scientific establishment fluctuates. But the two areas where trust is very high—and remains high—in the United States, is with the military, which perhaps isn't that surprising, but the other is in doctors and nurses. And that's true also across Europe as well. And I think maybe what professionals in those fields have in common is that they provide forms of physical protection of one kind or another. I think that the elites, the professions that defend humanity in its full-bodied, rounded, emotional, rational way are the centers of power and authority to which people turn when they're afraid in various ways. Now, you could say, therefore, that a pacifist version of populism, rather than the militaristic one, is one that extracts the caring spirit from that lesson. Because I do think that mobilization has to be part of our politics. We can't renounce both the opportunities and the feelings that mobilization offers people.

Betty: It's interesting because what you talk about in terms of protection—that is a very basic human need. In social service agencies and in mental health, we often refer to Maslow's hierarchy of needs, which is an ascending pyramid illustrating what we humans need and in what order of priority. And it shows we must care about food, shelter, clothing, before we tend to higher orders of need, like career aspirations or spiritual fulfillment. And protection and safety are in the tier of the most basic necessities. And maybe because of this necessity, they must trust—or they want to trust in the professions that are involved in the security and protection of their society and their physical health.

Michael: We're just out of time, but William, your points of slowing down to think, humanizing the truth, and placing a greater focus on protection and safety are great ones for us to end and reflect upon.

Betty: Well said, Michael. Thank you so much for joining us, William.

William: It's been a great pleasure. It's been very interesting.

Chapter 12
Trump on the Couch

Guest: Dr. Justin Frank
Episode Aired: March 11, 2019

Dr. Justin Frank is a former clinical professor of psychiatry at the George Washington University Medical Center and a physician with more than thirty years of experience in psychoanalysis. Justy has also been a contributor to Time Magazine, The Daily Beast, The HuffPost, *and* Salon. *He is also a best-selling author, most recently of* Trump on the Couch: Inside the Mind of the President.

In our conversation with Justy Frank, we asked him why he wrote Trump on the Couch. *His answer bears highlighting:*

> to help people understand and think about the person who they've elected to be their president. Even the guy who works at McDonald's has more of an evaluation about whether he's qualified when he gets a job there than a U.S. president does, so I was very interested in doing that.

By March 2019, the 22-month-long investigation of Trump and his 2016 campaign team by Special Counsel Robert Mueller for his Report on the Investigation into Russian Interference in the 2016 Presidential Election—*or the* Muller Report—*was concluding. On December 18, 2019, the first impeachment trial of Donald Trump regarding his abuses of power and obstruction of congressional inquiry into his attempts to seek damaging information about Democratic presidential candidate Joe Biden from foreign leaders, including Ukraine President Volodymyr Zelenskyy, began. Just over a year later, on January 13, 2021, an unprecedented second impeachment trial of Donald Trump commenced for his incitement of insurrection at the U.S. Capitol on January 6, 2021.*

Two years later, Trump became the first former president to be indicted on criminal charges, 34 in total, in New York State court for falsifying records masking "hush money" paid to porn star Stormy Daniels to silence her claims, one month before the 2016 presidential election, of having had sex with Trump. In June 2023, he was indicted in federal court for 37 felony charges for violating the Espionage Act, for retaining classified Defense Department documents, and for refusing to return them. On August 1, 2023, Donald Trump was indicted in federal district court in Washington, DC, for subverting the 2020 election results and for the events of January 6, 2021. The specific charges are for conspiracy to defraud the U.S., conspiracy to threaten others' rights, and obstruction of a proceeding before Congress. As of this writing, Donald Trump has been indicted on more than 90 federal and state criminal counts in four separate courts in Washington, DC, Florida, New York, and Georgia.[1]

This parade of historic and extreme political, criminal, and social transgressions by Trump, then and now, confirms much of what Justy explains about Trump's psychopathology: that emotionally and psychologically, he is like a relentless two-year-old who grabs for what he wants with no conception of limit, time, or reality. And yet, as of this writing in the summer of 2023, Donald Trump is far and away the leading candidate for the Republican Party nomination for the 2024 presidential elections. To consider some of the possible roots of this paradox, we refer to our conversations with Robert Jay Lifton (Chapter 21) on narrative necessities, Nancy Rosenblum (Chapter 10) on conspiracies, William Davies (Chapter 11) on the decline of truth in fact and expertise, Eric Ward (Chapter 14) on white nationalism, Antoine Banks (Chapter 15) on anger and racial politics, Lilliana Mason (Chapter 18) on toxic divides and Adrienne Hollis (Chapter 20) on the "syndemic" we sit within, blending the fracturing pressures of climate change, pandemic, and race relations.

Meanwhile, this comment by Justy is an important reminder of the dangers of Donald Trump as a public figure who dominates media attention, as a former—and possible future—president:

> He really makes it hard to think. He attacks. One of the main things that he does is he attacks thinking. He attacks your ability to think. The listener is either fact-checking or aghast at something

[1] Politico Staff, "Tracking the Trump Criminal Cases," *Politico*, accessed August 1, 2023, https://www.politico.com/interactives/2023/trump-criminal-investigations-cases-tracker-list/.

he says—and they are exhausted. That's part of it. You just give up. He makes people who must listen to him extremely anxious.

Robbed of the capacity to think, we lose our most powerful and sustainable defense against abuses of power, and we cannot exist freely. As citizens of a liberal democracy, we still have the power to mobilize against such encroachments on our minds. We would do well to see Justy's observation as a warning to protect our capacity to think, which is essential to protecting democracy itself.

Interview

Betty: As a podcast devoted to considering how psychology can shine a light on politics, we like to say that we put Trump and Trumpism on the couch in order to make America sane again. Today our guest is Dr. Justin Frank—who's asked me to call him Justy. He actually wrote a book about what it would be like to psychoanalyze Donald Trump. And I have to say, Justy, as an analyst, the first time I read your book title—*Trump on the Couch: Inside the Mind of the President,* I shuddered because I can't imagine Donald Trump on my couch. He'd be a nightmare to work with. Yet you wrote a whole book imagining what treating him would be like. What was it like to delve into the mind of Donald Trump?

Justin: Well, to be honest, it was something I didn't want to do initially, and I actually wrote that in the introduction to the book. And, like you, I couldn't imagine he would ever be my patient because A) he couldn't stay on the couch; B) he would disagree with most things I said; and C) if he weren't on the couch, he'd be banging on the door outside my office to get in. He'd be totally distracting and making ridiculous demands. That's who he is. He really doesn't have the ability to contain anxiety, which is one of the important things that a little child learns to do developmentally. He can't hold it in. He immediately has to express everything that makes him anxious. So I felt bombarded when I started doing this book.

Michael: Can I ask—why do it then?

Justin: I felt that it was important for three reasons. One is, when I do these analyses of presidents, I feel that the public knows much more than they think they do. We could understand even more if we just paid attention. It's pretty hard not to pay attention to Trump, but even paying attention to

Obama or Bush, we already knew a lot more than we thought. The second thing is to help people understand and think about the person who they've elected to be their president. Even the guy who works at McDonald's has more of an evaluation about whether he's qualified when he gets a job there than a U.S. president does, so I was very interested in doing that. And the third is, I just felt I had to. I don't really know exactly why, except that Donald Trump was so frightening. He reminded me a lot, initially, of George Bush on steroids—not very articulate, very much seeing the world in either/or, black-and-white colors, very simplistic. George W. Bush thinks you're either with us or against us. And Donald Trump is very similar to that. And so I was interested in the similarities. And as I wrote at the end of the Bush book, I said that if we don't deal with Bush directly, which Obama did not, in another few years we're going to have someone the same, only worse. And that's what happened.[2]

Michael: We should note that this is your third book on presidents, including *Bush on the Couch* and *Obama on the Couch*.[3]

Betty: Justy, I want to ask you about that. You have the unique perspective of writing about three presidents on the couch, albeit in a theoretical way. And you had talked about Obama having "obsessive bipartisan disorder." Did you hold both presidents, or all three presidents, in your mind as you were going through your assessment of Trump?

Justin: I do hold them in my mind, but sort of in the back of my mind, on the back burner. Because when I'm with a patient, I'm really with that patient, and I listen to them, and each session is a new fresh session. Yes, I remember things from previous sessions, but I'm really very much there. With Trump, it was pretty easy for it to be fresh because every day was something new and disturbing. I didn't need to hold Bush and Obama in mind particularly when I was writing about Trump. But I was certainly aware of the degree of health and competence that, say, Obama had compared to Trump's psychological health, but I also am very much aware of people's flaws. Everybody has them, including myself as the analyst. When this book

---

[2] Frank, J. (2006). *Bush on the Couch: Inside the mind of the U.S. president*. Politico Publishing.

[3] Frank, J. (2011). *Obama on the Couch: Inside the mind of the president*. Free Press.

came out, I sent some advance copies to my kids and my son Joey wrote on Instagram, "I just received dad's third book about himself and a President."

Betty: Right, exactly.

Justin: So, I think my son got it.

Michael: So what was it about Obama that caused him to seem frozen in your mind?

Justin: Well, Obama was really frozen at a very early age. His parents split by the time he was two, so he came from a very broken family. He only saw his father one more time in his life, when he was ten. And the other thing is that it was a mixed-race family. His mother was white; father was black. He was black, lighter-skinned than his father. He had this problem of trying to integrate different parts of himself, both racially and in terms of having an internal family, meaning a parental couple living inside of his head. When parents get divorced very early in a child's life, the child doesn't have as much of an internally containing couple in their heads where they can see that they have parents who both love them and can help them manage their feelings. So Obama was always trying to bring things together, and he denied a separateness in politics.

Michael: So he would insist, America's not really blue states and red states.

Justin: Right. And he really couldn't stand that split. He also believes in the triumph of reason over passion. And sometimes that does triumph. His mother made a great effort to keep his father alive in his mind. She played spirituals at home. She taught about the civil rights movement at home—lots of good things. But basically, he had to see that he was like Anne Frank, seeing people as basically good at heart. And it's just not true. They are good at heart too, but they're not only good at heart. None of us is.

Betty: So, in your experience of writing about Trump on the couch, do you read him differently from the Bush and Obama you wrote about?

Justin: Well, I read him differently because of his psychopathology—his lying, his destructiveness, his contempt for others, his misogyny, his racism, and his misuse of language. He can't spell. He can't use any kind of complex sentence structures or complex adjectives or nouns or ideas. These are all very serious issues. I saw him as very different from Bush and Obama. It was also very hard to focus on his past or on his childhood because he was so much in the present. He reminded me of somebody who makes so much noise, like I was saying about a patient banging on the door. He makes so much noise that you can't really stop and think. So, as opposed to Obama and Bush, it was very hard for me to step back and think about him. Bush actually did write his own memoir; then there were some other things written about him. His mother, Barbara, wrote something, and there is lots of literature about him. And Obama had this incredible memoir and a lot written about him. But there was not anything about Trump's childhood.

Betty: He was so "present tense"? Can you say more about that?

Justin: He really makes it hard to think. He attacks. One of the main things that he does is he attacks thinking. He attacks your ability to think. The listener is either fact-checking or aghast at something he says—and they are exhausted. That's part of it. You just give up. He makes people who must listen to him extremely anxious.

Michael: One of the things you said to Betty and me before we got going today was that you have read all of his tweets.

Justin: I have read all of his tweets.

Betty: What was that like?

Justin: Well, I would say it was pretty torturous.

Michael: How long did it take?

Justin: I would just read them every day. I didn't get a book full of them. That would have really killed me. I felt like I was a prisoner. I didn't go out of the house. I was still seeing patients. I was still working in the daytime and then reading all the stuff at night and on the weekends and writing. And it was really tiring.

Michael: How many tweets were there in the end? Did you know?

Justin: I wouldn't count, but there were thousands, thousands.

Betty: But this experience of not being able to think and being bombarded and crowded—we've been talking a lot about how the media and Trump are almost in collusion or working together, allowing public space for such bombardment. It is a bit of a perfect storm, especially with his tweets. The incessant flow of words from him, a lot of which don't make sense or are not true, creates an endless distraction. It is easy to see why he makes people anxious, so that they can't think. What is that?

Justin: It's like a two-year-old. One of my three children had ADD—or attention deficit disorder—and he would try to wake me up when he was two, even when I was sound asleep. And he was relentless. He wouldn't allow any kind of thought or sleep or anything. It was incessant. But he was two. And Trump is a grown man who is the president. But it's a very similar presentation of an incessant, relentless, machine-gun-like quality that makes it very hard to think.

The problem is, I was trained in a particular approach to psychoanalysis, which is called Kleinian—after Melanie Klein. Part of her approach involves the idea of projection, in which someone projects their own issues onto another person. It is like the pot calling the kettle black. When Bush, for instance, said, "I'm a uniter and not a divider," I would think he was a divider and not a uniter. It was unconscious—and projections only show up when they're unconscious. So, when Trump talks about "fake news," he means it—but he's the one who gives "fake news." That's an example of a projection. He's attributing something to someone else that he can't admit to. But, as I was trained in the Kleinian tradition, I was also very mindful of a thing I read from Klein. I hadn't thought about that in any interview until this second, but your questions are really good.

Michael: Almost as if Betty's a trained analyst herself.

Betty: Go figure.

Justin: It's totally great because there is this apocryphal story that when Melanie Klein was with someone she was supervising, the supervisee said to her, "My patient is projecting his confusion into me." And Klein said, "No dear, you are confused."[4]

Betty: (*laughing*) Right, right.

Justin: So, I've always wondered how much is me being confused by Trump, or how much is Trump confusing me. And it's very hard to tease those things apart.

Betty: Well, we're all stirred up by Trump in a way that is different from being stirred up by other public figures. There are a lot of provocative people in the media—some world leaders and other famous personalities, but Trump stirs us up in a very particular way. Do you think that he is putting some of his internal bombardment and his internal lack of boundaries onto us?

Justin: Yes, he's putting his internal lack of boundaries onto us. He's making us not trust ourselves. This is a very important thing. We don't always know what we're doing with him and how to deal with him. There's a really marvelous early paper written about the psychoanalysis of liars.[5] It turns out that lying is not something that develops later in life. It actually starts very early, and it's usually based on having been lied to by one's parents.

Betty: So, it's modeling, picking up on others' behaviors?

Justin: It's modeling. The liar is actually behaving like his or her parents, and they are also treating the people he's lying to as if they were the confused baby. So, we become the confused baby he lies to. And he lies to us incessantly while, at the same time, he's enraged with his own parents for lying to him in so many ways. Moreover he evacuates a lot of his anxiety onto us. The way he treats us is very destructive.

He's the first president in my lifetime who did not ever help us contain our anxieties. Every other president has been there partly to help us be saner because we all, as citizens, have worries and fears. Ever since 9/11, there have been even more fears, but there have always been fears and worries about

[4] Segal, H. (1982). Mrs. Klein, as I Knew Her. (paper presented at the Tavistock Clinic to celebrate the centenary of the birth of Melanie Klein, July 1982).
[5] O'Shaughnessy, E. (1990). Can a Liar Be Psychoanalysed? *International Journal of Psychoanalysis* 71, pp.187–95.

making a living, about all kinds of things. And this is the first president who doesn't help us contain our anxieties. Roosevelt was the best, when he had those fireside chats and famously said there was "nothing to fear but fear itself." But, by the way, the second sentence is the key in that speech when he defined fear as "nameless, unreasoning, unjustified terror, which paralyzes needed efforts to convert retreat into advance."[6]

Betty: That's striking.

Justin: And that's what happens.

Michael: Justy, you wrote in your book that "the pathological liar is driven by unconscious factors so powerful as to make it almost impossible not to lie. To the pathological liar, lying is an addiction and a perversion that unconsciously serves as a source of protection and power, defending against fears of rejection, blame, or loss while instilling a false sense of potency, control, and the ability to manipulate others."[7] Which is a lot of value for lying, a lot of bang for your buck.

Betty: A lot of motivation.

Michael: A lot of motivation. How can you be sure about all of those claims about what lying does? Because look, I'll be honest, I lie.

Justin: Everybody lies. But people don't lie as compulsively as Trump does. There are some who do. In fact, some people with learning disabilities lie more than others because they need to prove, or triumph, over the shame of having trouble reading or understanding material. So they act as if they know more. He exhibits an extreme version of that, as is evidenced by his saying, "I have the best brain and the biggest vocabulary."

Michael: "I'm a very stable genius."

Justin: Exactly. But everybody lies to some extent. We all do. And then we talk about the difference between a white lie to protect yourself or to not

[6] Franklin D. Roosevelt, Inaugural Address, March 4, 1933, The American Presidency Project, https://www.presidency.ucsb.edu/documents/inaugural-address-8.
[7] Frank, J. (2018). *Trump on the Couch*. Avery. p. 93.

hurt somebody you care about, like a person you know who gets a new hairdo and you don't want to say, "God, that's ugly." So you just lie. Is that evil? I don't think so.

But Trump lies as a way of mocking, unconsciously, his own parents. He's letting everybody know what it's like to be lied to. And I don't think that's conscious on his part. But I do think that he's letting us all know how hard it is to live in a world of lies because we don't know what to believe. We're busy fact-checking and doing all these crazy things. And he probably had to do that as a little kid to make sure that his mother would say, "I love you, but don't touch me."

Michael: I think lying may be the ultimate expression of power: "I can be president and get away with lying. And people can fact-check me, and it doesn't matter." That kind of lying may be the ultimate expression of power in our culture.

Justin: That's right. And lying *is* an expression of power. And the first lie that works is the one where you are able to lie to your mother and she believes you. Once that happens, you realize that you have power.

Betty: And privacy.

Justin: And privacy against the most powerful person in your world, which is your mother. And it also says that you are alone in the world because nobody can read your mind.

Betty: So, it's the ultimate act of separation.

Justin: Being able to lie and get away with it is the ultimate act of separation. And Trump has done that definitively. But he has to keep doing it because it's not satisfying enough for him. He doesn't feel separate enough, and he's too angry at his parents to stop. And by now, lying for him is second nature. It is natural for him to lie.

Betty: When I think about lying, not only is it an act of separation from the mother and an expression of individuality, but it is also isolating. This is a man who lies and lies and there's no authenticity. Where is his true self?

Justin: I don't know what his true self is, but I do know that the problem with his lying and the need to separate is that he's never been able to fully separate. If you look at pictures of his mother when she was in her sixties and then you look at him now, they actually have the same hairdo. It's really quite shocking. People wrote about that when he was first elected. And I've seen lots of pictures of it.

Michael: And separation is a necessary, healthy thing?

Justin: It's a necessary, healthy thing, but it's also a frightening thing, as Betty was saying. But separation also has to be relative. In other words, you can be dependent and need other people, but it's an interdependence. He doesn't understand interdependence because interdependence to him means that he can't think on his own. The reason he can't work with treaties and needs to get rid of all agreements, is that an agreement for Trump means giving up part of himself. This is the main reason why he's a bad dealmaker because he never gives up anything. For him, giving up something is a sign of weakness. He clings to his lying. He clings to being separate.

Michael: It is the thing that defines him.

Justin: He clings to power, and it defines him. And at the end of that chapter, I also said that he used to lie for power. He used to lie to convince people he was a good businessman, or he was richer than he was. But now I think he's lying in order to survive. And that's what's very scary.

Michael: And how is that different?

Justin: Well, it's more desperate. I think unconsciously Mueller represents Trump's father, and as Mueller gets closer, it's as if the father is closing in. Trump's father was the only person who really understood Trump. And he ended up having to send him to military school, which meant that the father said to himself, I'm assuming, "I can't cope. We can't deal with him. We have to send him away."

Betty: He's uncontainable.

Justin: He's uncontainable. "We have to send him to military school and…"

Michael: "...and maybe they can do something."

Justin: Yes. And he did try to contain him. Fred Trump sent him to this private school before he sent him to military school. He went on the board of trustees of that school to help Donald to work with the teachers and the faculty. His father was very devoted in that way. But he was unsuccessful. Donald was in detention every day.

Michael: Can I ask you then—what does all of that lying do to those closest to the liar?

Justin: What it does to the people close to the liar, who love and need the liar, is that there's a part of them that doesn't believe he's lying. Kellyanne Conway is an example. She makes a split and talks about "alternative facts." "Embedded" was a play about the Bush people in Iraq, and at one point, one of the reporters is talking about Bush and she says, "I know he's a liar, but I trust him."

Betty: So, it's the need to believe.

Justin: It's the need to believe.[8] And the problem is that, in the media now, people who oppose Trump and are concerned about him are fact-checking all the time. There's no point in doing fact-checking. It's a waste of time because he's always lying. And what happens when you fact-check is, paradoxically, it reinforces the idea that you can't believe he's lying. At some deep level, you're still shocked. Why would you fact-check otherwise? Who cares? That's who he is. We have to let go of the fantasy that he isn't lying.

Michael: Or you fact-check because you think that the intention is, somewhere, to tell the truth. I'm going to write an article for a magazine, and the fact-checker is going to come in to make sure I got it right, which is to say, my intention is to tell the truth.

Justin: But after a while, when you see that he has no intention to tell the truth—I think the fact-checkers who are opposing Trump and concerned

---

[8] See our conversation with Robert Jay Lifton (Chapter 21) on the concept of "narrative necessity," which describes how followers of a cult leader need to believe what that leader says, to capture a false reassurance.

about him have to give up trying to prove him a liar. It just doesn't work. You can't argue with a person who's a liar.

Betty: And yet, don't you think that's a normalization of his lying—what Robert Jay Lifton might call "a malignant normality?"[9] Meaning that if we just accept that he's not telling the truth all the time, what do we do with what he says? How do we ground ourselves in reality?

Justin: Well, we can't ground ourselves based on what he says. The one way that I've been able to ground myself with respect to Trump's lies, is to understand that with much of what he says, the truth can be found when we consider it all in terms of projection. So, when he talks about "fake news," he's talking about himself giving "fake news." When he talks about how low energy Jeb Bush is, he's talking about himself because he has low energy in terms of not ever wanting to look at any kind of briefings or any serious documents.

Betty: Seeing all that he says as projection is another way that we can approach his lies. We can read him in a different way.

Justin: Yes, but that's very important. We can read him in a different way, and we know how to do that. After a while, we can really understand that his accusation of fake news is really about himself.

Michael: Don't journalists and the press present a threat to his reality?

Justin: Yes, they represent reality to him. And that's something he cannot stand. He cannot accept the limitations of reality, which is why he's against regulations.[10] The reason he's against regulations has little to do with the functioning of businesses or corporations. It has to do with reality and how he hates a version of reality where you have to take other people into consideration, where you can't just grab something out of their hand or grab something under their dress or whatever it is you want. Reality means Trump can't just do what he wants to do. He can't stand that. And that's the

---

[9] Lifton, R. J. (1986/2000). *The Nazi Doctors: Medical killing and the psychology of genocide*. Basic Books.
[10] See our conversation in Chapter 21 with Robert Jay Lifton, "Sounding the Alarm: Cultism and Trump's Assault on Reality."

way he always has been. It's a very disturbing impulse problem that you see in young children, but they often grow out of it or their parents set limits or there's a way they can turn getting what they want into fantasy. Trump doesn't turn it into fantasy. If he thinks it, he does it. It's one thing to have a thought about wanting to do something, and another thing entirely to do it.

Betty: One thing you're pointing out, Justy, is Trump's ambivalence about boundaries and limits. And yet here we are with this campaign promise of a wall, and that is a concretization of a big limit.

Justin: Literally concrete.

Betty: Literally concrete—it's a big, beautiful, concrete wall.

Justin: A concrete concretization.

Betty: Yes. And so what is this wall in a man who doesn't have any limits, who is unbounded, is uncontained going back to when he was young?

Justin: There are several ways to cope with being uncontained. One of them is to project disturbing elements outside yourself and put them into someone else. So, as a two-year-old you suddenly become afraid of a parent, or afraid of the dark, or afraid of monsters—and you can have night terrors. The wall is an inner wall, and it's a wall to keep out danger and terror that is originally projected by the child.[11] He has to see himself as a good, powerful, strong boy, and strong man. And so everything that is potentially hurtful or destructive comes from outside.

Michael: Everything threatening comes from the other side of the wall.

Justin: Yes. Whether it's Mexicans, Muslims—his mother, his father, or most probably, projected parts of destructive aspects of himself...

Betty: ...that he can't acknowledge.

---

[11] See our conversation with Thomas Singer about "The Symbolic Power of Trump's Wall" (Chapter 29).

Justin: Yes. So, he will desperately cling to the wall because he doesn't have a choice. There's no point in negotiating about the wall with him. We have to find some way of dealing with him. But the fact is that he has a disability—he is emotionally disabled. And his disability is an inability to integrate different parts of himself. It's a refusal to look at himself. It's a refusal to integrate.

He desperately needs the wall, and the wall is a block. It's not like a wall that some people talk about as a "contact barrier" between disturbing fantasies that get modified in your head and turned into something different—or a new thought or a new idea. That's what we do in therapy. We help a person to face things about themselves or to think about things that bother or block them differently. They then find ways to convert them, to consider them as something new, so they can move them. Trump is too afraid of that and so he builds a wall against it. There's nothing porous. There's no self-reflection.

Betty: And there's no ability to make metaphors.

Justin: Exactly. There's no ability to make metaphors.

Betty: And this is where John Kelly or Lindsey Graham could talk about the wall as a metaphor. Kelly and Graham tried to turn what Trump was saying into a metaphor, and he refused. He insisted he was not making a metaphor.

Justin: Yes, Lindsay Graham can make metaphors. Trump cannot make a metaphor. The other people who watch over him can see the wall as a metaphor. They're right; it's a symbol of Trump's inner world. But it's not exactly a metaphor in the way we think of metaphors. It is actually a direct reflection of what his inner world is like. He has a very rigid inner wall that he has erected to protect himself.

Michael: I'm going to play this clip of Trump speaking about the wall and how he presents it to himself and to the world: I don't know how long we'll stick with the clip, but long enough for you to get a sense, because you said you didn't listen to the news last night, right?

Justin: Right.

Donald Trump: This morning, a number of people came out and said, you do need very strong border security. That includes a wall or whatever it is. A number of Democrats said that, but people don't like to report on it. We have tremendous unity in the Republican Party. It's really a beautiful thing to see. I don't think there'll be any break away because they know we need border security, and we have to have it. And the only way you're going to have border security, there's only one way. You can have all the technology in the world, I'm a professional at technology, but if you don't have a steel barrier or a wall of some kind, a strong, powerful wall, you're going to have human trafficking. You're going to have drugs pouring across the border. You're going to have MS13 and the gangs coming in. And we've done record apprehensions. We're doing a great job. But we need help. If we have the wall, we could have far fewer people working, in terms of border security, and doing an even better job. So, if we had the wall, we could have a tremendous saving. I feel, I really believe the steel barrier or wall would pay for itself every three or four months and maybe even better than that in terms of overall. So, that's it. Just a couple of things, Chris. I know the fake news likes to say it. When, during the campaign, I would say Mexico's going to pay for it. Obviously, I never said this, and I never meant they're going to write out a check. I said they're going to pay for it. They are. They are paying for it with the incredible deal we made called the United States, Mexico, and Canada, USMCA deal. It's a trade deal. It has to be approved by Congress. It probably will be, other than maybe they even hold that up because they want to have, you know, they want to do as much harm as they can, only because of the 2020 presidential election. So, Mexico is paying for the wall indirectly. And when I said Mexico will pay for the wall in front of thousands and thousands of people, obviously, they're not going to write a check, but they are paying for the wall indirectly, many, many times over by the really great trade deal...[12]

Michael: Basically, Trump stood up yesterday in front of everybody and said, "I never said that Mexico was going to pay for the wall."

Justin: Right. Which is not true. He did say it.

[12] Remarks on Border Security and an Exchange with Reporters Prior to Departure for McAllen, Texas, January 10, 2019; *CNN News*, "29 Outrageous Lines from Donald Trump's Wild, Impromptu News Conference on the White House Lawn," https://www.kbzk.com/cnn-us-politics/2019/01/10/39-outrageous-lines-from-donald-trumps-wild-impromptu-news-conference-on-the-white-house-lawn/.

Betty: And listening to that clip, I'm starting to experience that confusion you were talking about before.

Michael: So, can you talk about this moment for just a second?

Justin: Well, I can't talk about it for just a second, but I could talk about it for about an hour or two. First of all, one of the techniques used by liars is that they shift the meaning of the things they say. That's a very classic thing liars do. They say, "Well, you think I meant this, but actually that's not what I meant." It's a way of denying that they're lying by shifting the meaning. It's very Trump.

Betty: Well, in the world of trauma therapy, we call that gaslighting. So, he's gaslighting us.

Justin: Yes, he is gaslighting us, but he's also gaslighting himself. That's the thing that's so striking.

Betty: Say more about that.

Justin: When you lie over time, it also means that you're not interested in pursuing the truth. You don't want to find out what's real. The three of us, we're on a quest to understand more than we did before we started our conversation; that's our effort. When we stop making that effort in our lives, our minds start to wither and die because the quest for truth is, to the mind, like food is to the body. If you don't have it, your psyche will starve. And that is what has happened to Trump. We are seeing a person who has not had a quest for truth for decades, if not his entire life, and that's why he can't think. He doesn't know anything real.

Michael: And his psyche is starved?

Justin: And his psyche has starved. Yes. His psyche is really a tiny thing.

Betty: And is that what causes him to bombard us?

Justin: Yes.

Betty: And to cry out and constantly strive to gain attention because it's never enough?

Justin: Absolutely. Because Trump doesn't pursue truth and he doesn't face truth, he lives in what's called *segmental reality*. He lives in a digital world, not an analog world. So, he does not see the arc of a second hand going around the watch you're wearing. He sees the dates just flipping over: it's this now, it's that, it's this. There is no continuity. He actually doesn't always remember things that he says because the only place where there is a memory for it is on videotape...

Michael: ...or on Twitter.

Justin: Or on Twitter or whatever. Everybody is like that before they're eight months old. All babies are like that because they don't have words.

Michael: You actually write in your book that Trump is "completely in the present tense."

Justin: Yes.

Michael: "He's a digital thinker, not analog, functioning like a digital watch rather than one with a 12-hour face and a sweeping second hand that links events in the arc of time."[13]

Justin: That's exactly it. And to link events, you have to face your own need to mourn, your own need to deal with loss, your own need to realize that you are part of a big picture. Everything doesn't emanate from you. When everything is digital, you are the center and you're the only one. When you look at your baby who's crying, for those who have experienced their babies crying, it's like they've never been happy. They're just miserable. And then, when they're happy, it's like they've never cried. And they really act like that.

Michael: And that's how Trump experiences the world.

Justin: And that's how Trump experiences the world.

---

[13] Frank, J. (2018). *Trump on the Couch.* Avery. p. 223.

Betty: There's no continuous reality.

Justin: There's no continuous reality.

Michael: What happens if there is no past and there is no future? What happens?

Justin: Everything is the present.

Betty: And it's pretty terrifying. Just like with the baby, if you're in this terrifying moment of crying and you're hungry, you don't think it's ever going to end.

Justin: Yes, that's a great point. That's like the trauma theory you mentioned. When you're in the middle of something horrible, there's no past or future.

Betty: And to stay sane, you have to recruit your capacity to draw from the past or to know that you survived something before.

Michael: Or imagine a better future.

Justin: Or you can draw from something outside of your own experience to bring into your head and into your imagination or into something that you know about.

Betty: I think what's so traumatogenic, or what's so harmful about Trump, is this lack of concern for telling the truth, or for there being any truth. If there's no reality and there's no truth, experience is just what happens day to day to day to day. It's like Groundhog Day every day. We're redoing it and redoing it. If there's no continuity, there's nothing to reference. There's no reference point.

Justin: What this points out, though, is a couple of things. One is that, unconsciously, the three of us, and many more of us, have always believed in continuity and part of that's because of our own psychological growth and who we are. But part of it is also having a belief in continuity, rather than knowing for sure that continuity is necessarily a fact. It is still a belief.

What we have thought about—and so many people talk about this—are that the institutions of government are going to protect us. That's a fantasy about continuity. I wrote a while ago that it takes much longer to build a building than to blow it up. And we have built a lot of buildings in this country, along with passing lots of laws and creating lots of growth and enduring lots of struggles, from the Civil War to the Great Depression to World Wars I and II. We have endured lots of different traumas.

Michael: Add slavery to the list.

Justin: Yes, slavery, certainly. And so those are things that have been forged and built over time. But Trump can knock off the Supreme Court with a boom—or he can knock off Congress, boom. We don't think that's possible, but I think it is. And that's the scariest thing—that's why it's important to understand him. But at the same time, it's also important to know that at some point understanding has to give way to action because understanding alone is not going to change anything. I have one thing I want to read, which is written in 1941 before any of us were born. And it's about Donald Trump without using his name. So, I'll read it as if it's about Donald Trump.

Michael: Do you want to tell us who wrote it?

Justin: Yes, Budd Schulberg wrote this and it's from a novel called *What Makes Sammy Run?* It's highly worth reading. In the novel, Sammy is described this way, but I will substitute Trump for Sammy:

> *He was the smartest and stupidest human being I had ever met. He had a quick intelligence which he was able to use exclusively for the good and welfare of [Donald Trump]. And that kind of intelligence implies stupidity. Where other people might have one blind spot, [Trump's] mind was a mass of blind spots with only a single ray of light focused immediately ahead.*[14]

That's Sammy Glick. That's Donald Trump.

Betty: That's striking.

---

[14] Schulberg, B. (1941). *What Makes Sammy Run*. Random House. p. 9.

Michael: Since Trump appeared on the national stage, and certainly since he became president, commentators, presenters, journalists of all stripes have now stepped into your professional space of psychoanalysis. They offer analysis and diagnosis. We now have at the tip of our tongues words like *narcissist* and *pathological*—all of these terms of psychology.

Justin: Add *projection* to the list.

Michael: Yes—projection, a lot of words. What did they get right? What did they get wrong? How are they wrong in talking about it? Where is the danger in talking about Trump psychologically like this? We're doing it. How do you guys feel about the way the media has started to talk about Trump? I ask this because it seems they're at a loss. They don't know what to do and how to talk about it, so they're turning to folks like you.

Justin: No, they're not, though. They're turning *into* folks like me.

Betty: And yet I don't think they're turning *to* folks like us enough.

Justin: Agreed. They don't turn to us enough. I've never been on those programs. I was on a pundit program for a minute and a half. I said something that blew the host's mind. He looked and gasped when I said it.

Michael: What did you say?

Justin: I said that I thought Mueller was Trump's unconscious father figure. The interviewer looked like "Huh?"

Michael: You can't say that on television.

Justin: He'd never thought of it. And that was it. I was never invited back. That was a year ago.

Betty: Do you think it was because it was just too shocking, or do you think that it was too complex?

Justin: I think it's too shocking. But also, I think that people who are interviewers are much more comfortable having other pundits, who are not therapists, make generalizations. If you're a person who's a pundit and you have somebody like us on, you will be afraid that we're going to analyze you. And they become self-conscious. It's like, "Oh you're a psychiatrist. I guess I can't talk to you now."

Michael: What are they getting wrong?

Betty: Well, I think they make superficial analyses because it's not coming from a body of study or time spent in clinical work. The words are bandied about, and they're not used from the inside.

Justin: And that's very key. When I'm asked to give an opinion about Bernie Sanders or about anybody politically, I don't, because I'm only interested in analysis. I could give an opinion, but I don't want to use my expertise that way because I have to really get to know the person and do the in-depth work, not shoot from the hip.

Betty: One more thing, Justy, that you mentioned in your book that struck me is that Trump's psychology and psyche is being exposed for all of us to see. His words and his tweets are also fodder for Russian intelligence. And Russian intelligence traditionally uses the tools of psychoanalysis to assess what they are hearing. And you posit that they have viewed him as someone who is very malleable. If they are using these psychoanalytic tools, should we not do the same in our civic discourse?

Justin: Yes, I think we should use them about ourselves and maybe about the Russians as well.

Betty: We should use these tools. But if they're using them to manipulate our electoral system and our society, then we as a society need to understand more about how such tools work.

Justin: Now, I have to say that the CIA does use these tools, and we, too, have manipulated societies like Chile and Iran. We've overthrown governments by using all kinds of false information and false-flag operations. I don't think Russia is doing anything different from what we're doing. And that's not a false equivalence. I think it is an equivalence, but I think the danger is to just blame Russia for doing it.

Betty: If these tools are being used by our own and foreign intelligence agencies, however, then we, as citizens, ought to understand the nature of what's happening. We need to know what tools are being used to control or manipulate us or those in other countries.

Justin: Some of my former students are now psychoanalysts at the CIA.

Michael: As we start to wrap up, where do you think Trump's appeal comes from and how do we…

Justin: Oh my God. That's a big question.

Michael: Yeah. But seriously, it may seem self-evident to you, yet this is somebody who has enormous power and an enormous hold on a lot of people whom we don't want to belittle.

Justin: He's the kind of person who, when his child has night terrors, doesn't come into the room to give the child a flashlight. He turns on all the lights, proclaiming, "I'm going to save you." A healthy parent will give the child a flashlight to scare the goblins away, in effect saying, "You can do it yourself and I'll help you," as opposed to "I'm going to turn on all the lights and stun you with my power." Not only does Trump do that, but he scares the kids in the first place. And then he comes in and turns on the lights pretending to save them.

Michael: He's the goblin in the first place.

Justin: Right. So, the first thing to understand is that Trump is the alpha and the omega of night terrors. The second thing is that every single person has had some experiences with rejection when we were little—such as when parents go out, being made to wait too long for a pickup, some rejections being much worse than others. But some of the rejection hits deeper. It can be what we call *narcissistic rejection*, such as when you want to say something to your parent and they're not listening, or when you want to do something and they are dismissive. Trump is a victim of that, and he taps into that in so many people. He talks to his base about the Washington elites who don't pay attention to them or are blind, who are indifferent. And that's because Trump had indifferent parents, and he can tap into that in a way that's very powerful. It's important not to underestimate his power and connection. He is like a Franklin Roosevelt of the right, in terms of his ability to tap into feelings of not being heard, feelings of deep fears of there being dangerous perpetrators of violence in the world, feelings of being a victim suffering at the hands of unfair authorities. He is good at blaming other people while speaking to the insecurities of his base, all the while ensuring that he will protect them as no other can.

Betty: And yet there's a nonporousness to him where he cannot engage in dialogue or take in new ideas.

Justin: No, because that would be seen as weakness. I think that his taking in anything would immediately come up against his inner wall. I think his inner wall is actually expanding over time and blocks out even things that are close to the surface inside him.

Michael: In the end, do you have hope for the republic?

Justin: I have hope that we can accept the fact that we can't deal with a psychopath who is this relentless. You can't out-argue him. You can't out tweet him. You can't defeat him. You have to either impeach him or vote him out.

Betty: I think we have to titrate our own exposure to Trump in order to keep our own minds. As you said at the beginning, Justy, he just keeps banging on the door. On that happy note, thank you very much for this most enlightening interview.

Chapter 13
Delusions & Lies

Guest: Dr. Michael Tansey
Episode Aired: January 29, 2019

Dr. Michael Tansey is a former associate professor in clinical psychology at Northwestern University Medical School who has been a clinical psychologist in private practice in Chicago for nearly forty years, treating adults, adolescents, and couples. He has written numerous professional articles and coauthored a book on empathy and the therapeutic process. He is also among the coauthors of the New York Times bestseller, The Dangerous Case of Donald Trump.

When we spoke with Michael Tansey in January 2019, the "Washington Post *Fact Checker" had reported that Donald Trump, in 24 months as president, had made close to 10,000 false statements on myriad subjects—from the tax cuts he achieved, to the threats of illegal immigration, the "Russian hoax," and the size of the audience at his inauguration. By the time Trump left office in 2021, the* Washington Post *had tallied a total of 30,573 false or misleading claims he made in four years.[1] When we reached out to Michael at the beginning of 2019 to help us unpack the difference between delusions and lies in Trump's behavior, two concerns—one political, the other psychological—lay at core of our request:* What happens to an individual or a society when truth and reality are no longer valued by its leaders? *In* The Origins of Totalitarianism *and in "Truth and Politics," Hannah Arendt, an expert on trauma and authoritarianism, offers her observations:*

---

[1] Kessler, G., Kelly, M., Rizzo, S., Shapiro, L. & Dominquez, L. (2021). A Term of Untruths. *The Washington Post.* https://www.washingtonpost.com/politics/interactive/2021/timeline-trump-claims-as-president/?itid=lk_inline_manual_10.

The ideal subject of totalitarian rule is not the convinced Nazi or the dedicated communist, but people for whom the distinction between fact and fiction...true and false...no longer exist.[2]

The result of a consistent and total substitution of lies for factual truth is not that the lie will now be accepted as truth, and truth be defamed as lie, but that the sense by which we take our bearings in the real world—and the category of truth versus falsehood is among the mental means to this end—is being destroyed.[3]

Arendt's comments on the psychological roots and impacts of lying upon individuals and collectives informs our conversation with Michael. Such essential considerations on the functions and effects of lying deliver a deeper understanding of how it is crucial, not only for the health of a democracy, but also for an individual's sense of equilibrium and orientation in the world, to require that their civic leaders hew to a basic degree of truth telling.

Interview

Betty: Hi, Michael. Can I admit something to you?

Michael: Sure. Go ahead.

Betty: I'm kind of bored.

Michael: Bored?

Betty: By Donald Trump.

Michael: You're bored with Donald Trump?

Betty: Yes, I'm totally bored. I find him extremely repetitive. He says the same things over and over and over again. And I am just not that interested.

---

[2] Arendt, H. (1977). *The Origins of Totalitarianism.* Penguin. p. 459.
[3] Arendt, H. (1967). Truth and Politics. *The New Yorker.*

Michael: Right—so we're three episodes in, and you're bored of Donald Trump. I love this because I think "I am bored with you" might be the greatest insult you could hurl at Donald Trump.

Betty: Don't get me started. Let's welcome my friend and colleague, psychologist and psychoanalyst Dr. Michael Tansey. Thanks so much, Michael, for being on *Mind of State*. As a fellow psychoanalyst, I invite you to interpret this.

Michael Tansey: It's a pleasure to be here. As to your question, there is a phenomenon called *Trump fatigue*. And I think it's less about boredom, less about not caring, and more about having a sense of powerlessness at being able to do anything about it. I don't think it's that you don't care about these issues at all. I don't think that it's true boredom. I think it has more to do with a sense of powerlessness and fatigue because this stuff keeps coming at you again and again and again.

Betty: Too true. So my boredom is possibly "Trump fatigue"? That's what we psychoanalysts do—we look underneath the surface of what we're talking about to ask questions like "what could this boredom really mean?" We brought you to *Mind of State*, Michael, to talk about lying, which we could consider the ultimate in surface statements under which multiple alternate meanings or intentions exist. I'm getting roundabout, so Michael Tansey, can you talk to us about lying and your views on what's behind the ceaseless flow of lies coming from Donald Trump?

Michael: Because the thing is, Michael, we all lie, right?

Betty: And there are all different kinds of lies.

Michael Tansey: Sure.

Michael: But you seem to think it's qualifiedly different with Trump. His lying is not the same as mundane run-of-the mill white lies, or even more substantial ways of avoiding the truth.

Michael Tansey: Over the course of my intensive study of Donald Trump—and as an example of my focus, I continue to read his tweets every morning, which shows how utterly preoccupied I have been with him since he declared his candidacy for president in 2015—I think we have to distinguish between lies and falsehoods. *Lies* are a subset of *falsehoods*. It's rare when Donald Trump opens his mouth that the words he says actually match up with the truth. Even so, to help us grasp what is happening, it's important to see that there are two separate categories of not telling the truth that really need to be understood. It's central to understanding this man's personality makeup and the profound danger that we are all in with Trump as president. For years, I have been writing that we are not nearly as afraid as we should be.

Here's the deal on falsehoods. There are *strategic lies*—lies that serve an immediate purpose. "The dog ate my homework" is a classic example.

Michael: So when Betty says, "Michael, nice job on the podcast," that's a strategic lie?

Betty: Or a caring one.

Michael Tansey: That actually might be called a *white lie*, as opposed to Trump's brand of lies—like "I never met David Duke," or "I didn't call that country a shithole."

Michael: I'd like to share a list of lies that you published, Michael. They are listed in descending order of seriousness. So, Trump has, at different times, asserted that he owns an original Renoir, *The Sisters*, which is not true.[4]

Betty: *Two Sisters*.

Michael: *Two Sisters*, excuse me. He says he won the largest Electoral College victory since Ronald Reagan, which is not true. Barack Obama did with 322 electoral votes to Donald Trump's 300. There's his ugly, pernicious lie that he saw thousands of Muslims in New Jersey celebrating the collapse of the Twin Towers on 9/11.[5]

---

[4] Alm, D. (2017). Donald Trump Insisted He Owned a Renoir that's Hung in Chicago Museum Since 1933. *Forbes.* https://www.forbes.com/sites/davidalm/2017/10/19/donald-trump-insisted-he-owns-a-renoir-thats-hung-in-chicago-museum-since-1933/?sh=7ee7266610c3.

[5] Bancoff, C. (2015). What New Jersey Muslims Were Actually Doing on 9/11. *New York Magazine.* https://nymag.com/intelligencer/2015/12/what-nj-muslims-were-actually-doing-on-911.html.

Michael Tansey: These are *delusional falsehoods*, which reflect a psychotic detachment from reality. *Delusions* are rigidly held beliefs, despite irrefutable evidence to the contrary. With the falsehood about owning Renoir's *Two Sisters*, for example, he insists he owns that original painting, when it's hanging in the Art Institute of Chicago. I've seen it many times. He insists that Muslims celebrated the collapse of the twin towers on 9/11 in New Jersey. It simply didn't happen, and yet he pounds the table and insists that it did. As I have written, if he were wired up to a reliable lie detector test, *he* would believe that he would pass with flying colors. So, delusional falsehoods, when compared to strategic lies, are really very different.

Betty: So a delusion is a separation from reality that somebody believes in. They're not in reality, and yet they believe that their unreality is true. And therefore, it functions differently than a strategic lie.

Michael Tansey: When you think about the psychotic spectrum of disorders, which includes schizophrenia, the delusions fall under the descriptor "bizarre." Someone who is delusional might believe that Martians are infiltrating the United States. Trump believes that Muslims and Mexicans are infiltrating the United States. Someone might think, "Well, is that true? Maybe there's something to that." Because compared to Martians, it could be true, so there's a kind of pass on it as an untruth. When he says that the Central Park Five are guilty...[6]

Michael: For people listening, who don't know, this is a New York City story from the 1990s.

Michael Tansey: Yes, Trump pounds the table and insists, "They're guilty, they're guilty, they're guilty," despite the fact that the actual perpetrator, the man who committed the crime, came forth, his DNA evidence matches, he knows the details of the scene, and so on. Even after it's clear that these young men, after having spent eight to nine years in prison, are absolutely

---

[6] The Central Park Five refers to the five Black and Latino teenagers who were wrongly convicted of raping a white woman in New York City's Central Park in 1989. The police coerced confessions that the young men recanted two weeks later; however, they were tried and convicted. At the time, Donald Trump put out a full-page ad calling for the death penalty. The young men each spent between six and eleven years in jail and their convictions were vacated in 2002 after a serial rapist confessed to the crime and his DNA confirmed his guilt.

innocent, Trump insists otherwise.[7] So, now we have to look at the bigger picture. Throughout his run for the presidency—for example, just this morning there was a viral tape out about him saying—and it always starts with "I know more than all the fill-in-the-blanks"—this time it's U.S. military generals.

Michael: Or he says, "I'm an expert."

Michael Tansey: Well, it's more than "I am an expert." It's more like "I am the supreme authority." When he said, "I know more than all the generals," at the time, it seemed like hyperbole. Now with what has just happened with Mattis—James Mattis, Secretary of Defense—we now have to take it seriously, that Trump really thinks he does know more than all the generals.[8]

Michael: Can we pause for a second, because one of the things that I intuit in all of this is that he doesn't trust experts or facts, right? So Mattis can give him a briefing about Turkey, and the influence of Iran and Russia and the Kurds, and so on. And, for Trump, it's all about what he feels in his gut. His gut makes him the preeminent voice—the expert, the person who knows more, because what he feels strongly about matters more than facts.

Michael Tansey: It's way worse than that. How I would describe it—it's good for us to have a back-and-forth because it clarifies misunderstandings—not only in the public, but also, frankly, within my profession, where people simply don't get the profundity of psychotic detachment from reality. Here's the deal: with a delusional disorder, what is utterly mystifying is that on the surface, the symptoms of someone with this disorder sounds like a mythological creature that I'm making up. But this is an actual disorder that exists in the DSM-5 manual. And what is beguiling about it, is that on the surface, the person can seem charming, charismatic, high achieving, funny, etc. As long as they have underlying delusions, there is a psychotic

---

[7] Nguyen, T. (2016). Trump Still Thinks the Exonerated Central Park Five Are Guilty. *Vanity Fair*. https://www.vanityfair.com/news/2016/10/donald-trump-central-park-5.

[8] Secretary of Defense James Mattis resigned after Donald Trump announced he was removing all troops from Syria in December 2018. See Goldberg, J. (2019). The Man Who Couldn't Take It Anymore. *The Atlantic*. https://www.theatlantic.com/magazine/archive/2019/10/james-mattis-trump/596665/.

detachment from reality that's fixed. It's lifelong but doesn't typically show up unless the delusions are challenged.

A way to think about Trump is if we consider gaming—as in video-game playing. A video game is on a TV screen. You're playing away at it. But, say, you hear the doorbell ring. Or you can hear your mother call you for dinner. You can look at the clock and think, "I have to get to a meeting." There's still avid involvement, but you maintain connection with what's happening in the reality of your daily life outside the game. Take the video game *Oculus*, which perfectly captures what we're talking about here. *Oculus* has now evolved to a point where it's not only a three-dimensional video, it's audio as well.

Michael: For those who do not know, *Oculus Rift* is a virtual-reality game system where you put on the headsets...

Betty: ...and you're in the game.

Michael: You're immersed.

Betty: You're in the Matrix.

Michael Tansey: You are in the game. It's a virtual-reality game where a player wears a headset or goggles. They feel like they are in a 3D-gaming environment. From the outside you'll see a player reaching out, as if trying to catch actual things and so on. But it's full-on immersion in an alternate reality. When playing this kind of game, you don't know if the doorbell rings. You don't know if it's time for dinner. You don't know if someone has walked into the room. You are immersed, full-on, in your own alternate reality.

This helps clarify the distinction between Trump and a severe narcissist—what he is typically referred to as being. A severe narcissist finds it extremely difficult to empathize with another person. For someone of Donald Trump's nature, however, there is no person there to empathize with, any more than there is a spaceship flying overhead in a game of *Oculus*.

Michael: So there's nobody in the world other than Trump.

Michael Tansey: There's nobody other than Trump.

Betty: He's in his own reality; he's in his own 3D reality.

Michael Tansey: He is in his own reality, and all of these things out here are mere accouterments of his own full-on alternate reality.

Betty: Now that he's in the top seat of power in the world, as president of the United States, he holds a lot of authority. And there is an assumption that the person who holds that office is going to be accountable to the truth. Yet, here we are now in a situation where we have Trump who, as you're saying, Michael Tansey, doesn't even have a relationship with reality. It's beyond and separate from lying. This is a good distinction because we have been debating about truth and lies—the news-media outlets like the *New York Times* and the *Washington Post* have been keeping track of his lies, saying he's lying 70 percent of the time.[9] But according to your assessment, he doesn't care because he likely doesn't even know there's anything outside his version of reality.

Michael: I was also thinking of all of the press. The *Washington Post* refers to him as Pinocchio. All of the news media are tracking his lies.

Michael Tansey: I think they're keeping count—there's like 7,000 or 8,000.[10]

Michael: He's just hit some milestone. It's like some astronomical number per day. How is Trump lying this much? How does he keep pace with himself in this way? What you are saying is that he doesn't think he's lying. Is that fair?

Michael Tansey: No.

Michael: You think he knows he's lying?

---

[9] Leonhardt, D. & Thompson, S.A. (2017). Trump's Lies. *The New York Times*. https://www.nytimes.com/interactive/2017/06/23/opinion/trumps-lies.html.
Kessler, G., Rizzo, S., & Kelly, M. (2021). Trump's False or Misleading Claims Total 30,573 over 4 Years. *The Washington Post*. https://www.washingtonpost.com/politics/2021/01/24/trumps-false-or-misleading-claims-total-30573-over-four-years/.
[10] As of January 2019.

Michael Tansey: I think when he said, "I never met David Duke," and when he said, "I never called that country a shithole," with those versions of falsehoods, he knows he's lying. But when he says, "I know more than all the generals," he doesn't consider that as a lie.

Betty: So when he says that his inauguration was attended by as many people as Barack Obama's, does he presume that's truth?

Michael: Or how about the Electoral College? I mean, those are facts that you can prove.

Michael Tansey: Those are claims that enter Trump into the land of delusion. And this is so hard for people to grasp—they see him as seeming relatively sane or, at the most, like a narcissistic jerk who lies all the time and leave it at that.

Michael: And he's functioning, right?

Betty: That's the big debate. That some people call him delusional and therefore mentally ill, it...

Michael Tansey: ...gets him off the hook.

Betty: It also maligns those who are mentally ill.

Michael Tansey: I'm not concerned about that.

Betty: I know you aren't, but I'm just citing the opposing arguments, the negative impacts to calling him delusional or mentally ill. But what you're pointing out...

Michael Tansey: And I've never heard that from a patient, ever.

Betty: But what you're pointing out, Michael, is also the function of Donald Trump's various tactics with not telling the truth—meaning at a basic level he lies to defend himself. "I never met David Duke," or "I never said that." Those are knee-jerk ways to protect himself when he's faced by public demands that he explains controversial choices or extreme statements.

Michael Tansey: It's "the dog ate my homework" tactic—the strategic lies.

Betty: Right. "The dog ate my homework" means "I'm going to get away from being accountable for this however I can." And then, different from the strategic lies, are these expressions of grandiosity that reveal the world Trump must live within where he's everything—the alpha and the omega. Now how this functions or impacts the rest of us, the collective, the American public or the global public, is important. Because there is something to be seen in all of this. For those who don't care, he's subsisting very well with these 7,000 to 8,000-plus lies and counting. That the truth, which admittedly is not fixed—anyone can, of course, debate just what the truth is—but the truth of facts—meaning of recorded evidence, of reality witnessed by many—is not functioning in Trump and the public arena in the way most of us have ever seen before.

Michael Tansey: Yes. They are no longer functioning in the way that we need truth and facts to confirm our sense of reality. And this is the assault on the news—Trump's accusations of "fake news"—are about facts that conflict with Trump's reality. There is a role that these facts play in a functioning society. We're having this conversation on day—I don't know what it is now—but they are now measuring this federal government shutdown not in days, or weeks, but months.[11] This is because facts have stopped functioning or playing a central role in our culture, in our society. And we are suffering as a result.

Betty: There's an impasse between facts and fantasy.

Michael Tansey: Exactly. I think that's a better way to say it.

Betty: And fantasy could be another word for a system of lies. And Michael, you're pointing out the impact of the uses of this system of lies. There are different categories of lies…

---

[11] The federal government shutdown from December 22, 2018, to January 25, 2019, the longest shut down in history. Trump insisted that he would not reopen the government until Congress funded his border wall, but he finally relented.

Michael Tansey: I would say different kinds of *falsehoods*, of which there are *lies* and *delusions*. When Trump says, "I know more than all the generals," that's not a lie. It's a delusion. I don't think anyone can question that now.

But here's one point that I want to make about the shutdown, and this is what I mean to say overall about Donald Trump. He does not see other people as human beings to empathize with; they're ornaments or they're impediments. So when we think about the 800,000 people who are out there without a salary during this shutdown, and then the huge economic ripple effect suffered by retailers, restaurants, movie theaters, and so on, does Donald Trump think, with any measure of empathy or sympathy, any sense of feeling bad for the people who are really in hot water in all sorts of ways financially due to this shutdown? The answer is no. To him, they are ornaments or impediments; that's it. Same thing with children being ripped apart from their parents at the Mexican border. There is no sense of duty or obligation or responsibility or empathy because he sees it as "okay that's going to create pressure on the people who do care: the Democrats." And he's throwing temper tantrums because it's not working out that way; he's getting blowback. The monstrous nature of this man's personality organization is vastly underappreciated.

Betty: He doesn't care about anything, any damage to others, as long as he can get his deal for the wall pushed through.

Michael: The other thing in all of this is, which I'm fixated on, is the language that we use. It was initially so hard for the press to say in a direct way that Trump is lying. We all can remember how the press would say, "Well, that's not true. We're going to fact check it." Nobody could come out and say, "The guy's lying." What is our collective reluctance to say that Trump is lying? Why can't we call the fact out for what it is?

Michael Tansey: I think there are many aspects to that. We remember Charlottesville, and the shocking comments that Trump made—that there are good and fine people on both sides and both sides are to blame. That comment left people stunned that Trump could have possibly said something like that. I think Trump is so deviant from the norm, that we have never had to deal with anything like this before—ever. And as more and more irrefutable facts have arisen, we have continued to evolve. But the idea used to be "we can't say that because we don't really know."

Michael: And Michael and Betty, and all the other authors of *The Dangerous Case of Donald Trump*, have experienced something like this, too?[12] When the two of you and others have called Trump out, you've been chastised for doing so.

Betty: There are so many layers to this—sociocultural, political, philosophical. What comes to my mind is Robert J. Lifton's term *malignant normality*, and that the office of the president of the United States holds an incredible amount of weight and symbolism.[13] We depend on this office and its integrity for security, global and domestic. And to couple the authority and gravitas of the U.S. presidency with Trump's extreme, irresponsible, even nonsensical behavior is a shock to the American system. I think that even the U.S. news media, whose mandate it is to speak out whenever possible, however possible—I mean, we have First Amendment laws protecting their freedom of speech—but I sense they are not outside of the entrenched and even unconscious need to have the office of the presidency of the United States be a certain thing. It's an icon of security and safety. And if you say that the president is lying all the time, and not only that, that he may, in fact, be delusional, it is not just about Donald J. Trump anymore. It's about what structural flaws in our governmental system made room for this to happen. And now that it has, what can we do about it?

Michael: It's about the United States.

Betty: It's about faith. It's about the feeling of security and stability in the United States—by our own citizens and by the whole world. It's about everything.

Michael Tansey: It's about disbelief. People are thinking "this can't possibly be happening." Where have we heard that before? Prior to the election. Then, afterward, people thought, "He will most certainly make a soft pivot." You remember that idea?

---

[12] Lee, B. (Ed.). (2017/2019). *The Dangerous Case of Donald Trump: 27 psychiatrists and mental health experts assess a president.* Thomas Dunne Books.

[13] Lifton, R.J. (2017). "Our Witness to Malignant Normality" in *The Dangerous Case of Donald Trump: 27 psychiatrists and mental health experts assess a president.* (B. Lee, Ed.) Thomas Dunne Books. This piece was published as the foreword to the first edition.

Betty: You can look at this as a type of trauma response: it's a reaction from within a shocked state. And now, a year or so later, we're just coming out of the shock. We're still grappling with the impact of Trump's election, which is similar to the effect of hearing of something happening to somebody you know, something traumatic, horrible…

Michael: …or something terrible that was done to them.

Betty: Exactly. And when you hear of a terrible event, a crime or a perpetration—let's say it's happened to your coworker. You don't want to believe that that's happened, either. You may not want to tell other people that it happened because you don't want it to have been true in the first place. Admitting to the fact that such a terrible event happened to someone close to you could threaten to break apart everything in terms of what you believe to be "normal." It is very disruptive and destabilizing.

Michael: It's fascinating what you're saying, Betty, because it sounds to me very much that what you're talking about is identity. For all of us, the U.S. presidency is a symbol. It's something that we incorporate into our identity. And, for many, we have yet to have been able to find a way to incorporate the presidency of Donald Trump into who we are as Americans.

Betty: Definitely.

Michael: So we sit here, as Michael was saying, and we deny the lies. Or the nature of the falsehoods. We call them something else for a long time until we finally come out of it and start recognizing the trauma for what it is, of having a delusional person as president of the United States.

Betty: Exactly. And the disbelief, which Michael Tansey pointed to, is in line with the point you just made about identity. For many liberal Americans, there is an underlying sense of disbelief, akin to saying, "I'm not the kind of person to whom this kind of thing happens." You could swap in for this: "Americans are not the kind of people—the U.S. is not the kind of country where something like this happens." If you look at it in terms of survivors who are not wanting to speak out about the harm they sustained, or which they feel ashamed of, they may hide, deny, or dissociate that harm because they don't want it to define them. They may fear being seen as just that one thing—a survivor of an assault. This may be part of where we are as Americans, we cannot integrate it. So, we have to say, "This is not happening."

Michael: This is not who we are.

Betty: Right, this is not who we are. So, grappling with that unwanted reality takes a lot of time, time to reflect on just what's going on. And there's not a lot of time, nor are there the conditions to do so in our daily lives. There's a twenty-four-hour news cycle constantly going; there's each of our ever-available, ongoing social media channels and posts. That's where we're at.

Michael Tansey: The one thing that I want to add here is that, if, indeed, I am correct, that Trump has a psychotic core that is belied by this appearance of normality or functionality, if it is even normal or functional, it appears the walls are coming in on him. He's gotten himself into a fix with the shutdown. The Mueller investigation is becoming more and more compelling. All of that is coming down on his head. Enemies appear to be everywhere. In my view—and I've been saying this since before he was elected—that for Trump, the 2016 presidential election was about apocalypse, not politics. Let's remember—because people forget this, or they don't believe it—if he decides to launch nuclear missiles, as president, he can do that without any filtering process whatsoever. And they can be in the air in less than five minutes. People don't believe that, yet they need to know this fact. He can launch nuclear missiles. And politicians, like McConnell and Ryan, have opposed any legislation that would change the sole authority doctrine.[14].

And as he becomes increasingly delusional and paranoid, seeing enemies everywhere, he becomes more dangerous. Having worked at McLean Hospital, I've treated people who are in the midst of an extreme psychotic episode.[15] They would come in floridly psychotic, saying "I can't figure out if I'm Jesus Christ or Mozart or Jimi Hendrix and the CIA is after me." We don't know that Donald Trump will launch nuclear missiles, but we don't know that he won't. And other than a brief period with Richard Nixon,

---

[14] "Senator Markey and Rep. Lieu Announce Reintroduction of Bill to Limit U.S. President's Ability to Launch a Nuclear Weapon," January 19, 2021, https://www.markey.senate.gov/news/press-releases/01/19/2021/senator-markey-and-rep-lieu-announce-reintroduction-of-bill-to-limit-us-presidents-ability-to-start-a-nuclear-war.

[15] McClean is a psychiatric hospital in Belmont, Massachusetts.

that's never been a question of our being at risk of having a president who could take matters into his own hands before. It is a huge question now. Why? Because he is, as I've said, "crazy like a crazy, not crazy like a fox," which is to name the root causes of his manipulations and shrewdness.[16] His mentality is "if I am going down, since I am all that there is at the end of the day, and everything out there are simply ornaments or impediments to me," there is nothing to prevent him from taking the world down with him.

Michael: Well, on that high, lovely note…

Betty: …and that hopeful message…

Michael Tansey: Yeah, I have been referred to as Dr. Doom.

Betty: The key point here is that there is a very dangerous person in the White House who we have to consider and reconsider again and again, which is why we brought you on, Michael. Thanks for sharing your keen insights.

---

[16] Tansey, M. (2019). "'Why Crazy Like a Fox' versus 'Crazy like a Crazy' Really Matters: Delusional disorder, admiration of brutal dictators, the nuclear codes, and Trump" in *The Dangerous Case of Donald Trump* (Ed. B. Lee). Thomas Dunne Books. pp. 104–119 .

ANXIETIES OF RACE & DOMINANCE

Chapter 14
Justice, Rage, & Peace

Guest: Eric Ward
Aired: December 9, 2020

Eric K. Ward is a nationally recognized expert on the relationship between authoritarian movements, hate violence, and preserving inclusive democracy. In his 30-plus-years civil rights career, he has worked with community groups, government and business leaders, human rights activists, and philanthropists. Eric is executive director of the Western States Center. He's also a senior fellow with the Southern Poverty Law Center and Race Forward, and he's co-chair for the Proteus Fund.

In 2016, in the first week of Donald Trump's election as 45th president of the United States, the Southern Poverty Law Center (SPLC) reported that 701 incidents of hate crimes had occurred nationwide, all directly attributed to Trump's election.[1] The top three groups targeted in these attacks were immigrants, Blacks, and LGBTQ individuals. This surge in hate crimes proved to be a harbinger for a blossoming of white extremist violence during Trump's presidency.

During the next four years, some of the deadliest active shooter events in U.S. history occurred—including the October 27, 2018, Tree of Life Synagogue shooting in Pittsburg, Pennsylvania, where eleven people were killed; the February 14, 2018, mass shooting at Marjory Stoneman Douglas High School in Parkland, Florida, where 17 people—mostly teenagers—were killed; and the August 3, 2019, Walmart attack in El

---

[1] Hatewatch Staff, "Update: Incidents of Hateful Harassment Since Election Day Now Number 701," SPLC, November 18, 2016. https://www.splcenter.org/hatewatch/2016/11/18/update-incidents-hateful-harassment-election-day-now-number-701.

Paso, Texas, where 22 people were killed.[2] The perpetrators of all three mass shootings were white nationalist sympathizers who frequently touted antisemitic, anti-immigrant, and anti-Black views online.

Such hateful extremism contributes to a growing state of intense uncertainty, stress, and fear that has tightened its grip on the American psyche over the last decade. This prompted us to turn to Eric Ward to help us understand the mechanisms of white extremism and race-based hate, to consider ways we can stanch the growth of white nationalism, which nudges us toward authoritarianism. That white extremist leaders like Enrique Tarrio of the Proud Boys and Stewart Rhodes of the Oath Keepers have, in 2023, been convicted of seditious conspiracy for the key roles they played in leading the January 6, 2021 insurrection on the U.S. Capitol points to the direct threat white nationalism poses to the stability of American democracy and, therefore, to our collective sense of safety and well-being.

We begin our section on the Anxieties of Race & Dominance with this conversation because Eric's thoughtful reflections on the mechanisms and roots of white nationalism and racial animus in the U.S. relate to all the other conversations here on the American cultural complex of race and otherness. Themes he raises of how fear, anger, and stress operate within humans and drive a tendency to scapegoat minority groups also run through our discussions in this section with Dr. Antoine Banks on anger and racial politics, Drs. Susan Fiske and Peter Glick on antisemitism, Dr. Hawthorne Smith on anti-immigration sentiment, Dr. Liliana Mason on the mechanisms of political partisanship, Dr. Ashley Jardina on white identity politics, and Dr. Adrienne Hollis on climate justice. We imagine Eric, here, to moderate a virtual Mind of State panel discussion with these other experts. Collectively, they point out how crucial it is to pay attention to the ways fear, anxiety, and anger can drive harm and violence in civic life, often against immigrant or minority groups. As all of our guests warn, such internecine conflicts can stress U.S. democracy to the point of its collapse.

Interview

Betty: It's been a few weeks since the [2020] election, and I can say the exhaustion is truly setting in. In talking to friends and patients, I can now admit to myself that I'm done. I'm so done.

[2] Cai, W., Griggs, T., Gao, J., Love, J. & Ward, J. (2019). White Extremist Ideology Drives Many Deadly Shootings. *The New York Times.* https://www.nytimes.com/interactive/2019/08/04/us/white-extremist-active-shooter.html.

Jonathan: You know, you're not alone. There are plenty of people who are exhausted. They want to get in bed or maybe they just...

Betty: I don't want any more information. I don't want to turn on MSNBC. I don't want to hear a pundit. I don't want to read a headline. I don't want to think about a poll. I just don't want to.

Jonathan: I get it. We've been in a fight-or-flight mentality for the past four years. At the same time, there's another group out there who doesn't want to stop fighting. For them, the notion that all of a sudden the election is done, and it's settled, and Joe Biden is going to be president, so stop and lay down your arms, is anathema.

Betty: That is psychologically organic, meaning, you can't just shut that kind of energy down overnight. On both sides everybody has been up in arms and fiercely protecting themselves and their communities. It's a very defensive mentality. So the shift is hard. It's very hard.

Jonathan: In every cycle, political activists and campaigners have to shift from campaign to government. We have to shift from fighting to building. And that *is* really hard. But in this moment, we know that if we don't buckle down and focus on the work to be done on inclusively and constructively building, then we're going to squander the opportunity and suddenly find ourselves four years from now asking *what was that for?*

Betty: Yeah, I can see that we don't have much time to even take a breath, and we actually don't have time to keep fighting like this. It's too much. This election has been utterly depleting—all during the pandemic, no less. But here we are. This government has got to deal with the pandemic, an economic crisis, and a referendum on racial injustice. There's a massive amount of work—and repair—to be done.

Jonathan: At this moment, keeping focused on the agenda, keeping focused on getting some wins, keeping focused on pulling this country back together is all the more important.

Betty: It's a hard negotiation on how we walk the middle line. And that's exactly why we invited this next episode's guest, Eric Ward. Thanks for joining us on *Mind of State*, Eric.

Eric Ward: It's so great to be with you both. Thank you for inviting me.

Jonathan: Eric, you know, for the past four years or maybe longer, but certainly in the 2020 election, we have been locked in this struggle, this debate between the rise of authoritarianism on the one hand, and the urge to maintain and protect and preserve our participatory democracy on the other. It's a struggle that we're seeing, of course, in so many other countries all around the world. What I'm wondering in speaking with you is, how do you see the relationship between the rise of authoritarianism on the one hand and the rise of hatred and racism and bigotry on the other?

Eric: There's such a symbiotic relationship between the politics of authoritarianism and the scapegoating or dehumanizing of people. One of the reasons is that authoritarians build their political worldview or their narrative myth around the idea of being under attack—under the idea of an existential war that demands a strong response. Some of the language that I often hear from authoritarians is that society has been contaminated or infiltrated. And being able to tap into already existing forms of dehumanization just makes sense, particularly if you're Donald Trump, who I believe has leaned into a fully-fledged authoritarian program. You don't start that demonization or identification of an enemy by picking a broad target—for instance, folks who are left-handed. All of us know folks who are left-handed.

Jonathan: You're speaking to one.

Eric: Right. You're hearing from one right now. We all know someone who is left-handed. And so when an authoritarian, or Donald Trump and Trumpers, come out and say we're being invaded by left-handers, we're all like, "Well that's ridiculous, because I know Joe, he's left-handed. I know Christiane and she's left-handed." So you have to look for smaller groupings—and smaller groupings in American society are immigrants, Muslims, Jews, LGBTQ, African Americans. It's an easier grouping, because they are socially alienated already in our society because of historical forms of racism and other forms of prejudice. So this is why you see it. But it's critical to note. Authoritarianism is not successful unless it has an enemy at which to point society's emotional anger and anxiety toward.

Betty: I have a question about what you said about narrative. These authoritarians, or people with this propensity, seem to have something that comes up in a lot of our conversations—this *narrative need* to find an easy target. But what, in your view, having worked 30 years investigating, studying, and working with these extremist groups, what is their need to find a demon?

Eric: It's interesting. I actually have the same question, Betty. What are the ultimate drivers? Because I feel as a society, when we understand these drivers, we can attempt to interrupt them.

Betty: That's exactly right.

Eric: Or replace them with healthy drivers in our society. I wrestle with this. Over the last four years, of course, like everyone else, most Americans and folks living in American society and those impacted by such targeting have been doing a lot of thinking about what these drivers are. And my sense is there is a driver of demographic anxiety. Something is changing in the society fairly rapidly. Our society has experienced a significant amount of loss or societal-level trauma, and this triggers a feeling of scarcity. Now, I'm guessing, right? I'm not a mental health specialist. I want to be perfectly clear about that. But there seems to be the driver of scarcity, the fear of loss—whether it's loss of status, whether it's loss of understanding how to navigate a changing world, or it's the sense of perceived loss that comes from a sense of trauma. This doesn't drive authoritarianism, but it opens up the space for authoritarians in our society to try to organize that anxiety into political power.

That's what I believe we saw under the four years of Donald Trump—but it predates Donald Trump, too. We saw it at a lower level under Obama's administration, with the attacks on Barack Obama, Muslims, and others. And some suggest that it ties back directly to the events of 9/11. Our society was significantly traumatized on 9/11, and our nation's leaders didn't seek to address that trauma, except through political positioning and utilizing the tragedy to build power, rather than to heal lives and communities.

Jonathan: So, how does that trauma and that feeling of scarcity—which fuels racism or otherism—how does that narrow down and get focused in white supremacy and white nationalism? Because as I've listened to you and read your writings, it seems like white supremacy and white nationalism are very particular strains of racism. Could you talk about that a little bit?

Betty: And, Eric, you make a distinction between the two. So, in piggybacking off Jonathan, can you tell us what you see as the difference between white supremacy and white nationalism?

Eric: I do make a distinction, and it sounds weird, right? We often hear white supremacy and white nationalism used interchangeably. I offer a distinction because I think it helps us build proper responses, and building proper responses maintains our agency. In the face of authoritarianism, holding our own agency is essential for those of us who believe in democracy, for those of us who believe in human rights, and for those of us who believe in basic humanity. So, when we talk about white supremacy and white nationalism, we at Western States Center make a distinction between white nationalism and white supremacy. *White nationalism* is a social movement. *White supremacy* is a system of historic and present-day policies and practices. And we distinguish them from one another because they don't actually seek the same ends. I'll explain.

White supremacy has been with us in the United States since at least Bacon's Rebellion.[3] Some folks argue that white supremacy has been with us since the arrival of European colonialists and explorers to the Americas, going back to as early as 1492. White supremacy is a historic and present-based system of exploitation, and it was created as a narrative in which to organize society. This narrative was grounded on a concept called *white superiority*—the idea that one is superior based on their white skin, and that others are inferior because of their lack of white skin. The binary was white and black, whiteness being the closest to good and wholesomeness and black being the closest to evil and danger. It wasn't just Black folks, though, who suffered from white supremacy. The system had three pillars. Chattel slavery was one of them. The second was the theft and genocide of

---

[3] Bacon's Rebellion in 1676 was the last major uprising of enslaved blacks and white indentured servants in Colonial Virginia. One consequence of the failed rebellion was the intensification of African slavery and the social separation of blacks and whites in Virginia.

indigenous peoples and their lands. The third was the control of sexuality, primarily through the control of women. It was around these three things that American society organized itself. It is at least partially responsible for our being a powerful economy and country—because we were able to exploit the free labor of such a large portion of the population.

None of us are responsible for the creation of that system—none of us were here 500 years ago to set this up. At most, in terms of the existence of that practice, we're responsible for the fact that it continues to exist around us today. But this was white supremacy. It was challenged, I argue, in the 1960s civil rights movement—which defeated white supremacy as the rule of law. Now, that doesn't mean white supremacy does not still exist. But previous to the 1965 civil rights movement, white supremacy was primarily an uncontested space. It was how we viewed laws, culture, and economy—through this lens—and the civil rights movement disrupted that.

Now, imagine for a second, you are a person who was socialized and steeped in white supremacy and the belief that you were superior, just based on your white skin—and that Black people were inferior in every way, because of their dark skin. How, then, do you come to terms with the fact that you lost against folks you saw as inferior? It's just simply not possible. People don't shift their worldview so rapidly.

The answer was not going to be, "Well, I guess Black people are not inferior after all." So, instead, folks had to find another scapegoat. I talk about this in an essay called "Skin in the Game: How Antisemitism Fuels White Nationalism."[4] I won't lay out the full piece here, but what happens through a set of circumstances is that these white supremacists who perceive this loss of their system begin to look for someone to blame. And since it's not going to be Black people who they see as inferior, they look for another target. And due to hundreds of years of antisemitism, they choose the Jewish community as the answer, based on the notion that Jews operate as a secret cabal. I differentiate white supremacy from white nationalism and see them as two different things because the success of the civil rights movement in the 1960s gave birth to the white nationalist movement—long after white supremacy held sway for many generations in the prior history of the United States. If white supremacy is about exploitation, white

---

[4] "Skin in the Game: How Antisemitism Fuels White Nationalism" was published in *The Public Eye* (Summer 2017), https://politicalresearch.org/2017/06/29/skin-in-the-game-how-antisemitism-animates-white-nationalism.

nationalism is a social movement that has not yet fully come into its own, despite its heavy influence in our society.

White nationalists portray Jews as the reason that they lost white supremacy as an institution and as a narrative in America. They subsequently have blamed Jews for every perceived loss, whether it's the gains of women's rights, or labor rights, or immigrant rights, or the rights of Muslims and refugees in our society. White nationalists see themselves in an existential war with the Jewish community. This is a dangerous antisemitic worldview because it provides only one answer to the problem of the Jewish cabal—which is an ethnic cleansing that includes the cleansing of the Jewish community and people of color from the United States. So while white supremacy is about exploitation, white nationalism is a growing movement that seeks the removal of all people it perceives to be non-white from the United States—and that can only be done with violence. The goal is not to go back to the days of *Gone with the Wind*, despite the rhetoric of Make America Great Again—MAGA followers. The goal is not to go back to the days of slavery or the days of exploitation. It is about creating an all-white ethnic state.

Betty: So, Eric, do you feel like white supremacy and white nationalism are subsets or have Venn-diagram overlaps with each other? All white supremacists are not necessarily white nationalists. White nationalists seek ethnic cleansing and violence in a very extreme state. They advocate for a nationhood of only white people. White supremacists, however, may want a return to the days of *Gone with the Wind*. In your observations, do the two groups overlap? Are the nationalists recruiting the supremacists, so to speak?

Eric: Well, one of the things we know in the real world is that when a vision or a narrative meets with reality, it will often evolve in different ways. What I described to you captures the writings and thinking of the main theorists of the white nationalist movement. I sit within a human rights social movement, particularly in the progressive political left of that human rights movement, and sometimes we think we're the only folks who know how to form social movements. We understand our ecosystems, our think tanks, our activists, our policymakers, our researchers, and our cultural makers. But when it comes to the white nationalist movement, for some reason we think it's all driven by individual behavior—that this is a movement driven by hatred. What I like to remind folks is that the white nationalist movement isn't tapping into antisemitism or, quite frankly, racism or Islamophobia or any other form of bigotry because they're out there wanting to spread antisemitism. They're tapping into antisemitism and other forms of bigotry because it's useful for organizing.

As an organizer, you don't organize communities around things that you can't motivate them around. In his book, *Rules for Radicals* one of the first stories activist Saul Alinsky relates is one about organizing folks around a stoplight in their community because that's what folks cared about.[5] What the white nationalist movement gets, better than the rest of America—including the human rights movement—is just how prevalent antisemitism and racism and other forms of bigotry are in our society. I often say, Betty, these hate groups don't come to town bringing bigotry into our communities. They simply organize the prejudice that already exists in those communities. And it means one of the best ways that we can inoculate our communities is by addressing those deeper underlying issues—of alienation, trauma, and demographic anxiety. It makes our communities less susceptible to political theorists who are grounded around an exclusive idea of what American democracy should be, who see through the lens of a scarcity model rather than an inclusive democracy that's people-centered, transparent, and accountable.

But I think you're right. We have lots of stereotypes about the white nationalist movement. We see them as folks in rural areas drinking the six-pack of beer with the shotgun rack on the back of their truck. We think dropout, rural, poor. And certainly that exists because that exists in America, but interestingly enough the white nationalist movement does not disproportionately attract the working white poor or even people of color or even women. Who it predominantly attracts are upper-middle-class and upper-class white folks. A study that was done by Professor James Aho, a sociologist at the University of Idaho, remains one of the most comprehensive studies of the white nationalist movement.[6] He did it in the 1990s, just to give you an idea of how long ago that was. And what he found is that the members of the white nationalist movement in Idaho had a higher level of education than the general population of Idaho as a whole. It also had a higher level of income than the general population of Idaho as a whole and was more politically active. And so the truth is that the white

---

[5] Alinsky, S.K. (1989). *Rules for Radicals: A practical primer for realistic radicals.* Random House.
[6] Aho, J.A. (1990). *Politics of Righteousness: Idaho Christian patriotism.* University of Washington Press.

nationalist movement, except for the fact that it is disproportionately upper and middle class in its ranks, looks just like America. And I think that tells us something about the social movement, which is it looks just like every other social movement in America. It, however, has a vision of the United States being an all-white America, and there is only one way that that happens, and that's through violence.

Jonathan: So, if the movement on the right is one of homogeneity, the challenge on the left then is more complicated, because as you've articulated in your 21st-century civil rights movement conversation, we need to see Black Americans and Jewish Americans and Muslim Americans working together and understanding that the forces that hate them are unified against all of them. So, does the fact that the white supremacy movement is unified, drive the factions on the left apart or together?

Eric: I think it fractures the left, and this is one of the challenges that I wrestle with. And you can probably hear me doing the "uhh uhh" right now as I'm talking, because that's how much I actually wrestle with this question. Here's what I think—the white nationalist movement is only successful in America due to the collapse and the inability of the left and progressives in this country to show that they can build and lead a political consensus in this country. I think we can only effectively stop the white nationalist movement if we are able to break out of our own bubble, and that's hard, in authoritarian moments. We talk about the impact of authoritarian moments, and one of the impacts is the hardness of authoritarianism, the purity that is demanded by authoritarians.

None of our movements, none of our organizations and institutions escape this moment without being negatively impacted by the authoritarian thinking that has been pervasive in almost all of our waking lives over the last four years. And it's possible that it has put us in a mindset where we think the only way to respond to this hardness, is with our own hardness. And the only way that we can respond to the fanaticism of purity that has been demanded by the other side is with our own purity. And the problem is that neither hardness nor purity open up space for the heterogeneity that you describe, Jonathan—which is essential in our movement. It closes off the oxygen for that type of inclusiveness of different groups—be they Muslim, Jewish, Black, or White. It also undercuts the ability to keep a focus on what is important.

For four years, you've had first an authoritarian-leaning government, and then, in its final stages, an authoritarian government that politicized everything. There was no space to discuss values. You had to first stake out a political position, and you only knew who you agreed with based on a political position, on a partisan political position, rather than on an individual's or an organization's values. Values became not very important. So I worry. I worry that the toll of the past four years, the exhaustion of these four years, the horrifying months that occurred over these four years—each month was more horrifying than the next—has exhausted progressives and the left in terms of its willingness to lead the entire nation and not simply engage in building power for power's sake. I don't know if that makes sense.

Betty: It makes a lot of sense. What you point to is something that I think about with regard to trauma. If you don't deal with it, if we don't heal from our trauma, which you very accurately said was a consequence of 9/11, then it goes under the surface. We answered 9/11 with political responses, but we did not heal the nation in terms of going through it, facing it, feeling all the disparate and paradoxical feelings of hurt, loss, or blame. It festers. Another guest, Pauline Boss, who is a psychologist, said that we are a nation founded on unresolved loss. So you might say that we have had unresolved traumas going back to 500 years ago. That's what you're measuring.

And so now, authoritarianism offers this binary, this pure path. Such a narrative is a fantasy that promises "We know how to do it. We're going to do it. We're the son of God. We have all the answers and it's clear." But that's not realistic, as you put it. Reality is unclear. I think we're in a fractured, vicious cycle where we are compelled to fight, to break shit down, to blow shit up rather than build it up. I'm curious how you—as a person who has worked in this space for 30 years—face such hatred and not get sucked into this non-thinking, eye-for-an-eye revenge kind of mentality? Part of our exhaustion is that each side feels under threat and no one can think when backed into a corner. We're only going to react and strike out, and we can't create an inclusive democracy out of that.

Eric: I think that is really well said. You can't build. What I worry about is that we're missing the long arc in this moment. We're thinking in very short durations of three months—or one year, rather than in increments of 10 years—or even 60 or 70 years. Where do we want to be? It's very hard to find the space to think about the future beyond a very short time frame.

Betty: So hard.

Eric: But I know 2020 is fundamentally better in this country than 1920. And I absolutely know 2020 is better than 1820 in this country. And that doesn't mean that I think everything is marvelous. It doesn't mean that I'm ignoring the inequality and the injustice that exists in our society. What I'm noting is that we're in a better place. Now, why are we in that better place? As a person on the left and as a progressive, are we in a better place because capitalism made this a better place? I'm skeptical, though capitalism has had its own role to play, and I'll acknowledge that. Are we in a better place because folks who were bigoted decided "It's time to be in a better place"? No. We are in a better place because folks like me and folks like you and folks like those listening really struggled for generations, for hundreds of years, to get us to this point. And one of the things that the impact of authoritarian thinking does to our movement—in its insistence on purity and a unilateral narrative—is, when we look back, to disregard the work that people did for us to get us to this point. They died for it. They were beaten for it. They were ostracized for it. They were persecuted for it in ways that I can't even imagine.

If we are building a society that cannot acknowledge the work that got us to this point, how do we acknowledge the work that it's going to take to get us to 2120? And what type of democracy do we want or what type of society are we saying we want in 2120? And so I feel like that long-arc thinking is really important. I also think this is critically important—life has been unfair for the majority of Americans, for the majority of people of color, and for other marginalized communities in this country—for the majority of the world. Life is unfair. It is harsh in ways that are unnecessary. It costs in ways that are unnecessary. This has benefited a smaller grouping of folks in our society who have benefited from that privilege—whether they are male, whether they are straight, whether they are white—in lots of different ways. But the truth is that we're not seeking revenge here. That shouldn't be our goal, ever.

I realized I grew up in a pretty harsh punk music scene that I loved. But it was very violent. It was anxiety-producing. It was likely traumatizing in many ways, but probably less traumatizing than the world around me at the time. And I came to believe finally, not too long ago—10 years ago, maybe a little bit longer—that sometimes you don't get justice. And part of healing is trying to hold the loss that sometimes you have to let go of justice to get peace. Not all the justice; it doesn't mean that we give up accountability. But it means that at the end of the day—is our job all about holding people accountable, or is it about providing a vision of the world that we say people should live in? I'm no longer sure that those two things are necessarily synonymous with one another.

Those are some of the bigger questions that I wrestle with right now. At the end of the day, sometimes loss is loss, and we have to help folks mourn that loss, understand that we can't ever have that back. It's not coming back. We don't get our messed-up childhoods to do over again. And sometimes you just have to understand that it's gone. You have to mourn it. You can acknowledge it was unfair, but you can't keep seeking it at the cost of the rest of your life. And if I could backroad that comment to our movements right now, that is what I would be saying.

Jonathan: This shouldn't be about vengeance or settling scores. I agree with you that we need to act like winners and keep our eye on the prize. But isn't it important for the future to not settle scores, but to create some accountability, to recognize that we as a society don't find certain behaviors acceptable and lay down a marker so that we don't continue to turn the other cheek every time? If we go high when they go low, does that ultimately benefit us or do we have to actually create some form of accountability as we go?

Eric: It's the risk, and I don't know if we've ever done it. I think about South Africa. I was an anti-apartheid activist. I think about the years between 1985 and 1995 in South Africa. I don't remember the exact number, but I think somewhere around 18,000 or 24,000 South Africans were killed from political violence during those 10 years. Two-thirds of them happened in a two-year period between the release of Nelson Mandela and the passage of the South African constitution. I think about the different ideologies and tendencies in play, from the ANC (African National Congress) to the Afrikaner Party to the military and police intelligence services to Azania.[7] I think about all the bloodshed that happened. And I, as an activist at that point, I remember hearing the news that Nelson Mandela was going to be negotiating with de Klerk. I remember hearing that news, and I think about this because there are so many lessons.

---

[7] Azania is the indigenous name given to South Africa.

As an activist in the United States, I felt betrayed. And who was I to feel betrayed? It was not my lived life each and every day. I had no basis of experience to judge what was the right move there, what was the long arc that was trying to be achieved. And yet I found myself with this feeling of betrayal. And it probably took me 10 or 15 years to realize the hard choice that was made there. The hard, choiceless choice. Nelson Mandela and de Klerk had to decide—did they relegate South Africa to a generation of civil war? One of the things that happens in political movements is that we can become very nonchalant about political violence and what it means. And I think now is that these were two leaders who were not nonchalant about violence at all. I think they did the calculations, and both realized that whether it was a generational civil war or whether it was 40 years of grinding through the last vestiges of apartheid South Africa, that it was going to take the same amount of time to get to the same point. The question was, how many lives were they willing to lose over it?

And there were so many attempts to overturn that negotiation. And I think, at the end of the day, that historical memory—and the work of truth and reconciliation, are so critically important. I've grown up Black in America. I understand the rage. I have that rage. I feel it. It's always there below the surface. But that rage is never going to be fed. It has to be replaced with something. I came to realize that for Mandela and de Klerk, the truth was this: you don't negotiate peace with your friends; you negotiate peace with your enemies. And negotiating peace with your enemies is about ensuring that all people have a better life and that takes a lot of courage—it's a courageous risk. It takes a lot of courage to be vulnerable.

Betty: On both sides.

Eric: On both sides.

Betty: And as a last thing, Eric, you're talking about this rage, and it's something that I've been really curious about, through reading all your writings. Rage precludes thinking. It's a psycho-physical response. It's a physiological experience. And you have used it to fuel your work. It's clear. How do you think with rage—and how do we do this now, here, as we go forward and try and repair the last 4 years, the last 15 years—or whatever brought us to this point?

Eric: Here's what I think. My rage has definitely fueled my work, but mainly because I don't want other folks to feel that same rage. I'm just not down for building a world where my measurement of how amazing folks are is how much rage they can express. Folks who have actually experienced or been around real rage, who do you wish that on? You don't wish that on anyone. So I think this. I've tried to look at it in three different ways. What folks get to do in life is one thing, one thing in the pursuit of inclusive democracy. Whether that's racial equality or gender equity, whether that's dealing with the disparities of wealth in a society, whether it's strengthening participation. All of us get to pick one thing, whether it's taking care of our elders—which also would lessen the scarcity mentality in the society. Imagine if we were a society that didn't warehouse 75 percent of our people in the last 10 years of life? Not just warehoused, but ignored and shunned and treated as less than.

So I think about all the things folks can do over these next 4 years, over these next 60 years. And what I say is you just have to do one thing. You don't have to do everything that I'm doing. It can be one song. It could be a piece of art. Just do one thing. If everyone did one thing, rage would not be such a heavy driver within our movements, and it would connect us in such substantial ways. Not everyone needs to be a politico. I'm a politico. I like politics. But that's not everyone's gig, and it doesn't have to be. I'm also not an amazing gardener. It's not my passion, but there are people who are. That is what feeds them in life. And I think, what I want to say is: find that one thing that feeds you in life, then figure out one thing you can do with it that speaks to your values in this world. And I think we would all be stunned by how quickly our communities were transformed.

Jonathan: Eric, thank you so much for sharing your inspiration with us and for sharing your time with us. We appreciate you coming on *Mind of State*, and we wish you the best.

Eric: I appreciate you all. Thank you so much.

Betty: Thanks for joining us on this episode of *Mind of State* and thanks again to our guest, Eric Ward.

Chapter 15
Anger & Racial Politics

Dr. Antoine Banks
Episode Aired: April 1, 2019

Dr. Antoine Banks is a professor in the Department of Government and Politics at the University of Maryland. He is also the associate chair and director of the Government and Politics Experimental Lab. His research interests include racial and ethnic politics, emotions, political psychology, and public opinion. His book, Anger and Racial Politics: The Emotional Foundation of Racial Attitudes in America, *published by Cambridge University Press, explores the link between emotions and racial attitudes and the consequences it has for political preferences. His articles have appeared in journals such as the* American Journal of Political Science, Public Opinion Quarterly, Political Behavior, Political Analysis, *and* Political Psychology.

We were particularly eager to speak with Antoine Banks in 2019. He, too, saw the impact of psychology upon politics, and his political science research focused on the role emotions play in impacting political behavior—this made him a perfect guest for Mind of State.

What was striking to us—then and now—was a discovery Dr. Banks made in his investigations and described in his 2014 book Anger and Racial Politics: The Emotional Foundation of Racial Attitudes in America: *He found that whites, when made angry—even over topics that had* nothing to do with race or politics— *had more racialized political views. If, as Dr. Banks discovered, being angry made whites more politically extreme, especially around racialized issues, then here was another key to our entrenched and polarized divisions.*

Looking back on the 2016 presidential elections, Antoine had this observation to make:

There's been some data to show that 2016 levels of anger were higher than in any other previous presidential election year. And this was not just among Republicans, but Democrats as well. Trump's rhetoric not only made Republicans pretty angry at Democrats, but it definitely fueled Democrats' anger at Republicans. Both sides were angry, more so than any previous year. It's led to a lot of uncivil rhetoric, to racialized rhetoric. It's led to a lack of compromise. It's led to more polarization. The parties are seen as further apart than they have been in the past. In terms of trying to get legislation done that might help Americans, compromise is essential. We've had a much more difficult time doing that. Government has been shut down, fighting about what we're going to pass. These days we are venturing into new territory.

New territory, indeed. Dr. Banks's comments were not only salient in 2019, but also prescient about the future. Although he could not have predicted 2020's pandemic lockdown, the referendum on race sparked by George Floyd's murder, and the January 6, 2021, insurrection attempt on the Capitol by white nationalists, his insights describe the anger in American society that has only grown since 2019, pushing us further and further apart.

That "Stop the Steal" was the conspiracist notion that drove white nationalists to attack on January 6th revealed that by 2021 even the U.S. presidential election had become racialized. Here, Dr. Banks's research linking generalized anger and racialized politics becomes even more important, for he offers an emotional explanation to the scapegoating Eric Ward points to as a central underpinning of white nationalism. Because emotions defy reason, we start to see why truth and reality have no bearing upon those who are enraged. Since few would dispute that these are particularly enraging times, we could all apply Dr. Banks's insights and do what we can, when angry, to combat our tendency to go to political extremes.

Interview

Michael: We are excited to speak with Dr. Antoine Banks today because a few years back, in 2014, he wrote a book, *Anger and Racial Politics*, that was an amazingly prescient work. It saw something important in America that a lot of people missed, which was this unexpected link between anger, race, and public policy. The book focuses on how anger defines and even motivates a good portion of how white America, or some part of white America, thinks about race. Antoine, welcome to *Mind of State*.

Antoine: Thank you for that great introduction. I'm excited to be here.

Michael: What was so interesting about your book and the work you've done subsequent to that, is that you asked a really interesting outlier question that few others have asked, which is, if you put whites in an angry state that has nothing to do with race, will it still activate racial attitudes? In other words, does making white people angry cause race to play a larger role in our politics?

Why did you even think to ask that question? And then can we go from there to talk about what you found out.

Antoine: The reason I asked that question is because I wanted to be clear that emotion itself was driving the effect of race, not the attitudes or objects related to the emotion. So, if I made people angry about politics or made people angry about race, it's less clear whether the emotion itself is playing a role or whether it's the intensity they might feel about politics or their attitudes about race that's driving the effect.

In some ways it's a much cleaner test to show that it's the emotion as opposed to the intensity or just beliefs about race, which drives behavior. That was one reason I posed the question from an empirical standpoint. Another one was to show how strong the connection is between the two—to reveal that when people learn their attitudes, particularly about race, we find emotions play a big part of that. Because people have very strong attitudes about race, I expected the emotions to be just as strong.

Michael: So, the emotion can trigger thinking about race, even when the emotion is not inspired by the topic?

Antoine: Yes. To show this, I asked whites to write about things that made them feel angry—just things in their general life. It could be that their kids were not taking out the trash, or a partner was cheating on them, or they were being fired from their job—things that had nothing to do with race. Yet this still caused their racial attitudes to be more salient. That surprised a lot of people. But when you think about how mood, emotions, and memory work, it's not that surprising.

Betty: In terms of how angry emotions made race more salient, how did you discover that? What were you looking at, in terms of how people were stimulated when thinking about how their kids didn't take out the trash or about their argument with a spouse? Where did race come into that afterward and how did that clue you into the connection?

Antoine: Basically I first wanted to see what the effect of race was when emotions were absent. This was a baseline control condition I established. I had people write about things that made them feel relaxed. I wanted to see the relationship between this calm state and their existing racial attitudes— say, their positions on affirmative action, welfare, and government aid to Blacks. And I also looked at health care and immigration.

Betty: So you asked people about their positions on race-based or racially charged political policies when they were in a calm state?

Antoine: Yes. I wanted to see what the relationship was between their existing racial attitudes and positions on race. I wanted to get a sense of what this relationship would be, in a baseline state, which is, in this case, in a relaxed state. There's already a strong relationship between emotions and attitudes about race. When people who are racially resentful or conservative see a policy position dealing with race, that link is activated. My expectation was that, when I made people angry, that relationship would get even stronger. When I asked them to write about things that put them in an angry state, did I see a stronger connection between emotion and racial attitudes that was already there in a baseline condition? In other words, when in an angry state, caused by something other than race, did people with a preexisting negative attitude to race get stronger negative feelings about race?

And that's essentially what I've reported throughout the book. When I made whites angry, even if the cause of anger was not about race, it made the relationship that exists between people's views about race and policy much, much stronger.

Michael: Does making somebody angry turn them against a policy that they might otherwise support or not care about?

Antoine: No, it doesn't change their position. If you make someone angry, it's not going to make someone who has very hostile views toward Blacks become somewhat sympathetic to Blacks on policy positions. In fact, when you make people angry about something unrelated to race, they harden their positions about race. It makes them even more racially polarized and strengthens their more conservative position on, say, affirmative action or welfare than it would have been.

A good example of this is the healthcare debate where research by Tesler and Sears has shown that people's opinions on Obama's proposal, the Affordable Care Act, were in fact pretty racially polarized.[1] Racially resentful or prejudiced whites and racially liberal whites were pretty divided on the issue. What I find is that, when you infuse the debate with anger, the polarization increases significantly. It causes racial conservatives to take a more opposing position than they would have if anger wasn't present. And it causes racial liberals to take a more supportive position than they would if there wasn't anger.

Betty: Anger is a driver, a fuel for this fire. It causes white liberals to be even more liberal and causes white conservatives or those who have racial animus to be even more prejudiced.

Antoine: Yes. One impressive finding in the book is that even for issues that are already particularly polarized when it comes to race, anger magnifies that polarization even more. Making people angry increases their already racialized and polarized attitudes.

Michael: Emotion is something we've been discussing quite a bit on *Mind of State*. One of the surprises of our journey is that, when you enter into policy, you think it's all about rationality. You think it's about policy. You think it's all these adults making informed decisions. We do not pay enough attention to how emotion plays into politics. There's an example from 2010 you put in the book, an event that occurred on the eve of the Affordable Care Act vote in Congress. Representative John Lewis, who grew up in Alabama and represented Georgia's 5th Congressional District, is an American hero from the civil rights movement and the Student Nonviolent Coordinating Committee (SNCC). You recount an incident that's not from the civil rights era and has seemingly nothing to do with race. It's about healthcare reform. Here's the story from *McClatchyDC* on March 20, 2010:

---

[1] Tesler, M. (2012). "The Spillover of Racialization into Health Care: How President Obama Polarized Public Opinion by Racial Attitudes and Race." *American Journal of Political Science* 56, no. 3: 690–704. http://www.jstor.org/stable/23316014.

> Demonstrators outside the U.S. Capitol angry over the proposed health care bill shouted the N-word Saturday at U.S. Representative John Lewis, a Georgia congressman and a Civil Rights icon who was nearly beaten to death during a march in Alabama in the 1960s. The protesters also shouted obscenities at other members of the Congressional Black Caucus…spat upon [at least one Black lawmaker] and also used a slur as they confronted Rep. Barney Frank….an openly gay member of Congress…A colleague who was accompanying Lewis said people in the crowd responded by saying "Kill the bill, then the n-word."[2]

What the hell? I was floored when I heard this story. Is this what started your journey, Antoine?

Antoine: Actually, no. When I first got my job at the University of Maryland, my mom came to visit me, and I took her to the museums to learn about the history and culture that DC and the U.S. offers. And our visit there coincided with a Tea Party rally. It was the first one that I've ever been to and the thing that stood out to me was just how angry these people were. And this was not even part of the book I was working on at the time. I didn't have anything on health care or the Tea Party, but just to see the anger that was being espoused and the offensive signs they had made about Obama, showed me that this was something that I needed to look at more closely. And then, as the debate on health care grew and these incidents with John Lewis occurred, I saw the relationship between the Tea Party protests about Obamacare and my work connecting anger and race.

Betty: Antoine, I know you've written papers focusing on Black anger and politics, but for this particular study, why were you looking at whites, race, and anger?

Antoine: A motivating factor was to see whether racism is different from other explanations for opposition to racial policies. There's a debate and a discipline about whether one can distinguish between subtle forms of racism, which scholars and academics tend to refer to as *racial resentment* or

---

[2] William Douglas, "Racism, Homophobia Dominates Tea Party Protest over Health Care Bill," *McClatchyDC*, March 20, 2010.

symbolic racism or *modern racism*, and what we might call *race-neutral conservatism*. I am asking, can we distinguish between racially motivated politics and race-neutral conservatism?

Michael: I think it may be helpful to define the difference between old racism and more recent forms of racism.

Antoine: Pre–civil rights research has shown that the dominant view about prejudice was more biological in what people refer to as "old-fashioned" racism. In old-fashioned racism, Blacks and whites were viewed as biologically different. They could not be considered equal because of the assumed biological differences in race. Old-fashioned racism fueled Jim Crow and segregation and provided a reason for keeping the races separate. That type of thinking grew out of favor, particularly during the civil rights movement, when politicians took a strong stance against segregation, Jim Crow, and this old-fashioned version of racism. As a result, there was the debate about whether racism had gone away because these old-fashioned beliefs weren't there.

But then political scientists and psychologists became interested in whether a new form of racism had emerged and whether that new form of racism wasn't based so much on the notion of biological difference, but a difference in character and values. When we think about *symbolic racism* or *racial resentment*, it is not necessarily that whites harbor views that Blacks are biologically different. It's just that Blacks don't have the same character as whites—they don't work as hard, or they have a propensity for violence. That's what people would consider the attitudes exhibited by this new form of prejudice and racism.

Michael: So, the notion of symbolic racism is that after the post–civil rights movement of the 1950s and '60s, Blacks no longer faced prejudice or discrimination. Therefore their failure is their own fault.

Antoine: Yes.

Michael: They're unwilling to work hard like the rest of us.

Antoine: Yes.

Betty: So, we are looking at the '70s, '80s, and '90s as the time of the rise in symbolic racism when, for instance, during the Reagan era, people would speak of "welfare queens" and attack policies such as welfare, affirmative action, and more recently healthcare reform as enabling the bad habits of these welfare queens. In this regard, healthcare reform is interesting, since it started with Mitt Romney. How did healthcare reform become racialized?

Antoine: That's a great question. There have been two arguments proposed about how that occurred. One is that because Obama attached himself to the policy, it became racialized.

Betty: Simply because of the color of Obama's skin?

Antoine: It's what people refer to as the *spillover of race* and is actually called *the spillover of racialization theory*. Basically, Mark Tesler's argument is that any policy Obama attached himself to became racialized. Health care is a policy that Obama attached himself to and it has become racialized.

Another explanation for symbolic racism is the belief among a segment of whites that they are being discriminated against and that certain minority groups are getting privileges that whites had but are now unable to get. For those white people, this is very anger-inducing and frustrating. Many people who opposed affirmative action had this view. Affirmative action policies were designed as a way of remedying past injustices. We have been a country where, for hundreds of years, Blacks and whites were unequal. There were explicit forms of inequality. As a country, we've sought to rectify that inequality. There has been a debate about how to rectify inequality between whites and Blacks. Are we supposed to just put whites and Blacks on the same playing field and that should fix the problem? Or do we need to help Blacks move further ahead and give them a little bit more to right past wrongs? I think what some Republicans have done is to embrace the notion that pushing Black people ahead a little further hurts white people.

Betty: And this gets translated into the idea that affirmative action is actually a form of discrimination against whites. This obscures the history of slavery and its consequences, where Blacks have been historically subjugated and met with huge barriers to advancement at all levels. Now that they are given some advantages to rectify hundreds of years of historical disadvantage it is perceived as unfair discrimination against whites.

Antoine: Yes, that it's not fair. But to some whites, passing laws about equality was all that was needed. Others believed that to really accomplish equality, we need to give Blacks a leg up. But a lot of people have tried to demonize these types of efforts, and that has been very anger-inducing.

Betty: Antoine, you have mentioned in your writing that Trump is one of the angriest presidents ever. He injects a lot of anger into our social and political system. How do you think that impacts us as a society across the board—whites, Blacks, and other minorities?

Antoine: There's been some data to show that 2016 levels of anger were higher than in any other previous presidential election year. And this was not just among Republicans, but Democrats as well. Trump's rhetoric not only made Republicans pretty angry at Democrats, but it definitely fueled Democrats' anger at Republicans. Both sides were angry, more so than any previous year. It's led to a lot of uncivil rhetoric, to racialized rhetoric. It's led to a lack of compromise. It's led to more polarization. The parties are seen as further apart than they have been in the past. In terms of trying to get legislation done that might help Americans, compromise is essential. We've had a much more difficult time doing that. Government has been shut down, fighting about what we're going to pass. These days we are venturing into new territory.

Betty: I think Obama was quoted in his memoir as saying when he approaches white people, he has to speak slowly and make slow movements, in order to appear not threatening.

Michael: A Black man who is angry is a threat.

Betty: A Black man moving *quickly* is a threat.

Antoine: Obama was in a unique position when he ran for office because we were in the middle of the greatest recession since the Great Depression. In terms of economic factors, this plays an important role in whether people decide to vote for the incumbent party or not. Obama had that going for him. People had a very negative view of our position in terms of the Iraq War and terrorism. Many forecast models showed that mostly any Democrat would have won that election given the circumstances. So, Obama was able to have the right economic and foreign policy positions that allowed him to win. He was also very inspiring and hopeful. That motivated a lot of racial and ethnic minorities to turn out for him in unprecedented numbers. And his opponent, John McCain, was not really the kind to use anger as a tool or weapon to motivate his base. It will be really interesting going forward, to see how Democrats are going to think about using emotions to win the election. Trump is going to continue this anger appeal and message. It's going to be interesting to see how Democrats will counteract that. I think if it's a minority candidate, particularly a woman or Latino or African American, they have to be somewhat careful about the potential backlash they might get from using anger to appeal to people. I think Hillary was really careful in not conveying a lot of anger because she was concerned about such backlash.

Michael: Because then as a woman, you're shrill or you're bossy, all those negative sexist connotations. One of the things, Antoine, that you'd said to me before was that your advice to Democrats was not to talk about race, and I'm curious why you think that.

Antoine: I should be careful about that. Democratic candidates should talk about race in the primaries. But I think as they move to the general election, several indicators suggest that whites tend to hold racially conservative views. Talking to whites about race from a more liberal position might be detrimental to Democratic candidates. I think you might have to go back to the 1960s to find a past presidential election where race was an important, salient issue, and the Democrats won.

Betty: Where it was a part of John F. Kennedy's official platform.

Michael: It's an interesting thing that Democrats purposefully walked away from the South over the issue of race at that time. I think you're right that, after the Civil Rights Act of 1964 and the Voting Rights Act of 1965, many whites thought we had solved the problem of race. Then the next generation thought that Barack Obama's election to the presidency meant that we were in a "post-racial America." We are never beyond race.

Betty: Going back to Obama, he's a wonderful speaker. And he invoked emotions in his campaign speeches and in his ongoing speeches, but he rose on hope. That was his slogan, "Hope." I know, Antoine, that you've done research on the power of hope versus the power of anger. Can you tell us about that? Does hope have as much strength as anger to move people?

Antoine: I've looked at hope, more from the perspective of looking at African Americans and seeing whether hope about the Democratic Party and race cause Blacks to be more engaged or supportive of the Democratic Party. We don't find any evidence that hope causes Blacks to be more supportive of the Democratic Party. And what we mean by *supportive* is that they would be more likely to act on behalf of the Democratic Party. We think this might be because, at the time of the study, Blacks were feeling very pessimistic about race. The Tea Party rhetoric was at an all-time high. Opposition toward Obama was racialized, for example, with the birther movement. The optimism that Blacks felt in 2008 started to dissipate over time. The hopeful message didn't seem to be effective for them over time.

Betty: So, by your studies, hope is not necessarily as big of a motivator as anger?

Antoine: Most of my studies have looked at anger and how it has particularly negative effects when it comes to race. In terms of hope, I haven't really looked at that in terms of people's racial attitudes. I have looked at it in terms of participation, and we haven't found as strong an effect for hope as for anger, at least in the case of Blacks. We have combined hope with enthusiasm and pride, and in those studies it's harder for me to separate one emotion from another.

But when you feel hopeful, you have a sense that the goals that you're trying to reach in the future are achievable. I think that's what Obama did; he instilled the belief that the goals in terms of race and prosperity are very achievable. He influenced people to believe that they can reach those goals. People were motivated to come out and support him. Now, it remains to be seen whether other candidates can do that. In terms of my advice to a politician or presidential candidate who wants to be successful, you want your base to feel angry and hopeful, and the opponent's base to feel anxious about their candidate. When those factors occur, you have the greatest chance of winning in an election.

Betty: So anger can be a weapon for both sides of the aisle. It's a poison pill, or it's a motivating pill, depending on how you choose to look at it. How do you decode the emotional factor of anger and its effect on elections?

Antoine: I look to see whether some politicians or groups are more privileged to being angry than others. How does that maintain the inequalities we have between groups like Blacks and whites, or Latinos and whites—or even men and women. I look to see whether some groups are more privileged, and some groups are emotionally disadvantaged or constrained.

Betty: What do you mean by "privileged to be angry"?

Antoine: I mean, who is allowed to be angry? Are Bernie Sanders, Donald Trump, Howard Dean, and Ronald Reagan allowed to be angry? Do we not penalize them for being angry? Are Hillary Clinton, Barack Obama, Kamala Harris, and Cory Booker allowed to get angry?

If they are not allowed to express anger, that's important information, because anger has its benefits. It's a way to motivate your base; it's a way to seem more passionate about issues; it's a way to seem more competent as there's research to show that people who are angry are seen as stronger leaders. So, if certain groups are more privileged to be angry than others, and anger becomes a greater part of the rhetoric or national discourse on politics...

Michael: ...then you're disqualifying people from being effective candidates and good leaders.

Antoine: Yes. I think Hillary suffered from that because she had to be very poised and calm. She couldn't react with anger. And it had a negative impact on people's belief that she was a good leader, even though she had a lot of knowledge about policy.

Betty: We do want to remember she won the popular vote, which doesn't invalidate the fact that she was not a charismatic candidate.

Michael: I think that's really fascinating, Antoine, because it sounds like you have found that denying people human emotion—namely anger—in their presentation of themselves as political candidates, can be a way of handicapping, if not disqualifying them.

Betty: Well, I mean, is there a way to thread the needle? Can a Kamala Harris or a Cory Booker be angry?

Antoine: I think that the electorate is changing. The U.S. is becoming more diverse. As people of color enter in the electorate more, that dynamic might change. They might want to see their candidate angry. They might want to see someone passionate and emotional like them talk about the particular problems that their community is facing. It might not always be a detrimental or problematic strategy for women or people of color to show their anger as part of their political candidacy. Time will tell.

Betty: This understanding of how emotion—anger or hope—drives politics is essential. And that's what you've pointed out in your book and in conversation and in all your studies. It's so key. Thank you very much.

Antoine: I want to thank you for inviting me to be on your show. I've had a great time sharing my work.

Chapter 16
Why Everyone Hates the Jews

Guests: Susan Fiske and Peter Glick
Episode Aired: February 12, 2019

Susan Fiske is a Eugene Higgins professor of psychology and public affairs at Princeton University, where she investigates stereotypes and emotional prejudices. Susan is author of more than 350 publications, has won numerous scientific awards, and has been elected to the National Academy of Sciences. Peter Glick is the Henry Merritt Wriston professor at Lawrence University. In addition to many research articles, Peter has coauthored or coedited three books, including The Sage Handbook of Prejudice *and, with Laurie A. Rudman,* The Social Psychology of Gender: How Power and Intimacy Shape Gender Relationships.

In the two years before we spoke with Drs. Susan Fiske and Peter Glick, the U.S. had seen a disturbing uptick in hate crimes, especially those directed against Jews and Jewish institutions. From neo-Nazis chanting, "Jews will not replace us" during the Unite the Right rally in Charlottesville, Virginia, between August 11–12, 2017,[1] to the tragic mass murder of worshipping Jews by an avowed white nationalist at the Tree of Life Synagogue in Pittsburgh, Pennsylvania on October 27, 2018, American antisemitism seemed to take on a deadlier thrust. Seeking to understand the roots of this alarming rise, we turned to Dr. Fiske and Dr. Glick to ask, What drives antisemitism today, and how is it different from other kinds of prejudice and hate?

---

[1] Washington Post Staff, "Deconstructing the Symbols and Slogans Spotted in Charlottesville," *The Washington Post,* August 18, 2017, https://www.washingtonpost.com/graphics/2017/local/charlottesville-videos/.

In our conversation, they explain not only how prejudice operates, but that discrimination is not all one thing. By breaking discrimination down into its component parts, they describe that when a dominant group feels their power and privilege threatened by a minority group of "cold and competent" outsiders—like Jews—this creates the most extreme forms of bigotry. Fiske and Glick warn that in stressed sociopolitical circumstances, this bigotry can become violent and even genocidal, as was the case with the Holocaust in World War II and the Rwandan genocide in the 1990s.

Drs. Fiske and Glick's conversation with us on the components of discrimination and antisemitism connects with Eric Ward's Mind of State *discussion on the roots of white nationalism in Chapter 14 and Antoine Banks's insights on how anger drives racialized political attitudes in Chapter 15. All relate to Nancy Rosenblum's (Chapter 10) talk with us on the rise of conspiracism in the U.S. These interconnected themes lead us to highlight this exchange with Susan Glick:*

Susan: I would really pay attention to the disrespect that's implied in this preferential treatment [of non-white others] because being disrespected makes people enraged.

Betty: And shamed. They feel shamed.

Susan: You feel shame, but also pointing it outward, enraged. And especially so when the change is rapid and there isn't time to get used to the idea of being a minority population. When you have rapid change like this, people get anxious and angry and they want to break stuff.

Eric Ward, Antoine Banks, Susan Glick, and Peter Fiske all cite rage, disrespect, and fear of change as driving a sense of a loss of power and privilege felt among certain white Americans. Such anxieties lie at the roots of the January 6, 2021 insurrection attempt, reminding us of Eric Liu's statements in Chapter 23 in our Democracy at Risk *section. He said that as a democracy, we are indeed at a reckoning, and our ability to overcome our racism, our antisemitism—in sum, our anger about shifts of dominance and control in the U.S.—lies at the center of it.*

Interview

Michael: Susan and Peter, along with their colleague Amy Cuddy, have developed something they call the *stereotype content model*, which is what we want to discuss today. We're going to talk about what drives our prejudices from a psychological point of view and especially what drives antisemitism.

I think all of us have sensed a shift in tone in public discourse, whether we're talking about immigration or when "dog whistle" words like *globalist* come up—or when you see how George Soros is invoked by certain people. And then, of course, there was Charlottesville, with neo-Nazis marching, and most horrifically, the attack late last year at the Tree of Life synagogue where Shabbat worshippers were murdered by a neo-Nazi. I think it horrified all of us because it felt like an event more akin to Nazi Germany than the United States. But many people were talking about it as a kind of culmination of Donald Trump's nativist rhetoric and not only his unwillingness to distance himself from the neo-Nazis in Charlottesville, but also his reference to the "good people on both sides."[2] Betty and I invited Susan and Peter here as they have a more nuanced and useful explanation for some of what's going on.

But before we start, I thought maybe one thing we should do is first understand the problem and quantify it, especially in terms of antisemitism in America. The FBI reports that hate crimes targeting Jews and Jewish institutions between 2016 and 2017 have spiked about 37 percent. And there were about 7000 hate crimes reported in the U.S. in 2017, which was approximately a 17 percent increase year to year.[3] And religious-based hate crimes, the kinds we're talking about, constitute about 20 percent of the total number of hate crimes, with Jews and Jewish institutions being the most frequently targeted. They accounted for about 58 percent of all religious-based hate crimes. Muslims were the second most frequent, at about 18 percent. So what's the fuel of this uptick? The economy is doing reasonably well, although people are certainly being displaced. But this is not Germany in the 1930s, or Rwanda in the 1990s. What's going on?

---

[2] Rosie Gay, "Trump Defends White-Nationalist Protestors: 'Some Fine People on Both Sides,'" *The Atlantic,* August 15, 2017, https://www.theatlantic.com/politics/archive/2017/08/trump-defends-white-nationalist-protesters-some-very-fine-people-on-both-sides/537012/.

[3] The Antidefamation League H.E.A.T. Map is an interactive and customizable map detailing incidents of hate, antisemitism, terrorism, and extremism around the country. The map is updated monthly. See https://www.adl.org/resources/tools-to-track-hate/heat-map. The ADL Tracker provides the latest news on antisemitism at https://www.adl.org/adl-tracker. See also Vanessa Roma, "Antisemitic Incidents Are at an All-Time High, the ADL Reports," *NPR,* March 23, 2023, https://www.npr.org/2023/03/23/1165737405/antisemitism-statistics-report-2022-anti-defamation-league.

Peter: Although I think Trump in many ways is an amplifier or permitter of this, these hate crimes have roots that precede Trump and run deeper than him. You are right. It's not Weimar Germany where there was runaway inflation and people were burning money for fuel because it was worthless. But there is this sense of a changing culture and a fear that whites are going to be in the minority and that this will result in a fundamental shift in political power. This perception has been correlated with voter support for Trump. Brenda Major has a great study where she showed that if people are reminded that whites are going to be in the minority in so many years, they were more sympathetic toward Trump.[4] So there's an underlying fear of that change in culture and power. There is also this perception that minorities are doing better than middle-class whites and that they're getting special breaks. They are perceived, as Arlie Hochschild said, as line jumpers, that they've illegitimately moved ahead.[5]

All of this contributed to the emergence of the 1990s ideology of the white genocide conspiracy theory on the very far right in the white nationalist world. It connects the whole anti-immigrant impulse with a conspiracy theory that Jews are plotting the extinction of whites. In connection with your mention of George Soros, I didn't realize, when in Charlottesville the white nationalists were chanting, "Jews will not replace us," that the idea is not that Jews are replacing whites. Rather, the idea is that Jews are behind a conspiracy to bring Brown and Black immigrants into the U.S. to make whites the minority and to manipulate politics so that Democrats will be in charge. The immigrants are basically being used as stooges to bring about this takeover by the Democrats and Jews. Under this ideology, Black and Brown people are not seen as competent enough to carry this out by themselves. They are pawns in a conspiracy run by George Soros or other Jews. And so, it goes right back to the question of who is perceived to have the competence and influence to be able to do this.

Michael: I think it's interesting that you're mentioning Charlottesville. They were actually chanting two things. One was "you will not replace us," and two, "Jews will not replace us." Is that right, Peter?

---

[4] Brenda Major, Alison Blodorn, and Gregory Major Blascovich, "The Threat of Increasing Diversity: Why Many White Americans Support Trump in the 2016 Election," *Group Processes & Intergroup Relations* 21, no. 6 (2018): 931–940. https://doi.org/10.1177/1368430216677304.
[5] Hochschild, A. (2018). *Strangers in Their Own Land: Anger and mourning on the American right.* The New Press.

Peter: Yes. It's absolutely all interconnected in this grand conspiracy theory. In a lot of historical cases where there have been genocides, there were a lot of things happening in the society simultaneously—economic disaster along with cultural change. But as social psychologists, I think symbolic beliefs and culture change can generate fears that can be extremely powerful, even in circumstances where our recession wasn't nearly as bad as the depression that preceded the rise of the Nazis, for instance. Those forces can still be very powerful psychologically. And the other thing I want to say about this is that it's not just a lashing out randomly toward any vulnerable group. That's the kind of Freudian scapegoating idea, which observes when groups are worried about things, they tend to lash out against any group.

Michael: They project onto another group?

Peter: Yes, you project, and what you're projecting is your id, your unconscious impulses on some out-group because it's not acceptable in yourself. My interpretation of this, based on our model, is more that when you fear what's going on and it's occurring on a group-based level, such as the fear that "we" are no longer going to be the dominant and privileged group in society, that you then try to understand why it's happening. If it's a threat to you, it is adaptive to try to understand what the source is. But thinking about technological and social changes or other impersonal historical forces, doesn't really allow you to control this. If there's this one uncanny enemy behind all of this, however, a conspiracy by this enemy who's alien and untrustworthy, then it gives you something to focus on and to blame this whole thing on. And it also gives you a sense of control. There's a plan of action. You can think, "Yes, they're clever, but now we have unmasked them."

Michael: So it's not projection, which is the sort of classic Freudian way of understanding hate or prejudice.

Betty: Projection is a psychoanalytic concept, where we take what's in us that we can't meet and put it off on somebody else. But I don't think that's what Peter's talking about.

Michael: Right. So I think this is actually a good opportunity for us then to shift gears and to turn our focus to the *stereotype content model* that Susan and

Peter have created. It looks at this problem as a function of two different factors, unlike this classic psychoanalytic projection model.

Betty: Yes. The psychoanalytic model is intrapsychic. You have something in you, and you put it off on something else. But what Peter and Susan are doing, and Susan can clarify, is conducting research around how people look at friend or foe, how people see others, those very different from them.

Michael: Right. There are two factors here: whether a group is seen as warm or cold and whether they're seen as competent or incompetent. Susan, is that a fair way to start?

Susan: Yes. I think the easiest way to think about it is to ask, What do you need to know about a new group moving to your neighborhood? What people overwhelmingly tell us is that they want to know, can they be trusted? And so basically, you want to know what their intentions are. And it's kind of a miracle. I'm impressed by how much energy people put into trying to figure out other people's intentions. And the way we talk about it is if their intentions are benign toward you and your group, then you think of them as being warm, trustworthy, and friendly. And if they're not, if they're competitive, exploitative, or hostile, then they're cold. So once you figure out what their intentions are, the other thing you need to know is, Can they act on those intentions? Can they implement them? So, the second thing you need to know is whether they're competent or not. And it's really very simple; we're talking about group perception here. In the U.S., middle-class people, citizens, Christians, both men and women, to varying degrees, are seen as warm and competent. At the opposite extreme are groups that are seen as having no redeeming qualities, so they are seen as being untrustworthy and incompetent. All over the world, homeless people and refugees and undocumented migrants—people without an address, basically—are reacted to with contempt and disgust. They're basically dehumanized.

Betty: So this illuminates another way of looking at a global attitude toward immigrants, which is very useful—it explains why they are the ostracized and unwanted.

Susan: Yes.

Michael: And why we don't have sympathy for the refugees—because there's no warmth. They may not be, in your model, competent, but they're also not warm.

Susan: Yes. And I think part of it is that people don't trust people who don't have an address—that is, who aren't part of the community and aren't accountable because they could move on. So Bedouins and Roma, also known as gypsies, are likewise viewed with contempt and disgust. But there are different kinds of immigrants, and over time they take on different stereotypes. What's interesting in our model is not the "we're all good, they're all bad" part of it that I've just described, but the mixed combinations. So, for example, older people and people with disabilities are seen as well-intentioned, but incompetent. And people express pity toward them.

Betty: So, they would be warm, but incompetent. Low on the competence, but high on the warmth.

Susan: Yes. Pity says, "I feel sorry for you, but only as long as you're sort of below me. And if you become an activist, for example, then you become obnoxious and no longer pitiful."

Betty: So, there's a power dynamic.

Susan: There's definitely a power dynamic. And traditionally, ethnic groups are the butt of ethnic jokes. Depending on the era, it might have been Polish people or Irish people or Italians who have been seen as buffoons. People made jokes about them and did not understand why it was harmful.

Michael: High warmth, low competence.

Susan: Yes.

Michael: But they are not a threat.

Susan: No. Exactly. The other combination brings us to the main topic for today, which is groups that are seen as competent but untrustworthy—and they are the biggest threat to people who subscribe to the stereotypes. They're seen as having resources and the ability to act on their intentions, but they are not one of us and they do not share our values or our goals. All over the world, rich people are seen that way and so are outsider entrepreneurs who move somewhere and become successful locally. Jewish people have been seen this way all over the world. And Chinese people, in their own diaspora, are also seen this way.

Betty: Michael and I are bonding right now.

Susan: There is a particularly volatile emotional reaction that people have to these groups. It's envy. Envy says, "I admire you and you have something I would like. And in fact, I will take it away from you if I can, because you're not one of us."

Betty: This opens up a distinction between envy and jealousy. I think envy has an annihilating aspect to it; envy says, "I want to destroy you. I want to make it not possible for you to have what you have." Jealousy says simply "I covet what you have."

Susan: On that distinction, I think the resting state regarding envied groups is, when circumstances are stable, "going along to get along." Because these competent but untrustworthy entrepreneurs have resources. You shop at their stores; you do business with them. But if there's social breakdown or a demagogue who exploits the latent resentment, then these are the first people to be actively harmed. Genocide is often directed toward people with this combination, in this quadrant.

Michael: One of the things that you note, Susan, is that the Tutsi people in Rwanda were in this quadrant. The Tutsi population of Rwanda was a high-status minority group, and they were blamed for the country's severe economic problems. Is that what you're talking about? Is that one way to look at the genocide of the Tutsi people in Rwanda?

Susan: Exactly. And there are other cases of this. But tragically, the most common case of it really has been Jewish people.

Peter: Yes. I teach a course on the Holocaust, and one of the things I've looked at is various kinds of genocidal attacks historically. And it's often against these more privileged middleman minority groups, these successful entrepreneurial minorities. So one of the interesting things about Rwanda is, although it was a low-tech genocide, like other genocides, it was top down and organized. And the propaganda is something you can look at. It is amazingly similar to Nazi propaganda about Jews. The Tutsi were preferred by Belgian colonizers. They were more educated on average. They had higher status and more power and successful positions. There was a tremendous resentment against them. And it was when crashing coffee prices in Rwanda ruined the economy that this crisis emerged. It is this kind of minority group that gets blamed because they are seen as having the ability to influence these events. So it's very dangerous to be labeled with this kind of competence and success when you're also not trusted.

Michael: There is a danger in being perceived as a competent group.

Peter: Absolutely—there's a danger in it. Here's the way I put it: "Who thinks the Jews are especially clever?" There are two groups who do: Jews and antisemites. This is one thing they agree on, right? It's in-group pride for the Jews, but for antisemites, the idea is that Jews are so clever and conspiratorial that they can control world events. It goes along with an allergic reaction to a globalist view in which the Jews are seen as controlling the world. You've got to be extremely clever, competent, and powerful to be able to do that. That's the kind of enemy you need to destroy because that's an enemy you can't control. So this genocidal violence is legitimated by that view. It's not that other groups don't get attacked, but the groups that are seen as heading this conspiracy are especially dangerous. You can't enslave them. You have to destroy them.

Betty: So what you're saying with this keyword *clever*—which is a stand-in for *competence*—is that this tag is a double-edged sword. It's extremely potent because it holds power, as Susan said. Clever people are powerful, so this is made dangerous by a conspiracy theory. And this narrative becomes extremely powerful in terms of what people do with it in times of strife or scarcity—when the economy crashes or some kind of deleterious thing happens in a country.

Michael: Or you have a demagogue who's going to stoke these flames for the sake of power.

Susan: I want to go back to Arlie Hochschild's book that Peter referenced earlier. There are several ethnographies that have come out in the last few years by people who take seriously the circumstances of blue-collar rural people in the United States and are conducting investigations all over the country. What they have in common is this idea—and this is not drawn from the more extreme groups, but from the more moderate Trump supporters who see themselves as having been patient and hardworking—they value hard work. There's a moral respect for people who work hard, even if they're not making much money. Many of them have had jobs where they got injured, and they're on disability for the rest of their lives. But they want dignity and respect for their values and their hard work. And the story that Hochschild tells is about these people waiting in line for the American dream that's just over the hill. They've been working hard. They've been patient. They've been playing by the rules and standing in line. And then all of a sudden, these elites, people like us or maybe many Jewish people or maybe Obama, are ushered in front of them. Immigrants and women and minorities are seen as receiving preferential treatment.

Michael: And in that narrative, they are not earning it.

Betty: They have not waited in line.

Michael: And so they negate the hard work that I, as a blue-collar rural individual, have done.

Susan: I would really pay attention to the disrespect that's implied in this preferential treatment because being disrespected makes people enraged.

Betty: And shamed. They feel shamed.

Susan: You feel shame, but also pointing it outward, enraged. And especially so when the change is rapid and there isn't time to get used to the idea of being a minority population. When you have rapid change like this, people get anxious and angry, and they want to break stuff.

Michael: So how do you explain someone like Dylann Roof, who walked into the Emanuel AME Church in South Carolina and killed nine African

American parishioners? I mean, does this explain racism in America for you as well? Or is that a different dynamic?

Susan: Well, it depends on the social class of the African Americans. Black professionals are resented the way rich people and successful minorities of any kind are resented.

Michael: Jews.

Susan: And Jews.

Betty: So they are untrusted and have high competence.

Michael: So Obama is a Jew, basically.

Susan: Yes. Black Americans, who are low income, are in the same spot as poor white people. You know, I haven't done an analysis of what Dylann Roof was thinking or what he said before the incident, but...

Michael: Well, pretty much that they were going to take away his white identity. This was an annihilation dynamic.

Susan: So, it's a power struggle.

Michael: Correct.

Susan: You know, interestingly, the fascists in Italy in the 1930s had the same attitude. They put Jews and British people in the same quadrant and saw them as threats. And the cartoons that they drew were identical to the ones that are being drawn today.

Peter: I mean, one thing I want to say about this attitude about Jews and antisemitism: the more things change, the more they stay the same. You have to be a certain age to remember songs by Tom Lehrer, the math professor who wrote satirical songs that were very popular in the 1960s. One of his songs was "National Brotherhood Week." It contained a litany of all of these groups that dislike each other. You know—the Hindus hate the Muslims and vice versa. Protestants hate the Catholics. And the punchline is "and everybody hates the Jews." One of the things about antisemitism that's really difficult for Jewish people is why? Why does everyone hate us? We see ourselves as warm and competent, but it's really been about Jews' historically envied position for 2000 years for various different reasons. Circumstances have changed, but in ways that have always put them into this category—and now we have the antisemitism of the left.

Michael: Right. I was just going to ask about that.

Peter: It's rooted in a realistic conflict between Israel and Palestine. Of course, you can criticize Israeli policy—and Israel has a very right-wing government that I'm not happy about, but this now creates an antisemitic ideology with Jews as the oppressor. We saw this in some of the statements by leaders of the Women's March.[6] So, again, it's putting Jews in that envied space, or that elite space.

Michael: As you say, an envious prejudice.

Peter: So you get this weird combination of agreement on the left and the right—and they are strange bedfellows. You get it from both the Christian extremists and Islamic extremists. And in the West and even in the East, where there pretty much are no Jews, you can find some of these antisemitic conspiracy theories because they're about world finance. I grew up in Squirrel Hill,[7] and it was great, but the thing that worries me about antisemitism, especially when combined with where we're at culturally and technologically, is that via the internet we have all these different social realities. And this fragmentation of news sources and these bubbles that we live in make them echo chambers. This makes it really hard to convince people of there being different narratives. And when you combine that with the historical stereotypes baked into the culture and the background that can be reactivated when fears and worries are being stoked, it's dangerous. And I think one of the things that is stoking hatred is the fear of immigration.

---

[6] The Women's March on Washington first occurred the day after Donald Trump's inauguration in 2017. See also Anna North, "The Women's March Changed the American Left. Now Anti-Semitism Allegations Threaten the Groups Future," *Vox*, December 21, 2018, https://www.vox.com/identities/2018/12/21/18145176/feminism-womens-march-2018-2019-farrakhan-intersectionality.

[7] A Jewish neighborhood in Philadelphia.

Michael: Which Trump is fomenting.

Peter: Right. That's partly what has made antisemitic conspiracy theories grow and gain more attention and more traction out of this very small dark corner of the U.S. The other thing is that there is an asymmetry between competence and warmth perceptions. And this is a part of our theoretical perspective. We ask: what does it take to prove that you're competent, versus what it takes to prove that you're warm? In the example that Susan gave of railroad laborers, the Chinese are going to be perceived as mere laborers, rather than competent elites. But when they are entrepreneurs and child prodigies, and when they are 30 percent of the people getting college degrees in California's higher education system, then all of a sudden, they're competent. So the switch from being seen as incompetent to competent is relatively easy to make. Now changing warmth perceptions—that's more difficult. If people mistrust you, how do you prove that you're trustworthy and warm? Because you might have been perceived as having all sorts of nefarious reasons for acting trustworthy and warm. The whole conspiracy theory about Jews is also the stab-in-the-back theory—it's Judas's kiss.

Betty: You're always suspect.

Peter: We can think about this in terms of a marriage gone bad. Once, these two people loved each other and trusted each other. But then sometimes relationships go bad and that trust can't be restored. No matter what the one person who lost the trust of the other does, their actions might always be seen as being from ulterior motives. A conspiracy is a notoriously hard thing to disprove. By its very nature, a conspiracy is the secret thing that's been hidden.

Michael: Jonathan Swift said, "A lie can travel halfway around the world, while the truth is still putting on its shoes."[8] And I think that's what you're talking about.

Peter: Yes. And that's actually been empirically studied. Lies on Facebook or the internet actually do travel faster than the truth.

---

[8] Quote Investigator, https://quoteinvestigator.com/2014/07/13/truth/.

Betty: What Susan, and you, Peter, speak to by naming the internet as an amplifier of prejudice and as taking antisemitism out of the dark corners while exacerbating the bubbles of people who think the same thing and feed off each other, highlights the influence of this technological information revolution that we're in right now. We are online and in contact with each other in ways that we never have been in previous generations. This is a part of the perfect storm of amplification Trump uses so effectively. As competent elites, or as people who want to think about these things from all sides, how can we use your model of thinking about prejudice?

Susan: I would say that interdependence is the key. This is the kind of contact that both Peter and I experienced growing up. I grew up in Obama's neighborhood in Hyde Park in Chicago. Even as an adult, if your boss says the two of you are on a team together and your bonus depends on your performance, people get over it. They get over their in-group/out-group perceptions quite reliably when they need to. There's about 50 years' worth of research on the "contact hypothesis," which is not about food festivals and flags. It's about being on the same team with somebody and having shared goals that matter to you. And then people get to know each other better, and they get over their biases against each other. A lot of the people who are the most biased against Jewish people don't know anybody who's Jewish. And the same with Latin immigrants. The farther people are from the border, the more prejudiced they are against Mexicans.

Betty: So as we start up with the 2020 presidential election cycle, applying the contact hypothesis, would you say the task is for politicians, campaign managers, political leaders to use language that says we're on the same team, rather than reinforcing the polarized positions of right versus left?

Susan: Yes.

Peter: Absolutely.

Susan: And that we're a nation of immigrants.

Peter: Earlier, in a very sympathetic way, Susan captured that feeling among the eroding white middle class, the blue-collar heartland people. I live in that heartland now, where hardworking people feel that they have not been listened to and are the subject of derision from elites. For politicians and people with influence, breaking through that condescension is the crucial task.

Susan: We actually have data on this. If you watch high-powered, high-status people talking down to people with less power and less status, if they want to get along, they talk down. They patronize them. They use a dumber vocabulary. They don't talk about competence and achievement themes. They literally talk down, as if those with less status are dumb. So the stereotype is that the high-status person is smart, and the low-status person is less smart…

Michael: Or "incompetent," in your model?

Susan: Exactly. And people are no idiots. They realize they're being patronized.

Betty: So there's not a meeting of people with different socioeconomic statuses that's on the level. Power is pre-established in the way those of higher status treat people.

Michael: Is this how people perceived Hillary Clinton?

Susan: Yes.

Peter: Absolutely. Either you're patronizing or you're ridiculing, right? You're having contempt for us. So, her "basket of deplorables" comment was really damaging.

Michael: It was absolute confirmation that "yes, look, they think I'm incompetent. I'm an idiot. I'm unworthy."

Susan: It's never wrong to respect somebody else. That's my takeaway from this.

Michael: Especially if you're running for president.

Susan: We just want to be decent human beings.

Peter: We have to bring people in. But it's particularly tough, because one comment like that looms really large because people see it as revealing what you truly think. So all the nicey-nice stuff is not going to work. It's going to take a lot to make up for one negative comment.

Michael: That's the authentic moment.

Peter: Right. For Jewish people, when the Bernie Madoff scandal happened, I was like "oh my God, a bad Jew," like 99.9 percent of us can be great. And then you have that one scandal or now we have the Sackler family.[9]

Michael: And the Sackler family fuels the exact kind of antisemitic confirmation you're talking about.

Peter: That's exactly right. If it is a non-Jewish family, nobody notices that status. If it's malfeasance by a minority or group like the Jews who are marked as different, it's going to be picked up, at least in the mind of the right-wing extremist, the white nationalist…

Michael: You know, recently *The New York Times* had a big scandal with Alice Walker in the book review section, and I think we are mistaken if we talk about this only in the context of the political right, because the left is also susceptible to this.[10] She endorsed a book by a man named David Icke, who posits that the world is run by a secret cabal, literally of lizard people. Among other things in the book was not just Holocaust denial, but a belief that Jews funded the Holocaust. Much of the controversy wasn't just that she endorsed this very ugly antisemitic book, but that *The New York Times* put it out there without any context, any challenge, any note that this is ugly

---

[9] The Sackler family founded Purdue Pharma whose main drug was OxyContin, largely seen as the main contributor to the opioid epidemic that has ravaged millions across the United States. A court just granted the family immunity in exchange for a $6 billion opioid settlement. Samantha Delouya, "Court Grants Sackler Family Immunity in Exchange for a $6 Billion Opioid Settlement, *CNN Business,* May 30, 2023, https://www.cnn.com/2023/05/30/business/sackler-purdue-opioid-liability/index.html. However, on August 10, 2023, the Supreme Court blocked the agreement pending review. See Abbie VanSickle and Jan Hoffman, "Supreme Court Pauses Opioid Settlement with Sacklers Pending Review," *The New York Times,* August 10, 2023, https://www.nytimes.com/2023/08/10/us/supreme-court-purdue-pharma-opioid-settlement.html.

[10] "Alice Walker: By the Book," *The New York Times,* December 13, 2018, https://www.nytimes.com/2018/12/13/books/review/alice-walker-by-the-book.html.

antisemitic stuff. So people were mad, mostly at *The New York Times*, more than at Alice Walker, for effectively creating fertile ground for conspiracy theory. I mean, so it's not just coming from right-wing nutcases on the fringes. This is happening in the mainstream media, too.

Peter: That's all scary.

Betty: Indeed.

Peter: I think there is neglect on the part of *The New York Times*, rather than an active prejudice. And hopefully this stuff is still more on the fringes. The problem is that it's gaining some traction. And the more that fear is stoked, the more that we have these fragmented sources of news and social bubbles, the more that this might persist. Again, you can't disprove a conspiracy theory. It's really hard for somebody who believes it. They can say the Holocaust didn't happen. Well, you can say, "What about Auschwitz?" Then they come back with "Well, they constructed that stuff. They made it look that way. Of course they have a conspiracy, and they have influence and money, and so they're using this to political advantage." So these assertions have all got this internal logic that is really hard to stamp out. Hopefully, though, there is this counterreaction from the majority that once this stuff exposes itself, that it is not worth buying into and, in fact, maybe it is essential to react against it.

Susan: I would say a takeaway message is that people can be allies of groups that they don't belong to.

Michael: And we need to be vigilant about ways in which these conspiracies can seep in without us being aware of them.

Betty: And we can be vigilant about—as you said, Susan—about being human. That being decent and respectful to each other is not just a default mode, but it is actually quite difficult.

Michael: You know, we've had our guests bring up common themes. And I think one of the themes that is resonant, is that we as a society, as a country, are unsure of our story. There isn't a unifying story out there. And if we are the story that we tell about ourselves, and if, right now, there are a lot of competing stories about who we are, then that conflict—internal and external—is inevitable.

Susan: Yes.

Peter: That's really well put.

Chapter 17
The Perilous Path to Asylum

Guest: Dr. Hawthorne "Hawk" Smith
Episode Aired: March 19, 2019

Dr. Hawthorne "Hawk" Smith is a clinical psychologist and program director of the Bellevue Program for Survivors of Torture (PSOT), which provides comprehensive medical, legal, psychiatric, psychological, and social services for asylum seekers. He is also an associate clinical professor at the NYU School of Medicine in the Department of Psychiatry. Dr. Smith is a recipient of the Robin Hood Foundation's Hero Award and the International Youth Leadership Institute's W. E. B. Du Bois Award. He was a cofounding member of Nah We Yone, Inc., a nonprofit organization working with refugees and other displaced Africans in New York, and he helped coordinate the International Youth Leadership Institute (IYLI), a leadership program for marginalized New York City teens. Dr. Smith is also a professional musician, a saxophonist, and a vocalist with international experience.

Immigration policy has been a hot-button issue in the United States for decades, and when we spoke with Dr. Hawk Smith in March 2019, tensions were particularly high. Then-President Donald Trump had implemented a number of policies hostile to immigrants. This included the separation of families at the Mexico/U.S. border and the Muslim travel ban, which prevented citizens of several Muslim-majority countries from entering the U.S. And, from December 22, 2018 to January 25, 2019, the federal government experienced the longest shutdown in American history due to Trump's stalemate with Congress over funding for his border wall, intended to bar Mexican migrants from crossing the Mexico/U.S. border.

Four years later, partisan battles over immigration have only continued, if not intensified. In February 2023, the governor of Florida, Ron DeSantis, a Republican, sent an airplane full of Venezuelan asylum seekers to Massachusetts. A month later, the Republican governor of Texas, Greg Abbott, sent busloads of migrants to Washington, DC, New York, and Chicago. Both asserted that liberal-leaning states and cities like Massachusetts, Washington DC, New York, and Chicago, not Texas and Florida, should take on the burdens of immigrant influx as a consequence of their leniency on immigration. Democrats and immigration advocates counter-argued that DeSantis's and Abbott's acts were inhumane, opportunistic stunts designed to score political points with their conservative base.[1]

Rising above all this fragmenting noise, Dr. Hawk Smith's discussion with us touches upon the real-life complexities, confusions, and nuances of seeking asylum in the U.S. From within the trenches of the overwhelmed and overwhelming U.S. immigration process, Dr. Smith poses useful and re-orienting big-picture questions:

Maybe we need to have a conversation about who we are as a nation. Do we draw on this nationalistic momentum or do we adhere to what's written at the bottom of the Statue of Liberty? How do all of us who have immigration histories in our families—and we all do, some of us with forced immigration histories—deal with those who want in? Do we shut the door on those coming in who might be fleeing persecution? Is it a question of "us versus them," or is it a question of "us?" Are we spending so much time talking about "them"—those people, those aliens, those illegals—that we forget that we're talking about people who seek freedom, people who seek a better life and are trying to do something to help move this country forward? When does it become "us?" I think that we need to have those conversations in ways that aren't so tribalized...And in having those conversations, perhaps that's part of the key to unlocking some solutions in terms of how do we get more smartly placed resources to make this system—I won't say easier—but let's say, less difficult.

[1] Will Sennott, Zolan Kanno-Youngs, Eileen Sullivan, and Patricia Mazzell, "With Faraway Migrant Drop-Offs GOP Governors Are Doubling Down," *The New York Times*, September 15, 2022, https://www.nytimes.com/2022/09/15/us/desantis-abbott-migrants-immigration.html; David Kihara, "DeSantis, Abbott Taunt Democrats with Controversial Immigration Moves," Politico, July 19, 2023, https://www.politico.com/news/2023/07/19/desantis-abbott-immigration-00106902.

By pointing out that less-tribalized conversations are a key to rediscovering who we are and who we want to be as a nation, Dr. Smith joins with Susan Fiske and Peter Glick (Chapter 16), Scotty McClennan (Chapter 9), Anton Hart (Chapter 8), and Eric Liu (Chapter 23) in recognizing that respect, decency, and openness are central to this effort. Only then can we consider if it is our aim to fulfill the lines of the poem Dr. Smith cites, written at the bottom of the Statue of Liberty:

> Give me your tired, your poor,
> Your huddled masses yearning to breathe free,
> The wretched refuse of your teeming shore.
> Send these, the homeless, tempest-tost to me,
> I lift my lamp beside the golden door![2]

Interview

Betty: You know, when I read your bio and I get to "professional musician, saxophonist, and vocalist" on top of your work as a clinical psychologist, human rights advocate, and champion of marginalized and immigrant teens, I think you might just qualify for the title "Most Interesting Man in the World."

Hawthorne "Hawk" Smith: (*laughs*) I wasn't nervous until you gave me that introduction, but now...

Betty: (*laughs*) OK, I don't want to make you more nervous—so without further ado, let's get onto more serious topics. Hawthorne, or Hawk, as I know you to be, tell me about the new change in immigration policy. I know this is something you want to highlight—and it's very interesting.

Hawk: Yes. We're talking about the asylum process. And it's something I've been involved with, through the Program for Survivors of Torture, for these past 23 years.

We've seen a lot of recent changes that have been really daunting. We're seeing a system that is increasingly not systematic at all. People are paying a very severe and significant psychological cost while being involved in this

---

[2] Lazarus, E. (1883). "The New Colossus"

system. The programs have been identified by the acronyms FIFO and LIFO—FIFO stands for "first in first out, and LIFO for "last in first out."

To explain the system, let's assume, for example, Betty, you came to the States and applied for asylum three years ago. And I just show up today and I'm applying for asylum now. "First in first out," or FIFO, would signify that your case will be treated before mine, as a first-come-first-serve sort of thing, which makes logical sense.

Betty: And it's been an average of about a two- to three-year wait?

Hawk: Exactly, the system is very backlogged right now. But recently there has been a change in policy from FIFO to LIFO, or "last in *first* out," meaning that, even though you were here three years before me, if I come in and apply, my case will be treated first, before yours. The rationale behind this is the assumption that most people coming to the U.S. to apply for asylum are applying frivolously, and these cases really have no legal standing. With the understanding that the system is so backlogged right now, there is a fear on the part of the Trump administration that people will apply with frivolous cases just to get into the system. They will then be able to get employment authorization and other documents so they will be here in the country working for four or five years while they adjudicate their case. The new LIFO policy is basically an expression of the assumption that those who have applied for asylum in the U.S. are lying.

Betty: So the example you created, of my having been here three years waiting for asylum, would be cause for assuming I am a liar?

Michael: And you're also assumed to be a liar if you walk in the door today?

Hawk: While I don't want to prejudge what the government is saying, it does presume that among those people coming in seeking asylum, there are a lot of frivolous cases. LIFO allows the government to deal with "the last in first" as a way to get them out of the way, so they don't get into the system and get work authorization, etc.

Betty: I see.

Michael: Can you take a step back and tell us why, in your experience, someone seeks asylum? The assumption of the Trump administration seems to be that we should be turning all refugees away, that we should be working hard to deter people from even showing up at our door.

Hawk: Yes. And now to get to your initial question about who the people coming to seek asylum are—oftentimes I do trainings on this subject, and I'm speaking to a crowd that might not be as well-versed in what's going on. I start by asking a few questions. I ask people to raise their hands, for example, if they have ever voted in an election or if they have ever written a letter to the editor, which immediately dates me as an old guy. Or I'll ask, have they ever written a blog post? Or if anyone belongs to an identifiable religious group, or if they *don't* belong to an identifiable religious group? Do they identify as a woman? Do they have relatives or are they close to somebody who has a sexual orientation other than heterosexual?

Then I'll stop and say, "Okay you're probably wondering, who is this guy, and why is he asking all these intrusive and semi-inappropriate questions? The answer is that, if you raised your hand to any of those questions I just asked, I can say that the people we are treating at the Bellevue Program for Survivors of Torture are people just like you." We are not looking at an exotic "other" when we're looking at torture survivors or people who are fleeing persecution. It really is a question of a shared humanity.

Michael: There's the presumption that the people who are seeking refuge are going to be criminals or maybe even terrorists.

Hawk: Yes. There's a great deal of fear, and I think there's a lot of misunderstanding regarding who these people are. I think that it is extremely important in the discussion of asylum to look at what's written at the bottom of the Statue of Liberty: "Give me your tired, your poor, / Your huddled masses yearning to breathe free, / The wretched refuse of your teeming shore." These are the people this country has always supposedly stood for. These are the people coming and seeking solace and seeking safety under very harrowing circumstances. Literally, in the last two or three weeks, we have had families referred to us from detention centers in Laredo, Texas, along the border with Mexico, who were paroled on humanitarian grounds, but who were given their next address as 462 First Avenue, New York, New York. That's our address at Bellevue Hospital. They were just sent to us. And people coming from Central Africa who are detained at the border after a very long, arduous journey, but coming through the correct way and at the correct places, and then just being sent to us. Good luck, with no bus ticket, nothing, and they are forced to find a way to New York. We've had a couple of occasions where we've seen families arrive and come up to our offices on the seventh floor with suitcases. They are quite surprised to find out that we're not a hotel or hostel. And then we have to scramble.

Michael: And what are their experiences? Who are they?

Hawk: Often they have been involved in opposition politics against dictatorial regimes in their home countries, such as the Democratic Republic of the Congo, where there has been ongoing violence since 1997 for many really complex reasons. There are incredible natural resources in the eastern part of Congo, including uranium and cobalt, which is used in our cell phones. Those minerals are being exploited. And that is also where there's a great deal of violence. There has been a regime in place since late 2001 after the assassination of Kabila, the first president. The second president, his son, came in and trampled on the constitution by extending his presidency beyond the two-mandate limit. People are pushing back and those people who push back are horribly abused and detained and oftentimes forced to flee the country, often across the border into the country right next to it, where, again, as we always say, "If you're fleeing a war-torn, chaotic, impoverished nation, seems like four out of five times, you're crossing the border into another war-torn, chaotic, impoverished nation."
Betty: So it's a frying pan-into-the-fire kind of situation.

Hawk: Exactly. And then they hope that this will finally be the end of their journey. And what we are seeing now is that this country has become another frying pan.

Betty: We're becoming another frying pan, as evidenced by the language of the U.S. Citizenship and Immigration Services (USCIS): "paroled," "detained," "frivolous." It points to a criminalization of immigration and asylum seekers. And I want to ground us in the fact that these are people who have been subjugated in their own countries. They flee, coming to us with hopes of encountering a country that will improve their lives, and they get detained. And how long are they detained? Have the families who have arrived at your offices from the Democratic Republic of the Congo been detained?

Hawk: It can be a wide range. For a couple of the recent families that were just sent to us, the detention was not long at all. It was only a few days. We've had other clients from other countries who were detained for well over a year and, oftentimes, some of their cases were adjudicated while they were in detention.

So, again, as I mentioned up front, it is a system that is becoming less systematic and more capricious over time. This lack of control and lack of knowing what's coming next is also something that weighs heavily on the emotions of survivors. For people who have been here for three years and are still waiting for that initial asylum interview and now are being told that they're being placed at the end of the line, it is emotionally wrenching. It has a negative impact on their functioning, when everyday could be the day that they get the notice they're going to get an interview, and every day they go to the mailbox, every day to check that out. And it doesn't come. It doesn't come.

So they have no sense of control. They go to the USCIS website, and all they see is that their case is pending. They have no more information; all the while they're getting calls from their family back in their home country. This is one of the most wrenching things because we actually begin to see families disintegrate; they have been here for two-and-a-half, three years. There's no progress, and then someone back in their home country might begin to express doubt that a spouse might have found a new family asking, "Have you given up on us?" We deal with parents who have not seen their children for years. We view these wrenching images of what's going on at our southern border now. But for many of the family separations we don't have images of, are those people who came over the "correct" way and who have been sitting in this system for three years, while their children or their spouses are sitting behind a firewall in a very chaotic, dangerous place.

Betty: And once they get a hearing, what do they hope for? They're looking for a ratification of their asylum status? Then they can seek citizenship or seek work permits, a green card—a way to stay here?

Hawk: Yes. Often the asylum process moves so slowly now that one might be able to get employment authorization while still in process. I think that this points to some of the reasoning behind the LIFO policy—the government doesn't want people waiting in this long process and still able to work. They want to get the "frivolous" cases out. But what the asylum seekers want is a normalization of their status, so that they are considered to be here legally while their case is pending. And they are not illegal in any sense. They're not fully documented, but they are legal in the United States while their case is pending.

The first step is usually an asylum interview at the level of the asylum office. We find that it's a very high bar to get your asylum granted at the level of the asylum office, even with the assistance of our program. Oftentimes, we do a little stress inoculation with our clients by telling them that if you don't get it at that level, if you are referred to the immigration court, it doesn't mean they didn't believe your case. It doesn't mean that you have a weak case, but the asylum officers don't have the authority to grant asylum as readily as an immigration judge does.

Betty: Have you seen the number of cases approved go down in the last couple years?

Hawk: Yes, there are statistics showing that the level of approvals is going down. But what we are really struggling with is how slowly these cases are moving. Even if someone has a strong case, what might have taken two or three years before, now might easily take four or five years.

Michael: What's the cause of that? Is it just that the system is overloaded?

Hawk: The system is overloaded, and there have been times with the situation at the southern border that asylum officers have been relocated and sent there to deal with that situation. So we don't have as many asylum officers at Lyndhurst, New Jersey, or in Rosedale, Queens, where they adjudicate cases here in the New York Metropolitan area. Also, when people seeking asylum go to the asylum office and it doesn't work at that level, they are referred to immigration court, and it's at that level that they will see the immigration judge. That's where we have more of a chance to bring in expert witnesses who can provide affidavits. We help prepare people to tolerate what is generally intolerable in terms of the process, so they can hang in there.

I've heard statistics that only 25 to 40 percent of asylum cases that are adjudicated are actually successful. At our program, we have about a 97 percent success rate. Some of that is due to a selection bias, in that we are getting some of the more highly traumatized people. Also, we are able to provide the support to help them tolerate this process. We help provide medical and psychological affidavits. We can help get *pro bono* attorneys. We help solidify their cases. But, again, most people are not able to get to a program like ours. People are knocking on the door, and our waiting list is extensive.

Michael: How many people do you help right now?

Hawk: We helped between 400 to 500 people last year, in terms of active cases...

Michael: And how long is your waiting list?

Hawk: At the time, we had to push the pause button on our waiting list because of staffing issues. Our waiting list was approaching a year. For people in distress, and particularly now with this LIFO policy, some people coming in now are getting court notices that require them to be there in four to six weeks. At that point, they probably have not found a lawyer.

Betty: So they are ill-prepared for that hearing.

Hawk: Ill-prepared and perhaps they have fallen prey to some less-than-reputable services within the community. For instance a lot of my French-speaking clients talk about *les conseillers de la rue* or street lawyers who do a slipshod job. And if you go there now and your story is not airtight or there are contradictions, or things don't make sense, the bar is even higher.

Betty: So in a way, both policies— "last in first out," or "first in last out"— are hurting people on either ends of this waiting list. The people coming in first don't have the time to prepare a viable case in front of USCIS, and then the people who have been waiting are falling apart and not getting their hearings. They're being bumped to the back of the line. They're waiting even longer. This whole thing is a subjugation or a persecution of people who are seeking asylum. It's to harm them.

Hawk: Well, you're absolutely correct that people on both ends of this equation are suffering. I hesitate to go so far as to say that it's purposefully to harm them. But there is harm being committed; people are definitely suffering. I remember I had a group session—I run a support group for French-speaking African survivors that's been up and running for about 22 years now. And there was a particular session where a gentleman from Guinea said, "You know what, I'm done; I'm going home. My kids are calling me. I can't do anything for them. I'm going home. I know I'll be killed. I know as soon as the authorities find out that I'm back in the country, they will kill me."

Michael: What did he do that he thinks his life is in danger?

Hawk: He spoke up in terms of corruption. He spoke up in terms of human rights and the rights of women regarding FGC/M.

Michael: Female genital mutilation?

Hawk: That's correct. He spoke up on these issues, and he suffered greatly for it. Anyway, he was saying, "I'm ready to go home, because at this point, I can't hug my babies. And if I go home, I know they'll kill me, but maybe I'll have a few days. Maybe I'll have a couple of weeks where I can hug my babies, because I can't even do that now."

And people in the group really responded to support him with the different ways they shared their stories. For example, there was a gentleman from Brazzaville, Congo, who talked about when he first came to the United States and how he had set up a way to get into the airport. It had to be when a particular officer who had been bribed was there to get him on the plane, because he was being sought again for political opposition. And when it came time, he received the message, "Okay you need to get to the airport now. You need to be here within sixty minutes. We're flying." But his older son wasn't home. And he waited as long as he could. He couldn't wait any longer. He left. And when he got to the United States and he first activated his cell phone, all he saw were text messages from his son.

"Daddy, you didn't even say goodbye to me."

And so his first few days in this country, he just wandered around like a zombie. "How do I respond? My son."

So he shared this painful story, but then he was also able to talk about the fact that he has now successfully adjudicated his asylum case. He's in the process of trying to reunite with his family. What he said to the gentleman from Guinea, which I thought was very poignant, was, "You can no longer think about your family as the family you left behind. You have to think about the family that you're moving toward, that is in front of you, because if you place them in this context—that you're moving toward this, that you're working, you're going through this horrific pain right now, but they're in front of you—that will give you the strength to persevere. But if you think of them as behind you, you will drown." And it's this sort of insight, it's this sort of mutual support that our clients give one another. They can speak more poignantly to the suffering because they're involved in it. They're really walking in those shoes, and that's what we try to provide.

Michael: So that young gentleman who successfully adjudicated his case, he's the gentleman who came here and found the text messages from his son who he didn't say goodbye to?

Hawk: Yes.

Michael: In his future self, does he have any reasonable hope of reuniting with his family or not?

Hawk: Yes, that is in process now. This is one of the things that we really work with our clients on. As arduous as this is, one of the only tools we have left is this notion of hope that our clients have. And this person who was able to successfully adjudicate and get his asylum is now in the process of family reunification. There are things around DNA tests and tickets and visas, blah, blah, blah. But if an adult wins asylum, then their biological children under the age of 21 can be covered within that. So we're in the midst of trying to make that happen. And again, it's a question of resources. Even getting a family plane tickets from Brazzaville, Congo, to New York is not easy. Things like that.

Betty: And how many years have they been separated?

Hawk: It's been about five years.

Betty: So without any kind of policy change or persecution or attack on immigrants and immigration, this is the process that has been in place for decades. This is the challenge of seeking asylum in the United States.

Hawk: Yes, that's very accurate. But I do think that what has been happening recently turns up the temperature in terms of anxiety or the potential for hopelessness. For instance, street rumors get going that raise anxiety. We've had entire group sessions focus on a text going around that went viral: "Do not take the train up to 125th Street because they're rounding up all the Guineans on 125th Street and sending folks back to Guinea." And it wasn't true. But it's enough to make someone not want to leave their apartment, not come to their appointments, not go to work. It's getting in the way.

Betty: Not go to their hearing appointments, perhaps?

Hawk: Perhaps, that's right.

Betty: So where do you think these viral text messages and rumors are coming from? Is it from somebody in the community who gets anxious and hears something? Is it a result of our environment becoming very heightened and antagonistic toward immigrants? Are people hypervigilant about not getting stopped on the street and sent home in a second?

Hawk: Yes. I couldn't identify the particular source of the text, but I definitely think that the environment and the anxiety that is prevalent can increase the number of rumors that go around and, moreover, change the way they're heard. We work with different partners, like Lutheran Social Services, to provide "know your rights" trainings for our clients and inform them of what to do if someone approaches them on the street. What to do if someone knocks at their door and identifies themselves as an immigration officer. What sort of rights they have, for example, the right to ask for a warrant, the right to speak with their lawyer before engaging with immigration folks, perhaps even the right to use their phone to record what is happening. The training instructs them in the different sort of steps they can take. A lot of times what is being said in the neighborhood contradicts the notion that they have rights and tells them they are absolutely powerless. And we let them know that they do have legal status. You have applied. Your case is pending.

Michael: You can't just get kicked out.

Hawk: Exactly.

Michael: I'm curious, if you look back at the Obama years or, before that, to George W. Bush's administration—do you see those as the golden years? One of the things that the Obama administration missed was they were quite hard on immigrants. And I wonder if, in the Trump era, we look back and don't honestly assess that what we've actually been doing—which is being less than generous—for a very long time, regardless of which political party or administration has been in office.

Hawk: I think that's fair. I came into this work in 1995. There were landmark immigration laws passed in 1996 during the Clinton administration. It made things harder. We had the 12-month bar that was put into effect, which stipulated that, if you didn't apply within 12 months of arriving in the country, it made things much more difficult to adjudicate. I cannot point to any "golden era" with this asylum process. It has always been hard. It's always been an uphill struggle. Over the course of the time that I've done this work, I think the majority of cases I have seen go through this process have been denied. But now, there is more anxiety in a system that is becoming less systematic. I'm actually on call right now for an asylum hearing that was scheduled for this afternoon, but we just got notice yesterday that they switched it to this morning.

Betty: So it's just very idiosyncratic, spontaneous, and you just have to deal with these last-minute shifts?

Hawk: Folks are very powerless to change that, especially at the last minute. And you don't want to say, "Oh we're not available in the morning. Please reschedule the case," because then it might be a considerable amount of time before you have that opportunity again. One thing that seems to be systematic is that there were only a few people who they planned to deport. But then the courts overturned that because their notices to appear in immigration court didn't have a specific time or date. They were just "date to be determined." So the courts determined that it was impossible to calculate the amount of time someone has overstayed if they never had an appearance in immigration court. In response to that court ruling, what has happened in the last year or so is that we're actually beginning to see some people get notices to appear—whether before the asylum office or in the courts—with dates that are fictional. We've had people getting the date for an asylum appearance of September *31,* which, of course, is a date that doesn't exist, or they have been requested to come in at midnight, when the courts are closed.

Betty: And are they delivering these nonexistent dates and times on purpose?

Hawk: Yes, I think at first they were doing it to make sure that there was some date on paper by which they could calculate an applicant's overstaying and then move to deport them. But, of course, the courts started looking to see if it was a fictional date. The immigration authorities have since learned from their mistakes and people are now getting court notices or notices to appear before the asylum office with legitimate dates—but now, it is for appointment times that are not actually scheduled within the court calendar. So people might show up to see the asylum officer on a particular date to find they're not even on the docket. So this is something that lawyers are beginning to look at now.

Betty: So there's a date that the asylum seeker gets notice to come to court for, and yet there's no such appointment recorded within the court system.

Hawk: The immigration authorities didn't want to put a "date to be determined" on their notice because they know that might have ramifications later down the line. It's just another example of how this system is becoming less and less systematic, less and less reliable. Imagine being an asylum seeker and you get this letter. It says you must show up at this particular date. So you speak with your lawyers, who go onto the website and check. They see that you're not on the docket and they say, "You know what? Ignore that. You don't have to go that day." And the asylum seeker says, "Wait a minute. I have a letter that says I have to go." Again, this raises anxiety and the wish to push back, or to not go through the system at all. It feels like there's a lot of punishment or at least perceived punishment. People think, "I'm trying to do all these things the right way, but it doesn't seem like it's working out in my favor. They're giving me years to wait or they're rushing me before I can even get ready, or they're giving me a notice to appear for a hearing or an interview that doesn't even exist."

Betty: Hawk, do you think this is a breakdown of a system? Because we're seeing the temperature around immigration heat up. And, as you just said, it's always been bad. It's always been difficult to be an immigrant coming into the United States. And if we look back, what comes to mind for me is post-9/11. Immigration to the U.S. got really difficult post-9/11 because of the perception that people outside the U.S. were going to come here and do violence to Americans. At the time, immigration controls and airport security tightened enormously, and more people were detained. Even citizens with U.S. passports, who were profiled because they were brown people, were detained.

And now it seems worse. What's happening seems chaotic. What you describe of the immigration and asylum-seeking process sounds like an absurdist, dystopian bureaucracy for which a Cheshire Cat is the guide, pointing in different directions all at once. So where does this come from? Is Trump's scapegoating and overall othering of immigrants during his campaign and throughout his presidency creating more chaos in the USCIS system—or is this a result of ongoing historic negligence?

Hawk: I think there's no doubt that the issues surrounding immigration and asylum seekers are very active and very potent in the current political sphere. And they're being used in different ways, particularly by this administration.

But I also think that there are multiple factors contributing to what is happening now. There is more distress around the world, and people are trying to flee the strife in their homelands and come to this country. And our resources are not adequate to respond to that influx. We talk about the people who are coming in. We talk about the political aspect. Sometimes we forget to talk about the service providers in the immigration service who are caught in between.

I had the opportunity to do a training for the asylum office in Lyndhurst, New Jersey. The service providers also face an enormous amount of stress, anxiety, and pressure. There are people knocking on their doors who have been waiting for so long. And the service providers want to have more time to deal with the three or four cases they might have to deal with that day. They also feel constrained by some of the bureaucratic restrictions that they have to deal with. And they have to deal with how they are perceived.

I was giving a talk on provider wellness. And I asked folks, "When you go to a cocktail party or grab a beer with people you don't know, do you identify yourself as an asylum officer?" There were about 75 officers there, and maybe 5 or 6 raised their hands. Then I asked, "Well, do you identify what do you do for a living? How many say, 'I work for the government,' or something like that?" And maybe another dozen hands went up. And I asked, "Well how many of you make up some stuff—like, 'I'm an airplane pilot' or whatever?" And a bunch of hands went up, and there was a little bit of laughter. But at the same time, one of the officers said, "You know, it's funny. No one knows what we do. If you watch Fox News or you talk to someone who watches a lot of Fox News, they probably think that we're these people who are opening the doors and just letting anyone come in. But if you talk to someone who watches a lot of MSNBC they might say we're these draconian people who are just intent on ripping apart families. People don't know what it is that we do." It's just an example of the fact that everyone in this system is feeling overwhelmed and overwrought, and it's beyond politics.

Betty: If these asylum officers are lying about what they do, making stuff up so they can hide what their job actually is due to a grand misperception about what it is they do, then there seems to be a lot of shame and blame in this system. To the point of that officer's description of the opposite ways a Fox News watcher or an MSNBC viewer would see their job—both have one thing in common—they blame these officers for doing the worst thing imaginable when it comes to immigration. So there's blame and shame. And, of course, there's a lot of pain around the system—there are people waiting to get in, subject to these very mercurial changes in policies. They don't know at what time or what place their hearings will take place. And then there are these immigration agents meeting with them, and are these officers clear on what the system is? Are they also equally confused?

Hawk: You mention shame and pain. I would emphasize the pain more than the shame. When you're out in a social setting, if you are an asylum officer, do you really want to have this conversation with a stranger who's probably going to come at you from one way or the other? It's easier to say, "Let me be neutral." But I think that they are very well aware of what the limitations are. I think they are very well aware of where the potential pitfalls are. And they see the pain in the people who are applying face-to-face, the uncertainty of the cases where they know...if only a couple of other pieces of information were available, questions that remain unanswered could be resolved, and we would probably be able to grant at this level, but because we don't have the information, we can't. It has to go to the immigration court and this person is going to be in the process for another two to three years. And how do they feel about that? And they also fear making a mistake, of letting someone come in who might be dangerous or who is lying. They don't want to be taken advantage of.

I remember in New York, when we had a situation many years back with Amadou Diallo, who was gunned down in the vestibule of his building—out of 41 bullets, 19 hit him. He was a young African immigrant who just went for his wallet and the police thought it was a gun and they shot him down. And I remember in the aftermath of his murder, there was such a great outpouring of advocacy around the city and defending of his rights.

But what a lot of people didn't realize is that Amadou Diallo was here as an asylee. He claimed to have been from Mauritania and to have seen his parents killed in front of him. But then, after he was killed in a barrage of bullets, here come his parents from Guinea. His mom was quite the media celebrity. She was very dignified. But then it became very hard for anybody from Mauritania to go through the system for the next couple of years because there was always a sort of presupposition that they might not be telling the truth. Maybe this is someone from another country claiming to be from Mauritania.

Michael: I'm curious, what's your experience in terms of the counterpoint—the people in court who sit on the other side of the table? Are you looking at the asylum seekers and the court officials and saying to yourself, "We are entering into this in good faith?" Or are you seeing your counterparts inside the government acting in bad faith? Or is it just a system that's fundamentally broken because there aren't enough resources, there are too many displaced people fleeing all sorts of persecution, and there aren't enough days in a calendar year? What's your experience with the system itself? Is it just broken or is it actively resisting people who have a moral and humanitarian right?

Hawk: I think the system is overwhelmed. When I think of something that is broken, I think of something that is beyond repair—or so beyond its ability to function that it's almost better to do without it. I wouldn't go that far with our immigration system. From my point of view as a psychologist, as a human rights psychologist, not every client who comes to our program will get an affidavit from us, nor will we testify for them. There have been times when people have come in and said things that are demonstrably untrue. I only go to court, and I only write affidavits, for people with whom I've had clinical experience and who I find to be credible, who are here trying to heal themselves.

Michael: And how do you determine that? How do you differentiate them?

Hawk: One of the things that gives us an advantage at Bellevue is that we have a course of treatment with folks. We see them over time. We have been doing this for a long time and have become familiar with some of the history of many of the countries where our clients are coming from. I always give people the benefit of the doubt. We start there. But sometimes there's something egregiously wrong.

For example, someone who came to us from Guinea in 2010. There had been a huge riot and public rapes and people were killed at their 28th of September Stadium, named after a famous independence referendum on September 28, 1958. The riots and killings were actually on September 28, 2009. The man had a visa. He came to the United States on September 24, 2009, but was still telling the story of all the things he witnessed in person at the stadium and that he was locked up for months after the riots. His visa showed that he was in Brooklyn when the riots happened.

I can't go to court for that guy. When things are egregious, I won't go there. But I don't think that whoever knocks on the door fabricates facts as this man did. My assumption is to have good faith. It has to be good faith on our end. However, I cannot write an affidavit, and I cannot testify to something I have not observed or don't believe in. And I hope—and I'm knocking wood—that for the folks on the other side, the immigration officers, whatever their political point of view or leaning—I hope they come from a place of justice and a sort of clear-eyed weighing of the facts. I still do believe that exists.

Michael: What's interesting here is that one side says it's all fraud. The other side says everybody seeking asylum should get it. And what you're saying is that there is more nuance in these cases. We're so divided; we stopped listening to the details.

So with that example you just gave, that person was blatantly lying. But we are so divided on this and so many other issues that it causes me to think, if somebody hears that story, it validates the opinion that believes there's fraud rife throughout the immigration system; whereas somebody else is going to hear his story and say, "He must be here for some reason—he still should get asylum." There's such an emotional attachment to our politics; it seems to blinker us in situations like this.

Hawk: Yes. That particular case is an outlier. But what you said at the very beginning of that question is very important—that there is a great deal of nuance on both sides. We have immigration judges who are former Peace Corps volunteers and asylum officers who gravitate to this field because of a true concern for human rights and wanting to see people treated fairly. There are others who have much more of a defend-the-borders kind of mentality. That exists, too. There's a wide range of folks. I worked with an immigration judge who once said to me, "You know, there are some judges who grant almost 80 percent of the cases that come in front of them. There are other judges that only will grant 2 percent of the cases." And he said about both of those extremes, "Those are judges who don't work for a living."

Betty: Because they're not looking at the details of each case and thinking about it.

Hawk: It's almost like this preconceived notion.

Betty: Right, they've already decided. They say, "I'm going to approve" or "I'm going to disapprove" without thinking.

Hawk: Exactly. So there is a lot of nuance. And in terms of the conversation that's going on in our country—that it's all either the draconian folks who just want to block the borders from the hordes that are coming in, or those who feel that all asylum seekers are being treated terribly unfairly—those are extremes. If there's anything that comes from the conversation we're having today, I hope it is that people will think beyond that to the humanity of the person who is sitting in front of them. I remember working with a woman from Ethiopia. One very poignant thing she said was "Just imagine that I'm a person with no home, no family, no resources, and I'm asking if I can come to stay with you." In a very real way, that's where she was seated emotionally.

Getting back to the question you had about the gentleman who was in Brooklyn when he said he was at a riot in Guinea, there is certainly a potential that there were other traumatic things that happened in his life, but that's not what he came to us with. That's not what he was going to the government with. And if it's just judged on what he brought to us, he's going to have trouble. And again, that could be a problem with the street advice because some people have legitimate claims and then are told on the street, "That's not going to be enough for you. You need to exaggerate it."

Michael: Use this lie. You'll get in.

Hawk: Exactly. So that's part of the reason that we do as much as we can to get out there and educate in the public. And even in terms of the groups that we run, we let people know if there are things in your story or things in your past that you don't remember when you're asked about them, you need to say, "I don't remember." Or if there is a particular question that is asked, don't try to create anything if it's not part of your history, even if you think that this is what the officer or what the judge is looking for. These folks are very well-trained, and they will ask you the same question four or five different ways, and if it's inconsistent, they're going to think the whole thing is inconsistent. Tell your truth.

Michael: Truth will set you free.

Hawk: Well that's certainly what we hope. There is a challenge with traumatic memories and the fact that sometimes there are inconsistencies; people don't remember whether it was four people in a room or whether it was five people, which date, and all those sorts of things. One way I try to demystify this is to point out that the brain is not a library with books that are all neatly filed away. Perhaps under normal circumstances, there is something akin to a systematic filing away of memories. But when there's a situation of trauma or terror, the brain can be...

Betty: Flooded.

Hawk: And saying, "I don't know; things kind of hit the fan." And those traumatic memories, if they are books, are placed any which way, so that later on when you want to retrieve one and you go to the shelf where you think it would be, it's not there. You might not be able to recall everything that happened on a particular date. And then there are other times when you're just going around your life and you pick up a book without even looking for it. And there it is—it could be a flashback. It could be an intrusive thought if things are sort of scattered. So sometimes, if someone has some inconsistency in their story, that's not a deal-breaker. That might actually be something that is part and parcel of traumatic memory and how things are encoded and how things are expressed. And part of our job as psychological experts is to be there and help explain this so the person has a chance, and we can really get at the heart of what's going on.

Betty: Hawk, you made a clear distinction earlier between a system that is overwhelmed and one that is broken. Your sense is that our immigration system is very overwhelmed, but not yet broken. That still means there are too many people for the system to handle; there are not enough asylum officers or judges to meet the needs of all that's going on. How do we deal with this in terms of policy, so that it doesn't become a political football between those who watch Fox News and those who watch MSNBC? There is a real problem, if not a crisis—the system is so overwhelmed, it's becoming chaotic—or it is already chaotic. Even now, as we speak, you are on call because appointment dates and times with asylum officers or immigration courts are subject to very last-minute changes. This has a direct effect on peoples' lives and their mental health. On a policy level, what can be done to alleviate the bottlenecks and inefficiencies of an overwhelmed system? How do we create more roads on the highways, so the traffic isn't this bad?

Hawk: There are a couple of ways to look at that. Some of it is content in terms of policy and where resources go. And I know this is a huge issue. In terms of the security of the country right now—do we build a wall, or do we place these billions of dollars elsewhere, where it might be more effective? That's something for the politicians and social advocates to get into. I know that they are, but I think there's also process questions. So how do we talk about this? People don't recognize the nuances. They don't recognize that there are a lot of people who are doing not only a lot of thinking about this, but also feeling within this and they are trying to figure this out so that we can go forward.

Maybe we need to have a conversation about who we are as a nation? Do we draw on this nationalistic momentum or do we adhere to what's written at the bottom of the Statue of Liberty? How do all of us who have immigration histories in our families—and we all do, some of us with forced immigration histories—deal with those who want in? Do we shut the door on those coming in who might be fleeing persecution? Is it a question of "us versus them," or is it a question of "us?" Are we spending so much time talking about "them"—those people, those aliens, those illegals—that we forget that we're talking about people who seek freedom, people who seek a better life and are trying to do something to help move this country forward? When does it become "us?" I think that we need to have those conversations in ways that aren't so tribalized.

Betty: Right.

Hawk: And in having those conversations, perhaps that's part of the key to unlocking some solutions in terms of how do we get more smartly placed resources to make this system—I won't say easier—but let's say, less difficult.

Betty: Less backlogged, less chaotic, less absurd—it sounds like.

Hawk: More humanistic.

Betty: What you're saying is something that we've been hearing echo in several of our interviews—that there is a narrative that is changing. You point to the words at the bottom of the Statue of Liberty, and those words have framed a central theme of the narrative arc of the United States: "Give us your poor. Give us your cold. Give us your hungry." And as you put it—many of us have immigrant backgrounds or immigrant histories—most of us do. But there's a denial of this in these debates between folks with in-group and out-group status. People who have been here for a while, however they identify, might say that those now wanting in are "them." They may think, "We have what we have. We don't want to share what we got. Or we may have come here earlier needing help, but we do not want to share it with people who are coming now." Others feel "we don't have enough." There's a scarcity model in operation, and it clashes with this narrative of the United States as a beacon and a haven for the world's tired, poor, war-torn, and hungry, who seek a better way of life.

And, according to the Declaration of Independence, "all men are created equal." No one deserves to have more than another. So, Hawk, what you're pointing to is a very big-picture discussion. At the end of the day, one of the takeaways here is, perhaps, that we need to "expand the problem." That it is not just a process issue. We have to think about the big picture—

what we are as a nation, where we want to allocate our many resources, because we do have the resources to deal with this overwhelmed system. That's very intense.

Hawk: That is a lot. Sometimes I look at these issues in terms of the micro and the macro. And as we move through this enlarged space and consider the macro issues, I sometimes think that the best education in this set of complex problems is to be in the micro and have that experience. Whether one is advocating or volunteering, whether one is in the legal profession taking on some of these cases *pro bono*, or law students, or medical students, or psychology students, or psychiatric students, it may be best to get involved in this at a practical level and begin to understand what happens to asylum seekers. Then one will be better able to advocate from a place of some experience, of some contact. An immigration judge told me one time in an informal conversation that if I read *The New York Times* about an attack on a village and 1500 Congolese have had to flee across the border into Uganda, I get that. But when there's one woman who was among those 1500 who comes to court and tells what her experience was of that night, it almost becomes unbelievable because it's so shocking in its intimacy and its realness…

Michael: …and its inhumanity.

Hawk: Absolutely.

Betty: And it's personal. It's individual. It's not a number. It's not a statistic of people being shoved across the border.

Michael: How responsive is the system, then, to those people who are still dealing with their trauma from wherever they're fleeing? How much flexibility or sympathy or care does the system afford them? How much does it understand the psychological toll that they're still paying, which is why they're here seeking asylum?

Hawk: Two things with that. We've had a number of cases referred to us by asylum officers or even immigration judges where they've seen people decompensate in front of them and they're like, "You need assistance."

Michael: Decompensate?

Hawk: Fall apart.

Betty: Deteriorate. Have a breakdown.

Hawk: Deteriorate in front of me. But that has been the exception, as opposed to the rule. Oftentimes, it might be the legal teams who see that a person really needs help going through this process, to tolerate what is intolerable, and they may call us in.

The other thing I would say is that one of the diagnoses that gets bandied around a lot is post-traumatic stress disorder. But we are not just dealing with an isolated event of the impact of one really bad day that happened in Congo. We're dealing with recurrent and reinforcing stressors that tend to keep the trauma very much alive in the present. So we're not really dealing with the "post" of post-traumatic stress disorder. We are also looking at a disorder with symptoms that get amplified when someone who's been through the awful things we've been talking about—who has sustained the stress of coming here, not speaking the language, being the fourteenth person in a one-bedroom apartment, sleeping in shifts, and all these other hardships—wouldn't we expect them to have some difficulty sleeping?

Michael: Does the asylum system make accommodation for that? Or do they punish that?

Hawk: I think that there's a wide variation. I can cite cases from particular judges who weren't very conscious of that and others who are very open to this and actually will...

Michael: So it's not monolithic?

Hawk: It's not. There is a lot of nuance. We've spent a lot of time today looking at the limitations of the system because they're very real. But, in having conversations like this, we have an opportunity to open more eyes to what the barriers are, and what we can do to get over them in order to help these people who are very deserving of the assistance they seek.

Betty: And as far as I understand it, there's no systematized offering within the USCIS to deal with trauma, or complex trauma, in asylum seekers. They are purely legal and bureaucratic organizations. The individual judges may refer someone out for help, but there is no accommodation for the psychological impact of what asylum seekers have experienced and may continue to experience.

Hawk: That is correct. There is a national consortium for torture treatment programs scattered around the country. Bellevue is part of the consortium. There are different refugee resettlement agencies. But as I go around the country and do trainings at various places, the common theme is that there is a lack of adequate mental health support services for people. So I think raising awareness, doing what you people are doing here is a wonderful step. But it is going to be a long, long journey, and I remain optimistic that we can make progress.

If I can leave you with an anecdote from the Francophone group I run: an escaped slave from Mauritania asked the group what are the things that one needs, what are the characteristics one must have to change the world—or to at least survive in the world? I never thought they'd come to a consensus on this—it's a pretty deep question—but they did.

That night, they came up with three things. They said: wisdom, courage, and hope. And they went a little further and they said that, if you have two of these qualities, no matter which two, it's insufficient. Because if you're a courageous and hopeful person who lacks wisdom, you're going to go about your activities in an ineffective way and probably fail. If you're wise and hopeful, but you lack courage, then you're going to cross your arms and be trapped in a prison of inertia and never act on your ideas. With the people I work with, the wisdom is there, and the courage is there. What is hard to hold onto is hope. But then they went even further and mentioned that hope is not so much something you have. It's something you *do*. It's an attitude. It's a comportment. It's a way of leaning into the world and into a situation. And it's a capacity to hope—and perhaps most importantly—that capacity to hope can be shared. I find that a lot with our client base and how they help one another.

That's how I see our work at the program and what I do—we are actually helping people hold on to that hope. Even if it does take five years, even if there is a presupposition that your story isn't credible until you prove it to be credible and you stay in there and you hang in there. Your family can be in front of you. You can work toward that. You got to hang in. And that's kind of where we sit right now.

Michael: Beautifully said.

Hawk: Thank you.

Betty: Thank you so much for joining us, Hawk.

Hawk: It's my great pleasure. If someone wants to contact us, we have a web page which is https://www.survivorsoftorture.org/.

Chapter 18

Partisan Politics, Toxic Identities, Dangerous Divides

Guest: Dr. Lilliana Mason
Episode Aired: February 19, 2019

Dr. Lilliana Mason is the SNF Agora Institute Associate Professor of Political Science at Johns Hopkins University. She is the author of Uncivil Agreement: How Politics Became Our Identity *and coauthor (with Nathan Kalmoe) of* Radical American Partisanship: Mapping Violent Hostility, its Causes, and the Consequences for Democracy.

When people identify with a group so intensely that they want the group to win at all costs, what is really going on? What is it about winning itself that is so important? And how is group identity and the need to win impacting our contemporary politics—even American democracy itself?

In February 2019, these pressing questions emerged from the longest government shutdown in American history. Because the shutdown was a baffling and costly outcome of a partisan battle over President Trump's unrealistic desire to fund the construction of an anti-immigrant U.S./Mexico border wall, we sensed that greater psychological forces were at play. With Trump giving belligerent voice to ever-increasing social and political anxieties about immigration, race relations, and gender politics—we wondered just how politics, in-group affiliation, and partisanship had become such a toxic mix.

Inspired by the insights in her 2018 book, Uncivil Politics: How Politics Became Our Identity, *we turned to Dr. Lilliana Mason to help us understand the dynamics of "us versus them" partisanship. This in- or out-group binary has turned voting from being a considered choice about policies and candidate experience into a highly emotional pledge to help your party—or your "team"—win. Thus a candidate's lack of honesty, dearth of government experience, and even criminal background can be seen as beside the point. As long as they represent one's team, then they must win—at all costs. Yet, as the 2019 shutdown revealed, when government becomes like a professional wrestling ring for such partisan wins and losses, democracy cannot function.*

In our conversation, Dr. Mason clarifies just why winning is so fundamental and important to us:

>...imagine that you're having a bad day. Somebody at work said something mean or insulted you. You feel like you made a mistake. You did something wrong. You're not feeling particularly great about yourself that day. And then you find out that your favorite sports team has just won a game. You feel a little bit elevated because your group won. This is because your sense of identity, which is linked to your favorite sports team, rises because it has become your own individual status. Anytime you are feeling like you're losing, you can grab onto the status of a group that's winning, and you can feel better about yourself. It's a very basic sort of human need to feel good. There's almost nothing more basic than that.

We place Dr. Mason's chapter here, in the Anxieties about Race and Dominance *section, because her observations point to the origins, stresses, and impacts of identity upon American political behavior. She reminds us that these influences are dynamic, and that our current tendency to see party affiliation as a way to self-identify, was not the case 50 years ago:*

>...Through the 1970s and 1980s, political scientists thought about partisanship as a rational decision that people made based on the policy achievements of each party. People would look at the two parties and ask, "Which party has done better things or things that I like the most?" or "Which candidate do I trust, or which candidate do I like?" This presumes that people are making choices based on the pros and cons of the parties, or the candidates themselves.
>
>Then, in the early 1990s and early 2000s, we started thinking more about partisanship itself as a social identity. You feel like the people who are in your party are socially like you. And when you talk about your party, you say "we" and the party's status is connected to your sense of individual status. When the party wins

an election, you feel really great on an individual level. People feel emotions on behalf of their group. So, increasingly, we've been thinking about partisanship not just as a political choice, but also as an expression of a political identity that is linked to our own psychological wellbeing and linked to the identities that we have in addition to being partisans.

These observations add dimension to Sheldon Solomon's assertions in Chapter 2 that reminders of death and threat cause humans to unconsciously favor in-group affiliations. Indeed, the shifting tectonic plates of environmental crises, the pandemic, and other major demographic, social, and cultural changes pressure us existentially, and perhaps push us to affiliate more strongly with whatever political "teams" reflect our values. To combat an ever-increasing sense of helplessness and loss, we fight for our team's victory, sometimes at all costs. According to Mason and Solomon, we need these wins to feel good, to restore a sense of security. Yet, it may cause us all to lose American democracy itself.

Interview

Michael: If it feels like we are a nation torn between Republicans and Democrats, or red states and blue states, that's because we are. Today, we're going to talk to Dr. Lilliana Mason about the consequences of that division in our politics and in our public and private lives and how all of this gets wrapped up into our political identities. Lilliana offers some really fascinating research and data to show all the levels where differences manifest and how that causes us to see and behave around those who are different. Lilliana's book *Uncivil Agreement: How Politics Became Our Identity* is the wellspring for our conversation today. It is full of interesting statistics, insights, and social psychology experiments, which puts it right in our *Mind of State* wheelhouse. Lilliana, welcome.

Lilliana: Thanks so much for having me.

Michael: I want to start with a little bit of pop quiz for us, okay? Ask me anything you want about *Duck Dynasty*.

Betty: What?

Michael: It's a TV show. Lilliana, do you have a question for me about *Duck Dynasty*?

Lilliana: Yeah, okay—what's it about?

Betty: Who are the characters? What are their names?

Michael: I don't have an answer to any of your questions because I've never seen it. I failed that pop quiz.

Betty: Interesting, since you were the one giving it.

Michael: So, similarly, Betty, ask me any question you want about the TV show *Family Guy*.

Betty: Who are the characters and what is it about?

Michael: I don't know. I've never seen it. But I do know it's made by Seth MacFarlane and that there's a character, Stevie, who is a baby, but he talks like an adult. My college-age daughter watches it endlessly. And she's a very progressive Democratic who was a Hillary voter in 2016. And the real question to you, Lilliana, is what does this all mean? Because who cares what television shows we watch?

Betty: Or what would our preferences tell you about Michael or me?

Lilliana: So there was a study done in 2012 by TiVo that actually looked at the top ten network television shows and it broke viewership down by party, between Democrats and Republicans.[1] And what they found was that there was not a single show that was on both lists. Meaning, Democrats and Republicans watched very different television shows.

Michael: There was not one?

---

[1] Carter, B. (2012). Republicans Like Golf, Democrats Prefer Cartoons, TV Research Shows. *The New York Times*. https://archive.nytimes.com/mediadecoder.blogs.nytimes.com/2012/10/11/republicans-like-golf-democrats-prefer-cartoons-tv-research-suggests/.

Lilliana: No. In fact, you had to go really far below the top ten in order to find a show that both Democrats and Republicans liked.

Betty: Wow.

Lilliana: The reason that's important is that it indicates that there is a cultural difference between Democrats and Republicans. The watercooler conversations that we think of as our national American touchstones are often entertainment-based and television-based. If, as Democrats and Republicans, we're not watching the same shows, then we're not able to have these watercooler conversations. It puts up a divide between people who belong to different parties.

Betty: And when we talk about watercooler conversations, we could say they're our twenty-first century versions of gathering around the campfire. What would you say is the impact of not having these common interests, even if they're entertainment-based like *Family Guy* or *Duck Dynasty*? What does it mean that we can't come together and have these conversations?

Lilliana: Well, on a superficial level, it means that we're actually speaking different languages. If we have different cultural references, somebody will do a subtweet on Twitter referencing a commonly known thing within their political circle that the other side doesn't necessarily even understand. And so, from the 30,000-foot level, what that means is that we're speaking different languages from each other. And we are having a harder time as partisan opponents thinking of the other side as relatable and, basically, as human beings who have strengths and weaknesses and understandable faults. It makes it not only hard for us to communicate across the aisle politically, but also difficult for us to treat the other side with generosity because they seem very foreign to us.

Michael: So is there, then, no sense of common humanity? To quote *High School Musical,* is there no sense that we're all in this together? I brought up *Family Guy* and *Duck Dynasty* because they tend to be favored by Republicans and unknown by Democrats. This shows that the divisions between us are not just necessarily policy divisions, which is how we tend to think about splits. But these separations have seeped into, not just culture, but geography and faith. It reminds me of a phenomenal *New York Times* map after the

2016 election. It was very detailed, almost down to the level of individual streets.[2]

Lilliana: I remember that.

Michael: I typed in my current home address, the address of my childhood home outside of Chicago, and then my sister's address in Indiana. My current neighborhood in Brooklyn voted 92 percent for Hillary Clinton and 4.9 percent for Trump, which basically means we are in a deep, deep, deep, deep blue community. My childhood home was not nearly as pronounced. It was in suburban Chicago with 65 percent going for Hillary and 31 percent for Trump. Then in my sister's neighborhood outside of Indianapolis, the vote was split almost 50/50—46 percent Hillary, 45 percent Trump, with a sea of red nearby. What's so fascinating to me is what you've written about in your book, namely, that we've gone from being two parties that are a little bit different in a lot of ways to two parties that are very different in a few powerful ways.

Lilliana: Exactly.

Michael: What's going on? What do you mean by that?

Lilliana: So "a little bit different in a lot of ways" is basically the way that we want our party system to work. The parties should be distinguishable, and they should represent different interests and constituencies. That's natural and necessary. But what we've seen happening over the last couple decades is a shift from these multiple small differences between the parties to very important differences on social identities that are really crucial to people's sense of who they are. These social identities are about religion, race, and ideology. But also, there's a difference between an *ideology*, which is a set of policy preferences, and an *ideological identity*, which is identifying with people who are called liberals or conservatives.

Michael: So it's basically about which is "your team," and who you self-identify with.

---

[2] Bloch, M., Buchanan, L., Katz, J., & Quealy, K. (2018). An Extremely Detailed Map of the 2016 Election. *The New York Times*. https://www.nytimes.com/interactive/2018/upshot/election-2016-voting-precinct-maps.html.

Lilliana: Exactly. There used to be a mix of self-identified liberals and conservatives in both the Democratic and Republican parties. There used to be more of a racial mix in the two parties, and there used to be a religious mix within each of the two parties. Increasingly, what we are seeing is that the Republican Party is now almost entirely white and Christian, if not Evangelical, and self-identified as conservative. Whereas the Democratic Party is liberal, non-white, and non-religious, in general.

Betty: So, in essence, would you say that the moderates in each party have fallen away?

Lilliana: There's two different ways to look at it. One is that people are becoming more consistently identified with the "correct party." So, if you think of yourself as a liberal, it's increasingly clear that you don't belong in the Republican Party. And the Democratic Party is becoming more liberal because more liberals are moving into the Democratic Party. That's one way to look at it. That can also include people who call themselves liberal, but aren't extreme, who still hold relatively moderate issue positions. They just identify as liberal and think other liberals are people like them. Or there could be a situation in which the liberals in the Democratic Party are becoming more extreme in their policy preferences. And what I found is, actually, it's really the former rather than the latter. The parties are becoming more consistent in terms of identity, but they're not necessarily becoming more extreme in terms of their policy preferences.

Betty: That's interesting. And when you talk about ideological identity, I'm hearing something that you pointed to in the book about this being an emotionally grounded identification, that there's something about this that isn't just policy based, that these distinctions are driven not just by our thinking brain, but by our feeling selves.

Lilliana: Right. The way that I think about it is that you can actually measure ideology in two different ways. One way is to ask people, "When you talk about liberals, do you say 'we' rather than 'they'? To what extent do you identify as a conservative?" These are identification questions. Or you can ask people about their positions on six different really important policies, like health care and abortion. And what I have found—and other political scientists have also found—is that people's identity positions don't always match their policy positions. It's possible for self-identified liberals and conservatives to really dislike each other without actually having extremely different policy preferences. And the more strongly they identify with a group, the more they hate the other side, even if you hold constant all of their policy preferences—even if their policy preferences are not changing, or they have relatively moderate policy preferences or—and this is crazy—even if they have the wrong policy preferences. There is a relatively substantial group of conservatives who hold liberal policy preferences, meaning, to the left of the scale when you're looking at "what would you prefer the government to do?" And even among that group of people, the more strongly they identify as conservative, the more they hate liberals, even when they hold relatively liberal policies.

Michael: Right. This was crucial in the 2016 election. Everybody was talking about Trump not being a Republican. There were all these weird things, eminent domain and foreign policy questions, that didn't fit into the traditional Republican policy wheelhouse. And there was the expectation that those traditional Republicans who saw Trump as being outside the traditional Republican fold would peel off and vote for Hillary. And that never happened. They stayed within their tribe.

Lilliana: Right. For instance, he promised health care for everyone.

Michael: I have a friend in Virginia who is a former Marine, who has said to me on a number of occasions that he could never vote for a Democrat. It doesn't matter who the Republican is. It doesn't matter what the policy is. He's always a Republican, and he's never, ever voted anything other than Republican. And when the whole Russian scandal started to emerge, I had a friend say to me on social media, "Well, you know better Russia than the Democrats."

Betty: And that's something you mentioned in your book, Lilliana, that people will vote for their team or their party rather than for policy.

Lilliana: In fact, this is something George Washington warned us about in his farewell speech. He specifically said that if you allow parties or factions to form, people will be more loyal to their faction than they will be to the country as a whole. And that will allow foreign powers to take advantage of us. It will allow for cracks in our armor that other countries will be able to exploit. So we cannot allow these types of factions to form. Of course, as soon as Washington stepped down, there were parties that formed.

Michael: Let's take a turn because there's some social psychology behind all of this as well. Democrats and Republicans have grown so different from each other that cooperation is receding as a perceived value. We don't live in a country anymore where we value cooperation. We value winning, even if that means winning doesn't benefit us. I want to turn if we can, to a very interesting figure, Henri Tajfel. Some of the experiments that he was doing in the early 1960s really inform and help us understand the human motivation— the psychology—of what's going on in the political world today. He was trying to figure out early on, what's the baseline for group conflict?

Lilliana: Tajfel was a Polish Jew who fought the Nazis during World War II. He was captured and spent six years in a Nazi prison camp. And before he became a soldier in the war, he was studying to get his PhD in chemistry. When he emerged from the prison camp, he switched to a PhD in social psychology because he wanted to figure out what it was that could cause people to hate each other so much that the entire world could fight a war over it. That was his motivation.

Michael: To understand why the Holocaust happened and why World War II occurred.

Lilliana: Yes. How two groups of people could come to hate one another so much that they're willing to annihilate every single human on the other side.

Betty: So he wanted to know what would cause people to supersede humanity.

Lilliana: Right. Essentially to justify dehumanization. And so Tajfel decided to create a group identity for people that was so meaningless and so weak that there would be no conflict at all between that group and the out-group, the people who are not part of their group. His plan was to gradually increase the amount of conflict between this meaningless group and the outsiders until he found people becoming biased against the other side.

Michael: To try to determine the tipping point?

Lilliana: Yes, exactly. In order to create what he called "minimal group identities," he had people look at a picture full of dots and estimate the number of dots. Then he told them that they were either "overestimators" or "underestimators."[3] There was no difference in value. One group wasn't better than the other. They just found out they were in one group or the other. When they were doing the experiment, they were alone in a laboratory. They did not meet anybody else in the group. Then, later in the experiment, he asked them to perform an allocation task in which they were going to give out money to people. And each person got to decide how the money was allocated. In a few of these studies, he offered people a choice between what I call the "greater good condition," where he basically said, "You can choose for everybody to get five dollars or you can choose for your group, let's say you're an 'overestimator,' for the 'overestimators' to get four dollars and for the underestimators to only get three." Effectively, if you choose for your group to receive four dollars and the other group to receive three dollars, you're being punished or you're sacrificing part of the greater good and your own good for the victory of your group.

Michael: You're going to take a dollar less to give them two dollars less.

Betty: You're choosing to take a dollar less, to win. To get more than the other group.

Lilliana: Yes. To win.

Michael: And these dots, these were random?

Lilliana: Randomly assigned.

---

[3] Tajfel, H., Billig, M.G., Bundy, R.P., and Flament C. (1971). "Social Categorization and Intergroup Behaviour," *European Journal of Social Psychology* 1, no. 2: pp.149–178.

Michael: So, people literally were not even actual "overestimators" or actual "underestimators"?

Lilliana: No. But they didn't know that. In other versions of this experiment, he had them look at paintings, and he said, "You prefer paintings of Paul Klee over Kandinsky," or he said, "You're group W and you're group X." And in one of them, he actually said, "I am going to assign you random group numbers." And he actually told them they had been assigned randomly to different groups. And still these outcomes happened.[4]

Michael: That was the amazing one—where he said to them, "This is completely random. There's no meaning to this." Yet people still assigned meaning to the group. What's happening?

Lilliana: Right. He expected this to be the baseline condition—that people would obviously choose the greater good over the victory, with an added sacrifice. Even with these minimal identification groups, he actually found that people were reliably choosing the victory condition and sacrificing real resources to get the sense of winning. He couldn't get it to a point where people were willing to give up the sense of winning, even if it cost them money. Even in a minimal, meaningless, value-free, and brand-new group identity, Tajfel couldn't get people to stop being prejudiced against their out-group or privileging their new in-group. It's the winning that seemed most important to them. Tajfel was surprised and baffled by the fact that it was possible to find the same effect even when these groups were effectively meaningless.

Betty: What does that tell us? That, as human beings, we prefer to win rather than give each other equal good? Everybody can get five dollars, but we'd rather get four dollars, if we can get one dollar more than the people in the other group? The tribal brain tells us we like to win, but to me, this sounds like we also like to have power over another.

Lilliana: Yes. But it's not primarily about the power over another person or another group. Tajfel came up with what he called *social identity theory*. What Tajfel determined was that it wasn't so much about having power over

---

[4] Billig M., and Tajfel, H. (1973). "Social Categorization and Similarity in Intergroup Behaviour," *European Journal of Social Psychology* 3, no. 1: pp. 27–52.

another group. It was much more about feeling connected and feeling your basic sense of self-esteem or self-worth was intimately connected to the status of the group that you belonged to. Having your group lose is painful because your group status is connected to your own sense of whether you are a good person.

Betty: So, you'd rather have the distinction of being esteemed over another group than just have everybody be equal? But what is the meaning of winning? If you're talking about status, what does status mean then? "I've got more than them," so that bonds a group together? We have more money than the other group, even though overall we all have less money than we would have ended up with if we gave everybody five dollars.

Lilliana: We can run a thought experiment. If you just imagine that you're having a bad day. Somebody at work said something mean or insulted you. You feel like you made a mistake. You did something wrong. You're not feeling particularly great about yourself that day. And then you find out that your favorite sports team has just won a game. You feel a little bit elevated because your group won. This is because your sense of identity, which is linked to your favorite sports team, rises because it has become your own individual status. Anytime you are feeling like you're losing, you can grab onto the status of a group that's winning, and you can feel better about yourself. It's a very basic sort of human need to feel good. There's almost nothing more basic than that.

Michael: This makes me think about Trump and his MAGA followers— and even their hats. They are all about winning and about group identity.

Lilliana: That's where the book connects to politics. Through the 1970s and 1980s, political scientists thought about partisanship as a rational decision that people made based on the policy achievements of each party. People would look at the two parties and ask, "Which party has done better things or things that I like the most?" or "Which candidate do I trust, or which candidate do I like?" This presumes that people are making choices based on the pros and cons of the parties, or the candidates themselves.

Then, in the early 1990s and early 2000s, we started thinking more about partisanship itself as a social identity. You feel like the people who are in your party are socially like you. And when you talk about your party, you say "we" and the party's status is connected to your sense of individual status. When the party wins an election, you feel really great on an individual level. People feel emotions on behalf of their group. So, increasingly, we've been thinking about partisanship not just as a political choice, but also as an expression of a political identity that is linked to our own psychological wellbeing and linked to the identities that we have in addition to being partisans.

Michael: Liliana, as you were describing Tajfel's research, I was thinking that the best real-world example for me of what you're talking about was Mitch McConnell's behavior as Senate majority leader during Obama's administration. He took the position: "We're just going to obstruct and obstruct, even if it means our constituents get less health care, even if it means the levers of democracy are eroded. Because what matters most is winning."

Betty: Is that an example of what you're talking about, Liliana?

Lilliana: Yes, absolutely. And one of the examples that I use in the book is the 2013 government shutdown over Obamacare, which is relevant again. The cost to the U.S. economy of the shutdown was in the billions of dollars in 2013. And it's not just the costs of not having our government function, but also the opportunity costs to businesses, farmers, and entrepreneurs. There are billions and billions of dollars of cost and loss in having a government shutdown. And, usually, the shutdown itself is over something symbolic that was mainly about winning. The wall, itself, was a symbolic idea. And if Trump didn't get it, he didn't get to win. And similarly, in 2013, the shutdown was over Obamacare, which was already moving forward. There were no more legislative hurdles that could be placed in front of it. It had already been defended in front of the Supreme Court. And so the idea of shutting down the entire government at a cost of billions of dollars to the American electorate in order to feel like we are winning a little bit, sounds petty, but it's also accurate.

Michael: But it was about branding, too, right?

Lilliana: Yes. Exactly.

Betty: This echoes something we talked about in another podcast episode about Trump's wall: we discussed the symbolism of the wall and the symbolism of winning, which have become emotional drivers.[5] And since on *Mind of State*, we consider the mind and the emotions of states, be they political or internal, this is really central to the symbolism of the wall. Because Trump's wall is at least partly about winning to protect one's self-esteem. And what you, Lilliana, point out is that the notion of winning is more important than putting material benefits into the hands of as many people as possible.

Michael: Which is a main objective of a liberal democracy and its government. But governing doesn't matter anymore, right?

Lilliana: Exactly. Because a functional government requires compromise.

Betty: Right.

Lilliana: And compromise is the opposite of winning. In a compromise, literally no one wins.

Betty: Right. Everybody has to sacrifice something; they have to each lose something for the greater good to move forward.

Michael: You get something that you want, but you give up something as well. And if you see winning as an either/or proposition, you can't do it. This makes me wonder if we're in some grand Tajfel experiment ourselves. What if we have been randomly assigned parties or at least policy positions?

Lilliana: You know, people have done this in labs with policy positions. They haven't randomly assigned the party, but they have randomly assigned the policy position of the parties. Basically, in the experiments, policy positions have been switched.[6] For example, the policy of the Democrats and Republicans positions on welfare have been reversed and people reliably just take on the position of the party. Not only that, but they don't know that they've done it. So, when they are asked whether the party influenced their

[5] See Chapter 29, "The Symbolic Power of Trump's Wall."
[6] Cohen, G.L. (2003). Party Over Policy: The Dominating Impact of Group Influence on Political Beliefs. *Journal of Personality and Social Psychology 85*(5), 808–822.

position, they say "No." Then they are asked to provide reasons for their position and they come up with them. They create *post hoc* rationalizations for policy positions that, in fact, they have just been randomly assigned. The frightening thing is they are not aware that they've been assigned a position, or that they have been manipulated by their party's position. They come up with reasons to support their party's position or the position they've just been told their party holds on the spot. And they convince themselves that it is the correct position to hold. It is obviously not possible on every single issue, but certainly it is on things like tariffs or government surveillance.[7] And we've seen it happen on a widespread basis.[8]

Michael: In your book, you talk about a 2013 Pew Research study that found when George W. Bush was president and Republicans held the White House, 38 percent more Republicans than Democrats approved of NSA surveillance.[9] Under Obama, these percentages flipped. Suddenly, Republicans were 12 percent less supportive of NSA surveillance than Democrats. Yet the question prompts in the survey were exactly the same. The only thing that was different was the party that was occupying the White House.

Lilliana: Right. The government's policy hadn't changed either.

Betty: Lilliana, what you are saying is that support is more dependent on party than policy. People are choosing policy based on party affiliation. However they think that they're acting rationally, rather than tribally. They're behaving emotionally, but they *think* that they're acting rationally.

Lilliana: Correct. And this extends even to things that we think are objective, like perceptions of the economy's health.[10] Usually overnight,

---

[7] Yeyati, E.L., Moscovich, L., & Abuin, C. (2020). Leader over Policy? The Scope of Elite Influence on Policy Preferences. *Political Communication 37*(3), 1–25.

[8] Barber, M., & Pope, J.C. (2019). Does Party Trump Ideology? Disentangling Party and Ideology in America. *American Political Science Review 113*(1), 38–54.

[9] Pew Research Center, "Few See Adequate Limits on NSA Surveillance Program," July 26, 2013, https://www.pewresearch.org/politics/2013/07/26/few-see-adequate-limits-on-nsa-surveillance-program/.

[10] Pew Research Center, "Public's Views of Nation's Economy Remain Positive and Deeply Partisan," July 25, 2019, https://www.pewresearch.org/politics/2019/07/25/publics-views-of-nations-economy-remain-positive-and-deeply-partisan/.

when a new party wins the presidency, partisans' opinions about the health of the economy also completely switch.[11]

Betty: That's amazing.

Lilliana: If a Democrat is president, Democrats think the economy's doing much better than Republicans do, and vice versa.

Betty: Just because the party in power has changed, the opinions on what's going on—which has not changed—flips.

Lilliana: Right. The economy doesn't change overnight, but partisan opinions about the health of the economy do.

Michael: What does that mean? It's like how we feel about our country or how we feel about ourselves is dependent on whether our party is winning or losing, or how we perceive our party as winning or losing.

Lilliana: We want our party to be winning. If our party is in charge, then the country must be doing well, because our party does a good job of running the government. If our party has just taken over control of the government, we know that we are winners. We do a good job. Therefore, the economy must be doing great. And if the other party has just taken over control of the government, we know that they are losers. If they are in control, then the economy must be doing terribly because there is no way that those people could run the government in a way that's good for the economy.

Betty: The basic narrative for people of both parties has now become: if my party wins, they're good, and the economy is doing well, and the country is strong. If my party loses and the opposing party wins, then everything is bad. The narrative switches based on my party affiliation. This is how people behave.

Lilliana: Yes. And this actually goes back to one of the original works studying American political behavior. The book is called *The American Voter,*

---

[11] Gerber, A.S., & Huber, G.A. (2010). Partisanship, Political Control, and Economic Assessments. *American Journal of Political Science 54*(1), 153–173.

and it was originally published in 1960.[12] The authors called partisanship a "perceptual screen" and argue that our partisanship is like a screen that we're looking through that changes what we see wherever we go. The basic idea is that, depending on which party you affiliate with, you perceive a different reality.

Betty: The result, then, is there is no objective reality in this situation, even though we think we are working with realistic policies, facts, and decisions. How do we remove this screen?

Lilliana: We don't.

Betty: Uh oh.

Lilliana: The best-case scenario is that we have other identities that are relevant to us that represent a good portion of our sense of who we are, identities that are not associated with our party. If this is the case, the world can function, and we can attach our sense of self-worth to other identities that are completely unrelated to the success or failure of our party. That way we don't have to invest so much in the victory of the party itself. We can think about our church or our bowling league or our favorite football team...

Betty: ...or our family.

Lilliana: Yes. Those things can be the main drivers of our sense of who we are, as opposed to our identifications with a political party.

The problem that comes up, however, is when multiple identities are largely aligned. By that I mean when most of the people who are in group #1 are also in group #2, and you are members of both groups. For instance, many Republicans are Evangelicals, and most Evangelicals are Republican. Those are well-aligned identities. What happens is that the success or failure of either of those groups affects your sense of wellbeing. Because Evangelical is so strongly attached to, or aligned with, Republican identity, when there is an election, if the Republican Party wins, the Evangelicals also win, and the portion of your self-esteem that is connected to the Republican

[12] Campbell, A., Converse, P.E., Miller, W.E., & Stokes, D.E. (1960/1980). *The American Voter.* University Press.

Party feels good and the portion of your self-esteem that is connected to your Evangelical identity feels good.

Michael: A Democratic victory then, is an attack on your faith.

Lilliana: It's not so much an attack on your faith, but it is connected to your partisanship, which includes race and religion. And when all of those parts of you feel like they're losing at the same time, that's when the outcomes of elections become much more important than any individual piece of government legislation or even the greater good of the nation as a whole. You can't afford to lose such a large portion of your sense of who you are. So, as these identities line up along with party, the cost of losing the election feels greater.

Betty: That speaks to the potential for feeling a deep sense of threat not only on an identity level, but also on an existential level. Some of the studies that you quote say that in societies where there are such entrenched alignments along party lines, violence is likely.[13]

Michael: All this fuels anger and rage.

Lilliana: Right.

Betty: By your observations of what's going on, are we in increasing danger of such violence?

Lilliana: Yes. Those who study other countries have found that the chances of civil war increase as politics becomes polarized along racial, ethnic, or religious lines. That's what we're seeing in the U.S. I'm not saying that we are about to enter a civil war because we have very strong democratic institutions, which are certainly being tested, but many of them are holding up.

Yet the potential for political violence is not just created by the alignment between racial, religious, and partisan identities. Currently, I'm working with Nathan Kalmoe at Louisiana State University, and together we've been running some surveys asking Americans about their acceptance of political

---

[13] Marc Scarcelli, "Social Cleavages and Civil War Onset," *Ethnopolitics* 13, no. 2 (2014): 181–202; Joshua R. Gubler and Joel Sawat Selway, "Horizontal Inequality, Crosscutting Cleavages, and Civil War," *Journal of Conflict Resolution* 56, no. 2 (2012): 206–232.

violence.[14] Our main question is, "Do you think it would be acceptable to use political violence if your candidate were to lose the 2020 election?" And what we're finding is that the stronger people's partisanship, the more people are identified socially with their party and with their ideological label, the more they are willing to advocate for political violence. Around 5 to 10 percent of the electorate says, "Yes."[15]

Betty: That's very significant.

Lilliana: That's millions of people.

Betty: This is serious, Lilliana. In this screen that people have over their eyes, brought about by their loyalty to their party, they are willing to endorse winning at all costs, inclusive of political violence.

Lilliana: We ask twenty different questions in our survey, and one of them is about endorsing violence. Many of the questions are also things like, "How would you feel if you heard that a senator had died of cancer?" "Would you be happier if that senator was a Republican or a Democrat?" And we find people preferring out-group senators to die of cancer.

Michael: To die of cancer?

Lilliana: Yes, we find partisans wishing harm to someone who represents the opposite party.

Betty: This might also explain the immigration conflict that's going on because these, too, are out-groups. And, if you're affiliated with Trump and the Republican Party, then you are likely to see immigrants as an out-group, not a part of you, and so feel aggression toward them.

Lilliana: Not only that, most immigrants that we're talking about are Latino, and Latino voters in the U.S. have been up for grabs in terms of which party

[14] Nathan P. Kalmore is the author of *With Bullets and Ballets: Partisanship and Violence in America's Civil War* (Cambridge, UK: Cambridge University Press, 2020).
[15] These findings and others were ultimately published as a book in 2022: Kalmoe, N. & Mason, L. (2022). *Radical American Partisanship: Mapping violent hostility, its causes, & the consequences for democracy.* University of Chicago Press.

they align with. And, in fact, the post-2012 election GOP autopsy report specifically said we need to reach out to Latino voters in order to win more elections.

Michael: Right. And they are Catholic.

Betty: Also the Southwest is becoming majority Latino in population.

Lilliana: They are Catholic. They're pro-life. They have relatively conservative social positions, or at least the older generation does. But since Trump has become president, Latinos have become more reliably Democrats at this point. The Republican Party increasingly represents white people, and so white people are losing as well because brown immigrants have come in and they're joining the Democratic Party instead of the Republican Party.

Michael: "Replacing us."

Betty: That's the language.

Michael: Can I ask a different question? Many people I know experienced Hillary's loss to Trump as a kind of death. And I suspect that a lot of people went into therapy over the election. You saw that, right, Betty?

Betty: Oh, definitely. There was a surge across the country in people who sought therapy and continue to seek therapy due to having "Trump Stress Disorder." The election was experienced as a trauma by many, which I thought was confusing, because it wasn't as if anybody was harmed. It was a peaceful election. Nothing cataclysmic happened. But people felt it as a cataclysmic thing. Lilliana, is that an example of this win or lose phenomenon you are describing, in terms of identity and alignment with a party? How big of an impact does it have on us?

Lilliana: Yes. One way to think about this is to go back to the Tajfel experiments with groups that meant nothing. We learned that people were willing to sacrifice to win for a group they had just learned they were members of. But now imagine we are talking about a group that reflects the way you were raised. Your parents and your siblings are part of it. It's the church that you go to every week. It's your racial group that you identify with very strongly. These are really crucial parts of who you are. And so if you are willing to sacrifice for the victory of a tiny meaningless group, imagine how much more invested you are in the victory of these really central identities.

Betty: And in your current research, this is leading more people to endorse violence when their party loses. But to your point, Lilliana, this willingness to consider violence as an option has been happening for the last twenty years, so this last election is really a symptom, rather than a cause. Has the ante been upped in terms of the power of partisanship?

Lilliana: There were some political scientists who did a study after the 2012 election, asking Republicans how their emotional state was.[16] For a baseline of feelings about sadness and the pain of loss, they asked parents of small children how they felt after the tragedy at Sandy Hook. And they also asked Bostonians how they felt after the Boston Marathon bombing. They found that Republicans after 2012 felt sadder than those other two groups of people. The emotional stake based on the threat of losing the 2012 election was even stronger than how the parents of small children felt after hearing about Sandy Hook.

Betty: What you're pointing to, Lilliana, is a kind of political climate change. It's getting hotter and hotter. We're talking about Sandy Hook, and we're talking about partisan citizens wishing for the hypothetical death, from cancer, of opposition senators. According to what you're seeing and what you're looking at, are we headed into a hotter environment in the future?

Lilliana: There's no way to predict the future. It's important to think about emotions in a scientific way, and I like to think of emotions with an evolutionary psychology approach. We think about anger and enthusiasm as *approach emotions*. They are the type of emotions that get people moving. In contrast, anxiety is what we call an *avoidance emotion*. People who are feeling anxious often sit down and wait and don't do anything. In terms of politics and campaigning, we want people to be angry and enthusiastic. We don't want them to feel anxious. Or, at the very least if they're feeling anxious, we want them to also feel angry.

---

[16] Pierce, L., Rogers, T., & Snyder, J.A. (2016). Losing Hurts: The happiness impact of partisan electoral loss. *Journal of Experimental Political Science* 3(1), 44–59.

From an evolutionary perspective, one of the best ways to get people to respond to a threat with anger instead of anxiety is to make them feel like they have a strong group around them. I use a story to understand this: Imagine you are standing in the middle of a savanna and then you hear the roar of a lion. If you're all alone and unarmed, when you hear that lion roar you're probably going to hide because you're under threat and you have no group with you.

Michael: Fear overwhelms.

Lilliana: You're very vulnerable. You're anxious. You're scared. But if you're standing there with a huge group of people and everybody is armed, and they're ready to protect each other, you might go fight the lion. So you will respond to that roar with anger and excitement. Then, you'll go and attack.

Much of what Trump did was to take a bunch of people who felt lost and alone and gave them a group, he gave them a sense of identity. They went from feeling anxious and uncertain as to where their sense of threat was coming from, or whether they could even fight it, to having him point to where the threat was coming from, whether he was correct or not. He gave them a target and told them, "You have this group of supportive people around you. Together, we're going to fight this threat, whether it be immigrants or women or Muslims," or whatever the group was that he was attacking that week.

Michael: The lion is really a threat. But when you have a demagogue stand up and say this other person is a lion, and that other person is also a threat…

Lilliana: Right. This tree is a lion.

Michael: …whether they are or not.

Betty: Right. Rather than these very complicated globalization issues or financial services or realities…

Michael: …or just another human being. Just taking another human being and turning them into a carnivorous existential threat, all for the sake of preserving group identity and winning.

Betty: Well, I also think it's simpler. It's a simpler story. If you're afraid, and everything is changing around you, and there are all sorts of uncertainties in the world...

Michael: Politically the Republicans have used this to great effect. They stand up and say, "You're under threat, and you are special." The Democrats stand up and say, "I am competent."

Betty: There's a disconnect between what the Democrat says and a hunger for a more motivating emotion.

Michael: Like raw anger and emotion.

Betty: Lilliana, what your story about the lion and the savanna says to me, with my focus on trauma treatment, is that we are also talking about flight or fight and freeze responses. If you are frozen, which is the most terrified state a person can get into when they are under threat, this correlates with what you are talking about. Fight is still a threat response, but it's a motivated one. And it is very interesting that, in many of our interviews, we keep coming back to people having a deep sense of threat and of danger. We are not in a war, and we are not under active threat by an opposing force, but many people are feeling a sense of dire threat in the midst of great uncertainty.

Michael: And yet no common enemy.

Betty: We have no common enemy right now. In fact, we're in a very fragmented world. We are almost looking for a place to situate our sense of threat. And that's very interesting because it seems to be driving our politics, too.

Lilliana: The way to think about this from a social identity perspective is to say that these are not physical threats. These are threats to status. And maybe we are seeing a competition over victimhood. It's like "who gets to be under the most threatened status?" In that regard, men are particularly threatened by the idea that women are taking over. So whoever can claim the most threatened status can motivate the most people. It's not necessarily a threat to actual physical safety as much as it is a threat to an internal sense of self-worth, which can be even more frightening. If your sense of who you are, your superiority, or your status level is being threatened, everything else feels terrible.

Michael: It's exactly what you're saying. Identity politics is, in effect, Balkanizing us as a nation.

Lilliana: It is also important to point out a change with regard to identity politics. Democrats are usually the party that is being accused of playing identity politics. But, in fact, I think the difference between the ways that the Democrats are running elections, and that Republicans are running elections does reflect the fact that the nation, on average, holds liberal policy preferences and, on average, the nation calls itself conservative. So the average American is a person who identifies as conservative and yet prefers liberal policy preferences.

Betty: So are we actually more open and diverse than we think we are?

Lilliana: It is the policies that are crosscutting—and remember, policies don't matter as much as identity. Trump was promising health care to everybody, and that was really popular. People liked that. People would like to have health care. People would like to have Social Security, and people would like to have protection for themselves and their families if something goes wrong in their life.

In general, Democrats can run on policy-based campaigns because their policies are actually more popular. And Republicans, ironically, are forced to run more identity-based campaigns. They are forced to run on status threats, which are about who is coming after you and who is going to replace you. These types of status threats are especially compelling to traditionally high-status groups like men and white people. This creates groups of people who call themselves conservatives but prefer liberal policies. This focuses more on who they feel like they are, rather than what they actually want the government to do. The two parties are actually incentivized to run different types of campaigns. And the problem is that identity-based campaigns are much more exciting than policy-based campaigns. Identity-based campaigns actually get people moving and motivated much more effectively than the policy-based campaigns,

With the policy-based campaigns, people often feel they would like the policies, but they are usually not motivated to get up off their sofas to protest or work to mobilize people to vote or go volunteer for a campaign, just because they think that's a sensible policy position. However, if I think immigrants are coming to take my Minnesota summer house, then I'm definitely going to get up and vote.

Betty: Well, that speaks to the evolutionary brain or neuroscience because our fear centers and our threat centers drive us and will supersede our thought centers in the neocortex. The policies tend to appeal to the thinking part of the brain, but if we are under threat, then we're not going to be thinking. Does that mean the policy approach at this moment is not so effective?

Lilliana: Yes. Because the more animal part of the brain takes over when there's an apparent threat. In general, policy-based campaigning will work better for Democrats than it would for Republicans because their policies are less popular on average. But, in general, across the board, identity-based campaigning is more effective than policy-based campaigning because it gets at these very powerful kind of animal parts of our brains that do take over from our rational, thoughtful, cognitive processes.

Michael: So there are severe limits to the effectiveness of policy-based campaigns.

Betty: But are they mutually exclusive? Can you have an emotionally driven policy, or mix of the two? Does it have to be one or the other?

Lilliana: That is what Democrats should probably do, if they know how to do it.

Michael: That was what Obama did in 2008.

Lilliana: He went for enthusiasm, not anger.

Michael: Yes. It was a positive emotion, not a negative emotion, but there was a lot of emotion associated with the campaign that wasn't really policy driven. That campaign asked, "Who are we? Are we the kind of nation that can elect a Black man to be president?"

Betty: And that campaign had a candidate who had the personality to really motivate people.

Michael: Obama seemed like a really nice guy you could have a beer with. Liliana, this brings me to try to understand what had been driving us. For instance, how does race divide us? It has always divided us as a country, going back to when the Constitution was being written and the conflict emerged between the Declaration of Independence and the Constitution in terms of human rights and slavery. And then there was the Civil Rights Act of 1964 and the Voting Rights Act of 1965. I don't know if it's apocryphal or not, but Lyndon Johnson supposedly said, "We've just lost the South for a generation" after the Civil Rights Act passed. If it's not actually accurate, it certainly feels accurate. And he was proven to be right. Then, Nixon picks that up and goes with his "Southern strategy." At that moment, the two parties cleave both in terms of race and in terms of geography. Is that where all of this starts in the modern sense? Certainly, we had a civil war over this, too. But is that where all this starts?

Lilliana: It is almost like we had this 50-year perfect storm where we had the Civil Rights Act, which basically told white, conservative Southern Democrats that they did not belong in the Democratic Party anymore. But also, at that point, you couldn't find a single Republican in the South. Being a Democrat in the South was a very powerful political identity. These guys did not just become Republicans overnight; they hated the idea of being Republicans.

Michael: This is left over from Reconstruction.

Betty: This is historical. They were the carpetbaggers.

Lilliana: This is after the Civil War, itself. There were conflicts within the Democratic Party. The more conservative Southern Democrats started moving away from the Democratic Party. But still...

Michael: These were the Dixiecrats, right?[17]

---

[17] The Dixiecrats were a right-wing states' right faction of the Democratic Party in the 1948 election.

Lilliana: Yes. But they still identified as Democrats. It took a generation for them to really move over into the Republican Party. And during that time, we had a bunch of crosscutting identities. In the 1970s and 1980s, as this process was occurring, there was a lot of confusion in terms of which party represented which people. That was a time of relatively low polarization, at least partisan polarization, because the parties were sending unclear cues to people.

And then in the 1990s, or late 1980s, the religious right became politically active. They joined forces with the Republican Party, and all of their requests were included in the Republican Party platform by the year 2000. That was an even clearer clue as to which side you were supposed to be on. During the 1990s, we also had partisan cable news appear. And then we had the internet appear. Not only were the parties sending much clearer cues about who belongs with which party, which race and religion belongs with which party, but also those cues were being communicated in much more efficient ways. So, partisan news and the internet, eventually, were able to communicate who is "us" and who is "them" more clearly and efficiently than the three network news channels used to do.

Betty: I picked up on that in your book about media and social media; you said it's to the point that social clubs like Kiwanis and bowling leagues are disappearing. Now we seem to be finding those niches online in very narrow echo chambers. People are finding likeminded people online, all across the country. Do you agree that people are finding their identity groups online rather than with in-person groups in their actual communities and neighborhoods?

Lilliana: We're definitely having a lot more of our social interaction online and, in general, people tend to be less polite when they are not face to face with another human being. It's possible for people not only to connect with increasing numbers of likeminded people online, but also to attack people who are unlike them in a way that they never would do in a face-to-face environment.

For instance, on issues like guns and abortion, we're seeing that people are having identity-based connections to opinion groups on either side. It's like everything is becoming wrapped together into this huge identity thread. There is a difference between pro-choice and pro-life identity versus pro-choice and pro-life attitudes in terms of preferences for what the government should do. What gets people much more active in politics is the identification with the group pro-choice or pro-life, regardless of the extremity of their policy positions. I've also found that, and others have found that, gun ownership is becoming a real identity marker. The NRA has actually been intentionally fostering a sense of threat to gun owners in order to create an identity among gun owners so that they will be loyal.

Michael: Political consultants and all these groups are playing us because they benefit.

Lilliana: Any time you feel that your group is under threat, you tend to think of yourself more as a group member. We all have many group memberships. You may not be thinking about your hometown as a salient group membership right now, but if somebody were to walk up to you and say that everybody from your hometown is stupid, you would all of a sudden start thinking about yourself as a member of your hometown. By presenting these threats to people, it creates more of a sense of group identity and the desire to have one's group win. You can think, "I'm going to join the fight because I need that victory for myself. And I didn't even think of myself as a member of that group until you brought it up and made me feel threatened." The threat itself is actually creating more identification with groups than we had before.

Michael: And more activism is creating more emotion.

Betty: And threat galvanizes your identity. Threat galvanizes political identity, and it seems like political operatives are capitalizing on this.

Lilliana: Threat doesn't just galvanize identity, it also prioritizes identity. And I think that's really important.

Betty: That is really significant.

Lilliana: Because we have so many identities. I think that helps explain, for instance, a movement of Obama voters to Trump voters. It's not that they went from being not racist to being racist. It's that their white identity was not as salient earlier than it was once Trump started campaigning. And after Obama's second term, his race itself made whiteness much more salient.

And then Trump took that and ran with it. Ashley Jardina from George Mason University is coming out with a new book called *White Identity Politics*.[18] When she started writing this book people were saying that it didn't exist: "There is no white identity." The point is that it's not really about making an identity. It's about reminding people about the group that they are already a member of.

Michael: It becomes this echo chamber. This thing begins to propel itself forward, and there's no way to stop it.

Lilliana: It's a fight. And it's also what you see in these battles over victimhood. Who's the real victim in the Brett Kavanaugh situation? The ones who can credibly claim being victims are the ones who are able to point to a direct threat and that galvanizes and mobilizes people to think about that identity and to participate in politics on behalf of that identity. If men are under threat, then men get to be the ones who are galvanized, and male identity becomes extremely salient. And everybody thinks about their political participation based on whether or not their male identity is being threatened.

Betty: So, paradoxically, the threat to identity and the victimhood of race is empowering.

Lilliana: Absolutely.

Michael: We all traffic in our grievances. That is where we are right now.

Betty: In my field, we'd call that a *persecution complex*.

Lilliana: I would also like to add that because the divide between the parties is increasingly becoming a kind of social justice divide, the idea of grievance is used to amplify political activism. High-status groups, like men and white people, are now crying for social justice in the name of their own grievances.

---

[18] We interview Ashley Jardina in Chapter 19.

Betty: Unfortunately, though we could clearly go on, we have to end now. Lilliana, thank you so much for this enlightening, informative, and most stimulating discussion.

Lilliana: Thank you so much. It was fun.

Chapter 19
White Identity Politics

Guest: Ashley Jardina
Episode Aired: February 26, 2019

Ashley Jardina is an assistant professor of public policy at the Frank Batten School of Leadership and Public Policy at the University of Virginia. She studies the nature of racial attitudes and group identities and their influence on public opinion and political behavior. Her book, White Identity Politics, *explores the conditions under which white racial identification and white consciousness among white Americans are predictors of policies, political candidates, and attitudes toward racial and ethnic groups.*

In early 2019, when we were considering what subjects to explore on our first season of Mind of State, *the proposal that we explore white identity politics inspired debate. Why talk about white identity politics? What is it, and why does it matter? Was it just about the political mindsets of subcultures of white supremacists, like the KKK?*

Recalling that debate now, in 2023, such skepticism seems naive. Since then, it has become clear that white identity politics is a significant driver of our ongoing partisan divisions and of the anti-immigrant, misogynistic, and racialized perspectives that now define the policies and politics of the Republican Party. Conversations with season two guests like Michael Cohen have illuminated how Trump and the Republicans ran the 2020 election on identity politics—white identity politics—even more so than Democrats. And, of course, the conspiracism and white nationalism driving the January 6, 2021 insurrection reveals—as Susan Fiske and Peter Glick point out (Chapter 16)—how lethal in-group attitudes can become.

And so our conversation with Dr. Ashley Jardina about her 2019 book White Identity Politics *feels even more relevant today than when we spoke to her four years ago. She is concise about why white identity has become salient and how this relates to the ever-intensifying conflicts over immigration in the U.S.:*

For a huge swath of American history, whites have been the mainstream. They have not had to think about being white because whites have been the numerical majority. And, of course, they still are right now. But what's happening in the United States as it becomes more racially diverse is that the numerical majority of whites is on the decline. So whites are starting to think more about their racial group, largely because of the increase in racial diversity in the United States.

...If we were to go back to a period in which we weren't talking about population projections in which whites are going to be the minority, when we hadn't experienced a giant wave of immigration to the United States, we weren't talking about whiteness in the same way. I would argue that we wouldn't be talking about white identity politics in the same way. Whites, for the most part, were not thinking about their race as they are right now.

It is important to note that like Eric Ward, Dr. Jardina makes a distinction between white nationalists—those who want to wipe out people of other races and religions—and whites who are reluctant to give up the privileges they possess to those they perceive as "other":

There are many whites in the United States who don't hold high levels of racial animus. They don't feel a sense of negative attitudes toward people of color or Blacks. But, nevertheless, they feel attached to their group. They're worried about their group. What that means, in effect, is that they're willing to support policies that protect their group or benefit their group, often at the expense of people of color. But they're not motivated purely because they dislike people of color. We can think about this with regard to building the wall, for example. There are some people who want us to build a border wall because they dislike Latinos and don't want more of them in the country. There are other people who would prefer that we decrease levels of immigration because they are worried that the United States is going to look different. They ask themselves, "What does that mean for me? What does that mean for my family and my children? Does it mean that we won't have the same advantages that we had before?" Those are different arguments. They get us to the same place. I would also say that there's a way that politicians can use these differences strategically. And that is really problematic. We're less likely to censor them or notice traces of aggression when they use the language of white identity than when they use the language of racial prejudice.

While at the time, we felt there to be a "tomayto/tomahto" quality to distinctions between the overt racism of white nationalism and covert prejudice of white identity politics, today that distinction feels more relevant. Whites who worry about preserving their in-group privileges are not violent white extremists storming the Capitol—yet. But Jardina's note that politicians on the right can exploit the underlying racism of white identity politics with the seemingly more palatable language of self-protection, serves as a warning of the ways those in (or seeking) power can exploit anxieties of scarcity and instability. Again, this calls us to be vigilant of this troubling connection, particularly when it comes to dominant in-group attitudes like those that define white identity politics.

Interview

Betty: We're really happy to have you, Ashley, with us today on *Mind of State*.

Ashley: Thank you so much. I'm delighted to be here.

Betty: My first question is about the impetus for your book. Why did you want to do research and write a dissertation on white identity politics—and then, expand it into a book?

Ashley: For one, in my own personal life, in part due to having grown up in the South, I have been thinking a lot about the fact that, contrary to what many academics believe, white people do consciously think of themselves as being white. In graduate-school, I was doing work thinking about racial prejudice and white racial prejudice. Part of that literature essentially argued that white people don't really think about race in the same way that people in racial and ethnic minorities do, and it seemed to me that that wasn't entirely true. Of course, I couldn't have predicted then that the world would look the way it did in 2016 and the way it does today. But I did think that race matters to white people in a way that we hadn't really thought very thoroughly about in the social sciences—and in political science, in particular.

Betty: When you talk about people who you grew up with and that they think of themselves as white, what do you mean by that?

Ashley: They believe their race matters. They feel a certain attachment to it. They think it matters for how they go about their lives. They recognize that being white has afforded them some advantages, some privileges that they're happy to have. They worry about their racial group. They recognize that their friends are white and that their family members are white. They do, in fact, see race as important to them, and it means something to how they think about the political and social world.

Michael: I think that was the interesting thing about your book. Is it the traditional social science notion that whiteness almost doesn't exist, that it's not a category, even though we're asked to fill it in on lots of forms? Group identity isn't something that's quantifiable. When somebody does think about themselves as white, we tend to think they are an Aryan Nation person or they're part of the KKK. And your very nuanced, fascinating book asks us to think about it differently. Is that fair?

Ashley: Absolutely. That's an excellent assessment. There's a good reason why social scientists have argued that whiteness is invisible. For most of recent history, if you think in particular about the post–civil rights era, white people possessed unchallenged economic and social and political power disproportionately in the United States simply by way of being white and being the dominant group. White people didn't have to think about their race. It's not something that mattered to them in the way that we know it matters for people of color in the United States.

White peoples' lives are not determined largely by their race. The argument that I make is that, although that might be true, changing circumstances in the political environment have left many white people feeling like their racial group's privilege position is threatened. As the U.S. has become more racially diverse, in the wake of the election of the first Black president, suddenly, there are all these things in the political environment that have made whites start to consider their race it in a way that we might observe Black people and other people of color in United States thinking about their race.

Michael: It feels to me that even some people listening to this conversation might be wondering why even talk about white identity? There's a kind of resistance to it. Why study it? Why write about it? Why do a podcast about it? There's something almost unseemly about it, and it's also perhaps not "politically correct."

Betty: I think it is also a question of equating white identity with that of racial minorities. This might be a misinterpretation, but it could mean to some that white identity is the same as Black identity, which it is absolutely not. Or that of Asian Americans or Latinos.

Michael: But I think that is what Ashley's book is saying, it's becoming that.

Betty: Is that what you're saying, Ashley?

Ashley: No, I'm not saying that. There is an argument to be made that in some ways the psychological process is the same—that white identity is just like any other social identity. It's an attachment that people have to some social status that's in the environment. But it's not the same in that it certainly matters for outcomes that are quite different for people of color. We know that identities that are formed among subordinated groups or oppressed groups across societies are a function of the fact that members of those groups experience discrimination and subordination. For people of color, social identities have been a way to fight for equality and achieve greater political incorporation. So, certainly, white identity is not like that. Whites are a dominant group. But many of the factors that give rise to the development of any type of group identity are factors that are present in the formation of white identity. The major difference is the fact that white identity is an identity that's formed among a dominant group, a group of people based on race, who have a disproportionate share of social and economic power in society.

Michael: And that's your argument. That there are real political consequences. Donald Trump is as good an example as any of the consequences of white identity.

Ashley: Yes, absolutely. It matters.

Michael: I want to go to an anecdote that you tell in the book about a guy named Jim Boggess. He owns Jimbo's Deli in New Jersey, and he put up a sign in his window that read "Celebrate Your White Heritage in March, White History Month." If you are listening in and you hear that somebody put up a sign that says, "Celebrate your white heritage in March, White History Month," how does that make you feel? And Ashley, how do you read it? And why did you tell that story in the book? I thought it was fascinating, not the least of which is because when he talks, he doesn't seem like a bad guy.

Ashley: No. He seems well-intentioned, as are many white people who possess a sense of racial identity or think that whites ought to be able to celebrate whiteness. One of the things that I find is that in this subset of white people who do feel this sense of attachment matters to them, is the idea that they ought to be able to be proud to be white. They should be able to form organizations around their racial group. Now, of course, the problem with doing that is it ignores the fact that essentially every day we celebrate whiteness, to the detriment of other groups. Whiteness has been institutionalized. We don't have to have a "white history month."

Michael: Every month is white history month, right?

Ashley: Absolutely. It's a denial of the real structural inequality that we see across groups. But many white people don't really know about that or aren't aware of that. There is some degree of willful innocence or ignorance in this perspective, and it's an innocence that's problematic for achieving a more racially egalitarian society. And the other thing that's happening is that many whites are starting to believe that because they're being admonished for trying to form these organizations, this is more evidence that whites as a group are being discriminated against. Some whites believe they are being unfairly maligned or unfairly treated for being white and wanting to feel some sense of pride in their race. And again, that's a problem.

Betty: When you talk about the innocence of white people who don't know about this, I'm struck and even perturbed because there is the glaring fact of the history of slavery in the United States and…

Michael: …and Jim Crow.

Betty: And Jim Crow and segregation and is it possible that whites could be ignorant of this? Is this a result of the decline of historical knowledge in the United States?

Michael: When I think about somebody like Jim Boggess, I don't think he's denying that history or ignorant of it. When he was attacked for the sign, his response was that "no matter what you are—Muslim, Jewish, Black, white, gay, straight—you should be proud of what you are. I shouldn't have to feel bad about being white."[1] I don't think he's denying it in his mind.

Betty: No, but Ashley was speaking to the innocence of white people. Can you say more about that, Ashley?

Ashley: Absolutely. There are two important points here. One is that I do think that people are incredibly unaware of racism and the degree to which racism matters in American society. I think they're unaware of racial discrimination. When I talk to my students, I lay out the landscape of wealth inequality between Blacks and whites in the United States. I talk about discrimination in hiring. I talk about redlining and housing policy. And for many of my college students this is the first and only time they will have ever talked about these things in detail and the only time they will be exposed to talking about racial inequality in the United States. I do think that there is a lack of awareness among some white people. Of course, that's no accident. Our schools and institutions have failed to teach white students about the legacy of racism in the U.S.

But there's another thing that's going on here, that's even more insidious. Whites are starting to co-opt the language that racial and ethnic minorities have used as part of the development of their group identity, as part of their effort to try to achieve racial and political equality in the United States. This is language that states "we should celebrate our group. We should have these spaces. We should have these organizations." Many whites are saying, "We should be able to do that, too. They [meaning people of racial minorities] get to do it, so why can't we?"

Betty: That's the thing that I'm again caught on. I'm assuming your students who are hearing about this for the first time are white students

---

[1] Jardina, A.E. (2019). *White Identity Politics.* Cambridge University Press. p. 136.

because certainly students of color live this inequity and are highly aware of it. Either they've experienced racism, or they're aware that they're not part of the majority. But the insidiousness of co-opting the language of minority subjugation is interesting and disturbing because whites have not been discriminated against. To a degree, you're saying that whites are now experiencing subjugation. Or they feel they are. That's what's interesting to me because it's systemically untrue.

Michael: And that's what Jim Boggess expressed in his deli. When he comes under attack for being racist because of the sign, the other quote from Jim that I pulled from your book, Ashley, is "if there's any racial discrimination going on here, it's by people who are objecting to the sign because I'm white. I just want to be included. Why is this such a big deal? I don't get it."[2] So he feels like there's racism against him for celebrating his whiteness.

Betty: It's an interesting thing about the inclusion and the exclusion here. What is Jim feeling excluded from, that he wants to be included in, Ashley?

Ashley: He wants to be able to celebrate being white and to celebrate his race, just as he observes members of other races doing. But the problem is that it ignores the fact that we don't have a white history month for a reason. It ignores the fact that there are very real differences in the lived experiences of Blacks and whites in the United States and the fact that we don't need a white history month. We don't need whites to form all-white organizations. They do that already and have done that historically.

Betty: History *is* white history. It's mostly written by white people and men. I'm Asian American, but my parents were born and raised in China by way of Taiwan. And when I have visited Taiwan and China, I am part of a homogenous culture. But I grew up as a minority in the United States. It's a unique experience to have lived and been born here in the United States and lived with racism and lived with being a minority and being very, very aware that sometimes I'm the only Asian in the room. And then to go to a country where I'm like everybody else; I'm a part of the majority. And in China, being Asian is not something that folks think about. And that was highlighted for me by the fact that I was working with some patients who came to the

---

[2] Jardina, p. 136.

United States as students. They were really shocked to come here and start experiencing the minority experience that they'd never experienced before as Chinese nationals. Can you say something about this comparison—that in Asia, somebody who's Asian and born in an Asian country does not feel their race, at least in my anecdotal experience? And that American whites do feel their race. Is there something about the American context that is different?

Ashley: It's not that the American context is necessarily different. What you are describing coincides with the way that whites have operated and thought about race, even if we were to go back just ten years ago. The way in which identities and social identities often become salient is relative to something else. It begins when people start to think about their group because they are exposed to a contrast with their group.

For a huge swath of American history, whites have been the mainstream. They have not had to think about being white because whites have been the numerical majority. And, of course, they still are right now. But what's happening in the United States as it becomes more racially diverse is that the numerical majority of whites is on the decline. So whites are starting to think more about their racial group, largely because of the increase in racial diversity in the United States.

Michael: Which is why immigration is such a big topic.

Ashley: Right. If we were to go back to a period in which we weren't talking about population projections in which whites are going to be the minority, when we hadn't experienced a giant wave of immigration to the United States, we weren't talking about whiteness in the same way. I would argue that we wouldn't be talking about white identity politics in the same way. Whites, for the most part, were not thinking about their race as they are right now.

Michael: What is the driver for whites to be focusing on being white now? And to be clear, identifying as white is not the same thing as wanting to be in the Ku Klux Klan. Can you help us understand what you mean by white identity politics? I think a lot of people would think you're talking about racists, people who see whiteness as something racially superior. Can you make that distinction?

Ashley: I'm not talking about people who are members of the alt-right or card-carrying members of the KKK by any means. To be clear, those people are certainly very high on white identity. But actually, I'm talking about a much wider swath of the American population. If we look across surveys, we see that about 30 to 40 percent of whites in the United States possess a sense of identity. What I mean by that is that they feel an attachment to their group. They think that being white is important to them. It's important to who they are. And they feel some sense of commonality with other whites, and they feel, to some extent, proud to be white. I am not referring to people who want to join the KKK, but rather to those who think that being white affords them certain advantages that they're happy to have, and they're worried about the status of their group in an increasingly diverse country.

Betty: And when you talk about the awareness of being white, that's a racial distinction. But it obscures the fact that some people are Italian, some people are Irish, some people are Germans, and so on.

Michael: But those distinctions have gone away.

Betty: That does seem to be a trend over time. Have those national identities or cultural identities that come from having immigrated from outside the U.S., or from being descendants of immigrants from different countries, been flattened into whiteness?

Ashley: For many decades in the United States, for a big portion of the 20th century, we thought that those ethnic identities mattered for whites. They were consequential for some period of time. But, for the most part, whether someone is white, and they think of themselves as Italian or they have some Irish ancestry, those aren't especially politically consequential nowadays. I couldn't go out and ask somebody how important being Italian is to them and therefore have a good sense of who they were going to vote for in the upcoming election. Those identities just aren't as salient to people as they once were. There is certainly an argument that they have been folded under the general umbrella of a pan-European whiteness. When we think about white people in the United States, we think about people from Europe, generally.

Michael: Clearly, one of the big drivers in the current upsurge of a white identity movement is immigration. Previously American identity felt under assault by the waves of Irish, Italian, Polish, and German immigrants in the late 19th and early 20th century.

Betty: And there was a very anti-Catholic thread in the United States. The KKK is anti-Black, anti-Catholic, and anti-Jewish. We cannot forget John F. Kennedy was at risk for not being elected because of his Catholicism.

Michael: So, I assume, Ashley, if you were taking that survey in the late 1800s thru at least the mid-1900s, one's immigrant status would have had a profound impact on voting. And today, those particular identities have far less of an impact.

So, what are the consequences of the upsurge of white identity sentiment on our politics? How has white identity changed our politics? How has it changed our political life and our political discourse? Because it's more than just how people self-identify. It's also about how people behave out of that identity, how they vote out of that identity, and the policies that are chosen for our country based at least partially on white identity.

Ashley: I want to return to the early 1900s because immigration is such an important component of this story. It's really interesting that, at the time, people didn't think of the Irish or the Italians as white. There are plenty of historians who have thought about the fact that over the course of the 20th century, eventually Irish and Italians and other groups were subsumed under this label of whiteness. But if you go back and look at the conversations that we as a country were having in the 1920s about immigration and about race, and even if you go and look at the congressional record and what politicians were talking about prior to passing the Immigration Act of 1924, which put huge quotas and restricted immigration for most of the 20th century, they were talking about whiteness. They were having very explicit conversations about protecting and preserving America as a white nation. They used language like "we need to preserve the Nordic stock of the country." For most of American history, race and the definitions of whiteness and the definition of who gets to be considered American are deeply tied together. It's not surprising that once again, when we've experienced another wave of immigration from groups that aren't considered white by today's standards, that we are having these same conversations. I like to say that if we could go back and measure public opinion in the early 1920s and ask about white identity, we would have seen very similar results to what we've observed today.

Betty: And it's dynamic because back then whiteness did not include Irish and Italian Americans or Jewish Americans. Now the identity of whiteness includes all these different religions and ethnicities in this pan-European identity. I remember this about politician Eliot Spitzer when he was still a viable political figure here in New York City. Because he was so dynamic as New York attorney general, some folks were hoping that he would become the first Jewish president. That was going to be questionable because he was Jewish. And this was the case with Bernie Sanders as well. His identity as a Jew, even though he's white, was a factor in the 2016 campaign. In terms of how we define whiteness, as somebody who is non-white, I stand up...

Michael: Some have suggested that Latinos and Asians could eventually be considered white.

Betty: I resent that. I really do. I mean because it really denies my identity and my own experiences of racism. I think for people of color and people who have had to deal with the subjugation of racism, there's also an erasure of our cultural associations and our struggles against whiteness when it is said that Asians and Latinos could be eventually considered white. There's also a question of what "becoming white" even means. What you, Ashley, seem to point out is this: Whiteness is not a fixed thing. It's an idea. But what kind of idea is it, and how is it in flux?

Ashley: One of the key points that I try to hone in on in the book—and why this is so important—is how it relates to racial equality in the United States. It gets to the larger question about why we care about white identity politics in the first place. It's because the United States is organized along a racial hierarchy, where whites are at the top and other groups fall somewhere down in line.

Part of the effort to redefine whiteness over time is, in fact, part of an effort to allow whites to preserve their position at the top of the racial hierarchy. Some people see the story of the Irish and Italians and Jews becoming white as one of assimilation. But another argument is that it was a way for whites, in the face of feeling like their group was losing its numerical majority—just as they are today—to recapture or preserve their position at the top of this racial hierarchy. White identity politics is a problem for racial equality. It's not the same as prejudice in terms of an outwardly expressed psychological feeling of animus toward a group. But it's very much part of a system of racism and racial inequality, because very simply, whites who have this sense of identity do not want to give up their group's dominant and privileged status. They are very much seeking to maintain a system of inequality, even while simultaneously denying that racial inequality exists. And that's why it matters.

Michael: Implicit in all of this is that African Americans can never become white and are always held at the bottom by a system that discriminates through redlining or any number of other institutionalized and systemic racism. I want to shift a bit because perhaps one of the triggers in all of this was the election of Barack Obama. For a short while, there was a sense of hope that we had entered into a new era, that Obama's election meant we were post-racial—that we were finally accepting of Black people at the highest levels of our society. But, in your book, you quote Rush Limbaugh as saying, "I went to bed last night thinking we're outnumbered. I went to bed last night thinking we lost the country. I don't know how else to look at this." And you quote Bill O'Reilly as saying, "The white establishment is now the minority." How much of what you're seeing in terms of white identity is about the elevation of our first Black president?

Ashley: It's certainly one of the most important components of the story. It's hard to separate the confluence of events that have happened here. We have the election of the first Black president, which is, of course, deeply symbolic. And it's not just symbolic because of how meaningful it is for people of color in the United States. For many whites it became part of the narrative that the country, as they knew it, had changed. And, in fact, there's some reality to that perception. Obama won, in part, because the country had become more diverse and, in part, because so many people of color turned out to vote for him. I like to point out that in 2012, Obama had the lowest share of the white vote of any successful or victorious Democratic presidential candidate ever. Ever. Obama didn't win reelection thanks to white voters. The country had become more diverse.

Michael: He won because of people of color.

Betty: Because of a coalition.

Michael: A coalition of people of color that was sizable, if not the most significant part of the votes that put him in the White House. And that seems to have triggered a whole lot of things, including the birther lie and other discriminatory, racist reactions.

Betty: It also seems to have triggered the election of Donald Trump. There's a distinction in your book that differentiates people who think of racial minorities as out-groups. They have racial animus to out-group minorities, and you distinguish them from whites who are trying to protect their in-group status. For a person of color like me, I say "tomayto, tomahto." But you're trying to make a distinction and I want to understand how that distinction is useful.

Ashley: It's a very important question. I don't want to dismiss the significance of racial prejudice. Do I think the people like the Rush Limbaughs and Bill O'Reillys of the world are also probably racially prejudiced in addition to scoring quite high on white identity? Absolutely. I'm sure that's true. I don't spend a whole lot of time listening to either of them, but it seems to me that there's plenty of evidence that in addition to worrying about whites, they also don't have favorable views toward people of color in the United States. This is a distinction that matters to some extent, but also doesn't matter. It doesn't matter in that much of what we're observing with respect to the consequences of white identity looks a whole lot like the same things that we observe in the consequences of racial prejudice. But the psychological phenomena are different, and that does matter. And it also matters for how politicians talk about race and the extent to which they're able to use the politics of white identity to win elections.

There are many whites in the United States who don't hold high levels of racial animus. They don't feel a sense of negative attitudes toward people of color or Blacks. But, nevertheless, they feel attached to their group. They're worried about their group. What that means, in effect, is that they're willing to support policies that protect their group or benefit their group, often at the expense of people of color. But they're not motivated purely because they dislike people of color. We can think about this with regard to building the wall, for example. There are some people who want us to build a border wall because they dislike Latinos and don't want more of them in the country. There are other people who would prefer that we decrease levels of immigration because they are worried that the United States is going to look different. They ask themselves, "What does that mean for me? What does that mean for my family and my children? Does it mean that we won't have the same advantages that we had before?" Those are different arguments. They get us to the same place. I would also say that there's a way that politicians can use these differences strategically. And that is really problematic. We're less likely to censor them or notice traces of aggression when they use the language of white identity than when they use the language of racial prejudice.

Don't get me wrong. We're also in a political environment where it's clear that politicians can say egregious things about people of color and get away with it. But at the same time, it feels more palatable to people when politicians say things like, "We just need to protect Americans, or we need to make sure that white people are getting their fair share, that we're paying attention to the needs of white people."

Michael: Make America Great Again.

Ashley: Yes. Even when it's expressed as "we should worry about the competition in the country. We should worry about the effects of immigration." That sounds much more innocuous to people than this more inflammatory language of racial prejudice, but it has the same effect. It's just arriving at it from a different angle.

Betty: The positioning on it is still from a white perspective. Growing up as a child of recent immigrants I listened to the language used to justify the wall from a different perspective. "You don't belong here. We don't want you." I hear both messages loud and clear. And now among my patients and friends, I hear about people of color who were born here fearing for their citizenship. The symbolism of the wall can be seen as a dog whistle from the other side. And this is painful. It's also scary.

This is what I want to understand because this is where the partisanship starts to become really entrenched. How does understanding this nuance help the progressive side of the equation to address this growing trend toward white identity politics that can surely look like racism? And from many conversations we've had with other political scientists, historians, and social psychologists, Trump is a symptom of this trend, not a cause. Can you comment on that?

Ashley: Politicians on the right are far more likely to use racialized language of any kind, whether that's the language of white identity politics or to make more blatant racial appeals. As a country, we are increasingly divided along party lines not only with respect to race, but also with respect to racial attitudes. It's a strategy that Republicans use effectively. There's an argument that people make that implies that if Democrats could just hang on for a couple more years, enough people of color and certainly enough Latinos will dominate the electorate and vote. At that point the Democrats will be more likely to win elections. But the line that Democrats have to walk is a bit more precarious because they're in a position where they still need to win the favor of white voters. Many from the Democratic white base are, in fact, concerned about immigration and the demographic changes they're observing. The Democrats need to be mindful of the concerns of their white voters without simultaneously alienating people of color in the United States. In the short term, they are in a very tricky position.

But I think that we also have to think about just what it means for Republican politicians to play on race and use it as a political strategy. It's certainly not anything new, but it's troubling. We do observe whites in the United States co-opting the strategies of women and racial and ethnic minorities and Blacks, in particular, when it comes to identity politics. Identity politics traditionally have been a product of discrimination and subordination. They have been a tool that people of color, in particular, have used in order to achieve greater political power and political empowerment in the United States. They are a result of oppression and subordination. We wouldn't have identity politics to the same extent if we did, in fact, live in a more egalitarian society.

Betty: This is the language of conservatives about identity politics, that it's a tool and a tactic rather than expression that emerges due to sufferings and injustices of real structural oppression.

Michael: But if you don't identify as an African American, you don't assert your rights as an American. It's an important piece to racial equality that has been denied.

Ashley: Racial consciousness has been absolutely essential to the ability of people of color in the United States to organize politically, to seek out policies, and to fight for equal rights in society. It's a tool, but it's a tool that has been used in attempts to gain more equality in the United States. It is not just political strategy. It's also, in fact, the consequence of living a life in which your race or your gender overdetermines the outcomes in the way you experience your day-to-day life.

Betty: You would call it finding a way to speak and a way to find efficacy and to use the principles stated in the Declaration of Independence that all men are created equal...

Michael: And white people really don't need to use that language to get their fair share. They have it. They have more than their fair share, actually.

Betty: Correct. And the United States has had this bifurcated history where, on the one hand, we have an aspirational goal that all people are created equal and, on the other hand, our country was founded upon a system of slavery where white people were dominant, subjugating, and they enjoyed all the privileges of such an oppressive system.

Ashley: That's part of the problem with these critiques or these attacks on identity politics. They fail to recognize that the reason why important social cleavages and identity issues with respect to race have developed in the first place is because not all groups have been equal or had equal access to power and resources in American society. Part of the development of identity politics is grounded in the experience of racial discrimination against Black people who have worked together collectively to try to achieve political, social, and economic equality.

Michael: I'm curious, Ashley. How do you read Trump? How do you read Trump's election? Certainly when he started, people didn't take his candidacy seriously. Even his final victory in the Electoral College was a shock to many people who didn't think of him as a viable candidate. And yet it seems to me that white identity politics propelled him into the White House. Or at least that was a huge factor.

Ashley: You're right to say that. In some ways, Trump is a symptom, not a cause. We know that white identity politics and the sense of attachment that whites had toward their group mattered well before Trump. But if someone could write a playbook based on white identity politics, Trump knew exactly what to do. He knew exactly how to appeal to this particular subset of white voters. For one thing, he began his campaign by focusing almost entirely on the issue of immigration. If you go and look at Trump's campaign website in August 2015, when he was first launching his presidential bid, the only issue on his website was immigration reform. You can use the Wayback Machine to see what the website looked like in August 2015. Immigration was the only issue there.

The other interesting thing Trump did is that he departed from the traditional Republican platform when it came to supporting particular social welfare policies. For decades, Republicans have campaigned on trying to privatize Social Security, to cut back on Social Security, to cut back on Medicare. And what we know is that these policies are associated with whiteness. They disproportionately benefit whites in the United States. They also stand in contrast to other racialized policies, like welfare. They are seen as rewards for hard work, rather than government handouts. In this way, they are linked to whiteness and white people. Trump came along and said, "I'm not going to cut Social Security. I'm going to protect it. I'm not going to cut Medicare. We've got immigration. We've got the preservation of these particular social welfare policies. We've got this opposition to Obama."

Michael: Arguing again that Obama is not legitimate.

Ashley: Exactly. The whole birther movement. Trump appealed to the concerns about diversity, about changing demographics, and about protecting policies that benefit white Americans.

Michael:. One of the things you point out is that the protection of big government programs, like Social Security, was anathema in the Republican Party prior to Trump's campaign. There is a realignment in the party now around Trump and Trumpism. I think your book is so important because it recognizes how white identity issues have reshaped our politics and how we will be fighting over this question of identity in the decades ahead.

Betty: Do you see Trump as a reaction to Obama? You mentioned that Obama's coalition, which re-elected him in 2012, was not dominated by white votes. And here comes Trump as a reaction. Is Trump, as some people in the media have suggested, a last gasp? In your book, you look at the numbers and you do a lot of statistical analysis saying that, although the demographics are changing in the country, Democrats can wait this out.

Ashley: Whites still make up the disproportionate share of the electorate in presidential elections, and they will for some time. Obama was able to turn out people of color in far greater numbers than we'd seen in the past. So it's unclear whether that's going to happen again in 2020 or 2024, even if we have a person of color running as the Democratic candidate. Are they going to turn out people of color at the same rate? It's not clear that they will be able to do that. And if they can't, then more white voters will be voting. And it seems that people are going to continue to be concerned about issues like immigration. Anytime there is any sort of question about Trump's political legitimacy, he raises the issue of immigration. It rallies the white base. We've observed over and over again that it's an effective strategy.

Michael: It works because the Trump base feels their whiteness is under attack and, in the United States, race matters. This is a very fraught, emotional, important conversation because many whites were too quick to think that, after the Voting Rights Act and the Civil Rights Act, we had solved the problems of discrimination and institutional racism. You can't avoid the issue of race in America. And it's a really painful conversation to have.

Betty: I think something to talk about is the trauma of racism. I'm interested in hearing your thoughts on this, Ashley. The "tomayto, tomahto" aspect of identity politics that I mentioned earlier seems to come from the perspective of whites. It obscures the pain of racism to split hairs about whether we are dealing with racism or with the white fear of being a minority. Maybe whites are experiencing this trauma as well. But that kind of subjugation—where a person is reduced to a label—is that something that those advocating white identity are experiencing as well? The traumatic pain of being discriminated against for what you are rather than who you are?

Ashley: Of course, racism is a deep and significant problem in the United States. We don't have the conversations about it that we ought to be having.

It's also clear not only from my study of the development of white identity, generally, but also in my work on race and racism and in my own anecdotal experience teaching about race, that most whites don't really understand what racism does to people of color in the United States. But I think the danger of white identity politics is that it's allowing whites to claim that they too are experiencing discrimination, that they also know what it's like to be an oppressed group and that's certainly not the case. They do not experience the world in the way that Black people experience life in America by any means.

Betty: It's absolutely impossible.

Michael: I think what's so interesting about your work on white identity politics and its relationship to racism is that by identifying it, you run the risk of appearing as if you are endorsing it. That's obviously not what you're doing. It's clearly a significant phenomenon. It's a statistical phenomenon. You can quantify it. You can measure it. It's driving politics. And if we ignore it because it's uncomfortable, we ignore it at our own risk. So seeing it and talking about it is not the same thing as signing off on it. And I think that's really the great highwire and risky act that you've taken here, which is to go out and to say, "We need to have this conversation. We need to see that people are now identifying as white." But identifying as white no longer means going out and joining the Aryan Nation. As psychological, sociological, and political phenomena, white identity has mainstreamed, and it's being driven by a demographic shift in the United States. If we don't recognize it and we ignore it, we do so at our own risk.

Betty: I agree with everything Michael just said about white identity politics. But I come from the fields of psychology, psychoanalysis, and trauma. For whites to appropriate the language and the pain of what whites do not experience is egregious, at least for me personally. It's a trend, and we must pay attention to it. But it is creating a rift in the country. It has brought us Trump, who has spun this into an ever-consuming conflict. How do we get out of this? How do we emerge from this place that we've fallen into?

Ashley: I wish I had a definitive answer to that question because it's exactly the right question to ask. It's a hard one to answer because it requires us as a country to have real serious conversations about race. It would require whites to both understand that they have a disproportionate share of power and resources that they have to be willing to give up, and it also would require many hearts and minds to change when it comes to racism and racial prejudice. I want to go back to this point because I think this is where the distinction between white identity and racial prejudice is important. We often think of racism and racial prejudice as this feeling that some white people have. They just don't like people of color. And that's absolutely true.

But the other thing that's going on here and that I want people to understand is that there are many white people who don't feel this dislike or animus or hostility toward people of color, but nevertheless don't want to relinquish the privileges that they have as a result of being white. And they will fight to preserve those privileges and to maintain their power. And so therefore, they're helping to preserve a system of racial inequality in the country. This is an objective explanation, description, and observation of what white identity is about for many people. This is not a good thing for the world or for the country, especially if you care about racial equality.

Michael: And that's driving their identity.

Betty: In other interviews we have talked about this appropriation of being persecuted and a sense of grievance. White men feel put upon at this moment in history, and Trump is giving them a voice. There's a competition to being the most victimized in the country. And it seems to obscure true structural racism and inequality. It seems to be another example of the prevalence of perception versus fact.

Michael: I think that's exactly what Ashley is saying. I think we've also lost a sense of a common story. We are a nation of too many stories. We lack one unifying story that holds us all together. We seem to have lost a sense that we have something at stake in each other's equality and in the humanity of other people who may come from a different place than us or belong to a different race or have a different sexual orientation. We've lost that common thread.

Betty: We've lost a shared definition of our common humanity, like in our Declaration of Independence: that all people are created equal. That was our aspiration as the United States and that ideal brought a lot of people to this country. But we do not acknowledge that has not been the actual fact of American history.

Ashley: When you think about the history of the United States and you think about how central race has been to how we've come to be who we are as a country, I'm not sure the idea that we should all have a common story and should all be working together toward equality is something that we've aspired to. It's certainly not something that we have ever achieved, by any means. And clearly, we're at a point in time where it seems like we're more fractured with respect to race than ever. My less optimistic sense of the long view of American history is that we've never really gotten particularly close to that goal either.

Betty: Ashley, thank you so much for joining us. And good luck with your book. It's really interesting and provocative. And we loved having you on *Mind of State*.

Ashley: Yes, absolutely. Thank you.

Chapter 20
A "Syndemic"–Climate, Race & COVID-19

Guest: Adrienne Hollis
Episode Aired: January 6, 2021

Dr. Adrienne Hollis is the vice president for Environmental Justice, Health and Community Revitalization, and Conservation at the National Wildlife Federation. She's an environmental toxicologist and an environmental attorney. She was an associate professor in the Institute of Public Health at Florida A&M University and is an adjunct professor at the George Washington University Milken School of Public Health. So she's a bit of a triple threat: scientist, lawyer, and public health advocate.

When COVID-19 hit the U.S. in 2020, the country was beset not only with a global pandemic, but also an economic downturn, a historic uprising against racial injustice, and a series of massive wildfires and hurricanes. Terms like perfect storm, Armageddon, *and* end-of-days *were not too extreme to describe the confluence of so many cataclysmic events. We turned to Dr. Adrienne Hollis to explain how she saw their convergence as being far from coincidental, but in fact interconnected. Introducing the term* syndemic—*a situation in which two or more epidemics are concurrent, or serial—she convincingly argued we were undoubtedly in a syndemic and counted no less than five concurrent social, public health, and political epidemics impacting the U.S. at the beginning of 2021: the COVID-19 pandemic, systemic racism, climate change, environmental contamination, and economic crisis.*

In discussing this syndemic, Dr. Hollis observed how the pandemic sparked an unprecedented public reckoning with racism and environmental racism:

...somebody asked me right after Mr. Floyd was murdered, "Is it too soon to talk about environmental justice and what happened?"

I replied, "Absolutely not! How can you not talk about it?" I made the connection for myself between George Floyd's murder and public health. You can't talk about public health without talking about climate change, without talking about racism. Everything is connected. It's never too soon, but I think it can be a little too late. And I think the fact that so many people have passed because of COVID makes it late.

But now that people are listening; it's not too late. I think COVID opened people's eyes to a lot of things. I don't know why. I don't know what it is about COVID in particular that made people stand up and notice that people are being murdered or there is a lot of police brutality or that prisons don't have air conditioning and people are living in inhumane conditions. For instance, many homeless people don't have access to water. Before, we would give messages about this and nobody paid attention. Now communities that I work with are making a deliberate effort to provide running water to homeless populations, not only because of climate change, but also because at least homeless people can now wash their hands. At least we can do that for them in the middle of extreme heat during the day when their shelters are closed and there may be many COVID carriers around.

Nearly three years later, the connections Dr. Hollis made are still highly relevant. They point to the urgency of seeing the interrelationship between politics, economics, climate change, public health, mental health, and racism. Adding up these links, Dr. Hollis lands on an approach to how we shift the tide from within this syndemic approach:

We already know that just focusing on profit doesn't work. We had four years of that to the detriment of many people. We haven't focused just on people before. It seems that the best approach would be to incorporate everything—including profit, people, health, jobs. It's about bringing all the stakeholders to the table—your economist, your engineer, your community member, your small-business owner, your farm worker, your farm owner— everybody, because everybody has a stake in making this a success. I don't know how to do it, but I know I'm open to it, and I know it's necessary.

It is particularly fitting to end this section on the Anxieties of Race & Dominance *with Dr. Hollis's conversation because, we, too, have been seeing connections among the discussions we have had with our other guests, whether it be about race, gun control, teens and politics, or even the Syrian Civil War. Themes of truth versus lies, accountability versus blame, care versus negligence, belonging versus exclusion, and dominance versus oppression emerge from this confusing mix.*

Dr. Hollis teaches us that it is crucial to pay attention to these intersections. They illuminate causal, mutually reinforcing connections between intractable conflicts, and this shows us not only what matters, but also what is being obscured. Such neglect can result in mental and emotional stressors, with unattended-to traumas, fears, and anxieties leading to explosive anger, violence, and harm done to individuals and communities alike. As we approach another consequential presidential election season in 2024, it might even be that our democracy depends on our paying ever-closer attention to these interconnections.

Interview

Jonathan: When we were getting this season started and we were thinking about all the topics that we wanted to talk about, climate change popped to the top of the list. From a political standpoint, I go way beyond the Green New Deal. I'm thinking about all of the policy and legislative and legal measures that we can use to try to shape human behavior, so we can somehow pull back from the destruction that we're doing to our planet and to the human race.

Betty: Absolutely. Psychologically speaking, it's really interesting how these macro issues are coming into my sessions, into the individual conversations I'm having with people. Pictures of the San Francisco Bay Area looking like midnight at midday, hurricanes hitting Louisiana, and the feeling that we've got these multiple monumental crises bombarding us. It really can feel like it's Armageddon. And how we contend with that psychologically feels monumental.

Jonathan: So, here we are. We're looking at climate change. We think we've got an apt topic for our show that is about both psychology and politics, and then we hit something even richer, something even deeper.

Betty: Something that connects it all.

Jonathan: Right. And the term for this is *environmental racism*. That's where we landed and what we're talking about today is the connection between climate change and the impacts it has on communities that are already being disproportionately affected by economic injustice and racial injustice.

Betty: Local communities that are environmentally compromised.

Jonathan: Environmentally compromised for sure. And particularly when you think about how climate change has come together with the pandemic, with the George Floyd protests and the response of the Black Lives Matter movement. It seems like environmental racism is exactly right for us to talk about on *Mind of State*.

Betty: And to talk to us about it is an expert on the topic—thank you so much for joining us, Adrienne.

Adrienne Hollis: Thank you for having me. I'm excited to be here.

Jonathan: Tell us a little bit about your background and what drew you to the topic of climate change to begin with?

Adrienne: My background is in environmental health. I have a PhD in nutritional biochemistry, and I started working as a toxicologist looking at chemicals and how they affected the body. From there, I started working with communities and looking at how certain populations were affected by their environment more than others, and disproportionately so. For the past twenty plus years, my work has been on environmental justice. Climate change is a big part of that because environmental justice is intimately linked to systemic racism. With climate change, we see a lot of issues about people who were placed in living situations because of their race. And those are the areas that are most affected by climate change, first and worse.

Betty: As you were doing toxicology and looking at the communities most affected, you were drawn into the broader issues of environmental justice and systemic racism. And so, to a degree, you followed your instincts?

Adrienne: Well, Betty, actually, this focus has come full circle. When I was growing up, in Mobile, Alabama, there were only certain beaches we could go to where we were welcome as Black people. I remember my mom had bought me a two-piece bathing suit because when you're a certain age, it's not a bikini, it's a two-piece. It was white. I remember getting in the water for no more than five minutes, and when I came out, it was black. It was never white again. And then I began to notice some other things that stuck with me. A lot of people I knew had asthma when I was a kid, including my brother. And we didn't have enough money to get medication all the time. So my mom used to hold him over the bathtub and run the hot water to open up his airways. A lot of people did that back then because that's all we had. So regarding my interests, while I veered away from those memories and facts for a while, I then came back to them. But it's always been a part of me. I just didn't know what shape it would take professionally. I first had to go and get my degree, and then come back and apply it.

Jonathan: It's so interesting that while you've been acutely aware of these issues since you were a little kid, some sectors of the American public have been very slow to even acknowledge climate change, let alone environmental justice, as a legitimate scientific issue that we need to deal with.

Adrienne: I think that was just denial, just like there is denial about the whole racism issue. Because of where I lived in the South, there may not have been as much denial as there was in other places. But once things started to noticeably change in the weather, we became more aware. At Christmas, we used to wear shorts. And then, as time passed, we would wear coats and boots because it sometimes snowed at Christmas, People would question that. People were aware of things changing but didn't know enough about what was causing it. And then when we became more aware of what was happening, others weren't ready to call it "climate change." They figured that we are having a cold year this year, and it will go back to normal next year.

Jonathan: But it seems like even when the American public started to open its eyes, the conversation that brought climate change to light was more focused on climate refugees. The populations our minds went to first were living at the equator and on island nations. It was only much later that the general public in the United States started to think about the direct impacts of climate change on communities here in the United States.

Adrienne: What you're saying is true for some people, but for people who were already dealing with environmental contamination, climate change has just exacerbated something that has always been there. I do understand and agree with what you're saying for the general population who haven't had that other long-standing exposure to environmental contamination. The general population didn't pay real attention to that and didn't see it for what it was.

Betty: We have many forms of denial intersecting: the denial of structural racism, the denial of climate change—and, for many, the denial of the severity of the pandemic. There has been a denial or resistance to what science has been telling us. In your writings you introduce the term, *syndemic*. We at *Mind of State* got really excited about this word because it highlights the intersection of different elements we are equally concerned with. Tell us about how we're actually in a *syndemic*.

Jonathan: It's our word of the day.

Adrienne: It is my word of the year. I take every opportunity I can to say "syndemic." It's a real thing. It applies to so many things: climate change, mental health, and physical health. You could focus on climate change and look at its effects from the perspective of syndemic. But the syndemic that I always refer to, is the intersection of structural racism, climate change, and COVID-19. *Syndemic* is the occurrence of two or more concurrent or sequential epidemics. One of my friends and I have been thinking right now, there might be five.

Jonathan: God, I hope not.

Adrienne: I know, right? I was like wait a minute, why are we trying to get more?

Betty: But now that you mention it, there are five, aren't there?

Adrienne: Well, I can think of four that are disproportionately affecting people of color: COVID-19, systemic racism, climate change, environmental contamination. That's four.

Betty: Now there's an economic crisis.

Adrienne: There's another. There you are.

Betty: We found the five.

Adrienne: And we could go on. People don't think of all these things as being interrelated, but they are. I tell my students that everything's interrelated. You just have to start asking questions and think about it. You give me one thing, and I can run down a connection between that issue and everything else. And they started doing it. For instance, people think about asthma as just a medical or biological problem. No, start thinking about asthma in the context of what else is happening around you. What does asthma mean in the context of COVID? What does asthma mean in Lake Charles, Louisiana, where they had Hurricane Laura and then they had a Biolab fire all at the same time on a hot day.[1] They were told, "Shelter in place, don't open your windows and doors. Don't turn on your air conditioner." What does that do?

Betty: And what *does* that do, what are the long-lasting effects of that further on down the line?

Jonathan: Or what about Flint, Michigan? Is that solely a lead contamination problem?

Adrienne: Exactly, or is it a little bit more than that?

Betty: The question is, are we accountable and responsible to others or not? In the pandemic, if we wear a mask, we protect other people from whatever infection we might have. And if we don't, we could become super spreaders. We are all interdependent.

And now we must reckon with being in this perfect storm of these five major sociopolitical crises: systemic racism, climate change, environmental

---

[1] Rick Rojas, Manny Fernandez, and Richard Fausset, "Hurricane Laura Carves Destructive Path Across Louisiana," *The New York Times,* August 27, 2020, https://www.nytimes.com/2020/08/27/us/hurricane-laura-damage.html. Steven Mufson and Darryl Fears, "Wind, Rain and a Chemical Fire. Hurricane Laura Was Gone but the Crisis Wasn't Over, *The Washington Post,* August 27, 2020, https://www.washingtonpost.com/climate-environment/2020/08/27/hurricane-laura-fire-biolab/.

contamination, COVID-19, and economic crisis. And what you are saying, Adrienne, is they are all connected. They're not happening siloed, even though we tend to think of them in siloed ways. Maybe this is due to having a Western topic-specific way of thinking versus having a more holistic approach. I'm not sure of its roots. But it is really useful to say that these major problems are not separate—that they are interrelated. But this also can feel like an overwhelming tangle. As a climate change scientist, an expert on environmental justice, and a lawyer, where do your investigations begin?

Adrienne: Where it starts for me is with people. I look at what affects people, what all of these different things do to them. So that's where I begin. The primary question is always how does this affect the average person?

Our communities really have three questions to ask: What is it? How does it affect me? What can I do about it?

For instance, when I talk about COVID in the context of somebody who's already economically oppressed, I have to ask myself, "How is that going to affect them?" My brother is an essential worker, and when his restaurant closed, he wasn't given any money. I called about his rent, and I asked, "What are you guys doing? What break are you giving them?" They said, "Well, if they pay early they get 50 dollars off." And I said, "Well, 50 from zero is zero."

Betty: And paying early from zero is impossible.

Adrienne: Right, if you're not working. And this is all just indicative of the fact that we weren't ready.

Jonathan: Complex, interrelated, and intersectional problems take a tremendous amount of work, energy, coordination, and collaboration to break down. Are we structured in the right way to combat intersectional problems like this?

Adrienne: We weren't ready, Jonathan. We could be structured appropriately, if we had learned lessons from the past, such as from Hurricane Katrina. We could be ready for the next perfect storm because who's to say that this is never going to happen again.

Jonathan: Oh, it will.

Adrienne: Exactly. So, let's never be caught unaware again. I think we have what it takes to have everything in place, to be well-structured. We just haven't done it. And it does take time.

Betty: We didn't learn those lessons from Hurricane Katrina. I was thinking about Houston's collaborative response to Hurricane Harvey. They did bring together a consortium of different agencies. A coalition of competing agencies and interests worked together.

Because everybody got flooded, people had to come together from both sides of the aisle to rescue neighbors and even animals that were stranded in buildings. Now, a pandemic, and particularly something like COVID, is weirdly an abstract and isolated experience—even though it's concrete in that so many people are getting sick and dying every day. But it's different from experiencing, as a community, a hurricane with 80-mile-an-hour winds and the buildings around you falling down. I wonder what you think of that, Adrienne, in terms of how we might come together as communities, or how we might be forced to learn from our responses to this syndemic?

Adrienne: I think COVID is different. It may be scarier because it's stealthy. But I also don't think there are very many people left who have not been touched by COVID-19 in some way, either having lost family members or having had family members who were sick. I think that the lesson we need to learn is that we need to think broadly—by trying to understand the connections. We could begin by addressing the issues that existed before COVID—in the "before time," as I like to call it. If we had addressed structural racism and the effects of climate change and economic injustice, then I think we would have been a little bit better prepared for COVID. If people made enough money to have food, then they wouldn't have to stand in line because they were living check-to-check.

Jonathan: People who are most marginalized are among the most vulnerable and likely to be among the first ones hit. We do know that the Obama administration had a pandemic preparedness playbook. They wanted to hand it off to the Trump administration, but they showed no interest in it. But I wonder, as sophisticated and empathic as the Obama administration was, do you think their playbook addressed all of the intersectional issues, or was it mostly focused on dealing with a virus and a vaccine?

Adrienne: I have no idea. I haven't seen it, but I would hope that it addressed the interconnectedness of the syndemic phenomenon. I want to step back to your comment on vulnerable communities. That term is not my favorite. I feel like the communities aren't vulnerable. Rather, we have put them in vulnerable situations.

It is not just wording. Because in reality, these people bounce back. Even after Hurricane Katrina, when people were lost and they couldn't find family members and many were put on buses and evacuated, they bounced back. They didn't necessarily go back to the Lower Ninth Ward. Not everybody could go back. But those people are resilient in spirit and in their ability to fight. But the situation in which they were located made them vulnerable.

Jonathan: When I used the word *vulnerable* I didn't mean to imply that it was of their own volition or that they were just sitting there, waiting to be hit. There are communities that have been victimized, that have been cut out, that have been overlooked, that have not been listened to. And that's all I meant by my use of the word *vulnerable*.

Adrienne: I didn't mean you, personally. I just wanted to use this as an opportunity to point out how we can label a community as "vulnerable" as if it is a function of their weakness or lack of resiliency.

Jonathan: I appreciate that.

Adrienne: Because many communities point out how they are labeled "vulnerable" as if it is their own creation.

Betty: I also appreciate that you make that differentiation, Adrienne. The vulnerability is not inherent to the identity of the community but to the situation in which they find themselves. Furthermore, we all have a hand in the creation of that situation, and we can change it. Then the people who live there have a chance to heal or emerge from the vulnerable situation in which they have been placed. What do you think we learned from Hurricane Katrina and what do we still need to learn?

Adrienne: I will express my personal opinion. I think what we did right was what happened after Katrina, when people came together to help clean up and rebuild. I went down there because I'm from Mobile, which is only two-and-a-half hours away. I knew people there, and after talking to them, listening and helping, what impressed me was their resilience and the way people came together to help. It wasn't perfect. Some of the trailers that were provided were contaminated. People didn't get the financial assistance that they needed. But I was really impressed with the way that the citizenry responded, the way we all came together. And that is something that we've seen in COVID-19, some of that same behavior for which people are so grateful. What could have been different is that when people were told to evacuate they were directed to the Superdome.

Was there a way that people could have known that it wasn't going to be the safest place? I don't know. But I think that when things are built in the future, they need to be built with the possibility of "what if" this needs to serve as a shelter. And, in the future, we need to think about if we can do more adaptation to crises in addition to mitigation of them. Then I think we'd be in a better situation.

Betty: What do you think are the barriers to adaptation versus mitigation?

Adrienne: Financial considerations are really important because adaptation in the immediate run is more expensive, but in my opinion, in the long run, it pays for itself.

Betty: So do we need to be able to take a longer view in terms of our infrastructural investments? At times it must be really frustrating and disappointing for you and other activists to see people not do the right thing and realize that significant change is going to take a long, long time. And then a disaster comes, and you have to learn the same lessons over again. It must feel almost like you're rolling a boulder up a hill and getting crushed again as it rolls back down over you. How do you keep it going? What sustains you in this work?

Adrienne: That's a good question. Until I became too busy, I used to get together regularly with a group of my women friends. I had a Zoom line, and we'd gather online and talk on Saturdays. All of us were in the environmental field, but at different positions. One person was a secretary; somebody else was just starting out. We'd have a dean. We drew from different groups of people and would talk not only about how messed up the week was, but also about issues in general. We would solve all the world's problems. We would literally save the world. That was really sustaining. Also, at work, in my particular program area, to just talk about anything that wasn't work related helps. Just take that time out.

And then I call people who I know who are working in this area and we help each other. We lift each other up. The only way it works is to have other people support you, even if you don't want to burden your family all the time and have them worry that you are depressed. People who work with you are good to share with. Someone will notice I'm down and say, "Today was a bad day?" And I might reply, "Yeah. It sucked." I may tweet a colleague with "Sometimes I feel like I'm deliberately knocking my head up against a brick wall."

Betty: What you are working on is so big and multi-tentacled. It can echo what we do in trauma work. I work with sexual assault survivors, and we have long dark weeks, too. But it sounds like you debrief and share a mutual recognition of what you are going through.

Adrienne: Like a bitch session. Can we say that on the radio? I don't know.

Betty: Yes, you can.

Jonathan: On this one you can.

Adrienne: You know what's important? I have a group of friends from law school who don't do any of the stuff that I do. I get to talk to them about it, and they listen because this is something new to them. I listen to them, and they listen to me. Sometimes their fresh perspective is helpful, too. I think it's also just being able to talk to people who we don't work with every day all the time. And it's hard when you're in COVID, right? Stepping away is hard, and it's hard to make the distinction between work and home sometimes.

Jonathan: And we're so isolated. We're in our Zoom boxes. I want to take you back a bit in time and speak about a moment when we came out of our Zoom boxes and that was around George Floyd's murder. For me, it was a moment where the intersectional aspect of the syndemic of these multiple crises seemed to come together into stark relief for the American public and for the world. Given the focus of your work on environmental justice and environmental racism, I wonder if you could comment about how the COVID and George Floyd moment affected you?

Adrienne: You know, my initial feeling was just utter sadness because it took that moment for people to wake up. How sad!

Jonathan: Yes.

Adrienne: And how many people died before George Floyd? And then there was the realization that people were finally listening. People in the environmental justice community who have been doing this way longer than me—they've been talking and talking, and most of the time feeling like nobody was listening to them. And somebody asked me right after Mr. Floyd was murdered, "Is it too soon to talk about environmental justice and what happened?" I replied, "Absolutely not! How can you not talk about it?" I made the connection for myself between George Floyd's murder and public health. You can't talk about public health without talking about climate change, without talking about racism. Everything is connected. It's never too soon, but I think it can be a little too late. And I think the fact that so many people have passed because of COVID makes it late.

But now that people are listening; it's not too late. I think COVID opened people's eyes to a lot of things. I don't know why. I don't know what it is about COVID in particular that made people stand up and notice that people are being murdered or there is a lot of police brutality or that prisons don't have air conditioning and people are living in inhumane conditions. For instance, many homeless people don't have access to water. Before we would give messages about this, and nobody paid attention. Now communities that I work with are making a deliberate effort to provide running water to homeless populations, not only because of climate change, but also because at least homeless people can now wash their hands. At least we can do that for them in the middle of extreme heat during the day when their shelters are closed and there may be many COVID carriers around.

People just started thinking about these things. I don't know if it was because they were home all the time and had more time to listen or because people just got fed up. I think it was also social media that focused on George Floyd's murder, and everybody saw it. It isn't the first time people have seen something like this, but the man had his knee on his neck and nothing like that has happened before—on video. Putting it on social media for most people, particularly for people of color, was just reliving it and making it worse. It comes to a point where enough is enough.

People just reached that breaking point at the same time because of the incredible way things have been these last few years. It felt like the final straw.

Jonathan: And there have been record numbers of people marching and protesting, and they continue to do so. Are you feeling optimistic? Are you feeling that we have to keep the pressure on?

Adrienne: Well, you have the Trump supporters who are saying that the voting was rigged. They are also marching. But I feel like we are keeping the pressure on. There are a lot of people out there who have been working on voter suppression both before and after the election. They haven't stopped.

People are not only paying attention, but also commenting and writing letters and protesting in social media. And by social media, I mean more than just Twitter. People are definitely still putting on the pressure, and I don't think that's going to stop.

Jonathan: On the climate side, it seems like the Biden Harris administration is taking some dramatic steps, with John Kerry as climate czar, and Deb Haaland as secretary of the interior, and Gina McCarthy as head of domestic climate.[2] What's your response to these announcements, and what does it say about the future?

Adrienne: I think that we have to wait and see how all this plays out. I don't think this is the end. This is the beginning. And it is exciting on so many levels. Just from a diversity, inclusion, and racial issue standpoint, I see that we are beginning to address the unfair activities that have occurred these last four years of hell. Can I say that on the radio?

Betty: Yes, you can.

Jonathan: I'll say it again.

---

[2] She served from 2021–2022. Her deputy, Ali Zaidi, has been in the post since September 2022.

Adrienne: It's like waking up from a nightmare. When Deb Haaland was named, I was so excited. It's such a blessing in so many different ways. Now we have people who get it, who live it, who understand it. And that's what it's about. You have to have people in there who really have buy-in, who in some way have lived experiences of the problems as opposed to people who have been totally removed and couldn't care less or who have outside interests that are in conflict with their government responsibilities. So I'm hopeful.

Betty: When you were saying that sometimes it can feel like you were screaming and no one was listening, now you've got people who are not going to silence these issues, who have proven themselves to be listeners, and who have the ears to hear this. Do you feel like they, like you, see syndemics and the relationships between climate change, environmental justice, COVID, institutional racism, and our current economic situation?

Adrienne: I think they do because they are interconnected. There's no way that you can't be aware of it. Everybody's talking about it. Everybody's living it. You can't unmake it.

Right now Black people find themselves in dire economic circumstances. They have no economic choices. You know, that's the situation they've been put in, I'm going to say due to racism, but that's not always the case.

Sometimes it is due to something as basic as the gaps between rich people and poor people. And there's no consideration for poor people if you're very rich. When you might be thinking, "Hey I'm just trying to get mine. I'm not thinking about them." It's like a Marie Antoinette attitude: "Let them eat cake."

Betty: What you point to here is the class aspect of this, the huge splits between the haves and the have-nots. There are some people doing far better in the pandemic because they work in corporate environments, which is stunning and upsetting. It seems like there's not a full needs assessment in these stimulus packages, which still miss a bit of what is needed, who is hurt, what requires care. This refers us back to the work of Deva Woodly (Chapter 22), a political scientist and expert in grassroots movements. She studies Black Lives Matter and highlights its underlying philosophy of the *politics of care*, which has well-being rather than economics as its central focus. I wonder if you can see us shifting to numbers about health and suffering as a measure of well-being, rather than on stock market figures or other financial markers?

Adrienne: I think that you have to do them together. I don't think it's the one or the other sort of thing. I think there are going to be those who are more concerned about profits. We have seen that during COVID when people were buying up all of the paper towels and toilet paper and then selling them at a 700 percent increase in price.

But, we surely should have measures and an accounting of the suffering and illness that occurs as a result of environmental inequities. This requires its own needs assessment. We have to examine cumulative exposures to toxic substances in disadvantaged neighborhoods. And now we have to add other inequities related to increased risk as a result of the interaction of COVID, asthma, and particulate matter.

For example, let's do some calculations on how much it would cost to develop industrial-level systems with cleaner scrubbers for facilities that put toxic agents into the air of vulnerable neighborhoods. We are not going to move the people in those neighborhoods, so we need to make them safer.

Jonathan: Adrienne, do you think that the way the Green New Deal is structured addresses these intersectional issues or is it too siloed? Does it consider the needs assessment as you've described it?

Adrienne: I know the general framework of the Green New Deal, and I don't think it's siloed. In my opinion, it's the beginning of an intersectional approach. I know that it's going to incorporate a lot of different areas and entities and interests.

Jonathan: And an intersectional approach would take into account the profit motive as it concerns the climate and people and jobs?

Adrienne: We already know that just focusing on profit doesn't work. We had four years of that to the detriment of many people. We haven't focused just on people before. It seems that the best approach would be to incorporate everything—including profit, people, health, jobs. It's about bringing all the stakeholders to the table—your economist, your engineer, your community member, your small-business owner, your farm worker, your farm owner—everybody, because everybody has a stake in making this a success. I don't know how to do it, but I know I'm open to it, and I know it's necessary.

Betty: In terms of this human-centered approach to environmental justice and the syndemics of intersecting maladies, how can we address these problems in the future? What would be your top three steps?

Adrienne: The first thing I would do is establish trust and credibility. That includes having a trusted source for information who everybody can go to and know that this source speaks the truth and is transparent. And then, if people trust you or are beginning to trust you, you are going to get people participating and interacting with you on a more in-depth level. And you won't get so many people siloed. That would be the first thing. The very next thing is to address the economic impacts that we've seen with COVID-19 that we know extend far beyond the virus itself. We've got to get people some money so that we can then address the third thing, which is COVID-19 because people can't stay home.

For those who don't want to wear their mask, I think we might need a little federal action or start fining people. It's not about you. It's about the people you talk to, or you are exposed to. You know, I have a neighbor who doesn't wear a mask, and when I see him every day, I say, "You're welcome." And he just starts laughing. Then I say, "You're welcome because I'm wearing this mask for you." And then I say, "But you obviously don't give a damn about me because you're not wearing one." I'd talk to the people at the state and local level and health departments and see what we need to do in order to get people to wear their masks. People in other countries do it and it works. And I don't know what people need to be convinced. But, if we do those things, we're well on our way. We have a long way to go, and a lot of things to fix because a lot of things are broken.

Jonathan: I think you've laid out a fabulous recipe, the building blocks for a successful future. And we appreciate you coming to spend time with us on *Mind of State*. We look forward to continuing the conversation.

Adrienne: Thank you. I enjoyed it.

DEMOCRACY
AT RISK

Chapter 21
Sounding the Alarm: Cultism & the Loss of Reality

Guest: Robert Jay Lifton
Episode Aired: October 21, 2020

Dr. Robert Jay Lifton is a psychiatrist who has written numerous award-winning books on topics ranging from the survivors of Hiroshima to the doctors who performed medical experiments in Nazi concentration camps to the psychology of genocide. More broadly and most recently, he has focused on both political and religious zealotry, climate change, and cultism. He also taught at the City University of New York and Yale University.

When we spoke with Robert in the fall of 2020, he was 94 years old and had been applying psychology and psychoanalysis to the study of political history—specifically to examine the roots of war, authoritarianism, and genocide—for nearly 60 years. His 2019 book, Losing Reality: On Cults, Cultism, and the Mindset of Political and Religious Zealotry *joined a bibliography of 27 books, including* Thought Reform and the Psychology of Totalism: A Study of "Brainwashing" in China *(1961);* Death in Life: Survivors of Hiroshima, *which won a National Book Award in 1969 and* The Nazi Doctors: Medical Killing and the Psychology of Genocide *(1986).*

Robert's deep understanding of the mechanisms of how groups of people—even whole societies—can cede control to a religious guru, a cult leader, or a demagogue, prompted us to seek his insights on how vulnerable we in the United States were—and are—to a slippage into authoritarianism. Moreover, his unflinching ability to both face and delve into the harrowing details of the greatest atrocities of the 20th century also compelled us to ask for his help in thinking about what felt—and feels —unthinkable.

The United States now approaches the 2024 presidential election, in which Donald Trump is the leading Republican candidate to challenge incumbent president Joe Biden. Trump has survived two impeachment trials and faces criminal charges and investigations in New York, Georgia, and two federal district courts for corruption in New York, for interfering with the 2020 presidential election results in Georgia, and for conspiracy and illegally using the levers of government power to remain in office in Washington, DC. As of this writing, Donald Trump has been indicted on more than 90 federal and state criminal counts in four separate courts in Washington, DC, Florida, New York, and Georgia.

As we struggle to digest Trump and Trumpism's ongoing assault on reality and democracy, the traumas of the COVID-19 pandemic, George Floyd's 2020 murder, and the subsequent mobilization of the Black Lives Matter movement, along with the current impacts of climate change reflected in uncontrollable 2023 forest fires destroying millions of acres of wilderness in Northern Canada, Robert's words are both challenging and comforting:

> To the extent that we can rebuild while recognizing the very prominent difficulties and expressions of oppression and violence that have existed in American society—this could take us to a third place where we, as a society, would be viable in a more real sense. This would be a way of reconstituting American society that takes into account what we have tried to suppress.

It is significant that these sentiments—on how American society might rebuild based on a collective acknowledgment of past harms—are echoed by so many of our guests, such as Pauline Boss, in her conversation with us on "Ambiguous Loss" (Chapter 3), Judith Herman, in her discussion on "Collective Trauma" (Chapter 4), Betty Sue Flowers, in her talk on the "Economic Myth" (Chapter 27), Deva Woodly, in her discussion on the "Politics of Care" (Chapter 22), and Jessica Benjamin in her conversation on "Acknowledging Harm and Repairing the World" (Chapter 5). They all point out that we are at a threshold moment, one both excruciating and opportune. That they stress how crucial it is that American society reckon with its violent and oppressive past alerts us to how essential recognition of the truths of America's traumas are to its survival as a democracy.

Interview

Betty: Robert, we're in an anxious place right now. A very anxious and possibly dire place in terms of the state of our democracy. We have talked to you about Trump and his followers' assault on reality, which you've addressed cogently in your book *Losing Reality*.[1] It appears that we now sit in a time where reality seems to be assaulting Trump in the form of the COVID-19 pandemic. I wanted to get your sense of where we're at now. The presidential election is coming, and there's talk from Trump about not conceding to a peaceful transfer of power should he lose. What are your thoughts on where we are in reality, and what are the challenges to reality with respect to Trump?

Robert Jay Lifton: I'll start by stating things are in their most dire and yet completely accurate form, in my judgment. We are in a crisis of reality created by Trump. The central event that has caused the breakdown of reality in Trump is, of course, the coronavirus. That and other forces have resulted in a situation where the COVID crisis has joined forces with a climate crisis— the fires on the West Coast—and a social crisis, involving not just Black Lives Matter, but also the whole issue of oppression and inequality. All these come at a time when we have an administration that is both criminal and corrupt, and a president who engages readily and actively in what I would call *presidential killing*. The breakdown in reality can be looked at in terms of these multiple crises that have come at the same time.[2]

Trump's reality has always been solipsistic. By this I mean that his sense of reality is self-contained. It is the only reality that Trump experiences and needs. Such solipsism is enormously dangerous because it ignores the larger reality as experienced by many others, and it also ignores the requirements of evidence. Despite that, Trump has succeeded in creating a certain amount of confusion concerning his solipsistic reality. For instance, in the case of his conversation with the president of Ukraine, Volodymyr Zelensky, and his attempts to enlist Zelensky in connection with his own ostensibly electoral interests, it was easy to be confused by Trump's own interests and those of our national foreign policy. But when COVID-19 came along, everything changed, because COVID-19 is not something abstract. It is organic and bodily in the illnesses and deaths that it causes. And in that sense, Trump's reality system, or his efforts to impose his solipsistic reality and the falsehoods surrounding it, collapsed. Trump's solipsistic view of the

---

[1] Lifton, R.J. (2019). *Losing Reality: On cults, cultism, and the mindset of political and religious zealots.* The New Press.

[2] See also Adrienne Hollis on "A Syndemic Challenge: Climate, Race, and COVID," in Chapter 20.

world collapsed because the larger organic truth of the virus could not be denied.

There have been attempts to cover up the truth of the severity of the virus, to falsify numbers of illnesses and deaths, to have political hacks make decisions about handling the virus, and to reject and suppress the opinion of legitimate scientists and doctors. But despite all those efforts, the actuality of the physicality of the virus still predominates. And that has caused a desperate situation for Trump—in a way, a kind of surrender to the virus— and, certainly, a breakdown of his reality system, if not a breakdown of his individual behavior. He hasn't had that in a full sense, but there has been a breakdown in his solipsistic claims to reality.

Jonathan: Could you explain what you mean by "solipsistic reality?"

Robert: *Solipsistic* means individually based, and *solipsistic reality* has a specific meaning of being based only on what the self perceives and needs, not at all on the larger reality of other people. Or, as I said before, on evidence that we conventionally invoke in order to assert reality, especially in relation to the concrete reality of actual events. That's what solipsistic reality is.

Jonathan: So is Trump basically saying, "Who are you going to believe: me, or your lying eyes?" Is he making the assertion that what Trump says should be taken as truth, regardless of the evidence that's out there? Or is it that he believes what he says?

Robert: It's both. It certainly is an insistence that everyone believe in his falsehoods. We can make a distinction between lies and other kinds of falsehoods because he sometimes will consciously manipulate and falsify reality. But he also can come to believe in the falsehood of his solipsistic reality. Just look at the revelations in the Bob Woodward book on his presidency, particularly the contradiction between his recognizing, on the one hand, in private conversations the reality of the pandemic, while in public statements he tended to dismiss it and say it didn't exist.[3] It was a hoax, and it was going to go away any hour, so that we could open up the whole society and ignore it. It's quite possible for people in general to believe in antithetical concepts. These were antithetical ideas: "it was a terrible scourge" versus "it didn't

---

[3] Woodward, B. (2020). *Rage*. Simon and Schuster.

exist." In my judgment and from my experience with extreme situations, people can believe in such contradictory ideas. With Trump, that capacity is even greater than usual because by simultaneously believing in opposites, he can push forward elements of his solipsistic reality and elements of what he perceives he needs politically, which is to play down the virus. So, in that sense, these are both from Trump: what we can call manipulation of lies, which he knows to be lies, and the expression of solipsistic reality, where he believes in falsehoods.

For those who follow and support and believe in Donald Trump, one can see the two levels right there. First, do we believe the numbers? That's the manipulation of lies. And then second, if we do believe the numbers, there's a tendency to say, "It's not Trump's fault that the virus happened, and his political opponents are seeking to use the virus as a way to politically tarnish Donald Trump."

Jonathan: Can you say more about the historical context of your reference to how a supporting public can bend to the political narrative of a charismatic leader?

Robert: Yes. That becomes a deeply troubling and enormously significant question. And I would begin to answer it this way. There can be a cult-like pattern in Trump's relationship to many followers, and this can include prominent white-supremacist followers, although he certainly has followers other than white supremacists.

In addition to this cult-like relationship, there is a mafia-like relationship in Trump's takeover of the Republican Party. The Republican Party isn't really a party as we know one to be. It's a rogue group that has delegitimated any kind of opposition. This is in direct contrast with the American concept of *loyal opposition.*

This kind of following can fit anything Trump says into a positive narrative. I have spoken of the concept of "narrative necessity," which an earlier psychologist, Jerome Bruner, brought to narrative psychology.[4] Quite simply, *narrative necessity* explains situations in which there are deep contradictions to the positive aura of the leader and shows how followers can ignore them, falsify them, join in the falsifications, or say that they are the work of people who are antagonistic to the guru. Followers of a charismatic

---

[4] Lifton, R. J., & Rosenblum, N. (2022). Does Trump Believe His Own Lies? *Psychology Today* .

leader do this in order to perpetuate not only a positive narrative, but also a narrative of perfection.

There is some of this "narrative necessity" in the narrative surrounding Trump. And then there's another dimension. Although Trump is notoriously limited in his knowledge, he can be clever in certain forms of political and psychological manipulation. And he brings that cleverness together with an ugly arrogance in which he seeks not only to beat back those who question his narrative, but also to destroy them. And since he has such authority in his presidential standing, people are deeply afraid of him. And among Republicans, people not only fear him; they have, at the same time, cast their political lot with him and decided that he is their best hope for a political future. All of those elements define this relationship between Trump and his followers.

There's one more quality that is maybe even more important than the ones that I've mentioned. That has to do with a long-standing American pattern of anti-government sentiment, of distrust, not only in government, but also in governance of any kind. There is a pattern in our American psyche of what historians have called a *paranoid style*.[5] That paranoid style has to do with our frontier tradition. It has been recast or regenerated in recent times—certainly over the last few decades. This pertains to the practice in the Republican Party to reject any authenticity of the opposition. It sees any opposition as evil and conspiratorial, so that the pure and beautiful image of the group can be sustained. In other words, there is a long-standing element in American society best described as "settler civil society." "Settler civil societies" are born out of fighting with and destroying the society of a native population. And, on top of that, of course, has been our historical experience of slavery that reflected a reliance upon another form of violence. All of these embedded attitudes feed into the pattern that we're seeing today.

I reject the idea that it's simply a matter of "tribalism," which is often said. It's too easily said that "there's this tribe and that tribe"—it's a way of giving each tribe equal time. But, the Republican Party has gone in a direction that delegitimates any opposition. This delegitimization of any opposition moves us toward some version of having a strongman leader or dictatorship. It's fascinating that this movement has joined in with Trump's own traits. So, it's wrong to say that "this is only American society producing

---

[5] Hofstader, R. (2008). *The Paranoid Style in American Politics*. Penguin Random House Canada.

this and that, and Trump doesn't matter." That's not correct. Trump does matter because this delegitimization fits in with his solipsism and other traits. But it's also wrong to say that Trump alone corrodes democracy because Trump's influence relies on elements in American society that have been reactivated in recent decades and go back to its beginnings.

Jonathan: So many questions come to mind immediately. It's one thing for Trump to have run the first time as an outsider, with an anti-government mentality. But what confounds me is that he continues to run against the government and to gut the government's regulatory capability and its civil service capacity. Trump's running as "the anti-government outsider" *while* he's sitting behind the Resolute Desk in the Oval Office of The White House. I don't understand how he's able to carry that out—and how his followers continue to buy this line when he's sitting "where the buck has to stop." It stops with him, doesn't it?

Robert: Logically, yes, "the buck has to stop with him," but in terms of his followers' cult-like and mafia-like relationship to him, that's a very different story. So Trump continues to be, in a sense, the outsider who violates all norms of presidential behavior. There is even an attraction for some that he perverts presidential responsibility. Trump takes this duty, which is to care for and enhance the lives of the people and turns it on its head so that it permits the systematic killing of the people. Trump does this as a rogue and an outlier, rather than as a president, even though he is technically our president. But that doesn't mean that it's working. It's not working at all. And there is more and more accumulating in the minds of American people that Trump's behavior is wrong and simply, in a moral sense, unacceptable. That idea, that sense that he commits transgressions that democracy cannot sustain, is ever-increasing. And, as it increases, this causes more desperation in Trump and more extreme expressions of misbehavior on his part. This dynamic is very dangerous. But that doesn't mean that Trump succeeds in carrying forward this mythology of attacking the presidency (including his own) as a means of expressing his violent tendencies and his efforts to undermine our own reality.

Betty: Robert, you've said so much by pointing out that there is a kind of multifactorial historical, social, and psychological perfect storm in the collusion between Trump and his followers. This includes the "narrative necessity" of both sides needing one another—of his followers needing Trump and Trump needing his followers. I'm particularly interested in what you're thinking about in terms of Trump's desperation and the challenge that the reality of the COVID-19 pandemic sets against Trump's solipsistic fantasy. His solipsistic reality is playing itself out most darkly in its imposition on our own realities. Starkly put, Trump's effort to reject the truth and severity of the pandemic is costing lives every day.

Robert: It's one thing to reject truths about previous conversations, even when there is paperwork to confirm them. It's quite another thing to reject the truth of somebody being extremely ill or of 120,000 American deaths from COVID, a number that is greater than the total deaths in all of our recent wars.[6] As this truth becomes increasingly impossible to reject or to deny, there are consequences of growing opposition to Trump, which can be recognized by him and by the people around him. He then tries, ever more desperately, to take steps that will disprove this concrete, organic truth of the severe consequences of the virus. Those desperate steps can include opening up the whole society to greater social interaction, even at a moment of a deeply dangerous surge of the pandemic. This desperation also influences Trump's recent statements that he could resist a peaceful transition of power if he's defeated in the election and decides that the election was rigged.

The very impossibility of convincing the country of his falsehoods about the organic truths of the virus lead to ever more extreme expressions of criminality, including the refusal of peaceful transition of the presidency.

Jonathan: Robert, I want to come back to this question about the facts of the virus and the blame for the virus spreading. The numbers are the numbers. And there are undoubtedly some who minimize or dismiss those numbers, saying that they are not accurate. But by and large, people seem to accept the numbers, but they do not accept that Trump is to blame. They are saying that Trump intervened early and blocked travel from China and so forth. I wonder if you could talk a little bit about this.

---

[6] This was June 2020. As of July 2023, according to the CDC, there have 1,135,364 deaths from COVID in the United States alone. See https://covid.cdc.gov/covid-data-tracker/#datatracker-home.

Robert: I would say that the great majority of people put the blame on Trump. Of course, there is 35 to 45 percent of the population who reject *any* blame for Trump. That's deeply disturbing. But it does mean that 60 or 70 percent of Americans place the blame directly on Trump. This is a major issue in the 2020 election, because people in many related polls are deeply concerned about the economy and going out and working to bring home money and to have food on their tables. But they're even more concerned about illness and the death anxiety that is disseminated by the pandemic. It cannot be avoided. So, it is the pandemic that is breaking down Trump's claim to the truth of unreality in a way that no response to a prior claim could do. It's excruciating for us to hear these followers say, "It's not Trump's fault." To shift the blame and truly reverse reality, some Trump followers will even say it's the Obama administration's fault, or anyone else who is not Trump. But the strong majority of the country rejects that view and blames Trump for the death of tens of thousands of Americans. And that's what I mean by "presidential killing." This recognition may also be deadly to Trump's ambitions to sustain his presidency.

Betty: I see this almost in terms of what happens when an abusive predator begins to lose control of their relationship with a victim. The collusion between the two reaches a breaking point. This moment of separation is often the most dangerous. Could this be a metaphor for what might be happening as we head toward the election and see some sort of breaking point between Trump's hold on reality and how he does or does not let go of the presidency?

Robert: Well, I would say okay to the metaphor, but be careful about the precise details. Trump may be reaching a collision point as he recognizes that more and more of the country is increasingly aware of his falsehoods and his failure at what he knew to be the most challenging test of his presidency—the pandemic. In order to sustain his solipsistic falsehood, he has to create a narrative in which the opposite of what has happened is true. Namely, he has heroically combated COVID as no one else would have been able to do. Are all the lies and failures of the presidency breaking down—in terms of the domestic economy, in terms of his obeisance to Putin, in terms of his damaging prior alliances, in terms of his attractions to dictatorships internationally? All of this can be at issue as the COVID virus makes impossible Trump's solipsistic reality claims.

I would add it isn't only the virus. Look at the climate change issue now. It envelops everything. We think of climate change as incremental. Gradually it builds, and then it builds a little more, and it doesn't do anything for a very long time. Well, climate change is upon us, and it's not gradual. The wildfires in the West are a combination of extreme heat and drought. They are the most extreme fires ever experienced in those areas. Trump's criminality and presidential killing may be a little bit more indirect with respect to climate change, but he is contributing to something that is all-enveloping in its danger to our habitat. Trump's false claims to reality about climate change and especially in relation to COVID-19 are breaking down. His solipsistic reality has reaped the harvest of a pandemic that has been neglected or not treated as seriously as it should have been. He suppressed Dr. Fauci's warnings and policies of dealing with the pandemic as an expert in epidemiology, and he has also been negligent about climate change. Mother Nature is really challenging Trump's solipsistic reality. Still, 30 to 40 percent of the population supports Trump.

Jonathan: But there are people in the middle who are possibly undecided? How do we prevent a further slide into Trumpism? As you have pointed out, this may not begin or end with Trump, as there are preexisting social, historical, and psychological elements that have contributed to this perfect storm of his administration these last four years. Where do you see us being right now, Robert? We seem to be grappling with a slide into authoritarianism as Mother Nature is assaulting the solipsistic reality of a strongman who happens to be our president.

Robert: Mother Nature is not challenged by all this. What is challenged is the human habitat within Mother Nature. And what is challenged also is the human intervention with fossil fuels in relation to climate change and with what is done or not done in relation to the pandemic.

So our greatest concern now has to be short term: getting Trump and Trumpists out of office. Nothing is possible with them in office. Trump's statements of his intention to stay in office under certain conditions shows his sense of pending defeat and his sense that his transgressions are catching up with him.

My psychological and political judgment is that, even when Trump is gone, Democratic responses have to be strong. We have to consider changing rules involving the court and involving Republican abuse of situations that don't have clear constitutional rules. The plea for unity in the country has to be delayed until this terrible assault on our democracy is beaten back in a strong fashion. Having said that, we really need a return to governance.

Any democracy that has survived and done well by its people has offered them some kind of life-enhancing government. We see government in its best moments in our response to disaster. But we see it also when opportunities are offered for those at the lowest end of society economically, for some sort of safety valve that only a decent society could offer. And in an op-ed that I wrote with political theorist Nancy Rosenblum, we talk simply about the immorality of the Trump administration, which is obvious.[7] Everybody knows they are immoral. But we took that emphasis and used it exclusively in terms of how Joe McCarthy was termed by a man named [Joseph] Welch, an Army lawyer who voiced the words that seemed to represent the end of McCarthyism and his false crusade against communism.

Welch spoke of indecency, cruelty, and recklessness or carelessness, that is, being without care. And we show examples of each of these three failures in Trump's immoral administration. So, after Trump, we have to return to morality with toughness in a new administration. This means sensitive governance—which has disappeared in the Trump administration. This means governance that is life-enhancing to the people. That's a broad term, but one can look at policies and laws that will fit that category.

Jonathan: Morality is critically important to American norms of government. But morality is very hard to legislate and to write into policy. My question to you, Robert, is that you are here on *Mind of State* because you're both a psychiatrist and a student of history. What do you say to us today, in 2020 in America, as we teeter on the edge of potential authoritarianism and witness the erosion of democracy? What can history teach us? What can we do as a society to get back on track? How do we say that this will never happen again, and it will never happen here?

Robert: Well, I would begin to answer by saying that it's risky and inaccurate to say it could never happen here. Of course, it could happen here. Some kind of authoritarian government could happen anywhere and has happened throughout the world over the course of history. And that mistake can be

---

[7] Lifton R.J. & Rosenblum, N. (2020). Donald Trump: The immoralist. *New York Daily News*. *Mind of State* also interviewed Nancy Rosenblum on December 23, 2020. See Chapter 10, "Conspiracy without Theory."

made together with a kind of idealistic version of American purity, the idea of American exceptionalism being a form of decency that's different from that of any other country.

We've had struggles and nastiness, whether they are with Native Americans, whether in slavery, whether in frontier actions and violence, whether in waves of immigration, where each immigrant group has been victimized over the course of its integration or partial integration into American society.

So, it's never been a story of American perfection, although some American mythology places American perfection above the cruel, antagonistic, and less-moral world out there. This mythology requires us to come to terms with our history.[8] One of the demands of the Black Lives Matter movement, or even uprising, is that we must come to terms specifically with our relationship to slavery on every level. And that, of course, is inseparable from issues of oppression and inequality, which are still very active in this society. To the extent that we can rebuild while recognizing the very prominent difficulties and expressions of oppression and violence that have existed in American society—this could take us to a third place where we, as a society, would be viable in a more real sense. This would be a way of reconstituting American society that takes into account what we have tried to suppress.[9]

Betty: In terms of talking about the exceptionalism of the United States and how we need to be careful about that self-identity, there is an ideal that we were once great, and we need to go back to that. This feeds into the "Make America Great Again" slogans of the Trumpists. This points again to the idea of narrative necessity—that we are cast into the need for a certain self-replicating image. How can we, as psychologically minded people, encourage a more psychological attitude in others who are very concerned about the politics of the United States? How can we inform the movements and the debates and thoughts on American politics right now?

Robert: Well, right now, I think we can take actions in the House of Representatives to pass laws that help people, starting with a new bill to

[8] See also Jules Cashford on "When Myth Becomes History," in Chapter 28.
[9] See also Judith Herman on "Collective Trauma," in Chapter 4; Betty Sue Flowers on "The Economic Myth," in Chapter 27; Pauline Boss on "Ambiguous Loss," in Chapter 2; and Jessica Benjamin on "Acknowledging Harm and Repairing the World," in Chapter 5.

provide help for those affected by the pandemic. This would be in the form of economic help that is so desperately needed to provide for the states and all other sources of healing that's crucial in this epidemic. It also would include recognizing that Black lives have been threatened through our police system and through some of the subculture of police systems and other sources of white supremacy. It would be good to take a stand on this, while recognizing that it's a deep problem that doesn't go away overnight. And we also need to make clear what is at stake with climate change, by speaking out about what steps can be taken to support renewable energy. Climate change threatens our country and threatens the world. I think right now we need to speak and act in these ways, which includes a recognition of the value and importance of work and workers.

Jonathan: Robert, you've been so generous with your time and so thoughtful, both in reflection on history and on this present day. Do you have any last thoughts to wrap up this conversation?

Robert: My last thought for this conversation would be to say this is really a critical moment. All of us, as citizens, can embrace the role of what I call *witnessing*. As psychologists, part of the role of witnessing is to identify the increasing tendency to what I term *malignant normality* and to express alternatives in a way that promotes life enhancement. This involves everyone, even at modest levels, in small groups, in groups that one forms. It's a moment that needs the whole country. And I feel hopeful about its success.

Jonathan: Before we go, you raised a term that's most important for our audience. Please define *malignant normality*.

Robert: To put it starkly, *malignant normality* is a term I learned from my study of Nazi doctors.[10] The German doctor standing at the ramp in Auschwitz who decided which Jews to send to the death chambers wasn't breaking any law. He was just doing his job. That's what he was expected to do. That was the malignant normality of Nazi society.

Trump isn't a Nazi. He doesn't have enough of an ideology to be one. But he and those who stand with him do bring along a malignant normality of their own. And that malignant normality includes some of the things

---

[10] Lifton, R.J. (1988). *The Nazi Doctors: Medical killing and the psychology of genocide.* Basic Books.

I've been talking about—lying to the American people, presidential killing of his own people in the denial of the severity of the pandemic, obeisance to Putin and representing Putin and Russian interests rather than American interests, and disdain for ordinary people in favor of billionaires. So, this is the malignant normality Trump brings to us. The term really means a destructive form of behavior that is put forward as routine, as the norm. Malignant normality has to be uncovered and opposed.

Betty: And Robert, I really appreciate your evoking the witnessing professional or witnessing worker who can stand up against malignant normality and the assault on reality that Trump insists upon. It highlights the need to speak the truth as a grounding place against traumatizing people and events. You have reminded us of how we can stabilize ourselves in this time of great crisis on many levels and move forward in a productive fashion. Thank you so much for joining us. This conversation is so fruitful.

Robert: Thank you. It's been an interesting conversation for me as well.

Chapter 22
The Politics of Care

Guest: Dr. Deva Woodly
Originally aired: October 14, 2020

Deva Woodly is an associate professor of politics at The New School and the author of The Politics of Common Sense: How Social Movements Use Public Discourse to Change Politics and Win Acceptance. *Her current works include* Reckoning: Black Lives Matter *and* The Democratic Necessity of Social Movements.

In October 2020, our conversation with Dr. Woodly—an expert on social movements including Black Lives Matter—was particularly timely, due to the sustained BLM protests that had occurred throughout the summer and early fall in response to George Floyd's murder on May 25. It was later estimated that in 2020, as many as 26 million people took to the streets in more than 10,000 protests across the United States to protest police brutality against Black people.[1] The size, breadth, and depth of these largely peaceful protests made BLM the largest grassroots movement in U.S. history.[2]

We highlight two comments of Dr. Woodly's about the politics of care, *a core principle for the BLM movement, which became a root cause for its widespread appeal and impact on American politics and society:*

---

[1] U.S. Crisis Monitor Releases Full Data for 2020, ACLED, February 5, 2021, https://acleddata.com/2021/02/05/us-crisis-monitor-releases-full-data-for-2020/.
[2] Gause L. & Arora, M. (2021). Not All of Last Year's Black Lives Matters Protesters Supported Black Lives Matter. *The Washington Post.* https://www.washingtonpost.com/politics/2021/07/01/not-all-last-years-black-lives-matter-protesters-supported-black-lives-matter/.

A *politics of care* is about [our] orientation toward governance. It asks, "How do we collectively come to understand what people need, and then how do we distribute responsibility, so most people have what they need to live and thrive?"...

We're in an age in which people are yearning for a different way of relating to each other and the world. And the [Black Lives Matter] movement has come in and asked, *What if we do politics as though we want to live?* Not just to exist, not just to survive, not just to be running after the next coin. But what if we did politics as though we wanted to live together and enjoy our time on this planet?

By featuring our living, enjoying and thriving as the aim, rather than a byproduct, of government, the politics of care *is revolutionary in its human-centered common sense. That Dr. Woodly's statements about politics were stunning to us—then and now—reveals that such a focus is sorely lacking in our current way of operating in the U.S. The blossoming of the BLM movement during the darkest months of the COVID-19 pandemic could be seen as a collective call and craving for orienting ourselves around care, rather than power, profit, or individualism.*

Such insights on the yearnings Americans have for a government focused on a collective means to live and thrive are just as relevant today—if not more so—as when we recorded this episode in 2020. The evergreen nature of our conversation with Dr. Woodly points to how essential care is to the healthy functioning of American democracy and calls us to be mindful of it.

Interview

Betty: Hi, Jonathan. What's on your mind these days?

Jonathan: I'm thinking about politics. I'm talking about politics. Politics is on the brain all the time. And I'm watching a split screen where I see two things happening. On one side, I see our official political process, where people are registering to vote. They're getting their absentee ballots; they're getting their voting plan together. On the other side of the screen, I see a whole separate thing happening—an unofficial political process. I'm seeing the protests. I'm seeing the outrage. I'm seeing the petitioning. I'm seeing the handwringing and the buttons and the signs. People are saying, "Enough already. We need a change. There's something not working about our political process." And I'm wondering where and when those two streams are going to match up—or clash up?

Betty: You are not alone, Jonathan. Many of my clients are wondering the same thing. They are also asking themselves, "Do I join these grassroots protests? Do I vote? Do I get involved? If so, where do I get involved?" Because the feeling is, so much needs to change. But how do we do it?

Jonathan: I am frankly thrilled that politics is making its way into your sessions. That, to me, is a great mark of progress.

Betty: More and more people are really mulling over these questions, which I think is why you and I are having this conversation right now. And I think, with regard to how much political participation counts these days, the question, "What do I do, politically, and how does what I do make an impact?" is now something many more people are asking themselves.

Jonathan: Look, if people are grappling with whether their vote matters, then does it matter if they take to the streets?

Betty: Exactly. And yet there is a [Black Lives Matter] movement afoot that has brought millions of people into the streets. To talk about this and to put it into a social, political, and historical context is Dr. Deva Woodly. Thank you so much for joining us, Deva.

Deva Woodly: Oh, I'm so happy to be here. Thank you.

Betty: Deva, in my work as a therapist, I see a lot of people from myriad intersecting identities. And they have, in this moment, felt alternatively energized and also helpless. They don't know if marching, protesting, participating in rallies really does much. They are, of course, neither political scientists like yourself, nor are they students of political science. So, I wanted to ask you about this. You have written that social movements, protest, and rebellion are essential components of democracy. Your new book is saying that there is a democratic *necessity* to social movements. Can you unpack that for us a little bit?

Deva: Sure. My book argues—and honestly, all of my work up until this point has led me to believe—that we treat social movements in the wrong way when we're thinking about democracy. We treat social movements as episodic interruptions in the normal functioning of democratic politics. But that's not actually true empirically—or theoretically—in terms of the usefulness and purpose of social movements. Empirically, social movements have been around as long as democracies have been. And that's because social movements are actually a *part* of democracy. They're a feature, not a bug. They are the thing that democracies use to allow them to remain democracies, instead of devolving into oligarchies, because the tendency of all large institutions is to become self-serving. That is, they become institution-serving rather than mission-serving over time. And that's just like Max Weber's Iron Cage, right? You set up an institution, and eventually it has its own imperatives to preserve itself, more than to serve the mission for which it was first set up. Democracy is no exception. So, social movements are the phenomena that recall democracies to themselves and disrupt that oligarchic tendency.

Social movements are a democratic institution. We often think of the free press as a kind of fourth branch of government because they hold people and institutions to account. Well, think of social movements as a kind of fifth branch. Once we understand that social movements are a democratic institution the question about protests is one that is a little bit less fraught. Is a single protest going to change the way that business is done, the way that power is arranged, all at once? No, almost never. But over time, protests, combined with resonant messages, and the responses that they provoke and compel from decision makers, absolutely do change the way that things are run and have the potential to change the way power is arranged. So, it's a collective effort that happens over time. It's not the case that any one protest makes a decisive difference—unless it is extremely large and very, very disruptive. But cumulatively, over time, protests do make a difference, especially if they're of a size and a scope—that is, if they take place all across the geographic map and involve all sorts of people, as these last protests have. And that's, in part, because they change the way that people think about politics. They change what people think is possible, what people think are the problems, what people think are necessary to fix those problems, and the level of agency people believe that they have. It is a whole *process* of change, not an instant of change.

Jonathan: We can tend to be myopic and disregard the past. Can you give us a historical perspective on social movements and the interplay between protests in the street and government in the halls of power?

Deva: One of the books that I love to go to for the impact of protest is a classic from 1977 called *Poor People's Movements*, by Frances Fox Piven and Richard Cloward. The book contains case studies of several different American social movements that have made huge differences in terms of how governance is set up because of direct protests. It goes over labor strikes, such as the wildcat strikes in the early part of the 20th century, and how workers occupying their work sites and shutting them down—actions thought of as completely off the map, crazy radical things to do—and yet they actually were the things that led to the birth of the National Labor Relations Board, which led to the power to form unions and led to the ability for workers to have input on their working conditions, etc. But one of the things they say in that book is that these concessions are actually won in the moment of disruption. In the moment of direct action and protest, and then after the moment of direct action and protest, workers don't usually get any more concessions. What they then do is try to institutionalize the accommodations to whatever demands have been made. So, that's really important for people to be clear on. And I don't say that because it's not worth institutionalizing accommodations to demands—it absolutely is. But it's important for people to understand that you need both sides of that process. The disruption is necessary and essential—there is no change without disruption of the status quo.

Jonathan: Are you saying that the government, or the authorities, in embracing the call for reform, are somehow co-opting the power of the movement? Or is it always a tension—can they work together toward a constructive end?

Deva: What I mean is that they do work together toward a constructive end, but that the direct action and militant protest are a critical part of getting concessions. Now, getting those things institutionalized so they work for everyone is the process that follows—the institutionalization. I don't consider it co-optation. I just consider it the process of how social movements impact governance. Both of those sides are important. So it always annoys me when people are like, "What we really need is to be in the streets." Or, on the other hand, they say, "What we really need to do is appeal to elites." Well, there's no point in appealing to elites without people in the streets, right? But at the same time, people in the streets who are not willing to work with elites are also not going to be able to diffuse the benefits of the things that they have won.

Jonathan: Right. So, they're all core ingredients in the effort to change. You need militant protests in the streets. You need inside voices as well. Sometimes we see them coming together like the police taking a knee, or politicians at the front of the march, right?

Deva: Well, no. For me, not police taking a knee.

Jonathan: Okay, talk to us about that.

Deva: For example, in the Movement for Black Lives (M4BL), which is the movement that my current book is about, the organizers play both an outsider and governance game, meaning there is both vigorous organizing around direct action and militant street protest as well as an electoral justice project that's about electing new kinds of candidates at every level of government. It's also about pushing policy to allies in Congress who are not necessarily a part of the movement, but who are sympathetic to it, like Alexandria Ocasio-Cortez and Ayanna Pressley. This type of working with governance or working within the governance structure doesn't mean that symbolic actions by people who are already in government represents some kind of real alliance—only that you have to be willing to work in the register of that power with those decision makers, yet not take their gestures to be definitive. Only to understand that you have to work the policy side and the electoral side at the same time you're working in the streets.

Betty: When I look at a protest, I see an emotional response—a frustrated response. People protest because they cannot withstand what is happening anymore. They want to move and do something and speak out against an injustice or disenfranchisement. How does a movement become so organized that it bridges to connecting with people who are then looking at it in a more structural and organized way?

Deva: Well, organizers do that within social movements—that's their whole job.

Jonathan: Of course, President Obama famously started out as a community organizer.

Deva: Right. So, organizers are people who are in movements, who have made the connections, who work together, who study together, who are making connections between injustices, their causes, and their possible solutions. And they are the folks who galvanize others—not only to action, but also to understanding. And this movement has done so in a variety of different ways, both on- and off-line in a very large public conversation that's been facilitated by, although not limited to, social media. If you recall, in 2014 just the phrase "Black Lives Matter" was controversial. But the movement was not afraid to initiate a very large public conversation about structural racism in which they debunked or said what was wrong with the idea that "all lives matter" could stand in for "Black Lives Matter." This was a prolific conversation that was happening both online and in people's lives across time.

While in 2014 "Black Lives Matter" seemed shocking, after you talk about it for a while in the public discourse, the conversation grows beyond that—although not inevitably because it's the organizers and the movement initiating that conversation. Then more people who get it talk to even more people who then also get it. And then you have people independently producing memes and explainers and applying it to their own lives. So it becomes a part of the public discourse in a way that is comprehensible to everyone, even if everyone doesn't agree. But this takes time. So it matters that this happened five or six years after the first uprisings in Ferguson and the beginning of this iteration of the conversation about Black liberation and what that has to do with America becoming itself. People have learned over time. They have learned that "Oh, I wasn't quite sure what this meant, but now I feel like I know what this means. I feel like I know how to apply it in different cases." And don't forget—the empirical world also conspired to make everything that the movement claimed evidently true.

Jonathan: Yes. And there was video to prove it.

Deva: And there was video to prove it. But not only in the case of murder. I think it's also really important to consider the phenomena of the BBQ Beckys, along with the fact that the very same day George Floyd was horribly and viciously murdered by those cops, the Black bird watcher from Harvard, Christian Cooper, was also threatened with the white tears of Amy Cooper (no relation), who called the police as a deadly weapon against this man. This happened at the same time. So it was a vivid illustration of the argument that the movement has been making all along. That white supremacy operates on all of these different levels. And that it is harmful, all the way from vicious lethality to just changing your life chances. Just changing the way you're able to live your life. That's what structural racism is. That's what white supremacy does.

And it also made visible to a lot of white people who don't think of themselves as racist, how white supremacy is not about what's in their hearts. It's actually about the structures and practices that are already in place. As a white person, you can think of yourself as a nice person and still benefit from the fact that if you call the cops, they are not going to come and shoot you. And if you call the cops on someone who is Black, you can end their life even if you don't mean to. This has happened. So the empirical world provided vivid examples for the argument that the movement was making, and then the movement reinforced the argument. We see a ton of movement in public opinion polling on these questions over this time—precisely because people are coming to understand the argument that the movement is making.

Jonathan: So we've come into a perfect storm where forces have come together. It feels like we have hit a breakthrough moment. No doubt there will be steps backward and steps forward. This is a lifelong struggle. When I think about movements, I think about politics. And I wonder with other movements and other uses of language, if there is a political calculus that we need to think about in terms of political power. Because if you watched the first presidential debate of this 2020 election cycle, Trump attacked Biden by attacking Bernie Sanders and Elizabeth Warren. And he implied that Biden is not driving this train, but the "radical socialist left" is actually driving things. And I wonder, when we play to our base, are we at risk of undermining our objective because we play into the criticisms from the opposition? How do you balance the drive toward upholding our ideological purity with the pragmatic concerns of bringing the rest of society along?

Deva: I think you can approach it all pragmatically. It's a question of the terms of consideration, meaning what battle are you trying to win? Whoever won the Democratic nomination would have been called a "socialist."

Jonathan: For sure.

Deva: And even Bernie is not really a socialist.

Jonathan: Of course.

Deva: Not that there's anything wrong with that, again.

Jonathan: Yep.

Deva: I actually am not interested in the attacks of the other side. What I'm interested in is the message from our side and the values and beliefs that we hold to—and not in the service of purity. I'm not interested in a purist stance. What I am interested in is whether or not people on the left— or what is considered the left now, which, by historical standards, is not leftism, but just a position of providing basic care for people—are making an argument based on their values that can actually help people. Because we Democrats can have an unwillingness to stand in our values. So a lack of being able to deliver rights to people is part of the problem. I actually think that there's only a relatively small, older group of people who are really scared by socialism. People younger than 35 think socialism is fine and even people younger than 55 are split about it. It's people older than 65 who are still daunted by strong memories of what socialism was in the early 20th century. People of younger age groups are actually not that pressed about it. What they are skeptical of is whether the people who are promising them all this stuff can deliver it.

Jonathan: That is the question—how do you translate the power of a social movement into political power? Because if you're not translating slogans and marches into enduring policy change, then it's all sound and fury.

Deva: Yeah.

Betty: I think something that you're both referencing as well is that people have lost faith in politics and political discourse. It has all devolved into social media sound bites that get us to pay attention to outrageous statements rather than ground ourselves in discussions about our values of care. Deva, you have mentioned the word *care* many times. I know you have placed emphasis on the "politics of care" as a political philosophy. This intrigues me because it blends politics—which can become institutionalized and distanced from people, even though it is supposed to be about civic engagement—and care, which is about keying into and providing what people need. I think that this is the connection—the one between politics and care—that we are missing. Perhaps it is one that socialism promises as well. There is a collective control socialism implies that maybe older generations, under the shadow of the Cold War, are fearful of, and younger generations are not as chilled by this history. But what about the communication that this is a politics that's not forgetting the people themselves?

Deva: Well, that's what organizing is—or what it's supposed to be. For example, in the Movement for Black Lives, there is a wing of the movement that is about electoral justice. And the philosophy of the electoral justice side of the movement states, "We're not interested in supporting candidates who take our votes, yet do not remain accountable to our endorsement or labor." Instead, those on the electoral justice side of the movement see recruiting candidates for every level of office as central to their purpose. This is to convince people that what we can deliver does not start at the national level. You don't start by asking to address a national-level issue. The reality of federated governance is that much of the time what most people encounter is their local government. That is where they can see government at work— in the city council, in the school board, with the mayor, the district attorney, the judges. These are the people in government who directly impact our lives on a daily basis. And that's how we actually begin to learn how government works and what civic duty is good for.

So, people in the Movement for Black Lives started organizing in 2014 at the local level, recruiting people for local offices. If you look down-ballot, the opposite occurred versus what happened in the Obama years, when Obama won two national elections relatively easily, but the down-ballot was slaughtered. What has flipped is that while national elections have become structurally difficult for Democrats to win, steady gains have been made at local levels. This is including district attorneys, which were the first electoral targets of the movement. This is what I mean. All of this happens over time. We're in a culture where everything is supposed to happen instantaneously, or we're supposed to have some big heroic moment. The truth is the heroic work is the slog and in the trenches. That is what has been ongoing—it is in that moment where people flip the district attorney. And then marijuana prosecutions go down by 90 percent in their neighborhood. It is the moment when people begin to get hooked into the civic process where you can start to build power. And this building power is not just building power for a vote at the national level. It's also building power through increasing people's political literacy and their capacity to demand the things they actually need. They can do so because they have a better sense of what government is, what it can do, and what it ought to do for them.

This is how you develop a democratic citizenry—which, over the last more than half century, we have allowed to be decimated. That's the work—building a politically literate, democratic citizenry. It's really not about electing Democrats at the national level. I mean, we are certainly in a desperate situation at the moment. But the nature of grassroots political work is actually not about winning national elections. And that's why you don't have to worry about alienating this or that constituency. That's not the issue. The question is, are we building the kind of political power that can deliver for people? Also, are we changing people's expectations about what government can do? Are we making people feel efficacious? Now I'm on my soapbox because I'm a small *d* democratic true believer. That is my religion. I have seen what happens when people realize that they actually have power.

Jonathan: What do you say to people who believe that the most aggressive form of protest is to abstain? To people who protest by sitting out rather than lending legitimacy to what they consider to be a broken or corrupt process? Is there a place for abstention under the umbrella of political action?

Deva: Hmm. I don't think that abstention is an effective move. But at the same time, I also think that a part of what is broken about our democracy is that abstention can seem rational to many people. In an article I recently read, a young, potential Black Democratic voter was asked, "Are you going to vote—this year, of all years?" And this person said, "You know, I don't know. My parents voted, my grandparents voted—they fought and died to vote. And we're still poor and we're still in the same place. And we're still being terrorized by cops. I don't know if it matters." And empirically for many people, it doesn't matter. The national vote doesn't empirically, directly matter for their life chances—even though it empirically matters for the life chances of the whole collectivity.

Jonathan: That could comment on the legitimacy of voting, and it could also be a critique of the legitimacy of the forced choice, right? If there are two candidates or five candidates and you think that none of them adequately represent your interests, then you reject the very premise of choosing between flawed choices.

Deva: Yes, but I think it's more than just choices. I really think it's a kind of despair about the efficacy of governance at all. So it's good to have better choices, but it's better to actually show people their power. And that's something that usually happens at the local level before the national level. So that's why the organizing is so, so, so important. We discount organizing, and political campaigns have distorted what it means. Political campaigns think organizing is defined by flying into a place ten weeks before the election to knock on doors.

And it's great to knock on doors, but that's not what organizing is. Organizing takes years. It involves developing relationships with people around what they need and how they can be empowered to deliver it over the course of those years, not in ten weeks. That's what's key, not only for setting the goals you want met, but also for creating the kind of democratic polity that you need in order for self-governance to be possible. And that's the work that the Movement for Black Lives is doing. It is also the work of many different social movements that have arisen in the 21st century. #MeToo is doing this work. The Stoneman Douglas kids are doing it around gun control. The Sunrise Movement is doing this around climate change. This is the deep work of democracy.

Jonathan: And there are political movements on the right that are also working quite effectively at organizing. Who's playing it better: the right or the left?

Deva: I think that the right has been playing it better for seventy years. That is, empirically, they have been better. But that's because they believed in organizing and they also had a national institution for that organizing, which was the Church, which became the conservative church.

Jonathan: And they were building at the community level, right? As in "stacking," where you combine large minority populations with a greater number of white voters in order to ensure that districts are majority white.

Deva: Exactly. We have a roadmap for how this is done. But now I think that they're at a moment of fracturing. They're also at a moment where they are in the minority and have turned vicious in a way that is unappealing to most people. Although they have a lot of experience in organizing in this way, I think they're going to have more trouble organizing broadly, partly because they have become so odious.

Betty: When you describe what goes into the long slog of organizing—building relationships, gaining trust, making dialog with people so that needs can be determined—to me this is where politics and psychology, or psychotherapy, overlap. Because organizers, like therapists, must identify what people are hurting from or what they are missing, what they lack. And then over time, we figure out, in collaboration with the individuals we work with, what is the best thing, what is the best way for them to care for themselves, what is the best way to build support. It can take a long time.

To your point that people like that young Black voter can despair that change can even happen through this—or any—process, it takes a while to even convince people that living with less suffering is even possible. That young Black voter expressed intergenerational despair, and it's an outcome of intergenerational trauma. This made me wonder about the fact that the left has a coalition built that is much more diverse, and Black Lives Matter and the Movement for Black Lives have been instrumental, of late, in building these coalitions. They are including other people in the movement who are not directly impacted by police injustice but feel absolutely like they cannot bear witness to this any longer. With such effective grassroots organizing prompting many to feel moved or even empowered, how do we reach the guy who is saying he's in despair and doesn't want to vote? What do we say to someone who has seen generations of his family voting, yet they still find themselves in the same poverty-defined position?

Deva: You ask him to do other political work. That's the thing about organizing with a politics of care at the center. A politics of care is about your orientation toward governance. It asks, "How do we collectively come to understand what people need, and then how do we distribute responsibility, so most people have what they need to live and thrive?" It is not about demanding the vote from this person. It's asking him, "What is the biggest problem that you face in your life? Or what is the biggest challenge that your community faces?" And then it's to ask, "How do we step in? How do you step in? What would you do, what could you do if you had the support?" You don't ask for the vote because the vote is not what he needs.

Jonathan: Right. The vote is a transactional thing that you need from them.

Deva: So you stop asking for that. What you ask for instead is—and actually, it's not what you ask *for*, it's what you ask *about*— "What is the thing that your community needs?" Or "If you had the resources, what is the thing you would do first and what other resources do you think you might need?" Rather than asking for votes, let's start to think about what people have and what they need. I think this is part of what's appealing about the Movement for Black Lives and why it has so successfully worked with the #Metoo and Sunrise movements. All of that is because their guiding question is not, "What can you give me so that I can give you something else?" Instead they ask, "What do we all need to live and thrive?" And this was a question that was highlighted in the very beginning in a seemingly incidental way. If you all remember in 2014, when the Ferguson uprisings were just happening, all around the internet you started to see memes of that Audrey Lorde quote about self-care. Do you guys remember? "Caring for myself is not self-indulgence, it is self-preservation, and that is an act of political warfare."[3]

Betty: Yes, yes.

Deva: So, of course, self-care has been taken up and commodified and become about getting pedicures or whatever, instead of about caring for yourself while you're a revolutionary who has terminal cancer, which, of course, is what Audre Lorde was expressing. And the reason that quote about self-care struck such a chord—before it was synonymous with all

---

[3] Audrey Lorde, *A Burst of Light and Other Essays* (New York: Firebrand Books, 1988), 130.

these commodified things—is because we are living in an age, in a political economy, and in a kind of social logic in which nothing is supposed to be as important to anyone as their waged work. Everything else is secondary, both by necessity and also by the neoliberal logic that we operate under. And that's inhumane. It's especially inhumane to the poor, but it's actually also inhumane to a ton of other people who work for very high wages, but who still don't have any time for the human interactions in their life—nor any time to care for themselves. We're in an age in which people are yearning for a different way of relating to each other and the world. And the movement has come in and asked, *What if we do politics as though we want to live?* Not just to exist, not just to survive, not just to be running after the next coin. But what if we did politics as though we wanted to live together and enjoy our time on this planet?

Jonathan: Imagine that.

Betty: What a revolutionary thought!

Deva: I think that's just deeply resonant.

Jonathan: So, Deva, how far do we go? I mean, I'm all for "no justice, no peace." I march. I protest. I petition. I do all those things. How far do we go? Is it "give me liberty or give me death?" How disruptive do we need to be? How disruptive is it appropriate to be in this moment—or ever—in the social change business?

Deva: I don't know. People have to assess that for themselves. I think there are moments for physical, forceful revolution, as Frantz Fanon taught us. But there are also moments for revolutions that are mostly bloodless—that aren't directly born of war. For example, what happened in South Africa and the overturning of governance there. And then there are times for restructuring and a reorientation of structures in society, which is short of revolutionary, but still very significant. And then there are yet other times when what you need is a vigorous kind of reform or cleansing. It's situational. And people have to decide that together. And it's also a negotiation. It's not always path dependent. Sometimes things change as people go along.

I would say that, for now, in the American case and in places around the world where people have been marching and protesting—there are times for setting things on fire and taking down monuments—I feel comfortable with that level of engagement. Because people seem very clear about the kinds of transformation that they want, and they are really clear that they don't want it to be bloody. That's the thing—whenever people gnash their teeth about the violence of these protests, it's important to note that an estimated 25 to 30 million people were in the streets, just in the United States this summer. If people wanted to be violent, we would have been in a civil war, with bodies on the ground. Now we have bodies on the ground, but it's because of an infectious disease that the Trump administration refuses to do anything to control. The protest didn't even add to the spread of COVID-19. This is the epitome of peaceful protest. And I refuse to accept any other kind of characterization because a few buildings got set on fire. It's absolutely ridiculous. Given the scale of the protest, if violence was in any way in the purview of even 1 percent of the people who were in the street, we would have been looking at something very, very different from what we saw, which was mostly people—huge multiracial coalitions of people—marching with their children.

Betty: With masks on.

Deva: With masks on for the chance to live in a society they can be proud of.

Betty: Deva, you mentioned the COVID-19 pandemic. Right now, we sit in a time during which the pandemic is a driver, or a crucible, for all of this shift. It is causing us to reconsider many things because there's a lot that's going wrong, ways in which our government has not cared for us. Do you feel that these confluences of crises are pushing this drive toward asking *how do we live together?* And, as a consequence, what's next? How do we get out of this, or where do you see this going, in your wisdom, research, and observations as a political scientist?

Deva: Well, look, I can't tell you what the end of this is, but I agree that this is a critical juncture. This is one of those times in history that you read about. But the reassuring thing is that if you look back one hundred years, if you look at 1919, we're kind of in the same spot.

Betty: Tell us about that spot.

Deva: At the beginning of the 20th century, we were in the midst of a world war after a global pandemic, in the midst of uprisings for racial justice, and in the midst of trying to figure out a transition of power in the United States. Also, between the 19th and 20th centuries, we were trying to figure out how differently we would carry on with each other in the future. We were in the middle of the Bolshevik Revolution, and we were at the beginnings of what we now think of as the labor movement. It was also a critical juncture in which everything seemed to be changing all at once and nothing about how it turned out was inevitable. It was all contingent on the way people worked together to resolve the many problems that butted up against each other at that moment. Now, they didn't come up with any perfect solutions. And the solutions they did come up with have run their course. But this is the moment for us to set the terms of the 21st century. This is the moment in which we are doing so.

And the truth is, tumultuous as these times are, you don't get a chance to set the terms unless there is a critical juncture, like this, where people are open to change, and everything is on the table—for worse and for better. So while this is excruciating, it's also an incredible opportunity. Because this is the moment when we can decide everybody deserves a living wage, free health care, leisure time, etc. And we also are able to think about governance in terms of what do we need and how do we distribute responsibility so everyone can live and thrive? We have the opportunity to shift, so that we can invent in a human way—so that we can both share resources and innovate. This is the time that we can start to institutionalize those things. And it's important to do that in policy. But it's also about changing your mind about how government works and what it's supposed to be for. Because that's also what changed at the beginning of the 20th century. There began to be this idea that the government should provide enough stability so that people could reach prosperity—so that many people could reach prosperity. Before the 20th century or so, there had never been this kind of idea, that most people could be prosperous.

Betty: Yes, prosperity was only considered to be available to the upper classes.

Deva: It wasn't even on the board, right? The assumption was that most people were going to be poor and die young, and that's the way it would be. But then people changed their minds about what was possible. So they tried to put in place an apparatus that could make what they believed in possible, actually possible in the world, at least for some more people. We are now at the same moment. We have to decide what we believe is possible and then put in place the apparatus that makes it possible for most people. It's work—and it's terrifying. Don't get me wrong. We're in a terrifying moment. But critical junctures are always terrifying.

Jonathan: But you've framed it in an optimistic way. You've said we're at a critical juncture and change is possible.

Deva: There are international examples of different forms of leadership as well. I mean, look, Jacinda [Ardern] over in New Zealand is showing us the way, right?

Jonathan: Yes.

Deva: And people are learning from her. Especially with the key questions we now have hanging over us: Can we create a society in which people can live and thrive? And can we let the tradeoffs be ones that we're willing to deal with? And then we look around the world and see some examples of people like the prime minister of New Zealand who are making it work.

Betty: For me, one of the takeaways from what you've said is that these organizers and the organizing work they do show people that they have agency. And this is very important, both in terms of individual change and in terms of societal change. It's something people can lose sight of. So you need organizers and social movements to show people that they actually have agency in government—it's not just this monolith that people cannot change or get involved with.

Deva: Right. The Black Lives Matter movement has just had its first election of someone who was politicized and raised in the movement who has gone to Congress. Cori Bush just beat a thirty-year political dynasty in St. Louis and is now a new congressperson. And that follows a wave of people who weren't necessarily politicized in the movement, but who have been cultivated by the organizations that support the movement—people who have come out of Run for Something, the organization that recruits and supports young, diverse progressives; people who have come out of Higher Heights for America, which is a group that prepares women of color to run for office. So you don't tell people that they just have to be satisfied with the choices that are on the table. You go about the work of actually creating new choices—and that's already begun. And that does make me hopeful. You know, social movements have a logic, and this kind of change takes time. Right now we are in a huge moment of potentiality that people are trying to take advantage of, although outcomes are not guaranteed. And it is very stressful.

Betty: Yes—very, very stressful.

Jonathan: Especially when we're living in an era of minority rule.

Deva: That's right.

Betty: But I think what you, Deva, particularly emphasize right now is *agency*—that people can develop agency. They might not have it right now, but they can gain it and they can learn it and they can spread it. And that is really significant because I think there are a lot of people who feel very overwhelmed and, therefore, inactive or frozen. And that's very distressing.

Deva: I love your psychology analogy because the movement does take this perspective of "healing justice" really seriously. It comes out of the disability justice movement, but it also has roots in this idea that to be well is a process that takes time.

Betty: That's exactly right.

Deva: To make yourself well is a process that takes time. And political change is a course toward social wellness. So, of course, it's a process that takes time and you have to invest in it. I have not thought about it as being almost like the process of therapy, but it is.

Betty: There's a lot of confluence. I think that's the way people are connecting to it so readily and that's why it's so apt that it's called the *politics of care*. You know, it's not the "politics of progress" nor is it the "politics of industry."

Deva: Right.

Betty: And there are many similarities and parallels to psychotherapy.

Deva: Right, because the *process* is the thing. The outcome is not the thing. It's all about the process.

Betty: Exactly.

Deva: Because you don't quite know what wellness looks like at the beginning.

Betty: Right, so you find it along the way. You find what it feels like to feel good.

Deva: That's awesome.

Jonathan: Deva, thank you for making the choice to join us on *Mind of State*.

Deva: Thank you. It was a pleasure.

Chapter 23
Restoring Faith in Democracy

Guest: Eric Liu
Episode Aired: January 21, 2021

Eric Liu is the co-founder and CEO of Citizen University, which works at a grassroots level to build a culture of powerful and responsible citizenship in the United States. He is also the founding director of the Aspen Institute Citizenship and American Identity Program. He is the author of several acclaimed books, including Become America: Civic Sermons on Love, Responsibility, and Democracy. *Eric served as a White House speechwriter for President Bill Clinton and later as the president's Deputy Domestic Policy Advisor.*

When we posted our conversation with Eric Liu in late November 2020, two weeks after Election Day, it had been announced that Joe Biden defeated Donald Trump and was president-elect. Despite this, there remained a high level of anxiety among Americans about the stability of these results. It would not be until mid-December, when all Electoral College votes had been announced and it was clear Biden had captured 306 votes to Trump's 232, that some relief came. As the New York Times *reported:*

The normally rubber-stamp formality was followed avidly online in an extraordinary election year, one in which the incumbent, President Trump, refused to concede and incited supporters with baseless claims of a "rigged" vote. For some followers of the counting, it was a kind of replay of election night, but one in which the winner was assured.[1]

[1] Holder, J., Gabriel, T., & Paz, I. G. (2020). Biden's 306 Electoral Votes Make His Victory Official. *The New York Times.* https://www.nytimes.com/interactive/2020/12/14/us/elections/electoral-college-results.html.

The January 6, 2021, insurrection attempt upon the U.S. Capitol two weeks later revealed why such anxieties were valid. When over 2000 white nationalist Trump supporters, encouraged by Trump himself, violently tried to stop congressional ratification of 2020's presidential election results, there was no question that U.S. democracy was in crisis. Respect for our democratic election process was fraying and judging from the sense of conviction among the seditionists, would continue to do so.

More than three years later, in 2023, that crisis continues. As of this writing, Donald Trump has been indicted on more than 90 federal and state criminal counts in four separate courts in Washington, DC, Florida, New York, and Georgia. He has been indicted in U.S. federal district court in Washington, DC, for his part in trying to subvert the 2020 election results and for the events of January 6, 2021. The specific charges are for conspiracy to defraud the U.S., conspiracy to threaten others' rights, and obstruction of a proceeding before Congress. Trump has been indicted in Georgia for pressuring Georgia's secretary of state, Brad Raffensperger, in January 2021 to overturn his loss of votes in the state.[2] Nevertheless, Trump remains the frontrunner to win the Republican Party nomination in the upcoming 2024 presidential elections.

Against this backdrop of ongoing social and political instability in the U.S., Eric Liu offers a useful perspective of reason and realism. Turning to history, he reminds us that American democracy has always been a flawed work in progress:

> …we've gotten a little spoiled, those of us who were born after the Second World War, in this exceptional period when political differences were compressed and inclusion became a greater norm …But if you think about the betrayal of Reconstruction and what occurred in the United States after the corrupt compromise of 1877 that led to, depending on how you want to measure it—a half-century, or the better part of three generations—in which democracy was subverted in national politics, that has happened …and it could happen again.

Here Liu echoes Pauline Boss, Judith Herman, and Jessica Benjamin (Chapters 2, 3, and 4, respectively) in their observations of how unrecognized breaches in trust create repetitions of disavowed traumas. These denials, as Eric Ward (Chapter 14), Nancy Rosenblum (Chapter 10), and William Davies (Chapter 11) note, create structural weakness in liberal democracies, which can crack when social, political, and environmental

---

[2] Politico Staff, "Tracking the Trump Criminal Cases," *Politico*, updated August 1, 2023, https://www.politico.com/interactives/2023/trump-criminal-investigations-cases-tracker-list/.

pressures converge. Liu agrees with Robert Jay Lifton that U.S. democracy is in such a "convulsion":

> I do think we are in a constitutional crisis, a crisis of legitimacy, and that is fed by a single man who is occupying the presidency as the catalyst, but also by a great wave of people who respond to that catalyst…it was there before [Trump] and he galvanized it, and now he has activated it, and literally and figuratively weaponized it so that, even after he leaves office, those forces will still be there. The reckoning still is to come. And I believe we're not going to get anywhere in that reckoning unless we first attend to that base layer of rehumanizing our politics. Let me be very clear. I don't know if civic faith is going to be enough. I don't assume the United States is going to defy human history and be a perpetual experiment that runs forever. We might be coming toward the end of this experiment, but with every fiber of my being and every iota of my sense of purpose, I want to try to defer that collapse. And I want to try to be part of the renewal and the repair.

Eric Liu's passionate and yet realistic faith in democracy was not only reassuring, but a reminder—as expressed by so many of our guests—that the critical junction we sit in, created by what Adrienne Hollis (Chapter 20) named a "syndemic," is a call to action. Restoring faith in democracy depends upon effort, attention, and care—as Deva Woodly asserts in the previous chapter:

> We have the opportunity to shift, so that we can invent in a human way—so that we can both share resources and innovate. This is the time that we can start to institutionalize those things…it's also about changing your mind about how government works and what it's supposed to be for.

Interview

Jonathan: Eric, you've been out preaching the gospel of civic religion. Can you tell our listeners a little bit about what civic religion means?

Eric: At Citizen University, we like to say that democracy in the United States is a matter of belief in each other and in the possibility that this thing could actually work. We put it very simply: democracy works only if enough of us believe democracy works. When you consider that we are a nation that is bound together only by a creed—a set of ideas and ideals—we realize rather painfully and urgently during these times, how fragile and evanescent that mutual agreement is. So we think about this work as the work of sustaining and continuously finding new ways to rekindle a sense of civic faith, a belief that this common endeavor, this possibility of self-government, can work.

To believe in the idea of democracy is to recognize the values in the creed—words that we often say as clichés—liberty and justice for all, equal protection of the law, all people are created equal, and so on. At Citizen University, we sit with these words, interrogate them, and express our doubts about them, and also find ways in regular ritual gatherings to ask each other what these ideals call us to do. How do they require us to show up in our community, in our relationships, in our engagement in civic and community life?

The central program we have at Citizen University is called Civic Saturdays, which are a civic analogue to a faith gathering. It's not church or synagogue or mosque, but it has the flow and feel of people coming together because of a common faith, precisely because we believe that this stuff has to be rekindled and that belief has to be rekindled in the company of others where we can express our doubt, our fear, our concern, and where we can make meaning together in a time where so much in our national politics is undercutting that faith.

Betty: As you said, "Democracy works because enough people believe democracy works"; it is a faith-based thing. But right now it feels like we're having a crisis of faith about democracy. How do we deal with this crisis of faith? The language of religion really helps us galvanize and get behind civics, which can be dry. Your approach reminds us that democracy is a belief and a faith, something that gives us meaning. But right now, it seems like meaning is being taken away from democracy.

Eric: When we talk about civic religion, we do not mean blind faith, indoctrination, zealotry, or unerring dogma. To reckon with the ideas in the American creed is to recognize that there are perpetual tensions. If you take two elements of that creed—liberty and equality—those are not just mom and apple pie—nice things that we like. Those are things that are continuously in tension. And the debates that go on today, even in the midst of a cataclysmic pandemic, about whether wearing masks is too great an affront on our liberty, show that these are going to be continuously contested questions and ideas. The question of civic faith is one of enabling enough people to articulate their core values in a way where they can understand how others who have different priorities and values might see the world differently.

Jonathan: I'm all for trying to understand and empathize with the views of others in order to come together. But how do we repair the breach when it seems like, at this moment, there is a right and a wrong. There is not necessarily room for people to show up at a state house with guns and disrupt government function based on unfounded claims that an election was stolen. Two-thirds of the people who voted for Trump believe that this election was stolen. How do we repair the breach when we don't even agree on objective facts?

Eric: You are naming a central question, which is when you don't have agreement on objective facts or common reality, it becomes difficult, if not impossible, to sustain a union. That's just a fact. And we are experiencing that right now. I will say that I think the least effective way to try to re-create a sense of common fact is to tell people they're stupid.

Jonathan: But you have said we need less stupid arguments.

Eric: Well, yes. Our arguments are often very stupid and unsatisfyingly binary. But I think if you look at those two-thirds of Trump voters who believe that Donald Trump won the election and any evidence to the contrary is evidence of fraud, you will see a willfully stupid way of seeing the world. And to me, what's interesting and important about that, is what drives the willfulness, not the stupidity. What is leading those people to need to believe in that lie? I don't think you can change the minds of all of those two-thirds of people who voted for Trump. But I think you can change the minds of some of them. And the only way you do that is by actually getting to that base layer beneath the current arguments about the election to what it is that forms their worldview, what it is that leads them to react to reality this way and to respond to an authoritarian demagogue like Donald Trump the way they do.

Jonathan: You've been out on a listening tour, talking to people across red and blue affiliations, and in urban and rural settings to formulate your insights for common purpose. What are you hearing that we're not hearing and seeing? Because I understand the resentment and lack of faith in government. I understand feeling let down and left behind by the economy. That all makes perfect sense. But what are we missing?

Eric: I think it's really important and it's very difficult, even in a time of a constitutional-level crisis like this, to remember that the president is not the country. I always reject a formulation that calls this either "Trump's America" or now "Biden's America," or years ago, "Obama's America." America is a complex, contradictory ecosystem that will yield leaders of certain kinds at certain times. And Trump was as representative of America as Obama was and as Biden is, depending on what slice and what part of the swirl of this complex adaptive system you want to focus on.

But let's back up to consider *Our Common Purpose*, which is a report put out by the American Academy of Arts and Sciences, from a commission that I co-chaired with Danielle Allen of Harvard and Stephen Heintz of the Rockefeller Brothers Fund.[3] We were joined by 32 other commissioners, and we put together this report from all over the United States, from right and left. And we spent two years putting this set of recommendations together for reinventing American democracy.

Core to that endeavor were about 50 listening sessions around the United States in very different kinds of settings and domains with very different kinds of people: immigrants in Los Angeles, midshipmen at the Naval Academy, people in small rural towns and big cities. Jonathan, to your question, what we heard across the board, whether people were fans of the current president or not, is that people love this country. People love the idea of this country. They want to see America deliver on its ideals and its promise, number one. Number two, people are not as consumed as you or I might be with national politics. Instead, they are trying to figure out how to make things work in Scranton, Pennsylvania, or in Athens, Tennessee, or in San Bernardino, California, or wherever they might be.

The more local you get, you see the more relationship and trust matters. And the less you can get away with just simple mimicking of the words

---

[3] Commission on the Practice of Democratic Citizenship, *Our Common Purpose: Inventing American Democracy for the Twenty-First Century* (American Academy of Arts and Sciences, 2020), https://www.amacad.org/ourcommonpurpose/report.

that you see on social media or cable news commentary; because the more local you get, the more you actually have problems to deal with and solve. And simply rehearsing talking points from Fox or MSNBC won't cut it. So we did find that there are people all around the country who are trying to figure out, from the bottom up, from the inside out, and from the middle out, how to renew our system. But, at the same time, I do think we are in a constitutional crisis, a crisis of legitimacy, and that is fed by a single man who is occupying the presidency as the catalyst, but also by a great wave of people who respond to that catalyst. You can remove Donald Trump…

Jonathan: So it was there before Trump, and it will be there after him?

Eric: Well, it was there before him and he galvanized it, and now he has activated it, and literally and figuratively weaponized it so that, even after he leaves office, those forces will still be there. The reckoning still is to come. And I believe we're not going to get anywhere in that reckoning unless we first attend to that base layer of rehumanizing our politics. Let me be very clear. I don't know if civic faith is going to be enough. I don't assume the United States is going to defy human history and be a perpetual experiment that runs forever. We might be coming toward the end of this experiment, but with every fiber of my being and every iota of my sense of purpose, I want to try to defer that collapse. And I want to try to be part of the renewal and the repair.

Jonathan: Here's my issue, Eric. The common purpose doctrine seems to be all about fundamentally expanding the participation in democracy and faith in democratic values. But how do we convince a minoritarian government to cede power by making our democracy more participatory and more expansionist? I don't know how you do that.

Eric: I guess I don't wholly concede the premise. When you say a "minoritarian government," do you mean just by the design of the Constitution?

Jonathan: No, I mean, up until this recent election, we had an Electoral College that delivered a win to a president who was defeated in the popular vote. And we have a minority control of the Senate. So, why would Mitch McConnell ever agree to expand the franchise or expand the size of the House of Representatives? Power doesn't give up power without being forced to do so, right?

Eric: Yes, that's exactly right. Mitch McConnell probably won't ever do those things, but it is still up to the people of the United States to determine whether Mitch McConnell is Senate Majority Leader in perpetuity. So I think the kind of organizing that is going on in the United States right now shows that people recognize that they don't have to take as given, what is given. That is true on both sides of the political spectrum, by the way. Having record turnout in this presidential election guaranteed nothing except that we amplified our divisions. Meaning, therefore, that finally a pro-democracy majority took hold decisively. But there is no choice except to keep on organizing, number one. Number two, look at American history.

There are long stretches of American history when injustice was institutionalized and minoritarian power was operationalized generation upon generation. So we've gotten a little spoiled, those of us who were born after the Second World War, in this exceptional period when political differences were compressed, and inclusion became a greater norm. And we had what I think of as the third founding of the United States with the civil rights movement in the late 1960s, with the second founding having been with Reconstruction, following the Civil War. But if you think about the betrayal of Reconstruction and what occurred in the United States after the corrupt compromise of 1877 that led to,[4] depending on how you want to measure it—a half-century, or the better part of three generations, in which democracy was subverted in national politics—that has happened.

Jonathan: Yes.

Eric: And it could happen again. So, Jonathan, the premise of your question holds a little bit of disbelief, like "how could such badness happen?" And the answer is, badness is more the rule than the exception in American life. And the challenge we have right now is to keep it as the exception.
The report that we did at the American Academy, *Our Common Purpose,* includes 31 recommendations that span the gamut from institutional changes to other changes. But the big theory of action that undergirds the whole report is that in a society like ours, there's either going to be a virtuous cycle

---

[4] The compromise of 1877 came about as a way to settle the 1876 election when Democrats agreed not to block Rutherford B. Hayes's election if the Republicans agreed to withdraw all federal troops from the South, bringing an end to Reconstruction and leading to Jim Crow. History.com Editors, "Compromise of 1877," *History*, updated November 27, 2019, https://www.history.com/topics/us-presidents/compromise-of-1877.

or a vicious cycle between three things: our institutions, our civic culture, and our civil society.

When our political institutions are healthy, and there is a civic culture of, as you say, participation and inclusion, and civil society is robust and all kinds of clubs and associations and organizations are forming to engage people, that's a virtuous cycle. That's what we wish to set in motion. But when those things start to decay, they infect each other. When our institutions become captured and corrupted, that leads people to become cynical, which leads them to check out of civil society and stop showing up and joining. And that feeds a culture of cynicism and hyper-individualism and immediate gratification: people think, "I'm just going to get mine" in a zero-sum way. And that is the vicious cycle. And so much of, not only American history, but also the history of republics, tells you how difficult it is to sustain that virtuous cycle generation after generation. This is why our report isn't just an academic set of suggestions. It is an urgent call to action, recognizing the fragility of the moment that we are in right now.

Betty: As you said before, faith is a risk. You're not naive about the challenges. And what you're talking about is a lot of paradoxes. Even in the last four years, we've had more activism prompted by Trump than we've seen in at least fifteen years, if not for a whole generation. And, as a trauma therapist, I see intergenerational trauma operating, causing reactivity, dissociation, even paranoia. And here we are at a fourth founding, as you guys describe it. So viewing this through a psychological lens, I see this as a desire to move. Humans don't like to be frozen. They feel stuck. This impasse that we're having between the two parties of our political system is frustrating.

And yet both sides have articulated a faith in democracy by voting in record numbers. And so, how do we activate movement in a common direction or purpose that doesn't create another impasse again? And the love of the United States that shows up on both sides is at the core. How can we transmit this to both sides so that it's about not fighting each other? How do we get out of this political combat mentality and transform the vicious cycle to the virtuous cycle? People are moving at a grassroots level. People are moving in resistance, but we're not moving together as a nation.

Eric: I think it is worth saying that if I unpack my faith in democracy, what I actually mean more is a faith in democratic self-government. Democracy is a means, the idea of capturing something like the will of the people through a vote. Plenty of democracies have committed suicide through democratic elections—Germany in the Thirties being the most vivid example. And so just because a lot of people have voted for an authoritarian demagogue who might want to subvert democratic self-government doesn't mean that's great. I think we've got to get to a democratic culture in which people are entrusted with power to make decisions for themselves and entrusted to express what we think of at Citizen University as a complete notion of citizenship. The way we think about it, Power plus Character equals Citizenship.

We're focusing a lot, both in this conversation and in the United States right now, on Power, on being literate in Power and understanding how to move people and money and ideas to get what you want. But, if all you have is a literacy in Power and it's not coupled with some grounding in a moral ethical core, then you are just a really skilled *sociopath*. And we see that everywhere. And I don't use that word lightly. I choose that word very deliberately. You understand, you're a mental health expert, Betty. There is sociopathy afoot in the United States right now. There's sociopathy in the culture of indignant, intentional, non-wearing of masks. That is like declaring, "I don't care how much harm I may bring to others, so long as I feel unencumbered."

But I think we've got to cultivate the Character side of the equation. And that means being able to rekindle a belief in values like shared sacrifice, mutual obligation, service before self, and a cause greater than oneself. And I think the way we get to that, and the way we get to some of this reckoning with the trauma that you're describing, is by doing more together. Not talking about it, not arguing about it, not tweeting about it, but doing things and fixing things.

One of the core recommendations in *Our Common Purpose* is for a core expectation of national service, that every young person coming out of high school would choose a path of service, whether civilian or military. The reason why I'm a big believer in national service is that in the United States today, we don't have enough opportunities or experiences where we will come together with people who are unlike us, who see the world differently, who worship differently, who talk differently—where we come together, not to talk about our differences and have a diversity workshop, but actually to do a third thing that's not about me or you. It's in the doing of a third thing that we come to rehumanize each other and recognize that we do have common capacities, fears, hopes, and purpose.

Jonathan: Right. A barn-raising. It's not Democrats or Republicans. It's the community coming together to build a barn.

Eric: Yes, but, Jonathan, again, I grant that in today's culture, you have a group of people who are so hyper-individualistic and extremist in their libertarianism that it would be very hard to get them into the fold of agreeing to something like instituting national service. Yet, again, this is part of my faith. I take a longer view. I do believe that we are going through a convulsion right now, and I do believe it is possible, depending on how we show up and navigate this time, to invite people into a deeper sense of relationship and trust and mutual obligation at the level of where we live, not through mediated national politics. I do believe it is possible, in fact, still, to come out of this convulsive period with a sense that we must learn to coexist. That does not mean we have to agree on everything. And it can mean, in fact, that we can have better arguments. The Better Arguments Project that we're running is oriented toward that.[5]

Argument is okay, but what we've got to have as a shared premise is that this is a game of infinite-repeat-play, and you're going to win some and lose some. This is not a game in which the object is to wipe the other side off the face of the Earth, or to rig the rules permanently so that the other side atrophies and disappears. We must learn to coexist, and if you think about that, Betty, in terms of reckoning with trauma, then I think you cannot deny your way through trauma and the experience of it. You cannot just excise it and amputate it off your psyche. There's got to be a coexistence with the trauma and recognition that you, the body, the whole, has been changed by this, but we are still of a body. And I think that's what we're trying to promote at Citizen University. And I know it's hard and I know it's challenging, but I don't really see the alternative right now.

Betty: Having gone through two years of talking and listening to all the fine guests on *Mind of State*, I see there's a generational shift going on. Do you see that our prognosis is good, given what we see in our young people? They're very active, and they have taken to the streets on climate change. In the long view, looking at all the different generations of people who you and your team have spoken to, what do you see in terms of our possibilities for this collective faith, this ability to act, this grassroots possibility?

---

[5] See the Better Arguments Project at https://betterarguments.org.

Eric: I am net-hopeful about younger generations, both millennials and Gen Z, but I say "net-hopeful" because I think there are assets and deficits here. One of the great assets of the rising generations is this deep sense of idealism. They're not just digital natives; they are diversity natives and inclusion natives. This is a generation that has grown up in a hybridized, multiracial society and is super comfortable with that. And they are going to help us speed the reckoning with the way in which being American and being white are detaching. That has freaked out a lot of people, but I think this rising generation is equipped to handle it. On the deficit side, though, millennials and post-millennials have a shallower understanding and education in civic power. They don't have the knowledge, skills, habits, or practices of participating in a long-term way, beyond protest, in the process of self-government. That's a set of habits that needs to start getting cultivated rapidly.

What's hopeful about the surge of young people who have voted in this most recent election is that they're beginning to understand that it's not just a "one and done" effort; that if your concern is climate change, it's not just a matter of electing someone who's pro-addressing climate change. Now you've got to bring pressure to bear continuously to ensure that there are policies that get enacted that advance your agenda. The other thing that makes me concerned about the rising generations is that very little has been asked of most of them. This is not surprising, and it's not to blame them because the younger generations have grown up since the Great Recession in which "forever wars" have been subcontracted out to just 1 percent of Americans who we thank for their service and yet, again, nothing has been asked of the rest of us. They've grown up in a civic culture in decay, so it's not surprising to me that when you see these polls, the younger the generation, the less belief there is that democracy is inherently better than authoritarian or autocratic systems.

They don't have the faith because not a whole lot in their upbringing has reinforced that faith. So it is in spite of that that I remain "net hopeful" because they are learning to show up and they are teaching those of us in Gen X and older what it means to keep on believing and what it means to bring force and voice to the work of civic renewal and change.

I just want to close by saying I don't call myself an optimist. To me, optimism versus pessimism is a frame that is too much about spectatordom. It implies "I'm just watching this thing unfold" and "I think it's going to go okay," or "I think it's going to go terribly, but I'm just watching." To me, the better frame is not optimism, but hopefulness, because hope implies agency. And we all have agency and a hand in determining whether this republic is going to get another round and whether self-government is going to survive in the United States.

Betty: Your main theme is to take responsibility. Do something, join something, talk to some people, teach, say something. I think that is really a great theme and allows us to embody ourselves in the psychological sense. If we don't act, we can't be.

Eric: That's absolutely right.

Jonathan: I hope we're entering a more virtuous cycle at this point. Eric, you've pointed the way, and we really appreciate you coming and joining us on *Mind of State*.

Eric: Thank you for helping to make this conversation possible and being part of that wave, that awakening in civic life today.

Chapter 24

Can Voting & Democracy Survive the Internet?

Guest: Nate Persily
Episode aired: September 30, 2020

Nate Persily is the James B. McClatchy Professor of Law at Stanford Law School and the Director of the Stanford Cyber Policy Center. In his latest book, Social Media and Democracy, *Nate examines the impact of changing technology on democracy.*

Our interview with Nate Persily was posted six weeks before the 2020 presidential election, when then-Vice President Joe Biden challenged incumbent President Donald Trump's bid for re-election. Throughout the fall, anxieties about voter turnout, mail-ballot fraud, poll tampering, and violence at poll sites added to the strain of a highly contentious election season conducted during the COVID-19 pandemic. While Election Day—November 3, 2020—passed nonviolently and Joe Biden was elected president, Trump and his supporters refused to accept this result. Conspiracist "Stop the Steal" allegations by Trump and his most extreme supporters led to the January 6, 2021 siege on the U.S. Capitol to stop ratification of the 2020 election results. That all this followed our 2020 conversation with Nate—when we reflected upon concerns and anxieties about the security of voting and the stability of election results—reveals that the practice of democratic voting for elected leaders is still extremely vulnerable in the U.S., and its safety cannot be taken for granted.

Interview

Jonathan: I want to start off the conversation by speaking to this moment. Nate, your work focuses on the internet's impact on democracy, so we're hoping you're going to help ground us in some of the realities we're dealing with—social media, democracy, the health of voting—so we can process this moment a little more clearly and rationally.

Betty: Before we begin, Nate, can you tell us how you define "social media?"

Nate Persily: When we say social media, we refer to the peer-to-peer connection of information, mediated by an algorithm. Sometimes that algorithm can be very thin, such as text messaging through WhatsApp. Sometimes it's much thicker, such as Facebook's or Twitter's algorithms. The key feature that makes media social is that it's between users. And it's not being delivered and curated in the same way that media is when we're talking about TV and the like.

Jonathan: So you're really focused on the social space within the broader digital space. And is it safe to say that's mostly the major platforms— Facebook, Twitter, LinkedIn, TikTok, and Instagram, and so forth—or more the longtail?

Nate: I would add YouTube, which is also an important social media force. But Facebook is first among equals in terms of its impact on people's conversations. And when I say Facebook, I include Instagram and WhatsApp since that suite of products resides under one roof. But each product is different. So, when we talk about the beneficent or pernicious effects of social media, we have to be specific about the platform we're talking about. And the affordances of that platform. What is it about the way people interact on that platform that then has either consequences for their psychology—or for democracy?

Jonathan: So much of the concern is also about advertising—or paid content—in social media. Does your work also focus on paid social media?

Nate: Yes, both. I got interested in the effect of technology on democracy because of political advertising. Most of my work before seven or eight years ago was looking at the nuts and bolts of elections, whether it's political parties, redistricting, voting rights, or election administration. But then it became clear that the internet was going to fundamentally alter not just political conversation, but also political advertising. And this was at the same time that we were dealing with the famous Supreme Court case of

Citizens United, which upheld a corporation's right to run advertisements.[1] But very few people realize that case was about an on-demand movie. It wasn't actually about a political advertisement. That's relevant because it set the stage for many of these questions about whether it matters if people can download content as opposed to having it thrust in their face in a thirty-second television ad. I think the sort of technological questions that were implied by *Citizens United* were underappreciated, but they did hint toward what we are seeing today. And now, ten years later, we're dealing with billions of dollars that are being spent on targeted political advertising. And it's quickly going to replace television as the main mode of political communication.

Betty: From your research and assessments, how are we being impacted by these paid social media advertisements? If social media is peer-to-peer, then we're just interacting with each other on Facebook, Twitter, Instagram, etc.—and yet there are international corporations and other entities getting onto these platforms. How is this stirring us psychologically? How are we being influenced?

Nate: Well, I don't think we know yet the impact of online advertising on people's levels of anxiety or other psychological phenomena. But let me talk about some stuff that we do know. Let's take the Russian ads that were purchased in the 2016 election. We know that about 80 percent of those ads focused on issues of social division. So they were trying to inflame division, inflame passions on issues of race, religion, gun rights, immigration, and the like. There was very little subtlety in those ads. Now, I think that the influence of Russian ads, per se, has been blown out of proportion. I mean, they spent roughly 100,000 dollars on Facebook ads during that period. And if you could swing a presidential election with just 100,000 dollars' worth of paid ads, a lot of political consultants have been failing to do the same thing for some time. But having said that, when you spend 100,000 dollars on ads, it multiplies because of the social nature of the platform. It doesn't just end with the advertisement that's received by the viewer. It can get forwarded, then metastasize around the internet, which is why tens of millions of people ended up seeing those ads. But on the basic question of what makes social media different in terms of how it influences political anxiety, I would

---

[1] Citizens United v. Federal Election Commission, 558 U.S. 310 (2010).

put it this way: the social part of social media privileges virality. So the kind of communications and strategies and candidacies that are more likely to be forwarded are the ones that then get privileged in that atmosphere. And we do know that the kinds of communication that appeal to outrage and emotion generally are the ones that are more likely to be forwarded through social media. So whether it's advertising or organic content, if you try to evoke strong emotions, it's going to be privileged. That is exacerbated by the algorithms themselves that continue to feed you things that you've engaged with before. So if you find something engaging, then the algorithm is going to try to give you similar content in the future in order to keep you on the platform.

Betty: What you said about the virality of social media and the way things metastasize reminds me of something that you wrote back in 2017. You said, "What the Internet uniquely privileges above all else is a type of campaign message that appeals to outrage or otherwise grabs attention. The politics of never-ending spectacles cannot be healthy for democracy, nor can a porousness to outside influences that undercuts the sovereignty of a nation's elections. Democracy depends on the ability and the will of voters to base their political judgments on facts."[2] So with this virality, Nate, can you talk to us about how our own attention is almost betraying us? In a neurobiological way, we're drawn toward what is scary, fear-driven, or even angering. Our evolutionary brains will pay more attention to fear or anger-driven content. Are our brains being hacked by social media advertisements and is that affecting the democracy of the United States?

Nate: Well, emotions have always been part of democracy and politics. I'm not trying to undersell that. The question is whether we're processing information in a way that we can depend on and can evaluate the facts. If, instead, because of what we're seeing on our screens, candidates and strategies are adapting to that environment in the same way they would deal with entertainment, or fiction—that is not healthy for democratic deliberation and decision making. The blurring of news and entertainment happens online because the intermediaries are taken away. We have stripped the information environment of the social cues that we have in the off-

[2] Persily, N. (2017). The 2016 Presidential Election: Can democracy survive the internet? *Journal of Democracy 28*(2), 63–76, https://doi.org/10.1353/jod.2017.0025.

line world. For example, if you go to a supermarket checkout counter and you see a newspaper that says Hillary Clinton is involved in a pizza-related pedophile scandal, you can evaluate what kinds of newspapers are there as you go to the checkout counter. These are tabloids. You don't take them seriously. They're going to have stories about aliens and the like. When these stories come at you on your Facebook feed, stripped of all the other kinds of identifying information, you then are relying on it just like you would any other kind of communication because it comes at you in the same context as, say, your nephew's graduation video. A tabloid story about Beyoncé, a Paul Krugman op-ed, and a Breitbart story are all packaged essentially the same way, whether it's in search results on Google or Twitter's news feed or Facebook's news feed. So you lose some of the credibility cues that we have in the off-line world when they get repackaged in the online world.

Jonathan: Are you arguing that social media has hurt democracy? Of course, the original promise of the internet was to be the great equalizer. We were going to be in this massive, nonhierarchical, ongoing town-hall conversation, and everyone would have a say. But have we gone wrong?

Nate: I think what you're hitting on is that the most democratic features of the internet and social media actually pose real challenges to democracy. It is the leveling effect, the removal of intermediaries, the fact that we don't have guardrails on political conversation, which is both the great virtue of the internet and also its greatest challenge, when it comes to politics.

Just because we have these downsides to social media doesn't mean that the upsides still aren't there. And the way we're thinking about it in this discussion is very U.S.-focused. If you're living in an authoritarian regime, with top-down control of the information environment, clearly, having social media is a way of liberating information transfer from the authoritarian intermediaries. Even in democratic environments, it wasn't that long ago that we had four white males who were controlling the evening news and deciding what would be Truth. That definitely excluded large swaths of the population from being seen and heard by their peers. So it ends up being a mixed bag. We need to understand the downsides and try to amplify the upsides. Neither the utopians of the Internet age were correct, nor were those who were preaching it would bring on Apocalypse Now. These are tools that you need to harness to make sure that they have pro-democratic ends.

Jonathan: If we take a global view, how do we stack up? Are we healthier or less healthy than other democracies around the world?

Nate: We are unhealthy, but social media is just a small part of that right now. You need only look at people's faith in the democracy of the United States and how it's declined over the last five-plus years. These are worrying signs, let alone the fact that we have had, on two occasions in the last twenty years, and perhaps soon more, political leaders who get the minority of the vote, but end up ruling. So if you have a basic baseline of majority rule, we are not satisfying that. Also, there are other countries and electoral systems that are better capable of managing division. So our polarization is being channeled into the two-party system here, which is not healthy because it creates a dichotomous us-versus-them attitude, whereas in more pluralized electoral systems, you can have a greater diversity of parties, coalition building, and horse trading, which our political system doesn't allow.

Betty: In terms of the health of democracy and the fact that we, over the last twenty years, have seen only 50 percent of people, if that, vote in most popular elections like the presidential elections—tell us about people's faith in voting and how that is going to play out on Election Day this year.

Nate: I think you're going to see very high rates of turnout in this election, despite all the incredible obstacles, both intentional and partisan or unintentional and pandemic-related, that are being placed in people's way. We had a bit of a drop in 2016, but now people are pretty energized. And voter turnout has waxed and waned over the last twenty years. The Obama elections, the first one in particular, saw a surge in turnout.

There are many reasons for our comparatively low voter turnout as compared to the rest of the world. A lot of it has to do with the fact that we require people to re-register every time they move their address—and one out of four Americans moves every two years. So that aspect of our electoral system depresses turnout. The same is true with districted elections as opposed to proportional representation elections, and probably even the presidential system depresses it. But we also have more elections than almost any other country in the world. Maybe Switzerland is the only one that competes with us on that. So there is a bit of fatigue sometimes when it comes to voting. But I think this year we're going to see certainly 60 percent of eligible voters turn out. It may be more than that.

Jonathan: Your prediction of 60 percent voter turnout sounds like a more optimistic expectation than I'm hearing in other places. What do you know that we don't?

Nate: Well, it really depends on 60 percent of what, right? Is it 60 percent of the voting age population, the eligible voting population, or registered voters? We'll certainly have at least 60 percent of registered voters turning out. The historical statistics suggest only about half of the voting age population is going to turn out, but a lot of that includes people who are not eligible to vote, non-citizens, people who are in prison, and the like. And so I think it will still be a high turnout as compared to 2016, but it's still a shame that maybe 40 percent of those who could vote, don't turn out.

Betty: What's motivating us? Is it the pandemic? Is it the Black Lives Matter movement? Is it all of these multiple crises pushing us to seek change? Are we really looking for a "change election"? Jonathan often says that elections are either about "how do we change?" or about "how do we stay the same?" What are you seeing as the cause for the bump in voter turnout?

Nate: There are both push-and-pull reasons for turnout. One of them is that people either love or hate Donald Trump. And that ends up leading to emotional voting. Also, the political parties are energized and well-funded to get out the vote. But you're going to see more of those efforts in the battleground states, not necessarily overall. So, for example, we don't really know what the pandemic's voter-turnout effects are going to be for those who traditionally vote in person. Now people are going to not vote because of the health risk. There's also a lot of controversy over the basic mechanics of voting, whether you're talking about post office and absentee ballots or polling places and poll workers. That is a bit of a curve ball that we can't predict. You know, Democrats are not extremely enthusiastic about Joe Biden, but they are generally motivated to vote against Donald Trump. So the question is, does that emotion translate into a greater motivation to vote?

Jonathan: The question in my mind is, where does that motivation or lack of motivation rub up against the various forms of voter suppression and disenfranchisement? You talked about the mechanics, the structural or legal reasons why it's difficult for people to vote. But at the same time, you're expecting a higher-than-average turnout. I think the wildcard in this election is the indirect measures of disenfranchisement, the constant messaging about the lack of faith in our voting system. I'm wondering how those messages are going to affect voter turnout.

Nate: That's a very good question and we really don't know the answer. I think people are alienated. You have roughly half of the electorate saying they would not trust the outcome or that they're worried that the election will be rigged. Most of those are Democrats, but a sizable number of Republicans believe that as well. And it doesn't help that President Trump is raising that specter in his Twitter feed. But it's not clear that we have reached the levels that you see in developing democracies, where it almost leads to an election boycott of sorts—where people say, "Oh, well, my vote's not going to make a difference, so I'm not going to turn out." Many of the people who are most alienated are also, strangely enough, the most motivated, because they are angry at the system, and they are still willing to try to vote. But the jury is out on this. We don't know what voter turnout is going to look like this term. My prediction is that it's going to be quite high because of how engaged the groups are that work on this.

Betty: And there's still time. How do we encourage those folks to come out and vote if they're apathetic?

Nate: I think voter registration efforts begin the first week in September because there are a lot of people who have not been paying attention to this election, and they start paying attention, as surprising as it might be to us, after Labor Day. So there are all these NGOs (nongovernmental organizations) like Rock the Vote that are working to register more voters, and there will be millions of people who will register in September and October who will end up voting. We need to make sure as many people get contacted as possible.

Jonathan: Nate, do you think that the closeness of American elections—that some 70,000 votes made the difference in 2016—and the fact that twice in recent memory the winner of the popular vote has not actually won the election energizes people or turns them away?

Nate: I don't think it has a big effect on voter turnout. It definitely feeds into feelings of illegitimacy about the election, and that's a long-term concern of mine. So if we continue to have minority winners of the popular vote winning the Electoral College and becoming president, that poses a threat to the regime in some respects—but that's derived from the lack of confidence that people have in the electoral system in general. And a democracy is not healthy if the majority of its people don't trust its election outcomes. And we are hurtling toward that eventuality.

Jonathan: But that's a structural problem, right? Those in power don't give up power without it being taken from them. And if our constitutional process requires those in power to change the rules, how do we fix this problem?

Nate: The Electoral College is a very hard nut to crack. There are workarounds that people are trying to enact into state law. For example, there is something called the National Popular Vote Compact, which would lead states with large populations to commit to sending their electors based on the national popular vote as opposed to what happens in their states. But that is, for the most part, an academic enterprise these days. It's going to require a massive landslide election that would change the composition of the Senate, the House, and state legislatures to then effectuate that kind of constitutional change.

Jonathan: Where does technology fit into that question? That's your expertise—technology and voting, and the internet and voting. I think we initially thought that technology would improve our voting process. If we can bank by ATM, we should be able to vote from our mobile phones. Now it seems that we're rejecting technology. We want a paper trail. We don't trust the internet with our voting. Where do you think we are in terms of this nexus of technology and voting?

Nate: We are not going to vote over the internet anytime soon. You need robust confidence in the process in order to make that kind of move, which very few countries have. Estonia is one that's moved in that direction. You may see some internet voting in low-information local races, maybe some primary elections and the like. But you need only look at the debacle with the so-called Iowa caucus app. If you remember this from the Democratic caucuses, that even if something as simple as transferring information from the local caucus to the state database is that complicated, people are not going to be so trusting with their votes.

Now, you raise some other issues about technology and voting, like the voting machines themselves. For the most part, as you say, in the last decade, we've moved away from electronic voting machines, which were all the rage after the 2000 election debacle, where we replaced punch card ballots with more automated systems. But that's led to worries about the lack of a paper trail, lack of auditability, etc., so almost all jurisdictions have now moved to some kind of auditable paper trail. I served on the National Academy of Sciences panel dealing with the future of voting. One of the things we recommended was to make sure there's auditability, that you have a top-to-bottom check after every election to make sure the systems are working as intended. One thing—both in 2016 and in the run up to 2020—that we've now recognized is that focusing just on the voting machines is too myopic. That's because there's a lot of technology in the process—from the voter registration system to the electronic poll books to the election night reporting systems. If you worry about cybersecurity and the security of these systems, you have to worry not only about the act of voting, but also about all those other links in the chain. Particularly now that jurisdictions confronting the pandemic are buying all kinds of new technology—these are the things that worry me a little bit.

Jonathan: Speaking of what's worrying you, what Election Day scenario keeps you up at night? What's going to happen on November 3?

Nate: Well, first of all, the election has already begun, and that's because ballots are out. North Carolina mailed them out in the first week of September. So we should expect roughly half the votes to be cast even before November 3. The things that keep me up at night are the worst-case scenarios, which, I want to emphasize, are still low probability events, but they're a higher probability now than they've ever been. Issues of Election Day violence are things that keep me up at night because we have a greater risk of that happening now than we have had historically. I am also concerned with the relationship between the federal government and the states and local polling places. The president has threatened to use federal authority in this area, which is unprecedented. So those are the things that keep me up at night.

There's something called the election administrator's prayer, which is, "Oh God, whatever happens, please don't let it be close." Because if it's close, then all of the fragile aspects of our electoral system come into full view. And so if it's a close election that—for example—is determined by absentee ballots in the midwestern battleground states, that's the worst-case scenario because it will trigger a lot of conflict and litigation. Not to get too much into the constitutional machinery here, but we could end up with competing slates of electors for the Electoral College. And we've never really been in a situation like that. Given the polarization of our politics right now, it's not as if reason is going to win the day here and say, "Oh, yes, I recognize that my opponent has won." Instead, people will retreat into their tribes and process information that's more friendly to their outcome.

Betty: Nate, given that we're calling on you to ground us in the situation as it stands—so that we and our listeners don't spin off into election anxiety mode any sooner or any more than necessary—how do we put those guardrails up when we are on social media so that we can still use our minds and maintain our ability to reflect? Do we just unplug and not expose ourselves to the algorithms and the videos that attract our brains' fear and anger centers to focus on spectacle and outrage? How do we think about this and reflect rather than react?

Nate: Right now social media is pretty much mirroring what's happening on cable news, which is mirroring what's happening in larger society. So it's hard to escape polarizing and emotional information right now, whether it's about the fires in California, or the pandemic, or politics. I think those in a position of authority, whether in the media or politics, need to be vigilant about the problems that we see, but also emphasize that the basic infrastructure of democracy is going to work.

Let me take an example of something that came up over the summer, which is about the frailty of the Postal Service. A lot of people are worried that their ballot is not going to count if they drop it in the mail—that there will be political manipulation and the like. While we need to have congressional hearings that hold the postmaster general to account, we also need to make sure that everything on our own side is being done. If you talk to the local postal officials, they say this is not going to be as big a problem as it seems. However, that doesn't mean people should wait until the last minute to mail their ballot. The message that should be sent is this: if you're going to vote by mail, vote as early as possible, and that's the safest way to make sure your vote gets in on time. Because even before this last year of issues with the Postal Service, the post office has not delivered ballots on time in many elections, so if you wait until the last five to ten days to vote, you are risking that your ballot is not going to count. So people need to vote as early as possible. In other words—it is in your hands. You have the power to vote in a way that you know your vote is going to be counted. You just have to follow these rules.

Jonathan: Nate, how about people who are inclined to not vote by mail, but are planning to vote in person? I'm thinking about your work on the Healthy Elections Project. And I'm wondering what you can tell voters to reassure them about the medical health of voting in person. Are there some states that are better prepared? Do the same rules apply about masks and social distancing or is voting different?

Nate: What you're referring to is our work on the Stanford-MIT Healthy Elections Project. I sort of have dropped most of the cyberwork that I had expected to be dominant for this election, and instead I have really been focusing on the kind of work that I did when I was the research director of the Presidential Commission on Election Administration after the 2012 election. That was the bipartisan commission that President Obama's White House Counsel and Mitt Romney's counsel put together to deal with long lines on Election Day as well as the potential impact of natural disasters— like Hurricane Sandy—on voting. We didn't predict that we would have to deal with a pandemic in voting. So that was a void in that report. But some of the same lessons apply.

First of all, I want to urge people to vote early in person if they can. That is not only a safe way to get the vote counted, but it also relieves the burden on election officials—so we don't have the post-processing that is required for absentee ballots, and it relieves the stress of in-person voters on Election Day. But the electoral system has adopted the same kinds of safety measures that larger society has. You will see blue pieces of tape every six feet outside a polling place, and masks and hand sanitizer will be provided, along with disinfectant for the voting machines. The CDC and the Election Assistance Commission have prescribed all kinds of rules. So they're prepared for this. And I think that it does add to the anxiety, just as is true in any public setting that we engage in these days. But the election officials are prepared. And there are some new adaptations like this whole idea of arena voting, where you have some NBA teams contributing their arenas to make sure there's a lot of social distance when people vote.

Jonathan: When you think about the preparations that states have taken, we're so balkanized in our electoral system. Are there states that are doing it better or worse?

Nate: There are some states that were all vote by mail to begin with. Places like Washington, Oregon, Utah, Colorado, and Hawaii were 100 percent vote by mail. And so the pandemic doesn't really affect them all that much. I should add that in places like Colorado, while we call them vote-by-mail states, 75 percent of Colorado voters actually deposit their ballot into a drop box, not into a mailbox. Then there are states like California and Arizona. California has moved toward all vote by mail for this election. They're going to make ballots available to everybody through the mail, even though there will be some polling places. Arizona has historic rates of around 80 percent vote by mail. So they'll be able to adapt in ways that others can't.

The ones that are of concern are the battleground states in the Midwest where Wisconsin and Pennsylvania have historic rates of absentee balloting under 5 percent—Michigan, roughly 20 percent. Florida is actually quite well-adapted to this environment. They have historically had a third of their voters vote by mail, another third vote in person, and the final third vote on Election Day. It'll probably be roughly half who will vote by mail and maybe only 25 percent will vote in person on Election Day. Based on those historic rates of polling place versus absentee balloting, you'll have different rates of preparedness. But on the question of use of PPE (personal protective equipment like masks and gloves) and the adaptations of the polling places, everyone's getting the same instructions.

Betty: In the short term, Nate—even from your steady tone of voice—it sounds like we're doing everything we can. It's not chaotic. It's being managed, even in the high-infection-rate states. But in the longer term, looking beyond November 3, how do we consider our consumption of social media during elections? How can we be sane about this? How do we take some time so that we can choose leaders and take in our information about them in ways that allow us to really think about our choices, rather than just react to the latest online crisis? It sounds like you've been talking about a critique of the media.

Nate: Yes, there's some of that. And let me join that with Jonathan's question earlier about nightmare scenarios. One of the things that is concerning is— if it is a close election on election night where we don't really know the winner and it will be determined by the processing and counting of absentee ballots in the succeeding week—how do we deal with that uncertainty? That is the most anxious moment, where we don't know what the outcome is going to be. And if, at the same time, you have the candidates each declaring victory, or one of them declaring victory and the other waiting, that's particularly disconcerting, because then there will be allegations that the election has been rigged, that there was fraud, or even that these absentee ballots shouldn't be counted because they're somehow inherently tainted.

While you asked me about what to do afterward, there's a lot we can do now to try to inoculate ourselves from that anxiety. And that is to explain to people what that process is going to look like, what they can expect. We've often thought of putting something up on our website called "What to Expect When You're Expecting...Election Results." The idea is to say, this is not unnatural. This is how the process works. You should expect that they're verifying signatures on these mail-in ballots. They're giving people an opportunity, if there is a mismatch of their signature, to come in and cure it. Historically, this is how long it has taken. And that doesn't mean that there's manipulation. We need the election officials to be transparent about what they're doing, but at the same time, we need—and this is the hard part—we need this vote counting to occur under relative conditions of social peace, so that you don't have people trying to break down the doors of the canvassing boards and trying to interrupt the count.

Media organizations have a very important role to play here. Social media does as well. And I'll tell you, if you look at the Voting Information Center on Facebook, they have tried to provide information that will counteract some of the conspiracy-mongering you see. The truth is, only elites who really care about elections are going into the Voting Information Center. But what they are doing is they are also using the information that is there to then put alerts next to news articles that are referring to things like mail-in ballots. So they are trying to dilute the impact of the most incendiary items that might appear there. In addition, over the next month, you'll start seeing reminders from election officials, as well as a series of videos that

Facebook will be serving up at the top of your feed, on how to fill out your vote-by-mail ballot correctly so it's counted. Those are the kinds of things that we can do to manage expectations in the event there's a crisis.

Betty: Nate, when I asked you to join us, I wanted you to ground us—to be our voting doctor. And you've really done it. When my colleagues and I work with those who are traumatized, we aim to empower them and give them agency and information, so that they can do things for themselves. What you're doing is similar—you are telling us, as voters, what we can do and what we don't have to pay attention to, so we can just focus on our part and not be distracted by everybody else's—which helps reduce anxiety, so we remain calm. Thank you so much.

Nate: Thanks for having me.

Jonathan: We'll keep your words in mind as we approach Election Day, especially in the battleground states...

Nate: Yes—and repeat the election administrator's prayer, "Oh God, whatever happens, please don't let it be close."

Chapter 25
Analyzing the 2020 Election

Guest: Michael A. Cohen
Episode Aired: November 11, 2020

Michael A. Cohen is a political columnist at The Boston Globe. *He is the author of* Clear and Present Safety *and* American Maelstrom: The 1968 Election and the Politics of Division. *Michael has written for dozens of news outlets, including* The Guardian *and* Foreign Policy. *He previously worked as a speechwriter at the U.S. State Department and has been a lecturer at the Columbia University School of International and Public Affairs.*

Michael joined us on Mind of State a week after the 2020 presidential election when partisan tensions were still high, emotions were raw, and the collective energy was depleted. Americans were exhausted from the divisive campaign as well as the ongoing stress of the COVID-19 pandemic, the summer's historic Black Lives Matter protests, and what would become a record-breaking year of relentless climate-related events. In the absence of a viable vaccine for the virus, deaths rose at an astounding rate in the U.S. throughout the fall of 2020. According to the CDC, the weekly COVID-19 death rate would go from claiming 4,420 lives a week in early October to claiming 25,974 lives during the first week of January 2021.[1] Additionally, Americans were still reeling from the impact and outrage unleashed during the summer's Black Lives Matter protests, which brought as many as 26 million people into the streets nationwide to protest police brutality against Black people.[2] Also contributing to a sense of Armageddon in 2020, a record 22 separate

---

[1] COVID Data Tracker, CDC, https://covid.cdc.gov/covid-data-tracker/#trends_weekly-deaths_select_00.

[2] Gause, L. & Arora, M. (2021). Not All of Last Year's Black Lives Matters Protesters Supported Black Lives Matter. *The Washington Post.* https://www.washingtonpost.com/

billion-dollar natural and climate-related disasters occurred.[3] These included Hurricane Laura, a Category 4 hurricane in Louisiana late August, causing 42 deaths and costing $19 billion; and an unprecedented series of wildfires that burned in California, Oregon, and Washington State between August and December, claiming 46 lives and costing $16.5 billion in damages.

It is no surprise, then, that against this backdrop, the topic of safety and security arose in our post-election conversation with Michael. As we discuss, it is perhaps the conflation of security with identity that factors significantly into the partisan impasses that prevent the collaborative dialectic a healthy democracy depends upon. In other words, a challenge to identity becomes a challenge to existence, making constructive dialogue almost impossible.

This discussion relates directly to our conversations on partisan conflicts with Jessica Benjamin (Chapter 5), with Scotty McClennan on what dialogue between opposing groups requires (Chapter 9), with Eric Ward on the roots of white nationalism (Chapter 14), with Nancy Rosenblum on the causes of conspiracism (Chapter 10), with Lilliana Mason on the cultural roots of partisan thinking (Chapter 18), and with Ashley Jardina on the anxieties driving white identity politics (Chapter 19). Perhaps, as Michael Cohen notes, a serious reconsideration of our unconscious conflation of safety with identity is necessary, if not crucial, to help us revive American democracy.

Interview

Jonathan: Here we are in post-election land. We've been waiting for this day. I've been waiting for this day for four years.

Betty: You have been waiting for this day for four years, and I have been holding my breath for four years. I realized this only Sunday, after noticing how much more deeply I am breathing now.

Jonathan: There *was* a national exhale, wasn't there? Or even a global exhale. I mean, when I looked at the international headlines and I got calls from friends from all over the world, it seemed the world was watching and many people on the planet exhaled.

---

politics/2021/07/01/not-all-last-years-black-lives-matter-protesters-supported-black-lives-matter/.

[3] Smith, A.B. (2021). 2020 U.S. Billion-Dollar Weather and Climate Disasters in Historical Context. *Climate.gov.* https://www.climate.gov/disasters2020.

Betty: Yes! I went to international news outlets just to see what leaders like the president of Fiji said to Biden to congratulate him. For me, it took seeing the reactions of other people in countries around the world—and that they also expressed joy at Biden winning and relief that Trump lost, to prove that it's real. You've been predicting and you've been trying to keep us steady, by reading the exit poll numbers, Jonathan. But I didn't feel it was real until I got news of the official announcement by text over the weekend from a friend who caught the *New York Times* headline before I did. I was in the middle of a park with my kids, and I didn't know what to think. It hit me as a surprise, even though I knew it was coming.

Jonathan: This was a fascinating thing. From election night forward, the results were the same, right? Biden was ahead. Biden was up. His lead only grew. And not only that, it was exactly as it had been predicted. The Biden campaign was steadfast and consistent. The polling data was right. The numbers were coming in. Yet everyone seemed to need validation from Pennsylvania. And even though we knew the result, and even though the news media play no official role in this constitutional democracy, somehow people needed to hear news anchors declare that a state's votes had been called and that the 270 electoral-vote threshold had been crossed. They needed to hear the validation from independent news outlets that a winner had been called.

Betty: Before we get too carried away with this conversation, I'm going to introduce our next guest, who will only make it better. Michael A. Cohen is a friend of yours.

Jonathan: Indeed he is. Michael and I go back to the '92 war room, during the Clinton campaign. But it's interesting, because while Michael Cohen was a trench warrior in partisan politics, he then switched over to journalism, to being an observer of politics. And I think that's why it's great to have him on the show today because he is a keen observer of American and international politics.

Betty: Welcome to *Mind of State*, Michael.

Michael Cohen: Thanks. Great to be here.

Betty: So, Michael, we brought you on to be our post-election guest and commentator.

Michael: Okay. A lot of pressure right there, not going to lie to you.

Betty: We're going to start with one that comes from my side of things. I am a trauma therapist and a psychoanalyst, and I see people every week for their individual therapy sessions. And this election week has been exhausting for them, for me—for us all. And it sits on top of a particularly exhausting election season.

Michael: Yes.

Betty: You and Jonathan have both been former war-room campaigners from way back. How does somebody from inside a campaign like this sustain the energy? And how do you recommend that we all sustain the energy past this moment? Because I think we know, actually, that we're far from done.

Michael: Well, that's a great question, actually. I guess the way you do it is you have to keep your eyes on the prize and know that if you're successful in what you're doing, you're going to elect the next president. And, on a personal level, you may end up getting a job in the White House or working in the administration or achieving what you wanted to achieve. I think for the rest of us—it's funny, just today I was talking with somebody about whether we felt joy or relief over this. And I think it's a little bit more relief than joy. I mean, I obviously think a lot of people are pretty happy, pretty excited that Joe Biden's president. But I think they're even more excited that Donald Trump is no longer going to be president. I think it's been really difficult the last couple of weeks.

I was doing an interview with somebody a couple days ago, and she asked, "What happens to the Democratic Party if Trump wins?" And it stumped me because I didn't even think about that. I hadn't even thought about that possibility because it's just too awful to consider. And not just for the Democratic Party, but for the future of the country. So I've assumed for several months now that Biden's going to win. I haven't really wavered in that belief. But, in the back of my mind, I thought, if I'm wrong, well, there goes a pretty good democracy right there. It's not a small thing when you think about that possibility.

Jonathan: It's amazing too that there is no opportunity to stop and regain your energy. Because Trump is not stopping, and I'm not even talking about his contesting the election and all of those distractions. I'm talking about his gearing up for 2024. He's already indicated—and we sort of knew this was going to happen—that he's coming back. And we've got two run-off elections down in Georgia that are going to determine control of the Senate. So in a way, we can't stop. There's no stopping. We move from one focus to the next. And it's all about, as you said, keeping our eye on the prize. And the strategy will be different if we're going into a divided government than if we're going into a united government.

Michael: I personally feel like a big weight is off my shoulders as far as national politics go, and you're right, we still have Georgia coming up. But seeing Trump today, with these silly tweets and how he won't concede, it feels like a temper tantrum. It doesn't feel like anything real or substantial that's going to affect the outcome. So I hear what you're saying, but I think there's plenty of time to get angst-ridden over that. Right now, I feel that the country did what it needed to do, which was to stop this candidate from having four more years as president. We should celebrate because that, I think, is a really momentous accomplishment.

Betty: Michael, you had spoken about there being no time. You're thinking about the White House if you're in the campaign and if you're in Biden's campaign. And, Jonathan, you're thinking about how Trump's going to launch a counterattack right now. But for those of us outside this world of campaign politics, it's been an overstimulating and overwhelming bombardment. Just in the last week alone, from Monday through Saturday, everybody's been checking the election counts constantly. Doesn't matter whose side you're on.

Michael: Right.

Betty: Here's a question for you both—where do we find the time to make mental space? Because this is what Donald Trump precludes—mental space—with his constant noise and critique he shuts down the ability to think. He creates reactivity in others, and that is in all of what we've been seeing in the binaries and divisions of things. And as you're putting it, Michael, there's now relief with Biden's election. I'm always advocating with my patients to take time, to make no sudden moves. So is this possible right now? Can we take some time to take a breath and settle?

Michael: I personally have taken most of the week off to relax and decompress because I just don't want to think about politics for a little while. I'm still a junkie, so I'm going to write about my big takeaways from the election. But that, for me, is enjoyable. It's not so much that I have to worry about what's going to happen. And to your point about Trump being in all of our headspace, looking back on this election now, it was so completely about Donald Trump in every possible way. And he has been in our heads—at least if you follow politics like I do—he's been in our minds for the past four years. And to not have to worry about what he tweets is an incredible sense of relief. And I can't be alone in feeling that way.

Jonathan: I think we are going to have more time and the headspace, simply because we're going to have a different president. And one of the reasons is this: Donald Trump has governed from a chaotic standpoint. From moment to moment, there has been nothing consistent, nothing predictable, nothing policy-driven about his platform. There's no long game with Donald Trump. He lives and speaks in the moment. Now we're shifting to a political professional. It was reassuring just to see that the transition website went up yesterday, and the transition team came in place. Why? Because they've been planning for months, and it's predictable. And Joe Biden, I think, is going to instantly telegraph to the country and to the world, "You don't have to worry about five minutes from now because I'm going to lay out what the next three, six, nine, twelve months are going to look like. Here's our plan." And that gives me peace of mind.

Michael: I agree with all of that. But I'd add, too, that lack of headspace is a function of what happens under a president who's a malignant narcissist like Trump. Everything for Trump is about Trump, right? Everything. He can't live outside of his own ego.[4] And for anybody who's had an experience with a narcissist—as I have, not including Trump—it is the most dislocating experience because a malignant narcissist can cause you to question your own reality.

---

[4] See our conversations with psychoanalysts Justy Frank, in Chapter 12; Michael Tansey, in Chapter 13; and Robert Jay Lifton, in Chapter 21.

Betty: Yes. Absolutely. The truth is up for grabs.

Michael: From my own experience, it's the amount of gaslighting that goes on, the amount of deception and lying, and the lack of accountability. They just don't take responsibility. They're always the victim. They blame somebody else. There's no introspection at all, no self-awareness. And, under Trump's presidency, we've been living in that world. To not have to live in that world any longer, to not care what he says, is such a relief. I can say this for anyone else who has been in a relationship with a narcissist, it is incredibly difficult. And to be out of this is incredibly liberating.

Betty: Well, that makes me curious, Michael, because having had a relationship with a malignant narcissist and now having covered one for the past four years, you are in a similar position to one of my patients who has been traumatized. I work with survivors of domestic violence and sexual trauma, and in Trump, they see a predator in the White House. They hear him talk, and they see somebody who is a rank misogynist who railroads women. It's triggering for them. What did you have to do to not be sucked back into, not only the world of Donald Trump, but also the world of a person who just doesn't see you, who just sees a hall of mirrors that reflects their image back to themselves, who denies your existence, and who is overwhelming? This is what we've all experienced, but you had to cover it on the front lines.

Michael: Obviously it's exhausting. Part of it is, you kind of detach yourself from it a little bit, but you also appreciate and understand why he does the things that he does. I wrote a column five or six months ago, when Mary Trump's book *Too Much and Never Enough* came out, and the column basically said, "I feel sorry for Trump," and many of my liberal friends didn't care for that argument. But my basic point was that this is just a very sad and broken man who does terrible things because he doesn't understand why they're wrong and why they're terrible. I've understood that for a long time about him, and I've always said that about him. I feel a little sorry for him. Again, I don't like him, to put it mildly. But I also understand that his actions are somewhat uncontrollable by him.

So that makes it a little bit easier to write about Trump, with the understanding that this is not somebody who is doing this purposely. It also means that my outrage for those who enable his behavior is so much greater. That's where I have focused a lot of my writing over the past couple of years—on the enablers, the people who knew better and basically allowed this to happen. But I remember saying this early on in the Trump administration, after covering him on the campaign trail—that the thing about Trump is, you don't need to be a political scientist to understand him; you need to be a psychologist because what he does bears no relation to political science.

Jonathan: Over to you, Betty.

Betty: He really is, as you put it, a malignant narcissist. He has no interest in politics.

Michael: None.

Betty: To your point, Michael, the enablers bear great responsibility for this. So, how do you read what happened, because the downballot votes reflected a support of Republican ethos and policy. And by the last count, 68 million people still voted for Trump.

Jonathan: Look, we're a divided country, right? Maybe it'll be 70 million who have voted for Donald Trump, and that is disconcerting. We wanted a blue wave. We wanted to not just beat, but to vanquish Trump and the Trumpists. There's no question that's the attitude we went in with. But I think the Democratic Party is uniquely good at mourning a victory. The fact of the matter is, we won with the largest popular vote in U.S. history. We will have won with the same Electoral College vote, most likely, that Trump had in 2016. We made gains in the Senate, and we held on to the House. Yes, we lost some downballot races. Of course we did. And we've still got a long way to go. But the fact of the matter is, this was a win, any way you slice it. So I think we need to celebrate that win. And, of course, within the Democratic Party, we're always going to have the handwringing about "should we be more of the progressive wing of the party?" or "should we be more of the centrist wing of the party?" That's not a new conversation. We've been having it after every single election as long as I've been in politics. We'll continue to have it. It's a good constructive conversation for us to have. I want Democrats to be fighting about whether we should be more left or whether we should be more center within the left.

Michael: Can I add two things to that? One is, I totally agree that this is a pretty substantial victory. It's going to be a win with the largest margin over the last thirty years, except for 2008. It's going to be bigger than Obama's victory in 2012. So in that sense, it's a repudiation of Trump on a personal level.

Where I'm a little more glass-half-empty is in seeing that what this election showed—by the fact that it wasn't a landslide and the fact that a lot of Republican senators and representatives won—is that partisanship and polarization are the defining aspects of American politics today. And when I looked at the numbers, it was kind of crazy how much the vote for Senate candidates in both red and blue states mirrored the numbers for Trump. Trump brought out more voters. And there's no question Democrats brought out even more voters. That's why they won. But the level of turnout from Republicans is something that none of us saw coming.

Jonathan: I was thinking about the turnout and what struck me is that having a celebrity president—for better or for worse, and you know my choice between those two poles—but having a celebrity president engaged more Americans in politics than ever before. The fact that we had such a large turnout of the electorate reflects the fact that this election was moved beyond policy and beyond politics to attention-getting at the level of celebrity. It will be interesting to see if we can sustain that level of electorate engagement now that we're moving back into the professionalism, rather than the celebrity, of politics.

Michael: The reason that Democrats did so well this year is because Donald Trump was on the ticket. The reason why Republicans did better than we thought is because Donald Trump was on the ticket. And I think the question that we really don't know the answer to right now, which is going to be the defining question of the next two to four years, is who is advantaged more by Trump not being on the ticket, Democrats or Republicans? Or who's disadvantaged *less*, is actually a better way to look at it. The question is, will Republicans turn out in 2022 and 2024 if Trump isn't on the ticket? My guess is, they won't, not in the same numbers. But also, will Democrats be as motivated to come out and vote if they don't have to vote against Trump? The elections of 2018 and 2020 should be seen as a backlash against Trump. That's what defined American politics since 2016 or 2017. It was basically Democrats coming out in big numbers to resist Trump.

Jonathan: Do you think Trump is on the ballot in the Georgia Senate runoffs?

Michael: No, I don't. But I think socialism is on the ballot and that's probably a more powerful argument than whether we're going to get the filibuster, or pass a Green New Deal, or healthcare reform. Unfortunately, I think the negative argument is going to play out a little more effectively than the positive argument in the Georgia Senate race. So I'm pretty pessimistic that Democrats are going to win either one of those two seats.[5]

Betty: When you're talking, Michael, about 2018 and 2020 being "backlash elections," what I hear is that this is about reactivity. That we're voting *against* Donald Trump rather than we're voting *for* Joe Biden. This is resistance on both sides, marking the polarization you highlighted. This is the challenge I'm seeing from micro to macro, from the one-to-one to the societal—is how do people bridge this? You guys are keen observers of this split. And we've been talking about divisions for months, if not years. You wrote about it in your book, *Clear and Present Safety*—that this polarization was a threat to security because the United States is a less healthy democracy, which it absolutely is. We're already anticipating gridlock. You can't do anything in a gridlock. As an observer of politics, how do you see this as being bridged? Is it something that you've even considered?

Michael: I don't think it's going to be bridged. That's the thing. I hate to be so pessimistic, but the best hope Democrats had was to win back the Senate and to make a bunch of systematic changes that would allow for a more democratic political system. And I don't think that's going to happen. Maybe in 2022 Democrats can pick up some Senate seats; they have a better map than Republicans do. But I'm not overly optimistic about that, either. My Sunday column was basically making the argument that the 2020 election shows that this is a center-left country. Seven of the last eight presidential elections have been won in the popular vote by Democrats. That's never happened before in American politics—ever. There's no precedent for that.

---

[5] The Democrats won both seats in Georgia. Jon Ossoff defeated Republican incumbent David Perdue in a runoff and Rev. Raphael Warnock defeated Kelly Loeffler who had been appointed to fill the seat of retiring Senator Johnny Isakson in a special election. He then defeated Hershel Walker for a full term in 2022.

Over and over again, Democrats win the popular vote, but because of the structural impediments to governing in this country, they have only won the presidency five of those times. And the reality of this is that it's not just a question of how the Electoral College disadvantages Democrats and the Senate disadvantages Democrats. It's the entire political system. Somebody asked me awhile back, "What's the one change that you would make in the American political system?" And I said, "I'd get rid of the Senate." That's the one change that I would make. I'm serious. The best thing you could do in American politics is to get rid of the Senate.

Jonathan: I just want to get rid of McConnell.

Michael: That's fine. And I understand that.

Betty: It seems Michael wants to take it one step—or actually forty-nine—further.

Michael: Right. McConnell's a terrible person. But real change would be to get rid of the entire Senate.

Betty: I mean, the Senate has the same problem as the Electoral College, in the sense that it prioritizes or privileges minority rule.

Michael: Yes, that's exactly right.

Betty: You've got two senators from every state, no matter what the population is, which is really crazy when you think about California and New York as having the same Senate representation as Rhode Island.

Michael: Or Wyoming, which has less than a million people.

Jonathan: There's no good argument in favor of anti-democratic structures or principles. I think everyone knows that. There were rationalizations; there were justifications for the Electoral College and for the Senate. But those have long since become irrelevant.

Betty: And yet, as a realist, because I work from a Buddhist perspective—not in a religious sense, but more in a philosophical sense—if we don't deal with reality, then we go nowhere. So the reality is this: How do people work to deal with this minority rule? How do we start to seek out the cracks in the pavement or seek out the bridges that are available to us, even though, as you say, Michael, on a national level, it's not going to change? Do we just get stuck or freeze?

Jonathan: That's a big question. Michael, how do we bridge?

Michael: I wish I had a good answer for you on this one and I just don't. I'm sorry. I think sometimes, like you said, you have to accept reality as it is. And I think there's an uncomfortable reality that we have to consider, which is that at the end of the day, more than 70 million Americans thought that Trump should have four more years in office. And I saw a lot of people criticizing Democrats for not doing a good-enough ground game, not doing enough messaging. And those are certainly criticisms to be made. But at the end of the day, the voters do have a responsibility here. And the voters decided, many of them in red states, that they were okay with the way things are going in the country. They were okay with having a manifestly incompetent narcissist as president.

I'm really kind of obsessed with the Montana Senate race, which shows you just how fun I am at parties. But this is a race in which the Democrats thought they could win, and they recruited Steve Bullock, the Democratic governor who has won three times in a state that's quite red. He raised a ton of money—more money than his challenger—and he lost by ten points.

Jonathan: And he wanted to be president.

Michael: He wanted to be president. Yes. He couldn't win the Senate race.

Betty: Yeah, okay, so what about that?

Michael: He did better than Jon Tester, who is the Democratic senator there now. Tester won two years ago for reelection to his third term. He won by about two-and-a-half points. Bullock did better than him in this election, and better than Biden. The biggest gap between a Senate candidate and Biden—at least on the positive side for the Senate candidate—was in Montana. But the problem is that Republicans brought out about 75,000 to 80,000 more voters than they had in 2018. And I am convinced that's because of Trump.

I look at a state like South Carolina where everyone thought, "Oh Jamie Harrison's got a chance." He lost by ten points, almost identical to the margin that Biden lost by. At the end of the day, people said, "I'm voting for X if there's an R or D next to their name, and I'm not going to split my ticket." And I don't know how you get past that if you're Democrats. If Steve Bullock can't do well in a red state like Montana, then who's going to do well there? I don't know the answer to that.

Betty: And yet, with the split ticket—which you did write about, with respect to the split vote for Republican Senator Susan Collins and Biden in Maine—how does that work?

Michael: Okay, so I usually try to have an answer for every question. But for this, I have no idea. That is the most bonkers result in this election. Biden won Maine by nine points, and then Collins won by nine points in the Senate. It's crazy.

Betty: And they predicted that she would lose.

Jonathan: Look, Sara Gideon didn't run a great campaign.

Michael: Maybe, yes.

Jonathan: And Susan Collins is a Senate stalwart. I don't think we can draw a conclusion out of this, except for the fact that incumbency is damn powerful.

Michael: My colleagues at the *Globe* who cover Maine politics basically summed it up as saying, "Maine is weird." So that's why she won. I don't mean it as a criticism. They just have idiosyncratic politics, and they like to split their ticket. They like to be independent. And this gave them a chance to do that.

Jonathan: Even at the presidential Electoral College level, they split.

Michael: That's right, that's right. They're big into splitting.

Jonathan: Michael, I want to shift for a second, if we can, from this moment of presidential politics to backtrack just a second to your last book. You wrote *Clear and Present Safety* as an argument for why this world has never been in a more secure, or safe, place in the history of the world.[6] It's a great book. And then the pandemic happened.

Michael: Sure.

Jonathan: Pre-COVID you wrote a lot about the issues that we struggled with in 2020 in the U.S. and in the world—issues that were thematic in this election. If you were to return to the book today, what would the prologue to the next edition of the book say?

Michael: The big thing I would say is that I would have included more in the book about the threat from pandemics. But the key argument of the book was that Americans are scared of the wrong things. They're scared about terrorism. They're scared about nuclear weapons. They're scared about Russia, China, and North Korea, when in reality they should be scared about the fact that their healthcare system is terrible. They should be scared about the fact that they are politically polarized. They should be scared of the fact that we have too much gun violence and too many drug overdose deaths. And so pretty much everything that's happened, unfortunately, for the past eight months, has confirmed that argument. It really has. The key point is that the problems that we have are at home. They're not overseas.

And yes, I understand the pandemic came from overseas, but many countries in the world figured out a way to deal with the pandemic, and we didn't. And why? Because we don't have a healthcare system that can adequately respond to it. We are politically paralyzed, so we couldn't respond to it. And we have an ethos that says we shouldn't use the government to help people in times of need, the consequences of which we are seeing play out across the country right now.

So, unfortunately, we're going to spend half a trillion dollars on defense, when by far the biggest threat we've ever faced as a country came from a virus—not something you can shoot down with a missile. It is not

---

[6] Cohen, M. and Zenko, M. (2019). *Clear and Present Safety: Why the world has never been in a better place and why that matters to Americans.* Yale University Press.

something a tank can take on. And we were not ready for that. So that, to me, confirms the book's argument.

Jonathan: But during this election cycle, we've seen that even a virus can become politicized, and that wearing a mask has become a political signal.

Michael: Yeah, we made a big point in the book in saying that political polarization was a big threat to America. And I think this election has proved it.

Betty: You talk about national security as being this huge distraction, and that what we really need to focus on is human security.
Michael: Yes.

Betty: I wonder, if in the end, the 2020 elections will reflect the varying levels of security that different groups of people in this country need. People can consider security as "I want to have my freedom and I want to be able to not wear a mask" or "I want to be able to carry firearms." Security is interesting, psychologically, because it's one of our basic needs. We all want to be safe. When we feel a threat to ourselves, physical or psychological, we react in all sorts of ways that we cannot even be totally conscious of. I wonder what you think about that, Michael.

Michael: I'm just spit balling here because that's a great question and I haven't thought about it. But one thing that comes to mind is that, for a lot of people, security and identity have become somewhat conflated. What I mean is that after 2016, people talked about identity politics being a problem for Democrats, and from what we've seen in the last four years, identity politics—white identity politics—is actually so much stronger on the right than it is on the left. What I saw in Trump's rise was many white Americans feeling scared about larger cultural changes in the country and wanting to resist such change. I think many of the problems that we have right now are about that fundamental conflict.

I think the controversy about masks—with those not wanting to wear masks or others saying, "it's my freedom to wear a mask"—is really more about "I don't want the government telling me what to do." And it's not even just about not wanting government mandates. It's more an expression of "I don't like where the country is going, and if I give too much power to the government, then they're going to take my power away," or "they will take my influence away as a white person." I have to think this out a little bit more, but there's some kind of conflation there between identity and security. But I think that's a great question, and it's something worth thinking about.

Betty: I think identity, for many, in a psychological sense, *is* security. We can think, "If you take away my selfhood, if you take away who I am, then you annihilate me." So this could be where the flex point is.

Jonathan: I was just considering how heads must be exploding all around the Trump universe now, because our first female vice president is also our first Black vice president, and our first Indian vice president, and she is married to the first Jewish second gentleman. With Kamala Harris, a lot of glass ceilings were broken in this election, and identity is split wide open once again. But Michael, you're probably right. It looks like Trump gained among whites, including white women. It's hard to even fathom that, but that is true. And this happens in the midst of the ascendancy of Black Lives Matter and the importance of this issue. And rather than seeing Black Lives Matter as a unification against a historical injustice, it is seen by some as a challenge to the lives of others.

Michael: I'm going to disagree with you on this one.

Jonathan: Please go ahead.

Michael: We need to give white people some love. I really think we do. If you look at what happened this election, the story is that Black and Hispanic Americans did not come out in the same numbers as we expected for Biden and instead voted for Trump—and the election was in fact won in white suburbia. I take, for example, Detroit in Michigan.

Jonathan: And Philadelphia, too. Absolutely.

Michael: In Michigan, in Wisconsin, in Pennsylvania, in Florida, in Texas, in Georgia. I saw some numbers earlier today that there was a 10 percent increase in support for Biden in Atlanta proper. And there was a 20-something percent increase in the suburbs.

Now, I realize the suburbs are much more diverse. I shouldn't say "white suburbia," as if all people in suburbs are white, but the majority usually are. Michigan is another example. In Detroit, Trump actually did better than he did four years ago—if you can believe that. The big source of votes for Biden came in Oakland County, which is just north of Detroit, and is about 75 percent white. In Dane County in Wisconsin, Biden got more votes there, relative to Clinton, than he did in Milwaukee.

So I disagree a little bit. I do think that one takeaway from the election is that with the growth of the Black Lives Matter movement and the overt racism of Trump, there was a backlash among lots of white Americans, especially white males with college educations. But I think there's even some evidence that Biden did better than Clinton among white noncollege-educated Americans. So I do think we could be looking at a positive note on white voters.

Jonathan: Well, look, the electorate expanded. We had more people voting than ever before, so that threw off some of the dynamic, but Trump did increase his share of the white vote and the white women vote.

Michael: We don't know that for sure because we don't yet know all the exit poll numbers. And I don't know how accurate they really are. But you may be right about that.

Jonathan: Okay, so we'll stipulate, there is still some data to be gathered out there, and no doubt there are plenty of white people who probably said, "We've had enough, and this has gone too far and we have to dial this back." It was a repudiation of Trump in that regard. At the same time, if you look at the factors that were driving Trump voters, aside from the argument that somehow they believe Trump is better for the economy, then they were motivated by this argument about the looting, the rioting, and the crime in the cities that was going on during what were largely peaceful BLM demonstrations. People were also concerned about socialism.

Michael: I don't know about that.

Jonathan: They were concerned about violence in the cities.

Michael: I don't know about that either.

Jonathan: Well, not enough people, clearly, because he didn't win.

Michael: That's the point, though, right? If you look at Biden's support among Black and Hispanic voters—based on those numbers alone—he would not have won, especially when you consider the increase in vote totals that Trump got. So where do those additional votes come from that allowed Biden to beat Trump? It came from mainly white college-educated voters. I mean, some non-college-educated voters, but mostly white college-educated voters. Whether that's sustained, I don't know. But I think it's a pretty positive sign for Democrats that they were able to persuade a lot of voters who maybe didn't vote for Clinton in 2016, or who maybe stayed home in 2016, or who just didn't vote in general, to come out in 2020 and support their candidate.

Betty: I think what you're both saying is something that goes beyond politics. Whatever you may say—a person of color, a white person—the groups you belong to are not monolithic.

Michael: That's right.

Betty: I think there's more to be read in who did vote for Trump, especially the white women. My question is where did they vote? What was their socioeconomic background? To incorporate what you were saying, Michael—in terms of security equaling the sanctity of identity—who felt threatened, where, and how? Who felt like, "I'm going to have my way of life taken away from me?"

And it might offer a different kind of a story. Because if your selfhood is under stress—which is true for many people, for many different reasons right now—you're going to put it on somebody. You're going to look for who is taking that security away. Which is why, I think, Jonathan, the looting and the rioting became overblown—partially because of the media—but also because when people need something to hang on to, they're going to find something to blame, whether it was truly a real threat or not. One of our guests, Robert Jay Lifton (Chapter 21), talked about this, which is the "narrative necessity" people have to attach to a certain story of the way things are. Meaning people have a psychological need to attach to Trump, what he stands for and the false narratives he insists upon. They don't care whether he was saying fact or fiction, because he gave them a reason to feel like they were viable.

Michael: And they were recognized.

Betty: Exactly.

Michael: And validated.

Betty: Exactly.

Michael: I agree with all of what you said, but Miles Coleman, who's at Crystal Ball, put this map out on Twitter that was fascinating.[7] It showed the vote shift in some of the northeastern counties above the suburban counties in Pennsylvania, which are white working-class counties. And the vote shift was almost completely congruent with education levels. So the more educated the community was, the more likely they were to vote for Biden. The less educated, the more likely they would vote for Trump. In a way, you're seeing education become this pretty clear dividing line. Now, you could argue there are lots of reasons why that's the case. I think it has to do with economics.

Betty: Right.

Michael: If you don't have a college education, chances are, your job prospects are worse. This is the case for both white and Black Americans.

Betty: And you're in a vulnerable position in terms of having more stress.

Jonathan: How do you figure that Biden won among folks earning 100,000 dollars a year and less?

Michael: Because that's mainly African American voters, right? I mean, Clinton did the same thing in 2016. She won more of these votes than Trump did, because those are from largely minority voters.

---

[7] J. Michael Coleman, Sabato's Crystal Ball, https://centerforpolitics.org/crystalball/articles/author/j-miles-coleman/.

Jonathan: It certainly takes the air out of the argument that Democrats are a bunch of coastal elitists who are drinking cappuccinos.

Michael: It does.

Betty: It also highlights the issue of economic disparity, which you did write about, Michael. You said that economic disparity was a stressor in American democracy. Is that something that we can address in a different way rather than deal with it from within gridlock, which is unaddressable, really?

Michael: Well, there's something that's relative to this. There's a great study showing that Black Americans, even if they're worse off than white Americans, have been more optimistic about the economy because they come from a lower relative point.[8] So they view their economic achievements in greater terms than white Americans do, who may have just been treading water or even declined in economic status.

And so I do think a lot of this is identity politics for Black Americans, who can have their identities wrapped in the Democratic Party, especially for Black women, since they're very much conflated. I do also think many white Americans conflate their identity with the Republican Party. But white Americans and Black Americans might both be poor or might both be lower class, but each group may look at their relative position in very different terms. And I think that is a crucial difference in how we think about our economic opportunities in this country.

Jonathan: Where do you think the issue of gun control factored in this election? Because it was barely mentioned, whereas pre-pandemic, gun control was still a major issue.

Michael: I don't think any policy issue really mattered in this election. I don't think anything mattered. I think it all came down to whether you were with Trump or against Trump. That's been my view from the beginning, and I stick to that. I don't think the debates mattered. I don't think the conventions mattered. Maybe along the margins, sure. But, in general, I don't think anything really mattered. I don't think even COVID mattered all

---

[8] Carol Graham, "Why Are Black Poor Americans More Optimistic Than White Ones?" Brookings, January 30, 2018, https://www.brookings.edu/articles/why-are-black-poor-americans-more-optimistic-than-white-ones//

that much, to be honest. I know it sounds crazy to say that, but Biden led every poll this year, every poll headed back to the fall of 2019. The margin possibly expanded because of COVID. There may have been a backlash from people who were pissed off about all the closings and pissed off about the economy not doing so well because of COVID. I think at the end of the day, none of that stuff really mattered all that much. I know that sounds crazy to say it, but I think that's the case.

Jonathan: I think you're probably right. I mean, COVID might have been a motivator for those who believe in health care for all; it might have been a motivator for Trumpists who are using COVID as an excuse for the economy going down. But either way, it was in reaction to Trump. It was not about COVID itself.

Betty: It's interesting. He goes out as he comes in, making it all about him. And I think that is a mark of his psychopathology, frankly, that he sucks the attention of every person to himself, whether they are right or left. People could not stop watching him—whether it was in support of him or to make sure he didn't blow things up even more than he already had. His outrageousness just dominated, maybe to his own self-destruction, which is to your earlier point, Michael, that he doesn't know what he's doing. He is like a temper-tantruming child.

Jonathan: So maybe the pivot here is that we're going from a presidency about personality to a presidency that's actually about policy. What do you see as the future? Joe Biden is not a personality president. He's not a personality politician. He's about policies for people.

Michael: Disagree again.

Jonathan: Please.

Michael: I actually think that the advantage that Biden brought to the table was his personality, which was that he is seen as a good and decent man.

Jonathan: Oh, an empath, absolutely. So he brings trust, stability, confidence…

Betty: Accountability.

Jonathan: He's a professional. Yes, absolutely. He's an empath. But now going forward, that got him here and now he's got to govern.

Michael: That's the hard part. And the thing is, I think what it comes down to is results. At the end of the day, if the economy is doing better in four years, then he has a chance, if he'll be on the ticket in four years.

That's why I think it's so disappointing that Democrats could have engineered a situation in two years where the economy is doing great and COVID had largely gone away—maybe they can get the latter one with his Pfizer announcement, but improving the economy might be a little more difficult to pull off. Although the one thing I'll say that Biden has going for him is that if this vaccine is real and if it can be rolled out next year, you will see people's lives getting better and you will see the economy improve.

Betty: Yes, movement will happen.

Michael: Not much that should improve, but it will improve. And I think that could bode well for Biden and that's what I think he'll be judged on. Did he get rid of COVID? Did he improve the economy? Those are the things that politicians are usually judged by. Now, Republicans won't give him credit no matter what he does. But will he keep the voters who this time turned out for him? Possibly.

Betty: Michael, one of the things you said earlier on was that you've taken a break from politics this week, which as a political columnist, is pretty significant.

Michael: I mean, it's not a total break, but you know.

Betty: I think that's healthy. This has been a very, very intense and overwhelming time. And as early as 2016, I have been counseling my patients to put themselves on a news and notifications diet. That goes for professionals and amateurs alike, and for any of us fixated on what's been going on. I'm curious, how are you going to maintain your equilibrium once you get back into it for real?

Michael: It's a great question. I don't know. I think much of what fueled the things that I wrote about the last four years was outrage, anger, and frustration. And I was honored and humbled to have a platform where I could express those ideas to people. I imagine that I will still be outraged by things.

Betty: That's inevitable.

Jonathan: Safe prediction.

Michael: That's right. It's inevitable when you write about politics. It's inevitable when you're me, frankly, if I'm being honest about it.

Betty: Political columnist, voice of outrage.

Michael: Right. But I think there's a different kind of outrage. There's the outrage you feel when you hear that kids are being locked in cages, that's a real outrage. But when Mitch McConnell is blocking legislation, I will be outraged, but it's not the same. In the last couple of weeks of this election season. I felt a real sense of hopelessness—or, not hopelessness, but helplessness. COVID numbers are going up; Trump's making it worse; nothing's getting better. And you can just feel like "how can this go on?" And so I don't know that I'm going to feel that sense of helplessness and that's a pretty good feeling to have, I think, in terms of politics.

Jonathan: That is a fantastic upbeat note to end on.

Michael: Glad I could give you a kicker there at the end.

Betty: Thank you so much for joining us.

Michael: That was a pleasure. I really enjoyed the conversation. It was a lot of fun.

Chapter 26
Politics & the Teenage Mind

Guest: Dr. Lisa Damour
Episode Aired: April 16, 2019

Dr. Lisa Damour is a psychologist with an expertise in children and adolescents. She is the author of three New York Times best sellers: Untangled, Under Pressure, *and* The Emotional Lives of Teenagers. *She co-hosts the* Ask Lisa *podcast, works in collaboration with UNICEF, and is recognized as a thought leader by the American Psychological Association. Dr. Damour is also a regular contributor to the* New York Times *and* CBS News. *She was featured in a* New Yorker *interview with Jessica Winter, in "The Parent of a Teenager is an Emotional Garbage Can," on July 16, 2023.*

In February 2019, Slate editor and columnist Dahlia Lithwick published an email conversation with Lisa Damour titled, "How to Talk to Your Teens about Sex, Climate Change, and Existential Angst."[1] In that exchange, Lithwick spoke to her growing concerns about the ways intense social and political issues and events were impacting her and, as a consequence, her teenage son:

My kids seem to be growing up in a world of near-paralyzing cultural dread. They're trying to understand movements, like #BlackLivesMatter and #MeToo, while being flattened and numbed by school shootings, lockdowns, and protests. They can't seem to wriggle out from under the specter of authoritarianism that characterizes Trump's presidency. Or, as my 15-year-old put it

---

[1] Lithwick, D. (2019). How to Talk to Your Teens about Sex, Climate Change, and Existential Angst. *Slate.* https://slate.com/human-interest/2019/02/navigating-teen-anxiety-with-lisa-damour.html.

a few weeks ago, after yet another depressing dinner conversation: "Living with you guys has been very taxing on me. Your pessimism has been very crushing. Really, I'm just trying to bring back the love."

Lithwick's poignant comment about how the volatility of American politics was laying siege to her family's psychological well-being inspired us to seek out Lisa Damour on how best to hold this fragile line between psyche and polis both for ourselves and our children.

It is crucial to point out that just two months before we aired this episode, on February 14, 2019, an 18-year-old shooter with a history of mental health problems and extreme white-supremacist sympathies killed 17 people—mostly teenagers—with an AR-15-style semi-automatic rifle at Marjory Stoneman Douglas High School in Parkland, Florida. At the time, this was the deadliest school shooting in U.S. history. Such gun violence in schools has only grown. According to data analysts at Education Week, *who established a "School Shooting Tracker" in 2018 to document shootings perpetrated on grade K-12 school property resulting in injury or death, there were 24 school shootings in 2018 and 2019, ten in 2020 (during the pandemic lockdown), 35 in 2021, and 51 in 2022.[2] Of the attacks in 2022, the shooting on May 24 by a deeply troubled 18-year-old at Robb Elementary School in Uvalde, Texas, stands out. Among the 21 people killed, 19 were children aged 11 and younger.[3]*

Moreover, in late 2021, the American Academy of Pediatrics, the American Academy of Child and Adolescent Psychiatry, and the Children's Hospital Association issued a joint statement declaring a national state of emergency in children's mental health.[4] They cited rising suicide rates in children and young people aged ten to 24 across 2010–2020 as the reason for this declaration of emergency and identified two key drivers of the mental health crisis: our society's struggles with the COVID-19 pandemic and its conflicts over racial injustice. These alarming—if not devastating—facts alert us to the malignant and lethal impact toxic politics have upon both the bodies and the minds of our children, the most vulnerable members of our society.

---

[2] "School Shootings This Year: How Many and Where," *Education Week*, June 15, 2023, https://www.edweek.org/leadership/school-shootings-this-year-how-many-and-where/2023/01.

[3] "Uvalde School Shooter Left Trail of Warning Signs ahead of Attack," *PBS News Hour*, July 19, 2022, https://www.pbs.org/newshour/nation/uvalde-school-shooter-left-trail-of-warning-signs-ahead-of-attack.

[4] "AAP-AACAP-CHA Declaration of a National Emergency in Child and Adolescent Mental Health," American Academy of Pediatrics, October 19, 2021, https://www.aap.org/en/advocacy/child-and-adolescent-healthy-mental-development/aap-aacap-cha-declaration-of-a-national-emergency-in-child-and-adolescent-mental-health/.

Interview

Betty: I'm so pleased and honored to introduce this week's guest, whom I happen to have met in my late teens when we were both in college. Welcome to *Mind of State*, Lisa.

Lisa: Thank you for having me. I'm thrilled to be here.

Betty: In February, *Slate*'s columnist Dalia Lithwick spoke with you about how our anxiety as adults over all that is happening in politics and society impacts our teens' anxieties and states of mind, and this is a serious consideration. Ideally, our role as parents is to help our children regulate stress. So then in these volatile and stirring times, what are the adults to do? How do we juggle and contain our own stresses, so that we can help our kids—particularly our teens, who are becoming ever more aware of the world, as their brains develop into maturity. You've been traveling the country and focusing on this issue, especially as it impacts teen girls. You talk extensively about teen anxiety in your book, *Under Pressure*, so can you say something about all this?

Lisa: Sure. I'm a mom myself, so I also have to navigate this question of "how do I manage my own discomfort about whatever is going on politically in the context of life at home?" My older daughter is 15, and my younger daughter is 8, and my older daughter is very plugged-in and aware and tuned into the world around her. I think about this with different perspectives— both my clinical professional view and then also my life-at-home view. In terms of broader, cultural, political phenomena, I cannot find a justification for terrifying children. That's where I start. I've had conversations, at times, with parents who feel obliged to give a very unfiltered account to their child of their current state and gravity of their concerns, and it's left me feeling uneasy—and also uneasy about my own uneasiness with it, because a part of me feels like we should be honest with kids; we don't soft-pedal stuff.

And yet, kids are helpless. I know a lot of adults feel helpless, too. But at some level, we actually have more power. We're voting. We can donate to causes we care about. We're not entirely helpless. And that's how we manage much of our discomfort, whereas kids really are quite helpless. The job of adults is to shield them at times, if not often. As I've tried to navigate this, both clinically and as a mom, I've come to an uneasy peace with the idea that I don't need to give my kids a totally unfiltered accounting of my own anxieties about the current political state of affairs. They've got a lot on their plates already—which is the job of growing up. So, I need to raise, and help other people raise, kids who feel brave and not terrified. And that, I think, means that we have to do some titrating at times.

Betty: When you talk about titrating, Lisa, the question that jumped into my mind is how do we do that, given that teenagers are increasingly on the Internet getting information from their classmates, from social media, and various other online sources? We might not be able to control their access to stressful news and information. How do we contain these anxieties or these exposures to information that can stir them? How do we titrate this stress from the environment?

Lisa: I think we have a few different openings. One is, when they're coming to us directly about concerns. And for me, the way to thread the needle of being honest to kids without being necessarily frightening to them is to remember that all communication holds a few different channels within it. There are the words we say, and there's *how* we say the words. What I think parents can do quite artfully—and I think a lot of parents do this instinctively—is they say the truth to their children, but they do it in a tone that communicates that the child can trust that the adults are aware of the situation, are working on it, and are responsible for it.

For instance, say your child happens to have a really hard time with the Trump administration. And they have a really hard time with immigration policies and really feel uneasy about the news that is coming to them. A parent could address the depth of those concerns without unnecessarily stoking the child's discomfort—and there's a lot of discomfort to be had on those topics—by saying something like, "I know exactly what you're talking about," or "I agree with you. The state of immigration and the way people who are immigrating into the U.S. are being treated right now is something that none of us feels good about. And, you know, so many of us feel awful about it, and you're having the right reaction. What we have to hold out for is that these policies will change in time." Everything there is factually correct, empathic, and acknowledges the child's feelings. But that's a very different communication than a parent who says all of the exact same words in a fever pitch with anxiety just rippling through the tone of their voice.

So the same lyrics could have a very different impact, depending on the tune that parents sing or how they package them. We have to do this throughout the child-rearing years. I remember in a much more pedestrian example, I was driving and my younger daughter—maybe she was five—was in the backseat and she asked, "Are you going to die?" And I said, "Yeah." Then I waited and held my breath. And then she says, "Oh, this really funny thing happened the other day at school," and it was over. I was honest. I answered the question that was asked, but I also was very deliberate in my tone. I presented it as a matter-of-fact thing. And I don't know where the conversation would have gone if I had said, "Well, yes, but it's not something you need to worry about now," and taken it down that road. But we do have those options in our communications with our kids, to play with the nuances of tone and transmit a general sense that we grownups get it and are on it, as much as we can be right now, while also having factually correct conversations.

Betty: What you're talking about is something that we do clinically—which is to go with the affect as well as the content, to build communication with the emotions as well as the text. So, your daughter asked, "Are you going to die?" Or our teens come to us and ask about immigration or the Trump administration or the instability in the world, and what you're saying is that we can digest this for them and present it back to them in a way that's more stable than perhaps the ways in which they're taking it in. So this is a way to stabilize them against overwhelming information that their young minds may find far more intense than our adult minds do, and our adult minds certainly find it all quite overwhelming as it is.

How do we encourage this kind of open communication? Being a parent myself of younger kids, hearing about what bothers them can be a catch-as-catch-can prospect, as it was with your five-year-old daughter bringing up her concerns about mortality in the backseat on the way home. We can't often purposefully foster these conversations—kids of any age might roll their eyes when you sit them down and say, "Let's have a conversation about X, Y, Z." It often comes out spontaneously. So, with overwhelming information—like the recent mass shooting in New Zealand—with teens, particularly since they're more aware of the world and they're more exposed to news, how do you foster such open conversation?

Lisa: You wait for them to open the door. I think it is hard to have a conversation when we're the one driving the agenda, especially with adolescents. So, I would listen for them to say, "You know, did you see what happened?" If we observe that our child may be well aware of it and is quite uncomfortable about it, then we can say, "Hey did you see what happened on the news?" and open the door that way and see if they want to go there. But we have to follow their lead. And if they say "yeah," and they are ready to settle in to talk more about it, great. But I also think if a ninth grader says, "Yeah I saw it" and indicates that "while I saw it, it feels to me like it's on the other side of the world and even as it's really, really tragic, I also have a physics test tomorrow." In my mind, our kid has a right to focus on their physics test.

Michael: I encourage my kids to read the paper every single day. I have a 19-year-old freshman in college and a freshman in high school. I don't think that knowing about traumatic events is a problem for kids. They should not be exposed to it in kindergarten, but at some point, tragedies can and do happen. And, of course, we adults have to be there to support them, but in terms of the mass shooting in New Zealand, I made sure my kids read everything. I don't want them ignorant of that kind of hate.

Betty: And then do you have a conversation with them about it?

Michael: Of course. It's important for them to engage the world as it is. In the same way I make sure they read about Jim Crow and the history of lynching. Because I want to raise responsible citizens, and part of that is to be informed about all aspects of history and humanity. Lisa, one of the more toxic dynamics that I see in my teenage daughters and their friends is that there's no past tense. It's just a persistent present tense. It's, you know, the picture of the day.

There's just zero context. So, rather than shielding them, I want to keep giving them context. And I feel like I have to give it to them as history. I'll say, "Hey it was way worse here for a long time. And we owned people and sold them. And then after that was over, we passed laws that made it legal to lynch them. There were women who were not allowed to vote until 1920. Mississippi didn't pass the 13th Amendment abolishing slavery until 1995."[5]

---

[5] In 1995, when Mississippi finally ratified the 13th Amendment, they neglected to send the required paperwork to the Federal Register so it wasn't recorded officially until 2013. Eyder Peralta, "After Snafu, Mississippi Ratifies Amendment Abolishing Slavery," *NPR*, February 19, 2013, https://www.npr.org/sections/thetwo-way/2013/02/19/172432523/after-snafu-mississippi-ratifies-amendment-abolishing-slavery#:~:text=%22In%201865%2C%20Mississippi%20was%20among,the%20ratification%20was%20never%20recorded.

People get caught up in the present tense and create anxiety, thinking the sky is falling.

Betty: Is that something you see, Lisa, that teens lack context? And to address what you're talking about, Michael, my understanding is that this is not so much about shielding, but about interpreting. And how and if we interpret what comes in from the outside world for our kids, or do we just let them be exposed? We focus on politics here on *Mind of State*, but it really could be about anything. Kids can certainly encounter traumatic information and experiences. How do we as adults help them process this? Lisa, in terms of the current tensions in the world, are you seeing a lack of awareness of context in your teen patients and in conversations with teens and parents across the country?

Lisa: I don't know that I would call it that. I think, in many ways, teens are very attuned. I would say that my 15-year-old is the wonkiest person I know and very much uses social media as a place where she stays on top of things and follows the discourse she's pursuing. Every one of us has the risk of settling into our own little echo chamber. Adults and kids do it, where you're only connected online to people who agree with you. And then you get entrenched in that.

But I have two thoughts on what Michael was saying. One, there is a way to take a psychological turn on what he's describing, which is to say, he's helping his kids with the intellectualization—the defense of intellectualization. So they look at the news of the day. And then, Michael, you help them see it within the context of a broader historical scope. I have a friend whose husband is an academic in political science—this is a very, very liberal friend. And what she takes comfort in is that he, as a political scientist, looks at the Trump administration as a particularly unpleasant blip in this long historical trajectory. And that's comforting for her. And what we know about psychological defenses is that they act as emotional circuit breakers. They keep us from becoming overwhelmed by affectively charged information. I don't want to advocate from within a binary—meaning either you expose kids to stirring news, or you don't. That's not the question. I think the question is, how do we expose them in a way that includes enough context, data, broad historical scope, or adult perspective so that the news of the day—which can blow us all out of the water—does not do so to our kids?

The other thought I have is about what teenagers are exposed to in their school communities. I live in Shaker Heights, Ohio, which is a suburb of Cleveland, and I would say we are probably a very blue dot in a very red state. But that doesn't mean that our dot is entirely blue. My daughters both go to school with kids whose families are Trump supporters. They are in history and social studies classes with those kids. I am actually impressed by the fact that my daughter, when Trump was elected, was having more direct and engaged conversations with people who don't share her politics than I am having, ever. I am cautious about suggesting—at least with the teenagers that I have immediate contact with—I'm cautious about suggesting they have a narrow view. I remember I was talking to another mother in my community who herself is very liberal and her daughter is a dear friend of my daughter's. And I said something to her like, "You know, our girls are doing hand-to-hand combat at school with kids who don't agree with them. I mean, they're really in it," which I don't ever do.

Betty: And what kinds of conversations or debates do they find themselves in? Are they happening on the fly, are the teachers bringing topics up, or is it naturally happening, given the context of the subjects they're studying? I'm curious how they're negotiating these divisions face-to-face in ways that we, as adults, can choose not to. How are they navigating this?

Lisa: Well, the ones I hear about are much more on-the-fly conversations. I remember my daughter coming home and saying a kid in her class had accused Democrats of being hypocritical for saying they were feminists and yet not supporting Ivanka Trump's work. And my daughter said she quickly pointed out to him that the Democrats were the only party, the only major party, that had ever nominated a woman for president. She was ready. Then it went on to a broader conversation. And I remember asking, "Where was your teacher?" and she said, "Oh, we had a sub that day." So this is all going on in a garden-variety eighth-grade conversation. This part is fascinating to me because I do feel like my older daughter is way more engaged with people across the political aisle than I am.

Betty: And since this was back in middle school, and she's now 15, she's literally growing up within this blue/red divide and the debates that go with it.

Lisa: Yes.

Betty: And does she feel the polarization? I don't know if 10 years ago kids would have been having these conversations, at least not as starkly. In the macro sphere, in the adult world, these conversations are quite split, to the point where we don't often enter into the Fox News space if we're MSNBC people, or if we're Fox News people, we don't enter into the MSNBC space. We've had several interviews with people about perceptions of in-group or out-group status with each other, and about the greater tendencies people have toward sticking with their political tribe. But these kids are not there yet, but they have to engage because they're in class with kids whose families may hold opposing views. Your daughters are, as you put it, going to school with kids from Trump-supporting families. So, do they feel the lines, the divide?

Lisa: They do feel the lines, and our job, I think, as parents, is to hear them out, hear what happened at school today, to listen. Around here, especially given that we are in a really mixed environment, in terms of political views, something I'm working really hard as a parent to do is to prevent contempt. Liberals can be extraordinarily contemptuous of people who don't share their views—more so than people on other parts of the political spectrum. I try to always push my daughters to try to understand where somebody else might be coming from, even if they firmly disagree with their views. And I remember going on a long walk with my younger daughter and she asked, "How did Trump get elected?" She asked it flat out. And I really tried to give my best assessment of what did not appeal about Hillary to a large percentage of Americans. And I described what does appeal about Trump to a large percentage of Americans. And I tried to be neutral and yet to also say, "This is the piece we don't agree with" or "this is the piece we do agree with." But I aim to be balanced and not jump in with dismissive views, which can come faster and easier.

Betty: Which sounds like you aim to be less reactive, which is where contempt can come from—it's a desire to get rid of something quickly, to make a wholesale dismissal. But I'm curious, your younger daughter is eight, right? And she was asking, "How did Trump get elected?" two years ago, in 2016—so she was six or seven then?

Lisa: No, I think it was about a year ago that she asked this question, so she was seven-and-a-half.

Betty: What prompted the question?

Lisa: I have no idea. But something else happened with her, right when Trump did get elected, that gets back to that question of whether kids are having too much exposure to politics and what they are being exposed to—especially when they're little—and then how to keep such conversations going when the topics do come up. I don't know if that was after a period of her being anxious, but somehow it rose to the surface that she was really, really frightened about the elections. I think this was when the elections were going on. And she brought it up spontaneously on a walk. Again, we were on a walk and stuff started to bubble up. She told me a kid said on the playground that Mike Pence is going to kill all the children. So she had this really wild and terrifying story told to her, and I was so glad that she said it, because then I could address it. But that's the thing with little kids around the news. There's the news, and then there's what they think the news is. And so that's the other piece we have to manage as adults. Even if we think we're shielding them, they're picking up playground information. So, that's probably another moment where we might say, "There's what's in the news, and there is what you are hearing about what's on the news. Because those can be two very different things."

Betty: Absolutely.

Michael: What social media platforms are your kids on?

Lisa: My little one, none. My older one, for reasons I don't entirely understand, has never taken much of a liking to Instagram or Twitter. None of them use Facebook. So, I don't really think she spends much time on Instagram. She is on Pinterest, and she likes to watch YouTube videos. She's not deeply engaged in social media. What she does engage with is the memes Pinterest has, where kids put up memes about current events. It's a real hodgepodge. Some of it's about Beyoncé, and some of it's about Harry Potter, and some of it's about what's going on politically. So, she stays very engaged in that way. But the other thing is that we live in Shaker Heights, Ohio, and my daughter attends Shaker Heights Public School. She's a member of the student group on race relations, which is a 40-year-old institution at Shaker Heights Public Schools, which are unusually well-integrated schools. So she is constantly engaged in very political and thoughtful discussions around race relations at the school level, the community level, and the national level. I'm grateful to Shaker for creating this environment where the school is supporting very thoughtful discussions.

Betty: And the discussions are surrounding discrimination, implicit bias—these kinds of conversations?

Lisa: I think all of the above. They spend a lot of time looking at groups and disadvantages and microaggressions. And not only does she do programming—meetings and programming with kids her age—she then goes into the classrooms of the elementary and middle schools and does all of the programming for younger kids. Esteemed positions in the high school are to get to be the ones who are going and doing this with younger kids. And it's well done and thoughtful. She engages in that way very full on and keeps her social media a little bit to the side.

Betty: Ferguson was a while ago, so that event was well before her engagement in the anti-discrimination or the race-relations group at high school. But what about Black Lives Matter and the movements that are rising up in this polarized climate that we have in our adult spheres? There is a rise in anti-immigration and racism, showing up in marches and protests like the ones we saw in Charlottesville. How are your daughters, or your students and your teen patients, engaging with this information? How are they digesting this? What is it doing to their perceptions of themselves in the world?

Lisa: I see them very active with it, clinically and at home. I see an urgency on the kids' part to get their voices out there. I see them wearing many more t-shirts proclaiming Black Lives Matter, many more yard signs that kids are asking their families to put up. I've taken care of adolescents for 25 years, and I've never seen more politically engaged and active groups of teenagers than the ones we have right now.

Betty: Is that because of their families or is this all self-motivated, or a bit of both?

Lisa: No, it's coming from the kids. It's very much coming from the kids. I think they're frustrated with the grownups. Certainly on the liberal side, I think they feel a strong obligation to try to get their voice in. It's fascinating to see and remember how out-to-lunch I was politically as a teenager compared to how engaged my own ninth grader is.

Michael: How much is the environment—climate change, global warming—a factor in their world view?

Lisa: That is not a topic that I hear kids around here talking much about. Like, that one is not so clearly on my radar. Around me at least, it feels like kids are much more concerned about racial equity and social justice questions.

Michael: Why do you think that is? Shaker Heights is hardly a hotbed of racial discrimination.

Lisa: Everywhere is a hotbed of racial discrimination. For us, the high school itself has a 50-50 minority/white racial makeup. And it has a very long history of trying to think deeply and carefully about racial integration. Part of what makes it so front and center is our demographics. I travel around the country to other parts of the U.S. where I speak in front of public school audiences that are almost entirely white. So, I think, for students in less diverse communities, questions of racial equity and justice are easier for them to set to the side and not think about. Whereas I think because of the integration we have in Shaker Heights, questions of equity and justice are in front of the kids all the time.

Betty: Like you, Lisa, I was also a politically out-to-lunch teen, and now, kids are much more politically and socially engaged. What do you think are the factors to push them to act in ways that are different from what we experienced?

Lisa: First of all, I think they have a steady stream of their own information. When I think about us as teenagers, if we didn't watch the morning news with our parents, and if we didn't read the newspaper at night, we were sort of existing in our own little...

Betty: ...teenage bubble.

Lisa: Yes. Whereas now, thanks or no thanks to digital technology, kids have constant access to a steady stream of their own updates about the news, however it may come across to them. You know, it's particularly packaged for kids.

Betty: So, we now have kids who are more engaged across the board and impacted by the fact that, through their phones, they have constant access to information. And they are living online far more than we do, although we ourselves are quite attached to our devices. How do we manage, monitor, or help them navigate what can be an onslaught of media?

Lisa: Earlier on, I said there are two things parents could do to help kids. One is to think about how we handle our communications. The other is around helping kids not feel so helpless in the face of stuff that is scary. Some of the extremely uncomfortable conversations I've had clinically are with kids who are very scared of a school shooting. And that is a very hard conversation to have.

Michael: That's very real. That's a totally different set of fears than we contended with. I mean, I was motivated by seeing social injustice in the world and feeling like I should do something. The difference is that I never felt unsafe in school or any other public space. That's where we have failed our kids.

Lisa: There are ways, though, to help kids, in terms of addressing questions of helplessness. Setting to the side for a minute the concerns around guns, though I do want to return to it because it's so charged.

Betty: I do, too.

Lisa: But just even when kids are unhappy—say they're unhappy about the political state—I think we can say, "Hey this is in the long arc of history." And then I do think we can say, "But look, there are things you can do, even before you can vote. You know, if you're really interested in this, there are things we can do where your voice can be heard before you hit 18." And that's like a real template that we always use in psychology when kids are feeling sad. If a classmate's parent dies, we say, "Yes, it's incredibly sad. Do you want to write them a note?" We always look for something that the child can do to help them not feel helpless. So, I totally agree with you, Michael, that they may feel helpless, and they may not always even be helpless. As a result we can point them to ways they can exercise the power that they do have, even as kids.

But then, to take it to this question of school shootings. I mean, these are excruciating conversations because I'm terrified of it. The kids are terrified of it. It's not even an irrational fear, even if it's a very low base-rate fear. And even there, I have often found myself trying to help kids have some sense—and again, it's not complete by any measure—but some sense of what they could do. One thing I often will say to kids is "you know, in school settings, when you look at the data, the student who does the shooting is often broadcasting in advance that they have something like this in mind. So..." I will then say to them, "You guys have data. You make sure you get that data to the grownups, if you have information that makes you scared. You just let a grownup know." Again, it feels sorely inadequate. It's not enough. But I have found that is one little place where I can try to give a child a sense that it's not completely out of control, that there may be a piece of it that they may have some ability to change.

Betty: What you're talking about, Lisa, from my perspective of trauma treatment, is that you are taking them out of a frozen place of anxiety and giving them some empowering strengths—pointing to their strengths—so although they are children and their capacity to engage with voting etc. in the adult world is limited, they still have strengths and power. They have the strength to write a letter. They have the strength to tell an adult if they find something alarming. And they have the strength of tuning into their own instincts if they see something online that alarms them. That's something that, in terms of emotional intelligence, is an opportunity for us to say, "Tune into your instincts. Tune into those feelings that you may have, even though they may be just feelings and not based on any kind of overt evidence, but there's something there. And then an adult can take that in and help you with that." And hopefully not turn it into a five-alarm fire if it's not merited, but also to be able to collaborate because we don't have access to their world. We don't live in their online worlds. And if student shooters, past and, God forbid, future are active in ways that are patterned, then we can communicate mutually about what we see retrospectively and what the kids can do to help us about it.

But in terms of things like school shootings, this jumps me to something that is very on the ground for kids, especially but not exclusively for girls—and you addressed this in your book, *Under Pressure*. You wrote that half of all 8th to 11th grade girls have been sexually harassed. So, this is how #MeToo is not exclusively an adult topic that kids can be passively worried about. They are directly involved.

Lisa: Yes.

Betty: These stats, although maybe not surprising, are still harrowing, especially for me as a mother of a daughter who is now still very young. But I look ahead and then I think about my nieces and my friends' teenage daughters, and they have all reported experiencing harassment. And so, how do we help teens navigate a world where sexual harassment is present in their schools? And then they're seeing it in the Kavanaugh hearings, and it's not coming to a decision that favors the survivor. Is that something that impacted your patients? Is that something that you've had to grapple with at home and in the office?

Lisa: I wrote about the high levels of harassment that girls are facing, and this includes girls and also kids who don't identify as straight. They can also be subjected to high levels of harassment. This, for me, is one of those things where I feel that, for adults—and I acknowledge this in my own writing and you're talking about it now—it catches us up short. I think we are surprised by these high numbers. We are surprised by how garden-variety sexual harassment exists in the school day for a lot of middle and high schoolers. I think that part of why it catches us up short is that we don't think to ask about it, and the kids aren't going to bring it up with us. They feel shameful and odd, so they keep it to the side. We can carry on with a relatively low awareness of how much of this is going on.

In terms of what we do, I think the first thing is for us to acquaint ourselves with it. Like, get to know the real numbers, get to know the forms that harassment takes, and then, a first step probably is to bring it all under the anti-bullying behavior umbrella that already exists in most middle schools. You know that *bullying* is a term that's obviously had a lot of traction in recent years, and that's something schools are talking and thinking about it, and, in truth, sexual harassment is bullying with a sexualized twist. But it's essentially just bullying made weirder or more uncomfortable or more shaming for the recipient. I think that's a first step.

The other thing for girls that I have found important, which may seem like a small thing, but it feels like it's where we start, is confirming for them that this is wrong. I think they know it's wrong. They're aware that it's wrong, but it's uncomfortable for them or hard for them to always hold onto that. Or they question it because it can be so commonplace. And everybody around them can act like it's just part of the day. So, for us to ask, "You know, is this kind of stuff going on?" and they say, "Yeah, yeah, yeah," then I think we need to start by saying, "Okay, you know that this is completely out of bounds. This is a completely out of bounds thing to say to anybody, under any conditions."

Michael: In the world of my teen daughters, there is a lot of sexual shaming on social media, and it's oftentimes in "Finstas."

Betty: What's a Finsta?

Lisa: Fake Instagram. It's an Instagram account their parents don't know they have.

Betty: Okay, I'm out of the loop on that one.

Michael: For teens, this is where a lot of emotional damage is being done. Often parents don't know about Finstas. They think they're on top of things. They're never on top of things. They're Luddites compared to their children, even their young children.

Betty: So a fake Instagram—a Finsta—is an Instagram account a kid can create that is under a shadow name that the parents don't have access to. The account parents see is a red herring, and your Finsta is where you post what you actually want all your friends online to see?

Michael: Yes. Your "fake" Instagram account is real.

Betty: So, what are you seeing happening on Finstas?

Michael: Highly sexualized posts. Young girls putting themselves out there in ways that would make their parents aghast. Yet the real poison is in the comment threads. Both in the admiration and the bullying that happens. Those comments get passed around relentlessly. This happens so often under the radar of school administrators and of parents. Kids sustain these attacks and have to manage them on their own in the toxic environment of high school.

Betty: And your girls have come to you about them?

Michael: Yes, we talk about it all the time. My two daughters follow each other's Finstas, so it's out in the open.

Betty: Lisa, I'm curious to hear your thoughts on all of this.

Lisa: Part of what comes to my mind is developmental age. A 12-year-old putting up a sexy photo of herself is really different from, say, a 17-year-old doing the same thing. There are whole developmental universes that we want to try to understand here. And the word *power* keeps coming up for me again and again. There are also a couple different questions that arise. One is, is this a 12-year-old understanding how she exercises her power as a woman? She's aware that this gets attention. She's aware that this pulls people her way, whether they are admiring or criticizing her. But 12-year-olds are very interested in power—particularly social power, which is why it's when bullying begins. So, that's one way we want to frame this up.

Michael: I think that's right, because when my older daughter would post things that my wife or I would find—let's just say, less than appropriate—she accused us of being sexist. And I thought, "Wow that's really fascinating, because to me, you're objectifying yourself," which is my feminist approach.

Betty: And maybe an adult's way of looking at this.

Lisa: Or she's saying, "You're telling me my body is gorgeous, so I'm going to use my body and celebrate it, and everybody's gonna celebrate it with me."

Another teen practice where power also comes into play—and this is a topic where I feel like grownups have dropped the ball completely—is with sexting and on how we think about it. I know it's really complicated. But when I hear about a scenario where an eighth-grade boy says to a seventh-grade girl, "Send nudes." And that is the tamest, friendliest version of that kind of invite that I usually hear about. As soon as I hear that, I think, that's harassment; there's no power equality here. This is an eighth-grade boy and a seventh-grade girl, or it could even be a kid in the same class, but he's got a ton of social power. And so suddenly this request, which looks neutral on the surface and something she's free to ignore—to me feels so much more loaded. It is something that adults have not really engaged in a meaningful way. And then if the girl says "No," often it's not at all unusual for things to turn into what is, without question, harassment for inappropriate photos.

Betty: Lisa, to go back to the developmental piece of this—while we're talking about teens. To your point, development and maturity at age 12 is very different from development and maturity at age 17. And yet with all teens, we're dealing with kids with little impulse control because their brains are not fully formed. At the same time, they have access to this very potent sexual material and social media channels where this potent material can be trafficked or exchanged. How have we dropped the ball on all this, in your view?

Lisa: To go back to the inappropriate photos and the sharing of them, one place I feel we dropped the ball is that we save a lot of our critiques for the girls. We're like, "Why would she put up a photo like that?" We set to the side the fact that she was asked 40 times by a boy to do it. We don't make an issue of his constant requests, but we do make an issue of her finally giving in. I really think we need to revisit that piece.

A charged topic—one that's on fire and where we, as adults and parents, are not doing our job—is pornography. A lot of kids are learning about sex from looking at porn. And it's hard not to sound prudish, but I remember feeling like, "Oh, kids look at porn. It's just one of those things." Then several years ago, I was about to give a talk at a boys school in our community, and one of the mothers said, "You know, I think you should take a look at what the boys are looking at." And she sent me to PornHub. com, where I thought surely they will ask for a credit card or surely they will ask if I'm eighteen. So, I typed in PornHub.com, and I was floored, absolutely floored. And what I was floored by—what I saw—and again, I've had two children. I have been a practicing clinician for nearly 25 years.

I am no prude. What popped up on my screen was nine videos running simultaneously in this tiled gallery. Every one of them presents a video that looks like violent rape—really hardcore, graphic sex to the point of being grotesque. In what looked to me to be a really, really upsetting situation, the woman in the video seemed to be having a really good time. Moreover, every actor in these videos is an anatomical outlier—everyone, the men, the women had bodies like you've never seen in nature. So, I was drop-jawed looking at this. And I thought, what would it be to be a 10- or 11-year-old, and this is your introduction to sex?

Michael: That's also because we as adults don't know how to talk about sex with kids, right?

Lisa: Yes, I agree.

Michael: And, when you hit puberty, the last people you want to talk to about sex is with your parents. That's the worst thing in the world.

Lisa: And they're not going to bring it up, either.

Michael: So kids might go to PornHub to learn...

Betty: ...or out of curiosity, probably.

Michael: And pornography's been around since Pompeii. I remember walking through the ruins in Pompeii and the penises and everything graffitied all over the walls. But it is also dysmorphic and teaches kids nothing meaningful—socially or emotionally. They're not learning about love or about intimacy from porn.

Lisa: I would take it further. I would say that what I saw felt traumatizing and very different from passing around a *Playboy* magazine with your friends. And I have cared for kids who were traumatized by porn. The way it unfolded was that they were seven or eight and they went on a playdate or to a sleepover at a friend's house and some older sibling thought it would be funny to show the little kids porn. And the kid didn't sleep for six months and finally blurted out to their parents what happened.

Betty: It's overwhelming. Looking at it from the perspective of somebody who treats people who have been sexually assaulted, some during childhood—kids' brains literally cannot contain that kind of adult material. It's too much. It's not even in a language that children can digest. Kids have sexuality, but within a bandwidth that their minds, bodies, and perspectives on the world can handle. And that extra adult bandwidth in porn, with dysmorphic bodies and this violent, aggressive sex is very, very potent. So, then, Lisa, are they being passively exposed to this by having access to PornHub? By passive, I mean they are not exposed to it by a perpetrator flashing them or by somebody cornering them and getting off on showing a child sexual content. If it's just there for them to find, and yet it could create a shock close to that of a forced sexual encounter with someone much older, what do we do about that? How do we protect kids from such harmful shock?

Lisa: Keeping separate questions of self-regulation, here's what I did. Because I've been caring for kids where I'd heard these stories clinically, I made a rule with both of my kids that they were not to go on computers outside of our own home, at school or at someone else's house. I said, "If you're on a playdate and somebody says, 'Let's go do this,' you say, 'My parents say I can't go on other kid's computers.'" I'm not a particularly anxious parent but having cared for a couple of kids who had exposure to porn unfold in this particular way, that was one thing I did.

Another thing I did is that when my older daughter was negotiating for a smartphone, I told her, "My number one concern is that this will be the domain through which you see pornography, whether you're curious or somebody shows it to you." I said, "So there is a whole bunch of stuff I want to say to you about it before that time comes. A lot of what is out there is not loving, it is not kind." I quoted Dan Savage, saying "You know, pornography hates women." And I think that's a very good framing on it.

And then I said, "I don't want you to think that that is what sex is about, and what it has to be about. I want you to be very mindful that these are people who are electing to take pay to have sex in a public venue. This is just one corner of the sexual universe. That is not the sexual universe as a whole. And that corner has commerce involved." We were on a walk, so she didn't have to look at me. I said, "And just to be clear: that's not what's going down at our house, that really violent, weird stuff you're going to see. That's not our sexual lives in our own home. between your dad and me." Of course, at this point I'm sure she was ready to crawl out of her skin. But that's the way a lot of little kids look at it. They're like, "Oh my God, is that what's happening in my parents' bedroom?"

Betty: And how old was your daughter when you had the negotiation with the phone?

Lisa: 12. We had that conversation when she was 12.

Betty: And she knew what pornography was?

Lisa: She knew, yes. And I made a point to say to her, "*When* the day comes"—I said "when" the day comes, not "if" it comes. Because I know she will see it. I wish I didn't know that, but I do know that. So, I said, "When the day comes, you can ask me any question you want. I will answer it, no judgment. Don't worry. Don't feel like you have to walk around with questions that you can't get answers to."

Michael: But the genie is out of the bottle. Maybe you can tell your kid to not look at computers outside her home, but when she's 12, 13, 14, there's no way that's going to hold up.

Lisa: Yep. That's why I said, "When you see it."

Betty: And the genie may be out of the bottle, but we can talk about the genie and we can name it. It's when it's not namable, or recognized, like the worst monsters in good horror movies, it is much scarier when it's implied by shadows on a wall. When you actually see the monster, it suddenly has limits. It loses some of the power we give it by imagining the worst thing possible.

Michael: That's my take, which is, it's like media literacy, to get back to our earlier conversation about Trump or politics. One of the things you have to teach your kids is: What's the source of the information? Is it a rumor? Did you read it? Did you read two articles about it in two different sources? To teach them how to recognize the roots of the viral quality of our political environment right now. And I think that there's something of the same thing here when it comes to a very oversexualized society where pornography has seeped into everybody's cellphones and is everywhere, especially for a certain cohort of kids. And I think one of the things you have to do is teach them how to read it. Teach them, "Look, this isn't real. This is what it is, and this is why it exists. And this is what the industry is." Because if they can read behind it to see the matrix code, it loses its power.

Betty: It also loses its chaos. It's possibly less overwhelming. But what were you going to say, Lisa?

Lisa: Let's just keep going, which is to point out that we now show rape on TV—a lot.

Betty: Right, like with *Game of Thrones*.

Lisa: Yes. TV shows now have rape as a part of the story. And again, I think maybe it's because I work with this clinically, I'm more sensitized to it or I'm not desensitized, but I had to stop watching *Game of Thrones*. I said to myself, "I can't watch another rape. I just can't do it." Because if you've cared for people who have suffered from being raped...

Betty: ...it's not entertainment.

Lisa: And it was interesting with all of the hullabaloo with *13 Reasons Why*, which, when that came out clinicians everywhere were beside themselves about its impact on kids and the way in which it got way out ahead of the grownups.

Betty: And to orient people who might not know about *13 Reasons Why*, it's a young adult novel and Netflix series about suicide.[6]

Lisa: When Netflix released the series, kids had watched the entire thing before grownups even knew what it was. It's about a girl who takes her own life and then it unpacks retrospectively the events leading up to the suicide. Everybody was rightly really concerned about the messaging around suicide. The conversation that stayed with me the most was from talking with a bunch of ninth-grade girls. In *13 Reasons Why* there are rapes, and

---

[6] Asher, J. (2007). *Thirteen Reasons Why*. RazorBill. The novel was developed by Brian Yorky into a Netflix series, *13 Reasons Why* running four seasons.

they are very graphic—so graphic that an adult man said to me, "It was one of the most upsetting things I've ever seen." And I remember sitting with this group of ninth-grade girls and I said, "You guys, I hear there are rapes in this," and one girl in particular got this stricken look on her face and she said, "It was *awful*." She looked traumatized. And I thought, holy moly, when did this come into the culture that we just show graphic rape in content for teens?

Michael: My question is who is the adult at Netflix that thinks this is right? To show the rape of a minor?

Lisa: I know. I was on the ceiling about it.

Betty: I think one of the factors is, with shows like *Game of Thrones* and *13 Reasons Why*—which I did not know contained graphic rape scenes—everything is getting more extreme. To garner the maximum amount of attention, everything has to be ever more stimulating—the explosions, the violence, the spectacles. It seems our need for sensory overload has increased.

Michael: What killed me was *Game of Thrones* is at least labeled MA—for mature audiences—and is supposed to be for adults. But *13 Reasons Why* was literally targeted to teens.

Betty: To bring our conversation back to matters of "state" before we let you go, Lisa, what do we do with a president who has been accused sixteen times of sexual harassment and assault? There's a tacit endorsement of this violence against women with his election to president because these accusations came out before he was elected and had little impact on his electability. And that really upset my patients, some of whom were older adolescents, meaning in their early twenties, and they were devastated. How do we digest this ever-extreme escalation of sexualized content and violence for our kids? Because what you're talking about with the prevalence of sexting, sexual harassment of teen girls, and of rape culture in traditional and social media realms, even though it is grotesque, is a tacit endorsement and normalization of sexual sadism. Because it's Netflix, not PornHub, which isn't as openly acknowledged a place for entertainment as Netflix.

Lisa: First of all, we have to acknowledge that, yes, it's gotten louder and louder and louder. But child psychology has not changed. A kid's capacity to take in the world is what it's always been. It's not that somehow children are suddenly able to tolerate things they were not previously able to tolerate. So, I would say, and maybe I'm speaking for myself, I would say parents should take steps to try to filter some of it from reaching their children, especially younger kids. I don't think we should be like, "Well they're going to see it all, so we'll just hold on and see what happens next." I do think there's a lot to be said for trying to put up guardrails when we can. And then I think we get out in front of it, and we say, "When you see pornography, here's what you're going to see. Here's how we think about it as a family. Here's my availability to talk with you about it." And then we say, "You know, with regard to Trump and the question of his sexual history, here are our values as a family. This is what we believe." Articulate those values and whether they do or don't line up with any political or any public figure.

Again, so much comes through in how we say it. And kids do draw reassurance from grownups, and from feeling like "okay there are some grownups in the room." Maybe not as many grownups in the room, but there are *some* grownups in the room. And then I think the piece that we— and I'm thinking through this as we have this conversation as well—if the total stuff that feels out of control is getting louder, then the grownups need to get louder too, to reassure kids that they're not crazy, that this is not how things just go. That they're not having the wrong reaction to things.

Betty: Thank you, Lisa.

Lisa: You're welcome. Thanks for a great conversation.

THE IMPORTANCE OF MYTH IN POLITICS

Chapter 27
America's Economic Myth

Guest: Betty Sue Flowers
Episode Aired: October 7, 2020

Betty Sue Flowers, PhD, is a professor emerita (UT-Austin) and the former director of the Lyndon Baines Johnson Presidential Library. She is an international business consultant with publications on topics ranging from poetry therapy to human rights, including two books of poetry and four PBS tie-in books. Flowers was the series consultant for Joseph Campbell and the Power of Myth *and has served as a moderator for executive seminars at the Aspen Institute and as a consultant to governments, corporations, and institutions. Publications include the complete edition of Christina Rossetti's poetry,* Presence: Human Purpose and the Field of the Future *(coauthored), the essay "The American Dream and the Economic Myth," "The Primacy of People in a World of Nations" in* The Partnership Principle: New Forms of Governance in the 21st Century, *and the coedited* Realistic Hope: Facing Global Challenges.

We posted this conversation on October 7, 2020, one month before the 2020 presidential election. We invited Dr. Flowers onto Mind of State *to talk about her ideas on myth and how the stories we tell ourselves about who we are and what we value drive us—as individuals and as a collective. The American dream, for example, is a myth that has driven social and political behavior in the United States for generations. It has also been a source of fervent emotional belief that the U.S. is a land of opportunity and openness for all. In late 2020, however, from the midst of an unresolved pandemic, death rates rising and no working vaccine yet available, global economies stalled by work stoppages and supply chain problems, and protests supporting the Black Lives Matter movement over racial inequities in the U.S. staged throughout the world, anxieties ran very high about whether the 2020 election could occur safely and peacefully. All the stories we told ourselves of American democracy and its efficacy and resilience seemed to ring hollow. Since this conversation, events such as the January 6, 2021 siege on the U.S. Capitol, mass shootings—many of them politically and racially driven—as well as multiple climate disasters, continue to challenge assumptions of American stability. It is still relevant to interrogate, as Dr. Flowers does with us here, the archetypal myths that drive us and how they might guide us—or blind us—as we look to a future that is volatile at all levels.*

Interview

Betty: One thing preoccupying my patients is the dilemma, "Do I go to work, or do I stay home and stay safe? How safe or unsafe is it?"

Jonathan: We're also seeing this tension play out in the political sphere. The politicians and the candidates are forcing this unnatural dichotomy between health and wealth.

Betty: It's creating stress because no one really knows the appropriate way to think about this.

Jonathan: It's really a microcosm of the debate that's been going on for years. It's shaped by the stories that people are telling us, against how we interpret the data. And here to help us unpack this is Dr. Betty Sue Flowers.

Betty: Betty Sue, we brought you on to talk about myth. You write compellingly about the myths we swim in, here in the United States. You talk about the hero myth, the religious myth, the democratic myth, and the economic myth, which is the title of our show today. Before we get deeper into things, can you first describe how you define a myth and its purpose? And how a myth might function in a society, or a political system?

Betty Sue: Myths are stories we live by. They give us meaning. And in a culture, a large story of reality is always operating. I came across this idea of an economic myth when I watched newscasters on television—at the time, I was an English professor at the University of Texas. They were always turning to the economists to explain what was going on. And I thought, "Why the economists? My colleagues and I are experts in stories. Why let economists tell the stories of our reality? Why are they the ones who are telling us what's going on in the world?"

Then it struck me that Joseph Campbell was right when he said you could always tell the values of a society by its tallest buildings. In medieval times, the tallest buildings were churches and cathedrals. In the times of princes, they were castles. And now, it's bank and office buildings. So I thought, "Oh, we're in an economic myth. That's our story of reality."

Jonathan Kopp: Betty Sue, let me ask you to clarify. I used to think about myths as being untruths, but the way you've described them, myths seem to exist in our reality. So is a myth a story, or is it real?

Betty Sue: I don't make a claim about whether a story is true or not true. It's just a big story—even with the scientific myth, which I tend to see as true because of the process by which scientists come to their conclusions. But I call this a myth, too, because it's a large story of reality. We're very lucky that we were formed under a democratic or a scientific myth in this country— that is, the myth of the Enlightenment. That's how we got a nation under a constitution rather than a person like a king. And that's how we got the idea of, "Come, let us reason together in our polity, in our community." But unfortunately, we're not in that myth anymore. We're in an economic myth.

Betty: And so, what is it to be in an economic myth? What is this story that we tell ourselves—or the ways the economists tell the story about us?

Betty Sue: Economists have become the high priests of our culture. So we're told when the GDP (gross domestic product) rises, we're doing very well. And yet you can look around and see the homeless. You can see the enormous economic inequalities in our society, and something inside you says, "Actually we're not really doing that well, precisely because the supreme value of the economic myth is growth."

If we are lucky, there's a larger story that we may grow into, which I call the "ecological myth." It's a myth of health, where growth is a subset of health, but it's not the supreme value. So we're in this amazing transition point—a liminal period—between a myth of growth and an emerging myth of health in which growth is just a part of the bigger story. But we don't yet have the metrics to believe in that ecological myth.

Jonathan: So when you refer to the "economic myth," it sounds like it can have multiple manifestations, or submyths. You mentioned GDP, but it seems that our current president likes to point to the stock market as a measure for how we are doing. Is there a gap between the stock market myth and the rest of the economic myth?

Betty Sue: No, I would say the stock market is a metric of the economic myth, like GDP. The gross domestic product is composed of certain things that we consume and spend. So if you get a divorce and you have an operation the same year, you've contributed more to the GDP than if you grew cucumbers and sold them on the street corner.

Betty: I'm interested in what you just said about the liminal space we're in right now, where we are moving from a story of growth. That we are between this economic myth that drives us, which is focused on things—producing, making, and selling them—to a story of health, or an ecological myth, which is more concerned with nurturing our health and well-being. It seems resonant, as we're sitting in the middle of a pandemic where preserving our health is so all-consuming, it's stymying the economy. There's a big debate going on: Do we favor the economy over lives, or lives over the economy? Do we foster health or wealth? Can you say something about this liminal time and where we might see ourselves ending up? It seems up for grabs right now.

Betty Sue: It does. As someone who's been thinking about this economic myth for 25 years, I never imagined that we would have such a stark choice between valuing one over the other. Although I think the economy is part of health, health takes priority over wealth if we are going to become a better civilization for all people. I think we should choose health first and the economy will follow. If we choose the economy first, suffering will be unevenly distributed.

Jonathan: Do we even have to choose between health and wealth? About 20 years ago, your collaborator Bill Moyers did an interview with Bill Gates. And Bill Gates said back then that this choice between health and wealth is a false one, because if we invest in health, it begets wealth. How did we find ourselves in this binary, where we believe that one is a tradeoff for the other?

Betty Sue: Because we have such a narrow view of what the American dream is. We think it means to pursue property, and it's really to pursue happiness. And happiness is a byproduct of a lot of things, including serving your community. Above a certain minimal wealth standard, wealth doesn't produce any more happiness. So I think Bill Gates is exactly right. To be clear, I think he was talking about physical health, not health in the sense of wholeness. Even so, this choice between health and wealth *is* a false one. One of the things the economic myth should show us is that we're all interconnected. The economic myth is the first truly global myth because it depends on numbers and images, rather than language. So it is understood around the world. What this pandemic has shown us, in terms of both health and wealth, is that we're truly all interconnected. We always have been. But now we see it.

Betty: Betty Sue, can you say more about the images and the numbers that bind us globally over language? Can you make that distinction? How does that reflect our globalization?

Betty Sue: Well, the global economy is one in which multinational companies don't have a national home. For the most part, they operate everywhere, and they are the true institutions of this myth. And no matter what country I am from, I can understand your numbers, and you can understand mine. Value is quantitative rather than qualitative. My dollar is as good as your dollar. There are advantages to the economic myth. It is radically leveling. It shows us our interconnectedness. It could really wake us up to see just how deeply we're all globally interconnected. And then, if we moved into a new value system in which we were willing to sacrifice some of our individual wealth for the health of the collective whole, a true shift of value would occur.

Jonathan: If the economic myth is global, how does it transcend political systems? The economic myth must manifest itself quite differently in a capitalist system versus a socialist system or a communist system—or does it transcend the political?

Betty Sue: Right now, in our global system, the free flow of capital transcends individual political arrangements. But I think some societies have emphasized well-being over sheer economics, which is one reason they have been more willing to share the wealth among all their people, rather than just among those lucky enough to make it. I say "lucky enough" because there is a great deal of luck, as well as skill and will, involved in making money.

Betty: Here in the U.S., with ever more trade tariffs erected and visas revoked, there is this implication that we're isolated and it's best we retreat further from the rest of the world. But how is this possible against a growing reality that the world is ever more interconnected with the U.S. as a major hub? Does this reveal another myth driving the United States? Possibly a hero myth of rugged individualism? If so, how might this interact with the economic myth?

Betty Sue: The hero myth is a wonderful myth for sports events, but it doesn't work for nations because of how complex they are. If I'm in a boxing match with you, it's not that complex, even if we're both highly skilled. But the global economy is so complicated that if I slap a tariff on soybeans in China, it can affect a family in Iowa. We're so interconnected in ways we can't even see that the unintended consequences of throwing tariffs around are multiplied. You might have been able to do that in the 18th century—although I think Adam Smith would have argued then, that it, too, would constrain the growth you would want. But in the 21st century, it is a step backward in evolution. As my mother used to say, "Don't cut off your nose to spite your face."

Betty: There seems to be a story operating on one side of the political spectrum where the narrative objective is all about winning or losing. Donald Trump is obsessed with always winning, and he cannot tolerate the notion of losing. You write about the winning and the losing that emerges from the economic myth, as it overlaps with elements of the hero myth. I wanted to ask, why is winning and losing so compelling to us as Americans? Am I accurate to say that this is what so many of us are preoccupied with here in the United States?

Betty Sue: I think you're very accurate. If you see a nation as a kind of hero and you see yourself in a struggle, you're living out the only myth the media can tell stories from. And I say this as someone who taught literature. The medium of the hero myth is stories. So if you're doing a newscast, you're going to tell a story with a good guy and a bad guy—or describe events in terms of who's up or who's down. The very form of a news story is "story," which by definition includes conflict.

But the form of economics is not a story. It's more like a painting. It's more like an interconnected, woven tapestry. As a leader, if you are covered by the media, you will want to tell a hero story about yourself or your country. It's perhaps interesting as a form of storytelling, but not at all helpful as a way of creating policy. So the hero myth is great for entertainment, but life is much more complex than that—if you're trying to help families and if you're involved in politics.

Jonathan: There's the question of which myth predominates—economic myth or hero myth. Are we in the midst of a struggle to determine the terms by which we apply the economic myth? On one side, we have politicians arguing for capitalism in deregulated markets. On the other, from the far left of the Democratic Party, we have a call for a democratic socialist approach. Although both of these positions are about economics, they manifest themselves quite differently. However, they both seem to put a priority on the economic myth.

Betty Sue: I think the emerging myth, which I call the ecological myth, has a value and focus that overarches individual national economies, and even the global economy, and that is of the health of the Earth as a whole. So if you judged every action your country took by whether the policies actually helped the seventh generation or even helped our grandchildren—if you judged every policy on those grounds, you might not make the same decisions that you would make if you were focused on the short term and concerned with the GDP for this year, or the statistics for this year. So all the arguments about what form our economic system should take are very relevant. But an overarching value is what drives the myth of reality of any given time or place. And the value of the economic myth is growth, and the value of the ecological myth is the greater health of peoples, nations, and, of course, the Earth.

Jonathan: So where do you situate the Green New Deal, which merges elements of the economic myth with the ecological myth?

Betty Sue: I think it partakes of the value of the ecological myth. Yes, it inserts some of that value into an economic program. So from that perspective, you could say it's looking into the future. And I think it's no accident that a lot of young people are attracted by this because they're the ones who will be living into our future, either under a myth that allows them to thrive or one that looks forward to the death of the planet—if you're going to be apocalyptic.

Betty: I note that you highlight a key factor in how we consider how to proceed, which is time. You note there is a short-term view versus a long-term one in the ways we assess what we value over time, like the growth of our GDP versus the health of the planet. And there also seems to be a generational shift reflected in our thinking and our politics about climate change. At the same time there seems to be a portion of our country that is very compelled by the hero myth and seeing society in terms of good guys versus bad guys. Even our attitudes around gun control reflect this. It seems one side isn't listening to the other. When you're behaving out of a hero myth—good versus evil—drama and conflict are essential, whereas in an ecological myth, we see we are all in this together; we share one planet, and to save it, we have to all row in the same direction. In this scenario, conflict and drama are not central. They get in the way. So I wonder from within this moment of crisis, how these frameworks might help or cause people to retreat further into their opposing corners?

Betty Sue: I think in this country, we tend to misunderstand the hero myth and its origins in Greek mythology and Greek stories. The hero myth is really about excellence and about two people fighting to see who is the most excellent. And in that domain, you want your opponent to be as good as possible so that it brings out the best in you. So, when Achilles and Hector fight each other, they're both heroes, pushing each other to fight harder and better. Yet we tend to overlay the religious myth on top of the hero myth, so we don't just have two heroes fighting each other; we have a good guy and a bad guy.

Jonathan Kopp: Good and evil.

Betty Sue: Yes, good and evil.

Betty: Ah, I see.

Betty Sue: And that view belongs to the religious myth. When you mix up the two, you don't have competition as in sports, where that hero myth is still pure. If you mix the hero and religious myth, then you have this religious dominance of the fight—instead of the idea that we were founded in a democratic myth, where you argued to find truth, the way scientists or philosophers do. You don't declare one side good and one side evil, the way religious wars have been fought. So we've got our myths all confused in this country. We don't even see what we're doing. I don't think it helps either our politics or our economic structures to be so confused about the stories of reality and value that we tell each other.

Jonathan: If the hero myth dates back to the ancient Greeks, where does the economic myth come from? Did it emerge from capitalism or does it pre-date capitalism?

Betty Sue: It arises out of the scientific myth, the Enlightenment myth, because it really is a myth without values. It knows the price of everything and the value of nothing—as has often been said of capitalism. The economic myth arises out of a lack of religious hierarchy. It would never have been countenanced in medieval times, when we were in the religious myth in the West and there were strict standards of good and evil and right and wrong. We all still pay lip service to the religious myth, but it isn't what runs our country. So the economic myth has come out of the same 18th-century thinking that produced science and a philosophy that enshrined the Goddess of Reason in Notre Dame Cathedral during the French Revolution, when Catholic worship was forbidden. Every movement in history has good effects and bad effects. We live in such a mixed story with the economic myth—which means it has many good things as well as many bad things. But we have to expand that myth if we're going to go forward and continue to live on this planet.

Jonathan: Before we look forward, I want to keep talking a little bit more about the past because you're grounding us in Enlightenment thinking. This reminds me of some of your writings about the American dream and the founding of this country. I was struck by something that you wrote, which was that our pursuit of life, liberty, and the pursuit of happiness derives from an original notion, which was life, liberty, and the pursuit of property.

And I wondered—did we get it wrong?[1] Is property a proxy for happiness? And how have those two things gotten conflated?

Betty Sue: I think we can mistake property as what we have a right to pursue. But to be clear, happiness and property are not the same thing. And I think John Stuart Mill had it right when he said that happiness is a byproduct of something else. It's a byproduct of pursuing your dreams or the health of the community. While pursuing wealth can produce happiness, it's usually the pursuit that produces happiness and not the wealth. Wealth can create security. But happiness comes from other places.

Betty: This causes me to think of Maslow's hierarchy of needs—a classic psychological theory that defines what our basic human requirements are in terms of priority. Psychologist Abraham Maslow put all human needs into a pyramid model, and at the very bottom are basic physiological needs like shelter, food, and clothing. At the top are elements crucial for self-actualization like creativity, generativity, and spiritual understanding.

When I did refugee work, those first-tier needs were the things we had to focus on exclusively with clients, some of whom came to the U.S. with barely anything. Before we could attend to even helping a person find a job, we needed to help them meet these basic needs first. Because in order to go out and look for work, it was best if a person was not hungry or worried about needing clothes or a secure place to stay. So these basic needs and the others above, like job security, self-esteem, are building blocks for self-actualization, or happiness, but not happiness itself. As you say, wealth or money can be important for feeling secure—but it isn't happiness.

When did that become a seemingly fixed idea—that happiness *was* property, or security? If you look at car commercials, for example—they define happiness in terms of things. You buy the thing, and it will make you happy. We all know this is fleeting. From what you speak of, is the pursuit of a deeper happiness the process of finding a way to generate eudaimonic pleasure—or the enjoyment of a meaningful life—for yourself and others? And if so, then it is more of a process-oriented endeavor rather than an outcomes-based one. When did we get so stuck on ends and outcomes? Can you speak about how these myths have become so twisted up?

[1] Flowers, B.S. (2006). *The American Dream and the Economic Myth*. Fetzer Institute.

Betty Sue: I think it's human nature to try to find solutions to problems. It's one of our good attributes. And if the car commercial comes on and says get this particular car and you'll be happier, we try it out. Commercialism and consumerism exploit the gap between where we are and the better place we might be. Commercialism feeds on this basic evolutionary aspect of human beings, which is ever seeking to improve—it feeds on this strength and turns it into a weakness. So until we realize that I think we'll always be caught in that trap.

This is a time of crisis for many reasons. One of them is that because we like to solve problems, we like to have control, and we like to have it now. The pandemic is just flummoxing for us. We can't make it go away just by snapping our fingers. We can't manage this through will alone, in spite of what some of our leaders would like to think—that we can make it go away by pretending it's not here. This pandemic makes us come face to face with the fact that as human beings, we don't control the very grounding of our lives. We control a lot, but we don't control how we come into this world, what gender we are, where we are born. There's so much we don't control. So how do we come to terms with that? Philosophers and religious leaders of all times have tried to answer those questions.

Betty: It sounds like what you're saying is that crises expose what's been working and what hasn't. And as you said, there's not just the pandemic. There is an economic crisis. There is a referendum on racial injustice. There is a crisis of climate change. So all this challenges the way we have been living and calls a lot into question. These answers that we insist upon having point to our being a mastery culture—as one of our other guests, psychologist Pauline Boss, has noted. So how do we use myth to tell a new story about ourselves and make a deep shift?

Betty Sue: If we step back and think about the stories of our own lives, we'll see we're always in a story about reality that we tell ourselves. We are also shaped by the story of the future that we tell. But when you think about it, the story we tell about the future is always and only a fiction, by definition. And we can build a better fiction. It's the job of a leader to create a story of the future that's compelling. Moses's story was "I see a promised land," and Martin Luther King Jr.'s story was "I have a dream." The leader tells a story of the future that enables people to move forward and to deal with their lives with hope and efficacy. So the stories we tell about the future shape the present. I don't think we've been imaginative enough about our current story of the future. And this pandemic wakes us up to the possibility of telling a better story about our relationship to each other, and to the Earth.

Jonathan: If the story of the future is a fiction and the American dream is a fiction, there's an aspirational element to all of these things. Whether a political leader is calling for hope and change or whether they say they will make America great again, these stories are both trying to—in the most reductionistic way—promise a brighter future. The politician is always going to strive for optimism. They're going to try to sell a winning ticket. Trump is telling voters that if Biden is elected, we're going to have chaos and mayhem and riots. So can the myth be about selling a better future? Or can it be selling the avoidance of doom?

Betty Sue: Either. We've seen examples of both. We've seen Winston Churchill call on the will of the people, saying this is going to take blood, sweat, and tears. He wasn't making it easy. We've seen Franklin Roosevelt who told us "the only thing we have to fear is fear itself." And then there are those leaders who rule by fear and who say, "be very afraid" and "I alone can protect you" or "I alone can fix it." So there are two ways to move people— through love and hope, or through fear. And both are effective. It behooves us to know what string is being jerked in our own psyches by the stories we are being told about what reality is. Is the future going to be terrible unless we go with this leader, or that one? If we don't have fear, can we actually use our faith to build something, and build it better than it has ever been? That's the choice offered Americans in this particular election.

Jonathan: So when the story doesn't match up with what we see, then there's a dissonance when the politician says, "Don't believe your lying eyes. Trust me." We hear one thing, and we see another. How do we process the conflict between the reality that we're experiencing and the myth that we're being sold?

Betty Sue: I think both stories are always consonant, but they're consonant with different things. So someone who says "things are terrible and they're going to get worse unless…" tells a story consonant with your fears. If you're living in fear of change or fear of what's happening, or fear of the images you see on television, that is how you experience reality. So both candidates are telling stories that match people's vision of reality. It just depends on what reality you're in tune with. And they're both very powerful realities. The fear on the inside, or what you see as facts on the ground outside.

Betty: What you're saying reminds me of psychoanalyst Jerome Bruner's term "narrative need."[2] According to Bruner, we will stick with certain stories, whether realistic or not, which feed our psychic and emotional needs. So right now the narrative needs of people with very different perspectives and experiences are apparent in the conflicting stories folks are telling, with the same set of facts. Either Biden's going to allow us to rebuild better than ever, or he will squander our ability to be great again. Either Trump is going to erode U.S. democracy, or he is the agent of its salvation. Great swaths of people in this country are interpreting the facts of 2020 extremely differently. Some people are far more fearful or angry than others. How do we make ourselves aware—as we aim to do on this show—of how stories function and act on us, so that we can be more conscious of their influence? You essentially say myths drive us almost unconsciously—for example, we're being driven unconsciously by the economic myth. How do we raise our awareness—outside of talking about it on a podcast?

Betty Sue: Well, speaking about it here is one good way. It really is. Another good way is to realize the plotline of the stories you're telling about yourself. I have an exercise that I do where I have you find a partner and tell them the story of your life as a hero story and then as a victim story and then as if there were a purpose to life, and so on. The facts of your life are there, but you can put any genre of plot onto them you wish. The victim story is the same as the hero story, just with the agency reversed. So if we knew how to see and analyze the stories we're telling ourselves about reality, and if we could listen critically with an analytical mind to the stories that are being sold to us—whether sold to us to buy things or sold to us to vote for someone—then we would start to become more conscious. We could take the stories that are intended to move us and test them against the largest values we have—say, love and inclusiveness. If we tested these stories against the highest values we have, I think we would get clues as to which are the better stories to act on.

---

[2] Bruner, J. (1991). The Narrative Construction of Reality. *Critical Inquiry* 18(1), 1–21. DOI: 0093-1896/91/1801-0002.

Betty: You wrote about love as being a real component of how we move the economic myth into a far more collective and interconnected myth.[3] Can you say more about how love might move us differently from say, winning or losing—or being right or wrong—or being reasoned or irrational?

Betty Sue: To me, love is very closely connected to truth and beauty. One of the things artists show us is that anything can be appreciated. This is true of the beautiful diversity of this world. The way that difference is wonderful, and the way that we can stop and appreciate, rather than bully someone else with our way of being, is a way to express a kind of love. I'm always amused to see grandparents show pictures of their grandchildren. All babies look a little like Winston Churchill, yet the first thing grandparents say is "Aren't they beautiful?" The appreciation of beauty is akin to a form of objective love. The flower you find beautiful is not doing anything for you. That's not its purpose. It just is. And it's beautiful in its own being and diversity. I once worked in a science lab, and late one night, while I was transcribing a German scientific paper for the professor I worked for, I overheard the graduate students in the lab next door saying, "Oh, isn't it beautiful? Oh, it's so beautiful." And I thought, what in the world are they talking about? I went over and discovered they were talking about their laboratory animals, which were cockroaches from all over the world. They had looked at these darn cockroaches for so long that they made distinctions of beauty among them. That experience has really stayed with me. If we just look at anything long enough, we can appreciate its being in the world. Or as the poet Auden put it in "Precious Five," "Bless what there is for being."[4] If we fostered our ability to see beauty everywhere, we would have a world focused on appreciation for difference, not this addiction to perfection, according to what we narrowly think perfection should be.

Betty: What better place to end—on beauty and appreciation. We want to thank you, Betty Sue, so much for having this conversation with us. It's been a pleasure.

Betty Sue: It's been a pleasure for me, too. Thank you, Betty. And thank you, Jonathan.

---

[3] Flowers, B.S. (2006). *The American Dream and the Economic Myth*. Fetzer Institute.

[4] W. H. Auden, *Collected Shorter Poems* (London: Faber, 1966), 288.

Chapter 28
When Myth Becomes History

Guest: Jules Cashford
Episode Aired: January 20, 2021

Jules Cashford is a Jungian analyst who writes on mythology. She studied philosophy at St. Andrews University and postgraduate literature at Cambridge, where she was a Supervisor in Tragedy for Trinity College for some years. Her books include The Moon: Symbol of Transformation, The Mysteries of Osiris, *a translation of* The Homeric Hymns, *and (coauthored)* The Myth of the Goddess: Evolution of an Image. *She is the coeditor of* When the Soul Remembers Itself: Ancient Greece, Modern Psyche *and has made three films on* Gaia: Mother Goddess Earth, The Eleusinian Mysteries, *and* The Return of Gaia *and two films on Jan van Eyck.*

While our episode aired on January 20, 2021, we recorded the following conversation with Jules within ten days following the January 6, 2021 siege on the U.S. Capitol. This violent insurgency was instigated by right-wing Trump-supporting extremists whose goal was to stop the House of Representatives from ratifying the results of the 2020 presidential election, in which Joe Biden unseated Donald Trump. In our conversation with Jules, we aimed to recruit her expertise in myth, history, and the American Constitution to make sense of such chaos, where self-described "patriots" ransacked the U.S. Capitol and threatened elected members of Congress to stop ratification of election results that had been confirmed by all states to be fair and accurate.

At this writing, in the two years since the January 6, 2021 insurrection, the House Select Committee to Investigate the January 6 Attack thoroughly investigated the attack, identifying Donald Trump as one of the main instigators of the violence. With this awareness, our discussion with Jules about how dangerous it can be when myth becomes history—when individuals like Trump and his supporters conflate their grandiose stories about themselves with reality—takes on a deeper resonance. The January 6, 2021, siege is a prime example of a potent, psyche-polis collision, revealing the destabilization in society and government that can result when a people resort to violence to insist that their individual myths be recognized as universal reality.

Interview

Jonathan: I am exhausted, Betty. I don't mind telling you. I am glued to the TV. I'm watching every minute. I'm reading every article. I'm watching the videos as they continue to pour out from cellphones and other devices that were in the Capitol at that siege a couple of weeks ago on January 6, 2021. And the more we learn, the more I want to know, the more I want to understand what was going through the minds of these people. Why were they there? What were they hoping to achieve? It's incredibly unsettling.

Betty: Is it a shock, or are you over the shock?

Jonathan: You know, I'm afraid of the normalization of it, frankly. We need to be shocked. We need to be outraged. We need to recognize that this is not normal. We need heavy consequences and reckoning.

Betty: And I think we really need to think about this, as you are doing. You are trying to mull this over and look at everything. I'm doing the same thing. How could this be—and where did this come from? Because it didn't happen overnight.

Jonathan: And how do we prevent it from ever happening again? That's where the reckoning comes in. It's incredibly difficult to process because not only is there an overwhelming volume of content and conversation, but we are also experiencing it in real time. We don't yet have the objectivity of time and distance from these events that are ruling our lives at the moment.

Betty: That's the paradoxical nature of being overwhelmed. You're in it and you're consumed by it, and you're feeling it and flooded by it. And yet you can't have distance from it to think, which is our objective here—to be able to think about the chaos, to make sense of the nonsense.

Jonathan: What wonderful timing that we have an expert here who will help ground us with context for history, for mythology, and who has a remote detachment from these events, which may give a more nuanced understanding of what it is that we're experiencing. Jules Cashford joins us from her home in the UK. Thank you so much for being with us, Jules.

Jules Cashford: Well, thank you very much for inviting me. It's a great privilege.

Jonathan: You are an outside observer of American politics and an expert on myth and history. I wonder from your perspective, Jules, what is the view from abroad of Donald Trump's second impeachment and this seditionist siege on the Capitol? What does it look like to see insurrectionists in fur pelts and horned Viking helmets and warpaint storming the U.S. Capitol?

Jules: What a question! It looks absolutely incredible. It is something that we could never, ever, ever have believed. And yet somehow it is also something that we could have anticipated if we had begun at the beginning of Trump's presidency to see the divisiveness of the way that he thought—how, right at the beginning, he encouraged the "lock her up" chanting about Hillary Clinton. I suppose from abroad it's inconceivable anyone would say that about their opponent. We can be over-English and over-polite, which doesn't help, either. But the level of sneer is unprecedented. That it is acknowledged and applauded is what's so frightening. You sort of wonder if you haven't seen this coming all along. And then, of course, you can overdo that too. But it is a culmination. It doesn't come up completely out of the blue, does it?

Jonathan: I think it's really instructive for us to think back to the beginning of Trump's attacks on Hillary Clinton. I'm reminded of his attacks on Hillary when just last week, reportedly, Donald Trump said to his vice president, "Either you're a patriot or a pussy."

Jules: Yes.

Jonathan: The paradigm that Donald Trump is laying out there uses gender and sneer to attack Pence in a personal way that harkens back to those earliest attacks on Hillary Clinton.

Jules: He's bullying Pence in that moment, isn't he? He's threatening him because he dared to disagree with Trump.

Jonathan: Absolutely.

Jules: "If you don't go with me, you're going to be in trouble." And that's what he's said to so many people. And that's really what was happening in the Capitol. They weren't going with him.

Betty: Jules, from the perspective of the UK, you have written about liberty and freedom and the U.S. Constitution and the Statue of Liberty, which are icons of American democracy. Looking at this bullying, looking at this aggression, and through your expertise in myth and philosophy and history, how do you make sense of what is coming out? What is rooted in our attitudes about liberty and freedom here in the United States?

Jules: I think that freedom means various things to different groups of people in the United States. Perhaps the U.S. is more polarized because it's such a big country, and also because people live different kinds of lives, more so than, say, in England or Scotland or Wales. And you wonder if the people who Donald Trump appeals to have felt so disenfranchised, so lacking in the freedoms that more metropolitan people and—what we would call "the establishment" in England—enjoy. Trump supporters have felt sided out, really, and he spoke for them, and they enjoyed it. When I listened to his talks, I think, "Oh goodness, don't be so divisive." But from their point of view, they're thinking, "Someone's on our side for once. Nobody's been on our side."

If we are being psychological, we might want to see their embrace of Trump as a projection of their own sovereignty. At the same time, we also have to say that Trump projects his own sovereignty onto the Office of the President. He unites his supporters' projection of their sovereignty onto him with the projection of his own sovereignty onto the Office of the President. He's doing the really forbidden thing to do with archetypes—which is to identify yourself with one. That is to say that once Donald Trump, the man, has identified himself with the Office of the President, he becomes like a king. Therefore, he's not subject to the checks and balances that the rest of us are, as if he were a king in old England. But now, ironically, even in modern England the kings and queens are subject to checks and balances in their power. You asked me what it looks like from abroad, and it's astonishing to see that your president is acting like a king from old England, which is precisely what you Americans broke away from. You demanded freedom and wouldn't be colonized by a wretchedly miserable, disgraceful king. Your country is founded on freedom from an authoritarian ruler in the hopes that it would liberate our feelings and make us more welcome to life, rather than having to defend ourselves from a bad ruler.

Jonathan: And yet here we are. We elected this wretched king, right? And so it was democracy that brought us there. I'm struck by your writings, Jules, where you said in ancient cultures, the moral character of the leader was believed to have consequences for all the people and even for the land itself. So, what does it say about us in light of Donald Trump's moral failings?

Jules: Well, it's rich. It should start the other way round, really. I mean, what does it say about Trump, first? Because after all, this comes from Oedipus in ancient Greece. Even though he didn't know he was doing it, Oedipus made the mistake of killing his father and marrying his mother. And, therefore, the land of Thebes begins to die. He fights it, of course, as we would. He's then sent off to the Delphic oracle who gives him the truth of what has happened. We took the lesson that the land suffered from the king's failings. Of course, this could also be a myth for our time: the devastation of COVID-19 over the world might be warning all of us that we are failing in our relationship to Earth.

And I'm not sure that this isn't somehow particularly linked to Trump's priorities. I don't know, maybe you could tell me. Is there a link between that way of thinking in which the land suffers from the king's failings and the fact that Trump ignored the pandemic, and it has increased and everybody is suffering?

Betty: The metaphor, or the ancient story of Oedipus and the fact that Thebes suffers because he has done this dark crime, does perhaps mirror the fact that something was wrong in our land, which may have been made manifest by the COVID-19 pandemic. COVID-19 has exacerbated many issues in the United States, more so than in other parts of the world, shockingly to us. Not only has the pandemic illuminated the illness of the leader, but it has pointed out the previous illnesses in the land that were sitting there, illnesses that this leader has ignored for five years and may have been the result of his denials of these ills. We have this perennial debate as to whether Donald Trump is the cause or symptom of all of this. And that's a big question right now, after the January 6 insurrection. Was this attack last week because of Donald Trump? We can say yes, but weren't these issues already embedded before Trump's rise to power? Can you say more about what happens when a democratic leader over identifies with an archetype such as the king? What happens when history becomes myth? I think that is really an important concept, and it might help us hold what's going on a little bit better. Has history become a myth?

Jules: Yes, it's a very important question.

I think it brings us eventually to the problem of freedom. How do we interpret freedom—as a gift, or a right, or a responsibility, or all three and more? For instance, let's focus on just one example of what this could mean: the refusal of Trump's followers to wear face masks because he says so, because they are "free" not to wear the masks. Well, of course, everybody has that freedom not to, but that's just the first part of it. The second part never seems to follow, which is the responsibility to other people's freedom—that the people who come toward us with their masks also have a right to their freedom not to be possibly infected by our not wearing them. And it seems to me that what Trump has done is to inflate himself completely into the role of presidency, of kingship, of being all powerful. Of being the God, really, the One who can do whatever he likes and what he likes is right.

Betty: Indeed.

Jules: That's what we call an inflation. We can all get caught in it occasionally, can't we? And then, when we come back down from our inflation and look at ourselves afterward, at how "high and mighty" we were, we feel a bit ashamed of how ridiculous we were. But, with Trump, his inflation is a permanent state of being, and we can't wait until he comes down or topples down. If we listen to Trump's niece, this has always been the case.[1] His inflation has been fed by his family and by his money and by the way he deals with people. And by how he gets away with everything!

Jonathan: Right, lack of restraint in everything.

Jules: Yes, lack of restraint.

---

[1] Mary Trump, Trump's niece, is the daughter of Fred Trump, former President Trump's oldest brother. She published a book entitled *Too Much and Never Enough* (New York: Simon and Schuster, 2020) critical of Trump and the Trump family.

Jonathan: Just unchecked.

Jules: Yes, that's the shadow side of freedom, isn't it?

Jonathan: When we're talking about freedom as a concept in society, community, government, it has never been suggested by anyone that it should go unchecked. It's always been a regulated freedom. When did it get metastasized so that freedom means, "I can do whatever I goddamn please?"

Jules: Well, I think it's whatever Trump goddamn pleases. I mean Trump seems to believe that what he thinks is free *is* free. Don't you think? I'm quite sure that if Trump told everyone of the Republican troop to wear a mask, they would wear one.

Jonathan: Yes, I think that's right.

Jules: So it's directly linked to the inflation of the leader.

Betty: Stable governments are identified by their ability to have peaceful transitions of power. The events on January 6 show that we are not so stable anymore. We could not have a peaceful transition of power between Trump and Biden. Individuals who assert their freedom to not wear a mask—or members of Congress who insist on their freedom to carry a gun into the House chamber—these attitudes are not just borne from Donald Trump's cultish megalomania. Insistence on a relentless individualism versus taking collective responsibility is a tense dichotomy we have wrestled with in the United States for a long time. Is this uniquely American? There were people who stormed Congress wearing pelts and furs, and we wondered if this was some symbolic evocation of a Daniel Boone–like pioneer spirit of freedom retaking government. I wonder what you think about that, given that you've looked deeply at how things have become mythologized?

Jules: Yes, I certainly think that this is a return to the original wildness of freedom based on the attitude, "You can do whatever you feel like." And, as you say—relentless individualism—it's the same with the Second Amendment. It's almost like the Constitution is such a sacred text that it can't be rethought or adapted at all. Whereas we know that we're all evolving—

especially with weapons. I mean, the Second Amendment couldn't have dreamt of machine guns that could finish people off in Las Vegas with a bump stock attachment.[2] And yet if you try to say, "Could this be updated?" you get a "No that's my creed. That's my belief. It can't happen." And Trump, of course, endorsed that because that's what comes from his base. I mean, there is a kind of narcissistic internecine relationship with his base, whereby they feed off each other, don't you think?

Betty: Absolutely, absolutely.

Jules: And therefore, and if you can't update—and I don't exactly mean "update the Constitution" because that's obviously the wrong language—but if you can't sort of massage it a little bit into the future…

Jonathan: It's a dangerous period. I think what you're talking about is that the myth is overtaking actual history. To say that the Constitution is a sacred text is buying into the mythology of it because how can it be a sacred text if it has amendments written into it? The very fact that amendments exist demonstrates that the Constitution was not perfect, that it was mutable. The very fact that gun rights, to the extent that they exist at all in the Constitution, are embodied in the Second Amendment demonstrates that the Constitution is mutable and can evolve with time.

Betty: Right.

Jules: And that's even subject to different interpretations. It doesn't actually say everybody can have the right to bear arms.

Jonathan: No, absolutely not.

Jules: Yes, I think that's absolutely right. History has become mythical in the image of the—shall we say—inflated king who wants it that way. And that's terribly dangerous.

---

[2] This refers to the October 1, 2017, mass shooting at a music festival in which sixty people were killed and scores injured.

Jonathan: Right. So once myth gets confused with history, you've said that the myth becomes destructive.

Jules: Yes.

Jonathan: And I'm wondering if there are any examples that run counter to that maxim. I mean, is it the fate of every myth that it will inevitably become confused with real life and, therefore, always become destructive? Or are there some myths that actually work constructively?

Betty: Before that, can you describe some of the mechanisms by which it becomes dangerous when history becomes myth?

Jules: Joseph Campbell's *The Hero with a Thousand Faces* is brilliant on this, but basically a myth—like the myth of freedom and of the beautiful goddess of liberty—they reach down much deeper into our psyches than we probably realize.[3] We're moved by them, and then we get inspired. And it's that deep-down place where we have to go with an honest state of mind, or else it can overwhelm us and lead us to believe we can do whatever we feel like. We can justify what we do because we feel it so passionately. So, it's really about the relationship of the conscious to the unconscious that decides whether a myth is going to be destructive.

If the passion of the myth is allowed to go wherever it feels like, we're into different levels of the psyche, aren't we? We are in the mythic level, which is usually mediated to us through poetry or song or dance, etc. It requires a containment to it, perhaps because it, as it were, knows how dangerous it can be. If our own little stories suddenly become larger than ourselves, then that's very dangerous because we embody a level of the psyche that doesn't belong to us. We can do anything—like Hitler, we become all powerful. So, you can't possibly lose an election. It's got to have been stolen.

I don't know if Trump actually believes the election was stolen, but you could understand if he did, because it would come from this confusion, this conflation of myth and history. And myth and history should very much be kept apart. Usually myth dies once it comes into history, and you just carry on. Then you're not as inspired as you were once. But suppose myth doesn't die when it comes into history. Suppose it's fueled by a mythic person who's

---

[3] Campbell, J. (1959). *The Hero with a Thousand Faces*. Pantheon Books.

making that connection with the myth himself ultimately, that *he* is the myth. Then that myth can go anywhere. We have seen it throughout history. I mean, we've seen how the Third Reich came out of nowhere when Hitler came out of prison.

Betty: Right.

Jules: It's the rhetoric and the poetry of myth. What I'm trying to say is that the poetry of myth moves us beyond ourselves. And that's very dangerous if we attach it to a historical position that we want. Because then we get the worst of ourselves, which says, "What I want I should have," mixed up with some of the best of ourselves, which says, "Look, of course, everybody's born free; of course we should have freedom." It can get very confusing, especially if we have a leader who confuses them for us in everything he does and who praises us when we follow him.

Betty: I think it sounds like myth has a different tenor and function than fantasy. There's a way in which we can all imagine ourselves as heroes prevailing over dark forces or opposing forces in a metaphorical sense. But if it becomes concretized, if you actually imagine yourself as the, say, pioneering hero attacking what you conceive to be your enemies in the U.S. Capitol, that is not symbolic. That is a literal act.

Jules: Yes.

Betty: This conflation between myth and history is almost like a literalization of myth into actual events. This is dangerous because the power and the emotions that are wild and bigger than us can be destructive—and aggression, anger, and fear are best contained by art and interpreted and digested that way.

Jules: Yes, absolutely.

Betty: So then this is what's happening. We—or some people, through Donald Trump's permission or aegis—are concretizing these big feelings of aggression and frustration and making them real. They are acting them out.

Jonathan: Right. They existed long before Trump, but Trump uncorked the bottle. He brought them out and he said…

Jules: He ratified them.

Jonathan: Yes, he ratified them. Exactly. I wonder how damaged America is—within ourselves and in our world-standing—by this moment that has been the Donald Trump presidency. De Tocqueville said, "America is great because she is good, and if America ceases to be good, she will cease to be great." Have we lost our standing, or do we have an opportunity for redemption?

Jules: Well, of course, there's an opportunity for redemption, but I do think that something serious has to be done to separate from Donald Trump's actions. And it's really disheartening to see so many Republicans *not* thinking that. They have put their party beyond their country, and you can't do that at a time like this. I think if they don't do something radical like reject Trump then I think it will damage the standing of America—for Americans themselves, most primarily. This really matters much more than what anybody else thinks.

Betty: Well, the hypocrisy is writ large and, Jules, this is what you're addressing. Many Republicans gave ratification to the lie of the 2020 election "steal" by defending it in the House and in the Senate. The facts clearly show that it was not stolen. And yet these congressional members, they make it real by advocating for it. And so I wonder, Jules, if by turning a lie into reality, they are making myth into history.

Jules: Yes. Absolutely!

Betty: And that is where Donald Trump's alchemy, dark as it is, works in this mixed-up place we are in. He lost, but he won for some people. So you can't ever lose because all you need to do then is twist reality into the version you want it to be. Is that right, Jules? You're always in the myth. You're always myth-making.

Jules: Yeah, you're always in the right. Nothing else can happen. In many cases, honest people in Georgia went through every single vote by hand.

That's never mentioned. I find it fascinating that I haven't heard anybody come back with "yes, something was wrong, but they carried on three times, and by hand, and still Trump and his followers are accusing God knows how many people in Georgia of doing all that day's work and then another day and another day's for nothing. Are you assuming they're all lying? And why would they do that?"

Jonathan: Because people are only useful to Donald Trump as long as they agree with him. And then once they don't, even if it's because facts suggest that they shouldn't, then they become an obstacle.

Jules: Yes. It's almost like kindergarten. Whenever you win, there's no problem. But whenever somebody else does, then they cheat. I mean, it's one of the first lessons we learn, isn't it? That there's an objective reality.

Betty: It speaks to the primal nature of Trump's psychology, or his psyche. He's very toddler-like and that's been extensively commented upon. And his followers seem to join him in that infantile state, or he brings that out in them. And I wonder, Jules, looking at United States historically, in its mythology of prioritizing liberty and freedom—if we assess the moment we're sitting in, where this recent transition of power has not been peaceful, and our democracy is unstable, do you feel like we can recapture the distinction between history and myth?

Jules: Yes, of course! But it does seem important to trace every single lie, and reinstate, as it were, the factual level of things: evidence, proof, logic. Not just a statement that there is fraud—coming from a conviction that there must have been cheating or Trump would not have lost. In logic there's even a name for this kind of so-called argument—the *a priori argument*. What I hear quite a lot is that there's so many of these so-called arguments that people can't keep up with them.

Jonathan: It's a torrent.

Jules: And they can't say that's not true. How do you know? Oh, it's true. Well, what are your criteria? Oh, you don't need any. It's just that no one ever challenges him, as far as I can see, because they'd be kicked out by then. I mean, that's kingship, isn't it? No one ever gets to the end of it except his niece, who is wonderful, but he's never accountable. He's never asked to be accountable for anything. And no one ever asks the questions, that I can hear, except in tones of despair, but never personally to him. He never has to answer the question. And I've been thinking so much about how he never actually says anything. It's like a sort of movement on a dance floor. It's like a way to create a snare and an opposition and a further inflation of himself, and each time he talks, it's almost like he gets larger and larger.

Jonathan: But it's so transparent, isn't it? I mean, it's such an obvious grift. It's so obvious and facile that it continues to astound me.

Betty: And yet, interestingly, it's working. It worked.

Jonathan: And that this is the party of law and order that has not only cheated its way to this position, but now he's just overturned the table. He's no longer even cheating. They are just ransacking the Capitol.

Jules: The irony is that it takes a technical company to shut him up.

Betty: Right—you mean, Twitter and Facebook.

Jonathan: They should have done it four years ago.

Betty: There's a cynical view that they were making too much money on Trump's outrageousness up until this moment. There's little loss in cutting him off now that he's not going to be president anymore.

I think that's something to note—we are speaking on the advent of Joe Biden's presidency, and we are *still* talking about Donald Trump. I'm sure that's a mark of the continued impact of his psychopathology. However, in this moment in which so many historic things are happening, it's hard to even process. There's this raid on the U.S. Capitol, which is absolutely unprecedented; a second impeachment of a president of the United States, which is still hard for me to make sense of— "impeached again" just sounds like an absurdist joke. There is a question of a transition of power that is unstable in the United States. And we are obscuring the very interesting and monumental fact that we have just elected a first vice president who is a woman and a person of color. That almost gets left out altogether. And Joe

Biden is going to become the president with a majority rule in the Senate, which we didn't think was going to happen.

So, Jules, how do you consider all this with your perspectives on myth, politics, and history? How can we use your expertise to think about this differently and perhaps more creatively than, say, folks do on CNN and MSNBC and Fox News?

Jules: I would have thought it would start by stopping the obsession with what Trump says, thinks, and does, that he should just not be spoken of, if possible. If you can't count on the truth from someone then there isn't even a dialogue, and who needs another lie?

And leave it to the banks! I mean, there are other people whom he might listen to, as it were, because he has to. And I think what we're doing now, we have had to do, but we're at the end of it. We're nearly at the end of talking about Trump, hopefully...

Jonathan: Let's hope.

Betty: Yes.

Jules: Perhaps it should only be thought of as a mirror to something good that's happening from now on. I would have thought that the best thing that we could do is simply embrace Joe Biden and try to protect him and Kamala Harris from the people who will look for everything they can to run them down—in the name of Trump, presumably. But the thing is, Trump's *not* gone, is he? I mean, he's not going to go, unless he's sort of frozen out.

Betty: We may have to do something like banish him from our minds.

Jonathan: He whose name must not be mentioned.

Betty: Yeah, right.

Jules: Well, it's a start!

Betty: This is something that we have to mull over and have to think about as we put the lens of psychology onto politics. How do we think about this in a different way and make sense of such nonsense? I think your wisdom of not giving fuel to the attention-fire of Donald Trump might be a great way to conclude our conversation.

Jonathan: I have a question for the two of you, though, before we go, because I need insight from the mental health professionals. Given that the U.S. electorate, and perhaps the world, has become so addicted, for better and for worse, to the chaos that has defined the Trump era, how will our minds adapt, reset to the predictable boredom of a technocratic professional who is not keeping us at these manic levels of highs and lows with every news cycle? Are we capable of adapting back to some normal set of predictable behaviors and emotions, or are we going to need the fix?

Jules: I think one of the things that keeps us going on Trump is that we have the delusion that we can convince anyone through argument, and we are absolutely nuts to carry on thinking that. And I can't prevent myself from thinking about arguing with him every moment I see him. But I know at the same time it's wrong. So maybe we can actually just give up that obsession. Maybe we should just let it go and focus on curing people, on healing the pandemic.

When we're in these obsessional states, it helps when we do something most precise and particular. We set ourselves some limited goal, and we don't mind the noise, and we don't care if anybody agrees with us. We just do a little bit and then a little bit more. And it's a goal that's a good one. And that's enough, really. I think his inflation doesn't help our own anti-inflation on him. It almost becomes a kind of wrong relationship. Certainly, speaking for myself, I know, as some people raise their eyes when I start to talk about Trump. I definitely understand and I try not to, but you know what I mean, probably.

Betty: Absolutely.

Jules: I think just listening to Joe Biden's talk, it's very precise and particular, and it's measured. And if we just followed the next stage and tried to help people not be ill, that is enough, isn't it, to be getting on?

Jules: That would probably cure us a little, letting him go—do you think?

Betty: I think that's well said, Jules. What you're both pointing to is that there's an addictive quality to what has been going on. And so we need to recognize that—which is what we're doing right now—and detox. We have to go into rehab. That is, we need to start to take ourselves off this drug. It is a relief. And we have to take care, just like you were saying, Jules. Heal, take care of the pandemic, deal with healthcare, deal with the economic crisis, focus on wellness. And I think that will actually help settle the ills of all of this over-anxiety and uncontained aggression and rage. It sounds simplistic, but as you say Jules, Joe Biden himself is really focused on this. And I think it's the right way forward.

Jules: I think that's a beautiful way of putting it.

Jonathan: Thank you. It's a wonderful prescription. Thank you so much for joining us.

Jules: It's been lovely to talk to you. Really, it has.

Chapter 29
The Symbolic Power of Trump's Wall

Guest: Dr. Thomas Singer
Episode Aired: January 29, 2019

Thomas Singer, MD, is a Jungian psychoanalyst and psychiatrist with a lifelong interest in symbols. Tom is president of ARAS, the Archive for Research into Archetypal Symbolism. He has been researching cultural complexes in different parts of the world and written several books on the subject, including Cultural Complexes and the Soul of America, Europe's Many Souls, *and* Cultural Complexes in China, Japan, Korea, and Taiwan. *In addition, he coedited the Modern Greece/Ancient Psyche series.*

Although we posted this episode—our first—on January 29, 2019, it was recorded a couple of weeks earlier, during the first week of the year. At the time, the U.S. was less than a week into a government shutdown, the result of a dispute between President Trump and congressional Democrats over funding of a proposed wall along the U.S./ Mexico border intended to keep illegal immigrants from Mexico—whom Trump had frequently referred to as "rapists," "gang members," and "animals"—from entering the U.S.[1] It is key to remember he ran his 2016 presidential campaign on a harsh anti-immigrant platform, with a promise that he would build such a wall along the southern border of the U.S. To fulfill this promise, Trump refused to sign an appropriations bill funding the federal government until it included funds to build the wall. The shutdown was the longest in U.S. history, lasting more than a month—from December 22, 2018 until January 25, 2019. That the U.S. federal government was forced to a standstill,

---

[1] Oliphant, J. & Esposito, A. (2018). Trump Says 'Animal' Comment Refers to Criminals, Mexico Protests. *Reuters,* https://www.reuters.com/article/us-usa-immigration-mexico/ trump-says-animals-comment-refers-to-criminals-mexico-protests-idUSKCN1II2AT.

halting crucial services to millions and freezing the salaries of hundreds of thousands of government workers due to Trump's insistence on funding for a physical border wall was a prime example of a political event that had deep psychological drivers. We turned to Tom, an expert on psychology, myth, and politics, to break down the myriad meanings— symbolic, psychological, and political—of Trump's wall and help us make sense of such political nonsense.

Interview

Michael: Tom, why should we talk about symbols, or more to the point, why should we talk about the symbolism of Trump's wall? Why does it matter?

Thomas: The reason why talking about symbolism at all, and about the symbolism of Trump's wall, in particular, is important, is because the way we hear and think about the wall in the media's portrayal of the battle between Congress and the White House reveals that it is all about emotion. And the power of a symbol is its ability to tap into deep collective emotion, emotion in both the individual and large groups of people. Symbols are particularly good—and they have been, ever since humans have been roaming the Earth—at evoking deep emotions, which short circuit any kind of rational understanding or explanation of things. A symbolic understanding allows us to grasp that what we're responding to has deep emotional origins. It is the key to the emotionality of the responses people have to, say, the wall.

Michael: So, a symbol has meaning, right?

Tom: A symbol has more than one meaning. A sign would have just one meaning. If you see a red light, it means "don't go through this intersection." That's a sign. A symbol, on the other hand—like the cross or the swastika— has multiple meanings, even for one individual. A symbol carries meaning, and its capacity to carry many meanings simultaneously that evoke our deepest human emotions makes it extremely powerful. Currently, all you have to do is say, "the wall" and you're off to the races in terms of the emotionality and the multiple meanings that it evokes in many people.

Betty: Tom, are you saying that symbols drive us in the sense that they evoke our emotions?

Tom: Symbols do drive us in the same way as a locomotive would. If you look at the ancient cave paintings discovered in France and other parts of the world—in Australia and so on—they're all symbolic images. They're mostly about hunter-gatherers, and they're often magical, potent images, but also ritual actions that drive people to action and to deep feeling.

Michael: It's interesting. A second ago you said, "The wall." You just have to mention those words, and they evoke feelings of being either for or against keeping immigrants out of the U.S. But we don't say *a* wall. It's *the* wall, and it has already become an object, a physical thing, even though it hasn't been built.

Tom: That is a really important point, because it's as if "the wall" is already real to us in our individual and group psyche—even though the actual wall, as Trump envisions it, hasn't been built. It is as if it's already alive. And that's what a living symbol does. It comes alive, whether or not it actually exists physically.

Betty: How does it drive us? If you see a symbol, like the swastika or the cross—as you mentioned—and now there's the wall, what about these symbols moves us?

Tom: Well, it goes to the core of our deepest concerns, which, at their core, are about survival itself. If you can touch something in a group of people or an individual that calls into question their very survival, you can bet you're going to get a strong reaction. "The wall" is about survival, at least in many people's minds. It's about whether we continue to exist as a particular kind of America or not. So the wall actually is about American survival, as Trump has offered it to us.

Michael: And he's brilliant. As a Jungian, Tom, I'm curious about your analysis of how Trump talks about the wall—factually. Let me just stop for just a second and play a mashup of audio clips of Trump on the 2016 campaign trail talking about the wall.

> ***Donald Trump:*** *First of all, I want to build a wall. I will build a great, great wall. On day one, we will begin working on an impenetrable, physical, tall, powerful, beautiful southern border wall. And it's a real wall. This is a*

wall that's a heck of a lot higher than the ceiling. And we're going to have that big, beautiful door in the wall. They built the Great Wall of China. That's 13,000 miles. Here we actually need 1000 because we have natural barriers. The wall's probably 8 billion dollars, maybe 10 or 12 billion dollars. The wall is peanuts. Remember this, the wall will be paid for by Mexico. Mexico is going to pay for the wall 100 percent. And I would build a wall like nobody can build a wall. I build great buildings all over the world. What's more complicated is building a building that's 95 stories tall.

Tom: The first thing I want to say in listening to that tape, Michael, is I'm actually more impressed with the reaction of the crowd than I am with Trump's words, because what he's playing for is that tremendous emotional excitement that he generates in people, which we hear in these clips. People are thrilled by what Trump is saying.

That's what I mean by the emotionality of the symbol. Now, what I would say about Trump's use of that—it's interesting that he refers to the Great Wall of China, which was built well before the birth of Christ—I think two or three or four hundred years before the birth of Christ.[2] He's already comparing himself and his creation to one of the greatest creations in human history.

Michael: And that's in keeping with the man, isn't it? Not a lot of humility.

Tom: No, he is not known for his humility. He is known for his grandiosity or his sense of his own largeness and bigness. And he's equating himself with his ability to build as an individual, but to the people who are listening to him, that translates into our largeness as a nation and to "making America great again." So he has a lot going on in the wall. He's packing that all into the physical structure of the wall, which he compares to the Great Wall of China. And that's a symbol—that's the power of a symbol to move, to recruit the emotions.

Michael: It's fascinating because on the other side of this debate is a rational discussion—whether that's for a different notion of immigration policy or the fact that building a wall across the southern border of the

---

[2] The Great Wall of China was built over many centuries, from the 3rd century BCE to the 17th century CE.

U.S. is not practical or necessary. It's totally apples and oranges against what Trump and his supporters believe about this wall. To refer to evidence or information—you are talking past the people who show up at these rallies, who support Trump, who believe in the wall because they're not talking about facts. It seems "the wall" means something entirely different to them, which is well beyond rationality.

Tom: Yes, that's absolutely right. And the reason is that we're having a tremendous emotional debate in this country—a huge emotional debate— where there's very little room for actual rational dialogue, discourse, or exchange, because of the power of the emotionality. The reason you talk about symbols is to open up the discussion to include both the rational and the nonrational. You won't have a discussion until you let the nonrational in. And the symbol is carrying the nonrational.

We all need a sense of protective barriers between us and the unknown world, which is potentially dangerous, because it is outside of us. I was in Africa several years ago, and I witnessed a group of water buffalo under attack by a pride of lions. What was amazing to see was that the water buffaloes had a first line of defense. The old strong bulls created a protective barrier around the rest of the herd. And when a young water buffalo was separated by the lions, the bulls went out and pulled the young buffalo back in before the lions were able to eat it. What's even more amazing is that, when the older water buffalo in the defensive perimeter got tired, there was a second defensive line that came to replace them. Animals know about the need for a protective barrier. And what Trump's speaking to is our animal instinct about needing protective barriers. And this need gets concretized in the physical wall he wants to build, to protect us from dangerous attacks, whether they be from foreign drug dealers, criminals, terrorists, or whoever it is.

Michael: But the problem is that these beliefs about immigrants as foreign threats are often fictions. Trump is tapping into people's fears of "the other," and he's criminalizing people who are seeking refuge and asylum in the U.S. To build this wall, he's perverting and undermining the notion of America as a global beacon. You can't be a beacon for the world if you've closed yourself off. You can't perpetuate stories about streets paved with gold, about grandparents coming to America for opportunity, about immigrants coming to seek refuge from their homeland strife. I'm going to read a tweet.

Trump says, "Have Democrats finally realized the desperate need for border security and a wall on the southern border, need to stop drugs and human trafficking, gang members and criminals from coming into our country?"[3] Then he goes on, of course, to talk about the shutdown. "Do the Dems realize that most of the people not getting paid are Democrats?" It's a little silly, but it's also really pernicious, because he's made everybody on the other side of the wall—including whoever is opposed to it— "the other."

Tom: Yes. When I talk about the deep need for security and why the wall is so appealing to people, I'm not advocating or embracing Trump's notion of the wall. As a psychologist who understands the power of a symbol, I am trying to recognize what it is that moves people to embrace his ideas. It doesn't have to do with whether the origins of the fear are rational or not—often fears are not grounded in what's real. That's what makes them a powerful tool for people like Trump.

Betty: As you were saying before, you need to recruit both parts of the brain—the thinking and the emotional aspects of mind—to have a dialogue with folks who are driven by these emotions, who are compelled by these symbols. How do we do that? How do we have a dialogue with people who are very moved by this compelling notion of protection? I mean, I was even compelled by that wall speech. I'm surprised that I was. I even understand how emotion and fear operates on us. Trump's creating a negative fantasy— as you were both pointing out—and activating our survival brains. How do we use reality to ground us against being carried away by fear-based fantasy when it is used in these compelling ways?

Tom: That's a good reason to discuss symbols, because it helps to create the psychic space for people to begin to understand one another. And if you start off by saying to Trump supporters, "Everything you think and believe and feel is an illusion. It's not real. It's fear based. And you're crazy for embracing the idea of the wall…"

Michael: …then they hear it as an attack on them.

---

[3] Twitter, December 27, 2018

Betty: And they would probably feel insulted and think, "Oh, I'm not listening to them."

Tom: Yes. So you have to try to create a bridge, even if in today's climate, nobody is interested in creating bridges of mutual understanding. But my notion is, to create any kind of bridge of understanding, you need to walk around the symbol of the wall and talk about what it means. You need to consider the feelings that it evokes in people who are for or against it. That feels like an impossible task. But I don't know where else you begin.

Michael: You guys have brought up two provocative symbols—the symbol of the cross and the symbol of the swastika. But let's talk about America. As you guys were talking, I thought of the American flag, because it is a very powerful symbol, and it's been used politically as a very divisive symbol, which arguably, it should not be. I mean, we are all Americans. We can all have different emotional connections to our country. And yet the American flag is not a metaphor. It doesn't stand in for something else. It is its own living, breathing thing that has meaning for people. And it is so fascinating to me that we're now doing the same thing with the wall—and not even with a physical wall that exists—but a proposal for a wall, a heated conversation about a wall.

Betty: A fantasy wall.

Michael: A fantasy wall. But if you say a "fantasy wall"...

Betty: ...people get turned off.

Michael: Tom, what do you think? Am I wrong about this?

Tom: I think you're absolutely correct. In fact, the power of living symbols to move us with emotional reactivity is paralyzing the country. The symbol of the wall has brought the government to a standstill. It's amazing. But that's exactly the power of a symbol. It moves people because of its direct link to deep unconscious or preconscious or semiconscious emotional reactivity. You're in deep trouble when a group of people are seized by a collective emotion about which they can't think and there's no room to have discourse or dialog, yet that is exactly where we are. The symbol of the wall has shut down the government.

Michael: It's especially entrenched because it means security for some and it's a negative fantasy for others. If Trump gives up on the wall, by his own definition, he will have let the Mongol Horde through. He'll have physically imperiled the country. Yet on the other side stand those people who say that the symbol of the wall undermines the openness, the generosity, the freedom, the ideal of America as a refuge. It compromises the ideals of America, with which people are also emotionally caught. Those two things strike me as utterly incompatible. I don't see how we move forward.

Tom: That's precisely the point, Michael. That they are utterly incompatible, and the wall evokes the emotional reaction of their being utterly incompatible. It feels as though it can't be both. There is the need for security as opposed to the need for openness, warm heartedness, and generosity of spirit. They seem to be mutually exclusive. And when a symbol gets as concretized as that, you're stalemated.

Michael: You're immobilized.

Betty: Frozen.

Tom: I actually have the fantasy—and it's just a fantasy—that right now it's important for Trump to evoke and play with the symbol of the wall. And, as you suggested earlier, he is a master, because he needs his own wall right now. He is under ferocious attack, and it promises only to get worse in terms of the Mueller investigations and other House-led investigations.

So, when we talk about the wall at our southern border, we actually may be talking—this is one interpretation—about Trump's internal need for an impenetrable wall to protect his presidency. That is how confusing these things get. We may not even be talking about a wall to block immigrants at the southern border. The government may have come to a standstill because Trump personally is feeling so threatened and under attack that he is diverting and displacing this huge emotional energy onto something that was his original campaign promise, which was to get them—that is, immigrants—out of here. His very first campaign speeches were "to get them out of here." And the wall is the direct consequence of how powerfully people reacted to this declaration, whether it was against Latinos or Muslims or anybody who did not fit into his fantasy of who we are as a nation.

Betty: You were talking earlier, Tom, about this wall being protection against bodily threat, as a means for survival. Linking that to what you just said, this is not just about American survival. This is about Trump's own survival, or it has become enmeshed with it. It implies we are not surviving, because if we need to protect ourselves from attack, if we need to protect ourselves with a wall, that means there is a threatening force. Earlier you talked about our need for psychic space. Can you say more about what "psychic space" is?

Tom: If you're governed and motivated only by your deepest emotions, as you know well, Betty, it becomes impossible to have complex thoughts or to think at all because the emotion is so powerful. An emotion is not graciously inclusive. Emotion knows simply what it knows. If you're a fan of the New York Mets or the St. Louis Cardinals or whichever team you root for, you're not rooting for your opponent. You're only rooting for the victory of your own team. When you get emotionally engaged with an issue, the capacity for thinking diminishes, or it becomes so extremely oversimplified that there can be no discourse.

Michael: Tom, in John Kelly's[4] exit interviews he—and other people have mentioned this as well—has said, "Oh don't think about the wall as a wall. Think about the wall as a metaphor. Think about the wall as security. We know we're going to have drones and all these other high-tech things crossing over it." They have explicitly said, "The wall is a metaphor." Are they trying to find a way to walk back Trump's literal meaning? And are they going to be successful?

Tom: That was a very interesting set of exchanges about whether Trump was speaking literally and specifically about a physical wall. I agree, it was an attempt to walk it back and say, "Well it's just a metaphor." But then Trump immediately came back and said they misunderstood—he really is talking about a wall, a physical wall. He refused to let them walk him back because that is where his shrewdness comes through. He understands that the physical wall as a symbol should not be diluted into a metaphor because

---

[4] John Kelly was Trump's second Chief of Staff.

that's not where the emotional power of the symbol of a real wall lies. He wouldn't let them walk it back.

Michael: And metaphors and symbols are not the same.

Tom: Metaphors and symbols are not the same thing. A metaphor makes it more complex. It says, well, we have a wall here, and then we have some electronic devices there, and we have some more men over here. And that already makes it more complex. Whereas with a physical wall as a symbol, there's no complexity about it. It is what it is.

Michael: Right. Along these lines, I was thinking nobody gets all emotionally worked up over a metaphor, but you do get worked up over symbols. People get worked up over the flag as a powerful symbol. And the wall has become like that. If I can go back for just a second, you had said something that I found fascinating. You said Trump himself right now feels under assault with the Mueller investigation, the Democrats taking over Congress, the multiple subcommittees within Congress that are likely going to start subpoenaing him. Should we also be thinking about the wall in terms of the Russia investigation and all these other things happening to Trump? And if so, what hope do we have of shifting focus on Trump's wall? Are we going to keep having this conversation over and over again?

Tom: I think we are talking about multiple walls. There is the defensive wall that Trump has tried to build around himself in terms of the Russia case. And that does seem to be eroding, or at least there are cracks in that wall now. Things are quickening. The election of 2020 is suddenly upon us, and I think he wants to remobilize his base to get back to the core issues that they identified with.

But the wall is also not just about Trump, and it's not just about the United States. It's actually about the whole world. Europe is besieged with the same kinds of concerns about immigration. They are terribly afraid of what immigration means to their own societies. Trump is not just reflecting a peculiarly American symbolism and attitude over the very real challenges of immigration and migration, but his stance reflects a worldwide problem, which is how defensive do we have to become to protect our own interests? That's a basic, constant, and universal human concern about the tension between the individual versus the collective—and, in a related way, of psyche and polis.

Betty: I'm thinking about the fact of borders and walls and the global problem of human displacement and migration as it relates to globalization. What strikes me is how this symbol of a wall is so simple—it's even simplistic—in contrast to how complicated globalization is with multiple trade agreements between countries and multinational corporations who function as countries themselves. And the complexity of these things that we cannot fully understand unless we are experts—the financial markets, the 2007 derivatives meltdown, and then the burst of the housing market bubble, which I cite as the source of ongoing fears people have about the entire American economy nearly collapsing in ways in which few people can grasp, except for economists and experts on Wall Street.

Michael: And even if you do understand it, there's nothing you can do, right?

Betty: Exactly. And broadening it beyond Trump—Trump, himself, might equal simple, or a simple way of thinking. The wall is simple, and symbols are simple. And he may offer—or even represent—an antidote of simplicity against an increasingly complex and confusing world, which the internet and the information revolution has allowed us to know more about. I wonder, Tom, what you think of this—how the wall might also be compelling and comforting because it's so simple and uncomplicated?

Tom: I think you've nailed it, Betty. The first thing that comes to mind is that, while many of us oppose the wall for all the political and even philosophical reasons that we've already discussed, it's easy to overlook the positive function of a wall. As you were talking, Tibetan *thangkas* came to my mind, the paintings depicting a Buddhist deity or mandala. They're used for teaching and meditation. They sound very esoteric, but if you look at some of the deepest spiritual traditions in the religious world, in the religious mind, often when they represent what is most sacred, they are surrounded by a wall. You don't get access to what's most sacred without having protective barriers around it. That is what we in the Jungian world would call an archetype: what's sacred needs to be protected.

Betty: And why is that?

Tom: Because it's vulnerable. Because what is most sacred can easily be trashed. If you look at the news today about our national parks and the fact that there are no rangers or anybody else there, no support services because of the shutdown—they've literally been trashed. The garbage is overflowing, the toilets are overflowing.

In order to have a treasure, you need to protect it; otherwise, it gets trashed. Whether it's a physical treasure, like a national park, or a spiritual treasure, such as some sort of deep spiritual insight into the nature of being itself, or an emotional treasure, such as our own vulnerability and sanctity. These precious things require defensive walls for their protection. And if we're going to have an intelligent discussion about walls, we need to acknowledge that, in human history, there has been a positive function for walls. Those of us opposed to Trump's wall see it as evil or as negative, but to view it so reductively means we are really missing something.

And back to your point, Betty—which is that we are being assaulted by so many different ideas, by so much information, whether it be about the digital revolution or trade agreements—it's all way more complex than any one individual or group of individuals feels that it can manage. And in being so overwhelmed—including by the threat of extinction because of climate change—we find these facts to be unacceptably intolerable things to think about. So, we build walls around it. Climate denial is a kind of psychological wall against something that is unimaginable. And I do think the growing complexity of globalization and information and internet technology is deeply threatening to all of us. When you walk down the street and you see eight out of ten people on their cell phones, you wonder about the nature of human communication and relatedness.

Michael: All the things that you guys have been referring to—the walls in Tibet, which bring to mind the walls in Jerusalem—they are built around something that has meaning and value and is really precious. And in this context, if you say you don't want a wall, what you might be saying is, you don't value this thing. If you don't want a wall, you're saying you don't recognize how special, how precious, how totally unique it is and you're going to deface it. You're going to...

Betty: ...expose it.

Michael: Yes, expose it to the elements. Expose it to...

Betty: ...marauders.

Michael: Yes, to marauders. By opposing a wall to protect something, you miss its importance and the value it holds. And that is also a huge part of this conflict.

Betty: All this speaks to an emotional fragility that is present and a chief concern in our national psyche. The symbol of the wall captures an anxiety about our vulnerability, which is crucial to note, regardless of what we feel about it politically. What is curious is how Trump, in those audio clips, kept describing his imagined wall as "tall, powerful, beautiful...with a big, beautiful door"—it almost ceases to be a wall. I don't know what the beautiful door is supposed to be, but he has created this monolithic "beautiful" structure in all of our minds that he equates to protecting the preciousness of the United States. It's vague in articulation, but you are right, Tom, the emotion is distinct and spot on. He hits an emotional core. And maybe both sides of the political divide need to acknowledge the importance of this emotional core in order to have a truly productive conversation about this.

Michael: The interesting thing is also how symbols of walls have different meanings at different times. Prepping for this conversation I thought about Reagan's 1987 speech standing outside the Brandenburg Gate in West Berlin. I went back and listened to the speech he gave, calling for Gorbachev to tear down the Berlin Wall. He spoke of freedom—and how tearing down that wall would mean the expansion of global freedom. The Berlin Wall for Reagan was something drastically, dramatically different. The Soviet Union had built a wall to keep people in. For the longest time, we thought of walls as bad because of the Berlin Wall, and now we have a different world and we think of walls symbolically in a very, very different way.

Tom: Absolutely. The Berlin Wall was to keep people in. And Trump's Mexican wall is to keep people out. They serve entirely different functions. One we want to tear down, and the other we want to build, but both serve symbolically to address our precious freedom as we perceive it.

Michael: Let me ask you this last question, Tom. As you said earlier, the wall, or the symbol of the wall, has completely frozen and arrested the functioning of our government. If you were advising Democrats or Republicans in Congress on how to end this stalemate and get back to functioning, what advice would you give them in terms of how they talk about the wall or how to talk with each other about the wall, so we can all move forward?

Tom: I would advise our leaders to do what we've been doing here, which is to have a real and layered discussion about all the different meanings, perspectives, and implications of building such a wall. I would encourage consideration of both the positive and negative reactions and see if instead of having to be so concrete about whether or not to allocate 5 billion dollars for building a wall, they might reinitiate a serious discussion about immigration and immigration policies. All talk about the wall has, among other things, stopped any real serious discussion about how we're going to manage immigration in the future.

Betty: It's a distraction.

Tom: Exactly, it's a distraction.

Betty: We have to talk about the roots of the symbol in order to get past it.

Recommended Reading

Framework

Singer, T. (Ed.). (2023). *Cultural complexes of Australia: Placing psyche*. Routledge.

Singer, T. (Ed.). (2021). *Cultural complexes in China, Japan, Korea, and Taiwan: Spokes of the wheel*. Routledge.

Singer, T. (Ed.). (2020). *Cultural complexes and the soul of America*. Routledge.

Singer, T. & Rasche, J. (Eds.). (forthcoming 2024). *European cultural complexes in crisis: Jungian perspectives on Brexit and war*. Routledge.

Singer, T. (Ed.). (2023). *Latin American cultural complexes: South and soul*. Routledge.

Acknowledging Death, Trauma, Loss

Becker, E. (1973). *The denial of death*. Free Press.

Barnard, A. "Inside Syria's torture prisons: How Bashar al-Assad crushed dissent." *The New York Times*, May 11, 2019. https://www.nytimes.com/2019/05/11/world/middleeast/syria-torture-prisons.html.

Benjamin, J. (1988). *The bonds of love: Psychoanalysis, feminism, and the problem of Dominication*. Pantheon Books.

Benjamin, J. (2017). *Beyond doer and done to: Recognition theory, intersubjectivity, and the third*. Routledge.

Boss, P. (1999). *Ambiguous loss: Learning to live with unresolved grief*. Harvard University Press.

Boss, P. (2021). *The myth of closure: Ambiguous loss in a time of pandemic and change*. W. W. Norton & Co.

Doney, M. "The wolf and the dog." *Creative Nonfiction*, no. 73 (Fall 2020): https://creativenonfiction.org/writing/the-wolf-and-the-dog/.

Herman, J. (2000). *Father-daughter incest*. Harvard University Press.

Herman, J. (1997). *Trauma and recovery: The aftermath of violence—from domestic abuse to political terror*. Basic Books.

Herman, J. (2023). *Truth and repair: How trauma survivors envision justice.* Basic Books.

Hoffer, E. (1951/2010). *The true believer: Thoughts on the nature of mass movements.* Harper & Row.

Rothberg, M. (2019). *The implicated subject: Beyond victims and perpetrators.* Stanford University Press.

Solomon, S., Pyszczynski, T, & Greenberg, J. (2002). *In the wake of 9/11: The psychology of terror.* American Psychological Association.

Solomon, S., Pyszczynski, T, & Greenberg, J. (2016). *The worm at the core: On the role of death in life.* Penguin.

Wedeen, L. (1999/2015). *Ambiguities of domination: Politics, rhetoric, and symbols in contemporary Syria.* University of Chicago Press.

Why Truth Matters

Davies, W. (2015). *The happiness industry: How the government and big business sold us wellbeing.* Verso Press.

Davies, W. (2017). *The limits of neoliberalism: Authority, sovereignty and the logic of competition.* Sage Publications.

Davies, W. (2018). *Nervous states, democracy and the decline of reason.* W. W. Norton.

Davies, W. (2020). *This is not normal: The collapse of liberal Britain.* Verso Press.

Davies, W. "Why We Stopped Trusting Elites." *The Guardian*, November 29, 2018. https://www.theguardian.com/news/2018/nov/29/why-we-stopped-trusting-elites-the-new-populism.

Frank, J.A. (2006). *Bush on the couch: Inside the mind of the U.S. president.* Politico Publishing.

Frank, J.A. (2011). *Obama on the couch: Inside the mind of the president.* Free Press.

Frank, J.A. (2018). *Trump on the couch: Inside the mind of the president.* Penguin Random House.

Mayer, J. (2017). *Dark money: The hidden history of billionaires behind the rise of the radical right.* Anchor Books.

McLennan, S. (2009). *Jesus was a liberal: Reclaiming Christianity for all.* St. Martin's Press.

Oreskes, N. & Conway, E.M. (2010). *Merchants of doubt: How a handful of scientists obscured the truth on issues from tobacco smoke to global warming.* Bloomsbury Press.

Piketty, T. (2013). *Capitol in the twenty-first century.* A. Goldhammer (Trans). The Belknap Press of Harvard University Press.

Pinker, S. (2022). *Rationality: What it is, why it seems scare, and why it matters.* Penguin Random House.

Rosenblum, N.L. (2018). *Good neighbors: The democracy of everyday life in America.* Princeton University Press.

Rosenblum, N.L. (2010). *On the side of the angels: An appreciation of parties and partisanship.* Princeton University Press.

Rosenblum, N.L. & Muirhead, R. (2019). *A lot of people are saying: The new conspiracism and the assault on democracy.* Princeton University Press.

Lee, B. (Ed.) (2017/2019). *The dangerous case of Donald Trump: 27 psychiatrists and mental health experts access a president.* Thomas Dunne Books.

Tansey, M. (2019). "'Why crazy like a fox' versus 'crazy like a crazy' really matters: Delusional disorder, admiration of brutal dictators, the nuclear codes, and Trump." In *The dangerous case of Donald Trump*, (B. Lee, Ed.), pp. 104–119. Thomas Dunne Books.

Anxieties of Race & Dominance

Alinsky, S.K. (1989). *Rules for radicals: A practical primer for realistic radicals.* Random House.

Banks, A.J. (2014). *Anger and racial politics: The emotional foundation of racial attitudes in America.* Cambridge University Press.

Glick, P., Dovidio, J.F., Hewstone, M., & Eses, V.M. (Eds.). (2010). *The sage handbook of prejudice.* SAGE Publications.

Flick, P. & Rudman, L.A. (2010). The social psychology of gender: How power and intimacy shape gender relationships. The Guilford Press.

Fiske, S. (2018). *Social cognition: Selected works of Susan Fiske.* Routledge.

Jardina, A. (2019). *White identity politics.* Cambridge University Press.

Kalmoe, N. & Mason, L. (2022). *Radical American partisanship: Mapping violent hostility, its causes, & the consequences for democracy.* University of Chicago Press.

Mason, L. (2018). *Uncivil agreement: How politics became our identity.* University of Chicago Press.

Ward, E. "Skin in the game: How antisemitism fuels white nationalism." *The Public Eye* (Summer 2017), https://politicalresearch.org/2017/06/29/skin-in-the-game-how-antisemitism-animates-white-nationalism.

Democracy at Risk

Arendt, H. (1977). *The origins of totalitarianism.* Penguin.

Cohen, M. & Zenko, M. (2019). *Clear and present safety: Why the world has never been in a better place and why that matters to Americans.* Yale University Press.

Damour, L. (2016). *Untangled: Guiding teenage girls through the seven transitions into adulthood.* Ballentine Books.

Damour, L. (2023). *The emotional lives of teenagers.* Ballentine Books.

Damour, L. (2023). *Under pressure: Confronting the epidemic of stress and anxiety in girls.* Ballantine Books.

Hofstader, R. (2008). *The paranoid style in American politics.* Penguin Random House Canada.

Commission on the Practice of Democratic Citizenship. (2020). *Our common purpose: Inventing American democracy for the twenty-first century.* American Academy of Arts and Sciences. https://www.amacad.org/ourcommonpurpose/report.

Lifton, R.J. (1967). *Death in life: Survivors of Hiroshima.* Random House.

Lifton, R.J. (2019). *Losing reality: On cults, cultism, and the mindset of political and religious zealots.* The New Press.

Lifton, R.J. (1988/2000). *The Nazi doctors: Medical killing and the psychology of genocide.* Basic Books.

Lifton, R.J. (2014). *Thought reform and the psychology of totalism: A study of "brainwashing" in China.* The University of North Carolina Press.

Lui, E. (2019). *Become America: Civic sermons on love, responsibility and democracy.* Sasquatch Books.

Persily, N. & Tucker, J.A. (Eds.). (2020). *Social media and democracy: The state of the field, prospects for reform.* Cambridge University Press.

Piven, F.F. & Cloward, R. (1977). *Poor people's movements.* Vintage Books.

Woodly, D. (2015). *The politics of common sense: How social movements use public discourse to change politics and win acceptance.* Oxford University Press.

Woodly, D. (2022). *Reckoning: Black lives matter and the democratic necessity of social movements.* Oxford University Press.

Woodward, B. (2020). *Rage.* Simon and Schuster.

The Importance of Myth

Cashford, J. (Trans.) (2003). *The homeric hymns.* Penguin.

Cashford, J. (2016). *The moon: Symbol of transformation.* The Greystone Press.

Cashford, J. & Baring, A. (1993). *The myth of the goddess: Evolution of an image.* Penguin Books.

Flowers, B.S. (2004). "The primacy of people in a world of nations." In *The partnership principle: New forms of governance in the 21st century*. Archetype Publications.

Flowers, B.S. (2006). *The American dream and the economic myth*. Fetzer Institute.

Flowers, B.S., Seng, P, Scharmar C.O., & Joworski, J. (2008). *Presence: Human purpose and the field of the future*. SoL.

Flowers, B.S. & Wilkinson, A. (Eds.). (2018). *Realistic hope: Facing global challenges*. Amsterdam University Press.

Singer, T., Cashford, J., & Roque, C.S. (Eds.). (2019). *When the soul remembers itself: Ancient Greece, modern psyche*. Routledge.

Trump. M. (2020). *Too much and never enough*. Simon and Schuster.

www.ingramcontent.com/pod-product-compliance
Lightning Source LLC
Chambersburg PA
CBHW021805270326
41932CB00007B/56